ENDORSEMENTS FOR RAVEN DAVIES

"When David and Ted meet the Mistress they embark on a whirling adventure through spiritual realms and earthly lusts that transforms them both and enthralls the reader. "Between Here & There", by Raven Davies, is a sweeping, glorious gay love story like no other you've ever encountered. By turns comic and heartwarming, 'Between Here & There' is a story to engage the heart, mind, and soul. Be warned: once you begin, you won't be able to put it down."

Ralph Higgins for *Wayves Magazine*

"This new Canadian author is emerging as one of the most unique, independent, adventurous, thought provoking storytellers today."

Friction Fiction Books Inc.

"Raven Davies is one of the most original literary artists working today. Davies is successfully bridging the gulf between traditional fiction and the new, exciting world of Internet 'Slash' writing. With tremendous assurance and with great panache, Davies is giving readers an entirely fresh and fascinating reading experience. At this time of crossover literary technologies, Davies is emerging as a singular creative voice. This breathless, altogether remarkable storytelling makes for compelling reading."

Joseph Dispenza: spiritual counselor and author of *Healer, Older Man Younger Man, God On Your Own, The Way of the Traveler, Live Better Longer, The House of Alarcon*

"As a proofreader, it isn't often I am swept into a book, my mind too analytical to allow the story to interfere with my work. Resist as I may, Davies' 'Between Here and There', with its wonderfully wild adventures, crossover realities, and multi-faceted characters, carried me away into the thought-provoking world of David and Ted. Be prepared to fall headfirst into a riveting tale."

Leona Luba: Professional Proofreader

"Raven Davies brings unusual and exhilarating life to a unique work with a poetic style, imagination, and a keen eye for what lies beneath the surface of the human condition."

Warren Redman: *Achieving Personal Success, Listening Power, Portfolios for Development, Counseling Your Staff, Facilitation Skills for Team Development, Working Towards Independence, Finding Your Own Support, Creative Training*

'Between Here & There' is a well-crafted novel, combining romance, mystery, mysticism, and adventure. The writer takes us inside the character's emotions, showing an intensely complex range of fear, anger, love, need, desire, human curiosity, and so much more. The power of male love, shown through sex and intrigue, is blended together not only in the world as we know it, but the spirit realm as well. This makes for a thought provoking and interesting tale, which still has me reeling and thinking. The story is exciting, mature, and erotic, with a climax as surprising as any you will find. Truly an engaging, wildly imaginative story, I recommend this book highly."

5 stars on Amazon and Barnes & Noble by a reader from Tennessee

"Sexy and well written, a thought provoking novel. Constructed to make a coherent, powerful, and unusual statement. Found it intellectually stimulating, spiritually provocative, and entertaining to read. A definite page turner."

5 stars on Amazon and Barnes & Noble from a reader in San Miguel de Allende, Mexico

"Mystical role Playing, this book is a multi-stranded novel about a group of actors who find themselves involved in the adventure of a lifetime. Transported into another mystical dimension they become involved with mysterious beings of great power. Using their acting skills to perform in the games of these beings, they explore the inner landscapes of their own natures. A fascinating mix of mysticism, sensuality, and role play."

4 stars on Amazon.co.uk from a reader in Glasgow, United Kingdom

"I have enjoyed Raven's Slash stories for years. With Between Here & There, Raven's plots continue to be exciting, complex, and intense with deep psychological overtones. One is never sure where the stories are going to take you, leaving you on an emotional roller coaster. Many times Raven has woven Native spirituality and healing into the storylines, which lends an air of mysticism, which continues in here mystical theory in Between Here & There."

Lynda Perry: Registered Nurse and Cherokee Healer.

"This novel is amazing."

5 stars from David on Goodreads website.

"Raven Davies' wittings are a must read! This brilliant author does it again with her novel Between Here & There, delivering a story with elaborate scenery, in-depth character exploration, and titillating sex."

Faith Scruggs: writer and Raven Davies Fan

BETWEEN HERE & THERE

Revised Edition

RAVEN DAVIES

ISBN: 978-0-9866742-2-8

Printed in the United States of America

PROLOGUE

"The dark and the light, they exist side by side,
Sometimes overlapping; one explaining the other.
The darkened path is as illuminated as the lightened,
Only the fear of the dark keeps us from seeing our way."

Raven Davies 1996-02-07

CHAPTER 1

With a mere wave of her hand, the soft clouds dissipated in front of her. One could see the other side of the stars through her massive window, with a view of one reality turning into another, and another beyond that. A place of power, peace, and magic was her home, floating amongst the misty vapors of lavender set against a dark purple background. Embracing it all, she stood silently, dressed in burgundy velvet, the same shade of the wine within the pewter goblet she delicately held in her long, slender, white hand. It was time. The voices had been heard too often to go unheeded, but why did they beckon her with such urgency? Could they be the ones? A wistful smile crossed her face, remembering something from long ago, for those whom she would wait an eternity. It was a fleeting thought; one she had grown weary of pondering.

Her mane of raven hair danced in the breeze, which picked up in a gust and returned the swirl of clouds to veil her visions. A waft of a whisper snuffed out the candles, leaving her motionless in the dark. Her mind dwelt on two men whom she did not know, although there was an unmistakable connection. Green eyes stared up through her grand portal, while she contemplated on what should be. Her worry beads were her stars, glittering and falling through the never-ending darkness of her silent realm. Which one shone down upon their lost children? With a gentle sweep of her hand, she caressed her cheek, feathering back a few strands of the black silk that crossed the pale, ageless face. She would help these men, starting as the first rays of sun sparked Earths next dawning.

CHAPTER 2

Rain came down in torrents; and David LaCoix had reached his fill of a wasted day. The coffee, which he held, warmed his hands more than it quenched his nonexistent thirst. He sat wet, tired, cold, and now angry at having to wait for another take of a scene that would undoubtedly end up on the editor's floor. His reputation for being somewhat forgiving and generous on a set had long passed, replaced by his ire that, along with his star status (what remained of it), would be used to go on a rampage. The other side of his contradictory personality, he actually enjoyed exhibiting this one when warranted. David stomped through the mud in grim determination, not caring about the expensive leather boots, or the costly antique silver spurs he wore as part of his costume. Enough is enough, he kept reaffirming to himself; and the director had better prepare for his wrath.

"Carter!" LaCoix yelled through the chaos of constant chatter, the neighing of frightened horses, the movement of equipment, and the pounding rain. "We've had enough; everyone's tired of this shit. This is fucking ridiculous."

"Sorry, David, but every part of this movie has been screwed up by the weather. We can't wait for a goddamn sunny day to start over just for you." Equally irritate, the director lashed out at the man who could bring people in to see a film just because of his name, not a household one, but a respected moniker all the same.

"One more take, man; that's all I'm giving you, before heading to my trailer for a hot shower and a decent drink."

"Damn it, LaCoix, it's dangerous; and we need your close-up. I don't want any of you slipping underneath a fucking horse."

"All you need is one shot of the eleven of us riding around that outcrop of rocks. We've done it a half-dozen times; and you're still unhappy. The close-ups will be piss-poor, considering how mad I am at this moment."

"Okay, okay, you win. Give us a half-hour to get the crane and cameras back on line. George will have to use his experience to adjust the lighting for the lack of shadows."

"What the hell do you know about lighting, Richard? There's no damn way. Go with what we have, exactly like you've been doing the past three days. Come on, man; if you're worried about that little close-up of me and Barrett, we can do it another day."

"No. It's got to be exactly in these same conditions."

"Why don't you try it, and haven't you heard of a green-screen?" David hated pompous, young directors with little experience. His thoughts were always with the actors. "Let us do our jobs," he muttered under his breath.

"Okay, we'll hit you with a light from the jeep, carrying the camera that will take the shot."

"One camera--in a goddamn jeep--just one angle? Jesus Christ."

"David, piss off. One light may give us some creative off-the-wall effects, along with three or four different video side shots." Richard Carter was finally thinking, trying something new. At least David managed to get the man off his derriere and to start reacting to the circumstances and horrendous conditions plaguing the production. Delays lasted far too long.

"Once more, because that's all you're getting. We're all experienced actors, but your total lack of technical prowess has fucked us up royally."

"One shot. If we don't get it..."

"...no, *if*'s, one time, babe, and you're done. Make it right, and we'll do our part. Put a little rust remover on the crane; it's our best hope. Try a little on yourself; you've been out in this rain too long." He turned on his heels and headed to inform the others to start preparing: wardrobe and make-up needed checking. David LaCoix did not push his weight around unless forced; and it usually came with a far more violent crashing of objects than this minuscule display of words. Under his quiet exterior, he could be extremely volatile and unpredictable. Seldom unsettling in his work, and respected by all for his professionalism, what he may say in anger and frustration reputably meant a good idea. For now, he felt too tired for one of his famous, yet rare, blowouts.

The extraordinarily handsome blond had the sense of a practical man, but with all the idiosyncrasies that accompanied fame. The list was long: married twice, soon to be divorced twice, three kids between two wives, two alimony payments, three households to maintain, college money for his two boys, and now Rebecca--his young, beautiful fiancée--the unknown factor. An average man with normal problems, the decisive factor still existed: he was an actor. Instability and uncertainty inscribed itself into the nature of the beast: the job in hand, the failure before that, a film to follow, a surprising box office smash, or just another TV movie with no guts, not to mention the eternal question of age, and who would usurp him to steal another film. It had been his downfall three times, in three different smash hits that should have been his. He undeniably understood the complexities of his craft and had a screen presence, but he already saw another scene grabber in one of his young co-stars. It was difficult for David to even talk to the man, although Barrett appeared genuinely personable and very polite, not to mention knockdown-dead gorgeous. The cameras adored him.

LaCoix's confidence had dropped to an all time low, although his work continued to be impeccable. Too stressed to forget lines of intensity, he saw them uniquely as a reflection of his own emotions: fear, jealousy, depression, anger--no, not anger--fury. He had to face the facts: yes, he was still attractive enough for certain roles, with his natural blond hair and green eyes that flashed with a hint of insanity; both had become his trademark. Even his lower lip that pouted slightly and a wicked smile that lit up his entire face, when he allowed it to happen, all added to the charisma and mystery of the man. At forty-three, he was in the best physical shape of his life. Tall and lean, with a well-chiseled, finely honed body, nothing overdone, but just taut and sinewy, made him the perfect specimen for any camera lens. His gestures and movements made him elegant and graceful, agile and quick, adding to his already long résumé of talents and credentials.

The other ten actors in the scene sat idly on picnic benches, under a small canopy about to give way from the weight of the water it desperately tried to support. Huddled together, attempting to stay dry and warm, they indulged in quiet contemplation, while drinking copious amounts of hot coffee. It was not the best decision an actor could make, waiting in a downpour, dressed in almost immovable period costuming. The astute actor mused to himself, thinking it one of those rare times men acted like women, needing to ask a friend to accompany them to the powder room, and certainly not for a chat.

"One last attempt, in thirty minutes, and we're finished for the day. You boys okay with that?" He gave a heavy sigh, while seriously sizing up his cast members. Ten men, and only one he had met and worked with before; even the director was new to him, another rarity. "Shit, I'm getting too old to be fucking around in the mud, Jess. I feel like all my bones are creaking." He slumped down on the bench, immediately receiving another cup of unnecessary coffee. A loud roar of laughter came from the group, all suffering from being stiff and sore, cold and tired, and extremely bored. Very few frills came with a low budget, independent film.

"You're not the only one, LaCoix," Evans yelled out. One of his co-stars, this man was wildly talented, now coming into his own. The leading man admired Ray Evans, for being an all-round entertainer, and just fun to watch. Though David seldom sat with the group, or conversed at any level with the rest of the cast, the two that he did enjoy were Jess and Ray.

"Just another day in sunny Arizona; don't you just love it?" Jess Carmichael grinned into his steaming mug. A big, lovable bear, the oldest member of the group remained calm and patient through any crisis. David had only seen him angry once, and once had been enough. Several decades prior, on another set, a young, female actor was being taunted by a slimy young actor whose star had risen too brightly, too quickly. Everyone heard her scream and saw her run from behind one of the unstable sets, with her costume torn at the shoulder. Reaching to grab her, the young man stumbled out, laughing in his inebriation and lust. Jess did not hesitate to send the young star flying into kingdom-com, with a full backhanded swing across the pretty boy features. Pure fury in his attack, he immediately softened to comfort the frightened, humiliated girl.

The kid changed his ways dramatically after that particular afternoon, and became one of the more courteous actors in Hollywood, if womanizing, the occasional tantrum, and a once-in-a-while, public, drunken brawl were considered part of the guise of a Tinsel-town gentleman. The kid was David LaCoix, twenty years earlier, and now they could laugh about it. The trouncing taught him a lesson he would never forget, and now found himself happy and secure in the man's company, considering few people made him feel comfortable. David's intensity, in his profession, went beyond the script, spilling into his own life and relationships. His silent mannerisms frightened people, as did the infamous wicked look in his eyes, either dancing with angry fire or mischief, or straining in sad insanity. On occasion, drugs or alcohol enhanced the look, but this one physical attribute remained a constant in his persona.

The call came, sending half the cast to be buckled and belted, the other half to be puffed and powdered, as if it would do any good in the heavy drizzle. Cowboy hats were a nuisance and made lighting of the face difficult. They did keep, however, the make-up from dripping down the fronts of the costumes. This day provided a perfect test of waterproof cosmetics, causing David to smirk, knowing they continued to film in soft-focus. Good for his ego, the technology made him look ten years younger on screen. With that cheerful thought in mind, he strolled over to the make-up trailer. They would finally get this over with, allowing them to return to the warm sanctum of their temporary dwellings. Besides making the work difficult, the rain played depressing games within their heads; and even the happiest of dispositions grew weary and bedraggled.

LaCoix relaxed in a chair next to the sunniest: Theodore Barrett. The younger man was not his usual chatty self, a relief for the weary star. He closed his eyes, enjoying the feather-like touch of a woman's fingers, intricately reapplying the scraggly beard to his face, creating the perfect illusion. A simple look to achieve with an overnight growth, unfortunately, his natural beard was paradoxically very dark compared to his blond hair, eyebrows, lashes, and even his light brown pubic hair. Opening his eyes to view the results, he looked squarely into a pair of unearthly blue ones. The kid was astonishingly attractive, startling to even someone who still received endless second looks.

David stared back for only a moment, but quickly diverted his eyes to the magnifying mirror handed to him: details meant everything in this business. While studying his face for perfection of his character, he was very conscious that he made Barrett nervous, certainly subduing the kid's sprightly nature when in such close proximity. The older actor sensed a sadness in those blue eyes the first day they met, and he could not shake the feeling the young man acted a part laid out for him. Not his concern, he had enough sorrow in his heart, brooding about his youngest child: a five-year-old daughter whom he had not seen in several months. He had visitation rights; and his little girl spent weekends with him, when at home. This location shoot had made it impossible, raising his ire further, to lash out unexpectedly at the man in the chair next to him. "What in hell are you looking at, Barrett?"

The kid nearly jumped out of his seat at the harsh tonality of his chastisement. "Sorry, sir; just lost in thought. Didn't realize I was staring."

"Ouch, another knife through my ego. You're making me feel downright elderly; and here I thought you were mesmerized by my incredible good-looks and awesome presence?" David teased his usurper, trying to regain a hospitable, nonchalant atmosphere.

"I... I didn't mean any disrespect, Mr. LaCoix." The man may be enthusiastic and generally outgoing with everyone else, but he proved scared senseless of the older, somewhat sullen actor.

Embarrassed by his anger toward a man who seemed genuinely innocent and respectful, beyond the average young Hollywood star stud, LaCoix pulled back to redeem himself. "People call me David, Theo. Why don't you try it? We've been filming for months; lighten up a little. I'm not quite old enough to be your father, although I sure as hell feel like it today." David looked directly at the peculiar eyes, wondering just how frightened this young actor was.

"Yes, sir... I mean, David; and for some reason, people here are calling me Ted." Barrett looked away from the famous face, to contemplate the toes of his boots.

"So I noticed. Are you comfortable about riding around those rocks? It's a little slick." David did not see fear in the young man, but perhaps only a little star-struck. Chuckling within, he never considered himself, or even believed, he ranked *star* status. The blond turned his thoughts to idle business conversation, to allow this ray of sunshine to spark back to life.

"Sure, no problem; sounds like fun. It's been a total yawn these long weeks we've been here. A few thrills, no matter how small, would be some kind of diversion. Hate this waiting part. There has to be a better way to film without wasting all this time. I even hate the coffee, just to..."

"...piss after every cup?" David put on his best smile, receiving an understanding one in return.

"This weather makes that colossal problem worse." Ted could actually speak, although looking rather bashful in his attempt to avoid the famous green eyes scrutinizing him.

"It does at that, not to mention caffeine is a natural diuretic and purgative. Try to avoid the crap, or you'll end up with ulcers like the rest of us. Find something you like to do. Get a hobby, Ted."

"Yeah, right. Can't do that here, and I'm certainly not one for sitting around playing cards. I think I've seen every video we have available. At least it's constructive, studying other actors."

"Good ways to familiarize yourself with different acting styles, as well as directing techniques; but now you have me intrigued--a hobby you can't do here--a puzzle and I do love puzzles." David warmed up to the kid, happy to find Barrett able to converse without stumbling over his tongue.

"Well, you won't be hearing it from me. Hope this last take gets us back into our trailers to continue twiddling our thumbs."

"You're absolutely right, my boy; this has been one long shoot; but we should be finished within the next week, to return home for the last few interior shots." David leaned back and sighed, wondering where he could hang his hat and call it home. A shell of a townhouse awaited him, not yet furnished. The separation took place so quickly, he did not have time to find a secluded place to his liking; the Beverly Hills tradition of leasing begrudgingly hit his practical sense of wasting money. He loved the big homes he helped redesign for his two families that were to last forever. His lifestyle, once lavish and regal, now meant hiding out in an attached condominium, his own stupidity causing the entire situation. The thought of neighbors, on either side of his walls, scared him to stone. A sudden shiver swept down his spine. David LaCoix was ill prepared to surround himself with what he considered the *public*, and he felt vulnerable and completely naked.

"Are you okay?" The timid voice jolted the lost actor back into action.

"Yeah, let's get this show on the road. Come on, man, work awaits. You remember how we did the last take; your expression was perfect. Try to keep the same intensity and smugness. If they hadn't hit us with the wrong light, we'd be enjoying a drink and laughing about this horrendous day. So, here we go. Put that grimace back on your pretty face, Ted."

The younger man blushed, catching David by surprise. Those wondrous blue eyes dropped again to look for his boot tips. David had embarrassed the man, a difficult thing to do with crazed, young pups. It amused the older actor who caught the refreshing expression. The kid would go far if cuteness counted; and it most certainly did in their profession.

They both walked out and joined the rest of the crew. Their horses waited, allowing eleven men to mount up, as wranglers fussed over their animals' tack, shoes, buckles, and anything else that might have loosened. Once again, the director shouted out the same scenario they had heard a dozen times that day. "Okay, let's get this, boys; start slow. When you reach your first marker, make sure you're positioned correctly to get your horses into an easy lope. Stunt shots are done, so don't go racing off like lunatics, just to make me mad. Take it easy and be careful. David, Ted, when you turn, do it slowly. Got it?"

"Yeah, yeah, yeah, we've got it. We've got it up to here, man," David whispered under his breath, as the wheels of moviemaking started to turn. Cameras in jeeps, on cranes, in trucks, with stationary cameras on the left side, followed the riders with most of the lighting equipment turned off, except for that instant close-up, lasting only a matter of seconds. A difficult maneuver to accomplish, LaCoix and Barrett had to be completely synchronized, along with the thousand-pound, unpredictable animals they had to deal with and give directions to. The blond actor leaned down and patted his gelding's neck to reassure them both.

Eleven horses took off at an easy pace, with all the actors hitting their appropriate marks and taking the warning seriously. The two main stars turned at precisely the right moment with the perfect expressions, and then twisted back around to gaze at a fog patch falling before them.

"Keep going! Keep riding! Go! Keep going!" Directions were yelled through a megaphone; and the first five riders disappeared into the fog. It would be a brilliant shot, if everything went as planned technically. Excitement raced through the crew, believing they had done their jobs in capturing the mystic essence of the abrupt fall of mist that swallowed up the lead actors and their mounts. The round, of joyous shouting, stopped; immediately followed by hysterical shouting at the dreadful noise and the shaking of the earth underfoot. A rumbling of rocks and the deafening crash of boulders, falling in front of the last six riders, had them sliding to a halt, with their horses trying to retain their footing in the slippery mire of the road. Jeeps spun out of control, while drivers tried not to hit anything or anybody. Everyone appeared unscathed, having not yet counted heads. The unexplainable fog lifted, exposing a wall of rock covering the trail. The first five riders had vanished; chaos ensued. Cellular devices fumbled out of pockets; emergency calls collided in cyberspace to everyone and everybody. Five men were missing: Jess Carmichael, Ray Evans, Kevin Donaldson, Theodore Barrett, and David LaCoix.

CHAPTER 3

Five riders rode through the fog, oblivious to the shaking of falling rocks beneath their horses' hooves, and the thunderous noise of the slide. Experiencing a serene sense of floating, they continued on, not hearing the order to stop. What appeared to be mist felt refreshingly cool, yet strangely dry. They emerged into a landscape reminiscent of a Salvador Dali original; the eerie scene quickly brought them to a halt. Warm, arid air, with a hint of a breeze scented with lilacs, dried them to their bones. Five men sat motionless, viewing in wonder at what seemed surreal.

Theodore Barrett spoke first, trying to stay calm, but everyone heard the nervous crack in his soft, raspy voice. "We're dead!"

David stopped beside him. Hearing the fear in the voice of the younger man, he reached out a hesitant, but comforting hand. Disconcerted himself, the gesture relieved his own insecurity to feel another warm body. The older actor tightened his fingers around the skinny arm. "Easy, Ted. You can feel that, can't you?"

"Yeah, I'm okay, I think. This is so weird."

Ray Evans quietly whistled under his breath, pushing his hat back to get a clearer picture of the panoramic display. A series of statuesque rock formations surrounded them, donned in the hues of the pastel rainbow, with no earthly way to approach them. Spreading out before them, a large flat area, in the same hushed desert colors, seemed to disappear as quicksand, with nothing solid to stop a fall but a handful of beige talcum powder. All five noticed the peculiarity; all five declined to advance.

"What the hell?" Kevin Donaldson leaned forward in his saddle, trying to make out the terrain without his glasses. An outrageous rogue, in the form of a big tough guy, his boisterous enthusiasm obscured his emotion and sensitivity. This spectacle put him into reserve mode.

"Don't know, Kev, but we're not in Kansas anymore," Jess laughed and joked, feeling comfortable in this space, like he belonged there, and reveled in the pure essence of a life-giving force he could feel. Carmichael and Barrett were the two spiritual members of the group, although aspiring to very different religious and life philosophies. For Jess, he had found Nirvana or Shangri-la, and he heard the sounds before anyone else. Those whispers on the breeze, and the light crystal chimes floating through it, were talking about them. He did not understand the words, but felt the many eyes observing them.

With nothing said amongst the group, stunned silence replaced all thought. Each man heard a single voice telling them to remain quiet, to pause, and to let their minds drift in time and space. David tightened the pressure on Barrett's trembling arm. Scared beyond reason, the blue-eyed innocent faltered, nearly toppling off his horse, only saved by his idol's hold. The older actor steadied the man, feeling the tension and panic in the thin appendage. In contrast, LaCoix felt good; and for one of the rare times, in his life, was not thinking about himself, or his own troubles. The lightness of being, he thought, remembering a part of a movie title, which seemed the perfect description for the emotion coursing through him: happy, honestly happy.

The five scanned the craggy formations, watching them blur and transform in the haze of a heat-induced mirage. Beauty beyond reality, only an artist's eye for color and light could create such a masterpiece. A jewel of nature, the air filled with strange music, and scented with unlikely northern lilacs hanging on a steady breeze, freshening their faces, and intoxicating their senses.

One by one, an apparition of light flashed on one of the many ledges as a form took shape. Each ghostly figure appeared in diaphanous robes, camouflaged within their surroundings, but a glimmer of light could not be easily concealed. Different luminescence colors blinked from under the pastel shades of pinks, peaches, sands, mauves, and blues. Without the knowledge of what lay disguised, under the wispy shrouds, the five actors sat quietly mounted, waiting for proper introductions to be made by someone.

The still-life watercolor of light and grace shifted. One lone figure rose majestically: tall, elegant, and graceful. The arms lifted as if to fly; and in slow motion, the image floated to ground, landing with a slight bend of the knees. Fluttering down, she looked no more than a feather. Yards and yards of gossamer danced around her ankles until her robe came to rest, dusting the powdered cloud where she stood. The apparition, of the female persuasion, was clearly visible through the semi-transparent, ethereal illusion. She walked toward them, her bare feet barely touching earth. Draped in blush colored cloth, of the most exquisite and delicate of material, she allowed its many layers of lightness to catch and float with the slightest breath. The head covering, attached to the flittering attire, slipped off, revealing thick, raven tresses. A mass of shining curls fell to her waist, then feathered behind her as she approached. Well-disguised, only her hair, gently playing in the wind, contrasted against the soft-hued surroundings. The luxurious mane framed an attractive, ageless face, full of spirit and spirituality, serene yet sensual.

"A... an angel!" Ted stuttered.

A sharp ring harshly penetrated their inner ears, with an urgent demand for silence, but immediately replaced by the whisper of a melodic female voice filling their heads. With the green eyes of a Siamese feline, she smiled at them, seeing and watching them all at the same time. Instinctively or telepathically, they understood that any sound might hurt these frail figures unaccustomed to the crushing cacophony of the human voice, not in this beautiful place, not in this realm of mystery.

A gentle chiming, accompanied by the haunting sounds of the wind echoing through the rocks, rewarded their stillness. The lavender sky and soft white sunlight became their canopy; the pastel monuments of desert rock their only shade; and the five men were bedazzled. It cloaked them within an overwhelming comfort, but for the one. David kept his hand on his co-star, not understanding why he needed to reassure someone who had been an annoyance until this eventful day.

Theodore Barrett, without thought, dropped his reins and placed his shaking hand over the firm hold of LaCoix, and prayed to his God it would remain there. Convinced they were dead and held for questioning, he awaited his Lord's decision. How they died, he could not imagine; the only thing remembered was riding on a cloud and its mist smelling sweet and enticing. Now he sat in line for the pronouncement of judgment, along with his inspiration, David LaCoix, who saved him from passing out in terror.

The bewitching Fey smiled at each actor, speaking telepathically to only the person her eyes turned toward, mesmerizing that individual into a silent concentration of immense understanding. Starting at the beginning of the string of quiet horses, she languidly gazed up at Carmichael. Already in her world of spiritual enlightenment, the gentle bear would continue along his chosen path. Not one of the voices heard, he had earned his fondest wish through a lifetime of learning; and the magical entity smiled wistfully at him and nodded her head. All would be taken care of;

Jess Carmichael would reach his goal with little of her priceless help.

Ray Evans expressed a delightful smile, blatantly flirting, for his heart's amusement, with this unknown apparition. A man intoxicated with life, he required no assistance, but she could not resist his enormous dreams that included a vow never to sacrifice his family for want of them; an example of that sorrow pointed at the only blond rider on the second horse from the far end. She would allow Evans to glory in each wish asked, eliminating possible interference that may cause him to trip. His selfless, grandiose ambitions of a workaholic, and an extremely talented man, would do the rest. With a second nod of her black curls, she moved on with a wink.

Turning to the middle rider, she tilted her head in bewilderment. There was little to sense, his interior so different from his exterior. Donaldson's guise of a tough, brawling, roving-eyed male, of the human species, had her soon smiling brightly. Under the mask, she found a simple man with a sensitive Spirit, and a *let's get it done* attitude. His wishes were minimal, believing he had everything a man required. Not one of the two sad voices heard through her window, he would still receive a gift of a contented, happy life, without the need for the sinful façade. Cat's eyes twinkled to confirm her promise.

She glided over to the last two men, one of whom she recognized instantly. The tall, slender figure slipped her way between the horses carrying LaCoix and Barrett. The younger man she knew was frightened; and his world would be shaken soon enough. She looked up into the glistening, crystal green eyes of David LaCoix, smiling her warmest of smiles. She knew him intimately and tried not to laugh. How could it not be him? Her mistake to rectify, LaCoix had done his part attempting to contact her through every splinter of his broken heart.

'Let go of his arm,' came the silent request. Both men heard it and quickly glanced at each other for confirmation. Puzzled, LaCoix could also hear Barrett begging him not to let go. The woman won with a formidable trick, turning the slim arm to hot metal at a touch. Left with no alternative, David had to give in or be burned, releasing the shaking limb and fracturing the needed connection. She glanced at the last man in the line, to ensure he remained with them mentally. He immediately turned to face the other way; she allowed him the small respite for a moment in her time. Returning to LaCoix, a conversation developed between them. Thoughts, questions, and answers exploded at a cosmic rate, faster than mere words would allow.

'What is required to make your life perfect?'

'So that's what this is about: the granting of wishes. How many do we get, Genie?'

Not exactly, and a Genie? What an interesting thought and maybe you are correct. Go ahead, and you may find out.' The chimes of laughter tickled David's ears, as she urged him on to spill his secrets.

'Some honest joy and an end to years of emptiness.' LaCoix surprised himself with his first admission, but quickly changed his thinking. *'This is a remarkable place; I've never felt so comfortable. Perhaps that's the word I'm looking for--comfort--in everyone and all things in my life.'*

'Open your heart and eyes with the wonderment of a child, and you shall obtain it, but what you think is not your deepest need, Mr. LaCoix.'

'No, but being a rather private person, it's difficult to reveal dreams to a stranger. Since you know who I am, who are you?'

She hummed a haunting melody, of spring breezes rustling through silver-leafed trees, to tickle him once more. Such a sweet sound, David lost himself in the moment. The mysterious woman confirmed her knowing of his inner voice, and gratified herself in the sound of it. *'Now is not the time, but soon. Just know I am back with you. What is your life's most important goal that will bring you happiness and settle your inner turmoil?'*

'Tough question and you know of my confusion. Right now, I have mixed feelings as to what would bring me joy. I suppose, in all honesty, I still want fame and wealth, although money I have, but not in great abundance. Notoriety I have, but not honest respect. I want a reward or acknowledgment for all my work. An Oscar nomination would suffice, if I were asking for the rainbow. Just getting my teeth into a great part, for my peers to notice, or a string of box office hits to make me feel better about my acting would do the trick. I've worked a long time without the sound of applause. Am I making sense, or being selfish?'

'Yes, it makes perfect sense. Selfish you can be, but that will soon change. It is an unkind word in your reality, but there are times when humans need to center on themselves. Do not condemn yourself for it, as long as it does not harm others. It has taken you far in your career, but not in your personal life. What else? I believe you have buried something so deep, you cannot bring it out to view in the light.'

'I don't know who or what you are, but you already know.'

'Not precisely, unless you give me a few details. Bring it to the surface. It is buried deep inside your subconscious mind. Think it, Mr. LaCoix, and you may very well receive it.' The woman waited patiently, undisturbed at the random logic spinning in the blond head. One of her voices whispered on the wind, he would make it clear when he formulated his needs in thought.

'This is the hardest word a man can say or admit. I suppose the answer is love: a strong, enduring one, with someone who will stand by me, who needs just me, and who depends entirely on me to make them whole. I would sacrifice a lifetime to have someone love me for who I am, and not for what I have become--no money, no fame, no free trip to Hollywood--just one person for me alone, never to be used again. Can you do that? Can you find me a partner who I can trust with my life and heart with no hidden agenda, and without having to repeat the accursed word for an eternity to remind them of my feelings? I need somebody to hold, knowing they won't break my heart, or I theirs: not again. I desire someone real, who can reach in and make my toes curl up with just a glance.'

'You surprise me; I thought it might take more coaxing. It is a large request you ask, for you cannot alter the mind of another to match your own desires. Something will be asked of you. If you accept the opportunity, you may find that person; and the dreaded word should flow naturally from your lips. Through difficult work and understanding on your part, let it start by reviewing your lifestyle and attitude, to make you worthy of such adoration. You will also receive a good deal of money in the future. Learn to handle it yourself, with the help of a true friend in the knowing of these details. Only love carries the honesty to help you. Recognition, beyond dreams unimaginable, is also on your horizon, but not from the film that you are currently undertaking. Be patient, and your next feature will return you to your proper path. This one is for your young co-star to steal. Let him have it willingly, Mr. LaCoix, knowing what you know now. Be prepared for your rewards. With a great deal of self-analysis and emotional duress, fulfillment and happiness shall be yours. Can you handle both extremes?' With a tilt of her head and a cat's inquisitiveness, the seductress could not be denied.

David nodded, accepting the challenge. *'How will I know what opportunities to take? And stress, hell, I believe I thrive on it.'*

'You have a willing guide, and you know instinctively when to react. Raise that power within yourself, and all shall fall into place. You have already started.' She slowly turned toward the desperate man at the end of the line, when she heard David's last request.

'One thing--are you real--can I touch you before I go believing in the Powers-That-Be?'

'Good choice of words. You are already using your innate gifts. Perhaps those Powers-That-Be may grant you a private audience one day.' A long, slender, white hand reached up for him to take; and he accepted, shaking it firmly with the masculine version of the same hand. With the connection granted, the ethereal creature before him radiated warmth and love. David sat in awe at the intensity of the feeling. He wanted to express the same sensation, so foreign to what he had become. As the hand slipped out of his, he felt a loss, but the memory kept his heart and hopes alive. *'Could she be the one?'* LaCoix heard her laughter in his head. Smiling her most beguiling, she put a finger to her lips, a charming reminder to be careful what you thought in her presence.

The unearthly Fey turned her elegant head toward Theodore Barrett whose terror had him paralyzed, not knowing where to look. This was his test, one unexpected when he died. This angel scared him, although she looked and acted like one. Not the time to lose his faith, Ted prayed, and kept praying all the prayers of his youth, trying to fight the fearful demons circling him, and to embrace what was to be.

Forcing Barrett's head around to look directly at her, this one had her puzzled with his thoughts. He had intense dark blue irises, overly large for an adult, making him look like a frightened child. The woman gave him a sympathetic smile for reassurance. Cat's eyes met cobalt ones; she had him bewitched, while she tried to understand and make sense of his panic. *'What do you want most in your life, Child? Do not be frightened.'*

'To be home and safe, ma'am.'

'Soon, but you have a commitment to fulfill.'

'Are you an angel?'

'I expected you to surmise angels had wings. Good for you to see passed the absence of such adornment. You succeeded in your first test, if that is what you want to call this conversation, but an angel, Mr. Barrett! No. Do not confuse me with your mythology. Remember always this lesson: learn as much about a living creature, of any kind, before you speak or think in suppositions. You never know with whom you may be conversing. Insults come in many forms; even the most sublime can be a destructive force; and we try to negate them in my world. Perhaps one day, I shall introduce you to someone who does have wings. I am sure it will delight you; and they in turn shall be as honored.' Her words triggered memories of legends of long ago, but not the necessary details. This may be the start; unfortunately, it could be with one clinging to his rightful path by a fingernail. She had to get him through a state of brainwashed consciousness, embedded by the Fates' intent on destroying him, and into an awakening that could be as equally devastating to his psyche.

'Are you real?'

'What do you think?'

'You have to be. There's no other explanation.' Ted tried to look away, but her odd stare held him captive. Moving also seemed impossible. Held by forces he did not wish to know, they

prevented him from reaching the road to his heaven.

'My poor Child, you are confused. Let your mind wander into the unreality of your existence. If you believe in heaven, why not something higher? Perhaps there is something worse than your preconceived idea of Hell; something we can contemplate together, in a future time and another place. You are the other who calls. We have been searching for you. Unfortunately, you have been hidden from us for reasons unknown. Our guesses as to why would only confuse you further.'

'Why would you be looking for me?' The sapphire eyes grew wider, wondering if he should be questioning this intimidating creature.

'To answer the distress calls you have been transmitting into the universe. It is greatly disturbing to hear painful cries in the night asking for help. We are here now. Please tell me what will make you happy. You have been sad and hurt your entire life.'

'Happiness is an illusion, ma'am. My first thought would be to become the finest actor I can be. It's not for fame or fortune, but being the best at what I do. I want to make people feel things, to laugh and to cry.'

'Just as you do naturally. Perhaps life is the illusion. You have the talent, Mr. Barrett, and your achievements shall be great. I have a question for you. What if your first desire does not happen and your acting career no longer exists?' She watched him relax slightly, while he thought seriously of his possibilities.

'I will do the Lord's work, becoming a missionary for Christ.' A determined statement, he met her eyes without being forced.

'As I thought; and that would satisfy you?'

'Yes, spreading Christ's teachings is the ultimate sacrifice and reward.'

'Working for your Christ requires a sacrifice? What kind of being would ask such a thing?'

'You sacrifice your Soul to him, if you are a true believer.'

'That is a lot to ask, sacrificing something so priceless. Have you asked your Soul about this? Perhaps it would prefer to be sold to your devil. It sounds the same to me.' Again, that unnerving tilt of the black curly head and a puzzled look emphasized the question.

Completely adrift at her remarks, Ted did not comprehend her lack of knowledge in basic truths. Why would he ask his Soul? He was his Soul. They always divided you into heart, body, and Soul. Were they actually separate parts to the whole? No, his heart, mind, and Soul followed what he knew to be right and righteous. Sacrificing your Soul for the good could not compare to selling it out to evil. She spoke blasphemy. Christ would protect and guide him through life, whether as an actor or not.

'He will, will he? You truly believe you own your Soul? A very interesting, but misconstrued conversation you had with yourself, my Child. Whom were you trying to convince? Remember I hear all.'

'I believe in Christ; and he'll save me. I also believe my Soul and I are one in the same.' Theodore Barrett held his breath, watching the apparition grow in stature, to float upward until she looked at him eye-to-eye. She gave him another questioning stare he could not fathom. His heart started pounding; beads of perspiration coursed down his forehead. Anxious and fearful, he wondered what he had said in error. Rising further, and circling around behind him, she secured him under his arms with strong, willowy ones, and lifted him off his horse. They slowly levitated, higher and higher, into the surreal, cloudless, lavender sky.

'Do you like the view, Mr. Barrett? It is lovely up here.'

'Please put me down. You're playing games. This isn't possible.'

'I thought Christ was your protector. Can he save you from me?'

"You are Satan!" Ted blurted out, to be instantly hushed with a warning ring in his head.

'Now you are becoming tiresome, Mr. Barrett, confusing your mythology with the unreality of it all; but you do not understand that as yet.'

'Please. I'll do whatever you say. Just put me down.'

'What? You do not believe your Christ will save you?'

'Yes, I do. Of course I do. You're testing my faith.'

'Perhaps. How high do you think we are? You are a rock climber, from what I understand, and should be a good judge of altitude, or is that another lie from your biography, like your actual height and age?'

'About two hundred feet, and this isn't funny. Please stop.' Stunned that this woman, seeming to know all things, had read his biography, confirmed to the young man this had to be a hoax; an elaborate game arranged by Richard Carter.

'No, and this is not amusing to any of us, Child. Do you not think we know your fears? I read every thought in your head. Are we high enough to kill you, if I let you go?'

Ted clung to his only support and nodded in agreement. Dangling precariously, he looked down at his boots, feeling they weighed more than his entire body. Gravity pulled on his legs in frightening pain at the hip joints. Seemingly unconcerned of his plight, this demon of the devil floated like a leaf on a silent pond. The game had grown deadly serious; and he feared losing control of all his bodily functions.

'This is not a game, for there are no coincidences; and there are always reasons for what we do and have become.' She opened her warm, safe arms, and everyone heard the deafening scream of Theodore Barrett, echoing through the canyon, as he plummeted to earth. All sat frozen, stunned, and terrified, watching the rag-doll body twist and turn in mid-air.

An instant burst, then a continuous stream of pink-lit ribbons radiated from the figures forgotten amongst the rocks. Each took human form under their robes, but remained unrecognizable through the shifting haze of the mirage and the light focused under Barrett. The most powerful, of this strange happening, came from the single ray originating from the forehead of the ghostly form in flight. It centered on the location of lethal contact. With nanoseconds to spare, a cradle of clouds caught Ted, and rocked him back and forth in its forgiving power. The light beams came together, enfolding him, embracing the trembling young man five-feet off the ground, now visibly firm and hard. Gliding down, as if a damselfly caught in the sun's glow, all iridescence and glitter, she came to rest delicately at Ted's side, still controlling the pink illusion. Tilting her head in thoughtful amusement, the Fey looked into those terrified eyes. Something about those eyes--she tried to remember--it was a *knowing* she should understand. Uncertain of the young man's identity and worth, she filed her thoughts neatly in a reachable recess of her mental library. Time would tell. *'Who saved you, Mr. Barrett?'*

Ted thanked his God, his Christ, and the Archangels for his reprieve.

'Wrong answer, Child; open your eyes and look around. Try again.'

"Christ... Christ saved me. My God answered... answered my prayers, and made you save me." Ted spoke aloud, stuttering out his horror. He thought his heart had stopped on the way down, and he could not catch his breath. Embarrassment flooded his face, matching the pink light, upon the realization he had made a mess of himself during the terrifying fall. Was he still alive?

'Of course you are alive, but you are wrong again. Why do you persist in speaking? You should be sending your thanks to the beings surrounding us, including your friends. They saved you with their love and concern for your welfare. You are an unhappy man; and they want to see that rectified.'

'Only because Christ made them.'

The apparition of light and dark laughed that entrancing, charming sound, and shook her head of twisted, shiny curls so very, very black. Raising her arms, the pink cradle disappeared, landing Ted in a heap on the hard ground. *'We do not answer to your Christ, Mr. Barrett, or to any other of your earthly gods. Your friends, along with mine, saved you with their kind thoughts. You shall be the actor you wish to be, and lose the sadness you refuse to acknowledge because of your Christ. If you choose your opportunities carefully, you know what will make you happy. It is within your grasp if you are strong enough to admit to your true feelings. Stop hiding, Mr. Barrett. We shall talk again another day, time, and space. I believe you to be of some importance to us.'*

The surreal landscape disappeared; and Ted lay in the middle of a muddy road, soaked through to his skin, covered in his own filth. Back to being cold, wet, and stunned into human symptoms of shock, the others looked around to find themselves where they had been before the fog. Jess noticed it first, and pointed at the rock wall that separated them from their warm trailers and a bottle of whiskey. None could speak, but Donaldson managed to get off his horse to help a shaken, frightened, and mortified young man. With some doing and a few consoling whispers, Ted stood up, shaking and covered in sticky, disgusting humiliation. Paying no attention, Kevin gently helped him back onto his patient steed. The young man was close to catatonic; and the much bigger man did not hesitate to come to his aid, taking the horse's reins to lead Barrett out from behind the fortress wall.

With Carmichael taking the point, each man carefully picked their way through the fallen rubble, only to stumble into a frenzy of activity trying to find them. People screamed and cried, while desperately digging through the rocks with state-of-the-art equipment, and more impressively with their bare hands. Noted by LaCoix, it would not be forgotten, nor would the names and faces of the photographers and journalists getting in the way of the rescuers. They were etched in his memory for later use.

The missing men continued to pick their way carefully through the last few boulders, a fair distance from their entry point. Coming closer, the chaos subsided as the massive crowd silently watched the approach of five men whose faces were ashen gray, the color of the rain-filled sky. Shock and disbelief, clenched in drawn lines running down their strained faces, were captured for eternity by dozens of telephoto lenses. Not one man answered the questions flung at them. After dismounting, they stuck together in a phalanx, pushing away the wranglers, and shoving their way, *en masse*, to one of the many cars with a key in the ignition. Four of the survivors protected the fifth from everyone's sight, and quickly disappeared into the chosen vehicle that sped them back to the camp a mile away. Each man entered his designated quarters and closed his separate door behind him. Five bolts locked immediately from the inside.

CHAPTER 4

LaCoix locked his door, turned around, and leaned against the cool metal. A smile crossed his face remembering the touch of a hand. It was real; it had all been real. The offering had sent a surge of warmth and understanding straight into his heart, maybe his Soul, if he still had one. He wanted to remember the feeling. A moment's respite, from all his worries, filtered through him by a lingering scent of lilacs on an unexpected breeze through his back window. The sound of an ice cream truck broke his reverie; he shuddered, as his cellular phone rang the crazy tune he had programmed for the delight of his little girl. Now it drove him crazy; and he wanted to smash the device every time he heard the childish ring-tone. Thankfully, the contraption took a message silently, while he just stood against the door, looking at the hated object flashing the number of saved calls. Everyone, he knew, was trying to reach him.

David ignored it; he ignored everything he could, while stripping out of his wet costume. A torturous task without assistance, he struggled to free himself of the overly tight pants that now stuck to him with thick, clay mud. He swore under his breath, took in a lung full of freedom, and peeled off the last of the saturated garments. Shivering violently, he headed for the shower, only stopped by a loud barrage of banging against his door. Another sudden fright made his heart leap; his eyes rolled skyward in disgust and irritation, hearing Carter's voice calling through the portal to his sanctuary.

Yelling back, he told the director to speak with Carmichael, and leave him to his shower. He reached for his cigarettes, lit one, and took in a long, sensual drag that went straight to his head. The waterfall pulsated on full intensity; and he cranked it up to the hottest temperature his skin could tolerate. Standing just outside the stall, he let the rising steam penetrate his cold and shocked body, while quietly inhaling half his smoke before stubbing it out and stepping under the steaming comfort. The heat allowed him to relax and remember, thankful for their quick decision in the car, nominating Jess to handle Richard and the press.

It had been a strange conversation, during the one-mile drive back to safety and security guards, with Ray jumping for joy, expressing his excitement and enthusiasm over the experience, whatever it was. The speed, at which he took the one curve in the makeshift road, certainly indicated his feelings. Beside Ray, Jess sat in the passenger side, peacefully meditating. David sensed the tranquility radiating from his friend; the eldest of the group had clearly come back with a new revelation and wallowed in the essence of it. LaCoix envied the man's inner harmony, wanting it for himself, but having no idea how to obtain it. Although the car stunk of wet leather, horses, and human waste, he could at least tolerate Ted sitting next to him in the back. No one else minded except the young man himself. David grinned slyly at the embarrassment wrought on Barrett who had no need to be with this group of men; all had vowed silence. The journey to their trailers became part of the bizarre encounter; and the fading star just did not care. He felt too good, wanting to dive into that serene place behind the rocks, to remain there forever.

On the other side of the sullen victim of the strange apparition, Kevin tried to rally Ted with some reassuring words. Along with his confusion and humiliation, the kid appeared completely dazed. If he had blinked, since riding into the canyon, no one noticed. Four of the five agreed that some type of event took place, yet not knowing what, nor revealing their private conversations with the charismatic enchantress. Barrett said nothing in his frozen silence, while the rest unanimously appointed Jess to investigate the matter and to return with an answer. Kevin agreed to help Ted, while Ray headed for his shower, and then to his keyboard to commit forever, into his computer memory bank, the adventure he had experienced.

LaCoix only wanted privacy, to reflect on the spellbinding incident. The steam rose; all his aches, pains, and tension spiraled away down the drain. He leaned against the shower stall, letting the warmth stop the chills and staying the problems he faced, including the messages chronologically listed on the extremely annoying cellular. After dressing warmly, he turned the heat up to prevent the return of his shivers, as the coolness of evening approached. Raised in the Southwest, he hated the cold. Although his work forced him into severely hazardous climatic zones, Arizona and California encompassed his world; but there he stood, freezing in one of the hottest spots in the country. It had been an unusually dreary summer, extending into fall, giving their unique Western the somber ambiance of the original book.

With the hair blower on full blast, the straight, baby fine, blond hair was dried and ruffled into place; a fresh cigarette was lit; and a straight bourbon splashed into a glass. A couple of sips reinforced him to make the easiest duty call to his first wife and sons, and then a more fragile one to his estranged parents. His watch indicated six o'clock; what his family said, however, indicated the group had been missing for nearly three hours. It seemed to David that the event happened within minutes. Over too fast, he wanted more and still had questions to ask.

Pressing the programmed button, he placed the dreaded call to Susan and Holly. Speaking to his daughter first, relief lightened his load. Nothing had been said to her, and never would. Giggling with the joys of her day, she informed her father of everything she had done. David's pride visibly glowed the moment he heard her voice. Unspoiled and sweet of heart, at least Susan had done something right. He immediately chastised himself, knowing the blame for his marital problems lay entirely on his sordid actions, having been caught performing the most disgusting of lascivious acts on someone he barely knew. The thought and deed had mortified him, pushing him into a whirlwind affair to compensate for an overdose of depression. Even worse, the divorce still pended before his engagement, to his new flavor of the month, and the scandal hit the tabloids without authorization, hurting more than a few. His inexcusable perversion glowered back at him in the haunting words of the mystery woman. Hit with an instant revelation, his depraved past had to be reconciled with a change in attitude toward women. He adored them, at least thought he did, but he used them unmercifully. Time for reform, he vowed to become someone deserving the love promised.

Susan came on the line, sending her daughter away to speak privately. Half-crazed with worry, she yelled at him for not calling immediately. It had been an hour since she saw him on the news, soaking wet and pushing his way through the crowd. She finally stopped her frightened tirade, while David patiently listened, sipped his drink, and puffed on his smoke. The next few questions concerned his well-being, and what had happened. In his slow, quiet manner, he told her nothing, but said enough to stop her asking for more details. The five men had made up a tale of attempting to outrun the slide on hearing the initial rumble. They made it unscathed, but the fog rolled in, too thick to move in any direction. Remaining very close to keep warm, they found their way through the rubble, once the heavy whiteout dissipated. End of an unspectacular story, those involved were just left cold, wet, hungry, and a little shaken.

The conversation ended with a strange request to get back together. Seldom caught off guard, David stammered for a delay with a monumental decision, unprepared for the puzzling thought and unable to accept; a far too expensive diamond adorned another finger, and Rebecca was next on his list. The following brief dialogue stopped the woman's tears, leaving her happy he was safe, and looking forward to his return. A knock interrupted his scattered thoughts on the odd situation confronting him, again jumping into the fire with two women. His bewilderment grew over the rapid events that had taken place within a few months. Once more, a knuckle rap, and he turned to address another mysterious event of the day, promised by Jess' yell for entry. David opened the door to greet his welcomed friend who quickly stepped into the trailer. The tall blond jumped back a pace to avoid the flash bulbs and shouting reporters.

"What in hell are they doing so close?" David peeked through his shuttered blinds, stunned at the number advancing passed security to surround their living quarters in reminiscence of a siege.

"We're news, man," Jess chuckled with that certain serenity still aglow in his eyes. David knew that the older man, thirteen years his senior, laughed uproariously inside over the silly, unwarranted attention.

"Don't they have a war to cover, or something that actually affects the globe?" David refilled his glass and poured one for Jess. "So, what's up? How are the others faring?"

"Since I checked on everyone else, thought I'd look in on you."

"Was happier than hell, until I spoke to the important people in my life. They rushed my old man to Emergency, on the premature announcement of our demise. Apparently, the press considered us dead and buried. Damn them for putting our families and friends through hell before they knew anything. Richard probably called his publicist before he dialed 911. We should charge him for the extra publicity this should bring to his film."

"What's the going rate per hour for advertising? It's been on the news channel steadily since the event. I suppose a number of undeclared wars ceased-fire to watch our untimely deaths." Jess gently swirled the amber liquid in his glass, smiling at something only he could see in the bourbon, dancing and sparkling golden in the light. "How's your father? Nothing serious I hope?"

"Man, I haven't spoken to my folks in years, but something drew me to make the call. I wasn't aware Dad has a ticker problem, but he's okay. Upon hearing the news, his heart gave him a jolt. It shouldn't have happened; my final proof that Carter has shit for brains."

The big man laughed, deciding time had come to swallow the glistening liquid, while David lit up another cigarette in shaky hands and watched his own private display of a vice, filling the air with long streams of gray smoke, only to float away into a widening cloud the higher it reached. Chain-smoking since the separation, he used it to face another domestic problem looming precariously: Susan wanted him back, although Rebecca was his future. Again, the Fey's words blew through his mind, clearing cobwebs to reinforce the cruelty of scheduling the wedding the same day his divorce papers would be finalized. Becoming nauseous, he shifted gears, tossing those thoughts back into the recesses of his mind, by inquiring about the other three.

"Stopped to see Evans first, who's already rattling off the story for his memoirs. Donaldson's with Barrett; the kid's in bad shape. Why do I keep calling him a kid? The man's thirty years old."

"No, shit! He could pass for twenty! Doesn't look any older than my boys!" David was truly surprised at the man whom he had scrutinized in the make-up trailer and held firmly while in the Dali masterpiece. "What's wrong with him, besides being scared shitless? Pardon the pun," LaCoix asked with a concerned frown, but he had other things, too close to home, to debate in his head this night.

"He wouldn't answer the door, so we liberated the master key. We found him, still wet and filthy, sitting on the floor of his trailer. Ted is a strange little beggar. All these days of cold weather, he never once complained about his heater not working and no hot water. While Kevin helped him stand, I grabbed some of his clean clothes, and then we moved him over to Donaldson's digs. He 's now showered, dressed, and lying there, violently shaking, bundled up in a ton of blankets on Kev's couch. Hasn't said a word--not a murmur--and he hasn't moved. I felt like I was washing down a corpse."

"He's in shock. I'll be damned. Knew he was scared, but thought he'd be over it by now. The other day, I heard him talking to one of the others about a mountain climbing accident, which nearly claimed his life. Obviously this fall meant something more serious."

"Don't think it was the fall, David. The whole experience has him confused, considering the few statements he uttered aloud. I would suggest we call a doctor. Shock trauma can be serious."

"Would hate to explain this to a doctor; we'd all sound nuts." David got up to turn the thermostat higher. Just the thought of Barrett in a cold, tin box had him shivering again.

"We'll see how he fares through the night. At least Kevin seems able to help. He's got a soft heart that man."

"He came to Barrett's rescue fast enough. Good thing one of us can play mother."

"Thanks for the drink, LaCoix. I'll check on those two again, and make sure maintenance is working on Barrett's trailer. Are you okay for food, or do you want something brought over?" Jess slowly got up and donned his rain jacket. Strong as steel and built like a grizzly, the man simply took over without hesitation when things needed doing. His calm exterior reflected his serene heart and mind.

"Have something in the fridge, thanks. Don't want to be distracted tonight. I'd like to wallow in the feeling we experienced today; it felt too good to ignore the residual affect it leaves on a man."

"Glad you felt it, David: the ultimate serenity."

"Get out of here, before you get me into the lotus position and shaving my head." David missed the attempted pillow toss, while Jess laughed and exited the trailer. Flash bulbs blazed like shots from a silencer, while the clicking of cameras echoed like a barrage of gunfire ricocheting through the metal boxes that made up the camp.

Sighing heavily, David rose to bolt the door. Back to his drink, he could contemplate Susan's suggestion in peace. Living full-time with his daughter beckoned him, seriously considering the possibility; but anger and hostility were not good for a child, and what of Rebecca? Calling off the already disturbing engagement would create more havoc for him publicly and personally; hatred would come from all sides. His only relief came from knowing Holly loved him on their special days, and seemed happy and content with her mother. Susan, however, had him wondering. Did he ever love her as a person, or as a prize won for being David LaCoix? Another fancy charm on his bracelet, it allowed her into the realm of movie stars, parties, and cameras. They argued over their lifestyle incessantly, since David preferred intimate gatherings at home with friends, rather than warily expecting a sudden camera or microphone jammed up his nose. He hated it; Susan loved it. Then again, there he was, back at the heavy partying with his *bad boy* friends and the lovely

Rebecca on his arm. The young, sexy starlet added an even prettier gemstone to his overly encumbered wristband.

His mind turned to the enchantress. He closed his eyes, leaned back into the softest chair allotted him, and relived the understanding rapport that made his head spin. Whoever or whatever, she exuded an indescribable attractiveness in a surreal sense. No perfect features, but her expression illuminated an undeniable charm and beauty, much like Ted. At that odd thought, David remembered the unspoken words to allow Barrett to steal this picture. Snickering slyly, he knew the man already shone the brightest amongst the cast; the dailies proved that one fact.

His mind certainly not at rest this night, he waged a back and forth battle with no winners. First Susan and he shuddered in shame and guilt. Next, Holly popped into his head; and a laughing smile spread across his face with the joy she always captured within him. The luscious, young Rebecca, who made him feel young and virile, lingered in his mind, not knowing just what to think, tending to rattle his Spirit instead of cheering him up. The Fey--then the lovely lady Fey--the mysterious woman unveiled herself; and he glowed internally, feeling her vibrate through him. If he did not know better, he felt himself being fondled; he was that aroused. He shook it off, hoping the reverberating sensation came from a revelation like the one Jess had in the car. Barrett's image reappeared, bringing other intriguing thoughts, causing David to ponder on what had transpired between the young man and the woman, and why she intentionally dropped him. He loved mysteries, but this one seemed too obscure to be solvable, considering he barely knew Ted except for the rumors.

A Christian Fundamentalist, Barrett participated in several male groups centered on the family, with strict adherence to the wife remaining at home, maintaining the household, and raising children. The fanatical sect was not popular, with their pontification of literally interpreted beliefs and continual barrage of irritating dogma. From one of the conversations, which David had overheard, the young man's faith remained the true one, and all others were held in contempt and damnation. Jess had a field day with Ted, considering his very opposite eastern philosophies and tranquil meditative states. Mr. Carmichael enjoyed their *tête-à-tête* encounters, watching the man reach zero tolerance, and depart the area with the older man laughing at him. Unkind in Barrett's sad eyes, but a fascinating debate for Jess, they left no middle ground to accept even a minor change in beliefs. With no right or wrong answers, a huge wall prevented Ted from discussing it further. Religion appeared serious business to someone so young.

David's mind spun out of control, returning to Susan and Rebecca. After several hours of his head leaping between here and there, he stood up, wobbled a bit, and tried to find something edible. While dinner warmed, his fifth or was it his sixth bourbon splashed into a glass. He set it back down. *'Enough of that, Mr. LaCoix,'* he thought to himself. The only thing he did that night was to decide not to decide, until he had a chance to talk to both women face-to-face. Ignoring the grisly substance called a microwave dinner, he went to bed. The liquor put him into a fitful sleep of dreams and images all intermingled. He saw and felt them all: the bewitching touch of understanding from the apparition's hand, the tension he sensed in Barrett's arm, the sweetness of his little girl's embrace, the anxious moments during Susan's verbal battles, and then the brashness of Rebecca's sexual passion.

David LaCoix's life had changed with the intimacy of a slender, white hand; his new journey had begun; while a raven-haired seductress, in burgundy velvet, rubbed her ringed fingers together in the darkness, warming up with what might be. The devilishly handsome blond she knew and had left alone too long. She picked up her drink and took a contemplative sip of her ambrosia, while stroking the cool metal stem of the goblet. Theodore Barrett, the wild card, had been brainwashed from birth. Left completely alone in an overpopulated world, he came close to slipping through the cracks; they had almost lost him. The woman sighed heavily; and the Cosmos waited tentatively.

CHAPTER 5

His head hurt, as if beaten by a sledgehammer. Unfortunately, he knew why. He had not drunk that much in years, and David was furious with himself. After such a wonderful experience the day before, he had allowed himself to be seduced by the intoxication of bourbon. With no one else to blame, he rubbed his temples and swore aloud for his idiocy. He slowly rolled over, opened his eyes to squint into the torturous brightness, and glanced at his watch. Nine o'clock: he was late, very late. Picking up his cellular, he quickly rang Richard to apologize, only to find they had the day off, but to stay close for news.

Curious, David climbed out of his warm bed, shaved, showered, dressed, and cautiously stepped out of his door. The flash bulbs were gone, replaced by a peaceful calm over the entire area. Sensing the same radiant feeling on meeting the Fey, his seldom seen smile returned. He pulled out a cigarette to enjoy the calming effect of nicotine, while watching the sunshine dry the impassable bog. The desert floor had turned into an ugly mess; and he never failed to sink into the mire on stepping off the temporary boarded walkway. The morning heat, of a southern autumn day, felt good on his face; he stretched out to greet the Arizona sun. He dragged back on his smoke, thinking about coffee. What he smelled cooking, along with his hunger, drove him onward to the caterer's trailer, believing food would cure his headache and stop the pain surging through his ulcers. He stopped short, turned, and headed back to his own shelter; too many people with too many questions, he shut the door behind him.

An ice cream truck seemed to be passing through his living quarters every fifteen minutes; and he quickly looked at the incoming number suspiciously. With some relief, he flipped open the demon machine to greet Jess; coffee, Carmichael, and Carter were on their way. The first two were appreciated; the third was not. David slumped into a chair and dialed a happier number while he waited. He called Holly every morning to wish her a sunshiny day, reassuring both father and daughter a good start with a giggle.

Jess and Richard walked in on his second call to his father. Sentimentality raced through him, hearing his old man's voice, comforting in its familiarity. Once so easy to talk to his dad, so long ago, but a half a lifetime of exchanging occasional polite, dishonest greetings always ended in selfish sadness. Things changed after both men feared for the life of the other. Today, David wanted to cry, listening to the frail, tired voice hesitantly expressing concern for his only child's near catastrophe. Choking up, he asked his father the same question. A minor attack, his old man had returned home within hours, currently testing a new diet bestowed upon him by worried doctors. He would be fine. David lingered with the last of his cigarette smoke in his lungs, slowly releasing the call and the blue-gray cloud, along with the weight on his overburdened heart. Perhaps a few fences could be mended; and one small family of three rebuilt.

"Thanks for the day off, Carter. What did we do to deserve this?" David did not look at the troublesome director while downing a half glass of thick, creamy milk, to ease the uprising in his stomach.

"You damn near died: all five of you! I lost ten years off my life yesterday, thanks to you, and now another ten this morning."

"You're not that old, Richard. What's happened?" David remained quiet, listening to the agitated voice expressing concern by blaming the actors for a natural occurrence, or a supernatural one. It gave him cause to ponder. His mind came back to the ranting of a very upset man.

"You tell him, Carmichael. I'm too angry to talk." The young director did look a little red faced; his frustration certainly showed with the pacing and repeated slamming of his right fist into his left palm.

"Barrett's packing and departing the picture."

"He's what? Has he left yet?" The sullen calmness switched instantly to mounting anger.

"No, he left Kevin's place at dawn, knocked on Richard's door, told him the blessed news, slipped quietly back into his trailer, and barricaded the door from inside." Nothing bothered Jess, believing everything took care of itself at the appropriate time. You had to wait and watch what unfolded.

"Shit, he can't do this. No way he's pulling a stunt like this." David remembered the woman's prediction, and his ire peaked. He would not allow Barrett to destroy the picture, along with a rising career. Shocked over his sudden concern for someone he barely knew, it had to be the words of the strange apparition, and his wish for his own star in cement. He bit his lip at the selfish thought, considering this may be part of her suggestion to turn his life around. Whatever he felt or desired hinged on the pivotal role of Barrett making this movie.

"We've tried talking to him, but the son-of-a-bitch just keeps requesting a car and someone to drive him to Tucson for a flight back to San Diego. On top of that, a new producer is on his way, one whom purchased the rights to the film and all the contracts. If Barrett walks, he'll be taking a huge new backer with him, leaving me with the clean up." While wearing down a path in the carpet, Richard visualized his work melting in the flames of a garbage dumpster.

David's new guide came to the fore, forcing him to do something. He could hear her voice urging him on. Barrett's ticket to stardom could wash away in a desperate moment with only regret to follow. Too late, to recast the part, it would end up in lawyers' hands, to dwindle away the production money, leaving everyone else to dangle in the breeze. The news of a new buyer, backer, and producer, appearing out of nowhere, seemed a touch bizarre, but it could mean a better film with more guts. Barrett had to come into line.

"Damn and I was just beginning to like him." The lanky blond got up, his cigarettes and coffee in hand, and headed out from his trailer, leaving Jess and Richard to ponder a young innocent matching wit with a ferocious lion. If anyone could get to Barrett, it was David LaCoix. The kid did not hide the fact he idolized the tarnished star, to the point of stumbling over lines in every scene they made together. David's adeptness at his craft, however, allowed him to take mistaken lines thrown at him and react to them as if scripted. The spontaneous affect made Barrett's nervous performance that much better.

LaCoix remained steady, cogitating on what to say. How could he make someone, who he did not know, do something he did not want to do? Not his forte, he had no sympathy for temperamental baby stars; his cigarette was just not long enough. He pulled out another, stopped to light it, and with those long legs, strode over to Barrett's trailer. Puffing on an adult's needed pacifier, he stopped at the door to convince himself he could do it. Not the first time someone had bolted from a picture; he had tried it himself once. The departure of his co-star would have been a relief at the start of filming; however, the raven-haired enchantress had turned that around. With no need for jealous rivalry, it would feel good to see the earnest young man (well, not as young as he thought) get his chance. Maybe he still had part of his Soul after all, and he grinned earnestly as he stepped up to the white metal door. There was no answer to his first tap, or to his second. He sucked in his breath, and with his best acting ability, lowered his voice. Sounding non-threatening, non-judgmental, non-patronizing, and certainly non-disciplinarian, he quietly called through the locked barrier, "Ted, it's LaCoix. Let me in."

"Go away." A muffled sound came through the door, only to re-ignite the flame outside.

"Throwing a promising career away is something to talk about." David waited, letting Ted think about it. He heard the bolt pull back, allowing him entry. Once inside, the door was immediately slammed and locked behind him, making the one headlining star feel like a hostage held for ransom; he was probably only worth a '59 Chevrolet convertible, intrinsically necessary for driving over a cliff. Ted turned his back to finish his telephone call, with a series of *yes dear, no dear, I'm trying*, and a *yes ma'am*; the last comment drew a wide-eyed glance not seen. An odd thing to say to your wife, LaCoix sent the remark back into those same recesses with his other problems he had to address.

"Sorry, my wife."

"Isn't it always?" There was a definite sigh in LaCoix's tone.

"You should know." There was a marked sarcasm in Barrett's utterance.

"Guess I should, but down to business. Why are you making a hasty retreat from this film, which promises to be your first step into notoriety?"

Taken aback at the confident statement coming from his idol, Ted stopped packing to turn around. With a frown and a questioning glare, he looked at David for the first time. "What makes you say that?"

"A little bird with curly, black feathers told me."

"I... I don't want to talk about it. It didn't happen. It... it was an illusion... a trick." Ted's voice grew higher and angrier, cracking at each word, sticking in his throat throughout the short tirade, and exposing a slight speech impediment. A hint of a corrected stutter emerged, something that undoubtedly took years to rectify, yet never revealing itself in a rehearsed line.

"It happened, Barrett--a miraculous illusion--if that's what it was. I feel very much alive today, remembering the comfort in her touch. Just stepping outside, the radiance is still there."

"Sorry, I didn't feel that splendid while waiting for gravity to pulverize me. She tried to kill me, you ass-hole."

"I've been wondering about that. None of us has revealed our secret conversation with her, keeping it locked away in a private place in order to remember the sensation. Something about your little head-chat with the woman was different. It certainly bothered her when you yelled out something about her being Satan, and that Christ would save you."

"It's none of your business. Jesus saved me from her treachery, that's all that counts. Now get lost, I'm out of here." The quick, jabbing attacks left no room for discussion.

A puzzle came into play, and nothing could deter David from finding out what lay behind the fury and rapid departure. "Would you please stop packing, and, if possible, think. What will the ramifications be, if you run away? The picture will die just when new money has suddenly dropped from the sky. Do you want that? Sounds pretty selfish for someone whose Christ just saved him. Can't you see further than yourself, Ted? After our short talk yesterday, I expected you to have enjoyed the adventure, particularly the fall."

"A fall? Is that what you call attempted murder? Shit. My leaving goes deeper than your drugged brain can deal with, LaCoix; and this superficial picture of life, and my success or lack of it, has no meaning in the grand scheme of things." No longer neatly folding his clothes, to place them into the large backpack, Ted hurled what remained across the room, only to squash them tightly into the soft container.

"What the hell does that mean?" At this stage, David refused to start a debate, which would ultimately turn into an argument over drugs and alcohol.

"My wife and I are meeting my parents at the Retreat. I need to refocus after what happened yesterday." Finished packing, Ted slammed down the diet soda he had been sipping, and slumped into a chair looking dejected, defeated, miserable, angry, and scared. His blue eyes magnified every emotion the man felt.

"You told your wife? Are you nuts? We all had an agreement. Christ, Barrett, where is your head?" Now David's ire raised several notches. A vow of secrecy had been understood, not to share the phantasmagoric happenstance outside the confines of the five.

"Of course I told her. That's how marriages work, but you don't know much about that."

David's eyes widened at the uncharacteristic snarl from Barrett. A snapping turtle was not a creature he wished to fight. He pulled out a cigarette and clicked down hard on the silver engraved lighter. A large flame burst off the wick, lighting every inch of his tense face, nearly singeing his eyebrows. He merely squinted through the rising smoke, considering his next move. He did not have one.

"Put that thing out. Didn't you read the sign on the door? Of course not, your fist was covering it while you hammered on it."

"Go to hell. Now you're overreacting to my knocking on the door. You're evacuating the premises; I'll do as I damn well please." David could do a decent imitation of the infamous amphibian himself.

"Seems that's what you do best."

David looked at the younger man from beneath his golden lashes, and glared menacingly at him; green angry eyes met smoldering blue ones. He had to dismiss his hurt feelings and change strategy. "Ted, my boy, you are acting like a jackass. Why? Who came up with the idea of hiding out at a retreat, and what kind of retreat?"

"My mother, then Karen made the arrangements. It belongs to my church; and why is that any concern of yours?"

"Your wife, now your mother? Fuck. What do they know about contracts, legal and professional ethics, responsibility to commitment, and the fact you won't have a nickel to your goddamn name after the lawyers get through with you? Are they acting as your agents now?"

"I've been taught those traits all my life, but this is different. It's better to vanquish the devil and live in poverty, than to prostitute yourself for material gain." Ted sat back in the chair, arms crossed over his chest in confident defiance.

Sitting down, while taking a stubborn stance, made Barrett an easy target; David jumped at the advantage given him. He moved forward to tower over the smaller man, and then very slowly and deliberately leaned down, issuing a low growl in his throat, while grasping either arm of the chair with his hands. Ted visibly squirmed in discomfort. "Now, aren't we just on our high-horse and spouting shit from the wrong end. So, the rest of us are now whores. Thank you so much for that insight. The others will be pleased to hear our profession has been downgraded. Listen up, you: the number of people affected by your little spat, with your so-called devil, is immense and hurtful. Tell me this, Mr. Barrett, out of curiosity, when she lifted you off your horse and carried you into the air, what did she feel like?" The menacing-looking actor used an abrupt and bizarre question that only an abstraction could answer; making people reverse course in thinking usually worked to settle things down.

"I don't remember, and get out of my face! Take a dozen paces backward and shut the door behind you. If you recall, she dropped me from two-hundred feet. Memory fails a man when the ground is coming to meet you at a speed you can't comprehend. The dumb blond title sure fits you, LaCoix."

"I refuse to continue this debate, if you resort to name-calling. Shame on you for the inability to be a forgiving Christian. Come on, Barrett, I touched her hand, never before feeling that kind of spirit surge through me. Tell me what it was like. Think back to her first touch." David calmed himself, and sat down in front of his attacker who immediately leaned forward to study his exposed toes in his sandals.

"Nothing; it felt like nothing. I can't remember."

"It felt consoling and understanding, until you pissed her off." David maintained his glare, as Ted tried shrinking into the smallest of earth's creatures, to get away from the green-eyed monster's penetrating heat. Beyond thinking straight, he could not control his words or actions.

"She's a follower of the Devil, maybe even Satan herself!"

"Bullshit. Don't see you suffering from any burn marks. You're making this up in your head, and you're scared. Although a weird experience for all of us, the only one running away is you. Why?"

"She was testing me; and I don't know if I passed or failed. Fuck, what am I supposed to say? I am scared, because judgment came down on everything I deem holy. She taunted me, asking questions I had no answers for; at least not the ones she wanted. I forgot my faith, David. Can't you understand the significance of that? I'm confused and just want to go home." Blue eyes fearfully peeked out, from under thick, dark lashes, into fiery green ones. The pain exposed in those sapphire crystals melted a selfish heart; the flame extinguished. LaCoix had no idea how to console another man, and avoided uncomfortable crying scenes if he could. Hearing Ted take in a deep breath, and seeing him rub his face, quelled his fears. There would be no tears as Barrett stoically sucked it back.

"Come on, man, I'm asking you to stay. You need this picture. If you won't do it for yourself, look out the window at the people who will be out of work and out of pocket."

Bewildered and still in shock, Ted returned to the obsessive habit of looking down at his shuffling feet. It gave him time to pause when unsure of how to react. His quiet, timid voice uttered shakily, "She felt warm and soft. As we went up, I could feel her strength; it felt good; it really did; but she frightened me. God, David, I've never been that terrified." The young actor could not look up, in fear of breaking down. The magical event, which the other four had reveled in, was killing the fifth mentally. Besides his family wanting him home, something else seemed astir. Ted felt like a tug-of-war rope stretched to the maximum.

"It's okay to be fearful of the unknown. It's part of the rush in life, giving us the spark to survive. But why this woman, Ted?"

"I don't know. I didn't know what she wanted from me."

"Maybe nothing." David languidly stood up, stretched, and pondered the peace spread before him outside the window, as he came to his own realizations. Perhaps they all shared a grand illusion that meant nothing.

"After she released me, and I landed on the ground, she said I'd be the actor I've always wanted to be. Do you think I can believe her?" A look upward sadly questioned the green eyes; David said nothing. The conversation abruptly halted when a phone went off, which Ted rudely answered instead of letting the machine take the message. After another similar one-sided discussion of *yes* and *no* answers, and a farewell of *Go with Christ*, the young man hung up.

The rude action lit a match under the tall stick of dynamite, fusing that instant temper, rumored yet rarely displayed. "Do you act on everything your wife tells you, or was that your mother this time?" David's annoyance erupted when someone disrespectfully allowed a telephone call to take precedence over a business meeting, particularly with him. It wasted his time, and it was his turn in line. Both parties flared at the simple attack.

"My wife, and we're partners; something you should learn, after hearing yours caught you cavorting with your new babe. You make me sick; and I idolized you. You're the reason I did this picture, to learn from the master, even if he is a part-time drunk, gets his famous wild eyes from drugs, and treats women like whores, or is it the other way around, prostituting yourself for pleasure and for gain. After this bitch broke up your marriage, all you've done is complain about missing your little girl. By the time this latest brunette is finished taking you for a ride, you won't have enough money to put Holly through college. You won't have to worry though, because you'll have another, maybe a redhead on your arm, and she'll probably be younger than your daughter. Never took you for a fool, man, but that's what you are--an aging, arrogant fool--playing on Glitter Town's Carousel."

The anger intensified, jolting David to the bone. No one dared insult him in such a manner. He said nothing, feeling the steam bursting out of his ears. Listening to the truth, buried in illogical reasoning, was far too upsetting. He had never come to terms with his first divorce caused by his depravity, and now a second one. Turning sharply to look anywhere besides the insolence of one who knew nothing, he lit another cigarette and quietly departed the overly warm trailer, now fully functional. His attempt to sway Barrett had gone badly, and he walked away infuriated, depressed, and humiliated by his known usurper: a little twerp of an upstart. Seething through his clenched teeth, he kicked over a deck chair, sitting on the covered walkway, and stomped back to his own temporary quarters; his smoking cigarette never left his lips. He felt like a fire-breathing dragon, and now he looked like one.

LaCoix flung open his door, knocking the still pacing Carter off his feet, crashing him to the floor. He glared at the director who immediately rolled, leapt to his feet, and veered away from the taller man's reach. Heading straight for the bar, David grabbed a bottle, but a large hand covered his, staying his nerves and anger. With a heavy heart, he leaned back against the gentle man's chest. "Thanks Jess."

"No problem. Come, sit down, and eat what's left of your cold breakfast. I suppose he has your ulcer acting up, as well as your ire. I wish you'd consider seeing a doctor. There's a simple cure now, just by taking pills and a liquid for two weeks. You'd finally stop doubling over." Carmichael liked LaCoix, and he had seen him travel down many a dark road in the past. It would not happen again, especially one generated by some prima-donna spreading his wings not yet earned. He felt his friend's need, knowing the man welcomed his calming influence. David did, and he obediently sat down to pick at a piece of dry toast and the rest of his milk.

"I'm fine, Jess, and just to ease your worry, I'll see a doctor as soon as I'm home, wherever that is."

"Good, I'll text you the name of a good one, but it sounds like you're personal life is also aggravating your condition. Best do something about your lifestyle, LaCoix."

"You sound like... never mind... we'll discuss that later. For now, I just don't know how to deal with someone like Barrett. You know I'm useless with the rational part of life. He talks the talk, full of good and cheery thoughts, but he strikes like a goddamn viper when he's..." David pushed the plate away and slumped back in the chair, thinking of a way to describe the scene-stealer.

"...scared, confused, the nature of all creatures when cornered? Perhaps that's how Ted feels, reaching a junction as to what is right and proper. I assume you gave him something to contemplate. You're not exactly quiet and aloof when you have important matters to discuss."

"Didn't say anything that either of you wouldn't have tried. Same old shit. Putting people out of work, tangling up his friends with strict contracts, losing his respectability as a responsible actor, what else could I say?" David rubbed his face to erase the anger. Raking his hair out of his eyes helped ease the strained frown lines in his forehead.

"Nothing I can think of." Jess took a sip of his coffee, understanding completely.

"Okay you two, we have to think fast. David, I have to meet with this new producer in fifteen minutes. Is there any hope?" Carter settled down and started to think, desperate to come up with some way of delaying the situation until Barrett came around, if he ever did.

"All I can tell you, Richard, is that he's acting exactly the way Jess described, which I increased tenfold. Maybe releasing his anger toward me helped. Just don't know."

"Cut through your façade and hurt your pride, did he?" Jess chuckled lightly, amused that their staunch Christian co-star had goaded David into a guilt reaction.

"Sure as hell did, but he spoke the truth, which hurts even more. I have an idea that may buy us some time. Yell through his door that he'll have to make his own transportation arrangements, considering he no longer works on the project. It will take hours to get a rental car here from Tucson; and Barrett probably has no idea of our exact location. He'll be stuck here for the rest of the day. Have security keep their eyes on the cars, securing the keys, and have the trailer watched. Let him come in and out, but no escaping through a window. He may be acting like a jackass, but he's not stupid." David finally smirked with a crooked upturn to his lips; it felt good to foil a man making a major mistake.

"Didn't know you were so devious; I admire that in a man." Jess snickered, very pleased with the idea.

"Thanks, David; sounds like a plan. Security will be notified immediately." Richard appeared relieved, although other things lay in wait on his return to his office.

"Should be enough time to let him think it through, or get mad enough to talk to one of us, even if it is the temper tantrum of the century." A flash of his teeth indicated David's resolve.

"That's you, LaCoix, not Barrett." Jess laughed and whacked David on the shoulder, nearly toppling the slighter man off his chair.

"As you said, Jess, when a wild creature is cornered, the fangs come out. Well, this Leo is not backing down from an outraged baby mouse."

Richard left quickly; and Jess soon followed to take in the serenity of the day, which David had enjoyed earlier. The depressed blond wanted that feeling back, but Ted's remarks hurt deep and cut raw. Once an alcoholic and cocaine addict, he had them conquered until last night. It took him a long time, and a great deal of therapy, to rid himself of the Hollywood *bad boy* image. A small lapse of too much bourbon would not happen again; and drugs could not claim to be the source of his insanity filled trademark eyes; they were his alone, inherited from his mother.

Women--now that was an accurate statement--he had to admit it, considering the speed at which he fell in lust with Rebecca. David stepped directly into the muck, with only a wink on her part as an instant boost to his faltering ego. Typical Hollywood madness, falling in love with your co-star, he jumped in headfirst--the wrong head--to be witnessed by Susan who walked in on the mindless, sleazy, lickerish sex. Luckily, Holly had been behind her, missing the scorching moment. An unfortunate circumstance to have a judge as a father-in-law, divorce papers arrived later that day. End of a marriage--end of a love story-- Rebecca took him home as a trophy. He made himself sick thinking about it.

LaCoix did not want to be that man, so insecure he had to prove to be younger and more virile than his true years, by latching onto a beautiful, younger woman who used him to step up the ladder into the glittering lights that beckoned for cruder, more outrageous behavior, and spurred on by an undaunted press. Thinking more clearly, he realized that was exactly what Rebecca wanted--career advancement--and what better way than on the arm, and in bed, with someone who supposedly had some notoriety in the industry. He remembered a small piece of his own past, and now felt nauseously ill, mortally wounded with the truth. They played each other very effectively: David wanting Rebecca's young body and her beautiful presence beside him to make him look good; and in return, she received offers because of her new connection. For a real kick in the guts, her career prospects deemed more lucrative than his did. He could probably hold onto her for maybe a year.

LaCoix and his friends seemed unable to grasp the concept that they lived in a fantasy world of users and abusers. They all played the same insidious game on Ted's *Glitter Town Carousel*; the perfect term for the musical-ride that they clung to, but who actually enjoyed it? One could not say, even if they knew. David's practical side kicked in, seeing how bewitching the entire industry beckoned the bright, innocent eyes, and even the ones who knew better, now requiring reading glasses. It was easy to be caught in its spell; fame made you feel immortal. Fairy tales and riches, falling stars and overdoses, the latter appeared the commonest way to jump off the whirling horses permanently. Living and working, in a normal fashion, proved irreconcilable in their miniscule, inbred world. At a certain level of notoriety, what you did not have or desired, someone could and would provide for you.

David lay on his stomach on the couch, his head resting against his crossed arms, and his mind going over the night before. Susan wanted him back; Rebecca waited for him; and today he did not want either woman. With a deep sigh of despair, he exhaled into his pillow, imagining himself as an old man with a cute kitten on his arm; while Holly, now fully grown with a life of her own, frowned and scowled at him. David LaCoix had lost; Hollywood had won. He would not become that man; he would not.

One tap on the clanking metal, he yelled *Enter* without moving his position. He did not care who stepped across his threshold. Being caught in his own misery made him vulnerable, he cared little at that moment. Wallowing--he loved to wallow occasionally in self-pity and self-loathing--even for a short while, and today he did feel bad. A raspy, apologetic voice interrupted his sulking.

"I'm sorry, David. I'm so sorry for what I said. I've never been so cruel to anyone in my life. God, forgive me."

"You spoke believing your accusations true, Ted; and God doesn't need to forgive you for that, so don't even ask him. It hurt, but I'll live." LaCoix sat up, his elbows on his knees, his chin resting in his cupped hands, and his eyes still closed.

"I'll fulfill my contract. Richard knows, but he's furious with me. I'm disgusted with myself for disrupting the serene day you mentioned. There is a calming presence out there. I felt it." The tremor of the voice, and the trivial chatter about the day, did not sound like Barrett, but David ignored the oddities while massaging some feeling back into his face.

"Yes, Ted, there is." LaCoix finally dropped his hands to face the man; he froze. "What the fucking hell?"

The young actor stepped back, tears welling up in his eyes; and David knew the man already regretted what he had done. His co-star looked a fright. The long extensions, worn as part of his character and meticulously woven throughout his short hair, had been hacked off, and not gently. A mess of jagged spikes, Ted appeared to have been attacked by an uncontrollable weedwhacker.

"Don't cry, man. Shit, don't cry. Just tell me what you did."

Barrett took in a deep breath and remained in control. "I don't cry. What do you take me for? I was so angry with myself, and my phone just kept ringing and ringing. My mother insisted I hurry and leave, and then Karen, and... Then I knew, in my heart and head, I couldn't leave... you... you were right about hurting everyone. I rang Richard immediately, and then... Christ, David, I picked up a knife and started sawing off my hair. I don't know when insanity hit, or even what I did until... oh, man, they'll never be able to fix it. I've really screwed up." Ted had his hands in his hair; LaCoix recognized the frenzy building.

"They'll make it right; it's their job." David got up to take a closer look at the catastrophe, and felt sick to his stomach for the distraught actor. He stopped, hearing a small whimper accompanied by a desperate sigh.

"My life is as fucked up as yours, and I keep hearing the lady's voice. I don't know what to think or do. Someone else controls my life. Thirty years old, and I'm still caged." A heavier sigh escaped; the control faltered with tears spilling down a face that did not move or wrinkle up. The stunning, dark-blue eyes, awash with utter despair, had LaCoix hypnotized. He almost hit the floor with the final defeated call for help. "Why did you let go of my arm? Why?"

The older actor gaped at Ted in astonishment, reflecting on those last words. He saw one of his boys falling apart in a crisis, and he hurt for this lost Spirit. Paternal instinct, what little he had, took over. Without hesitation, he put his arms around the traumatized man, to allow tormented tears soak into his T-shirt. Ted leaned into him, but did not hold on; David was thankful for an unwanted bonding. After the shaking subsided, the concerned blond pushed the mess of a man away, steadied him gently, walked him slowly to the couch, and helped him lie down under a warm cover. Nothing was said; nothing had to be said.

David took a seat, next to the sofa, and leaned forward to stare down at the fallen creature. "I heard your request to hang on, Ted, but she forced me to let go. I couldn't help you."

"You were my last earth-bound contact. I thought it was the end. Sorry, I shouldn't have asked such a stupid question."

"It's okay. I just don't understand why you didn't have the same pleasurable experience as the rest of us. Nevertheless, today is a happier day, and you made the right decision to finish the picture. Have you cancelled your plans with your family?"

"Not yet. I can't pick up the phone." Hands started pulling at the blanket to cover half his face, only to expose those peculiar blue orbs that forced you into their depths.

"Do they scare you that much?" David gently reacted to the gesture, pulling back the cover to hear the man.

"No, it's just that I've never disobeyed them before."

"What kind of power do they hold over you? I can understand the disappointment thing, story of my life, but disobedience. You're not a child." This came as a stunning revelation to David as to the psyche of the next superstar. Besides being a ray of sunshine to the world, and a viper when cornered, Barrett was shy, emotional, and chronically depressed, if David's assumptions were correct. From experience, you learned to put on a show to ease everyone else's worry, but it did not stop your own downward spiral.

"Not in their eyes. They've never wanted me to be an actor. It's a sinful profession, filled with unmentionable evil. I curse too much, I take the Lord's name in vain, I sometimes drink, all because I'm surrounded by it, but that's just an excuse. I'm living a lie, but don't know what else to do." Ted's eyes lowered to look at where his toes should be. The sadness of a defeated man, and a lonely one, emerged.

"What about your wife? She married you, knowing what you had chosen for a career. How can they be making demands on you now? You've been in the business since you were a kid. My God, man, you couldn't help but pick up the vernacular. Profanity goes with the dialogue of every conversation you have in this business."

"The church arranged my marriage, and they thought I'd grow out of my infatuation with the theatre, but I never did."

"An arranged marriage! Holy shit!" David fell back in his chair and wondered if he wanted to hear the rest of this overwhelming saga. The fact came out so easily, his head almost spun around at the thought of the archaic institution of selective pairings, similar to finding the right stallion for your brood mare. It made him cringe, not to mention sick, and his ulcer burned.

"It's our way; and I do love Karen. I think I do, but I love acting more. It's the only time I feel like me."

"I think you've been acting your whole life, Barrett." Returning to a forward position, David tried to understand this man of contradictions.

"That's what she said."

"Who?"

"The lady... the Lady of the Rocks." Ted's shaking started again, forcing David to retrieve another blanket from his bedroom.

"Lovely name for our mysterious beauty."

"Seems appropriate considering. Thanks for the extra covers. Don't understand why I'm so cold and thirsty. I feel like shit." Ted snuggled in deeper, absorbing any warmth offered.

"You've been in shock since we met your *Lady of the Rocks*. I think we should call a doctor."

"No, don't do that." The abruptness in the voice stopped David immediately.

"Okay. Steady there, man. Have you eaten?"

"No, not hungry. Feel sick to my stomach. Could do with a drink."

David reached down and felt the cold, clammy forehead, a symptom of emotional trauma, not to mention the shivers, the nausea, and the thirst. "I'm going to call Jess to bring us some food. He knows a few things about first aid. Our enchantress really did a number on you. Still with me, Ted?" With no answer but the chattering of teeth, he quickly grabbed his cellular and dialed out. LaCoix issued a quiet alert to Carmichael who appeared before he snapped the handy device shut. The two older men went into action: rolling Ted onto his back, raising his feet, and bundling him up further. Heat billowed through the vents to help the shivers, while a few bites of non-salted crackers were eaten under protest. With no further argument, their patient dozed off, and the cold sweats seemed to subside. Neither man could tell if Ted had passed out or fallen asleep.

"Thanks for coming, Jess. I wasn't sure what to do."

"It's worse than last night. Rest is the best thing for him. He should be exhausted in this state."

"He's so nervous and agitated, yet he's been acting the happiest and cheeriest of us all, until yesterday. I can't keep up with his mood changes. Man, he's all over the place."

"Understandable. From the few words he said, yesterday's event put his Christianity into a tailspin. Hard on such a staunch believer. Strange how he looks at Christ as his savior, yet it doesn't seem to be giving him any peace. His psyche is in confusion."

"I thought I read something in those peculiar eyes. Maybe I'm learning something from you, old man." David teased, waiting to be decked or hugged. Jess just smiled, and the two men sat back in their chairs at the table, quietly talking while they left Ted to rest.

Finishing off something healthier than bourbon, the two old friends left the sleeping man-child for a leisurely stroll to enjoy the essence of a beautiful day. Happy to be out in the fresh air, they relaxed in the tranquility--no chatter, no clanking of garbage cans and dishes, no movement of heavy equipment--just quietly listening to nature sounds with a great deal of smiling. The rumor of Ted's departure now crushed; talk of the rockslide subsided; and no reporters lurked behind trailers or cacti. Positively blissful, they meandered their way around the temporary village and a little further into the desert landscape.

The warm air eased the tension of weary shoulders, and returned the land to its natural dry state. David's body embraced the heat as he stretched his arms to capture the sun's rays. Inhaling eucalyptus, cypress, cactus blooms, horses, and leather enticed his senses to waken. He loved this arid, desolate land, and wondered why he had never built a house in his natural desert homeland. A huge smile crossed his face with his first life-altering decision: he would live quietly, on his own, to learn whom David LaCoix was, to mend many broken fences, and to thrill in his new plans and attitude. A sudden surge of unexplainable joy swept through him, from head to toe, as the female voice, whispering in his head, approved.

He confided in Jess of his need for a drastic change, and what he intended to do. Walking back to their trailers, Carmichael could see in the bright, smiling face and dancing eyes that this may be LaCoix's most honest, sanest decision that the actor had ever made. It seemed, to the older man, his friend needed to get away from his seclusion in Beverly Hills, and to live a more realistic lifestyle. With broad grins of reflected sunlight, they made their way to where the bog had been. They came to a sudden halt: three magnificent horses stood patiently waiting in front of Carter's office. Both men took in a deep breath and held it, admiring the exquisite, unearthly creatures.

The horses stood quietly, all three similar in looks, but the middle steed posed impressively. He turned a perfectly proportioned head, with one glistening amber eye focused directly on David. Dark charcoal gray with hints of silver tips brushed through the animal's coat, while the mane and tail captured their imaginations and attention. Both curly, and so very, very long, the tail hung perfectly to rest on the ground, to be easily stepped on by the manicured hooves that shone lacquer black. A wind-tossed mane fell down the right side of its neck, cascading at an angle to the knee, at its longest point. With another gust of air, it blew the long forelock off the extraordinary face, while the delicate pink nose, with nostrils flaring, sniffed at the breeze that brought the scent of LaCoix to the wondrous creature. The horse seemed to recognize him; the blond-headed human felt it. A connection of profound understanding fused between man and beast, each sending powerful signals of admiration and reverence to the other. Green eyes caught the blink of an amber eye; and David suddenly entered *the knowing*. In a burst of excited energy, his revelation of partial comprehension increased his happiness one-hundredfold. *The knowing*--he heard it in his head--it was important and it must be remembered.

Filled with the magic of the day, and questions so deep they rattled him, David's future lay ahead with new goals, a new state of mind, and with the blink of a horse's eye, he knew his decisions were correct. A signal of approval, with a sacred word implanted--*the knowing*--he would be moving home, returning to live under his Arizona sky.

Turning away in a hypnotic state of wonderment, he bid Jess farewell and ventured back to see how his trailer guest had slept. He quietly opened the door to hear Ted fidgeting and talking in his sleep. Only uttering a jumble of *no* and *stop*, a whimper, and a whine, the young man suddenly sat bolt upright, causing David to jump back a step.

"You okay, Ted? Man, you could give a guy a coronary doing that." A hand covered a heart for effect; and LaCoix caught his breath while leaning heavily against the wall.

"Yeah, I think so. Where am I?" Confusion remained obvious, but the tone sounded relatively normal.

"My trailer. Do you always get nightmares? You talk and moan a great deal in your sleep." David hid his worried frown by heading over to make sure enough coffee remained for two.

"Can't get rid of them. I sleep alone most of the time, and not for great lengths. Did I say anything intelligible? What's happening?" Ted's hands went to his face to erase the last fragments of a frightening awakening.

David did a double take, but kept his mouth shut over what was none of his business. "Just incomprehensible words. It seems, Mr. Barrett, you are the quandary of the day, but you're sounding better. How about some coffee and fresh air? You're missing this beautiful day, and there's something outside you might like to see." David lied behind his actor's smile, watching Ted stagger over to the kitchen counter. Pity, for the still-shaken victim, overcame the taller man, and he gently steadied the trembling hand trying to grasp the coffee pot. "Here, let me do that. I think you're over the worst."

"The worst of what?"

"You went into shock a few hours ago. Don't you remember? I guess that's part of it. Jess helped, since I'm pathetic during a crisis."

"I can't remember anything, except... Ah, shit, I made an ass out of myself. Sorry, I can't remember ever losing it like that, not since I was about six." Ted looked away, his hands sweeping through the mess of what remained of his hair. Embarrassed at the remembered tears and the hatchet job, he stopped his urge to dash out the door.

"It's just between you and me. Panic happens to all us macho types on occasion. You've had a hell of a time this past day and a half. How are you honestly feeling: a little confused and out of focus?" David placed the hot mug in the shaking hands and held both firm, until Ted steadied himself enough to stop spillage.

"Exactly. Man, it seems like I'm looking down a long tunnel, not seeing or hearing what's happening around me. Thanks, coffee smells good."

"Things will slowly become clearer, given a little time to rest. We've all experienced emotional trauma at some stage in our lives, and we do manage to go on." Picking up his own refill, David tried to avoid looking at the other leading man by staring into the steam rising into his face. If another trigger shot hit Ted, the older actor was ill prepared to deal with a sudden attack.

"This isn't supposed to happen to me." A return to studying his feet and a waver in his quiet voice, the fragility of Ted's emotions easily surfaced for anyone's viewing.

"Why should you be so special?"

Barrett turned and looked at him with those big blue eyes full of sadness and answers that he could not reveal. His mouth opened to say something, but stopped short and shook his head.

David resisted pressing for more information and ushered Ted out the door. A little fresh air, the peaceful feeling, and something beautiful to look at may cheer up the stricken man. It did. Enthralled with the unusual horses, Ted connected immediately with the exquisite mare. Another bright, corrected Hollywood smile wrinkled up the once sad face, and he laughed. For David, it brought the chimes back, and he delighted at the sound. Everything seemed to be returning to normal, with the young man's pronouncement of returning to his trailer to unpack, to call Karen, and to cancel his mother's plans. David made the inquiry if he needed help; but Ted made the decision to take on the entire Barrett army himself. His smile changed to grim determination, but fear filled those eyes that could not get any wider. Wishing him luck, LaCoix watched the man leave to fight his demons via telephone.

Another cigarette, slipped out of its protective pouch, was placed between the infamous pouting lips. Leaning against the outside wall of his trailer, David contemplated his next move toward restructuring his life. A huge smile could not be hidden, as he expelled the smoke and watched it drift lazily on a hair-ruffling breeze. He had made a number of decisions, which he vowed to keep. His families, his future home, his relationship with Rebecca, and his new attitude toward life and work would fall into place naturally. Without a speck of doubt, and filled with relief and eagerness to start, David disappeared inside, straight to his secret telephone list. He mused to himself in his excitement; his bright countenance lighting up the luxury trailer.

Close by she hovered; those long slender hands rubbed together once more, feeling the joy of success. A hidden eavesdropper smiled down on her charges, musing over her latest title: *The Lady of the Rocks*. She felt a power shift, seeing new pathways open for each, and her heart filled with exhilaration at their starting markers. Her entrusted Spirits were coming to their own conclusions, with a whiff of a scent, a strange *knowing* glance, and a few secret tears.

CHAPTER 6

Settling at the built-in desk, David picked up his lifeline to the world, checked the eighteen messages left, and ignored them all. The important ones had been handled earlier. Happily, he scanned through his address book, full of famous names, and called a few acquaintances residing in Arizona. Reuniting with old friends sparked new interest and lively discussions, culminating in a small list of distinguished, knowledgeable realtors, and a bonus of scheduled meetings with a number of casting directors with whom he and his agent had lost contact. Things were looking up for David LaCoix, both in lifestyle and work possibilities.

After several hours, he completed his scribbling of copious notes regarding everything and everybody. He put his feet on the desk; his chair tilted backward; his arms supported the back of his head; and his smile helped the sun brighten the day. David had not felt this good in years, uncontrollably giddy in his excitement. A rap on his door warranted a welcoming command to enter.

The metal portal opened, without the usual squeak, and a breath of fresh air blew in, mingled with a remembered scent. David immediately reached forward to save the tiny yellow bits of notepaper that skittered across the desk and flew through the air. As he struggled with the mini-twister and the sticky notes, he heard it. First, the faint sounds of whispering on the unexpected wisp of wind, and then the chimes. He froze in his chair. Another sound rustled with the same little whirlwind--the sound of butterfly wings--thousands of them. David still had not reacted or asked who had entered. The sound of a female voice, soft and melodic, filled his thoughts with pleasant memories, until he realized words were spoken aloud and directed at him.

"Mr. LaCoix?"

David turned sharply to squint at a silhouetted figure. Difficult to discern who it may be, dressed from head to toe in black against the bright light of an early afternoon sun, he only sensed the identity of the figure. A lean, elongated shadow touched him, stretching harmlessly from the statuesque female standing in the threshold of his sanctuary. With a quick up and down look, he recognized a distinctive slouched, cowboy hat pulled down over unseen eyes, and covering the top of the dark, curly hair that hung passed the waist. Her curls matched the mane of the exquisite horse standing just outside. Silver loops dropped from her ears, flickering in the bright light, and casting prisms across the room. A rather revealing shirt, rolled up to the elbows, emphasized a vaguely familiar hand that reached out in greeting. The light breeze fluttered the black gossamer around her upper body, revealing the outline of the woman who stood quietly waiting. More sparkling silver buckled around her thin waist, hardly a necessary adornment to hold up the tight black denims, partially hidden under a pair of perfectly fitted chinks, fringed below the knee and up the side. They just covered the top of the high riding boots, trimmed down the side in the same fluttering thin strips. Butterfly wings were the sound they made on the disruptive breeze, rustling the fine bands of black suede to bedazzle the stunned actor. LaCoix was speechless.

"Have I interrupted you? I wanted to meet you personally, and to schedule a meeting with you and Mr. Barrett." Her voice floated, lyrically lingering in the air, filling the room with a haunting sweetness, again sending David adrift on a lilac scented cloud. The woman dropped her hand, not offended by the man's surprise, or lack of response to her gesture of a handshake.

"I'm sorry. You are?"

"Your new producer. We need to discuss a film that has gone terribly awry. May I come in?" The woman stepped forward and closed the door. Jumping to his feet, in the normal masculine response, dictated by society upon the entrance of a lady and the introduction thereof, David felt a little perplexed, recognizing the face but not the reality of the person. There were similarities, but as many differences. Aristocratic in demeanor, she radiated the same spirit and sensuality, the scent and the sound, and the feeling of tranquility that filled his awareness with subtle thoughts of nature's serenity. The same sense he had enjoyed all that morning returned, forgetting the short interlude with his roller-coaster riding co-star.

This face, in the true light of reality, appeared a little older, just as wise, but more determined and forthright. David shook his head, assuredly knowing that this could not be the same vision, although as attractive and equally seductive in her manner. The extended body of an El Greco painting, the face of unknown nationality, green eyes full of wisdom, and all that hair, which he wished to run his fingers threw, had David LaCoix falling instantly in love.

Mysterious women intrigued him, but they seemed unimpressed with his abundant, dangerous charms. He had never captured a heart of the intelligent, elegant, or sophisticated. Thinking with more clarity, he realized how plastic his two mannequin wives looked in comparison; and Rebecca had suddenly become toxic waste in his eyes, and as impossible to dump. Certainly beautiful, his fiancée now took on the look of a sexy, long-legged kitten, with dresses too short and a hooker's demeanor. With a sad sigh of his own conscience, he knew he rated no better. Standing so still, this unknown woman smiled at him with no judgment, seeming to understand. He startled out of his thoughts; the voice continued quietly speaking; and under the influence of the lyrical sound, he knew what his new future would hold. Change--David would change to attract the love who the other mysterious woman suggested he wait for--second best would never be an option.

"I would like a synopsis of how you see this picture as a critic, and how to make it more powerful. Could you ask Mr. Barrett to do the same? We could all meet tomorrow evening at eight o'clock, in your trailer, if you desire a lengthy intrusion."

David refocused on the amused eyes and cleared his throat to answer. "I'd enjoy the company, along with tackling the monumental task of helping rewrite the screenplay to coincide with what the writer, of the novel, had in mind. After reading the story several times, the subject matter seems far more intense than the drivel of the first script. The author had much to say; and we haven't even scratched the surface."

"I agree, Mr. LaCoix; the current script is a typical Hollywood travesty and an insult to the original author. What he went through, as a young man, altered his life; we mean to replicate his horror. I believe we can carry this movie to its more alluring and dramatic climax. It will take only a few scenes to correct, but they will be intense."

David laughed at the thought of the controversial story. It intrigued him because of the time setting, changing the modern history of the true story to a Western adventure. The scenario seemed a likely possibility happening in the ruthless American frontier, where law scattered in the dust of a desert outpost, and life meant only survival. "I don't know if we can go that far, but I'll jot down some notes."

"Could you tell your co-star of our plan? I doubt if the young man has read the original novel. I do hope he surprises us."

"It would surprise me as well, as the book would horrify him." After their last conversation,

David also questioned the likelihood of Ted reading such titillating and brutally frank literature.

"I need his feedback nonetheless. A lot will depend on his capabilities, and his willingness to do certain things." The woman in black searched deeply into his eyes, looking for something besides an answer about Barrett. David, uncharacteristically, looked down to avoid the penetrating stare.

"He has the talent, but doesn't know it yet. I'm certain you'll face rejection on just how much of his physical attributes he must display." LaCoix smiled up to meet a grin as wickedly mischievous as his own.

"I agree. A little incentive may help. Tomorrow evening then?"

"Fine, Ms... I'm sorry; did you tell me your name?"

"No. Good day, Mr. LaCoix." Leaving quickly, with David watching entranced, she joined her two anonymous companions. With a graceful flying motion, she leaped onto the back of the middle horse, to land like the feather he remembered drifting to ground the day before. The three loped away in a vision of manes and tails, tangling with the long hair of each rider, feathering in strands of black ribbon twisting in the wind. They disappeared into the mirage of quivering haze under a bright sun.

Wild with excitement, David finally received his hoped for screenplay. Retrieving his cigarette from the full ashtray, he took a long drag. Intoxicated by everything changing, David felt silly and stupid with renewed enthusiasm, to the point of laughing and giggling aloud. A tinkling of wind chimes, lingering on the breeze, calmed his Spirit into a peaceful state once more; and he wondered where the enchanting musical notes came from. He wanted to keep them forever near, to charm him whenever the melancholy hit. With his new beginning, he would vanquish his self-absorbed pity, never allowing the insidious feeling to hurt him again, and he continued to laugh and clap his hands together in unabashed delight.

Reality jarred him out of his thoughts. He had a great deal to do, although not fully comprehending what had happened. The excited actor rang Barrett: busy line. He then called Carter: out of range. Back to his main source of information--Carmichael--he finally received an answer. The excited blond rattled off his unusual encounter with someone who looked much like the mysterious apparition, along with the good news of a partial rewrite for the picture.

Jess responded in kind with the strange goings on at the location. Carter and crew were gone, with only the cast remaining, while a new crew busily packed things up to take to their new location. An unusual group, they said little, and never made eye contact. While these strangers continued with the move, the cast would have a few days off. Carmichael's day brightened further, hearing of the additional scenes. Being a truly gifted and well-trained, repertory-style actor, he fully recognized the injustice done to a film based on what a naïve young man would do as a result of a long-term hostage situation. The novel held a powerful message of someone coping under degrading, torturous circumstances.

"I'm glad the film will now incorporate your love of insane, psycho drama. Dangerous is your middle name," Jess laughed at the joy he heard on the other end of the line. It had been a long time, perhaps never, since his old friend abounded in such profound happiness.

"Think I would have done a better job than Tony? Too bad I'd just emerged into the light of day." David laughed, considering overlooked for the remake.

"Speaking of babies, how's Ted?"

"Better, I think. He left hours ago to explain things to his family, although he's not one for confrontation with the Barrett clan. I've been trying to reach him, but his call has been record-breaking in length."

"At least he's willing to stay. His hair was a shocker."

"Talk about a sudden attack of madness. I'm concerned about his call to his wife; she could change his mind. I've never seen a grown man, or met one who seems so..."

"...vulnerable and submissive?" Jess filled in David's sentiments.

"You have that right. Strange way to live, but I'm probably no better in a different way."

"Can't interfere with another man's choices, LaCoix; although, I have taken my best shot with you. By the way, I saw the dailies of yesterday's shoot, which almost culminated in our burial. The scene's dynamite, or perhaps I should use the terms powerful and ghostly. Best bit of technical work, or luck, I've seen in a long time. They're saying it will be the last scene. Instead of riding into the sunset, we'll be the only cowpokes ever to gallop away into the fog. Both men laughed, both men feeling the same experience of the day.

David grinned devilishly; a hint of madness increased the sparkle in his eyes, lighting up his entire face. He finished his conversation with Jess and disconnected the line. Richard Carter was gone; everything had changed; things grew more interesting and exciting as this extraordinary day raced by. The sun finally spread its last brilliance across the expanse of desert; and he took the time to take in a burst of its energy through his back window. The sunset was beautiful; and David LaCoix finished his picture-perfect afternoon deciding on finding a new home, a new lease on life, and a simpler way of just being. With a script to help rewrite, and this last touch of nature's ever-changing watercolor background, he could not be more willing to start. Blessing him with renewed vigor, the vanishing yellow disk blazed across his handsome features and turned his blond hair to gold. Was this a gift from Ted's *Lady of the Rocks*? He wondered and thanked her anyway.

Lingering for a moment, absorbing her words, which continued to haunt him, he suddenly dashed for the door. In his enthusiasm, he had forgotten his co-star, whom he had tried countless times to contact, only to ignore it as a tough afternoon for Ted to deal with the strange Barrett family. After an absurd amount of time, David became wary at another busy signal. Lighting a fresh cigarette on the run, he headed for Ted's trailer, to get him off the phone and to deal with what they had been hired to do: make a great feature film.

David banged hard on the door and yelled the occupant's name: no answer. The older man dreaded the thought of his co-star diving headfirst into an endless chasm of dementia. He turned the knob and found the door opened smoothly to the slightest pressure. Calling Barrett's name, he entered. Looking around the tidy accommodations, signs of life were noted: an open can of diet soda and a partially nibbled chocolate bar left on the counter.

"Okay, Barrett. Come out come out wherever you are?" David teased into the emptiness of a hollow sounding trailer. It made him chuckle, remembering his favorite game played with Holly. He expressed the glory of this day in his voice, smile, and contagious laughter. Heading down the narrow passage into the private areas, he found the bedroom door slightly ajar, enough space for a curious feline to sneak a peek. At the end of the bed, Ted sat motionless. The young man stared at his cellular, listening to the dial tone growing louder, until it started squealing in pain for release.

"Ted, turn off your phone. You're killing it."

"Shit, you scared me! Don't you knock?"

"I did. Sorry, but we have work to do, my boy."

"Stop calling me that. I hate it. You sound like my father." Ted's unwarranted anger lashed out at the one not responsible. Something was terribly wrong.

"I gather things didn't go well. What happened? Promise I won't call you whatever it was I said."

"Your boy. You say that every time we talk. I don't want to talk to you as if you're... Oh shit, I'm going to..."

After a long hesitation and no eye contact, David threw his cigarette out the window to turn quietly to face another installment of the sad epic of Barrett's life. Completely disgruntled at the change in Ted's mood and the unanswered questions, he tried again. "Do you want to start from the beginning, or at the cliffhanger from which you left me hanging?"

"I spoke to them all. They were unhappy with my decision to stay, but I got around my mother with the commitment thing."

"At least they seem to understand your situation. It's a start."

"Not really; I have to go home sometime." Such sadness and despair in the voice truly mystified David as to what this young man faced alone. He had never really cared about his fellow cast members, except his leading ladies whom were another matter, but this man had him engaged in a puzzle.

"And what of the home front?" David raised his eyebrows with a question to Barrett. The man continued to watch the tiny instrument in his hand, waiting for it to explode in his face.

"I... we're..." Ted jumped off the bed and headed for the bathroom, leaving David to listen to a man heaving up the little he had ingested that day. A ghostly creature reappeared, to sit down heavily on the bed. Elbows rested on shaky knees, and trembling hands hid swollen eyes.

"Now for the cliffhanger, I presume?" David sat down beside Ted, and although not physically in contact, he could certainly feel the tremor running through the smaller body.

"I thought I heard something in Karen's voice when they were deciding my future. She wanted to tell me when I got home, but with the arguing... Christ, what a mess." Ted took a deep breath and sat up a little straighter, letting his hands drop between his knees. He looked distant and perplexed. Carefully watching his co-star settling his stomach and his nervous quivering, LaCoix could only wait patiently, until Ted confessed, "David, I'm... I'm going to be... be a... Christ, I can't even say it... a father."

Before the older actor could give him a congratulatory slap on the back, Ted scurried back into the bathroom. Baffled, LaCoix shook his head and followed him. While Barrett hung over the toilet, he rinsed out a cool cloth, filled a glass with mouthwash, and waited. LaCoix had seen a lot in his life, but never such an overt reaction to becoming a parent. Not knowing Mrs. Barrett, he was grateful she did not see this display.

"Okay, Ted, let's get you on your feet. Now, rinse your mouth and look at me." The younger man turned to face him, obediently and as trusting as his five-year-old daughter. Closing his amazing eyes, he allowed David to wash the sickened, ashen face. This was not a happy new father-to-be. "Do you want to lie down, or do you think you can handle sitting for a while? I need to talk to you about the film, if you're up to it."

"Yeah, a comfortable chair would be fine. I'm feeling better, I think."

The three-time father could not be more thrilled at a friend having a baby. He remembered his happiness at the announcement of Holly's impending birth, although it did cause his first divorce and the alienation of his sons who had brought him the same joy when they occasionally grouped together. Melancholy swept through him for an agonizing instant. Reason dawned on him that his joy of having children only masked the giddiness as a male-stud reaction, which disappeared in a flash when the full implications became apparent. His free Spirit, of wanton behavior, destroyed his first family, as it did the second. He loved his children, but did he really want them? Shaking his head, he smiled inwardly, knowing to the depths of his being that his new life would change his relationships. His families would be reconciled in some manner; he would give it his best shot. His boys had turned into decent young men without him; perhaps Holly would also benefit with his absence. Becoming a father took no brains, but being a good parent was another matter. Barrett would have been better off without his domineering mother, a strange, idle thought that came to mind. He contemplated the young man who slumped in the chair, looking as if hit by a stun gun. Would Ted make a good father, with his emotions running white-water rapids, just below the surface, and his kayak constantly overturned? Barrett could easily drown in the responsibility of keeping upright.

"Congratulations, Ted; we should celebrate. We have a few things to raise our glasses to; but I think you need to talk about this pending blessed event. You're certainly unhappy about the news, my friend."

"Your friend? After everything I've said to you?"

"Only friends can get that mad at me, and get away with telling me the truth. Today has been especially exciting for me, with a newfound purpose. I'm starting over, Ted. You pushed me into action with your brutal comments I needed to hear. Now, with this new baby on the way, your life is going to change drastically as well." Maybe, with a little of his own enthusiasm, David could coax a smile on the sullen, boyish face.

"It's not the drastic change I wanted to make, particularly after making a serious, personal decision. Any hope of that coming to light is gone--*poof*--faster than a puff of your smoke. With a single statement, my life collapses into ruins. Shit, man, things seem decided for me before I can turn around. Guess I'm happy. I'm supposed to be. That's why we get married, to reproduce and carry on the human race for the Lord."

"That doesn't sound like a jubilant father." David desperately wanted to cut to the chase in this bizarre discussion, wanting to dig deeper into Ted's anxieties. He quietly refrained from hitting the man with insults to his unbending philosophy of life. This was not the time; and he was not the one to do it.

"You know my beliefs are strong enough to bind my marriage forever, and it has to be my future: a faithful husband, a good father, and a generous, obedient son. I no longer have a choice with a baby. It's the end of everything I dreamed about." Ted visibly attempted not to break down. More weight crushed those shoulders than a new family addition.

"There are always choices, Ted. So, you broke a rule today by staying. You say you love your wife, but do you honestly? Sounds like you were trying to convince yourself, but if you do love her, then why aren't you happy about this child? How can this affect your personal dreams?" David led him out of the bathroom into the sitting room. A little shaky, the young man maintained his balance.

"Never mind. I'm excited; and you're right. Just too many things are happening at once, and I'm losing it, man. Hell, I feel like I've been twisted into a knot and pulled inside out." Barrett switched the subject gracefully; and David smiled inwardly, recognizing a lie by the lack of eye contact and the nervous drumming of fingers on the arms of a chair his co-star occupied.

"Your hair may be an indication of your mood." David laughed and pulled a couple of beer bottles out of Ted's fridge.

"I'm already a basket case, and now a beer? That'll do wonders for my stomach."

"Always does for mine. It's the fizz and the foam. So are you going to tell me or not?"

"The thought of a baby was never an issue until it became a reality. We're supposed to have children, but I tried so hard to prevent it. Difficult to explain, LaCoix, I just know what's expected of me."

"Let me try. You were forced into a marriage by your parents and church to procreate, but you don't want children. You say you love your wife, but act as if you're afraid of her, sleeping alone and not in her arms. I'm assuming you didn't want to marry Karen, considering the thousands of women, on this planet, whom would gladly accept any carnal offering from you, even for the thrill of jumping your scrawny bones for one night. Every female on location is mesmerized by your good looks and sunny façade. Sorry, you're right; I am confused. What am I missing?"

"Just me, I guess."

David looked down into the astonishing eyes, becoming more familiar up close, and seeing the mist forming over them. The sorrow and despair no longer lurked in their depths, as the entire face strained with suppressed sadness. He and Jess had only presumed the possibility, but reality struck. "What do you want to do, Barrett? You said you came to a decision, which now can never be. Is it because of the baby?"

"An impossible dream never to come true. Enough said. Tell me why you're here. You were in a great mood when you came in. Sorry I spoiled it." Again, Ted flipped subjects, and left David dangling without an answer. This time he would let it pass.

"Nothing can ruin my happiness at the moment, although I'm worried about you."

"Really? Thought you didn't like me." Ted looked up in complete surprise. He really had no idea of what people thought of him. Socially inept at understanding body language and verbal innuendo, he watched the outside world go by in a blur through a tiny porthole from the confines of a family too tight and a church too repressive.

"Behind this disreputable façade, I do occasionally have a soft heart. We'll have to finish this conversation when you're feeling better and have come to terms with the idea. Now, for some different good news: the new producer wants our thoughts on how to make this film as explosive as the novel. Are you willing to take it further?"

Immediately on his feet, Ted ignored the overwhelming need to purge, and clapped his hands together. Enthusiasm could not be controlled; and a beam of sunshine radiated through his mesmerizing smile. "I'm ready! Oh, man, am I ready! Couldn't believe the minimalist final script, and my disappointment on receiving it. But, wow, this is great!"

"How far will you go to keep this film viable? It's full of eroticism."

"The love scenes and nudity? I've done it before, but not to great critiques for my performance, unfortunately. Sex is always simulated anyway, along with those horrible frontal patches they paste on you. Find it the most boring part of acting; it's my downfall. Can't even get enthused about it."

"I've always found love scenes the most fun, and the most arduous."

"You would, and look what it's cost you. Sorry, David, I didn't mean that, but you're one hell of an exhibitionist in your films, and crazy enough to try anything. You'll have to advise me on this, and stop me from giggling through the scenes, or fucking them up with the right groan in the wrong place. I've never played a convincing love scene in my career. I'll need a coach." Ted grinned shyly, imploring the more experienced actor for help.

David's relief bubbled over in his wicked grin, enjoying himself with his new friend who also appeared gloriously happy over a rewrite. Ted had returned to whatever normal meant for Theodore Barrett; while LaCoix drew comfort in arriving before the kid had done something far more hazardous with the knife. The younger man released his nightmare of the revelation of fatherhood, when his interest picked up and spun him around by his first love: acting.

"When do you want to start? We have a meeting with this woman at eight tomorrow night."

"Now seems perfect. Sounds like an interesting challenge. No one's ever asked for my opinion on a script before; and I sure don't feel like being alone thinking about... I still can't say it."

"We won't even talk about it. I like this happier side of you. Right then, my trailer in fifteen minutes. Grab some paper and a pen, your copy of the book, and the old script. I'll get some dinner from the caterers sent over. What would you like?"

"Maybe some spineless soup and crackers. Don't want to keep getting sick." Ted smiled broadly, to receive a quirky grin and a wink in return.

David exited, turning momentarily to watch his co-star search for supplies. It had been an odd, confusing conversation; and he wondered about the troubled actor's life. Certainly not one he wanted, but with luck, Ted may face a day that LaCoix was experiencing; a moment to turn your life around and make you feel good in every DNA molecule of your body. Tonight he would keep the anxious man working, until tired enough to fall asleep on his couch, where he could be watched over. He doubted Ted would last but a few hours after another devastating shock. Barrett teetered too close to the edge; David had been there more than once.

Only the beaming blond-haired actor, who headed for his trailer to order food, heard the sigh whispered on the early evening breeze. Chiming sounds filled his head, creating a twinge of embarrassment upon hearing a *'thank you'* for his selfless act of protecting his would-be rival.

The grateful woman's arms stretched out to carry breathless, loving kisses across the vast chasm of darkness to each of the awakening Spirits whom lay within her hands. For one, the change would be rapid; it made her heart beat faster. The blue-eyed man-child, however, needed cautious handling. His immaturity showed in the fragility of his psyche, so hidden from everyone. With a wistful smile, she looked out to scan her stars; the aristocratic Lady, in burgundy velvet, returned to her nightly watch. With a wave of her hand, she filled her window with a shroud of pastel colored clouds; the portal opened to all in need.

CHAPTER 7

David watched the sun break through the open door of his metal abode. Orange, red, and flashing gold filled the sky; and the former desert dweller remembered the heat that the brilliant hues bestowed; the blinding reflection already bounced off the hard, sand floor into his squinting eyes. He had not wanted yesterday to end, or the night blessed with the excitement created by that special day. The blissful state of a dream remained; and even a snort of cocaine could not match this natural high. The only man drugged that night slept fitfully on his couch, shivering nonstop under the many warm, spare blankets found in LaCoix's trailer.

A successful evening for David, he had brought a little laughter into another actor's troubled life. Chuckling through the parts of the book too explicit for conservative film-makng, they came up with plausible alternatives. Ted continued to surprise LaCoix with his eagerness to insert some of the controversial subject matter, rallying the older actor to recognize his usurper's creative intellect, quite the opposite of his *Peter Pan* persona that occasionally emerged. Troubled over the younger man, possibly changing his mind when shooting started, convinced David to watch him closely through the night. Even in a drug induced slumber, brought on by a mild sleeping pill secretly dissolved in a cup of hot sweet chocolate, the man whimpered and cried out.

Returning inside, LaCoix quietly closed the door, poured his third cup of the morning's hot brew, and stood looking down at the head of uneven spikes and tangled waves. Still in shock, Barrett had bravely fought off the symptoms, finally succumbing to his weariness with David's devious aid. The lead actor had quietly laid the fading figure out, taking off his sandals, and tucking him in snugly. Although the chills persisted, Ted had refused to change, from his Venice Beach, baggy garb, into something warmer, leaving David to believe his co-star would never grow up.

With another cigarette lit, he looked about the trailer, immediately calling housekeeping to restore order before their new employer arrived. For now, Ted could sleep his disturbing dreams, while David fastidiously placed their paperwork in order. The two men had done their job; and he felt a certain pride of accomplishment. A small moan returned his attention to the couch. The tossing body needed more sleep; and David kept still, to prevent startling his overnight guest.

The conversation of the previous afternoon continued to nag at him. Voluntary entrapment seemed the only description for Ted's predicament. David had spent his adult existence in confusion; he could relate to that; but this family's problems seemed worse than his own ridiculous situation. Letting his mind wander, the first thing that came to mind was abuse, physically and mentally, or worse, sexually. Sounding inappropriate for a person raised in a strict Fundamentalist Christian family, LaCoix believed the isolationist attitude of cults could cause mental problems, leaving a child a misfit in mainstream society, along with the guilt created if he stepped out of line, even accidentally. He could not presume anything, not knowing Ted's background, except for the few snippets mentioned in one of their sparring forays the day before. Barrett was not his main concern, however, and David turned his mind back to his own agenda. Before doing so, he used his own blanket, off his bed, to tuck around the young man, and quietly departed his quarters, carrying two cellular phones, a pen, and a pad of paper. Strolling over to partake in an early breakfast, under the warm morning glow, he happily found Ray, Kevin, and Jess, leisurely enjoying a meal outside the caterer's trailer.

"Hey, David, haven't seen you since our run in with the phantasmal, as well as the changes in the past two days. How's the kid?" Donaldson prattled on, while stuffing his face with bacon and eggs. The very tall man ate copious amounts of food, yet stayed slim and in fighting condition without lifting a finger. He had an envious metabolism.

"Morning all. Barrett is sleeping and needs to stay that way. I'm wondering if we should call a doctor. He had another wicked eye-opener yesterday."

"What now?" Carmichael slowly peeled a sacrificial orange, while leaning back and balancing on the back legs of his chair.

"He'll tell you when he's ready, but he sure has me confused. If he was Catholic or Jewish, I'd say he needs a priest or a rabbi, but I'm clueless about his religion, or whom to call."

"Ted's that bad?" Honest concern lay in the question posed by Ray Evans, emphasized by his deep forehead lines.

"Wait until you see his hair." Jess grinned, his eyes never leaving the luscious orange object to be ingested and enjoyed in all its sweetness. The thought of the bright sphere had the eldest of the group comparing the wondrous morsel to Barrett; a man who had built a thick, protective barrier to encase the sweet, fragile person lost inside. A whimsical orange-painted fence on first sight, it appeared cheerful and glorious. The second glance proved no gate existed to pass through, yet conversely, so easily smashed. Theodore Barrett shone like morning sunshine, with the only window into the sadness through those big blue eyes and his occasional displays of timidity. His contemplation on Barrett, and the man's continuing aversion to what happened, was interrupted by Evans frown and worry.

"I've been so busy writing, I haven't ventured out of my trailer since the rockslide, or whatever we experienced. So, Barrett's in worse shape; and no one has discovered any hint of what really happened." Ray had not seen the others, except Jess, since the appearance of the magical illusion and the wild ride back to their trailers. This early morning gathering was the first time a discussion opened on the mystery.

"Nope, not a thing. Drove to the scene of the crime and found nary a trace of what we witnessed. The landscape, the slide, everything about the place is different from what we saw; if we actually all remember the same thing." Jess slipped into his natural element, discussing the metaphysical and the mind's ability to perceive things differently than the projected norm.

"The event had to mean something. Did you all smell the overpowering aroma of lilacs?" Ray questioned, and nods of agreement came from the other three. "Okay, what about the figures in the high rocks? We all saw them, right?"

"I did," Kevin replied, pushing his plate away, satisfied with breakfast, and now fully prepared to discuss the sensations he had experienced and the impact of the phenomenon.

"And they shone under those robes, or am I totally crazy?" David's confidence grew, gratified to hear confirmation of what he instinctively knew.

"A light flickered with the slightest movement; I'd agree with that." Jess leaned forward, his elbows on the table, and his fingers twisting a coffee mug around and around. His reflection grew deeper with the unreality of it all.

"And then those sounds and the energy; I never want to forget the overwhelming sensation of harmony," Donaldson piped in with his most influential remembrance and wishful desire.

"I've spent most of my time attempting to describe that feeling of serenity, Kev, and then the woman! My God, I couldn't find words to describe the telepathic conversation we had."

"She was real, Ray. Her hand gripped solid, warm, and powerful. Sent shivers up my spine, it felt so..." David closed his eyes with a look of euphoric, satisfied bliss, and left Carmichael to finish.

"...Your mind is in the head of your dick, LaCoix." The big bear laughed, finishing the started sentence, while visualizing his friend entrancing a Fey. It would serve him right.

"Hey, it's true. Needed a smoke as soon as she let go." David's famous smile burst forth; four men laughed long and hard. They all experienced something--hearing, smelling, and remembering the same things--an immediate unburdening for each. "By the way, Ted has officially entitled her with a moniker: *The Lady of the Rocks*. He's terrified of her, and yet there you have it. Rather Christian oriented, and who uses the word lady these days?"

"Sounds like Barrett. I'm surprised he can even refer to her. I believe we'll never find out what we came away with individually. Perhaps, just a rare moment in time and space, beyond our comprehension, to someday be explained when least expected." Jess continued to lead them into a spiritual world, of which, the others had no understanding.

"Think it's already begun, Jess. My life has certainly changed; at least I'm trying to put things in order. Haven't felt this good in years; and it began with the touch of her hand. Man, it was extreme." David leaned forward and lit up for the benefit of his never-ending need for nicotine.

"One possible explanation: we were given a quick pass into another dimension, only to be witnessed but once. Unfortunately, it had quite the opposite effect on Barrett." Carmichael's worry about their youngest showed in the etched lines of his face.

Evans reaffirmed his opinion over the occurrence, wishing to ease everyone's concern. "There was probably a reason for that as well, Jess, if we take your philosophical stand on the matter. I'm curious about all our futures; and if wishes do come true." Ray finished the last of his coffee and set it on the table beside the cellular phones. One of the two suddenly went off. Not the sound of an ice cream truck, the ringer made all four men jump. Everyone seemed spooked with the subject matter discussed: ghost stories over breakfast.

"Barrett's phone: I didn't want anything to wake him, so I grabbed both cells. What's that sound it's making? It's worse than the shriek it makes when it's left on. Think I'll just take a few messages." David's eyes flashed mischievously; and a wicked grin crossed his face.

"Up to no good, LaCoix? I'm out of here. See you all later. By the way, I think it's a hymn." Ray headed out with Kevin to walk off their meals, leaving David and Jess staring at the phone.

"A hymn! That's just great. Now I feel like I'm defiling something. I'll probably be struck by lightning." David picked up the phone and glared at it, waiting to be burned on the spot.

"That was Zeus, not Ted's God. Go ahead. Maybe you'll find out something." Jess smiled back and leaned into David, enabling them both to listen to the conversation. Crazed green eyes rolled, wondering if Zeus and God were one in the same, as David pushed the talk button. "Hello."

"I'm sorry, is this not Theo's number?" An excited female voice, yet conversely demanding, rattled both men in its tone.

"Yes it is. He is unavailable at present. Can I give him a message?" David played at being very polite, not knowing what to say, or if he should give himself away.

"Who is this?" The voice became harsh, with a cutting cruelty. As actors, aware of the nuances of the human voice, Jess and David understood the anger in the question.

"Who are you to be asking?" A quick comeback, David met Jess' eyes for a nod of approval. The cadence of innocent questioning usually foiled a verbal attack.

"His wife. Now, who are you, and where is Theo?" Upset or angry--a hard call--Mrs. Barrett forced David's hand.

"This is David LaCoix, ma'am." His voice oozed kindness and quiet confidence.

"Oh, my, I am sorry for being so forward. My husband speaks highly of you." Jess turned away to stop himself from laughing at her honest surprise and awe-struck tone.

"How very kind of him; and it's a pleasure to meet you. Your husband worked late last night, and he's exhausted. He has a meeting this evening, which requires his complete attention. Unless it is extremely important, I would suggest we leave him to rest." David primed himself to see just how demanding this woman could be; unfortunately, his name got in the way.

"Of course, Mr. LaCoix. Is he feeling all right? Does he seem excited since yesterday afternoon?" Without giving anything away, Karen Barrett strove to learn of her husband's reaction to the news of the pregnancy. It had David wondering how Ted initially responded when first told. He certainly could not divulge the man's true emotions after the initial announcement.

"I don't know him well enough to judge. He seemed in good spirits while working last night." David did not lie; the two men did enjoy their task; and the older actor certainly did not know the person sleeping on his couch. Barrett remained a stranger to him; a paradox disguised in the form of a likable young man.

"Please ask him to call me when he awakes, if not an inconvenience?"

"I'd be happy to, but I wouldn't expect a call today. We're on a very tight schedule."

"When he can then. Wish him a lovely morning."

"I'll relay your message. You have a good day as well. Good-bye." David clicked the off button and turned to look at Jess. "So, what do you think? Sounded a tad overbearing at first."

"Your name pulled the proverbial rug out from under her. Face it, LaCoix; you scare the crap out of people." Jess laughed and slowly walked away, leaving David to write down the message and take care of his own business dealings and family contacts.

With morning rituals taken care of, and business handled with a number of new possibilities, David's face wrinkled up superciliously at the offer of reading new screenplay. Written by a well-known screenwriter of dramatic epics, this particular film promised characters with copious bouts of sparring and mentally challenging dialogue. Excitement raced through him, hoping for the opportunity to audition for the possible lead of the major production. At this stage in his career, such starring roles seldom crossed his desk.

David finally tackled all his messages quickly and politely. Several hours had passed since his last call to Rebecca. With six messages left on his intentionally switched-off phone, he knew the mood that would be steaming on the other end of the line. Premenstrual Syndrome never bothered his first wife, except for a few days of slight mood swings; Susan seemed to handle it medicinally, with little problem; but Rebecca became a flaming nightmare. They had known each other only a short time; but he clearly recognized an oncoming attack of nature's making, when hormones suddenly surged through the sexy, young body. What a relief it would be, he thought, to love someone who did not create hell in your life once a month. He prepared himself to endure at least three or four days of blistering conversations about nothing. Just the thought spoiled everything gained in the last few days. Out in the middle of his desert, he refused to be embarrassed by the hurtful remarks, which she may or may not retract with a teasing giggle a week later.

Barrett's phone rang only once the entire morning; and David mused to think how Ted's family networking must be kept well informed of his comings and goings with a single call. His mirth gave into a soft chuckle, remembering the startled voice of Karen Barrett when he introduced himself. Smugness evaporated quickly when he looked up to see the man in question bolt out of his trailer, hand over his mouth, and running for his own facilities. He spotted Jess in the man's path, and yelled for him to save the flying figure before he tripped in his panicked dash. Grabbing the phones and his pad of notes, he rushed over to help. Except for his children's welfare, this obligation of caring needed cultivating into his character. He arrived to hear the nauseating sound of Ted being violently sick, while Jess watched attentively from the bathroom door. Laying down his armful of electronics and paper, David motioned his old friend to come over. "Is this another sign of mental trauma: sick before dinner last evening, and on and off again all night? He needs a doctor."

"No, I don't!" Ted stepped out, bracing himself against the doorjamb, waiting for his head to stop spinning, or having it smash to the floor like a ripe melon.

"You look like hell, Ted--bed--now." Jess ordered sternly and headed toward the much smaller man.

"I feel half-past dead. I'm so cold my teeth are chattering."

"And you're dripping in sweat, still in shock from the day you won't talk about. If you don't want a doctor, David and I will have to do what we can."

"I'm okay, just need more sleep. What time is it? Why am I so cold?"

"Nearly noon and you're sick. How many times do we have to say it?" LaCoix walked over and felt the cold, damp forehead, while Jess supported the swaying body. "Do you have something warmer to wear; maybe a sweat suit or something to sleep in?" The blond's kind demeanor changed to impatience with the continuous denial.

"In the bottom drawer; but I just need more rest and I'll be fine."

"I think a warm shower would help," Jess suggested.

"No way. Just lay me down to die in peace." Near collapsing, the idea of standing in a shower, or fainting in a bath, did not compel Ted to do either.

"I'll help." The eldest extended a hand that was adamantly rejected.

"To do what: kill me or let me drown myself in a bath? I can do the latter alone, Mr. Carmichael." Ted tried to smile, but it quickly disappeared when his knees buckled. Prepared for the eventuality, the older man caught him before he hit the ground.

"Okay, son, but you don't know how ill you are. This is serious, Barrett. Did you find those clothes, David?"

"Think so. Are you sure, these are yours? They look big enough for Donaldson." LaCoix held up the navy sweatshirt, confirming it would fit any of the frontline of the Greenbay Packers.

"Hate tight clothes," Ted complained, not knowing what else to say, outnumbered by two much larger, healthier men; one he dared not refuse, while the other fussed over him like a frantic mother. Jess set him on the edge of the bed, steadying him with a massive hand on his shoulder.

"That's obvious in everything you wear. Strip out of those damp clothes, and that means everything." David turned toward the man, ready to rub him down with a towel to generate some body heat. With Jess' help, it would take seconds.

"I don't think so. Toss them on the bed, and I'll manage."

"Thought you said nude scenes didn't bother you." David hesitantly laughed, while Barrett glared at him.

"On stage, not manhandled!"

"Manhandled? Were we planning such a thing, Jess?" The tall blond smiled wickedly, receiving a huge toothy grin back from his mentor.

"Hadn't planned on it, but it could be arranged." Carmichael chuckled at the modesty, and bid his leave until Ted finished dressing.

"I'll grab a face cloth for you while you're changing. You are one stubborn jackass, Barrett. What woke you up? You should have slept for hours."

"Your fax machine; it wouldn't stop. What do you mean I should have slept for hours? I've told you before I don't sleep much." Ted managed to lift his head high enough to squint suspiciously at his idol.

"Slipped you a sleeping pill last night, to keep you from wearing a hole in my floor."

"You what! I'm not supposed to take drugs! You've contaminated me! How could you do that?" More torment streamed out, creating deep guilt in David with no idea why. Unlike taking care of one of his children, this time he had done an extremely poor job.

"You held it together last night, but I couldn't get you settled. If we weren't working, you paced or puked. I thought you needed a decent rest."

"We're not supposed to take medication; and I shouldn't be drinking beer either. Besides, you don't know a damn thing about me." Ted's ire flared, but very little fire remained.

"Guess I don't, and the deeds done. Who's going to find out? You really do need a doctor, or a therapist."

"No." The anger refused to abate, but the voice grew weaker. Barrett was truly upset about the innocent little sedative.

"Don't tell me your faith doesn't believe in doctors?" David did not receive an answer, but only a sad whisper.

"Christ will know."

"Sorry I slipped you a Mickey, but you needed sleep. Now I'm here to ensure you're well enough for our meeting tonight. Hurry up; I'll be right back. If your Christ wants to blame someone, I'll volunteer." David left Ted to peel off the sweat-drenched clothes, sticking to every part of him, and to fumble into fresh ones. Expediously, the blond actor joined Jess in the kitchenette and just shook his head in defeat. "What do we do? He's a mess."

"Once he's changed, we'll set him up like we did the day before. He should be extremely tired just from shock, and if you drugged him with something his system isn't used to, he'll be out for a while. You should be more careful, LaCoix; the pill could've killed him."

"Never thought about it. They're not even mine, but Holly's from her tonsillectomy. I don't know why I still carry them. One baby's pill shouldn't hurt him, and why can't he sleep if traumatized? He should have collapsed long before we started work last night."

"Probably kept moving to finish whatever work deemed so necessary. He's a very conscientious man. As for the drug, it may be the reason he's throwing everything up. What made him start this again, or hasn't he recovered from his first bout?" Two heads came together over the counter, trying to figure out the strange idiosyncrasies of someone they barely knew.

"Can't tell you, but he's been bombarded with earth shattering news from every direction."

The two older men walked in to find Ted curled in a ball on top of the bed. He shook violently, but still had not covered himself with a blanket. Ignoring possible ramifications, Jess simply hoisted him off the bed like a small child, much to the man's indignation, while David pulled back the sheets and blankets. With much arguing, but little struggle, they placed Ted in the same position: legs elevated on pillows, body tucked in with layers of woolen blankets, and the forehead wiped clean of sweat. Looking down at the ghostly face, all they saw were black rings framing exhausted blue eyes--those peculiar eyes--so beautiful, but not normal. They were large when opened wide, with irises filling the entire spheres. Startling to look at, those spectacular eyes took the entire cast and crew a few days to stop staring in wonder. Even more unusual, they were the color of dark, sparkling blue sapphires, fringed with long, thick, black lashes, bedazzling every female, along with many of the male members of the group. Ted never acknowledged a single look, remaining the same charming innocent throughout the shoot, until two days ago. Now fear seemed to rule Theodore Barrett's life.

"Feeling better, son?" Carmichael asked quietly, lost in the blue vision.

"Yeah, thanks. Just tired."

"Thanks Jess; I'll stay with him. We'll see you later."

The big bear departed with a questioning, bemused smile, unprepared for LaCoix to volunteer the tending of their failing new star.

"Okay, Barrett, anything else you need?"

"Yes... no... Nothing thanks."

"Sounds like one of those nothings that means something important. We're worried about you. Is there someone you can confide in: a minister or holy man of your faith? You're having a particularly difficult time. Wish you'd change your mind about a doctor."

"Can't do that. There isn't anyone. Thanks for asking."

"I thought you belonged to a fundamentalist church of some kind?"

"I do, but it's family based."

"That means you keep all your own secrets and your own council, unless you tell your parents. Sounds like a hard life to lead, unable to speak and share with an impartial individual. I know there are many things I've done, or thought of, which my family would not approve of. Even after all these years, they don't understand my actions; and I certainly can't share some of them. To tell you the truth, my old man and I have hardly exchanged two polite words to each other in over twenty years, until he had his minor heart attack over the rockslide. I hope to rectify the situation, and finally introduce my folks to their grandchildren."

"Wish I could do the complete opposite. There are elders I could talk to, but they would pass it on to my parents." Ted's melancholy statement, his bloodshot eyes, and the small quiver of a lower lip broke David's heart.

"You're tired, Barrett. We'll talk later, when you're feeling up to it." The leading man steered away from helping others in distress, preferring to be the focal point himself; and yet, he seemed automatically drawn to care for this person. The thought scared him.

"You'd talk to me?"

"What have we been doing?" Again, David's heart thumped at the sadness. Out of his element, the self-proclaimed arrogant bastard had no idea how to advise this man. It would normally throw him into a flash fire of fury, not understanding someone who could not help himself. Barrett appeared to have created the scenario. On seeing him curled in a ball, David concluded that Ted had waited for the desperate attention. Perhaps, Ted did not complain about his trailer problems, expecting someone to rescue him, or too embarrassed to ask. A weak voice woke him from his thoughts.

"Guess I've told you more than anyone else, except my brothers."

"Are they unhappy as well?" The words came out before David thought.

"Who said we weren't happy? How could you say that? We've been given every opportunity asked for; even some they disapproved of." Ted retaliated, the lip quivering even more.

"In the last two days, you've mentioned things that have bruised this stone cold heart. You're getting upset and should be sleeping, not talking to me." David added another cover and pulled it high around the thin neck. "Now, shut up, and I'll leave you to nap."

"Don't go."

"Pardon?"

"Why did I say that? Oh, man." Barrett turned away; an unsteady hand hid his shame.

With a resigned sigh, David sat on the edge of the bed, forcing Ted's tired head around, while biting his own lower lip when he looked down at a face scrunched tight to avoid further humiliation. He saw a troubled kid, no matter what the age, and he put his hand on the cheek that remained silky smooth after forty-eight hours without a shave. The skin felt delicate to the touch, and he delighted in the feel. "Don't go weird on me, Ted. Just close your incredible eyes, I'll be here when you wake up."

"Don't know why I said that. Now I've made a fool... a fool of myself." The old stutter could not be controlled.

Fully frustrated, David clenched his famous jaw over his inability to help. He had only the gift of an actor's vocabulary, and hoped his reassuring words would not embarrass the man. "You're scared and rightly so. Everyone needs someone close-by when lost and unwell. If it makes you feel better, I'm happy to stay. A lot has happened in a few days, most of it overwhelming; and you've had your share. Please, just sleep."

The blue eyes closed with the command and a quiet touch to his cheek. Within minutes, the turmoil gave way to slumber. LaCoix sat, believing the man too troubled to work. It felt peculiar to be protecting this annoying Spirit, one who should be turning to his indisputable faith in times of stress. His mind wandered back to the apparition, the *Lady of the Rocks*, and her different handling of Ted. From the moment they entered the fog, the fun-loving piece of sunshine, which drove him crazy, changed into a shattered fragment of a woeful waif, confused and very much alone. What had happened during those indiscernible moments of terror Ted faced alone? David let out a disturbed sigh and shook his head. Curious, but not wanting to know, he found himself fingering the spikes of perspiration-dampened hair. His actions more than surprised him.

An afternoon to kill, he peered out the bedroom window, looking for something to do while he waited. A smile appeared, remembering what Ted said about the fax machine. It would be the promised screenplay; the one he needed to brighten his dulling star. Quietly departing, he rushed over to his own trailer, grabbed the important document, and returned to keep his promise.

The day grew scorching hot as predicted. Once back in the confines of Ted's domain, the stifling central heating hit him; and he considered replacing it with air conditioning. He stopped short, remembering the chilled figure in the bedroom and made his way to check on his charge. A quick hand to the forehead and a simple diagnosis meant no cool air that afternoon. David slipped into the one chair in the room, put his feet on the bed, and started to read page after exciting page. An explosive story, it had been written for him. Having never done a period piece of such magnitude, he knew instinctively how to portray an unidentifiable character that straddled a line between good and bad. A thriller, a horror, and a mystery drama with a moral, the story wove into one. On that thought, his face lit up with excitement; his eyes closed to envision each scene unfold, finally succumbing to mental fatigue.

Alone in her chambers, the woman could not hear two of her voices. The younger man, though in trouble, had someone special keeping him at rest. LaCoix, also silent, happily slipped away from her mind, melding readily within her hands. The shifting phase had started. Altering her image with a thought, she dressed more casually in garb not to alarm the mortals. Vigilantly watching through her window, she silently stood, allowing a fresh breeze to brush out the tangled mane. Their meeting would be interesting; yet she wondered how to deal with the young, broken Spirit. She would not interfere this night, but allow the game to unfold naturally.

CHAPTER 8

Beginning to come around, from a deep sleep without nightmares, Ted felt secure for the first time since arriving on location, which seemed so far away and so disconnected from what he knew. Even while his credentials grew, he never experienced another job that took him away from his tight family safety net. Blue eyes flashed open, remembering those dreaded words: *I'm pregnant, Theo*. Staring at the ceiling, he calmed the terror facing him; he had to stop and accept his new role in life, while wishing for a miracle. His eyes lowered to see his legs elevated and wearing apparel he hated. Something had happened that he was unaware of; the overwhelming heat in the trailer made him nauseous. Attacking the sweatshirt first, he pulled it off, not bothering to get up. Warm droplets of perspiration slowly dried off his chest; his anxiety quieted to a silent scream; the strong presence of another had him suddenly holding his breath.

Ted looked to his right. Propped up in the chair, next to his bed, sat David LaCoix--the man he had admired since his youth--a man so underrated, Barrett's heart broke for the perseverance to survive in a cut-throat industry. The remarkable face softened in sleep, still extremely handsome and young looking for his age. Barrett had heard the whisperings of David's sordid reputation as a womanizer, mean drunk, and drug user; but every performance, executed by this actor, bordered on perfection. The young man had not witnessed the ugly side of the infamous star: no anger, no fighting, no snarling, and no wanton sexual depravity toward the few women of the cast or crew. As for a drug addiction, it appeared rooted in nicotine and single bourbon to finish off his day. Ted had not given LaCoix the benefit of the doubt, accusing him of something rumored. Deeply ashamed for his cruelty, he felt unworthy to be in the man's presence; considering the once front-cover David LaCoix took the time to help him through crisis after crisis. Barrett remained in star-struck awe and a little frightened of the intense actor.

Quietly struggling to sit up, explosions went off in his head. Remembering Jess and David's comments regarding shock trauma, his beliefs could not accept the diagnosis. Mental instability and physical frailty were unacceptable flaws by his church, rendering his headache not real, but a creation of his God to teach a lesson or a reward into heaven. Doctors were not permitted to save lives, insufficiently strong to deal with reality; medical science had no right to interfere in God's business. At the sound of a quiet voice, the pain hit the top of his head, coming close to nullifying the belief.

"You're awake. Feeling better?" His idol came out of an afternoon nap far too chipper, and certainly not helpful to a Christian in torture.

"David! What are you doing here?" A little disoriented, Ted questioned the first person he ever admitted anything to, now regretting every word said and those few tears fallen.

"Well, Mr. Barrett, you asked. I promised to stay with you, and I did. It appears you're over the chills, enabling us to turn on the air conditioner. It's hotter than great sex in here. You obviously need something for your head, but I suppose an aspirin isn't possible either."

"I asked you to stay?" Startled and mortified, Ted shook his head at the recommended medication; the action made his face scrunch up in more pain.

LaCoix nodded, rose from his chair, stretched, and yawned. He turned to catch a glimpse of the slight chest, rising up and down too fast, and noticed how much smaller Ted compared to himself. His co-star consisted of only bone with little mass. Acutely fine tuned muscles, of the thinnest titanium wire, gave him some definition. The naturally pale skin contrasted wildly with the rich, dark-brown hair found only on his head. One would expect some body tufts, but this man looked freshly waxed from top to bottom, possibly including parts that made him cringe at the thought. Not even a dusting of peach fuzz, Ted appeared as smooth as the fairest child. David quieted his tone for his charge, as the kid still appeared unwell. "What are we going to do about your headache?"

"Didn't I hear you use herbal oils or something? I can use nature's remedies."

"Witch doctor medicine? If you're sure, I have a concoction you can massage into your temples. Takes about ten minutes to give you some relief." David left, found his lifesaving pack of herbs and oils that Susan made especially for him, picked out the correct mix, and returned to toss the small vial at the man sitting semi-naked on the bed. Ted's reflexes were quick, and his hands came away from his pounding head to snatch the healing oil out of the air. "Nice catch. Hurry, we don't have much time before our meeting. I'm off to shower and change. Sure you're okay?" David watched intently and saw the resolve in the strained face of a man remembering the unhappier portion of his day.

"Why do I have to keep telling you I'm fine?" Ted's hint of a childish temper amused David. He had been baby-sitting *Peter Pan*.

"Because I'm concerned. It's six, and we have two hours to eat and freshen up. Now, start rubbing that stuff into your temples."

"Oh!" The boyish face dropped to look at his hands fidgeting with the small bottle of strange smelling oil.

Peter Pan had definitely emerged; and David smiled at the exclamation as he headed for the door. On a sudden thought, he returned to sit on the end of the bed.

"What?" The younger man startled, immediately on guard, not understanding David's sudden serious posturing. Those crazed green eyes stared straight through him like a sinful X-ray machine.

"You told me you had no one to talk to, but if you need someone, who's very understanding and who you feel comfortable with, why don't you sit down with Jess?"

"No, absolutely not. He laughs at me and my beliefs."

"That's nonsense, Barrett. If you would stop being so defensive in your conversations about your faith, you might find some neutral ground. I suggested Carmichael, because he's my mentor and confidant, seeing me through many hard times. He's even decked me once or twice, but he understands without judgment."

"No, you're my mentor."

"Me?" The proclamation nearly toppled David off the bed.

"I've told you things I shouldn't have. Now you know too much."

"Sounds rather ominous. Should I be shaking in my boots and looking over my shoulder for a hit man?" David laughed at the potentially serious threat, if it had come from someone else.

"Of course not. It's just... it's... Shit, I just don't need anybody. I'm fine, I'm happy, and my life's on track."

"If you say so. I'll see you at eight in my trailer. Don't be late."

"David, if I did need someone to speak with, would you listen?"

"I have so far. As for you being happy and on track, that's bullshit. Now hurry up." LaCoix rose from the bed and turned away. His broad smile returned, believing that this devout Christian could lie his beguiling face off. Heading back to his own trailer at high speed, he lit a cigarette on the run. Now in a rush, he jumped in the shower to prepare for their meeting, and to come up with the appropriate wording to fax the famous director that he wished an audition. Now paramount in his mind, the role was his goal; and his catnap gave him a slight adrenaline rush, which pumped his heart with renewed excitement over the current production, promising to unfold in a new light.

Barrett followed orders precisely; LaCoix did the same; and at exactly ten to eight, the blond-haired lead actor opened his door to a clean and somewhat healthier looking second lead. A fright fell over Ted's face, meeting eyes flashing with anger. He had seen the flame only once, and he deserved it. Something was wrong; he wished to beam elsewhere in a *Star Trek* second.

"Damn, Ted, if you start shivering on me, so inappropriately dressed for a desert night, I'll smack you to kingdom-come. I swear to god, I'll do it."

"What's got you so pissed?" Ted's feigned smile disappeared; his depression returned instantly. Looking into an angry snarl, and a curled lip of disgust, was not what he needed.

"First, I'm nervous about this meeting. Secondly, if you have another anxiety attack, I'm going to call a fucking doctor, whether you want one or not. Thirdly, you're still upset, sick, and not dressed warm enough for a desert night, or properly attired to meet our new producer. Casual, yes, but you look like a bum. Start acting your age, if you want to be taken seriously by your peers and business associates. No wonder everyone perceives you as a silly kid."

"Gee, thanks, but no one handed me a set of etiquette rules when I arrived in Hollywood. What's wrong with this?" Ted looked down, spreading his arms out for his own and David's full inspection, completely miffed at the insult.

"Did you call your wife?"

"No, I couldn't deal with it."

"That's just perfect. Although I suggested you'd be busy today, she'll still call, if you don't return her greeting. Damn women." David turned sharply at the sound of an ice cream truck, looked at the caller's number and answered immediately, while turning to flash his eyes back at Ted. As David said good night to Holly, he pulled out a woolen pullover and threw it at the man standing in baggy shorts, sandals, and an oversized U.S.C. T-shirt. The older actor, feeling the onrush of the cooler evening, had already turned the air conditioner off. Dressed in tight black jeans, a matching cashmere turtleneck pulled up slightly at the forearms, and finished off with matching black socks, and loafers, handsome could not qualify as a description for this man of white-blond hair and finely chiseled features. He turned heads when he desired the attention, and he knew exactly how to do it. On a sweet note to his daughter, the call ended with the sharp snap of the cellular phone, making Ted jump with the ferocity of the action. David did not look at him, but placed the device on the waiting table with their papers. LaCoix appeared ready for business.

"You sure can be a grouch; and I don't need your fucking sweater either." Tantrum would be exchanged for tantrum, if it came down to more orders and insults that hurt.

"You will, and you should be dressed with some dignity to meet your new boss. Do you always look like discarded garbage littering the beach?"

"Sorry I offend you. Maybe, you should explain to me what a man dresses like these days: basic black only. Where's your string of pearls?" Ted grew more nervous the more violent the argument became, and the more insults he received from the man who had been so kind that day.

He prepared himself to duck, if the ugly side of the notorious actor came brawling forth.

"Good one, Barrett; I simply want this meeting to go well. Are you up for it?"

"Why wouldn't I?"

"Shit, I never get a straight answer from anyone. Did I tell you our producer's another woman?"

"I don't remember, as if it matters; but why are you degrading women so harshly tonight? I thought they were one of your favorite toys. Problems on one of your domestic home fronts?"

"Shut up, and call your wife, so she doesn't interrupt us. I'd normally shut mine off during a business meeting, but I'm expecting an important call, and not from Rebecca who's the problem. I can't stand it when she's going through this once-a-month, beat-the-crap-out-of-men shit. She drags me down with her."

"Then you bitch to those around you. I'm beginning to think men suffer from the same thing, like false labor pains. You sure do, LaCoix. Do pregnant women get PMS?"

"Oh, fuck, I forgot about your situation, Ted. No, of course not: female reproductive system, remember? Even through morning sickness, they're usually happy campers when pregnant, unlike one pending father I know." David's voice immediately softened; his demeanor became more sympathetic.

"It was unexpected; that's all."

"Obviously, now call her, and get it over with. I have a feeling this woman will be on time."

"Is she as formidable as you're making her sound?"

"No, Ted, she's not. I'm being very unfair to both of you. She's a lovely, tranquil person, quite mysterious; and I don't even know her name. As for you, I apologize for ranting, but please put on my sweater. No more shaking and shivering, okay?"

"Since you asked politely, I may just do that."

"Thank you for doing an old man a favor. Now call your wife."

Ted quickly rang Karen, reassuring her of his good health and his excitement over her news. He repeated his happiness over the announcement twice, but on the final note of *Go with Christ* and the hanging up of the call, he stood motionless, staring at the phone. Becoming a fine actor, Barrett already claimed the title of a great liar. David shook his head even more perplexed.

A tap on the door had LaCoix taking a deep breath. One of his reasons for worrying stood beside the table in an oversized T-shirt, with sparrow legs sticking out from khaki cargo shorts, which were four sizes too big. The older actor wanted to see Ted's initial reaction of the uncanny resemblance of this woman to the mysterious high-flyer that dropped his co-star. Opening the door, a sense of well-being swept over him, with the gentlest of a lilac-scented breeze; his anger instantly mellowed. The woman looked entrancing, comfortably dressed in those formidable black denims and a pink velvet turtleneck, so soft you wanted to curl into it. Her mass of tangled hair sprang from a bizarre gizmo at the top of her head, to cascade in curly strands to her shoulders. She looked younger and even more attractive in the casual gear, right down to the slightly scuffed tennis shoes and the wild twinkle in her emerald eyes. She cast a spell over him; the greeting of a firm handshake felt the same; he held back the gasp.

"Please, come in." David turned to look at Ted who scrutinized their guest with an intake of breath. Sapphire eyes widened to their fullest, but he showed no further indication that she may be the same woman.

"Good evening, Mr. Barrett." The melodic voice enveloped them in a cloud of new spring green; the tinkling sound of fine crystal shards danced in the faint breeze of an alpine meadow.

"Ma'am." Ted shook her bejeweled hand and offered her a chair. His stare, through thick eyelashes and a squint, alluded to some recognition. This woman, with a penchant for extraordinarily elegant and large rings, had the same facial appearance and long lean body of their apparition, without the ethereal look. Ted took it well; the host finally exhaled.

"Can I get you something to drink?"

"Gin and tonic, thank you." She continued to study the younger man, while reassuring him with a look to mesmerize and nurture. Amazingly, Ted returned the look inquisitively, illustrating he did have pinwheels spinning in his head, attempting to sort out the identity of the woman.

"You have remarkable eyes, Mr. Barrett. We shall have to use them."

"Thank you, ma'am, but please call me Theodore... or Theo... or Ted."

"If that is what you wish; Theo it will be. I do believe you should put on some warmer clothing, as I do not desire you turning blue while we work." With a drink placed in her outstretched hand, the crackling of ice against glass broke the disquieting exchange of looks. On receiving her thank you, David came to his senses, handing Ted his usual soda, and then sitting down with his bourbon in one hand and a smoke in the other.

"Addicted are you, Mr. LaCoix?" A teasing comment, emphasized by a wicked, knowing smile, she baited him into something unknown.

"To many things I'm afraid, Ms.?" He waited for the hook.

"Mistress, for now."

"Unusual, and it's David. Thank you for confirming my sentiments to Mr. Barrett about these cold desert nights."

"David... a strong ancient name of power. It is nice to meet you both; and yes, I am concerned for this man's health. You have to keep your strength up, Theo, to get through the rest of the picture. Speaking of which, here are the new scenes. Please read the latest version before we discuss it further. We have plenty of time. If you made notes, now would be a convenient time for me to review your ideas. I am sure you have come up with your own unique interpretations of the characters."

"Right down to business; I like that." David smiled at her and received a beautiful one in return. Two pairs of green eyes flashed at each other in a curious flirtation of wills. Something more to this woman, he sensed a strong likeness to himself in some regard, causing him to shiver.

"You are a fire sign, David, as am I. This should be entertaining. We have much to discuss tonight, or do we argue to see who is dominant?" A soft chuckle and another mischievous smile flashed at the handsome blond. From a happy look, to one a little more surprised, she turned to face the boyish features continuing to scrutinize her. "The first thing I must ask, however, is what fascinating explanation do you have for your hair, Theo?"

The young man sank back in his chair, not knowing what to say at the unexpected question. He had forgotten the mess he created and looked at his mentor for help. Receiving only a shrug, he felt very alone. With no logic behind his actions, Barrett had no explanation. "I don't know; it just happened."

"Just like that? How peculiar. Perhaps we are dealing with magic. Well, we shall have to rectify the situation tonight."

"How?" Two male voices blended in unison, knowing the task difficult to correct, and certain scenes needed more than a stable wig.

"If magic caused the new look, then magic can restore the original one." Her laughter taunted and frightened at the same time. The Mistress accepted their notes and started analyzing the requested suggestions, ignoring the two men gazing at her with their mouths open. Ted and David looked at each other, shrugged, and commenced their own study of the new scenes, with connecting general information and set-ups.

Silence stilled the threesome for several hours, except for the sound of turning pages and the unnerving tapping of a pen against wood. Occasionally, David looked up to see the Mistress smiling, jotting down small notes on their sheets of paper. His attention would then turn to watch the stunned face of his co-star, whose blue eyes grew more frantic with every word read; and his mouth gaped upon studying each page, which he repeatedly turned back to reread. David refurbished his bourbon and finished off his once full pack of cigarettes. A jingling of ice in an empty glass broke the unnerving silence; David had to speak. "Amazing: this equals the intensity and intimacy of the book, but how do you propose to simulate the erotic scenes? The notes, on the side of the love scenes, have a dozen cameras on the set; and they all, or the majority of them, call for close-ups of our private parts, and doing very *risqué* things."

Ted listened to his co-star intently. His puzzlement increased to alarming proportions; and LaCoix seemed equally aghast at the camera angles suggested. This could not be simulated. Scared into silence, the younger actor knew precisely what this kind of technical set-up meant: the rumored new location probably lay hidden at the end of a dark alley, in an abandoned warehouse, on a rat-infested bed, with dirty, cum-covered sheets. Barrett nearly gagged at the thought.

Realization of the acting ability required for these scenes caught David off stride as well. Particularly difficult for Ted, it would be an emotional ordeal in many ways. The two men peered questioningly at each other in confusion; they must be misinterpreting the technical data.

"It will not be simulated, or rehearsed, and no body-doubles. The first time we shoot will also be the last; and the scenes marked in red, we propose to capture in one take. We are counting on it."

"Impossible! We can't do this!" Horror-stricken at the thought, David looked at the Mistress, then at Ted--two opposite ends of right and righteous--one smiling like a Cheshire cat, the other ready to run.

Unable to believe his eyes or ears, Barrett sat dumbstruck. His role deemed too riveting to give up, and yet, to perform such an explicit sexual act, this he could not do. Besides the embarrassment, he had his faith and reputation to uphold.

"Of course you can, David; both of you can. Opportunity knocks on the rarest of occasions, Gentlemen."

At the Mistress' reminder of what the mystery woman had said, LaCoix slumped back in his chair, not knowing what to do next. The ice cream truck rang, and without thinking, or looking at the number, he answered; something he would have never done if not shocked to his core.

"Hello." David knew instantly he had irritated the woman, with a call of little consequence: one of Rebecca's ranting sprees of trivial, hateful problems concerning him, her immediate family, and her closest friends. He tried to end the interruption graciously, but after the stunning revelation of what his future held, he had trouble listening to the babble.

The Mistress looked questioningly at Ted who tumbled out the words without thinking. "It's his fiancée; PMS alert."

Ted saw it first, then David: the Mistress' eyes suddenly flashed crimson. She held out her hand for the black communication device; the tiny piece of electronic equipment was obediently placed in the long, slender hand. As the mysterious eyes returned to normal, accompanied by her smile, serenity once again settled over the two surprised men. She listened to a few seconds of the tirade and turned to the unnerved blond actor. "What is her name?" The tonality of her voice signaled subtle anger; the Mistress was not amused with the person yelling into her sensitive ear.

"Rebecca." LaCoix sat very still, wondering what would happen next and shuddering over what went before.

"Thank you. Quiet, Rebecca; you have said enough. You shall receive this warning only once, or suffer the consequences from beyond what you know in this reality. Your handsome beau is currently in the middle of an extremely important meeting, and he needs his wits about him. This intrusion of no importance and vindictive innuendo has caused us all undue stress, for you are not the only one presently in turmoil. I suggest you think before speaking. A woman, who uses the physical phenomenon of hormonal change (blessed upon the female gender of the human species) to abuse others, with outrageous name-calling and pain-inducing words, is only a silly, spoiled child. With the medical profession putting a name to a simple human condition, it has allowed certain individuals, such as you, to misbehave incredulously. I will not allow you to harass my actors via insolent verbiage. Be accountable for your obnoxious behavior toward the innocent, Rebecca, before you lose friends, family, and any chance of happiness with a man. Do not phone again. Mr. LaCoix will call you in his own good time; and I would suggest you be kinder and gentler, or you will lose him; perhaps you already have. Forgiveness will not be forthcoming, for the unkind remarks that you have thrown at David, not this time; and this discord will be a reminder for him as well, not to give in to your acidic tongue next month. There is no sympathy for you here. Good night." The Mistress disconnected the call without touching the apparatus, while two men gasped at the electrical flash from a bejeweled finger.

"Fuck, give me that. Now you've done it. She's very fragile during this time." David spouted angrily, not caring who was present to hear his profanity and panic.

"As are you. No one deserves such verbal aggression, no matter what the mood. Some women use the erroneous diagnosis, as an excuse to behave abominably, and to say anything they please to hurt and torment. Your Rebecca is stating what she truly feels, only to retract the critical, unkind comments later. I never took you for a fool, Mr. LaCoix; no man should put up with it. Nature's ways do not initiate such outbursts of hate; it is in opposition to Natural Law. Now, back to business."

David said nothing, remembering what he had wished for a few days earlier. Since this woman did not tolerate such behavior in her own gender, why should he.

"Excuse me, ma'am, but... but how... how did you do that with the phone?" Ted commenced shaking, his hands no longer able to hold the pen that landed on the floor. The woman looked at him with the compassion of a mother upon her only child. Ted was a man-child, whose forehead grew feverish, dotted with beads of perspiration, and his pouting lip aquiver, waiting for the sky to fall upon him.

"You don't believe in magic, do you, Theo?" A simple question was asked sweetly, accompanied by a little mirth to make the nervous man, who still appeared upset, feel a little more at ease.

"Of course not."

"Do you believe in *mind over matter*?"

"Like what?" Ted settled a little, charmed by the melodic voice, to focus on the question asked; whether out of interest or fear could not be ascertained.

"Have you had a prayer answered?"

"Once, as a child."

"Tell me."

"My brother became very ill, almost to the point of dying; but we kept praying and praying to Jesus for help." Throughout the painful memory, the older man's hand reached out to wipe Ted's sweating brow. Barrett remained motionless, but shivering. He was not ready for what may come; David sensed it.

"When you prayed, how did you see your ailing brother?" The Mistress tried to maintain eye contact; her softness swept away much of the fear filling the room from both men.

"I saw us playing games and having fun."

"That is positive visualization, Theo: powerful mental magic, whether you pray, chant, meditate, or cast a spell. They are the same thing: *mind over matter*. You saw him as he should be, healthy and happy, not deathly ill; a very wise thing for one so young." The Mistress rubbed his hands, which now clenched around each other. Ted allowed the gesture without flinching, while David took the opportunity to stop the conversation, before his co-star brought Christ back into the mix. Too late, the Mistress brought it up first. "Why did you pray to Jesus and not your God who is more powerful? It is just an idle question, Child."

"Don't know. Guess it's because we're Christian."

"I will accept that for now, but consider this. Praying to an unknown increases your visualization of the outcome you desire--*mind over matter*--remember that always."

"Well, it's going to take some time to get my mind over this matter." David pulled out another cigarette from a new packet and inhaled deeply, while tapping the opened script before him. He glanced at Ted who fell into contemplation over the Mistress' statement. No time for *Bible* studies, consideration of what they were being asked to do deemed more relevant.

"The roles have become much deeper, thus harder to portray; and I am sure you are being underpaid for this film. A common phrase, David, one I know you have heard: *everyone has a price*. What is yours?"

"Hell if I know. All of a sudden I have to perform something completely unnatural to me; something I've never done."

"Oh, please, David, you cannot lie to me. I am sure in your youth, a few flirtatious casting calls, gone too far, earned you a number of roles."

"What? First you insult Rebecca, then Ted, now me!" David leaned forward and snarled at her.

With the calmest of smiles, she flicked her wrist. The angry blond flew across the room, landing heavily against the far cupboards. Stunned, open-mouthed silence shattered two men; Ted froze where he sat. The Mistress slowly got up, gracefully walked over to a very startled action hero, and raised him off the floor and onto his feet with the lightest touch to one arm. He did not resist, or attempt to get up himself.

"Turn, please. With such a thick skull, the lump will be small."

"What happened?" Dazed at the unexpected bashing that came out of nowhere, David put his hand to the back of his head. The woman's touch stopped the pain and eradicated any bump, if there had been one.

"Rebecca learned a lesson; Ted received praise, not insult; and you became rude, getting angry over the truth."

"How did you throw me like that?"

"Me? I did not touch you." The Mistress turned to smile and wink at Ted, unfortunately not easing the young man's frightened astonishment.

"Well, someone did. It's certainly not a habit of mine to fly through the air fifteen feet, to hit a treacherous wall of cabinets with metal handles, just for kicks."

"Magic is very real, David. Now, we have upset your co-star, making this the opportune time to take a break and deal with his hair. This should relax you both." The strange woman beckoned the younger man to move, by wiggling one of her many ringed fingers.

A static back and forth motion of Ted's head commenced, indicating his disagreement. "What... what do you plan to do? I don't... I don't understand what you did to David. I don't want any part of this." Ted remained fixed in his chair, while the oncoming anxiety attack became intensely visible to a rattled LaCoix who felt as catatonic as his friend. Unwilling to upset the woman further, he remained cemented to the floor, unable to hastily run to the young man's aid and rush him out of the trailer.

"We are going to fix your hair. It will feel wonderful; I promise."

"No, you did something to his phone and tossed him across the room; then these scenes we have to do; I can't; I won't."

"No further discussion until we get you both settled, starting with the machete job. Experiencing, and even watching the procedure, tends to immerse a person into a world of dreams. After a gentle scalp massage, we can partake in some quiet time." The Mistress smiled at her charges reassuringly; they accepted her request to sit in the appropriate places. Ted eased himself out of his chair to slip onto the one offered. David saw the slight wobble and hesitation, praying this would calm the approaching attack. Still shaken, the blond actor had no idea what or whom threw him across the room, but he acknowledged the fact, that if this was not the same strange creature behind the fog, then it had to be her demonic twin sister. For the first time in days, his sense of serenity dwindled; LaCoix also grew fearful.

Holding his breath, Ted closed his eyes at the first touch; and as promised, David felt the sensual strokes running up the back of the other man's neck and into his own hair. At that moment, he would have killed to be in Barrett's place, and he gave himself a shake. Returning to his half-empty glass and opening another package of smokes, sitting next to the one just opened, he looked up into a disapproving face.

"Enjoy your last cigarette and your final drink, David. No more alcohol or drugs when you report for work." A smile teased him, and the hands, working on Ted's hair, had him agreeing without any other thought but the touch and the sensation quivering through his body. The room grew hotter, as did he, mesmerized at the sight of Ted and the Mistress, feeling it all without a caress of a hand.

"You think I can stop that easily?" David coughed and stammered, trying to compose the erection rising out of control.

"No, but I want you in a foul mood for a couple of scenes. I do believe the lack of these addictive substances, along with Rebecca's bad attitude, should put you in character."

"You know too much." David squinted at her from under his blond lashes; his lips curled to let out a faint growl of dismay at the misery he would face.

"A few things, besides the usual, like your co-star may feel ill at the smell of you when in such close proximity. Are you accustomed to cigarette smoke, Theo?"

"Don't mind. Guess I'm just used to David."

"You have been that close to him; and his scent is not offensive?"

"Shit, what a subject to be discussing. Do I stink to you, Ted? I thought you hated my smoking?" David's mood changed to extremely testy at these personal questions.

"No, you smell really good to me." Ted blurted his truth; his eyes opened in a flash to look at a surprised LaCoix; he had said too much. The lids closed in humiliation, a blush ran from his neck into his cheeks, while the sensuous hands kept moving, caressing his scalp, and fingering out lengthier strands of hair. Equally mortifying was the sensation stirring within the confines of his shorts, and his eyes again opened as he inhaled deeply. His thick, dark brown locks felt longer, tickling his forehead and feathering down his cheeks. The reaction, across from him, was not surprise at what he said, but his hair left David with his mouth open! Ted jolted forward, stood up, and scrambled to the bathroom for a look.

The Mistress leaned nonchalantly against the wall with a sly grin; her green eyes danced the devil's dance. LaCoix sat speechless, but heard Ted yelling his name.

"This is your opportunity to prove your acting credentials, by helping our frightened man-child. He is disturbingly fragile and needs consoling. Go to him and try to calm his anxiety."

"What the hell am I supposed to do with him? This is probably the push to send him diving head first into a bottomless chasm. He's been in shock since the day you dropped him, and don't deny it. Fuck, he needs a doctor or a priest--whatever--anyone would be better than this selfish bastard. I could cause more harm than good." LaCoix glared menacingly, aghast at the supposition he could aid his usurper through another trial. Not his responsibility or his desire, fear of mentally damaging the young man's teetering psyche created a greater concern. The shriek, coming from the bathroom, increased in momentum, as did the horror heard between each cry for help. Gulping, choking sounds became unbearable to tolerate. The normally controlled actor looked in the direction of the echo chamber, and then at the Mistress, his eyes reflecting his dire concern and confusion.

"Recognizing you may hurt him signals that you are the correct person to aid him, as you care; and he calls for your presence."

"Fuck." LaCoix darted for the bathroom as if scorched. Openly indignant at what this crazed woman had done to them both, a sudden insight flashed through his befuddled brain: the reasoning became immediately clear. The scenario had nothing to do with the Mistress or his acting ability, but a test of his sensitivity toward another. Dismissing his selfishness and forced into a drastic situation, his adolescent behavior had to stop, or Ted would be vanquished. Not a magic trick, it became a deadly game for the life and mental stability of both men.

The Mistress held back, watching LaCoix awaken to a real test of his humanity. A turning point for both actors, they had to bond for the film, and what better way than a little comforting with soothing words. David would come through, even if acted out. She knew everything about the blond-haired man, particularly why his life had run amuck. Her fault: his life required intervention.

An entirely different problem, Barrett exhibited extreme sensitivity, far more than she had anticipated. This episode of panic added to her puzzlement on how to handle his delicate situation. She had read his mind; she knew part of his emptiness; she would try to fill the void in his heart. The parts missing would be found; only the Fates could jeopardize her plans. The inner pain, he dealt with daily, tortured him; and Ted bore the problem alone. Now, knowing more about the man-child, the Mistress wondered how she missed the connection, or if it even possible. She would find out details covertly through another. Refilling her glass with a thought, slipping into a comfortable chair, and closing her eyes, she watched them in her mind. The two men would never know she saw and heard everything transpiring between them. The Mistress she was; her power engulfed them silently and without notice; they remained safe for now.

CHAPTER 9

"Jesus Christ, what's happening to you, son?" David raked his fingers through his corn-silk locks, while taking a couple of deep breaths in preparation. He found Ted crammed between the toilet and the vanity, incessantly babbling gibberish, gazing into nothingness, trembling uncontrollably, and trying, in his shocked ranting, to understand what had occurred. Barrett pulled at the magical, long, luxurious hair, attempting to tear it out by the roots. Scared out of his mind, he lost control and soiled himself--not knowing, not feeling, not crying-- albeit endless tears streaked down a white death mask.

David stepped toward the Jacuzzi tub and turned on the hot water. By the time he wedged Ted out of his awkward position, the water would be the perfect temperature. A quick scan, he spotted Susan's treasure trove of medicinal oils--scents for every mental and comforting need imaginable--and they worked. Many had come in handy: eucalyptus for his allergies, the headache oil that helped Ted, but he searched for something special. Once found, he emptied half the vial into the filling tub and turned on the jets. The entire room steamed with the mind-altering and calming affects of jasmine and narcissus. He shut off the taps and turned with a sigh of deep sorrow, to look pitifully at a man who could no longer recognize the famous face. A short pace forward by David had Ted cringing like a frightened rabbit, sinking deeper into his burrow. With little effort, the older actor gently slipped off the sandals, only to look up into the petrified eyes that could not blink away the tears.

"Come on, Teddy; I'm putting you in the bath where you can relax. You don't even understand me; do you, Babe? I'm sorry I got you into this mess, as you've become very ill and certainly unprepared for more." David shook his head, feeling guilty over his knowledge that the younger man remained in shock when the meeting started, and now seemed beyond handling.

"Please don't hurt me. Christ, help me. Christ doesn't know, does he?" Ted blurted something at least intelligible, allowing David to converse at a basic level.

"Know what, Baby?" His voice quieted, treating a grown man, with words he would use on his daughter.

"Satan's real. Christ, save me. Where are you?" The tears turned to cries of alarm.

LaCoix assumed a role never acted out: a mother. He put his one knee on the toilet seat and made a successful attempt to get an arm around Ted's back. Once managed, he placed his other arm under the bent knees, and with all his strength, raised the smaller man out of his hiding place. He felt every vertebra in his spine strain, even hearing one crack, but he secured Barrett within his arms. Struggling to remain stable, every muscle burned, as he used the support of a cold, tile wall. Clothes and all, he lowered the clinging body into the foaming, pulsating water, submerging the thin figure into the bubbling depths. More yells for help echoed throughout the trailer.

"Okay, let go; let go, man. Is it too hot?" With no response, David methodically removed the ruined cashmere sweater, the clinging T-shirt, and then quickly set to work on the shorts. Zippers and buttons were difficult to undo underwater, particularly with another pair of hands fending you off. Without underwear for a little security, it became more difficult to protect the delicate areas easily pinched. With the major task completed, David took a deep breath, steadied his nerves, and wistfully smiled at the stripped body, never expecting Ted to be naked under his pants. With a stretch of his back, he stood for a few seconds, threw the wet garments in the hamper, and with some reluctance, started a task he had never performed. David remembered the many times Jess had forced him into an ice cold shower when drunk or overdosing on something, and then scrubbing the skin off him until he yelled for a reprieve. If his long time mentor and friend could do it, so could he. From head to toe, he soaped the quivering, tense body with no hint of embarrassment; simply a job that needed doing, he was the only one available.

With his superficial problems washed away, Ted's ramblings, of deeply ingrained fears, continued undeterred. David forced him to lean forward to inhale the sedating fragrance. Squeezing the bubbling sponge, he spent ten minutes indulging a knotted body with a soothing massage of the neck, shoulders, and back, with the added benefit of silence. The ranting had stopped. After a quick rinse, he hoisted Ted to his feet, helping him move one leg at a time out of the tub, and steadying someone who remained adrift. Reaching behind him for a towel, he turned too late to save the young man from slithering down the wall, landing unscathed on the floor, where the fallen victim coiled into a fetal position. David sighed and began removing the shiny beads of water from the rangy body, and drying out the magical new hair. The effort took all his patience; emotional exhaustion finished him off. He stopped long enough to get his strength back before his next task of maneuvering Ted to the bedroom and dressing the shattered man.

The struggle continued. Ted lay shivering on David's bed, while the weary blond went back to raking his fingers through his own hair. What next? Nothing came to mind in dealing with a new situation. Desperation yelled at him to call Jess, or ring for a doctor. The ordeal made no sense, thinking back to the Mistress' words; if truly a test of his acting ability, he felt ill prepared for such an insidious experiment. The problem, lying catatonic, required more than acting ability; he only had his heart, which had been ripped apart by the sadness and fear that filled the once ray of sunshine. Ted had turned into a fragile firefly whose light had died.

Dripping wet himself, David took a few minutes to rest and change into his signature black, and not once did Ted veer his attention toward him. Unused to being ignored, the heroic leading man sadly smiled within, believing, even with another male, he warranted some attention. Out came that strange actor's ego to get in his way, and that ego had better start working on someone else's devastated psyche.

For Ted, the Mistress had kindly laid out a pair of LaCoix's faded jeans, sneakers, and a pair of warm socks, along with a navy cotton turtleneck, and a light blue cable knit sweater. After another accomplishment of dressing the man, David stepped back, overcome with what he saw before him. Barrett looked extraordinarily handsome, almost beautiful, with his still damp, magic hair hanging in wet waves. An innocent vision in blue, the color of the clothing accentuated the dark sapphire eyes; the look of an *enfant perdus* emerged with a natural pout and an empty stare. Ted looked no more than nineteen, close in age to his sons.

"Feeling better?"

"Yes sir."

"Come on, Ted; where are you, son? Do you know who I am?" David placed his hands on the smaller man's shoulders, leaning down slightly to be swallowed up by the vacant blue orbs leading to eternity. They blinked a couple of times, and a little life came back, long enough for David to try again. "Look at me and tell me where you are."

"I'm not sure." Ted looked around, showing signs of conscious life.

"What do you want to do?" LaCoix gave him a little shake to focus the blue eyes into his green ones.

"I'm cold?" A strange question to utter, Barrett asked for confirmation of an abstract David could not decipher.

"Your hair's still wet, maybe that's the reason. I'll blow dry it for you." David plugged in the electronic device everyone seemed to need, but not knowing how to use it on Ted's new mane. Holly's desire to have her long blonde hair brushed came to mind.

Ted watched the switch turn on with puzzlement. Remembering a flash of light doing the same thing, he shivered not understanding anything. If he had the power, he would run, but there seemed nowhere to go in his absent head.

"Can you count the brushstrokes for me? Start with one, and we'll see how many it takes to get this mop shiny and dry."

Barrett began counting in rhythm, concentrating intently, until David finished. Stumbling their way down the corridor, the smaller man slowly returned to semi-coherent, but required urging to move one leg at a time. If he saw the Mistress, he gave no recognition of her presence, but quietly sat opposite the woman whom had caused his distress. LaCoix gazed piteously at the woman, begging her for help. She put her finger to her lips, issuing a silent order to ignore her. A hard request to accommodate, David continued, "That wasn't so bad, Teddy, but let's finish brushing your hair."

"Why? Didn't I cut it off?" Barrett looked bewildered at the suggestion; although leaving LaCoix gratified on hearing an intelligible question, unfortunately one too fearful to answer. Grabbing the hands, before they reached the brunet head to discover the mystery that could send the young actor hurtling backward, David again looked at the Mistress for help, only to receive a confirming smile in return.

"Your hair is longer now, remember?" David waited for another explosive fit, while continuing his grip on the struggling hands. He received an agitated shake of a head in response. "Come on, Baby, please remember. What's my name? Look at me, and tell me." Exhausted from lack of sleep and great exertion, he pleaded for Barrett to make sense. He never felt so useless. At least with the birth of Holly and his sons, he had stayed rooted beside his wives, although deathly ill and trying not to watch.

"I can't remember. My head feels fuzzy; and I'm cold. I should be home; they're expecting me." Ted looked around, as if searching for a coat and a recognizable door.

"You're supposed to be here, with me, shooting a film. Don't you remember?" Acting and films often made a good start with Barrett, when nothing else worked; love for his art appeared his strongest motivator.

"Oh, yeah, a Western." Ted's focus returned to the blond individual standing over him.

"Good man. Now, what's my name?"

"David LaCoix!" The look and sound were of surprise and awe, as if they had never met.

"Yes I am; and you're starting to come back. Are you seeing things clearer?" Receiving a breakthrough, David could only ask questions to keep Ted thinking.

"I'm not sure. What happened? Why are you here?" He had already forgotten the movie.

"The Western we're making; and you're with me because you've had another shock, and so have I. You're shivering, and I'm feeling cold as well. Let me sit next to you and pull this blanket over us." With some nervousness on David's part at the closeness, he had nothing better to offer a man who seemed mentally detached from everything that went before. He finally settled his own frightened heart, pulling Ted into an embrace while sitting side-by-side.

Barrett could smell the familiarity of bourbon and cigarette smoke, creating more lucidity. "I'm confused and don't feel well."

Without thought or embarrassment, David pulled him closer; and without hesitation, Ted laid his head on the black-clad shoulder to stop the room from spinning. Unfortunately, the change of position brought his stare directly into the mysterious green orbs of the Mistress; his chilling whispers started slowly, growing faster and faster. Barrett reached another point of panic, and turned away from the unwanted terror. David allowed him to twist on top of him, until he settled with his small behind between the longer legs, and his body turned to press his chest against the warmer one. Knees bent over the taller man's left thigh, as two arms wrapped around his neck. The change upset David, wishing that the Mistress, whoever she was, would help him out of this delicate entanglement. A single movement by Ted also had him thankful for his quick reflexes, avoiding a crushing assault on parts not built for the purpose. He thanked his own children for giving him those instinctive, evasive maneuvers. The whispering continued, with words, rushing passed the corn-colored hair, into an ear attempting to grasp their meaning; he was losing Barrett to a place he could not enter. Decades since LaCoix entered a church, except for marriages and funerals, he thought he heard the repetition of Psalms and slightly familiar passages from the *Bible.* He let Ted ramble, while thanking the Mistress for tucking several more blankets around them both. With one arm around the smaller back, he took his free hand and started caressing the long, brown hair that smelled intoxicating and felt like silk. Every color of the autumn spectrum shone in the waves, enhanced by the glow of golden lamps suddenly turned on by an unseen force.

"Easy, Ted, shush now. It's David; you're safe." Silence filled the room, as the smaller, shaking body succumbed to the fatigue of shock, the comforting hold, and the stroking of his head by an equally tired, unqualified caregiver.

"You did an excellent job, David." The Mistress broke the silence, while placing a steaming hot cup of liquid beside the shaken actor whom remained awake.

"Did I pass your test? Damn you, he's extremely unbalanced for any more craziness. How could you scare him so badly?" Whispered in anger, LaCoix proved, to their vindictive producer, that he did have a heart and feelings for someone other than himself.

The Mistress was very pleased, but still unfinished. "Were you scared?"

"No, not really, until I saw him hiding. He's a broken man; and you wanted me to act the part of his savior. Well, I couldn't. I did what any human would do for another."

"You passed, David; your actions were exactly what I wanted from you: to follow your heart, not your pride and ego. I must apologize for not realizing how close he stands on the precipice, but it will be to his advantage later, and to yours."

"How can you play with a mind so frail? This is beyond cruel." David wanted to carry the sleeping creature back to his own trailer, and send Jess to watch over him. He would deal with this new, sadistic producer himself.

"Dispiteous, perhaps, but for the greater good."

"The greater good! How trite is that?"

"Theo is stronger than you think. Only his guilt, created by his upbringing and faith, has given him a heavy burden, for his life is not as he wishes. You reacted with anger and curiosity, after flying across the room and watching his hair grow through simple manipulation. Perhaps surprised, your mind stayed open to new thinking. What Theo believes impossible, my efforts contradicts his beliefs: a reality based on abstracts. His brainwashing runs deep; and you and I have an opportunity to open a door, allowing him to question things without losing his basic life philosophy. Surprising to me that humanity believes in intangibles, and yet, they do not believe in magic." The Mistress wandered into her own thoughts of the idiocy of humankind, until a male, panic-laden voice interrupted her contemplation.

"Why should we interfere in his beliefs? I don't know who he really is. In fact, why am I suddenly included in all this shit, besides getting him through this picture? If I was the type to run from a film, I'd be gone in a heartbeat." David's ire raged at the complacency offered toward a man close to being institutionalized. No hospitals--he remembered--his concern blew holes in his head thinking how Ted's church would deal with a semi-catatonic, adult child.

"I can see it is a moral dilemma in your eyes; and you do not know him. He does need a friend, however, and you seem to have accepted the position. For some of us, the reason for interference is a necessity when you hear the cries for help coming from the same source. The continuing calls become imperative for us to act. Until this man faces what he is and needs, he may end up in the morgue, dying alone in a locked car, filling with carbon monoxide." The Mistress slipped back into her seat, with her own mug of sweet, hot ambrosia warming her hands.

"Barrett would never do that, because of his beliefs, since everything he does echoes the sentiment." David kept staring at the green eyes that held lifetimes of wisdom and learning, but of what: good or evil. She pulled him into a vortex of immense power; he could not resist her seduction. The last of his fight centered on the continual stroking of the disturbed actor in his arms, as if holding Ted made him safer, using Barrett's God for protection from this strange being.

"Those are the ones who usually break first, leaving their loved ones unprepared and not understanding. All humans play roles they believe appropriate, not what their mind--their inner subconscious *knowing*--tells them. A difficult concept to grasp, people reject their unique humanity and the meaning of their existence. We all have certain powers. I manipulate material objects, as can you, if you develop that part of your mental being. To read minds and thoughts, you already have spoken to someone telepathically, but cannot receive the same kind of transmission unless in a controlled environment. All beings, sentient or not, broadcast continually, silently and alone, not realizing who hears their messages. A good Tarot Card reader is empathic. They understand and can visualize what you are thinking, and they surprise you with something only known to yourself. When they predict your future, they simply reconfirm the goal that you have already set. They are starting the journey of relearning the abilities of the first ones, long past forgotten; and those latent talents, within all humans, are now returning. A slow process in the beginning, hindered by church, state, social mores, and cultural bigotry, one-by-one they shall evolve."

"Who are you? Why should I believe anything you say or do? Your words sound like New Age mumbo-jumbo; and I heard enough from my second wife."

"I am a Caretaker, attempting to rectify misguided individuals pushed off track by the forces of the Fates, with only disaster looming in their future. Perhaps I keep people from falling off their life's path. Do not scoff at those of the New Age, albeit much is wrong with their theories, like all religions and philosophies; however, those involved continue to piece together a complex puzzle with few clues. Ironically, the term *New Age* means the study of ancient wisdoms, but they do not go back far enough. Like other ideologies, they unfortunately learn through other's written words--some right, some wrong--and do not listen to their own *knowing*."

"And that includes me: the part about falling off my path?" David hung tighter to his safety net, and the comforting strokes through the slippery mane, to keep from losing his mind.

"Yes, but unlike Theo, you are already making strides in preparation. I had nothing to do with your *awakening*, except to shake your hand, if that is what started this renewed interest in living fully with nature and not artificially." Pink velvet clad arms wrapped around her long legs, with her graceful hands still holding a glass filled with the unknown liquid. A finger swirled around the rim, hypnotically calming her distress over the mistakes she had made this night.

"What do you mean by the *knowing*? That's the word I sensed from your magnificent horse; and you've used it several times."

"Your own subconscious truth, nothing more."

"I assume it's an art, difficult to learn. Listening to your inner-self seems a frightening thought, considering we're often wrong."

"You are listening to the wrong voice. Once you are in communication with the correct one, the sensation is indescribable. When the portal opens, a flood of information, difficult at first to comprehend, awakens your Spirit to put your own life's puzzle together." A flicker of black eyelashes blew away the steam off the hot liquid, unveiling those green eyes that penetrated straight through LaCoix.

"So, you are the chimes in the wind. I believe you to be our mystery woman; you truly are Ted's *Lady of the Rocks*."

"A peculiar title, but an honored one. Drink while the ambrosia remains hot. We have other matters to discuss."

"Nice change of topic: very subtle." David sarcastically lashed out, still unnerved by the five-foot eight-inch leech attached to him. Not his idea of a formal production meeting, perhaps the intimacy rendered as a casting couch scenario. Sipping the drink, he closed his eyes; his racing heart began to slow down; tranquility filtered through him.

"Theo will awaken soon, but I must know how you feel about this picture and the rewrite. I can tell you two things. This picture will place Barrett amongst the ranks of superstars, with your help; and you shall be swept along in his new fame, adding to your own notoriety. The second item, as a reward for aiding your co-star, is Rod Morris' call, giving you the part of a lifetime."

"Shit, he called? Hell yes, I'll accept!" David's sudden instinct to jump halted, feeling the weight on his lap. Wild, darting eyes showed the emotions of joy and excitement at the news. He had waited countless years for an opportunity of this magnitude.

"Good, as the film appears written for you, to reap the overdue accolades deserved and desired. I surmised your affirmative response, and told him you would discuss details with him at his ranch in Arizona. He left his number. A confirming reply deems appropriate, as does an expeditious meeting, since he returns to England in a few days. They are in the midst of preparatory work, anxiously waiting a final decision for the lead. Your name came up in a conversation with Ethan Peerce; and I hear Mr. Morris did a few handsprings in his excitement. You need a new agent, David." The Mistress smiled at the man who wanted to dance, yet hindered by an unconscious pile of skin and bones.

"Ethan Peerce! Holy shit! Whatever he said, I must send my thanks. What made him think of me; I've never met the man?"

"Obviously he has seen something in your screen presence, which made him believe you would fit the character. It certainly is not Mr. Peerce's style of acting. For now, your obligation is to fulfill this young man's dreams."

"Anything! Shit, I don't know what to say. When does Rod require my presence?"

"When I am finished with you, and at the proper moment in your space and time. Now, drink up, for we have much to do."

A quiet peace settled inside the trailer, as the woman curled up in her chair like a lazy feline, while David effortlessly held Ted who slept unperturbed in his arms. Never in his wildest imaginings would he believe himself in such a position. His paternal instincts fell into play with his co-star, the same feeling when consoling Holly, or one of his boys. The soothing gesture made him realize he could be a better father to his children, and that change would happen. The strangest part of his revelation: everything felt right, sitting with these two strangers, and LaCoix had no reservations of starting first. "To business then, if these scenes aren't simulated, you want us to perform the acts. The question is why, because I don't know if I can act my way through the blatant sexuality?" David flashed his dangerous eyes at the woman across from him. He tried to be quiet for Ted, but his ire resurfaced with the remembered insinuation of his moral character.

The Mistress made up for her disturbing remarks quickly; her eyes glittered back in defiance, but not in anger. "I am sorry about the casting remark. Just know that when I say something, the words are not without total thought, but a well-versed statement to catch a reaction. I need to know you both, along with your toleration levels. As for the love scenes, you will perform the action. Every detail, every emotion, and every sound heard will be filmed and recorded. Be assured that only a few of my people will be around for these scenes. With no direction, you both shall be left to interpret the love scenes and in several diverse situations. Anything you deem inappropriate will be destroyed in front of you."

"It still doesn't answer the question why. The set-ups for the cameras appear pornographic!" David sounded like Ted when in a dilemma of shocking news.

"The reason is simple. The film industry gives the public little credit, with love scenes bordering on the predictable, but for the exceptional few. Your audience realizes the fact, knowing every sound and embrace has no passion, only meaningless platitude. Few actors hide their lives, becoming more open and thus talked about. Fans know every detail about them through rumor and open dialogue, leaving only the true persona lurking inside the recesses of an actor's heart. Even the continuing Hollywood square dance, of changing partners, seems part of those simulated scenes, as you well know; and the stack of cards, called marriages, come tumbling down within the make-believe world created with a co-star and carried out too far off-camera. We want the essence of reality, not the crudity, or the sick curiosity of a new relationship starting and an old one ending. It makes great publicity for a film, but an expensive sacrifice for the actors and their families. Sex is a wondrous, powerful part of life; we mean to show that intercourse and love naturally coincide."

"Thanks for reminding me of my indiscretions; but the sudden closeness, of a co-star, makes real-life evaporate, and a new relationship begins. The idea sounds like actors are extremely shallow as a group." He rested his head against the back of the couch, taking in as much air as allowed by the weight on his chest.

"Everyone is a complex individual, uniquely his or her own Spirit. The intimacy seems an excuse, however, for a lifestyle not worthy of you or your peers; similar to Rebecca's excuse for dispiteous behavior."

David remained silent; committing sodomy with a man, in front of a camera, seemed of greater concern.

"Since love scenes have become trite and not even titillating, except under the watchful eye of a few gifted directors and editor; our intention, for actors, is to experience the emotion of love. Look at the scene as a one-night stand, and then return to normalcy. There will be no choreographed body movements and scripted sighs, all hidden under dubious shadowed lighting to eliminate any change of color pigmentation that naturally occurs to the skin. Are you that quiet in the throes of sexual intercourse, and your voice-overs done with the proper passion? Do you not sweat when working at such an elevated heart rate?"

"Excuse me?" Pelted by a repeating revolver, each hit embedded in the logical part of LaCoix's brain.

"Pornography is very vocal, David, and since it is not love-making, the sounds are totally out of place by very bad exhibitionists. Most humans give off little whimpers or groans in their pleasure--pleasure being the appropriate term--do you not agree?"

"I guess." A rarity in his life, David glowed crimson, flushing with a slight arousal from the conversation with such a blatantly frank woman.

"Your public wants to fast-forward those mediocre scenes, unless they can see some skin and body parts, and not those of body doubles. Fans adore an actor for their physical attributes and their ability to capture their attention sexually. A scene of a fade-out, with two lovers on a beach, no longer stimulates or attracts a sophisticated audience with today's morals and knowledge. Charisma makes stars, rather than their talent, only recognized later. That said; we have a picture where love transforms and molds the characters into the beings they later become, which is the essence of the book. How can we make such a scene beautiful and erotic, where the emotions, felt at a first touch, grow intensely real and nervously played out? We want to show that single moment of fear and wonder of a first kiss between two people who have come together under extraordinary circumstances. For all your extreme talents, David, we must face the fact--this script needs the emotion of a virgin's first encounter--Theodore's first encounter. Of course, the scene will feel awkward, tense, and frightening, to become exciting, soft, and gentle. You can bring that out in him. I know he will react exactly as the book describes, while you delve deeply into your character: the man who makes him feel special."

David closed his eyes, desperately craving a smoke. She truly wanted him to help Ted, but this leading man, with so many women after him, wondered if he could become aroused on cue over the one he held. With no inhibiting crotch covers or sexual drug depressants, the shoot would be a nightmare. "I don't know. This is extremely difficult. The whole rewrite has such power; the emotions run so high; I can't refuse the challenge, but I must." David opened his eyes and gave the woman a look of complete disappointment.

"You know what the 'A' list is averaging. What would your price be?"

"Hell if I know. I'm making less with every low budget movie I make, and I doubt if Barrett's even getting a fraction of the pittance in my contract. We're receiving only a small percentile of what the big guns score. Besides me, what about Ted; he doesn't care about money." David hid his sudden excitement at what may be offered. His thoughts tangled, wondering how much worth his dignity held.

"Theo cares about this role and the greatness this picture may achieve. Would you take sixty million dollars, plus a generous royalty percentage, knowing it requires full body exposure, including the act itself, without the finite detail? We wish to capture the true emotion felt and the essence of the experience. You and Theo have the final word on editing, although I believe you shall be amazed with the results."

"Sixty million for one picture! Jesus Christ!" David's heart nearly jumped out of his throat, and his shock skyrocketed. He calmly wiped the cool, damp beads streaking down his forehead, while his mind fumbled with an unimaginable offer of money, to commit a sexual act in front of cameras and real people. His dilemma increased one-hundredfold, thinking of every repercussion if he accepted.

"I can guarantee you double for your next feature film; and Theo's status and remuneration will escalate within the same sums."

"Holy shit! Sixty million! One-hundred-twenty million? I can't believe it. If you scare up that much cash for both pictures, and make sure the movies, from this point on, are all features, with pay-cheques in that range, you may have a deal. Whatever Ted wants; you match. He may go higher to redeem himself with his Lord and Master; major convincing is in your hands. And lastly, we do not become overnight gay porn stars." He had done it, selling himself for millions, and wondering if he should have asked for more. Now committed, panic set in, which he tried to hide within his jabbering for conditions.

"Theo's faith may be our greatest challenge; but I believe more than one force pulls him into this character. All is agreed, if you wish this arrangement?"

"You said that a few days ago. Are you going to tell me how you created that illusion?" Now confident of the woman's identity, with his wishes being granted, her presence even had him searching for new opportunities, and deciding to wait for the love that she had promised. His greed and need for notoriety came straight at him; he would not miss the catch. The love would come at the proper time, as per the Mistress' words. His thoughts were interrupted and his question left unanswered, when Ted softly moaned, struggling deeper into David's chest for warmth. Like a child, he slowly awoke.

"Hey Teddy, are you with us, son?" David let him wriggle a little, trying to come out of a shock induced sleep.

Only a sigh, the eyes fluttered open to look up into a concerned green pair. He pulled himself awake, and pushed away from the intimacy of the body holding him. "What's happened? What are we doing?"

"It's okay. You just fell asleep for a short while. Settle back down; you still feel cold." David pulled him back into his warm chest and caressed the hair once more. "How are you feeling?" Oddly, David refused to release his captive, holding tight in fear of the bargained agreement: a great deal of money from a stranger with even stranger ideas.

"Confused; foolish; why am I sitting on you? Why are you calling me Teddy?" Completely disoriented, the smaller figure struggled to sit straight again, and returned to gaze at David in disbelief at the strange position in which he awoke.

"Just a nickname you may have had as a kid."

"It's not my real name. They changed it."

"Of course, the Actors' Guild, but I think it's cute. Teddy... Teddy Barrett... Teddy Bear!" David laughed aloud, and spontaneously tickled the ribs under the blanket. With an embarrassing giggle and a blushing face from the man still not awake, Barrett came back into real time at a remarkable rate.

"Cute! Please don't call me that; I'll never live it down. Never thought of the name thing, and now I think it's time to return to Theo."

"No way, since the cast has dubbed you Ted; and your family and strangers only call you Theodore. Feeling up to talking about the picture?" The rapidity in mood changes cautioned David, having witnessed a number in the last few days. Ted seemed lucid with the trivial conversation, passing the time of day with a friend, and sharing a silly secret, while easing the tension permeating throughout the trailer.

"Guess so, if she stops freaking me out." Ted tried to avoid meeting the eyes of the woman, sitting on the opposite side of the table, but now he had to turn to face the silent smile, which beamed happily at the pair.

Extremely pleased over David's ability to override Ted's vulnerable emotions, with a few simple gestures and words, the Mistress spoke, cautiously formulating her words, "I am sorry for frightening you, Child. I thought I had explained what I could do. My fault entirely, for not making myself clear. For now, I do believe your hair is in proper order." The tall, slender woman stood, walked over to find a cup, and returned with fresh brew for Ted, when David realized he had finished his and could use a refill. His mug filled at the thought; his heart skipped a few frantic beats. After another taste of the unusual beverage, serenity returned. He wished upon every star, reflecting its light off his metal abode, the drink would keep Barrett from exploding into a worse condition. He sat ready, holding a keg of dynamite sweating in the sun.

"*Mind over matter* you said, visualizing what you want. While running your fingers through my hair, you imagined how long it should be, and what it would look like when finished. I'm sorry for misunderstanding, but my hair can't be real. It unnerves me, because it's too easy for you. Doesn't that make you dangerous?" One of the longest monologues Ted had made in days, his usual tirades aimed like shotgun blasts at David's heart and ego. Without a stutter of nervousness, the man absorbed the thought of the power of the mind.

The Mistress laughed, delighted her rising star settled quickly, back in good form and humor. He also understood more than he let on through the assumptions he made. "Some people would consider me dangerous; but I can also stop a rock from landing on your head. So you tell me."

"Now that truly scares me, believing you could throw the rock or catch it; and it's solely your decision." Ted finished the powerful potion and set down his mug without moving from his position. Whether the ambrosia helped or hindered, it brought him into the real world coherent and lucid.

"Freestyle rock-climbing is your favorite sport; every handhold and foothold is your decision; and the step up, down, or sideways must be correct. Each attempt makes your heart race with excitement. My actions can be a risk or a safety net; the choice is always yours. You will understand soon; and I hope not to add to your fears. Remember, you also possess the same abilities, having experienced positive thoughts toward your brother's return to good health." She gave him a beautiful smile, full of radiance and warmth that could melt ice in an Arctic storm. Her man-child, with the fragile Spirit, already thought in the *knowing*, but unaware of his gift. Deep within, she glowed with pride at his instincts.

"Yeah, right, as long as you don't subtly change the subject on him." Both the woman and David laughed, leaving the brunet in bewilderment. "It's okay, Ted; the Mistress and I spoke of the additional money we'd earn for these intimate scenes, and whether we're capable of performing. For the amount offered, I'd be willing, if you are." David left his co-star to clench his hands, understanding Ted could spook, but an arm reluctantly released from around the frailer shoulders.

"What would be your price, Theo?" The Mistress effortlessly curled up, embraced her bent legs, and rested her chin on top of her knees. Unable to sway his answer, being his choice alone, she waited while exchanging glances with another set of eyes flashing green for go.

"I can't do it at any price. I'm against sexually explicit acts on film, having stood in front of people, denouncing it. How can I justify my participation in a sordid attempt to make this picture viable?" Ted looked into David's face, waiting for a reason to agree.

"We approve the final edited version. Besides, we discussed the risky measures to bring this picture to life. We do make love in several scenes, but the details of the act will be eliminated. She only wants the emotion we experience, not the explicit visuals." They stared at each other for what seemed forever, both men thinking different aspects of the situation.

"But it's for real, man, in front of cameras! You and I doing..."

"...the doing being the biggest difficulty. Can we do it?" David sighed and leaned back with his eyes closed. His mind whirled with ways of getting around the sex scenes.

"Could you make love to me, David?" The direct question had the older man sitting upright and in stuttering mode.

"I... I don't know, but yes, I... I think so. Could you respond to me without having a stroke or feeling raped?"

"Man, this is beyond anything I've ever been asked to do. I just don't know how I'll react." Ted looked straight ahead, mulling over the scenario nervously, while two others watched his profile with fingers crossed.

"Has a man ever made love to you, or have you ever kissed another man?" David tried to soften his tone, caught off his mark by the interrogative expression suddenly turned toward him. He watched the lips, so close to his own, start to pout and quiver. A small sliver of an opening took in a hint of a sigh; the hollowed out cheeks took on a slight blush. Surprised, LaCoix could not understand the following answer, in denial of the need.

"No, never." Ted looked more embarrassed than indignant.

"That's what we want Child--innocence--the reactions of a first-time experience. No rehearsal for the kiss, or the act, but a spontaneous, sweet respite between two people, yet so intensely involved with the other that an audience will feel the emotion rushing through their entire beings. With a gentle seduction, two men save each other from their lonely, desperate lives. We want that special something to break the barriers and hearts of even the homophobic, as accomplished by the book."

"The role is so amazing, but committing sodomy with David? Man, this is hard. I want this part, and may be convinced, if we received a large remuneration; something closer to what well-known actors earn, without sacrificing their bodies. I still don't know."

"How does sixty-million sound?" David grinned smugly.

"Sixty-million! Fuck! Guess that's the optimum word, isn't it?"

"You got it." David and the Mistress laughed heartily over the statement, as it looked more promising that the young man would agree. They waited for the shock to set in; but this was business; this was acting; and this was the only thing Ted could cope with emotionally.

"Wow! Nobody deserves that amount. Hell, I'm not being paid a half million, let alone sixty. I don't mean to sound greedy, but shit!"

"It will make you the actor promised, Theo, and another secret for you: who knows what those top rated actors did, or did not do, to earn their twenty odd million?" The woman laughed her haunting melody and winked at them both. Now she had them wondering, and she giggled harder, watching the two look at each other thinking the same thing.

Two heads returned to gaze at her in amazement and complete surprise. David squinted at her suspiciously from under those flirtatious blond lashes. "You're not insinuating that..."

"...Of course not. People will do anything for the right price. You just never know which sacrifice they made. If extreme talent were the only key, we would have a different group of superstars than those that bring in box office revenue. Only they know for sure; and we could not possibly presume to guess. Now, stop running those names off in your head; I am surprised and ashamed of you both at such thoughts." The Mistress found their surprise terribly amusing, reading the list in their heads of who, what, and where, and continued to chuckle with her hand over her mouth. Her eyes danced in pure delight at the libelous thoughts.

"And you know who, don't you, however, that's an assumption on my part, and shouldn't suggest such a thing, nor should you. You are an outrageously wicked woman." LaCoix laughed along, knowing a few confirmed rumors.

"Sorry, David; shall we get back to Theo and what his answer might be? Well, Mr. Barrett, what is your decision?"

"Okay, but no one else knows." Ted returned to the matter at hand, and sounded more confident than he had since meeting his *Lady of the Rocks.*

All three agreed, shook hands, and the Mistress departed, stating she had further business to attend to on the morrow. The timing deemed appropriate for both David and Ted to take a few days off, to get over the shock, and clear up any personal business. Filming would commence in three days, and the appropriate transport and directions were given to the Mistress' chosen location. She assured Ted that the studio lay in the desert, far away from any dark alleys and dirty rooms. Making the location easily accessible, by road and by helicopter, she felt elated that the two men accepted the challenge. The blue-eyed man-child came around to his chosen future as an actor, rising above the incredible boundaries that blocked his way, and awakening into the light of new possibilities of the *knowing*. David had already started. Smiling and happy, time came for great care and even greater caution. She began to fit Theo into her own puzzle, while she maneuvered David along his original chosen path. Her moment's excitement stopped: LaCoix and Barrett agreed too easily.

CHAPTER 10

"David?"

"Yeah?"

"Why are we sitting like this?"

"We... I... Hell, it seemed appropriate at the time." David pushed Ted off, unceremoniously landing him on the floor. The older man rose and walked away, stretching out his numb and overworked muscles. Sitting there, entangled with Barrett, now felt extremely uncomfortable, particularly with the departure of the Mistress.

"Ouch! Thanks a lot. What do you mean by appropriate? I'm confused. Did I hear sixty-million dollars, or was I hallucinating? Feel like I've been walking through a mine field, and I think I've stepped on my share." Ted rolled into a sitting position and rubbed his face, wondering at everything heard.

"Good description of your evening; and you, Mr. Barrett, amaze me. You recover from an emotional breakdown in a blink of an amber eye. Man, you scare me; you're so up and down. Believing I'm volatile; you're off the map." David returned to the couch with his usual bourbon and a diet soda for Ted.

"Me? You're the one rambling. Just tell me what was real and what was not. Ouch!" Ted eased himself off the floor and rubbed his butt where he had hit the unforgiving floor. With little padding covering his behind, he gratefully sank into the soft seat beside David. He sat quietly, turning to look at the tall blond who squinted at him out of the corner of his concerned eyes. The older of the two melted into the sadness of the peculiar blue ones full of hidden mysteries. They could not bounce back from the turmoil within, unlike his mental and verbal gymnastics. As an actor, the young man could assume the look and sound of normalcy, but not those eyes. David shook his head, contemplating how to tell the man what went before.

"Ted, are you afraid of her?" David offered the soda -can to his co-star, who refused it with a quick shake of his new mane.

"Damn right I am."

"Why?"

"She can do the physically impossible. Just look at my hair, and I know she tossed you across the room." Ted clenched his fists, a sure sign of nervousness.

"At least you can admit to those miracles." David pointed to the wavy head, while Ted looked skyward at the strand falling over his one eye.

"Unbelievable, isn't it?" Barrett hesitantly touched his hair, confirming its permanence with a slight tug and small yelp.

"Yes it is; and for a great deal of money, you agreed to do what she asked. Can you handle the truth of what happened here tonight, without ending in a puddle on the floor?" David swirled the bourbon in his glass, remembering how much smoother the woman's beverage tasted, only to realize he poured the unwanted drink by habit. Attempting to think of something other than Ted diving into an abyss upon the full realization of what lay in wait, he downed half of the liquid in one gulp.

"What are you talking about?" The young man grew annoyed at the slow pace of incoming answers to his many questions. LaCoix could beat a bush to death.

"You remember me flying across the room, and that did hurt by the way. You know about your hair; what else do you remember?"

"Her conversation with your fiancée; which I rather liked." Ted actually smiled in his smugness over David's reputed wanton behavior, and the women involved. "Oh, yeah, she turned off the phone with a spark from her finger."

"What a trip we had tonight. Are you okay with these strange happenings?" David leaned back and turned his head to scrutinize the profile frowning in contemplation.

"No, they scared me to the point of pissing my pants. You can't tell me you weren't shaken." Innocence turned to experience for confirmation.

David could not lie to such honesty in those pools of blue. Shaking himself to answer, he withdrew from the quicksand that pulled him ever deeper. "No, I wasn't; and she asked me the same thing. I admit to being surprised and intrigued. Do you remember your reaction?"

"No." Ted looked sheepishly down, noticing the different clothes he wore. He touched his hair again and squinted questioningly at David.

"Do you honestly remember the last few days, Ted? This is important."

"Not really. Like I said, I've been fighting my way through a mine field, and there are just too many underfoot, if that makes sense."

The sad picture could break a heart, and repeating each occurrence would not help. Sighing and leaning forward, LaCoix set his glass on the side table. For unknown reasons, he grasped one of Ted's hands, and studied it carefully in an attempt to calm his own frazzled neural transmitters. Another fit had to be thwarted; he had to tread carefully.

"What are you doing? Let go." Ted came forward, wanting his hand back. He tried to pull away, but the pressure intensified. Nerves started to short-circuit, and more explosives lay too close to the surface.

"You've gone through one mental trauma after another; and I'm worried about you. Tell me now if you're unable to deal with these new scenes. I don't even know if you remember the rewrite."

Ted watched the hands, entrapping his own, puzzled by the statement and the action. He searched David's troubled expression for something tangible to focus on, and intently studied each line of the older actor's frowning face. From the end of a long dark tunnel, he heard his mentor speaking to him.

"No fussing. Promise me, Teddy."

"You're scaring the hell out of me. What did I do tonight? Where did these clothes come from?" The man, in pale blue, pulled at the sweater and peered down at the expensive item. A catch of a scent, the pullover belonged to David.

"You remember the Mistress fixing your hair?"

"Yeah, sort of: *mind over matter*. I can see the results and feel them. Does that count?"

"Don't be cute; this is serious. After doing your hair, what happened?"

"I remember nothing, until she asked us to make love for an incredible amount of money. That can't be true. She was joking, right? She's just a wealthy voyeur, willing to pay us for fulfilling a fantasy." Panic replaced bewilderment; and if a land mine went off now, he would not hear it.

"Sixty-million and she wasn't joking. If a voyeur, she certainly has the money to satisfy her lust; and you agreed to participate, Barrett. How can we work together, if you go into shock with every new surprise? You haven't recovered from the first few."

"I don't go into shock; you've been told that before. Christ protects me from insanity, saving me from stress and fear." Ted's agitation intensified; and David could not understand an attitude denying a truth.

"So, Christ put you in the bathroom, hiding in a corner, babbling like an idiot; and yes, you did piss your pants. If that's his treatment for shock, I wouldn't be asking for his help again." David held his co-star's hand tighter to stop the trembling, while two pair of wild eyes connected, the green sparklers willing the blue ones to stay strong.

"I did?" The brunet looked away, fighting any kind of flashback, as LaCoix's head spun with assumptions seen in the troubled face, but dared not reiterate those imaginings of horror he felt.

"Yes, and you put up a struggle to free you from your tight fetal position, scrunched between two immovable objects. Finally managed to get you into the bath, cleaned up, changed both of us into dry clothes, and came out here to sit with the Mistress. She helped cover us with blankets; and you ended up coiled around me like some deranged snake. Fuck, you were so damn cold; and I needed the closeness to fend off the same shock symptoms. Never have I been asked to take responsibility for someone in your condition. You gave me a hell of a fright, my friend. I didn't know what to do, except hold on to keep us both from falling apart."

"Man, I can't remember any of it. Sorry, I just don't believe it, David. It's not me."

"You were the only one in the bathroom with me, Babe, so you tell me who helped you?"

"You sound like the woman who dropped me. Please don't tell anyone. If they ever found out... if they knew... Christ, help me... the baby!" Ready to bolt, Ted felt two strong hands grab him and flip him onto his back.

David pressed the small body into the cushioning and snarled. The weary blond had had enough. "Stop squirming and look at me. This is what I mean; don't break down now. We're professionals and can do the scenes. When you get back from visiting your wife, we'll talk about the baby. Maybe your feelings will change. Promise me you'll go home, talk to Karen, and relax. With this much emotion, you should breeze through the new script we're being paid highly to perform." David eased up on the chokehold, and leaned away from the man still pinned at the neck by a strong forearm.

"You're strangling me. Let go. I've sold my Soul for mega bucks; that's why Christ didn't help me."

LaCoix nearly burst a vein in his forehead at the comment, and growled viciously at a frightened man; but who did Ted fear most: David or Christ? At this point, little mattered to the man, as he angrily gripped the brunet by the shoulders, shook him violently, and slammed his head against the soft seating of the sofa. The younger man's frightened eyes prevented a brutal assault with a fist; however, Ted believed oblivion preferable to the comments that hurt too deeply.

"No more of this crap, Barrett. I'd like to slap you silly. Christ wasn't here when you made your decision, or to help you out of your hiding place, nor when you heard the news of the baby. Considering the state you've fallen into, you must realize your God didn't show, to flutter down from heaven to alleviate your dementia. Damn it, Ted, you even admitted he didn't save you."

"You were there; he saved me through you." Extremely passive and incomprehensible, the answer irritated the explosive actor further.

"Bullshit; that's lunacy. You're crazy if you believe otherwise. Yes, I was there; but you have to take responsibility for your decisions and what transpired. Christ doesn't lead me around to do his bidding. If we had to wait for him tonight, you'd have ended up in a psyche ward; and you sure as hell wouldn't agree to sixty-million dollars for a few days work, playing parts that neither of us have had much experience with." David released Ted, leaving him stunned, in a half-opine position, against the back of the couch.

"What's happening to me?" The quiet question was not an act; the fire, lit under David, needed time to flicker out. Another assault of spontaneous anger, on the part of a steaming Leo, stopped the anxiety attack building in a confused man afraid of rationalization.

"Obviously too much. You're a grown man, but there you sit, blaming everyone but yourself. Stop asking stupid questions, Barrett, because there are no answers. If there were, you wouldn't listen. Grow up." David put his hands on either side of the startled, tormented face, making sure Ted had stayed his panic. A change of thought and a cooling off period deemed necessary. The blond let go, stood erect, and tried to smile unsuccessfully. "It's okay; just think logically, without further theological rhetoric. I think we've had enough of the Spirit World for one night."

"Okay," Ted quietly whispered.

Again, the submissive tone had LaCoix wanting to lunge at him with another barrage of fury. David hated the sound of any man giving in; but Barrett's hurtful words, from days ago, heightened the consternation of the older actor. Wondering which was worse, David had to settle the argument, knowing Ted incapable of instigating a resolution. "Good; a few days off and maybe you'll be able to talk about what's ahead. Get yourself thoroughly entrenched in the forgiveness of your Christ, while you're in San Diego. Perhaps his awesome powers will help you with the baby situation. I'm staying here, to look for property and catch up with some old friends, including a director who offered me the lead in his next picture. It's a hell of an opportunity." David's face turned from frustration to jubilation, remembering the moment of his confirmation as the lead in a period-piece drama.

Ted frowned and stood up with a slight wobble. Pacing to get the circulation back in his cramped legs, no acknowledgment of what David said came forth. After a few minutes of blessed quiet, he suddenly leered at the man with narrowing eyes of mistrust. "What did you mean when you said neither of us has had much experience? Were you implying something about me?"

David startled at the cryptic question, and blurted out something he never expected to reveal, "No, I was talking about me."

"You?" Ted abruptly stopped to stare into his idol's inner being.

"No one knows my secret; and you better have the decency to keep your mouth shut; or so help me God, I'll tell your wife exactly how you feel about the baby," David snapped, upset he alluded to a dark past, but assured his threat would keep Barrett silent. With his finger pointed up his co-star's nose, along with a vicious glare into terrified eyes, he need not worry about his monumental indiscretion.

"Maybe I don't need to know." Ted tried to look away, scrunching up his face in pain at the unmerciful grip squeezing his upper arms.

"Sit down and shut up. You need to know, to realize I won't hurt you during the intimate scenes. One call for Christ's help, from this point until we've finished filming, you'll have scars up your ass to remember me by." David shoved him back onto the couch and glared down at Ted, as if nothing but a worm.

"It's going to hurt anyway."

David calmed himself, coming to rest directly in front of the person who now could ruin his career with an innuendo. "A little the first time, unless you're willing and help me. Younger than you, married with two baby boys, and in constant motion auditioning for my big break, I read for a casting crew who introduced me to a very famous director. Before I no longer glittered as his golden boy, I got my foot in the door, by allowing him to fuck me for a couple of years: anytime, anywhere, on his command. Talk about selling your Soul to the devil, I did it, and have been working ever since, never regretting the experience. Even maintained my first marriage through the affair, although difficult, but I got choice roles for a while and lots of money, not to mention expensive gifts. I prostituted myself, Ted. Now what do you think of me?" David questioned the disbelieving face. He could not deal with the disappointment, and returned to a standing position, to fixate on the ice rattling against the glass he picked up in his shaking hand.

Ted's mouth dropped, inhaling short breaths, and improvising a great imitation of a feeding goldfish. All David could do was chuckle at the naïve expression he faced and at his own stupidity. He needed a countermove. "Stop staring at me, as if I've confessed to murder. It's not as if it hasn't happened to others, and more frequently than you can imagine. It's Hollywood, for Christ's sake, Ted. A good portion of our industry's population is gay or bi."

"Are you?"

"After such an affair, guess I'm bi. I prefer women, but the occasional male has certainly caught my eye. If that makes me bisexual, then that's what I am. It doesn't bother me, so it sure as hell shouldn't upset you."

"How could you tolerate it? I don't understand. Did you love him?" Ted seemed overly curious; and the older man tilted his head in a questioning posture, trying to understand the reaction, instead of the disgust he expected.

"In a way, I suppose I did, whatever love means between two men using each other. We're all a bunch of vampires in this profession, searching for life-sustaining blood, and if you have to suck cock or expose your ass skyward, then so be it."

"How do you live with yourself, doing something so unnatural?"

"Being that adored made the experience pleasurable; and the sex became a risky adventure. I met everyone on your *Glitter Town Carousel*. I've worked hard and steady since. Maybe not major films, but averaging two or three a year ain't bad."

"Why did you tell me?" Ted slumped forward, his face in his hands.

"You needed to understand, that when we do these scenes, I'm experienced enough to help you, and to make it as painless and beautiful as possible. You have to help by willing yourself to submit. Our biggest problem remains as to whether we can rise to the occasion; and I mean that literally." David laid his hand on a downcast head, feeling as dejected.

"It's true; it's finally sinking in. We're going to... oh man... can I react to your cues? What do we do?"

"You tell me. I'm a firm believer that the majority of young men, through a certain age range, are bisexual, accepting any offer of a gentle touch and a promise of sexual gratification, if done properly." David did not want this conversation, but better now before cameras rolled. He sat down beside Ted and stared through the window at the same bright star, which his co-star was probably wishing upon.

"You're kidding?"

"Not at this stage, Barrett. Think about sex from a physical perspective. Where's a man's erogenous zone, besides the normal: between his ass and scrotum, right? There's also some hidden in the anal canal, and thus the need to jerk off while taking a shit."

"You're disgusting." Ted screwed up his face and leaned away, as if David carried the plague.

"Don't look at me that way. Probably the reason men carry *Hustler* into the bathroom and take root for half an hour. It happens, and you know it." LaCoix gave him the same scrunched up face in retaliation, and slouched back into the softness of the couch.

"I don't know. Everybody's different." Ted mimicked the move backward, maintaining the intense eye contact. Both heads were supported by the softness of the couch; both men needed to learn and be heard; and both wrinkled up faces softened.

"There are some things that are indisputable: the prostate and urethra rest against the wall of your rectum, and how many women are willing to stimulate either for you: next to none, except for the very adventuresome. What I've experienced, read, and been told, from both gay and straight friends, your ass does have sensitive nerves in certain areas. Denied by many doctors, refusing to study the phenomenon, seem ignorant of this anomaly. Now then, women's G-spots are exterior, and what do we do; we ignore her needs, and just dive in, ramming the hell out of her. No wonder they get frustrated with us, and we with them. Neither participant is being satisfied completely. As for oral sex, who cares who's sucking your cock, as long as they're good at it, which should make another man preferable, knowing what a man enjoys."

"So you're saying that we have this whole thing backward; and gays have more sexual satisfaction than straights?"

"Not saying that's true, but the physical incongruities make me wonder." David finished his drink in one gulp, his last for the night, in case he confessed to something uglier.

"And you think you can turn me on with a finger up my ass? Get real. I still don't know why I accepted. I can't do this." Ted pushed himself up, nearly making it to the door, when a hand grabbed his shoulder. The action seemed a constant source of communication with the young man: Ted running and David stopping him.

"Barrett listen, really listen. This movie, even with the bizarre and provocative subject matter, is going to be a blockbuster; and you know it. We both need something incredibly dynamic for our careers. If filmed correctly, and I believe this woman has the capability to make it so; it's our ticket, man. If I have to fuck the life out of you to do it, we do it. You just tell me how to touch you before we start. I guarantee I'll turn you on and have you screaming for more. Your attitudes, toward your marriage, your faith, and to this new baby, are more foreign to me than sleeping with another man." Back to snapping turtle mode, David upset himself at the unwarranted attack. He had mishandled the delicate conversation.

"You don't know anything about me; and now I know more about you than I wanted to, including your high expectations of your sexual prowess." Another feisty comeback by the butterfly, set to fly away, smacked LaCoix in the face.

"Forgetting the boast, let's go down the list again of your peculiarities. I think I have a few more to add."

"Heard your analysis of my head space before; don't need to hear it again." Ted turned, reaching for the doorknob to escape, unintentionally lighting another fuse.

David abruptly latched onto the brunet's upper right arm, and spun him around, shaking him harder. "Shut up and take notes this time. You're trapped by something you refuse share. You were forced to marry someone you barely knew, arranged by a church with no leaders. You belong to a religion, in which, you can't confide your deepest worries and sorrows, without it spreading throughout your entire cult. To top it off, the reason to get married is to have children; and you're in complete distress over the eventuality. You're distraught, almost to the point of dementia, believing that the woman, who is giving you a huge breakthrough film, is Satan. You still believe Jesus will save you, when he hasn't been around the last few days. Tell me, Ted, what's swirling around in that head of yours? You are one enormous contradiction to me, and shouldn't even be in this business, if the little you have told me has any basis. Overly sensitive people usually make fine actors, pulling on those emotions to create their characters; but you are unbelievable. Remember, my friend, this is acting. You can do it, if you remember that one factor: become the character and how he felt."

"How dare you call my faith a cult!" Ted hissed at him like a venomous viper.

"Shit, is that all you heard? Sorry, I'll retract that part of my statement. Hell, I wouldn't want to upset you again. Now, tell me what else I said. You don't remember a fucking thing, do you?" David let go of the tense body, with a vicious shove backward, and turned away.

Crashing against the door, Ted hurled himself forward, swinging David around, coming nose-to-nose with the man. Barrett finally fought back, defending himself like a true man. "Shut up, you son-of-bitch. The only thing I want is to become a good actor, but I didn't think it would come at such a high price."

"What price, Ted, sixty-million or your Soul? Don't believe it's either. The whole thing's a crock made up in your head. Until you start confiding in someone, you'll lose it, man. To be that actor lies right in front of you, to make people cry along with titillating the hell out of them. With your *Lady of the Rocks* sitting in front of us tonight, I had a hard-on just reading the script. Good name for her, Barrett." David quickly turned away, trying to regain his composure by using his co-star's trick. Furious with himself, for telling the devout Christian of his past, he now snarled at a man who could snap mentally with just the wrong word.

A timid voice came from a head bent in shame and disbelief, "Can we talk after I get back, David? Maybe I'll feel better after talking to Karen and getting everything that's happened out of my head, so I can just focus on our task. I promise I won't screw this up, but I'm terrified."

"So am I. I'll see you in a few days." David wanted this evening to end, and calmly absorb the massively absurd commitment on his own time. Also in a state of bewilderment, he wished he could confide in Jess. With that out of the question, the woman came to mind, reminding him of an ancient seer, holding the secrets of the universe. Her memory held him spellbound, wondering if he could confide in a stranger, with whom he had a strange connection. He felt in juxtaposition with himself about the Mistress. Deep in his own mind of confusion, he dismissed Ted entirely and startled at the call of his name. He turned to face the downcast stare. "I thought you left?"

"You're not going home to see Holly, or even Rebecca?"

"No, I need to be here, to get on with my plans. There seems to be some urgency in starting, as if the sky is about to burst; and I'll be taken out to sea in the backwash if I don't get things rolling. I have new and old business to take care of."

"I thought Holly meant everything to you?"

"Stop pushing my buttons, Barrett. My daughter is my world, but I can feel myself changing, and I hope it's for the better. I sense Holly will be an integral part of my plans. Why am I explaining myself to you? I wonder if Jess has left." Again, David turned away, dismissing the man, or trying to, as he rummaged through the nearest closet for his pack. He only needed enough for a weekend of possible surprises; Housekeeping would forward the rest of his gear.

"Sorry, David, but I was just asking, not judging. Mr. Carmichael does keep you balanced, doesn't he?" Having enraged the lion, he softened his tone. The younger man also needed a mentor to calm his own distraught Spirit; he required David's approval.

"Yes, he does. Jess just listens and asks the right questions, making you believe that you've figured it out yourself. I think the Mistress does the same thing."

"You asked how to get a reaction from me to do these scenes. This might be a stupid idea; and I don't know if it would work, but..." Ted stumbled, not finishing what needed saying, and certainly unable to face David with his unusual request. Shuffling his feet, staring at his toes, seemed the best solution.

"What do you have in mind? Don't turn bashful now."

"This is really lame, and I don't want to upset you further. I'll see you in a few days." Once again, Ted headed for the exit, with his thin shoulders hanging in defeat.

David sighed, stepped forward, shut the opening door, and pulled his co-star around. Not knowing what he wanted, the taller actor looked weary and felt just as lost. The problems escalated beyond his ability to cope. "I'm not mad, Ted, only frustrated. What is it? Any idea would be a start."

"You'll think it stupid."

"Maybe, maybe not; just tell me." David watched *Peter Pan* emerge, and he had to be as gentle as he would with Holly, perhaps gentler. Since the Mistress entered his trailer, in such peace, the evening had rapidly spiraled downward. He had to stay calm and listen, without blowing another circuit in his brain.

"My character goes through hell, finally seeing his savior in the man holding him hostage. They fall in love under strange circumstances." Ted's eyes finally met the tired green ones.

"More complex, but close to my understanding of the plot."

"As normal people, we have no feelings of hero worship, or hostage trauma." Ted's difficulties grew, explaining a simplistic problem--the two men did not know each other--period.

"You're breaking my heart; I thought I was your hero." David chuckled a little nervously, wondering which direction Ted headed.

"Please don't laugh at me. This is hard enough." Ted squinted at him; his hands, once again, in tightly strained fists, clenched to his sides.

"Sorry, go ahead." David bit his lower lip to cover the bemused smile he held back. Whatever Barrett had in mind would probably delight the older actor. One big surprise package, he waited for his co-star to burst with pretty bubbles and sorrowful tears.

"If we're to do these unnatural acts, we must come to terms with you and me personally."

David watched the man fumbling for words, looking down at the floor, shifting his feet, and increasing the pressure of his hands until the knuckles turned white. The taller actor waited patiently for the next part.

"When I get back, would it be possible for you to act differently toward me, to become..."

"...You're getting nervous, Ted, which makes me very nervous. What are you asking? Do you want me to stay clear of you?" Unequivocally disappointed with that prospect, David again waited.

"No, quite the opposite. It's a bad idea anyway."

"Ted, you have me confused. When you return, how am I to treat you? Just say it: simple and direct."

"Okay. Could you care for me, sort of?" Ted looked up with those eyes desperately pleading for help.

"I do care about you." David stepped back. He felt hurt Ted would think otherwise, and confused at why he would feel that way toward the younger man.

"No, differently, something to get us in the mood for... you know... affectionate caring."

"Like flirting with you?" David's heart melted at the bashful request, but delighted at the prospect. A notorious flirt by nature, he loved to play the game.

"Oh, man, just kill me now; it would be less painful." Ted tried to get out the door barricaded by a stronger, longer arm.

"Makes perfect sense to act out a blossoming relationship to some degree, enough to learn a little about each other by innocent dating." The older man hid his mirth, and genuinely thought it a good idea, if he could pull it off, and if Barrett was receptive. For reasons unknown, he wanted to know everything about this unique character: how his troubled mind worked, why a young life posed such a paradox, and solve a mystery in the process.

"I'm sorry I said anything. I feel like an idiot. Do men actually date?" Ted gazed up from under those lush eyelashes into an amused face. It only added to his humiliation.

"Did I laugh, and yes, gay men date. They even marry, in some states, adopt children, and live average, normal lives. They don't just hang out in bars with dubious, dark, backrooms. Now then, when you get back, we'll add a touch of romance without anyone knowing the wiser: a few dinners together, long talks, a little handholding, and some gentle hugging. Although I'm not naturally a touchy, feely person, I can offer you affection. After these few wild days, I think we've become friends, and I do enjoy your company. I'll change from this cold-hearted son-of-a-bitch and become a better listener. Is that what you're asking?"

"I guess. You shouldn't have to change because of me. I like you the way you are. You're unpredictable and dangerously wicked. It's part of your charm." Ted teased, growing a little bolder, with a silly, embarrassed grin that crinkled and softened his strained face.

"You're already flirting with me, Teddy Bear. A Leo needs that kind of stroking; you're a natural. I think your idea sounds excellent, a little unorthodox, but fun all the same. Let's try and see what happens. If we're to make love, I better know what you like, including all your tender spots and how to seduce you." LaCoix graciously accepted the compliments that made him feel unique, and promised, to himself, to be extra vigilant over the unstable young man. His mood lightened immediately.

"Oh brother--seduction--I don't know what I like, or even if someone has tried to seduce me. Body signals are a foreign language to me. To tell you a secret, I'm not very experienced with women either. Karen's been the only one, and she's just as naïve. Guess I'm the touchy, feely kind, but never get a chance to express or experience it. Displays of affection..."

"...are frowned upon by your church. I'd certainly believe you to be a touchy, ticklish character. I bet you know exactly what you like, if you let your imagination loose. Be ready to tell me when you get back."

"Will you explain to me how I can attract you?"

Caught completely off his starting mark, by another unexpected request, David laughed off the implications and agreed to think of something. He finally pushed Ted out the door, wished him good night and a *bon voyage*. The blond head rested on the back of the door; the green eyes closed. Baffled at the last question, he understood the reasoning behind it, but not how it was put into words. Every sentence, spoken this night, whirled in his head, out of control like a tumble dryer, similar to the feeling experienced when he read the new script. Making love to another man returned his thoughts to his own seduction so many years prior. Smiling, he remembered the motion picture, which launched his career, smugly dangled in front of his face, in exchange for two years of loving sexual favors. Unfortunately, LaCoix had no such currency, and he doubted his acting ability to lust over his co-star. Not averse to sexual gratification, with almost anyone in a skirt, without the love part, it had been a while since he had been with a man. He would have to start looking at Ted differently, and come to terms with it, not letting it spin out of control. Being a needy creature, he easily succumbed to any type of erotica; but Ted was a virgin in this form of relationship, not to mention his lack of experience in the heterosexual arena. A heart could break, even the one beating against his chest. Rubbing his face, he felt damp beads of sweat, and recognized the symptoms of his own buried terror. He grabbed his leather jacket, picked up his smokes, and headed out for fresh air.

The night lay dark and still, except for the howls of coyotes passing messages back and forth under a half moon; LaCoix drew in a lungful of home. By tomorrow afternoon, all signs of the large encampment would be gone, devoured by heavy machinery and desert forces, left as if undisturbed for the sidewinders and scorpions. Another deep breath of purifying desert air, he watched the last trailer light dim. Ted had gone to bed; LaCoix had to ensure the man returned to finish the film. Imperative to them both, somehow he knew it as fact. A hint of chimes rang quietly, a rustle of wind fluttered his straight blond locks, and the scent of lilacs wafted passed; she had to be close. The Mistress stood beside him and smiled at his sudden heart-stopping jump.

"Shit, you scared me."

"In such peace and serenity, I thought you would have heard my footfall."

"Your footfall? I don't think your feet ever touch the ground."

"*Touché*. Perhaps I assumed that years of martial arts training increased your senses, or perhaps I caught you deep in thought. I suggest you enjoy those cigarettes and treat yourself while doing business the next couple of days. You have much to do and many people to see." The Mistress mused to herself at the unnerving confession this man had made to their man-child. A brave and honest statement, it proved a junction to a possible new future for the fading star.

"It appears I do. Can't wait to meet with Morris and old friends, making a new start, and with luck, finding a place to build a home--just mine--sounds exciting."

"I believe you are ready to move on. Take your time and find the perfect spot. Perhaps, the land you seek lies over there. You seem to be gazing at a parcel a few miles south, toward that unusual rockslide."

"It's a fine possibility, Mistress, if blessed with underground water and availability. One other thing, you have the strangest name. I'm sorry, but it makes me uncomfortable."

The Mistress laughed sweetly, charmed by the honesty of the man. "I am so used to the title that I forget its connotation to humans. Many call me *Your Ladyship*, and your co-star has alluded to it on a few occasions, along with a special title he has bestowed."

"Way too formal for this laid back California type."

"You choose then; I am sure I will delight in a new moniker. You forget that you soon will be an Arizona type again, out of the glitter of those so-called thousand stars. Too bad you cannot see them for the smog."

"Sarcasm? There's more to you than you let on. You believe us a false society as well?"

"In the most extraordinary of ways; and the saddest part is the world follows your example. Rather tragic in many respects." The beautiful head looked up at the real stars decorating the black sky.

"Well, we agree on something."

"Yes we do, and now about my name." Turning back, she smiled and waited for something as unique as LaCoix's persona. She refused to read the thoughts of another when it offered a happy surprise. A new name bestowed gave her pleasure. No one missed entitling her with something of significance to them alone; and she loved the perplexing wonder of each creative thought.

"If I'm correct, we met under the most perfect colored sky. The only word to describe the soft hue is lavender. What do you think, Lavender?"

"A good choice for the group of you; I like it very much. Shades of purple do have a certain meaning to me, which you will discover."

"How many names do you go by?" David kept on rambling, while contemplating her last statement and his own imagery. Under lavender skies: the saying had a sense of the surreal that they had all experienced; and it was her sky, however she manifested the illusion.

"You are a curious one. I wish our wistful young friend could develop a more inquisitive nature."

"A change of subject again; damn you're good at that; and thanks for releasing me from my agreement not to smoke."

"Perhaps, it is a little early for you to stop, considering you are visiting old friends." Both shared a little laughter; flirtatious eyes lingered long; her Ladyship broke the spell. They both turned to look at the rockslide that started the conversation. "Take in this wonderful night air and picture your new home in every detail, Mr. LaCoix. A helicopter shall arrive in the morning, to take you to Tucson, where a car and driver will be waiting."

"Thanks, that's very generous of you; but I'd rather drive myself. This is my home state; I know almost every road, rock, and canyon."

"As you wish: a red convertible for your mid-life crisis." She giggled softly, thinking of what pleased a man, no matter the age.

"Damn right. If I'm going through a change, might as well be in the appropriate style, before I trade it in for a Jeep Wrangler."

"You suit a Jeep. You appear behind the wheel of one in most of your films. Good night, David."

"Have a peaceful night yourself, Lavender." He smiled to himself and turned to follow her path into the darkness. She disappeared before he had spun around. Left alone and feeling one-hundred percent better, he took his first drag on a long overdue smoke. Filling his head and lungs with nicotine, he felt satisfied with his decisions. Everything would turn out; he had no doubts.

Shivering from the breeze, which decided to play in the sand on the desert floor, David welcomed the little dust devils dancing off the walkway for his own entertainment. His smile broadened. Soon he could watch these mini wind-bursts pirouette every night, and listen to the wind sing through the cypress and eucalyptus that would surround his new home. He could see exactly what he wanted, and as Lavender suggested, he closed his eyes to visualize every detail. Tranquil and happy again, he turned to do his last chore for the night, to clean up the mess left in the bathroom. His romantic mood turned to one of the chaos called reality; he sighed while stubbing out his pacifier.

To his amazement, he opened the door to find the room spotless, with a tub full of hot foaming water, clean towels laying close by, the scent of heavenly lilac lingering in the air, and a small set of crystal chimes left hanging near the window, tinkling their soft melody, all waiting just for him. This strange woman knew what he needed and seemed to be an endless source of surprises. He was smitten with the lovely Lady Lavender.

Looking down, now at peace with an evening that had veered slightly from her plan, the Mistress took a deep breath in the purple mist and held it, letting extra oxygen fill her lungs to awaken the deep resources in her head. She had her handsome leading man on a corrected path, finding his own way. He would stumble, but David LaCoix seemed eager to begin; she expected nothing less. A small glimmer of acceptance appeared in the man-child; only a glimmer, it sparked a light of hope. She heard him throughout the long night, calling for those who would not appear. Theodore Barrett relied heavily on outside forces to sustain him, and not his own mind. The Mistress knew he would take the hardest road. A spell of tranquility, sent on a whispered kiss, caressed the heart of her young charge. He would need her love on reaching San Diego.

CHAPTER 11

The famous LaCoix smile could not get broader, exposing the slight flaw of his corrected overbite, and erasing the seductive stubborn pout of his lower lip in its relaxed state. Sun-bleached hair fluttered over his face, while dark sunglasses protected his eyes. Flying in his freedom, he raced the topless red car along a straight patch of desert road, leaving a cloud of sand to drift through the hot air, like a vapor trail in the sky. David had a perfect three days of impromptu parties, meetings with old friends, new opportunities offered and accepted, and half-dozen properties to view. Off to a grand restart of life, he felt euphoric driving through his home state, acting like a teenager, and trying to forget that day: the horrible day, so long ago, culminating in a violent argument with his father.

He had left, that very moment, for what he thought would be forever, beckoned on by the bright lights promised by those strangers from Hollywood. Although his mother attempted to mend the deep rift between father and son, the chasm grew too wide to jump. Spending his last free time with his folks changed everything on this special day. A lifetime since things had been comfortable; the house, once filled with constant laughter, returned to past yesterdays that morning. His father, now fully recovered from David's mistaken demise, waited nervously for his son since the dawn. On seeing his golden boy, his arms stretched out to welcome him at the top of the porch; and David ran down the same path, of his youth, into more warmth than he could remember. He was home, and he felt what he had missed. Embraced firmly in LaCoix Senior's steel strong arms, his father refused to let go of the weary Spirit.

Those few precious minutes made David more resolute, to find his place under the Arizona sky and live a life of normalcy. With his future in flux, he planned to resolve the past week's dramas, fully empowered to rectify each one: Rebecca, Holly and Susan, his boys, the graphic scenes to be performed, the bizarre events with the paradox called Barrett, and of course, the mystery of the enchanting Lady Lavender.

David drew closer, feeling the calm, and chuckling happily to himself, as he tore up the road in the fiery, Italian cabriolet, feeling life return to his Spirit, and knowing, deep inside, that his world grew richer in all ways. One of his passions had been cars, but had never indulged in the formality of racing, like some of his peers. Street version, daredevil mayhem, and open desert raceways were his claim to the ridiculous part of his youth. A scandalous whim, to indulge in fun, added to his giddiness. The sensation stretched from his toes to the top of his head, turning on a heated arousal, and tempting him to pull off the deserted road to relieve the pressure inside his jeans. He laughed, recognizing what a fast, red, sports car did for a man, and he let out a scream of pure pleasure and primal howling.

Planning his arrival to be the first, he wished to view the unknown location during daylight hours. Like a mirage, in the middle of the Sahara, a large sprawling village appeared to float above the desert floor. Shimmering, then fading, only caught in the wavering light, gave the illusion that nothing existed. As he approached, his smile instantly disappeared. He slammed on the brakes, coming to a halt after skidding sideways a number of heart-stopping yards, filling the car, and covering him with road dust. Taking off the sunglasses and coughing out unwanted sand from his throat, he stared in amazement through the gates. This was not a studio or a location camp, but a home, growing with a life of its own. The spread extended in every direction, each building intertwined with garden passageways leading further into depths of green foliage and pastel colored flowers, and continuing through the many recesses of one level structures. Each turn of his head changed the vista, with only one constant: the wrought iron gate and stonewall, which had appeared out of nowhere, blocking any further progress. Lucky not to have hit the formidable barrier, he thanked his quick reflexes for saving his neck.

David whipped his head around at the call of his name, to see a rakish figure approach the passenger side of the steaming machine. Devilishly handsome, with long black hair and a perfectly trimmed goatee and mustache, the man looked familiar, yet unrecognizable. Suddenly, this strange creature hopped into the expensive rental and pointed nonchalantly at the gate, motioning David to drive onward. With a flick of a bracelet-covered wrist, the gate opened without a sound, and a magical sight spread before LaCoix. Other figures appeared here and there, again seemingly familiar faces, from what he could see at a distance, but names eluded him. He should know them, but grew increasingly baffled at his inability to recognize one.

The longhaired man, beside him, had a British accent, full of humor and good sport. He also admired the shiny toy that David had been playing with the past few days, but issued a direct request to take the car no further than inside the gate. David's gear had been packed and moved by Housekeeping three days previous, leaving only his backpack and the many large shopping bags, filled with surprises for Mr. Barrett, to tote. Remembering his promise, he spent sleepless nights contemplating what the younger man had requested. As an actor, his first priority, for any role, went into researching the character; however, Ted's hint could not be studied via the Internet. With no one to discuss courting a straight man by a bisexual one, he forged ahead, with a useless script, with no words, and no direction. Feeling ridiculous, he decided to start the old-fashioned way.

His charming welcoming committee of one aided him with the many parcels, and quietly accompanied David on the long walk to the main entrance, without an utterance of the strange items bulging from their wrappings. Changing direction, the two men strolled along a flower-laden path, that's trelliswork dripped with purple wisteria and pink climbing roses. Sightseeing on the trek, they stopped at a cleverly hidden adobe cottage with two doors, some distance from the central building. Completely turned around by the layout, if this man, who neglected to introduce himself, had not been his guide, David would be forever lost amidst the gardens, camouflaged dwellings, waterfalls, and trickling streams. With a turn of a latch, the man opened a door into a spacious suite. Decor presented an eclectic taste, with items of furniture and art from around the world. Antiques, too old to contemplate, mixed with state of the art luxuries, mingled in a basic Southwest style, plus the oddities of a Gothic castle. Luxurious, tasteful, and comfortable, the suite rated far higher than a tin trailer, or other accommodation endured while on location. As cozy as his imagined home, he wallowed in its welcome.

David inquired as to Barrett's accommodations, and hid his smile when informed Ted' is suite attached to his own quarters through the second door. The others would arrive late evening, leaving David with a few chores before the reunion, including reading the note received from the lighthearted Brit, who jammed his hands into his pockets and breezed away, with the long, languid strides of a dancer, while merrily whistling. The peace he radiated seemed to shine out in rays from his tall, thin frame, much like the contagious feeling of Lavender; the smile brightened on David's face.

Handwritten in a very distinctive style, perhaps of ancient origin, made the reading of the note difficult, but held an intriguing invitation for an evening's repast to end his special day. With a contented sigh, and before the call for dinner, he took the time to investigate the mirage and kick over a few rocks. The marvel of architecture and landscaping captured his sense of adventure and chronic curiosity, considering that the vista, viewed while driving, appeared to float.

The suite came first, checked thoroughly by discerning eyes, from beehive fireplace to the emperor-size bed, to the open windows filling the rooms with the sweet scent of jasmine. He loved the smell, enticing the adventurer to exit his temporary home, to take in the exotic scents and sights. Barrett would be his neighbor, in the suite attached to his, with the next double guesthouse a distance away. The possibility of a lengthy walk persuaded him to forego his boots for more comfortable sneakers, as the oasis appeared to have no boundaries, and conversely, no way out.

His mischievous side came into play, overriding his thoughts of captivity. Thinking about Ted's request, he turned the latch to the younger man's quarters; the door opened; David invited himself in. Similar in design to his designated quarters, the entire cottage fit his flirtatious plans, including the lockable door between the two suites. Returning to his side of the dwelling, he unpacked one large shopping bag, carefully pulling out a large, delicate surprise, still intact and arranged carefully with a card. Once again, he slipped into Barrett's quarters. The happily scheming blond began enjoying the planned adventure, believing his first gift would embarrass his young friend unmercifully. However, if Ted had experienced more sorrow, perhaps a small joke, made of their playful flirtation, would offer a little solace. David looked skyward, not knowing what he believed in, or if he ever did. The lack of tangible evidence did not prevent him from asking anyone, who might be listening, to have Ted return as the ray of sunshine he had first met, and not the melancholy Spirit who left his trailer three nights previously.

Ready and curious to meet his new employer for a third time, LaCoix followed his guide through a dark passage, with only bracketed candles to light the way. Led to a marble, open-air sanctuary, filled with white flowers, silver foliage, and more candles, his astonishment showed, in his wide-eyed expression of disbelief at the never-ending body of water, which lay as still as a mirrored surface. A physical impossibility, he stared in awe, and then gazed quizzically at the Mistress, approaching from the few stairs rising from the water's edge. The dashing, leading man waited for an improbable explanation, and for the feel of warmth of the extended hand. The illusion approached, in a gown drifting and fluttering with every motion made, mimicking the ebb and flow of the gold-green, reflective sea, a perfect match for the seductive eyes. Tonight demanded David's best behavior; and he remembered, without having to act, everything learned to play a distinguished gentleman.

"Good evening, Mr. LaCoix. Beautiful, is it not?"

"Absolutely, Mistress Lavender, and you look as enchanting this glorious night. May I escort you to your chair?"

"Thank you, kind sir. It is a pleasure to have the honor of a gentleman joining me for a quiet evening's repast, in my favorite moon garden."

"The pleasure is mine. Always a source of delight, you continue to amaze me. A contradiction in so many ways, I count on your surprises to be a wonder."

"I accept the gracious compliment and savor it."

David offered his arm; and they slowly made their way to a table, covered with crystal, pewter, and roses of black. He held out a chair, on which Lavender floated effortlessly to rest upon the soft surface. Her fluid and elegant movements mesmerized her guest, whose thoughts veered to a minimalist in flight, like a delicate but lethal condor. Being the perfect escort this night, he helped push her chair forward, and then gently lifted the long mane of wild curls over the back, leaving them uncrushed if she leaned against the high-backed furniture. Thrown back in time, with a lady of the court, he felt out of character in his California-style blazer and cotton pants. He needed his tuxedo, a shirt with a collar rising over his chin, with lace cuffs dangling from the wrists, and a long velvet waistcoat. Where was his high, black riding-boots when he needed them? The vision in front of him triggered his sense of the macabre: a Gothic Mystic, a Fey of the Night, a bewitching Enchantress, or an unearthly creature of unleashed power.

"Thank you. Few men think of such a needed gesture and a romantic one." Her beautiful white hand, covered in emerald jewels, sparkling with moonlight, bedazzled him. With the elegance of a Queen, she picked up her serviette and feathered it over her lap.

"Perhaps I favor long hair, and enjoy the opportunity to pleasure in its sweet smell and soft texture." David caught his breath at the majesty of her gesture, but did not miss a line.

Her Ladyship smiled and laughed softly in her now familiar way. She reached for a pewter goblet and looked across the table with a beguiling smile. David gently slipped the stem of his own vessel through his long fingers. A soft chime was heard, when two exquisitely crafted goblets met with a whispered toast to friendship and new beginnings.

"Were you able to make the most of your time off? Did you find the perfect place?" Her eyes peered over the rim, as she took her first sip.

"Yes and yes. The property is available; and my offer accepted. Soon to be a new landowner, I must ask how this magnificent place came to be, and how you found it. It can't be real, considering this part of the world has no large body of water."

"Does it not feel real?"

"Everything looks and feels very real; but I know Arizona; and an ocean is not on our map."

"I must admit the location is a hidden, sacred sanctuary, for only those who need its tranquility and protection. La Rosa Negra reveals itself to answer a man's most haunting questions and troubles. Although given directions to find it, tomorrow the road shall lead elsewhere. That is all I can tell you. Make yourself comfortable within its beauty and share the wonders that make this home--this realm of light and knowledge--this living generous organism. If you accept its secrets and open your heart to everything said, no matter how different the ideology, you will always find your way back. Even in times of great distress and confusion, we are here to help."

"Sounds mysterious and don't fully understand, Lavender, but I have this crazy notion that me and Mr. Barrett are your pet projects." David could not veer his attention from those all-knowing eyes; and his own startling green ones quieted, softening with the bewitching Fey's smile.

"I would not call you projects or pets, only people going through major changes in their lives. You are two of many. Your intuition is surfacing, but you found your own path with one sincere gesture. If you stumble, or wish to discuss anything, I am at your disposal, along with a number of Holy men, of different backgrounds and philosophies, with whom you may feel more comfortable. As you already stated, I tend to scare you; a serious understatement when it comes to Theo."

"You may surprise me, but you are intriguing. Every occurrence, of the last week, astounds me. I feel ten years younger, starting over; and you're right about the opportunities coming forth.

You're the guide promised me--confess--let me in on a few of your secrets." Enchanted by her presence, David had one option, to tease her, with his flirtatious mannerisms, to obtain answers.

"Perhaps, perhaps not, as I am only here if you fall, when one of the Fates attempts to interfere with your life's quest. In reality, you are your own guide--forever alone--no matter the number of personal attachments you make. Take the credit when you have done something well, and accept the full responsibility for any chaos you leave behind. No one else deserves the applause, or the blame. Hold that thought always in your mind. Part of something you are already learning, I am gratified at your willingness to break old habits. Making up with your father was a courageous step and necessary for your future." A bell rang without a finger raised; and dinner appeared before them. The disruption did not nullify the intensity of the conversation, or the comfort of each involved.

"How did you know? Besides, it's time to get on with a more fulfilling life, without all the artificial crap. I thought the *L.A. Freeway* was my driving force; but it's constantly congested, keeping one at a standstill half a lifetime. My chosen predicament created a person who drinks too much, abuses drugs, and makes the same sordid mistakes that I see my friends plunging into. Attempting to stay young forever, while constantly searching for attention, within the public eye, is a full-time and hellish job. Overall, we may be shallow people, and as you stated, we knowingly manipulate a rather naïve world into thinking we're gods. With innocent, unthinking people hanging on our every nonsensical word, I rather disgust myself, and no longer wish to feel that way. Perhaps, it's the reason I'm drawn to Barrett who takes me away from myself."

"Yes, our new friend, who is a gifted Spirit, floats free, yet wonders where and if he can land. I know much of what and how you feel. You are seeing people in a different way, not to be used and abused, but cared for and nurtured. Do you think you can sustain the trust of those who look up to you?" The question sounded like a dare; David's face lit up at another challenge.

"I can only promise to pursue my goals with the best of intentions and hard work, for my own sanity."

"Heartfelt words spoken with determination, you will make it, my friend. I believe you already feel the magic of La Rosa Negra, and will help Mr. Barrett deal with its mysteries. I have no objections to you sharing our conversations with him, at least those you believe of importance. He needs a teacher he respects."

"When the opportunity presents itself, I'll try. What I said is true, Lavender; and the philosophy you spoke of earlier sounds Taoist."

"Very basic Taoist, which continues to be a rule of nature, no matter what the philosophy, except for the few more grandiose religions, which our man-child clings to. Take your rewards when deserved and be grateful, always knowing that you alone must clean up your failures."

"Sounds simple, yet people get very silly about compliments, and appear selfish if they take all the credit. Then again, the same individuals seldom admit to their mistakes." Another sip from the goblet of wine, which never diminished, David became fully aware this would be an evening of learning; his eyes never left the beguiling face; his proper interpretation of every nuance required his attention.

"A paradox within your society, I regret to say. Women turn a *devoir* into a harassing statement, such as the word *Lady*; and men give all the credit for their talent to a god or prophet, as do your athletes when interviewed after a game. Perhaps the confusion rests in human DNA.

One truly wonders how men and women manage to come together and live happily-ever-after."

"On the most part, I don't think they do. Ted and I discussed the incongruities between the genders, after you left my trailer, that very strange night an eternity ago. I hope our species is not unique in its confusion between love and lust, friendships and relationships. It doesn't sound complimentary to mankind as a whole."

"Your species does not have the exclusive rights to the stated situation. Kind, meaningful words are tossed aside, when they should be embraced. I took to heart your comments of this evening. They were from your inner Spirit; and whether deserved, I cannot deny your feelings behind them. Accepting is politeness, and returning them when the time is right. When you and Ted win accolades for your achievements, simply accept them graciously. Do not thank everyone for doing a job that they were paid to do. Credit for their work comes with their own applause for being the best, as you alone deserve the reward bestowed upon an actor."

"Many people make an actor look good. Are we to ignore them?"

"For the most part, considering I am asking you to contemplate who truly creates a great performance. It is you alone, and perhaps a gifted director. The creation you bring to life should be brilliant and intense without make-up, costumes, special effects, lighting, setting, and on and on. I believe you hate working with celebrity status stars, as opposed to *real actors*. They are the ones who require the plumage, and the necessity to thank everyone under the sun. Rare acting talents, such as yourself, need only a well-crafted script, a poignant character, a bare stage, a minimalist director, and your own charismatic presence. Your talent makes the audience see what is not there. That is acting."

"Thank you for confirming my consternation. You're being very philosophical tonight. Is there something I can do to lighten your mood?" The startling green eyes flashed and flirted, and his famous grin teased a laugh out of the Mistress.

"I believe you just did. I thought you preferred young, whimsical beauties to older women." She taunted back, and her own green eyes stared deeply into the matching ones across the table, searching his mind, digging into his subconscious being, trying to find the parts she had missed for so many years. David noticed, for just a brief moment, the return of the cat's eyes of the *Lady of the Rocks*, and he shivered slightly.

"I don't seem to attract sophisticated, beautiful women such as yourself. Those of intellect and fine breeding do not readily succumb to what I thought were my many attributes, which, according to you, I should be proud of and happy with." A slight mood shift into the melancholy overcame David; he suddenly grew quiet.

A teasing tone, and an awesome smile, to spark a candle to light, returned his equally contagious grin. "Come now, David, you collect--I believe you call them--charms. You are a handsome, dangerous risk-taker, the perfect adventurer for the majority of women. Do not let it go to your head, for it has been your downfall in the past. You must decide whether you desire a permanent relationship, or to continue playing in a sandbox full of kittens."

"Lord, I hope not! It does sound sleazy and grotesque when put in those terms."

"It does at that; and I would ask you refrain from using that term within this environment."

"I'm sorry; a dreadful habit, whether one does, or does not believe in one higher power."

"Quite correct. How easy it entraps to form unwanted habits, but we must accept everyone here, whether we agree with them or not. Not our place to change one's faith, we must honor all.

Only the beliefs in those faiths need rectifying, coming to one's own conclusions."

"It's Ted's future that concerns you; his beliefs do not justify his faith."

"Very good, David, you are getting closer. We believe him an innocent snatched at birth, baptized, and brainwashed without choice. Children, especially infants, have no understanding of spirituality; or where their natural path will lead. The act of baptism is a cruel symbol hung heavily around their necks, before they can decide for themselves, suffocating them forever, and filling their lives with guilt if a pattern changes. The ritual becomes a permanent brand, embedded in their subconscious mind, that they belong to this group and beware of all others. My personal opinion only, and as a Caretaker, any initiation ritual of a child, offering their Soul to a false power, should be fended off with all due deliberation until adulthood, after all philosophies have been studied. For instance, would you hand your child over to a stranger; one you think you know, but have no proof of their reliability?"

"Never."

"Exactly. A child's path starts after some life experience, when the inner *knowing* of each unique individual surfaces. Perhaps you would live in a more tolerant world, if children were left free to wander in the Spirit World alone. As for Theodore Barrett, those with no right to interfere tore him from his path. We hope it is not too late for him."

"So, you believe baptism mentally abusive, and thus Ted's suffering."

"Only one part of his trials; the Fates willed him into his dreadfully confused state. What makes you feel guilty, David? You know what is right and proper, represented by all philosophies. You do not rob, rape, or murder--a strict code of the Cosmos--therefore what causes your guilt?"

"Considering my upbringing in a non-spiritual environment, my folks left me to find my own path, as you put it. I was christened into something or other, obviously of little importance to me or my family, just the right thing to do at the time, I guess. My biggest remorse would be the fight with my father so long ago, which doesn't sound like something one could blame on being baptized. Now, my licentious behavior, as an adult, buries me in a bottomless chasm of guilt."

"The fight with your father may have been warranted, not knowing on whom to rest the blame, or whether a catalyst to speed your departure. Perhaps your regret comes from one of the commandments you learned: *Honor thy Father and thy Mother*. Your subconscious mind took that in, and kept reinforcing the guilt, until it became the wall between you."

"Perhaps; but I wouldn't know, considering the time it took to rectify. I'll never forgive myself."

"Why not? You had a wonderful time with your father this morning, and he with you. Past culpability clings to you both, which is extremely destructive. The time comes to discuss such things with your father. Man to man, I think you can now accomplish a greater bond. You are both ready, considering he thought you forever lost; and you nearly lost him. Ponder this for your contrition: *Thou shalt not commit adultery*."

"Ouch! You're not subtle with your jabs either. I'm never sure what you mean; but as to my wanton behavior, no one can forgive me, until I correct my various family predicaments, starting with the deeply ingrained problem with Dad. In his remaining years, I wish to strengthen our new bond, by explaining and regretting my stupidity, over a few beers. Mom, I fear, I hurt the worst. She had nothing to do with it; and yet, I discarded her feelings in my anger toward Dad, and embarrassed her unmercifully with my public scandals. This morning we all fell apart, deciding to rebuild a family. I do love the old guy and my Mom."

"Of course you do. I am overjoyed to hear you say those words and mean them. You need these precious people, and so do your children. As for understanding me, I do over extend my explanations, and I am sorry for that. I seldom have guests to talk with on a different level than the nurturing Caretaker. Would you care for a glass of something rare and exotic?"

"Always happy to try something once, and if unsure, willing to try a second time."

"Your eagerness to delve into the unique and dangerous delights me. *Saluté*, my friend." Glasses rang out the same soft ring of a small metal bell; and a quiet, less intense conversation continued for several more hours. While slowly ingesting their gourmet dinners, David noticed how little the Mistress ate, coming to believe she thrived on her ambrosia. He, however, indulged in everything offered, including the delicate rare wine that tasted of a remembered night in his trailer, calming his Spirit. He felt the cooling breeze off the still water, fluttering the blond hair across his forehead, and tinkling chimes echoed lightly in his head. Forever present, they surrounded the beautiful Lady Lavender. She was the chimes; so soft and melodic, only trained ears could hear the sound. He felt wonderful in her company, lost in time of long ago.

The two elongated El Greco figures stood to stretch, slowly meandering down the few steps to the water's edge. It was real. The water lie still and felt lukewarm to the touch. A small upturn of the lips, he thought of the enticement of a quick skinny-dip. On second thought, he decided this woman would adamantly oppose such a suggestion, and had already read the retraction in his head. She did her own thing, in her own space and time, and probably very much alone. The thought saddened him, but created a revelation that nearly knocked him over. This woman remained forever alone, in her mysterious world.

"Careful, David, I lost you momentarily. You almost fell in the water; and I do not swim."

"You could always fish me out with a flick of your wrist." He smiled wickedly at her and laughed, but pulled away from the water. "Your ambrosia makes me a little lightheaded. Tonight has been overwhelming. Thanks for sharing, Lavender, and confirming some of my thoughts. As an aside, my second wife and I agreed not to baptize my daughter." Again, David flashed his wickedest grin, and received a familiar one in return.

"I know."

"Thought you might. I enjoyed this evening very much." David lived in a perfect dream this evening, even after proving the water real and the flowers had texture and scent.

"I can hear the metal dragonflies landing. The others shall settle in their quarters soon, as will Mr. Barrett. You must secure him in this environment, making him feel at ease. This place of solitude and foreign sanctity will frighten our man-child; I sense him fending off something very terrifying. What it could be is not yet clear."

"How do you know these things? Who are you, and how do you create these illusions? Quite baffling, it makes working with you difficult."

"Illusion or reality: until you believe there is more to time and space, then illusions they will always be, and your reality will only exist as two dimensional. Expand your borders by imagining your reality; and you shall instantly come into the *knowing*. Remember, I am simply a Caretaker, with guests arriving. I also enjoyed your company tonight, David, and anyone would be lucky to have you in their life. Do not sell yourself short, for many people love you, some of whom would surprise you, and they are real. Even a number of your fans probably fit your criteria, yet I venture to guess you never read one word of their mail. Such a pity, since actors have access to the largest dating service imaginable. Read some of the letters yourself; you might want to correspond with a few intellectual types. Who knows, you could even learn that actors are not the only creative, intuitive types you think yourselves to be. Many humans write to known faces just to correspond, being far more isolated in their lives than you and your friends." Lavender laughed her whispering song and blinked her devastating eyes in mischief.

"I would like to spend more time with you. Having completely mystified me, I still feel very comfortable and happy in your presence."

"You may not always, David, for I can be a tough taskmaster. I will be near when needed, no matter the situation; and I promise not to leave you alone again, lost in the web of your life. Remember to whisper my name, or think of me in your handsome head, and I will come. All will gather in the morning. As clocks and watches are worthless to us, you will come to know how time and space work within the labyrinth. Welcome Theo for me, and make sure he is well and calm before you leave him. Until the morrow, have a good-night, David." Lavender turned and walked away into the shadows of lush foliage adorning the marble lookout. David watched the slender figure slowly depart, not hearing a footfall, and before she vanished, called out. She stopped and turned, seeming to float before him.

"Lavender--the roses--they're black?"

"Yes, pure black and very rare, as is each person invited into this sanctuary. You have entered my home, La Rosa Negra. Good night, my friend; may your dreams come true." With a last wish, she vanished into the darkness; and David climbed the short set of steps to gaze down at the fragile flowers still fresh on the table. He felt the presence of someone at his side, ready to lead him back to his quarters. The shrouded figure reached down, gently picked up one of the precious blossoms, and handed it to him, granting his simple wish for one of his own. Standing motionless, still staring, and taking in the sight to remember this wonderland, he remained spellbound and moonstruck.

"Like every delicate flower, Mr. LaCoix, treat all those around you in like manner. You never know to whom you may be speaking; and each life is a unique entity." The raven-haired Englishman smiled knowingly at him, and silently escorted him back to his dwelling. David held the black rose gently, a priceless species not to be bruised between his nail-bitten fingers. With a simple good night, he entered his side of the vine-covered adobe to take care of the flower. Gentleness and kindness raced through his heart at the thought of all those he loved. A warm seduction, for a life that had run amok, the velvet softness of a black petal slipped across the back of his hand. He suddenly became aware of his own emotions and feelings toward others, reminding him of the day when a grand Andalusian, with an amber eye, had encircled him with its enchantment. His once cold, sullen expression brightened into a loving, peaceful face, easing the aging lines, and turning the lips upward at the corners. Switching his attention to something just as delicate in structure and fragile mentally, he left his domicile to see if Ted found his surprise.

The Mistress looked over the now misting ocean of water. It had been a long time since she felt an attraction to a human with such a devil-may-care attitude, much like her own. Curiosity--extreme curiosity they both shared--but her responsibilities dampened that wild part of her. She had forgotten this important mortal and vowed to correct her mistake. LaCoix stirred memories of a long past love, and lives snatched away from her. Settling into her own chambers, she pushed back the thoughts of the handsome blond. Rightful paths wrongfully altered; she had David's to correct. Only the Fates could change his future, and they were forces beyond her control. She knew them well. Slipping into her throne-size chair, she gazed through the open window to view her many realms, hidden within a black sky full of sparkling stars. With her favorite pewter goblet dangling precariously between her ringed fingers, she listened for her name, and heard it called repeatedly. The cries were countless, the names endless. Shadows played with the light, through the increasing veil of mist over her starry night, which lightened her mood back to a serene state of grace. She smiled, just to have remembered those feelings for a brief moment.

CHAPTER 12

Lights glowed dimly from within the quarters adjoining David's; and the older actor returned in a mischievous and randy mood after his *tête-à-tête* with the lovely Lady Lavender. She had him curled around her bejeweled finger; and he wondered at the possibility of charming his way into the woman's life. Not knowing who or what she may be, and understanding even less of what she said, his comfort level elevated higher in her company than with any other. Few dared get close to the rather reclusive and somewhat belligerent actor; but he certainly planned to allow the Mistress entry, to indulge his pleasure of further conversations and much more if accepted. The entire ambiance of her home intimated that of the macabre: from the first sense of the surreal in the garden of soft-hued blossoms and moving water, to the shrouded figures he should recognize. Completely smitten and very curious, he had to find out everything, including the strange reference to the *knowing*--the opening of your subconscious mind--but to what?

Smiling happily to himself, he wished for luck with his gift to Barrett. If the outcome of this film depended on seducing a man, he had better have started appropriately. Two raps on the door created a harried rustling sound inside, and a water faucet quickly turned on, then off. The door opened a crack, to silhouette the longhaired actor's head against the golden light of lamps and candles, flickering and dancing shadows on the far wall. Barrett said nothing.

"Great to see you, Ted; can I come in?" A sincere smile accompanied the honest request. Unsure of the cool reception, David stood impatiently, straining to see through the darkness hiding his co-star's mood.

"I'm tired. I'll see you in the morning." The door started to close; but the fast thinker, with the reflexes of a cat, jammed his foot between the door and its frame before it latched.

"Sorry, but I know that tone of voice. Now, let me in."

A nod acknowledged the concerned frown. Ted turned away, permitting the anxious blond entry. Right on his heels, David followed the dejected figure to the table adorned with dozens of white roses. One blossom, in particular, had been pulled free of the enormous bouquet, and placed atop the handpicked, sentimental card lying open on the shiny wooden surface. Half a flower's petals lay scattered over the terracotta tiles underfoot, plucked out one-by-one from the once perfect bloom. David scanned the room that revealed the story: Ted had been sitting there since arriving, his bag left by the door, with everything still in order, except for one flower, and a chair sprinkled with a few more white petals.

On further inspection, David did a once over of the younger man, seeing a distinct change. Not just the luxurious hair reaching halfway down his back, but his attire was different: the pale denims fit almost too snug; the fine cotton sweater of fresh white covered a checkered, navy, preppie shirt, exposed only at the collar and cuffs; and the loafers shone shiny new. Ted looked no more than sixteen from the rear; the entire ensemble flattered the slight build, creating an eye-catching figure, as if anything could enhance Barrett's extraordinary good looks. David took in a deep breath, with a lingering, appreciative viewing from top to bottom, quite spellbound at the new image, but also recognizing the stance Ted assumed when in distress, unable to face a problem of major consequence. The astute actor, a master of subtle body language in front of a camera, knew his young co-star more than he realized.

"I'm sorry you don't like them."

"What? The roses? Oh, I do; I really like them. You surprised me; that's all."

"Do you intend to annihilate them all?" Correct in his assessment, David planned solving the puzzle with patience.

"An old nursery rhyme, someone taught me, came to mind." Ted refused to look up from his fingering of another petal he picked off his chair. Disappointment over something seemed likely to LaCoix; and he sensed the dilemma grew stronger than the powerful perfume of the roses.

"I hoped you'd like white. What was the rhyme: *she loves me, she loves me not?*" Watching for a reaction of some kind, LaCoix received only polite, quiet answers.

"Something like that; and I do like white. I've never received flowers before. Feels strange, and I don't know what to say."

"Always thought it very special when people gave me flowers, for no particular reason. White stands for purity and innocence. I thought it appropriate for our first romantic trip into this adventure. I didn't mean to embarrass you."

"Please, David, don't laugh at me. This is the nicest thing that's happened to me, since... Well, I'm a little overcome with..." Ted slumped down into the seat he had been occupying, and started toying with the poor rose, which waited to be unmercifully stripped of its remaining petals.

LaCoix pulled out the closest chair, bringing it over to settle right next to the nervous, unhappy, younger man. He slowly sat down and laid a hand on the downcast head. He still had not been acknowledged by eye contact. "What happened?"

A gentle nurturing, of the brunet waves, enticed a low, quivering sigh. "Just been a really bad couple of days."

"How's Karen?"

"Happy, just like you said, but if I had to keep my plastic smile on, for one more second, I'd have suffocated."

"Still not happy about the baby?"

"Nope. If I could just stay here forever, in this maze of no return, I'd be happy to lie down and die amongst the flowers and the scent of..."

"...Of what? You keep stopping in mid-sentence."

"Nothing. Forget it."

"Again, one of those nothings. For God's sake, Ted, you can't say something is nothing in the same breath you insinuate dying. You scare me." David tried his next move with a hand under the chin to turn the hidden face. Barrett immediately pulled away, to look in the opposite direction, a grown man's simple defiance at an intimate yet child-soothing gesture.

"Please don't do that. I don't know what to tell you, David, but thanks for this treasured card and the awesome roses. They're special."

"Sounds like you're giving up on your idea; and I have all these surprises for you. I thought you'd think the flowers sufficiently ardent of me." With nothing left to do but jest and wait, the first lead actor leaned on the table with his arms crossed for support. Playing with a few discarded petals would keep him busy until Barrett decided to open up a dialogue. The stillness stifled further dialogue from LaCoix.

"The gift was romantic; but now I feel stupid asking you to do something so ridiculous. I want to leave, to run away; but then again, how do you get out of this place? I'd be lost forever, never finding the exit, and even if I did find my way out, where would I go?" The desperation of the voice hit David first, and then the meaning sank in. Green eyes darted back and forth over the profile, panicking at the real possibility of a suicide attempt.

"Listen, Ted, because I'll lock you up, or put a chain around your ankles, before you attempt to run. Look at me." David again reached under the chin, forcing the tense face around to make eye contact. The hopeless look shattered the blond's stalwart heart into fragments. The thought, of the young man making a futile attempt to wash away telltale stains and puffy eyes, he could not handle. "Tears? Why, man? What happened? You have to tell someone."

"Just life and I won't run. I've hung on for the past three days, until I read your note, and then I fell into my own trap. You called me a friend; and I don't have many. It's becoming a bad habit, this crying shit. Feel like a jackass, and all I can say is sorry. How weak is that?" Ted picked up the rose to smell its dying fragrance, but dropped it instantly with a yelp. The flower got its revenge, pricking Ted's finger in retaliation for the severe mutilation. "Ouch! I thought thorns were trimmed."

"Here, let me see. Haven't you heard the tradition that everything beautiful always has a dangerous side, thus one thorn remains in every bouquet of roses? It reminds us nothing is as it appears." David raised Ted's hand to examine the small puncture, and the crimson drop on the index finger. Under the spell of a sudden urge, which came upon him at the oddest times, and from under the long golden lashes, he gazed into the astonished blue sapphires. He put the finger delicately to his lips, inserted it sensually into his mouth, never releasing the languid stare of his dreamy green crystals. Cleaning the blood off with a flick of his tongue, he soothed the hurt with a slow withdrawal.

"David!" Taken aback, Ted had no idea how to react.

An instant rush of awkwardness was quickly diffused by the perpetrator of the seductive gesture, cooling down the sensitive nature of the act. Staring at the finger intently, David kissed it for lack of an explanation. Purely innocent, the enticement lingered in LaCoix's head. "All better; the thorn stayed with the treacherous rose and not in this tasty pointer. Are you okay?" David placed the now trembling hand on the table, attempting to disguise his erotic action as common first aid. He smiled sympathetically at the injured, tormented face, now dazed by his extremely suggestive conduct. Why he kept getting sudden bouts of being fondled, had him perplexed, and wondered if it deemed him abnormal. Something he experienced his entire life, it still surprised him, and usually got him into trouble with somebody. He may be in trouble now, and leaned back in his chair, not giving up his gaze at the young man who sat disbelievingly, yet not pulling away.

"David!" Ted tried to sound shocked, but the astute actor's fine-tuned ears caught the tone of a pleased sigh.

"I think you said that. Now, start again. What's upsetting you; and there's no need to be sorry?" The seducer smiled into the very startled, frightened face, straining between mixed emotions over the not-so-innocent moment. Tears started to well-up in the blue eyes, searching for something to look at except the older man.

"I thought you'd be here, waiting for me," Ted blurted his first admittance, but suddenly sprang to his feet, knocking over his chair, and fleeing for his life toward the door, with his mentor right behind him. Suddenly spun around, a stronger force made him stop and face what he could not. "David, leave me alone. I just want to die. Don't you understand? It seems the only way out of the two colossal mistakes I've made, maybe three." Ted caved in, falling against his pillar of support; David readily embraced what he had learned to foresee.

"I didn't know, Ted, or I'd have been here. An invitation, to dine with our producer, delayed my return. Please, don't talk or think of drastic actions. Besides, this is your room; and I believe, we'd get lost, venturing into the darkness." David stayed his concern over the threat, wildly contemplating his next move, while quiet sobs dampened his shirt collar and two hands clutched the lapels of his blazer. "Okay, Barrett, you're coming with me. I'm not leaving you alone tonight: no arguing, no fussing, no nothing. I doubt these few mistakes warrant killing yourself."

Ted pulled away and shook his head; but David refused to accept options. Remembering the words heard twice that evening, he reiterated them, in his own way, to a man struggling for liberation from life. "Listen to me, Barrett, you're a rare and precious being, and like that beautiful, treacherous rose, you also have something lurking under your perfect smile that is not always plastic. You're a good man, Ted, inside and out. You hide behind your dazzling welcome, except for those who take the time to look closely; we do see your sadness. You hold a dark secret; so please, let me help keep your problem from consuming you. Come with me, and I'll show you an object as unique and priceless as Theodore Barrett."

LaCoix had no doubt of Ted's depression, or his embarrassment that made him unreachable. Something unknown had vanquished him on his return home, leaving the older man wondering about his own distress over the situation, and giving him only one choice of ushering the silent figure into his quarters via the connecting door. Sitting his charge down, he took three steps to retrieve the dark wonder bestowed freely, now safely displayed in a crystal goblet full of clear, life-giving liquid. The blackest of velvet captured the light, absorbing its energy to enhance the absence of color.

"A black rose! I've never seen one, except in books, as they're normally just very dark red, but this is real! The hobby you inquired about is growing roses; and this one's perfect." Ted's enthusiasm gave David cheer. He had found something, to which his friend could relate.

"One of the rarest flowers in the world, it doesn't hide its dark secret in the shadows of the night, but revels in the bright light of day. It's as glorious as the light itself, even in its richness of black. You believe your dark secret is bad, or something the devil hatched up. Nothing in nature is evil, just dark and mysterious, like this magnificent rose. Your life is precious, Barrett, so no more threats." Surprised at his words, David believed they came from elsewhere.

Ted turned his attention to the lips uttering sounds he could not comprehend or focus on. He had upset his only friend, and regretted adding another burden upon the man; but his mind flew from exuberance to depression, unable to control either. His idol wanted and searched for answers; he had few to offer. "I won't say it again."

"Or attempt it? Promise me." The green eyes flashed wildly at the thought of this special person ending his life; a man willing to give up for inexplicable reasons. David's logic could not imagine the problems Barrett faced, but if he received a promise, he knew Ted would survive. Lavender had been correct: Theodore Barrett stood with his toes over the precipice, very capable of jumping.

"I can't promise anything, so don't ask."

"Can't accept that, Barrett. You're going against my beliefs, and probably your own. I'll be afraid, every moment you're not in sight, that you'll do something stupid. Now, give me your word." David yanked Ted out of the chair and shook him. Again, a few tears started, but with a single nod of the head, an agreement cemented between the two. The non-touching LaCoix hugged him, gripping him in a full body press, until the nerves of both men settled. This time, Ted returned the embrace, putting his arms around David's back and holding on as delicate as a feather. Barrett was a gentle creature and one of a kind. After the feelings felt over the Mistress, which aroused the nervous blond, the idea of making love to a high-strung, emotional train-wreck would not be difficult or unpleasant. David continued the rocking motion, allowing Ted to decide when to let go. Crazed green eyes never blinked, darting madly about the room in terror of what might have been, while the sapphires orbs remained clenched tightly, to hide a grown man's cry.

Barrett's head finally pulled away from its hiding place, his eyes opened so full of blue, they made David shiver. A raspy, sultry voice thanked LaCoix for his concern and the kindness expressed. The words did not quell one man's shaking over Ted's desire for an early demise, but eased David's tension by finding another diversion. "I have something else for you." David feigned a bright, ear-to-ear grin at the sullen face.

"You've given me enough, just by putting up with me. If I start crying again, just deck me." Ted pulled away, scrubbing his face hard with his hands, turning his cheeks pink, while sucking back his lingering sorrow.

"If that's what you want, but I'm not the reputed abusive type insinuated in the tabloids. I think we'll find another way; and since you scared the hell out of me, you're staying here tonight. The bed in there is big enough for six men, so I'm willing to share it, if you behave?" Laughing with gratification on hearing the soft chuckle behind him, David headed for his large stack of packages.

"I suppose I don't have a choice."

"You always have choices, Barrett, but not tonight. I'm a light sleeper, so don't even think about sneaking out. Now, close your eyes."

"This is really stupid. We're both acting ridiculous." Ted clenched his eyelids tightly, but remained crimson with shame that his unconscious death threat resulted in being chaperoned.

"I know, but surprises are fun; and you, my future major star, need some joy in your life." With much glee in his eyes, David approached Ted who stood quietly, waiting nervously. A tickle to his nose, then something fuzzy drawn across his cheek, made the child-like eyes flash open in bewilderment. A real smile shone through; a glimmer of hope sparkled forth to calm the older man's apprehension.

"A teddy bear! The baby's first present."

"Hell, no, it's for you. Look at the size of the damn thing. It's almost as tall as you, the biggest one I could find. Figured you needed something cuddly to sleep with, to confide in, and to share your secrets."

"Bet he's a good listener. What a big bear, and so soft. Always wanted one of these Gundt stuffed animals when I was a kid. Thanks, man. He's not wired with recording devices, is he?" Ted gave him a teasing smile and a happy chuckle; LaCoix's unnerving co-star returned to a sunbeam.

"It never crossed my mind." David winked at him, and the famously wicked grin grew.

"Yeah, right."

The response sounded normal, and the chiding had LaCoix feeling better. He might sleep this night. "When I spotted him, I thought he'd make a good friend for you. It's late, Ted, and I think you've had enough tonight. I'll get you something to wear, assuming you sleep *au naturel,* considering your lack of briefs."

After the emotional flurry, David delighted in his favorite game of watching the man blush and shuffle in embarrassment. He followed Ted into the large, comfortable bedroom, where he searched through his things, stored neatly in the drawers of an elegant cabinet. His rummaging produced a pair of black silk pajamas, given to him by Rebecca for sexy, scantily clad, boudoir romps. He sighed heavily at the thought, while tossing the slippery, knee-length shirt, with side slits, to Ted, while he changed into the loose-fitting bottoms. Sex came second, on David's list, after breathing; and his lust played tricks on his addictive mind, already experiencing nicotine withdrawal. The well-chiseled torso flexed slightly when he stretched, pulling each bone, vertebra, tendon, and muscle back into alignment. One more look out the garden window, to smell the enchanting jasmine, he turned to dim the lights and climb into the enormous bed. Exceedingly tired, and his head swimming with lecherous imaginings of Lavender and frightening ones of Barrett, the man in question suddenly caught his eye, meticulously doing up the long string of buttons from top to bottom. The combined thoughts had David reeling, the urge becoming too strong; but he had to hold this man together, not scare him off. With sexual pleasure abated, his sudden sadness rooted internally, unsure of whom his next partner would be. Not his first priority, he focused on Ted, whose life appeared unraveling, although the longhaired brunet pulled himself back from the edge one more time and reached happily for his new bear.

"Is our sleeping arrangement uncomfortable for you?" David's voice lowered and softened, as if on cue for a dimly lit rendezvous, but determined not to back down from helping Ted through a possible ghastly night.

"Nope, spent my childhood sleeping with my brothers; and being a rock climber and compulsive camper, you get used to sharing a two-man tent, which are a tight fit. Just hope I don't wake you up."

"Your nightmares?"

"How did you know?"

"At the other location, Jess and I watched you sleep, while in a constant shocked state. You fidget constantly, Ted. With a guard on duty, maybe you can get some rest." Comfortably lying on his back, David closed his eyes, ready for the deep slumber he desired. An intuitive sense of intense scrutiny made him turn his head and blink.

Ted stared at him. The man, who had decided the bear made a perfect companion to wrap his entire body around, thanked him with a smile. An enormous stuffed toy appeared the correct choice.

"Cozy?" David chuckled to see the big blue eyes sparkling, even in the dark.

"Yeah, I like this bear. He deserves a name. How about Sir Edmund?"

"Sir Edmund Hillary? Sounds appropriate, Teddy Bear." David disguised his mirth at a grown man accepting a toy and naming it.

"Stop calling me that. Ted is hard enough."

"Not a chance; it suits you. Go to sleep."

"Great. Well, Sir Edmund, we won't be talking to Mr. LaCoix again, if he continues calling me names. Perhaps, we'll find an appropriate nickname for David."

"I don't think so, but I'm glad you feel better."

"I do; thanks." The smaller man snuggled deeper into the bear, feeling the furry creature's soft coat tickling the inside of this legs. The huggable toy saved his bony knees and ankles from bruising when locked together; David would never know what this one comfort meant.

"Since you won't tell me what's troubling you, explain your fascination for rock climbing. Do you scale peaks with full gear, or bare-handed, fight-for-your-life climbing?" Attempting to befriend this man in a normal fashion, David thought it best to know him at his happiest. Ted's adventures, in the wilds of mountainous terrain, appeared to be his fondest memories.

"It's awesome, man; but I do both, depending how long the climb."

"I suppose you do it *because it's there*." David chuckled at the normal comeback, hoping he would get something more descriptive from an actor.

"Free-form rock climbing, with no ropes or safety nets, sets you free. At times, the risk reaches terrifying, making the adrenaline rush so intense, your heart almost stops. Can't beat the feeling of reaching the top with one last effort, standing on the precipice, with your arms outstretched, you can almost fly you're so free, absolutely alone and free."

"Means a lot to you: freedom."

"Means everything, and the risk: one mistake and you die. Survival, man, and you'll understand when you've experienced the thrill. What do you do for fun, LaCoix? Thought you'd be some kind of risk taker. You're sure fit enough, if you can lug me around."

"You're a featherweight, Barrett. As for risk taking, certainly nothing as death defying as your passion, except for women. Now they put the X on extreme sport: mentally, physically, and financially. Over the years of making action films, however, I've been trained in many forms of martial arts, and I do enjoy kickboxing. More fun than lifting weights or running to stay in shape, the sport has the bonus of an opponent to knock you senseless."

"Sounds dangerous. Broken anything?"

"It happens, but that's part of the fun. Now mysteries, those I do love--mental puzzles--like this place. What do you think, Ted, a risk or a haven?"

"It's a labyrinth with no way out."

"I'm sure there's an exit, but I think your mind opens the gate. Sounds strange, but the place may only be an illusion you must learn to see through. Sorry, I'm speaking in cryptic messages like your *Lady of the Rocks*. Interesting you likened it to a labyrinth; that's what the Mistress called it. Good guess, Barrett."

"You really like her?" Ted questioned from between two bear ears.

"Lavender?"

"Is that her real name?"

"No, just one of many I gather; and yes, the woman does intrigue me." David returned to stare at the ceiling, closing his eyes to see the vision in deep sea green appear in his mind's eye.

"Oh." The eyes dimmed their luster, diverting downward, finally to hide behind closed lids.

David turned to frown at the expression, allowing a glimpse of Ted's eyes misting over in the light of a half moon. *"Oh?* What does *Oh* mean?"

"She's trying to destroy me, to disrupt every belief I have. She's the woman who dropped me."

"I don't know, Ted; I haven't figured out that mystery either. Don't get upset about our weird circumstances. You're too tired for more, so close your eyes, and then I can shut mine." David diverted a potential panic attack in a shared bed, where he lay half-naked alongside his co-star. He imagined a wrestling match with a hysterical wildcat in slippery silk; and the thought, as well as the direct look, had him perspiring.

"No, I've come to terms with that. She won't scare me again. With renewed faith in Jesus Christ, he'll help me."

Sounding like a calculated affirmation, it was immediately discounted. "That's not the sense you gave me when you wouldn't let me in tonight." LaCoix rolled onto his side, getting a better position to question the stare. The change created a polar reaction on the other side of the bed, when Ted looked skyward to count ceiling bricks.

"It's too long a story, but I'm glad you barged in, since I feel out of place here, and then to see the roses."

"As I did at first, but I'm happy you're feeling better about the Mistress. I warn you, however, not to call for Christ. Even the other prophets and gods are not mentioned by name here. All religions and life philosophies appear as acceptable here, and on an equal basis, with no fanaticism shown. I distinctly got the hint that this place is one of toleration and learning of other faiths. You never know whom you may be speaking with, therefore, accepting what's offered freely, and answering truthfully when asked. If you don't, she'll squash you like a bug."

"That's why she dropped me. I asked for Christ's help, yet all those lights in the rocks, which looked like hooded people, were probably Pagan worshippers." A quick snap of the head, blue eyes penetrated straight through David, expressing a wide-eyed realization that he now dwelt amongst the unholy.

"Someone or something broke your fall with pink light. Now that was an inspired effect. If you asked for Christ, it could be the reason she let go, if she is the same woman. She's certainly sensitive toward organized religions; and I can't tell if she honors or abhors them. Whatever her reasons, she issued a request to stop calling other philosophies *Pagan*. Your religion is considered as such to a great percentage of the world's population." David continued to watch the expressive face for anything that may erupt into an anxiety attack. In the last few days, a word could set off his co-star who hung by his fingertips from an abyss too many fathoms deep to contemplate.

"But that's what they are, worshipping false gods." Ted refused to stop voicing his concerns. Christianity surrounded him from the moment of conception.

David succumbed, knowing Ted would not heed his warning, or discontinue the conversation. "To you maybe. Don't you think it's even remotely interesting what others believe in and why?" Wishing for a Lavender miracle, LaCoix wanted to hear a hint of curiosity, but he unwittingly fell into Ted's ballpark.

"No, ours is the true faith."

"Maybe, but the wonder remains, at least for me. May sound strange, Ted, but with everything that has happened, I feel great. I'm just going with the flow, amazed that this old, arrogant bastard may change into someone he likes." David relaxed and returned to lying on his back, allowing Ted to take up his favorite position wrapped around his new bear. The cuteness of his co-star amused LaCoix, thinking how much the man needed the toy, or was Ted truly *Peter Pan*. Perhaps, a loving person could help as easily, given a chance. He wished on a star for Ted to find someone gentle. A soft voice broke his thoughts and made him chuckle lightly.

"You're not old and arrogant. I like you, even when you're grouchy."

"Grouchy? I best discard that attribute, especially after I'm settled in my new place, one of my choosing."

"You're going to be lonely, David."

"No more than usual. It's time for reflection and focusing on me as a human being, instead of some false, fading, box-office idol. How stupid we all are, thinking that acting serves a purpose in life, to persuade people to do things, to say things, to buy things, and even to influence people politically. As a group, do you believe we're that smart? Hard work and luck finds fame, and then we demand special treatment: don't stare, don't come near, don't touch. We're made of priceless porcelain, and we might fucking break. What crap, but that's who we are, craving and thriving on adoration, and yet we don't even read our fan mail from those who keep us working. The studio, a publicist, or an assistant reads it, and then sends our devotees a form letter and an 8 X 10 glossy. All we wish to know is when the number of letters decline. Lavender reminded me of our immaturity tonight, and she's right. Depresses me to think we get more press time than a bombing, a war, an earthquake, not to mention the millions of unfortunate victims. Shit is happening all over the world, away from our safe haven. Who do we think we are? Does recognition go to our heads like an addiction, and falling out of favor the ultimate ruination, with death easier than withdrawal? Besides our egos, where are our priorities, Ted? People who put their lives on the line daily, like firemen, policemen, the military, they're paid a fraction of what we earn. Not all of us are on an equal pay level, but we still get the minimum for any picture or cameo we make. For a small walk-on, we make more than they do in a year, even a lifetime. We turn into the heroes when we rush in with a few supportive words and our tax-deductible chequebooks. What kind of deal is that? Too ugly to even think about."

"I've never heard you prattle on for so long, LaCoix. As a whole, we probably do take ourselves too seriously; but I've never reached that pinnacle of stardom to know. I agree that the work doesn't justify the money received and all the attention lavished on a few. You have to look at it for what it is: a huge business. The 'A' players bring in the dollars, so why should only the production company take the profit or loss. It's a double-edged sword. We make them or break them, and sometimes overpaid to make sure it's not the latter."

"Now, who's being practical? Business graduate from where: Harvard? Well, you're on your way with this venture, deciding if we're heroes or fools."

"U.C.L.A. majoring in theatre arts with a minor in business, plus a few other degrees. Just hope to keep acting. Are you going to finish from where we went adrift into the madness you live in daily. I'm still safe from notoriety, remember?"

"The lonely thing? Remains unknown for now, since I'm off to England when we wrap this picture. I'll be gone for four or five months, possibly longer."

"I'm sorry, I forgot. I didn't even congratulate you."

"Don't worry about it. I'm looking forward to being part of a grandiose production; besides, you were mentally preoccupied when I mentioned it." David came back to gaze at a remorseful Ted who seemed deep in thought about his rambling monologue on all things offensive in Hollywood. He had not wanted to instill his anger into someone so naïve, but he refused to put up with false platitudes. "Sleep, Ted. Life is changing for us both. Better rest for the next chapter."

"You're right, but now you have me curious. I didn't think you thought about our profession in such derogatory terms. I'd like to be good enough to warrant your respect."

"I don't have any doubts about you, just a general thought of the industry as a whole. I'm the stupid blond actor with a notorious reputation, my head full of cotton, and only interested in who is wearing Armani this year. God, why do people adore us, let alone put up with our bullshit. Must admit, my personality demands attention, but the incongruities seem insidious. We don't do anything but entertain. What's so fucking special about that?" David contemplated his statements, knowing how people, within the business, treated him. The dumb blond myth in Hollywood also applied to men; and he had been type cast for a long time. Certainly not an Einstein, he did have opinions on certain matters, but no one ever listened or cared, so he stopped sharing. Playing the jackass caused problems in the past, but also gained him many rewards by manipulating unsuspecting, pompous fools. David considered himself street smart with a couple of university degrees in the dramatic arts to back him up. He suddenly drew in a deep breath, remembering what her Ladyship said about taking care of his money. How was he to accomplish the feat, without the slightest idea of stocks, bonds, or any other kind of banking shrewdness? He used countless credit cards, and that was all he knew. Numbers and money were not his *forte*.

"What are you thinking, David? I lost you for a moment."

"Sorry, did you say something?"

"Just that I don't consider you stupid. We act out parts that don't represent our true natures for the public. I guess I haven't had to create a different persona yet."

"You will, and what will that be, Ted?"

"Don't know. Probably the same way I've always acted."

"So, you admit it? You display a sunshine personality for the world, your family, your wife, for everyone but me. Why is that?"

"Don't know, but for some reason, you've been there for me through the madness I want to forget. Maybe I just trust you. Can we leave it at that?"

"Thanks, Ted; I haven't heard a kinder compliment in a long time. I'm the bad one, set on a course of self-destruction, and have caused confusion and chaos wherever I stayed too long. My intention is to rectify that part of my life. By starting fresh, a new home, away from your *Glitter Town Carousel*, maybe I can fuse three families together, and build a montage that makes me happy as well."

"I'm glad for you, David, and will miss you when this picture wraps." Barrett's voice did not disguise his true sentiment; the not so dumb blond turned to acknowledge the sweetness of the feeling.

"I'll miss you too, as well as worry about you?" With no answer from the younger man, David's concern level once again bounced off the wooden beamed and brick roof. Green eyes looked into the sad blue ones, recognizing Ted did need a friend, and with the impending intimacy, of the movie, perhaps he could relent to become the young man's mentor and confidant. A vow made, he would be there for Theodore Barrett when called upon. "Well, it's going to be a long day tomorrow. Are you comfortable enough to sleep?"

"Sir Edmund and I are just fine. Do you know how often you talk to me like I'm twelve?"

"No, I wasn't aware of doing that. Sorry." David surprised himself, wondering if he treated his grown sons in the same manner as he did Holly.

"It's the sound of caring, so I don't mind. You can stop worrying."

"Don't think so, not for a while. Besides, it's nice to be concerned about someone other than myself. I was getting downright selfish before our rockslide episode. Good night, Mr. Barrett and Sir Edmund."

"Night, David."

Just outside, the breeze sighed through the encroaching foliage, entering their open window and drifting in with the soothing, dreaming scent of jasmine. Both men fell into a natural, deep slumber. The Mistress rose from her chair and retired to her own chambers. The man-child flexed his stoic façade once more, ready for one new door to open. She felt his fear disappear immediately upon the embrace of the older man. A source of amusement for her, she watched the changes taking place in one, and a small broach of willingness in the other. Perhaps she had done the right thing, leaving LaCoix to fight solitary for most of his adult life. His strength of will and clearly defined opinions were his alone.

After snuffing out the remaining candles, she stepped into the mist, disappearing into her own realm where she could regain her strength and continue to listen for cries of help from beyond. At least two of her charges lay safe, one unknowingly protecting the other. A remembered look in the blue eyes of the youngest, she knew the importance of the missing pieces in the paradoxical puzzle of the man. Smiling, with a renewed certainty, she would discover the mystery of his identity. Tonight, few voices disturbed her reverie. While two men slept, her realm lay quiet this first night of beginnings. All her guests faded into timelessness, by the wind-ruffled jasmine and its mind-altering exotic scent.

CHAPTER 13

David woke first, rolling over in a dazed, intoxicated state from the overpowering scent blowing through the window. At the sight of Theodore Barrett, he abruptly came into full consciousness. The younger man laid motionless the entire night, in the same position David last saw him. As the fog of dreamtime cleared from LaCoix's brain, he remembered why his co-star shared his bed, and almost laughed aloud. His gift remained crushed within thin, sinewy arms, and a sweet face, barely showing an overnight growth of a beard, and snuggled between two big bear ears.

The tall blond stretched and caught another compelling smell; the heady aroma of morning coffee beckoned, considering the black brew sufficed as the one addiction left to sustain him. Lavender thought of everything for their comfort; and if he did not know better, he would believe she wielded the ray of light, splashing across his face, as a signal to get out of bed. He watched the beam slowly reach across the long distance to touch his bed partner. Ted groaned slightly with the warm, bright ribbon, flickering and tickling his fine features, making his nose wrinkle up with some displeasure. The gentle hand of nature woke the young man to welcome a new day.

David mused, in fascination, at the struggle of an adult's body untangling itself from around a bear, while fisted hands rubbed the eyes before the bright blue orbs opened to view the splendor of color beyond the window. Ted's emotions, from a bright sunbeam to a thunderous lightning storm, continued to puzzle the man, worry the man, and delight the man. "Hey, Ted, wake up."

"Yeah, I'm awake. Man, did I sleep!" Ted sat up and leaned back against the headboard, looking a little bewildered.

"I thought you killed Sir Edmund, considering your choke hold around his neck. You didn't move an inch all night, and must be aching like a coiled snake cramped up in the cold."

"I've never slept through an entire night. Are you sure I didn't wake you at some point? I usually scare the crap out of my camping buddies." Turning his head, Ted peered into the amused face. His idol languidly lay there, gazing directly at him with those serene green eyes half-closed. The disheveled blond head, and the firm body of a kick boxer, would be a sexual fantasy for any woman. Grinning sheepishly, Ted tried to ignore the relaxed mouth opening a sliver and exhaling faint whistles of air.

"Had the best sleep I've had in years, and now coffee summons."

"Too bad." The soft whisper went unnoticed.

Pulling themselves out of the comfort of their twilight time into the dawn, two men headed for their own bathroom facilities. Ten minutes later, David emerged showered, shaved, and immaculately dressed in black denims and matching shirt, happily pouring coffee for two. He found the note slipped under his front door, stating that breakfast would be at his convenience, with directions to the main kitchen. Chuckling softly, he wondered why Lavender addressed the invitation only to him, believing she knew exactly where Ted had spent the night. The same note, however, did appear under his co-star's door. Nothing remained hidden from this woman; David's mirth grew at the thought of her reading his wild imaginings. Seeming to know all, Lavender did adhere to discretion, with polite mannerisms, formal speech, and impeccable etiquette, and yet so contemporary in outlook toward the controversial book. She certainly was not the voyeur Ted had suggested. With a rap on the outside door, an invitation to enter, the younger actor entered to face a crooked smile.

"Thought it appropriate to use your main entrance, rather than barging in unexpectedly."

"Barrett, you are a kick; use either door. Privacy becomes obsolete when you have kids; get use to it. Here's some brew. Shall we start again? Good morning, Mr. Barrett." David winked at him and received a bashful smile in return.

"Morning, Mr. LaCoix. Thanks for putting up with me last night. I feel a hundred percent better today; and those roses nearly knocked me over when I walked into my suite. Good thing I love the fragrance. Both gifts were very thoughtful."

"You're welcome. Leave the inside door open, so we can both enjoy the aroma."

"You bet, but please tell me if I'm invading your space." Ted displayed his timidity; his dancing feet shuffled slightly before he strode over to open the connecting door.

"Forgot to tell you how good you looked last night and now today. I did notice, Ted; you did some major shopping over three days." David caught the embarrassment in the nervous look, searching for a getaway. Barrett made a stunning impact in his body-hugging jeans and form-fitting T-shirt of navy blue, which showed off his taut, slender structure very effectively. The man now looked delicate for his five-foot eight-inch frame. Studying the man more closely, David recognized what he saw: a rock climber's limber body of skin and bones. Ted resembled a spider: all arms, legs, and eyes.

"Guess I did, and it got me out of the house. Thought I needed a change of image, since you broached the subject. My agent agreed and helped me refine my style. You didn't answer my question, so I..." Ted stopped in mid-thought; however, David laughed on this occasion, completely understanding what the man wanted to say. LaCoix had remembered the question; Ted's new look could hold anyone spellbound.

"Yes, your new duds are attractive. You look terrific, Barrett."

"How many shades of pink can I turn? I'm becoming an expert in burying myself in shame."

"Buying you flowers and a bear made me feel silly, but I'm glad I did; and as part of your plan, you tried as well. You like the roses and Sir Edmund; I approve of your choice of style." David leaned against the lower cupboards, appraising the figure from under his blond lashes. Sipping his second cup of coffee gave him a covert opportunity to scrutinize Barrett's striking persona. "I surmise that your new clothes aren't as comfortable as your usual attire."

"They feel quite good, actually; but the first time I wore them in San Diego, I felt like a guppy in a goldfish bowl. The stares I received made me wonder if I looked fat or stupid." Far from vain, Ted had plunged, full throttle, into making himself more attractive, and now doing the unthinkable, rectifying any imperfections with a fleeting glance in the mirror.

"Stupid--no; fat--never; sexy--absolutely. Here's your coffee. The looks received probably came from both sexes. You have to watch those sailors in San Diego," LaCoix teased; and Ted's face brightened to scarlet; his head came down to study his toes; and his search, for a full-length mirror, forgotten.

"You must be starving, LaCoix. Let's go and see what the plans are for today."

"You're on. As for eating, I haven't seen you keep anything down for a week; and the way you behaved last night, I doubt your stomach has been treated to a decent meal in days. You do eat, don't you?"

"When I'm hungry."

"Good man, as our day begins." A portal to the unknown opened; a grandiose gesture, of a sweep of an arm, invited Ted to step through first. Once outside, David reached for the smaller hand, to squeeze it playfully, continuing the lighthearted mood he had initiated. Barrett looked around in apprehension, returning his surprised gaze back to David. Snickering at the expression his gesture received, the older man let go. A perfect day to amble along the directed route, outlined in rows of spiked delphiniums and tall yellow daisies, the two welcomed Kevin and Ray emerging from another connecting path. With greetings happily exchanged, and comments expressed about Ted's long locks quickly dispelled with new extensions, they arrived at their destination, before the magic hair became an issue. The whimsical Englishman, whom David still could not identify, cordially invited them in to an elegant foyer. For David, the recognition of men passing by became an annoying game of who was who.

"Cast is to your left, crew to the right. Lavender will join the actors this morning. Welcome, Gentlemen." Brimming with charm and a hint of mischief, the expression on the man's face promised something miraculous; both David and Ray caught the surprise. An inner glow of light instantaneously radiated from the man, disappearing as quickly with a change of expression on his handsome face. Two men recognized one of the figures in the rocks, and each nodded acknowledgment to the other. Neither mentioned the sighting, but both understood they could experience a flash from anyone living in La Rosa Negra.

They entered their designated eating area, to sit, at a very large table, with the actors needed for the last few scenes. Another famous star finally made his first appearance, to meet and speak with the others, and to become acquainted with Lavender. At a table of men, one black rose handled them all.

Being his first meeting with the famous face, of the man who played the Marshall and the father of Ted's character, David thrilled at the chance to share a few comments with one of his own heroes, regretting deeply at having only one scene together. They took their seats; introductions made; and Lavender took over the session. They ate a healthy breakfast; each served what they enjoyed, or whatever special diets or non-diets they followed. Fruit and yogurt seemed the mainstay of the Californians, bagels and condiments for the New Yorkers, and bacon and eggs for the likes of Kevin Donaldson.

Much to David's annoyance, Lavender restricted Ted to a regiment of supplements and a nibbling of fruit and vegetables. She did express her unhappiness of adding to his miseries, but the young actor would be undressed for the rest of the shoot. Staying true to character, he had to appear half-starved through a few scenes. The schedule, however, would move along rapidly, impeding David from coming to his defense. Seeing Ted lose many pounds, since the incident in the rocks, LaCoix faced the warning glance, a dagger of blood red from the green eyes, to back away. A quick reminder of who was in charge, the old adage, of *a tough taskmaster,* came into full light.

The Mistress wanted to commence filming immediately. The ten outlaws and one hostage would start with a brutal assault on Barrett who appeared eager to begin; however, David watched him carefully, noticing the slight strain in the raspy voice. Theoretically, the scene should be a three set-up scenario; each accomplished over several days, if everything went correctly, which seldom occurred. Lavender issued an order for a continual roll; eleven men sat motionless. Something new for most, they could only see the technical impossibility, with cast and crew crashing into expensive cameras and booms, capable of picking up the sound of a feather whisked across a dusty table.

This was live theatre; and if you did not know your lines, your improvisational skills required spontaneity, not to mention quick reflexes for different camera angles. Baffled at the idea, they all stayed quiet. David slowly analyzed their situation and ran the scene through his head: no rehearsal, no retakes, no breaks, and no mistakes. First, Ted would be blindfolded and pushed into the hideout; second, he would be stripped and shoved into a small cage; and the last maneuver, the ten outlaws laughing over the successful kidnapping of Ted's character *Jay*, who would sit frozen in terror.

With the scene set and looks of bewilderment, the actors headed down a path, to a wrought-iron gate, leading outside the compound to more buildings. An enormous studio, recognizable by the lack of windows, seemed to appear out of the haze of blistering desert heat. Inside the structure, the cabin shots would catch the action, with no detail left amiss, including the perfect look of the outdoors, lighting the interior of the shanty. Appearing as a work of magic, the wonderment continued: stepping into the light, you would swear you stood outside, with birds twittering and leaves rustling, but stepping out of the light, you viewed only the cabin.

The interior, of the shanty, filled with the smallest of cameras, miniature booms, and multitudes of miniscule colored hooded lights, with only one now shining like a solar orb over the entire set. Everything seemed to move freely in space, without a wire seen. The two-inch roving eyes moved smoothly and quickly in space, to catch the action and to follow each actor separately. Even the walls of the set came down remotely and returned to position in a blink of an amber eye, allowing full shots of the interior space from any angle. Standing behind their equipment, computer magicians, cloaked in darkness, appeared to run the shoot remotely, except for the actors and the meager direction that seemed planted in their heads. The scenario deemed a technical marvel, if it worked. Too unimaginable and no time to think, the actors arrived in Wardrobe and Make-up before they could get a better look.

With costumes resurrected, the actor's quickly dressed and make-up precisely applied. Once finished, David now stood on the set porch, unable to remember a single face in either department. A total blur of too fast and too much, he forced his concentration back to a scene that demanded perfection. After seeing Ted, sleeping quietly as a baby with Sir Edmund, the situation laid heavily on his mind that he had to abuse this man unmercifully, and for many days of shooting. Craving a smoke made him edgier; the taste of a small cigarillo, which his character required, made the problem worse. Forbidden to inhale even a puff, he was well into angry mode. Remembering his last conversation with Rebecca and the storm, which turned into a hurricane the day after the one-sided conversation with Lavender, had him growling and ready. The clenched jaw, the crazed eyes, the long confident strides, and the constant chewing on the smoking cigarillo, scared everyone.

As they shuffled into their first positions, to hustle their hostage up the porch and through the door, David reminded himself of each character name. He whispered them, worried his skill at improvisation had disappeared many years before; names the hardest thing to remember. So many roles played, over so many years, he went through the current list of players. "Ted is Jay, Jacob Weaver. I'm Dusty Slade. Okay, Jess is Jackson, Ray is O'Reilly, and Kevin is Frank. Shit, what the hell are we doing?" He sighed heavily and shifted the annoying wide-brimmed black hat to fit snugger on his head.

An interruption, of his concentration, caused him to squint more menacingly; his lips curled into a nasty snarl. Abruptly, the order came, to take their marks and to keep to the script through the segment without stopping. The technical equipment, never seen before, would take care of the rest: an unsettling statement for the cast. A recap of their jobs was listened by all: express the emotion, create the action, and remember the dialogue as if in front of a live audience. For the first time in their careers, someone asked them to be actors; the idea frightened more than a few. Large inhales of air calmed frayed nerves, as the word rang out, "Action."

"Get 'im through the door, and don't hurt 'im." Slade barked, while getting his duster caught in the door. Cursing, he yanked at it, tearing the garment without hesitation. "Shit, just stole the damn thing." A perfect ad-lib mumbled created more anger.

"Why the hell not? Wouldn't mind beatin' the crap outta the son-of-a-bitch, for the trouble he's caused." Frustration grew in Frank, who struggled with a squirming, groaning Jay. With little fight remaining, a tied, gagged, blindfolded kid was forcibly shoved through the door.

"Welcome to your new home, Babyface. Can't believe you're a lawman." O'Reilly pulled off the bandanna to look into two terrified eyes and a muffled plea from under the leather muzzle.

"Just strip 'im down and get 'im the cage. Stop fussin' with the boy. He's as valuable as gold." Slade quietly uttered the command; the lower the head gunman's voice became, the more dangerous he looked. He did not glance at his hostage and ignored the pleading cries, while he ordered another of his men to rustle up dinner. They had been on a long hard ride, but outwitted the boy's father for what promised to be the last time. His plan would stop the chase, if he remained cautious. The persistent Marshall, bound to capture him, had been thwarted again; now Slade held the man's precious only son as protection. A crazed smirk spread over his lips at the thought. The close-up of the twisted snarl, the vindictive thinking, and those dangerous squinting eyes would definitely be used.

Screams of terror, filtered through the gag, caused Jay to choke and gag. With his pleas ignored, the outlaws cut away his clothing, stripped him naked, and forced him into the small metal cage, just large enough for a hound. Jay huddled in the corner, his eyes wide with fright and tears. He could only sit, bent over on his knees, and if his arms were untied, from behind his back, he could curl into a ball onto his side. Beaten and bleeding, still bound hand and mouth, and now naked, cold, and unable to breath, he tried to hide his shame and horror. The kid knew he had no means of escape--not now, maybe never--and his anxiety showed in the quivering, natural perspiration, and frantic eyes.

"Okay, boy, here's the deal. We'll take the bindings off, if ya stop that infernal screamin'. Ya ain't hurt bad, so there's no need for the ruckus. You'll stay in there, except when nature calls, with someone watching you every second. We'll keep ya alive, as our defense against your daddy. Ya hearin' me, boy?" Slade squatted, glaring unmercifully at the kid, who looked like a blue-eyed fawn caught in the glare of a flickering fire. Someone came around behind, removing the ties cutting into Jay's wrists and mouth, incurring a sharp painful yelp, as feeling rushed back into his face. After hours with the bone crushing leather strap digging painfully into his face, he could now breathe properly; the real screaming started, jolting everyone in the cabin. Another mind jarring ad-lib began; the scene became another; everyone immediately adjusted.

"Let me out! Let me out!" Tears, shrieks, and the pushing and pulling at the metal bars created a spontaneous, ugly roar of laughter. O'Reilly grabbed a stick and started pounding on the thin, steel lid, causing an unbearable cacophonous racket in everyone's ears. Jay's screams grew louder and shriller, while covering his ears to squelch the clanking.

"Ya like that, Babyface? Do ya like music? I can keep goin', long as ya keep singin' them screechin' songs." A horrid little man, far too handsome, Jim O'Reilly learned early in life how to protect himself. No one suspected he belonged to Slade's notorious gang, and easily slipped in and out of towns to scout for problems and all the intricate details for a well-run heist. An endless source of ideas and mean enough to carry out the most incredulous of deeds, O'Reilly came fully into character with Jay's ad-lib.

"Stop! Please stop!" Horror etched in the kid's face; and he grabbed the bars to peer toward the door leading to freedom. Alone and lost, scared and beaten, no one could save him. Tears washed his face, creating glittering pools of liquid blue, haunting and stunning everyone.

"Cut. Well done everyone. Very well done."

"Get me out of here! Help me! Let me out!" Ted's hysteria grew, as he clawed insanely at the metal roof, making his hands bleed. David and Kevin raced to pull him out of his backbreaking position and help him to his feet. The smaller man, still naked and shrieking like the banshee of death, lurched out of their grasps and sprinted out the door into the artificial sunlight. Shivering violently, the fleeing figure ran straight into Lavender's engulfing embrace. Someone quickly secured a robe, while the Mistress tenderly covered the quivering body, staying his panic, and holding him with firm, loving arms. With David looking on helplessly, she shook her head at his worried face and led Ted away. The discreet woman and the frightened man came to rest, sitting quietly outside the studio walls, to bask in the full light of the mid-day sun, and the pleasure of seeing the horizon until it reached forever.

She spoke softly while examining his bleeding fingers. No permanent damage, she quickly placed her hand over one, then the other. Cuts and scratches disappeared into soft flesh, without any notice by the injured party. The anxiety attack demanded a different approach. "Hush, Theo, take deep breaths. What happened? You performed impeccably; everyone reacted on cue to your improvisation. They are piecing the scene together this very moment; and the look you emoted at the end appeared outstanding. What has upset you? Control you shaking, keep inhaling, for you are finished for today, and you acted splendidly."

"I wasn't... wasn't acting... I... I was..."

"...remembering? I know."

"Life here's so strange. I've had nightmares all my life, until last night. But then this scene..."

"...felt familiar to you. Hush, Child. Take another deep breath and look around. Look at this open space in front of us. You are free of the cage. Now, tell me about your nightmares?"

"I wish I could, but they're not clear. I can't go in there again; I just can't; I'm sorry."

"Remember the cage remains your stage for many scenes. That initial reaction we talked about: you did precisely what we desired. Do not be ashamed of your fear. Bring it forth to exaggerate Jay's emotions." Lavender kept one arm around the shivering body, although the temperature outside fired desert hot; and the terry towel robe absorbed copious amounts of fear-driven perspiration. Held modestly in place, with her comforting grip, the covering kept him from further panic in his nudity.

"Are you afraid of anything, Mistress: spiders, snakes, sharks?" Ted tried to speak, choking out words to stop the cries.

"Fellow creatures, much maligned, but yes, some things frighten me. Everything and everyone has fears. An essential part of life, fear increases your survival skills--the essence of being--all of us our prey to stronger, more lethal beings."

"Guess you could tell I'm afraid of small spaces." Ted shyly pulled away, embarrassed by the overwhelming, loving arms, holding all the warmth the world could offer. Feigning his best plastic smile at the sympathetic face, he rubbed his own to dry the remaining tears. With his manhood in jeopardy, for something he could not explain, he gathered himself together. Lavender, however, had no such inhibitions.

"There is always a reason for claustrophobia."

Adamantly denying the problem his church refused to acknowledge, Ted snapped at her quite unexpectedly, "No, I'm not! I don't have phobias!"

"Okay, Child; you have had enough for today."

"Jesus will get me through tomorrow. I'll visualize my prayers appropriately." The second statement induced pride in Lavender; Ted opened a crack to the *knowing.*

"Sometimes another person, who you can confide in, is a quicker resource than waiting for a prayer to be answered or manifested. You have already admitted to a problem. Time presents itself to expose the frightening secret, lurking in your subconscious mind, to release the fear and the terrifying nightmares. We all have two sides: the dark and the light walk hand-in-hand, one enhancing and explaining the other. The darkened path is as illuminated as the lightened; only the fear of the dark keeps us from seeing our way. Once the fear disappears, you find beauty in both sides of nature. Embrace them, Child, disposing the fear, of any mystery, by seeing the beauty."

"David tried to explain the same thing to me last night and failed miserably, or I did. I only know the dark side is evil; and you must detach yourself from it. Are you light or dark, good or evil?"

"Listen closely, Theo, to everything one says to you, and not the parts indoctrinated into your non-thinking. Dark is not the same thing as evil. I am both light and dark, and may be good and bad, but never evil, for it is a manmade concept shown in the breakdown of a being's mind. Remember how pretty the jasmine looked last night, under the half-moon. Dark, as well as enchanting, no evil hid itself within its beauty. Now, you have stopped shaking and appear lucid; are you feeling better?"

"Yes, thanks; I'm sorry I panicked. Did I ruin anything? My screams were probably too harsh for the mikes."

"No, Child, you were brilliant. Amazing how an adrenaline rush creates an actor. By early evening, we shall see the results; maybe then you will believe me."

"Yes, ma'am, I understand dailies are very rough; but editing takes time. How can your technicians produce a finished scene so fast? With so many cameras, and so many things happening, they must have thousands of feet of film to review."

"My crew has enormous capabilities, plus a little magic."

"You're unlike anyone I've ever met. You're a Spirit or something."

"Something, yes, and call me Lavender. My new name has spread through your group, thanks to Mr. LaCoix."

"Your admission came too easily. You wish to rob me of my faith."

"No, only to strengthen it with truth; and we are all Spirits, Theo. If you have faith in your Christ, so be it; but I would ask you to listen to everyone around you. We teach understanding from all angles, like the cameras around you today. Be open and willing to hear different points of view; perhaps one has a piece of information you are missing in your own puzzle. Think of it as improvising your beliefs with new truths, when you run across something befitting your faith."

"That would be a sacrilege to me. You are trying to change my beliefs!" Immediately defensive, Ted forgot another lesson.

"No, Mr. Barrett, you continue to hear only what you wish to hear. Make sure you have all the facts before traveling down your own road. Clarify your beliefs to strengthen your faith. You decide which are right for you. Go through them, studying each carefully, and feeling it inside, deep within your *knowing*."

"My what?"

"Not yet, my dear, exhausted Child. Mr. LaCoix continues to pace, becoming very nervous. He worries a great deal about you. Go now, and get some rest before tea time, when we shall all gather to witness the results of our collaboration of talents."

"Yes, ma'am, and I'll try your suggestion. You won't hurt me, if I my beliefs remain the same? I'm sorry, but to be honest, you scare me."

"I frighten many people, including your friend whom waits. I would never hurt you for trying. Keep an open mind and heart." The Mistress laughed her most melodic; so endearing and warm, her voice forced a shy grin to appear, softening the tightly clenched jaw and the mournful look on Ted's face.

She helped him to his feet and held him for a moment of needed reassurance. Approximately four inches shorter than this elongated creature, he felt comfortable in her arms. His head hit her shoulder precisely at the same spot of David's. Lavender never appeared this tall by looking at her, but when he needed her strength, she grew in stature to hold him exactly how he needed to be consoled. Although grateful, Ted's mind whirled, remembering just how much strength this Spirit had. Seeing her as a manmade illusion or ghostly apparition, after her careful handling of his sorry heart, his mind only thought of more trickery, until he felt himself in LaCoix's familiar grasp and held in the comfort of his own reality.

"You were absolutely brilliant, Ted! Are you okay? You sure get into a part when the time presents itself. Man, did we have to switch gears when you started screaming." David squeezed Ted in a moment of excitement and relief, before saying good-bye to Lavender, and then gently pushing Ted away, to get him dressed more respectfully in the white robe.

"I'm okay; just takes me a bit to come out of character. Your ad-lib with the coat, however, almost cracked me up." Ted lied, not looking at his new confidant. David, however, had a keen sense of him, as he watched the young man hide the truth.

"Damn thing got snared during a nicotine fit, instantly making me angry, possibly throwing everyone out of rhythm. Let's get you back to your quarters to wash off those painted bruises. You're walking a bit strange, Barrett. Did you get hurt in the melee?" David noticed the lean forward, and the slow, short strides on their way back through the wrought-iron gate.

"I think Ray and Kev went crazy tearing my clothes off. They snagged more than my dick. The loudest screams, under the gag, came from our tussle over the clothes." Ted smiled, obviously not fussed at the manhandling.

"They impressively reacted to your plight. Do you need a doctor? Sorry, I forgot your no doctor rule."

"I'm fine, just sore. Nicks will be gone by morning, but the blue and black make-up is no longer fake."

"Everyone got into their roles, picking up on your lead. Can't wait to see what they captured in the dailies with all that equipment. Shit, this crew is amazing. I've got to see how they do it."

"Did notice how wild you looked. You make a great villain, LaCoix." Ted laughed with a devilish grin.

"And you make a great victim." David chuckled in return, but stopped immediately with the clenching of his co-star's mouth, and the sadness suddenly springing from under the dark, thick lashes.

"Do you think that's what I am?" Ted stopped, turning abruptly to glare into alarmed eyes, and demanding an answer.

"In the part, yes. What did you think I meant?"

"Nothing." Ted turned and headed down the path under his own power.

"Great, another *nothing*. That word's used more than any other in your entire vocabulary, leaving me dangling with no explanation. Just once, answer me directly, and stop with the cliffhangers, or to be continued, especially when I'm least expecting it. I hate waiting for decent sequels, especially when I headlined the original, only to be overlooked for the same role in a mediocre Part Two." The blond actor continued to rage, finally catching up to the determined figure, who slapped away any physical help to get to his quarters and away from the day.

"David, it's just me. I open my mouth before I think, knowing I've said too much and have to stop; but then you get mad; and everybody else is annoyed with me; but I still can't answer." Ted nearly passed out from lack of oxygen, after ranting a complete non-explanation, with words coming out in a static series, like a repeating revolver.

"Slow down. Shit, you're still wound up, and your springs are ready to snap."

"You're right. I do leave people dangling, but it's become a habit. I speak without really saying anything and catch myself saying something that I shouldn't. I'm always trapped." The habitual stance and motion started: head down, feet shuffling back and forth, hands clenched in fists, and then something unseen kicked with his toe.

"We need help communicating. I'm not good with unspoken truths, Ted, particularly ones so obviously close to the surface, which need expressing. I also don't want you to shut down on me and not say anything. Maybe you'll eventually feel comfortable enough to tell someone, even if it's Sir Edmund."

"Okay, I'll try to concentrate on what I say, and what I need to say. But you, LaCoix, have to promise to be more direct, instead of hitting that infernal bush with a two-by-four."

"Deal. You start opening up; and I'll get to the point. Now, have a shower and a nap. Come get me after your rest, whenever tea time is."

"Get used to it, if you're going to England and in the company of high society. Tea time is 4:00 p.m.; and they call it *High Tea*."

"No watches, remember?" David's bright countenance returned, and he shook his head thinking about the unbelievable magic he witnessed and participated in that morning.

"Yeah, time's weird here. Do you think it's part of one grand illusion? I believe Lavender is.

She told me she was a Spirit. What kind do you think she meant?" Ted stood at his door, wishing for the truth.

"I always use the term Spirit when describing someone's inner being. I figure the term refers to us all; and Lavender happens to be the wildest one we know. If an illusion, she has me puzzled with her strength, warmth, and kindness, certainly not a cold, skeletal, ghostly type. Now go, we'll talk later." David watched Ted closely, to ensure the younger man safe and happily secure in his quarters. Newly found respect glowed across the handsome, age-lined face. His co-star proved the picture belonged to him this day; and for reasons unknown, to the once selfish actor, he felt immensely proud of his friend.

David cleaned up and paced around his suite. The action took place so fast, with everyone doing their part, the shoot seemed impossible; one take and they finished in an explosion of emotion. Not a sound from the crew or a director, their only audience came from the serious faces hidden behind computer monitors, with their hands flying at the speed of light. He wanted to see them at work; then again, Lavender created miracles. Magic or trickery, she truly was the Mistress of the macabre--a dark, unexplainable apparition--unfathomable as the black rose given.

His pacing came to a halt at the unexpected tap on his door. He happily opened it to greet Jess Carmichael. Many days had passed, since the two old friends put their feet up and relaxed, spinning a yarn or two. Today, however, the conversation triggered more animation on David's part. With many things to discuss, he needed to converse, and his usual subtle demeanor bubbled over with enthusiasm.

"Well, Mr. LaCoix, congratulations. Great bit of acting on everyone's part this morning, and our young friend finally hit his stride in spectacular fashion. Hope this crazy way of shooting works, to capture the expressions and not the chaos."

"Thanks. We all got into the action, and how exciting was that, although a little over zealous at times." David chuckled.

"Why? What happened? Something wrong with Barrett?" A worried face looked up, creating an even larger smile on the blond leading man.

"Funny how Ted's name comes up when someone insinuates a problem. The kid's going to get a peculiar reputation if this keeps up. He did, however, sustain a few bruises, not to mention cuts to a delicate area." David smirked and winked, while inviting Jess to a cold drink and a seat.

"No wonder he fought so hard." Jess grimaced, as he found a comfortable chair.

"Says he's fine, but he's pretty banged up. Forget he seldom complains about anything; and he wouldn't have mentioned the problem unless asked why he couldn't stand erect. Secretive little beggar, although he should be napping right now, if he listened to Lavender."

"Probably will, considering he looked exhausted after we released him, although he disappeared in record time."

"Wasn't that wild? Bare-assed naked, flying like Yogi Bear with a pit bull after him; and all we did in such a short time. Man, I'm exhilarated by the whole few minutes it took; theatre on film, unlike anything we've ever seen; a four dimensional concept for an actor without a greenscreen." David sat across from his old confidant, beaming with never before seen fervor.

"Hard to believe this entire venue. Felt like being on stage again, and loved the spontaneity of the dialogue. I'd swear Barrett wasn't acting, but mentally felt the fear of the cage."

"Think you're right, but I'm not spreading that tidbit around. He's had enough, and if he does fear confinement, we'll have to act fast to get him out before he totally freaks. Agreed?" A pleading look, from the infamous face, received a smile and a nod.

"At least one of us will be around when he's caged. You two have grown closer, with a certain understanding between you. It's nice to see. I think he needs your guidance, LaCoix. I can't believe I even suggested that of you." Jess chortled when his friend sat back in mock disappointment, only to laugh harder at the hurt look lasting a second.

"Why's that? Oh, right, but that old son-of-a-bitch is fading away. Barrett and I have shared a few secrets in the last while; and he has me worried. I'm concerned for him, as to whether or not he can pull this off."

"He will, but he's showing his true colors. Highly emotional little sport, but sure can put on a performance when called upon. So what else has been happening?"

"This place we're nestled within for one. What do you make of it, Jess: illusion or real? Ted thinks it's a labyrinth with no exit."

"Feels very spiritual: peaceful, tranquil, enticing to all the senses. The different aromas linger and float on the slightest breath of a breeze, twirling and spinning their way through the gardens. The touch and texture, of every surface, feels smooth as silk or cold as marble, while some have razor-like barbs. As for the colors, they are truly magnificent, from soft pastels to violent reds and oranges, all in perfect harmony. Quite extraordinary, and then the sounds, they're back, David. The chorus of humming insects; and they're not flying creatures, but the medley of voices spoken in hushed whispers. There are people we know here, my friend; and they all seem devoted to the Mistress."

"I thought so as well, but can't recall where I've seen them, or their names. Can you? It's the damnedest thing. Which reminds me, Ray and I noticed at breakfast, that these *familiar strangers* glow or flash, or radiate a hint of light."

"Like the rock people. Noticed it once and sensed he dropped his guard for a moment; he's been the only one I've recognized. This may sound crazy; but I think they cloak themselves within an aura, which we can't see through, when at their highest level of inner being. When hit by an emotion, which conflicts with their serenity, their façade crumbles until they can re-adjust."

"You're scaring me. What are we doing here; and where is here?"

"The others leave tomorrow night after the final fillers. Ray, Kevin, and I are needed for a few more days; but our mystery Lady insinuated it would take some time to do a series of interior scenes. I can only assume it's for Ted and your benefit. I don't know why, just a gut feeling."

"Your gut feelings are usually spot-on, Jess. Why us though?"

"No idea, LaCoix, but I suggest you keep going with the flow, like you've been doing. Try to behave, unlike your usual *modus operandi,* when it comes to the frustration of not being in control. Her promises are coming true, so I don't doubt anything she says." Jess sipped his drink, and then withdrew from the crystal rim with a secret grin on his face.

"You're right, and you think she's the same woman as well?"

"Most definitely."

"At least I'm not alone in that. I must admit, some of the things we talked about are happening. I don't know what she asked of you; but it's weird how my life started to come together, and a once in a lifetime offer of a new film. It has to be the big one, Jess." David peered into Carmichael's twinkling eyes, finally noticing the supercilious grin. "What?"

"Congratulations on winning the role. I know how badly you wanted it. As far as my goals and aspirations, she fulfilled them with this picture; and after these last few days of shooting, I'll be able to do exactly as I wish. I'm retiring from this insane life, LaCoix, comfortable and happy; I intend to start immediately upon returning home."

"No shit, that's great news, but you'll be missed, old man. Where will I turn to have my ass kicked when needed?"

"You'll be fine. Besides, I won't be far away, except when Eva and I are traveling. It's time; I'm passing the baton to you, LaCoix. Take care of our troubled young friend."

"Good luck, Jess, but I don't know about this baton thing. I'll try since you asked. Receive all the positive vibes you can from this place while you're here. It's your kind of magical paradise, and it seems to be contagious. I've never felt so at peace with myself, since we met the Mistress. Simply can't be explained, but I'm curious to find out why and what it means."

"No one can, or they're unwilling to. Perhaps our fair Lady only knows the answer."

"That's a scary thought."

"What is?" Both David and Jess jumped in surprise when Ted struggled his way through the connecting door. Rubbing sleep from his eyes with both fists, he even had childish habits; and David could only grin and shake his head, thinking of *Peter Pan*.

"I thought you planned on resting this afternoon." David quickly changed the subject, amazed that their young friend appeared after such a short time. Jess arrived fifteen minutes previously; and he had left Ted a few minutes before, to clean off the make-up.

"I did; and you're talking to me like I'm twelve again. I showered, and then fell asleep. Feel like I've been out for hours." The exchange of glances, between Jess and David, was spotted instantly. "What?"

"I left you about a half-hour ago, Ted. Isn't that right, Jess?"

"Couldn't be much longer since we heard them yell *Cut*."

"You're both wrong. I don't usually nap, but I know I slept for a few hours. My shower took longer than twenty minutes, trying to scrub this body paint off, only to find it wasn't. Now I'm red and sore all over." Ted sat down, slowly waking. His timing seemed plausible, considering how disheveled he looked.

"How bad are your battle wounds?" David beamed paternally.

"I'll survive. So, how long have you been here, Jess?" Another exchange of glances between the older men; Ted actually initiated a conversation with Carmichael.

"I honestly have no idea, son."

"Think it's the time space thing that Lavender mentioned. No clocks or watches, so we're out of sync." David tried to reassure a sleepy face that refused to smile.

"What are we supposed to do then? Maybe it's tea time." An innocent but accurate statement, again Ted drew a surprised stare from the older two.

"It still feels like early afternoon to me, but I'm not betting my life on it. You could be our signal, Barrett. Are you game to venture forth with us, Jess? Shall we stroll down the garden promenade to wherever it leads, in our garden party whites, to partake in the luxury of a High Tea ritual?"

"And what do you know about proper English etiquette, LaCoix?" Jess delighted in David's uncharacteristic comments and laughed aloud. Never once would he expect the California based actor to acknowledge an obscure ritual of another country, let alone care. Well-traveled for business purposes, his friend appeared disinterested in absorbing the cultures he ventured into for a movie project. David's self-centered arrogance exuded another erroneous character flaw, for in reality, he just did not have time to indulge in exploration while on location. Jess took comfort in knowing his friend's reputation protected his true nature, but he did enjoy teasing the man for being a dumb blond.

"From our astute Mr. Barrett who looks like we pulled him out of a backpack."

"Do I need to change or something?" Still adrift and urged on by the other two, Ted used David's bathroom to brush out his clothes, comb his hair, and wash his face. He emerged presentable and alert.

"Ready?" David desperately wanted to call him *Peter*, but bit his lip and held back his mirth.

Ted smiled brightly; and the three men headed up the same pathway, where they had started their adventure at daybreak. Paying close attention, David was relieved to see their youngest walking straight, unencumbered by any damage sustained earlier. Something magical awaited the three; the smiling blond actor could barely contain his excitement.

CHAPTER 14

Entering through the familiar double-doors, the three men walked, reaching a room that should have ended seaside, if David's recollection was accurate. Life at La Rosa Negra, although slowly being accepted, continued to be a series of unsettling unknowns. An amazing vista, of an English country garden, spread before them, just beyond the classic Tudor paned windows. The interior remained cool, with lush northern foliage growing outside, although the studio appeared surrounded by sweltering desert heat. Flipping this miracle into the back of his mind, David scanned the room to count heads. Everyone appeared present, including a few new faces he soon learned to be technical crew.

Flowers graced every table; tea, cakes, and finger sandwiches were displayed lavishly for their choosing. A delightful scene of a world long past, David buried the need to laugh aloud at the strangeness of a High Tea. Happily participating in an ancient ritual, and in the politest of manner, the room filled with uncouth, crazy actors. He caught a glimpse of Lavender, motherly slapping Ted's hand. Only a morsel of chocolate deprived, the substitution constituted an unappetizing, dry cracker. On her departure, David watched the rising new star covertly return the biscuit to the table, touching nothing else. With a head downcast, Ted returned to contemplate the toes of his loafers; the reaction appeared his only alternative. Taking pity on the man, David headed toward him, wondering why Barrett discarded the salted savory.

A cheery voice called for everyone's attention; and the forever-present Englishman be divided the party into two groups, accommodating the technicians to give the cast an overall look at their operation. Upon finishing, all would reunite in the screening room, to view the scene shot that day. David had waited anxiously for this event, and turned immediately to follow the closest computer wizard, forgetting Ted and his dilemma. A gentle hand against his chest stopped him, while a second hand reached out and caught his co-star's arm before he raced to witness the creation of magic.

"I am sorry, Gentlemen, but you will go with the last group. The Mistress wishes your presence. Please follow me." The bearded rake of a man smiled rather wistfully and led them to a door. Opening another portal, without knocking, he ushered them inside, and then quietly shut it behind him.

Lavender waited in a small sitting room, with several doors leading to unknown recesses in the continually changing structure. Most disorienting, the interruption added an angry edge to David's craving for a cigarette, along with Ted's general anxiety over unexplainable events. The older of the two grew grievously miffed; a technical marvel, he desperately wanted to witness, had been delayed for something of probable trite importance. He abruptly switched gears upon viewing the eyes of the person who summoned them. Lavender had become gravely serious.

"When were you last tested for an STD or HIV, Mr. LaCoix?" The blunt question staggered the actor, but being as fast with his tongue as he was his feet, he managed a flippant come back.

"And just why is that of importance to you?" David teased in his most seductive voice; but her green eyes stared menacingly from under unblinking lashes.

"This is not a joke. It is of your co-star's concern; and I shall ask him the same question." Not holding back the demand, she intensified her brutally frank necessity of knowing.

"This is ridiculous, but if your curiosity needs satisfying, I received my second set of results before arriving at the first location. They were negative; and because you'll ask, Rebecca and I are safe sex fanatics, even when caught in that degrading, compromising position by Susan. Does that suffice?" A whip of a snarl hid in every word, but Lavender ignored the bruised ego she felt in the annoyed actor.

"No, but thank you. What of you, Mr. Barrett?"

"What?" Ted's mouth gaped open, perplexed and embarrassed by the intimate question.

"Have you been tested?"

"It's none of your business. There's no way I could be infected." Land mines went off in Ted's head at the scandalous insinuations that opposed his beliefs.

"How do we prove it, Theo? Please explain." Adamant, Lavender wanted a direct answer, no longer coddling her favorite child.

"I've only had sex with my wife; and she with me."

"Both virgins! I knew it, and still can't believe it!" The confession confirmed David's assumptions; but it remained a mystery for someone with the sex appeal of Barrett, and the length of his career, starting in his early-teens, how he had not succumbed to some beauty to entice him into bed. One could only wonder at a virgin working in one of the most casually sex-oriented industries and licentious societies on the planet. A percentage of them certainly gave in to satisfy their craving for their one big break, if unrelated to someone influential. Fending off predators for a young lifetime, Ted rose as a major inspiration to LaCoix who admired the decency of the man. Piranha would have devoured him in a second, if given the chance.

"It's true! It is!" Ted looked from one face to the other, unnerved by David's whimsical grin, and the strict determination in the woman's face.

"I believe you; but we do not know your wife."

"We've been married for nearly four years; I would know. We grew up within the same church, with the same beliefs: no premarital sex." To the strict fundamentalist, this edict was never to be broken; and this conversation abruptly closed on his part.

"In any case, you both must visit our healer. A quick examination will confirm, with certainty, that neither of you carry anything to be passed on to the other."

"Shit! Not only are we doing the complete act, but no protection. Aren't you taking this too far?" David's scowl deepened the furrows in his forehead. Upset by the notion, he had lost a number of friends to the epidemic, straight and gay, male and female; the very idea boded heavily on his psyche.

"Condoms would have been available during this period of time of syphilis and gonorrhea outbreaks; but your characters are unlikely candidates to stop at the local pharmacy, while thieving and pillaging a small town. Besides the historical incongruity, we wish to film you in your natural state, which means every fold and protruding tendon. You have protected yourselves, but I must insist. The doctor will only take five minutes with each of you." Her quiet, underlying tone indicated a no toleration argument.

"No doctors. No." Ted retreated backward to the exit door.

"I am sorry, Theo, I used the wrong term. Who cared for you, after falling as a child and cutting your knee?" The terror in his eyes softened her tone.

"Our faith healer," Ted obediently answered.

"Who mended your broken bones during a death defying escapade on a mountain top, or when you and your brothers fell off your bikes as youngsters?"

"Our faith healer."

"Well, that is exactly who will care for you: a physician in psychic phenomenon and a mystic healer. As a Buddhist Monk, he holds great skill in his hands and vast amounts of ancient healing knowledge."

"No, he's a witch doctor, a Pagan worshiper, not a faith healer."

"You are becoming tiresome, Mr. Barrett. To many people, your faith healer classifies as a witch doctor; so I will hear no more insults toward the man you are about to meet. Would it help, knowing you need not disrobe, or be touched physically? You simply lie there, close your eyes, and feel the heat of a warm light, or a sudden cold flash. The procedure is nothing to fear, Theodore. If you are afraid to go in alone, perhaps Mr. LaCoix will accompany you." Lavender restrained from flashing a red warning signal at the stubborn man.

"I'll go first, Ted, and then I'll hold your hand if necessary."

At David's sarcastic smirk, and feeling completely mortified, Ted agreed to go in alone. Fifteen minutes later, both men were pronounced disease free; neither carried the virus. They quickly departed to join the last sightseeing tour of the studio, leaving Lavender standing beside the persimmon and saffron robed figure. After exchanging the crucial information telepathically, she exited through another door, into a dark private chamber of candles and celestial music. Standing amongst the flickering flames, she puzzled over what she already suspected and feared. David had to be convinced to stop smoking and drinking. His damaged liver, stomach, and lungs grew weaker daily. Exercise, fresh air, and restraint would aid his battle, but the chronic mental exhaustion, plaguing him, needed more than medical science and healing hands to cure. He hid his condition well; she hoped his plans, to change his lifestyle, would rectify the problems.

Her burden, called Theodore Barrett, weighed heavier. Mentally on the edge of a breakdown, holding back too many secrets, along with his wandering thoughts of suicide and his parasitic behavior toward LaCoix, reaffirmed what she had known for some time. The baby added to his duress; but she remained uninformed as to why. Concerned and furious, at the same time, she wondered where his childhood Spirit Keeper had been. Her questions would be answered this night, as to the many healed broken bones and the mental terror of small spaces he displayed this day. Something else battled within the small frame that the Monk could not identify. Another unwanted worry, she hoped Ted would confide his secrets to David. Not her place to inform a person of another's misfortunes, the older actor must subtly confront Barrett. Now more acquainted with the congenial side of one of her leading actors, she surmised he would take the initiative. Far too curious and his mind working at a feverish pitch, David would uncover the hidden puzzle. For now, show time drew near; and the Mistress passed through the mist, silently entering the screening room.

Laughter and excitement filled the intimate theatre, where cast and crew gathered. David and Jess incessantly badgered one technician, deeply involved in the process they had just witnessed. If it worked, the footage would be unlike anything ever seen; moviemaking would become a faster, more spontaneous process for actors. Trained professionals would become the norm, leaving less room for direction, allowing more freedom for said directors to see the overall picture and finite details, without having to coddle untalented and ill-prepared actors through something they should know instinctively. Success would finally be based on talent, charisma, and above all, those innate, sensitive, intuitive responses to cues gone awry. Actors, not faces, would supersede, eradicating the insidious celebrity status of no consequence. LaCoix laughed silently, thinking of the backlash to the likes of Rebecca.

The Mistress gazed about the room, very pleased at the anticipation of what they all accomplished that morning. Smiling with some measure of satisfaction, she continued to watch David with Jess. The usual quiet hands gestured wildly, without the ever-present cigarette in one hand, while chewing the nails of the other. It reminded her of Ted, whose hands moved in constant animation, either wringing them or clenching them into fists in compulsive nervousness. Her eyes came to rest on the young man, sitting quietly alone; and she made her way through the mass of bodies to sit next to him.

"Are you feeling unwell, Theo? Did you get some rest?" Her soft voice initially went unheard, but the repeated call of his name brought the man into the now. "There you are. I certainly caught you deep in thought. Did you not find the tour of interest?"

"Yes, very much, but I'm not good with electrical or mechanical gizmos. I even have trouble with a toaster." Ted tried to smile, but could not bring forth even his plastic one. A heavy depression had settled over him after meeting the healer; and more quicksand pulled him downward on his lone return from the studio walkabout.

"What gives you pleasure when you are home?" Unable to reach into his mind through her favorite method of direct eye contact, she stared straight ahead and listened to his unspoken words.

"Renovating the house, taking out the trash, the usual domestic stuff." Minimal conversation, with an underlying current of something hidden, the man clouded his thoughts from her, not realizing the empowering capability or concern it caused. Of tremendous significance to the Mistress, this happened rarely, and only with a special few. Maybe, just maybe, they had found another.

"The usual stuff, which does not include toasters." Lavender received a faint chuckle and a nod of his head in acknowledgment.

"Trying to make things grow is a hobby, I guess."

"You like to garden?" Lavender sounded surprised.

"Takes me outside where I'm more comfortable. Love fresh air, sunshine, bright colors, the feel of dirt, and the fragrance of everything. Even in winter, you can smell the pines and the snap of cold when it almost burns the inside of your nostrils. Have you ever seen one of those spectacular northern mornings, full of ice prisms reflecting every color against a background of the purest white? Nothing takes my breath away as the sight of hoarfrost when the sun rises, causing the leafless branches to glitter. From trees to barbed-wire fences, the extravaganza adorns everything with fragile crystals. Nothing manmade can duplicate the look or the feeling." Ted's face softened with the telling; and his mind floated back to the last time he skied with a friend, climbing under the stillness of a full moon, skiing downhill at speed, as if dancing on diamonds. He wondered if his child would experience the thrill of such magical beauty. His passion, for such moments, shone through his eyes.

"It sounds like you experience another world when you ski, just like mountain climbing."

"Different kind of excitement, but equally as inspiring. Perhaps a reason for my devotion to God for his kindness. Who else could create such imagery?"

"The perfection of nature certainly makes one wonder, Child, but expand the mystery beyond your teachings. Now, you said you like to get dirt under your nails. What are you bringing to life to make the world more beautiful?" Lavender shifted in her seat, forcing him to look at her. Their conversation, so unlike their first meeting, felt pleasant; Ted's fear dissipated through the gray veil into his happier memories.

"It's a stupid hobby for a man; but I love to grow roses. David showed me a black one last night; the most perfect blossom I've ever seen." Ted gave the woman a half-grin with his confession, showing his true sentiments, and then faded into his lonely contemplation once more.

"Far from stupid, as roses take great patience and deliberation to nurture. Some of the foremost rose developers are male, considering the treachery of the flower, albeit magnificent. A great challenge to grow black ones in California, your hobby may take all your visualization skills to materialize them into reality."

"I'll try it when I go..."

"...home. Please do, and send me a message, in your head, if you succeed. Now, what of your evenings? Do you go out for dinner or the theatre? Do you enjoy music and dancing?" Lavender pried for answers already known, wishing to be wrong. It would not be the first time, having a few other beings on her mind.

"*Bible* readings three times a week, church on Sunday, and the occasional rally of Christian men, if I'm available. I know you disapprove, but that's how I was raised. Otherwise, I watch movies to study other actors interpret their roles to make a scene moving." A down and up emotion, one of pain and one of pleasure, Lavender witnessed the thoughts alluded to by David and the Monk. Something had to be done; but the Mistress dismissed the use of antidepressants.

"I shall not trouble you about your faith, Child, being the one thing that brings you peace and uplifts your Spirit. Enough on that subject, for now, but do you ever go out just for fun?"

"Trips to mountain climb, ski, or camp, depending on the season, making sure they work around my auditions and possible call-backs. I do love hiking, getting lost in the wilderness. All the seasons nurture different colors, like a painting that's real. Leaves are my favorite things to watch and play with in my head. Sometimes I hear them whispering to me, like a thousand-voice chorus in harmony. The quivering aspen I marvel at the most. Each gray under-leaf shimmers silver and rustles in the bright sun on the slightest breeze, making those chiming sounds that seem to surround you, Lavender. Before one of those storms, when they reflect light back against a darkening sky, I can't tell you how awesome I feel. Their leaves change back and forth, quivering in anticipation of an onslaught of wind and rain; now that's a tree with drama." Ted closed his eyes and a slight smile appeared, enjoying the image remembered.

Lavender finally heard the happier side of Barrett, enjoying every image he created. "You make it sound wondrous, Theo; and I sense the peaceful feeling you receive. If you ever work for a cause, perhaps, saving those silver leaves and ice diamonds deems favorable to you."

"I just might one day."

"One day can be too late in your precarious world; but you will know when you are ready to undertake such a task. Does your wife go with you on these excursions, to share your painted landscapes?"

"Rarely, although Karen's athletic and keeps in shape, she prefers home to the outdoors. We seldom share such thoughts, but the glory stays in my head, seeing the world in a different way than others. I think you're the first one I've told. It doesn't matter, since she hates me climbing and never comes to watch. I prefer the freedom without boundaries." Ted refocused on his shoes, deep in his own world of nature's magic.

Lavender visualized and felt Ted's need for such breathtaking splendors. A romantic dreamer, with a vivid, poetic imagination, he pierced her being, sensing his thoughts of never experiencing such joy again, and yet there he sat, remembering every detail of his experiences. Talking about his delights, only for a few minutes, he stored the images as only memories.

"Thank you for sharing, Theo. You paint wonderful images with your words; and I am certain you can picture anything described to you in a like manner, which may come in handy one day. As for your high-risk nature, I certainly understand your wife's concern regarding your safety. I also empathize with wanting something truly yours alone, especially nature's solace. Everyone needs space; and your choice, of precarious sports, appears fitting."

"Not for long, Lavender. Karen's pregnant." More defeat, the shoulders crumbled forward, with hands hiding the troubled face.

"I know."

"How; did LaCoix tell you?" Ted's sad countenance immediately changed to consternation; his back stiffened to look directly at her.

"No, he keeps your secrets. No one else knows; and my knowing matters little. Why will a baby hinder you from doing what you treasure?"

"Responsibility to always be there." The blue eyes returned to the floor; and Lavender sadly watched the man wishing for an escape from his proclaimed duty.

"You cannot be with a child all the time." If Ted faltered, he had to tell someone; and she tried to coax him to say what needed telling.

"It's imperative." The body, which sat so still when describing the joys of his life, started to tremble.

"Why?" A hand reached for the shaking one and thankfully received. A touch of the Mistress gave him the power to settle his uncontrollable anxiety.

"It's a necessity for me; and I probably should announce the fact, but I'm unable to admit I failed." Ted finally raised his head to look at the blank screen in front of him. Another empty canvas waiting for color, he sensed the blankness described his life.

"Failure, what an odd thing to say; although I do understand you have not adjusted to the idea."

"I've been trying, especially during our few days off, but..." Ted trailed off, his eyes veiled in the thought of all his days being gray, without a silver lining in any overcast cloud.

"...you do not want this baby, but there is more."

"You probably already know and can explain it better than me." Ted snapped back with an unsteady voice. Lavender could see the sudden panic in his face when she hit a nerve and a contradiction; Ted had to protect a baby he did not want. A large piece of the puzzle shifted into place; but she would soon have the facts. Dropping the unsettling discussion, she put her hand over the two fists, which had formed into a tight ball. Her man-child suddenly quivered again, like the last leaf taken by one of his winter winds, mentally ready to blow away to Neverland, or left to decay through the winter, rotting in a mire of once living plants and debris. Lavender grew gravely concerned at his sorry plight, and attempted to radiate her warmth into his chilled body.

"You are cold, Theo. Someone will fetch a heavier sweater for you. In the meantime, you require something to warm you up. We shall cheat on your diet and order a mug of hot chocolate for you. It seemed the only taste you desired at tea."

"I'd like that, but when are we going to start?"

"Good question, as we should have commenced much earlier. Wait here while I investigate the delay." The Mistress arose, but before she turned away, a tentative hand held her back, and she lovingly did not retaliate at the surprise touch.

"Lavender, what did the healer really find?"

The misty blue eyes disturbed her; she granted his request with partial truths. "If you are asking the reason for your melancholy, you have already given me an answer. Although extremely underweight, you appear in good physical health. The scratches received today started healing without the Monk's help. Besides the many old scars of breaks and injuries sustained, as one learns to take risks, you are fine. Malnutrition has caused brittleness of your bones. After the next few days, you must start eating properly and get plenty of sunshine; lack of both is part of your problem, physically and mentally." The Mistress hid a great deal of what she knew, but left only tidbits for Ted to hear. Enough for now, her own knowledge made her cringe at the agony he continued to fight, facing it alone, and not understanding what or why.

Ted's head dropped at the quick synopsis. She knew--they probably all knew--he hid his face in his hands to disguise more sorrow.

Lavender turned him around and leaned toward him. "I know you have been extremely upset since my arrival. Perhaps, after seeing your performance today, your tension will ease. Believe in your true talent and enjoy your chocolate drink when it arrives. I must take my leave."

"Thanks and I'm fine." Ted went still, his hands fisted in his lap, and a white line encircled the clenched lips. Another lie, but he had told so many.

"Physically, you manage nicely. You heal amazingly fast, Theo. Now, on with the excitement you created today." Lavender slowly stood erect, physically towering over the slouching man. She hated the symbolism and the reaction it created. A ruffle of his long, brown hair eased the moment, as she quickly departed in search of LaCoix. The announcement finally came; everyone took a seat.

"Please, take care of Theo, David. He needs quiet company in his current state. His descent, into an abyss, increases; and he requires support." Two pair of green eyes exchanged a concerned message; and David immediately found Ted and the chair relinquished by Lavender, allowing him to sit next to his co-star and to help Ted into a sweater. Someone handed the younger man a cup of hot chocolate, and the young man closed his eyes, taking in the scent and warmth, while ignoring his exuberant comrade. The next few minutes would be Ted's start or undoing as an adult actor. In his heart, he knew he needed the older man's presence; and on cue, a covert hand rested on his thigh. Barrett emerged back into the frightful world with the strong, reassuring pressure of David LaCoix.

CHAPTER 15

"You ready for this, Ted? I'm overwhelmed with what we saw and did today. The implication, of this new technology, is your wish coming true: no more waiting, twiddling your thumbs. Now we'll see the results." LaCoix excelled at masking his vocal tension, while waiting for a sign, from his hand, that Ted's shivering had subsided.

"Yeah, I guess."

"What's wrong? I seemed to have lost you during the tour." David squinted at him, attempting to read the somber mind. The steam rising from the mug made eye contact impossible: a fog looking into a fog. Growing increasingly disquieted, the older man could only surmise, as his imagination ran wildly amuck.

"You were busy asking questions; so I headed back to read over tomorrow's action. It's going to get ugly."

"I know; but tonight's free, to eat dinner quietly in my quarters and forget about the scene."

"Maybe." The onslaught of depression fully alarmed David, knowing Lavender's assessment deemed correct; Ted was not a trivial game to handle lightly. Nothing further needed saying, as the dailies flickered on the large viewing screen. Everyone went still; astonishment swept through the audience. Dailies these were not, but a polished, edited, finished scene. Lasting only minutes, the emotion and intensity, pace and consistency, spellbound them all. A flawless, masterly work entranced the cast; the extreme close-up, of two familiar blue eyes, peering out from between the metal bars, haunted and disturbed all. Jay's terror and sorrow, seen in the two sapphire stones, likened to a fortuneteller's crystal ball. For David and Lavender, they revealed far more, showing symbols of Ted's hidden secrets as another film unto itself, transposed on a blue-screen background.

David's heart crashed to the floor, and the stalwart actor shed a tear that he quickly wiped away. He turned to look at an unusually resolute Barrett when the lights came up. The audience scrambled to their feet, clapping and cheering; congratulations passed throughout the crowd; and then the focus turned to Jess, Ray, Kevin, David, and finally Ted. The young actor proved his acting skill and the merits received.

Ted's first congratulatory hug came from David, with the obligatory manly thumping of each other's backs; and the older actor stepped back in honor of the new star being whisked away by many hands. LaCoix looked up to exchange knowing stares at her Ladyship. Shedding sparkling mauve droplets, glittering of light, her tears cascaded like the quietest waterfall down her face; the Mistress also saw the distressing images in the bluest eyes. A hand to LaCoix's own face confirmed he spilled more than one tear. Their man-child stole the show, and with a nod from Lavender, David squeezed through the mayhem to rescue the shiny new, but reluctant star, whose saddest spheres glistening with moisture.

"Get me out of here, David." Ted whispered frantically, wincing at another powerful slap on his back and a bone-crushing handshake. The noise reached beyond his hearing endurance; but once free, he covered his ears to still his throbbing head.

"Thanks, guys; congratulations to all for a great job. If you would make way, Mr. Barrett and I have another scene to study. Please excuse our early departure." The actor, with the most influence in the crowd, wore his best Hollywood smile to open a narrow pathway. As accolades continued, David gently controlled a dazed Ted to the nearest exit. With LaCoix's right hand on the small of the new superstar's back, and his left hand lightly gripping the upper left arm, the two men quickly departed, meeting Lavender just outside the door. Moving quickly, following her floating, long strides, the co-stars hustled after the flying figure. Once outside their accommodations, she agreed they deserved a quiet night and would send dinner to David's quarters. Unfortunately, for Ted, his meal would be medicinal. With a wish for a pleasant evening, she left them in their peaceful surrounds. They waved good-bye and stepped into Barrett's quarters; the smell of roses nearly knocked David over.

"Whoa, man, I really overdid the flower power!"

"They're strong all right." Desperate to get away from the barrage of what he believed undeserved praise, Barrett needed concrete confirmation, and addressed his mentor with a puzzled gaze. "Tell me the truth. Was I that good, or did editing fix my mistakes?"

"You were that good, Ted; unbelievably good."

"No, tell me honestly, was it me or this new technical magic?" The young star could not separate his acting from reality; he empathized with his character more than he wanted people to realize.

"With only one take, they couldn't possibly enhance anyone's performance, but certainly edited the piece extraordinarily well. I love this mode of filming: the spontaneity of live theatre, but from angles an audience can't see. It felt right and amazed me; and you, Ted, created an outstanding, compelling performance. I'll never forget the last image of you."

"We're working with Brant Gray tomorrow. What if I can't live up to what I did today and make some stupid mistake with a legend?" Ted stood directly in front of him, nervously doing the Barrett shuffle.

"Makes me nervous as well, particularly because of your position. My horse better stand quietly." David sympathized over what awaited the young man, and sweated over his own part of the intimate action. Turning away to hide his trepidation, he walked to the table on the pretense of inspecting the condition of the white blooms. They remained intact.

"Lavender will quiet the animal." Ted met David's surprised glance.

Of course, the rider, of the Andalusian stallion with the amber eyes, would keep them safe. The *knowing* started coming into focus for David, opening his mind to instinctive thought. "You're right; everything will be fine. I tend to over worry; especially with your hands tied to the saddle horn. You could get hurt if anything goes wrong."

"Nothing will happen; besides, a potential risk gets the adrenaline pumping. I don't have any lines anyway; the dialogue's between you and Gray."

"We have words to help us; but you have to use every inch of your body to express the emotions wrought on Jay. Tough job, Ted, as true acting on film is showing, not hearing. It's a strange scene. I couldn't figure out why Jay had to be naked on the horse. Didn't make sense to me, when I read the book; still doesn't." A master at turning things around, David hit Barrett's intellectual side, wishing to change the melancholy of uncertainty.

"Prove to the father you haven't injured his son; but the gag, the tied hands, and the gun to his head, show Jay's old man that Slade's capable of hurting or killing his kid. His nudity reinforces the terror and humiliation endured under Dusty's hands; and in the dialogue, between Slade and the father, Jay now knows he's a permanent hostage. His horror, and his father's fury and duress, increase when Slade grabs him by the genitals and threatens to crush the last of the family jewels. If the Marshall doesn't agree, he would witness the excruciating pain of his son castrated by squeezing his balls until they rupture in a man's strong hand, destroying his ability to procreate. The kid would survive as a eunuch; and the father would learn of Slade's treachery with horrendous consequences. Pretty well thought out, I'd say."

"Makes sense; but it disturbs me how an innocent, like Jay, could be treated so abominably, just to cripple his father emotionally. And the grab..."

"...will hurt. Remember I'm still tender, so be careful. I'm not used to being touched, which should please the Mistress." Ted tried to make light of the action, which would prove Slade's hostility and devious mind. He prayed he could deal with the abuse, believing David too hesitant to try. A quick change in subject was needed, to forget the next day's dilemma. "What do you want to do tonight?"

"Just a quiet evening, to slow the pace down. How about a movie, while snuggling on the couch?" David returned from his inspection, bringing a white beauty to caress a sensitive cheek.

"What? Hey, that tickles."

"Remember our plan? Besides, I need to hold someone tonight. You have Sir Edmund; unfortunately, I didn't purchase two bears, but I thought I already had one?"

"Oh, brother, when you make a deal, you stick to it. I've never been held by a man."

"Yes, you have. Over the last week, a man has held you, bathed you, and comforted you. Snuggling, through a film, will comfort us both." David continued flirting with the rose, making Ted squirm and rethinking their plan.

"Guess I need someone too, but please stop with the rose. You're making me nervous." With a snicker creating a worse situation, the younger man fended off the fragile object of playfulness.

"And I was just warming up. Okay, Ted, you pick a movie, while I answer my door. I think dinner's arrived."

"Oh, great, I'm supposed to lose more weight in a hurry. There goes the hot chocolate I had. Wonder what the mystic Monk has in store. You better be eating gruel as well; or I'll be really pissed." Ted kept grumbling about the pagan healer, as he tailed David from one bedroom into another and on into the living area. An unknown personage entered, swiftly setting two meals at the table, covered with silver lids to keep them hot, or hide a horrible surprise. As he thanked the man, David was handed a note, with a message that made the older man sigh.

"Well, Ted, your life won't be improving." LaCoix stepped forward and laid his hand on the bony shoulder. "You're about to lose another ten pounds tonight. I hope they know what they're asking. You're thin enough to play Jay in his most emaciated state."

"Gee, thanks. Emaciated? I don't think so, but ten pounds! Are they going to make me puke and shit all night? I don't feel all that well now. I've never lost that much weight so fast." Ted came around to peek over David's shoulder to confirm the ugly news.

"According to this, after you drink the fluid, which they have so deviously prepared, you'll have about three hours for the cells in your body to absorb the required amount of nutrients. After that, you'll have an hour of purging. This makes no sense, considering drinking this crap will make you sick as a dog."

"Jesus Christ, help me."

"Good time to call his name, but we'll manage. Damn, ten pounds in an hour and this healer says you'll feel fine afterward and get a good night's sleep. Like to see that happen." David cringed at the thought. His co-star's mental state remained precarious after his entrapment, and now a new torture.

"What's this we, white-man? Let's lie instead." Ted grabbed the note, scrunched it up, and scanned for a trashcan. The note ended up in the massive bouquet of white. "Another thorn in the roses, LaCoix."

"Nice toss, Tonto, but I think they'll notice. At least I'll be in the adjoining room, if needed."

"I can barf my guts out by myself, thank you very much, Kemosabe."

"Go find the longest epic you can; and I'll put a few necessary items in your bathroom, to make this sojourn into hell more convenient and comfortable." David headed back into Ted's quarters and looked around. First, plenty of face towels piled next to the sink, with mouthwash and soap close by. He found the least scented of the bunch, not wishing to create more havoc with the wrong aroma. The toilet seat came down and the toilet lid left up. Searching a little further, he found a lightweight, large basin to place by the toilet in easy reach. This type of purging would feel like six-hours of food poisoning rolled into an hour. He hated himself for not taking a stand against such abuse perpetrated on so many actors, but nothing compared to the severity of what the note predicted. Mentally prepared to assist Ted through the night, his concern still showed.

David emerged to find Ted adjusting the quality of a DVD. The smaller man had arranged the stuffed sofa with pillows and secured a comfortable place to rest their feet. Through all his doubts, Barrett appeared willing to cozy up with the notorious blond actor whose wicked grin swept over his face. He saw sadness in the blue eyes, but his priority remained, to support Ted through a new hell.

"This place--you said she calls it La Rosa Negra--I wonder why only men reside here. Reminds me of our all-male Christian group for family unity, but we have our reasons for segregation. I wonder what would've happened, if I had been your female co-star." Ted's quick mind brought up unusual clues David had missed.

"Never thought of it, but you're right. We'll ask her tomorrow."

"Not me. She helped me today; but we're not that close." Ted peered at the man from under his dark lashes, determined not to enrage the Mistress.

"Coward. So, what's the movie and what are we eating?" David headed for the table and waited for his companion to join him.

"*Ben Hur*, with green goop for me and something tastier for you."

"Hamburger and fries?" LaCoix teased, having discovered Ted's favorite food. The youngest always asked for the fast food at the caterer's trailer, only to hastily change his mind and sit down with a coffee. Looking back, David could not recall Barrett eating much of anything, let alone a triple-decker with fries.

"You should be so lucky." Ted sat down, nearly gagging at the sight of a glass milkshake container filled with exactly what he had described.

Very hungry himself, LaCoix tried hard not to appear enjoying every morsel of his exotic meal. He ate slowly and methodically, while the victim, of this cruel act, sipped and choked down every swallow of the gruesome mixture. Ted did finish, as did David, and they settled in, side-by-side on the sofa, to watch a film made long before either man had seen the light of day. The loud, crackling static, from the old movie, gave them a jump-start, immediately adjusted by remote.

With legs stretched and feet elevated, two friends settled back to watch Barrett's favorite classic; one LaCoix had seen once on television, many years earlier.

The epic began, while the youngest man shyly allowed the eldest to put his arms around him; his head eventually rested comfortably against a warm upper chest; and he held the gasp stuck in his throat when a cheek came to rest against his luxurious, magic hair. Quietly holding onto the moment, he felt the blond-haired actor inhale his presence and attempted not to tense. LaCoix lingered, smelling the residual essence of herbal shampoo, fresh cut grass, and ferns, and seeming to enjoy the proximity of another body after a month of celibacy. Unconsciously for David, but nervously felt and accepted by Ted, his wiry arms were stroked, generating heat within the youngest, while giving the older man the connection he needed. Both men finally relaxed and lazily entwined to see the chariots fly around the Coliseum.

Warm and pleasurable, Ted released his fear of the innocent fatherly embrace, unbeknownst or understood by David, while internally bracing for a night of hell, and a long day 's shoot with a series of intense scenes. Promising to be a torturous twenty-four hours, games bounced in the minds of both men. The youngest lost his bashfulness, snuggling closer, and absorbing the radiant heat for comfort, from the strong arms that willingly secured him.

"What a great example of how far we've come technically since the filming of this piece. Things sure have changed." David smiled down at the top of Ted's head, which turned sideways under his chin, ignoring the credits rolling passed.

"Do you want to hear something funny? My parents allowed my brothers and me to watch Heston's movies on television, particularly the Biblical ones. We secretly wagered on the minutes, from the opening shot, to when he exposed his chest." The smirking chortle vibrated through another's covered chest, but the warm breath penetrated the few layers, titillating the one who did not want to be aroused at that moment.

"So, you three did have your wicked moments; shame on you. What was Heston's average?" A calming conversation, about nothing, slowed the onrush of another unwarranted and unwanted arousal, which David came to expect.

"Less than five minutes." Ted laughed harder and got an unexpected squeeze for his childhood antics.

"How are you feeling?"

"So far so good. I've never heard a man's heart beat before. Actually, I haven't heard anyone's heart beat this closely. It has a nice rhythm; I like it." The blue eyes grew larger, looking upward while listening to this miracle of nature and counting off the beat in his breathless voice. "The music of Native Americans is set to the heart's double beat. Their dancing also mimics the earth breathing."

"Really, I've learned something new today. How did you know?"

"Research for a film. As a tree hugger and loving the outdoors, I thought if special enough to remember."

"You must love the sound of your wife's heart against your chest or ear: two hearts beating as one." Becoming used to these intimate, revealing secrets, innocently iterated, they proved Ted's naïveté to David. The man seemed to have never been touched in an affectionate manner, let alone sex.

"Nope, this is my first experience. I would have remembered such a unique sound."

"You said you were virgins when you got married, but come on, Ted, you do make love to your wife. Besides, your family must have hugged the daylights out of a cutie like you."

"Cute again, and twelve, but I don't think Karen and I make love. In our faith, sex is for reproducing; so we don't spend time pleasuring each other, if that's what you're insinuating. We procreate when it's her time."

"No, shit. You're a young man, full of sexual passion and need, and you've never made love for fun: never touched every part of her skin, to smell her, to taste her? I'll be damned. You two are missing one of the great wonders of life. Making love should be sweet and innocent, loving and kind, sensual and exciting. My God, Ted, you really are a virgin, for the most part. All you've ever done is stick your dick in your wife and come on command. You're used like a goddamn stud. At least horses bite and kick in some type of foreplay and fun. How are you turned on to do what you have to do? You must use the one-inch on-switch between your legs, but you probably don't know where that is or what it is. Do you play with yourself? Don't answer that. If no, I'll have a coronary."

"Leave me alone. Of course I can satisfy myself, and with greater pleasure and more eroticism than you can imagine. Damn, LaCoix, I can't explain my beliefs about sex." Ted appeared truly upset, as was David. Pushing his body into a standing position, the youngest grabbed the remote, and snapped off the television.

"Surprises me your church allows masturbation; but I'm not saying another word. You're still a complete contradiction to me, Ted; I think you always will be. Nothing more will be said of the matter." David rose slowly, stretching out his longer body, which had held a small, but grown man for just under three hours.

"Just stop jumping down my neck about sex. Dealing with what's coming up, literally and figuratively, I don't need a reminder of my church's condemnation; or your criticism that I'm a sexually ambiguous freak." A slight pout with the ire, *Peter Pan* reappeared. David wondered who was who.

"I'm sorry for overreacting to the sweet sentiment of listening to this now broken heart. I don't know your situation; my arrogant judgment ill founded. You asked me to smack you if you cried again. Well, you're invited to deck me, if I say something you find offensive."

"You're forgiven; and I've also hurt you with my words. I apologize."

"All is forgotten. I suggest you head for bed and prepare for what your green goop creates. I'll tidy our mess and be right there."

"You worry too much." Ted laughed off the intense conversation, but remembered every word that hurt deeply. He needed David this night of shedding weight, knowing from experience just how sick he may become. "If this goes as badly as the note inferred, LaCoix, I think I'll be sleeping in the raw tonight. Don't let the sight of this beached whale frighten you." Again, the same laugh did not erase the distress of the older man who received a sweeping revelation: Ted did not know how thin he was, nor had he received a truly satisfying liaison. More problems reared up; David had to face them in whatever manner he could. If it required warm, strong arms, he had two available.

"Good idea; the less you have to deal with the better; and stop thinking you're fat. You're anything but, considering I've seen enough of you to know what you look like." David tried to chuckle his way out of Ted's serious condition, unable to understand a possible eating disorder.

One thing seemed certain; Barrett did not lack for endurance to get through a horrible scene, and the energy to take off like a deer. "Hold on, Barrett." The figure, once again in flight, spun around in the doorway to look back expectantly at LaCoix. "I have to say that you blew me away today. You're my friend, Ted, and those were not empty words about your brilliant performance. They also apply to getting through today's brutality. Don't take this as patronizing, but I'm proud of the way you handled everything, including allowing the examination by the healer."

"The one that's trying to kill me? Did I tell you that he knew about my broken bones? My arms have been fractured so many times, I don't even remember the current count, but he did."

"I'm complimenting you, Barrett. You're evading the gesture." Why David had to bestow more praise, he did not know, only believing his thoughts were required by this man, and necessary to repeat them. If a mentor, he had to be sincere with his statements.

"I'm sorry, thank you. I'm not used to receiving credit or support, at least not from someone important to me." Ted commenced his habitual shuffle; David could only smile to hide his own melancholy.

"Well, that ancient man told me bluntly to stop smoking and drinking. I had already decided to take the drastic step to alter my lifestyle. Must admit withdrawal hasn't been too bad."

"I'm glad, since you've stopped snarling at me, at least not noticeably annoyed."

"If I snarl, there's probably a good reason, Barrett. Now, get into bed; I'll be there shortly."

Ted departed quickly, hearing the fake, low growl accompanied by a soft chuckle. Unfortunately, David was not laughing. He could only see those eyes, revealing dangerous secrets on the strange bluescreen and wanting to know the meaning behind what he had seen. It hinted at a possible explanation of the mystery man's unnerving idiosyncrasies.

Given a few minutes, he slowly straightened out his living quarters, found the black silk pajamas, changed into the bottoms for rescue missions, and entered Ted's room. The man's clothes lay in a heap; and David heard the beginning of the purge. Shaking his head, he willed himself to wait until needed, while keeping busy picking up and folding the dashing new image.

Fifteen minutes, then twenty went by. The toilet flushed repeatedly, and still he heard no call. Thirty minutes, and a weak cry, between heaves, barely caught his ear. He rushed in to see a grotesque fountain, continuously spewing from Ted's mouth, inhibiting his ability to breathe. Tears ran down the pale face, and sweat dripped off the frail, shivering body. The toilet continually echoed with the sound of moving fluid, passing through a body that could not control itself, except a hand on the plunger, and the other hand on an overflowing basin.

David ran for another bucket from his own suite, furious he had not entered earlier. Unable to summon his support system, the victim of the atrocity could only keep his mouth open, to allow more hideous liquid to gush out of his system. David quickly replaced the first basin, only to stop and watch greenish liquid cascade like a Roman fountain out of an open-mouthed cherub. The number of fast trips, back and forth, was lost to a count; but he finally returned to an empty basin and a man barely able to breathe.

Swaying slightly, Barrett's eyes floated upward, ready to pass out from the exertion and lack of oxygen. It took his last will to remain sitting after being sick for too long. The purge continued freely from other orifices, while David cooled the fevered brow with a cool, wet cloth, and smoothed back the long hair hanging in sweat-drenched hanks. Too ill to notice how hard he cried, the failing creature continued to waver. Every pore, every duct, every opening of his body oozed or spewed some type of bodily fluid, even a little blood from his nose and ears. Horrified, the older man could only count down the time: forty-five minutes, fifteen to go if accurate.

Squatting in front of the white ghost, David could not speak in his rage toward the Monk and Lavender. This was torture; Barrett did not know who held his heaving shoulders, ready to collapse forward from the strain. A steadying hand returned to his forehead, supporting the drooped head. Wringing wet and feverish, Ted shook with the unknown pain he had endured during his life, but his mentor knew nothing of a worse condition than the green goop. David felt ill himself, watching a beautiful, delicate body continue to disintegrate. Seemingly over, the final basin was emptied and rinsed, while Ted, barely able to move, tended to his own hygiene. Upon completion and slick with perspiration, he sat there, gasping for needed air and unconsciously whimpering from a body in shock.

LaCoix quickly ran a bath and easily maneuvered the wispy creature into its comforting warmth, while he cleared up what little mess remained. Jasmine filled the air, with its perfume, coming through the open window, miraculously sweeping away the odorous remains of illness. With the bathroom airy and fresh, both men relaxed, performing a less stressful task. With hair and body washed and dried, teeth cleaned and mouth washed, a very unsteady Ted leaned against a supporting wall, ready to take his first step out of hell, to lie down in the warmth of his bed, and to hold tightly to a sympathetic bear.

"I'll go pull down the covers on your bed. Do you need something to wear?"

"No, thanks, just need to stand for a few seconds to regain my equilibrium. I might have to run in here again."

"Maybe you should sit down then, until I get things ready in the bedroom. I'll add more blankets." Not happy about this idea, David looked up and down at the man, whose eyes closed and his breathing continued to labor.

"This is better. I've been sitting for over an hour; and both my butt and asshole hurt like hell." Ted's exhaustion now overtook the ravaged body.

"I bet they do, not to mention that scratchy voice. You're completely dehydrated. I'll get you a cold bottle of water, as soon as you're comfortable. Hold onto something, and don't move or talk. You're a mess, Baby Bear."

"No shit." Ted let the wall support his head, ignoring the new childish nickname. Never, in his thirty years, had he felt this sick. Weakness in his trembling legs made them give way; and he tried to lock his knees in place.

"Pretty accurate, I'd say." With his co-star's humor returning, David chuckled and headed out the door, only to hear a crash and an outpouring of profanity, accompanied by a painful groan.

"Ted!" Back in an instant, David hoisted the crumpled figure onto his feet. A hard fall, the bony body landed on solid ceramic flooring, which did not allow for a bounce.

"My arm's broken. Ouch!"

"Are you sure?"

"Of course I'm sure; I heard it snap. Don't touch it; this one's bad. Don't think I can heal it."

"I shouldn't have left you. Did you faint or lose your balance?" LaCoix heard only the problem, not the impossible and extraordinary proclamation.

"Weak knees."

David felt guilty at leaving Ted alone, and blamed himself for the incident. It took little effort to pick the smaller man up and carry him in his arms. As light as a handful of dust, his co-star looked like the walking dead. Set carefully in a soft chair, the dazed victim held his arm, while LaCoix quickly prepared the bed, never losing sight of the man grimacing in pain. Badly shaken over his stupidity, a picture of Ted in his torment kept running through his head, adding to his disgust of what he had done and not done to help. Everything tried went wrong in his frightened mind. "Okay, let's get you comfortable in bed and have a look at your arm."

"Can't believe I've done it again. How am I going to hide this from the cameras? David, my hands must be tied tomorrow! What am I going to do?" A panicked victim, of Lavender's Fates, cried out in alarm.

David, however, only thought of broken bones taking six weeks to mend, too long a wait to finish the picture and on to his next. He stopped immediately, chastising himself for being a selfish bastard for thinking only of himself, and ignoring his friend's plight. It added to the guilt, creating chaos in the once stoic LaCoix. "It's not your fault. I'm going to find the Monk." Frantic, he could not move or think fast enough.

"How? There are no lights, and the pathways close in at night. We're alone, David." Ted's sore throat filled the room with more fear.

"Lavender said we could call for her." Frenzied green eyes met the trepidation of the blue ones.

"She also said *mind over matter*; visualize the results of what you need. Together we could try to get the healer to come. Maybe that's how I heal things. I've done it with simple hairline fractures."

"No shit? Sounds impossible, but you mentioned something to that effect immediately after falling."

"I don't know how, but I told you how many bones I've broken; and they sometimes mend within a few days; but this one might be trouble."

"Jesus, what are you going to tell me next? Okay, visualization seemed her secret for the tricks in the trailer, but does it work on someone's mind? Can you concentrate on healing yourself? Anything's worth a try. Maybe we should call for the Monk. So, we have to imagine the results, and what would those be?" Bumbling out an alien idea, David could think of nothing logical. He had an injured man, a very sick one, with no way of obtaining assistance; they could not even reach Jess' dwelling in the dark. Not in his wildest dreams would he have imagined that this place of harmony was a deathtrap; his head spun to the lesson of the black rose and Ted's thorn.

Equally unnerved over his utterance, Barrett mistakenly grew up believing that healing one's own injuries a common practice, and not worth mentioning, considering he did not know how he accomplished the feats. Only as an adult did he learn that the practice deemed a strange phenomenon, and certainly not a blessing in the eyes of his church. His gift remained hidden as his redeemer; this latest break, however, was a compound fracture. In a complete dilemma, his brain told him he needed the Monk. His heart said to summon the man with the Mistress' method, but his spirituality screamed witchcraft: he knew it, felt it, but did not know what else to try. Thinking logically, he believed this would be like praying; and with David helping, maybe they could manifest their own reality. The technique worked for Lavender; but she remained a mystery of power. They had to attempt the impossible, or suffer the consequences in the morning. "We need to see the Monk, standing beside me, smiling, knowing there's nothing wrong. We have to believe my arm's normal."

"I can do that. Seems like we should be chanting something. Fuck, this is bizarre!" David sat beside him on the bed, shaking his head in disbelief.

"I know, but I hurt like hell. What was his name?" Barrett grimaced and arched his neck up from the pillow supporting his head.

"Easy, Ted, take a few deep breaths. Let's just call him the Monk, and keep chanting for his immediate presence. Hold my hand and concentrate. Let go of the pain, Baby." David started his short two-line chant of saffron robes appearing, and soon Ted joined in. The worried green eyes closed, easing his alarm over the swelling and bleeding arm. Concentrating only on what they decided upon, he discarded how ridiculous he felt. Length of time did not matter, but a rap on Ted's door had David racing to open it.

"It's you! It worked! I don't believe it. Come in. We need your expertise immediately." David grabbed the ancient's arm, almost catapulting him into Ted's bedroom with one quick maneuver. The healer's frail, thin legs could only scurry along, sometimes off the ground in the blond's haste.

"What has happened? Did the purge go badly?" The Monk appeared unnerved, certainly unaware of being conjured up.

"He fell and broke his arm; the purge left him too weak to stand."

"I am sorry. This was unexpected."

With a healing touch, the bone was set in place, the wound healed over, the swelling calmed, although the pain remained and would for some time. Quickly informed of Ted's predicament for the morning's scene, the healer announced he could only desensitize it, and reduce the swelling and bruising. It still required time to set; but with that impossibility, the old man would bind the arm in place when not in front of a camera, and continue the healing process through the power of light. Two men nodded, mystified by the last comment, but certainly understanding the binding process. They agreed the Monk should stay close, until the completion of the shoot. For this night, he could keep the swelling calm, if Ted promised to lie still. Without doubt, an exhausted Barrett would dream the dreams of the dead, intoxicated by the overpowering mixture of jasmine and roses.

David walked the old man to the door, and returned immediately to the injured, unhappy party in the bed. "Will you be all right on your own?"

"Where's Sir Edmund?"

"I'll get him. He's still sitting on my bed." David left and picked up the huge bear, smiling at the sympathetic face; a face that kept secret cries hidden. A question uttered in a whisper at the inquisitive brown eyes, "Has he told you anything, my fuzzy friend?" Without an answer, the weary man, taking on too much responsibility, returned and sat on the edge of the massive bed in easy reach of the younger one. "Here's your bed buddy. He'll be good to rest your arm on."

"Good thinking. Besides, I need a bed-buddy tonight. I hurt like hell, David, and still feel like shit. Damn brittle bones. The small fractures are easy to deal with, but these major ones, Lord, help me. I'll never make it to the bathroom alone. Wake me up from this nightmare, LaCoix."

"Maybe I better stay. You never admit to discomfort, so you must be hurting big time."

"Would you? I feel so weak, if I have to make a charge for the toilet, I'll probably fall and break the other one. Sorry, I'm acting like a stupid kid over another break."

"Of course I'll stay, and don't feel badly for asking. We men are known for being big babies when we're sick. I know I am, enjoying all the fussing and loving I get when I'm ill. You have every right to want some support. I'll just slip into the other side."

"Could you stay closer to me, like you did earlier on the couch?" Ted pushed his face into the bear, humiliated at his need for another gesture of affection.

"Feeling very insecure, aren't we? Are you sure?" David held back his surprise. He was only there to support an ailing friend, not a comforting body to hold the man together.

"I can't believe I asked. Maybe I'll just slither away, before I make a bigger jackass out of myself. I'm sorry, David; I'm hurt, cold, tired, and need the feel of family, or a friend. I shouldn't have put you in such an awkward position." Ted's plea melted the last of a frozen heart. The fear, both men experienced, passed within a tender embrace and a request granted.

"We've been through too much to be uncomfortable. Besides, you did the best imitation of Linda Blair, in *The Exorcist,* I've ever seen. Waited for your head to spin a round, with a tongue jumping out to grab me around the neck." David's lighthearted humor worked; and the past two hours of drama ebbed between here and there.

"Gee, thanks, and she never did that with her tongue. Man, life sucks. Every opening in my body leaked, like one of those wild water and light shows, but in a rainbow of putrid colors and more violent water action. Did I cry?"

"Yes, but as part of the purge. You didn't cry for the sake of it. You had me worried when your nose and ears started bleeding; you also stopped breathing a few times. I tried to get you to blow the crap out of your nose, but you didn't have the strength. You could have suffocated." A repetition of the event burned fire hot in David. His wrath would release on the morrow.

"Bet that's when my head started aching. A touch by the healer helped. Just wish he concentrated more on my stomach." Ted lost his embarrassment, wishing David to hurry into bed. Warmth he needed; an affectionate touch he needed; and some soothing words he needed, rather than a replay of his performance in the perfect sound booth of a bathroom.

"Still feel bad, hunh?" David got in on the other side and wriggled over the massive bed to press his body against the back of the smaller, naked one. "How's that feel? Too close?"

"Fine, I guess."

"You guess? Do you realize the number of women who would kill to be in your position?"

"Men as well, probably."

"Some." David laughed, while shifting closer to get more comfortable, and to help restrain the broken appendage.

"Thanks, LaCoix; are you sure about this arrangement?"

"As long as you're okay? Thanks for including me amongst needed family and friends. I care about your welfare, Ted, and I'd like to see you return to the annoying ray of sunshine that I first met. I'm beginning to miss him."

"He's been replaced by a forward idiot who's acting like a baby."

"I like both sides of you. You're a nice balance of fun and sensitivity. Now, let's get some sleep and try not to move your arm." Along with those hopes, David prayed to every god man had created, to allow him to sleep without having one of his unexpected arousals.

"It hurts too much to sleep. Your voice will help. Talk to me about anything--a story--how about describing this house you're building? I might as well shame myself directly to hell, but I'm scared, David."

"I know, Teddy Bear. Too many wicked experiences, you've had a hell of a day; and it's over. Stomach feeling better?"

"Don't have one anymore, and I'm twelve again. Go ahead, while I close my eyes to envision the entire layout."

"You're on. Now, shut up and lie still. I'm right here, just like holding my sons when they were ailing and twelve." David needed a little comforting himself. Trapped, with someone sick and injured, with no access for aid, had his adrenaline pumping into a heart that could not withstand another jolt. With a request to detail his current passion, he settled down and commenced describing every image of his new home. The voice mesmerized his co-star who captured the picture as he dozed off, comfortably secure in a hug from his friend and mentor. Two men, two opposites, two sets of different problems, both collided in a space, where the Arizona desert merged with a magical kingdom called La Rosa Negra.

The Lady opened her eyes and smiled. Two men had learned an important lesson in visualization, and joined in their need to create enough energy to manifest their desire in the real world. Ted's arm would mend, as it had done so many times in the past, while David stood by like a rock, unselfish and giving with no hidden agenda. Lavender's hands came together in her pleasure. Tomorrow would come soon enough, but for these two weary men, she would delay the next sunrise in her realm of light and dark. A velvet mist arose, cooling and moistening the air to enrich her gardens, as her domain continued to grow. One errand to attend to, she disappeared into a cloud, looking for the Barrett brothers' childhood Spirit Keepers. They had some explaining to do.

CHAPTER 16

David sat alone in the small room outside the healer's door, where he waited for the swelling to go down in Ted's damaged appendage. His fault that Barrett had an excruciating day, he proposed to end the man's suffering that evening, if only for a small token of food and friendly camaraderie. David had seen Lavender once that morning; but for the first time, she did not greet him or anyone else. Grim determination, under a concealing smile, disguised her emotions of frustration and anger. This was not their *Lady of the Rocks*; and he wondered what could be so horrendous to change this woman's countenance and serene demeanor.

The day had not started well and continued to decline rapidly. David had woken to a sun-filled room with his head resting on Sir Edmund's soft belly, and another body draped over both he and the bear. A handsome head, sleeping fitfully on his chest, could not be soothed by the few tender strokes to the long mane. A sudden onrush of upsetting words, uttered in sleep, had Ted thrashing about. One swing of the broken forearm followed, alerting them both into a rude awakening. The youngest rolled to sit bolt upright, while rocking violently back and forth, and clutching the broken arm to his sunken chest, in a compensatory action to ease his agony. Cussing wildly at his injury, he turned the bright sunny morning into a profanity of blue haze.

Nothing had been said of the nightmares; they were part of what David saw in the bluescreen of tear-filled eyes. Nothing had been said of the position in which they found themselves upon awakening. Nothing had been said while the Monk held the arm causing so much pain; and nothing had been said while watching the swelling magically go down. Ted remained very ill and weak, saying little to nothing at all.

David's disquietude had started at the sight of the smaller man dragging himself out of bed. Thin as a stick, even his pelvic bones protruded from under the pale skin. On wobbly legs, Ted timorously greeted him with a few words, and then headed for the bathroom holding onto the wall for support. The blond could do nothing but clean himself and dress in fresh garments. Returning, he found Ted slumped in a chair, dressed only in a robe, apparently ready to leave for the set. The attire made sense, considering he would spend the day filming *sans* clothing. David did convince him to put on a pair of boxers and some sandals, at least to maintain some decorum at breakfast and in the studio when not shooting. With no argument, Ted had nodded, peering up to expose his gaunt face and the black circles surrounding those special blue eyes. His cheekbones and jaw line stuck out at sharp, piercing angles, casting deep shadows in the sunken hollows of his face. Barrett had lost more than ten pounds.

There would be food on his plate this morning, if David had to throw a major fit. About to stand his ground on the matter, the ghostly face turned and the head shook; the wisp of a creature could not look at food, much less tolerate the thought of ingesting even a supplement. He nibbled a piece of dried toast, while Kevin, Ray, and Jess masked their horror at the sight of their once beam of sunshine. They all had eaten in silence.

The cast departed for one major scene between Slade, Jay, and the Marshall. All the actors were necessary, to be seen from various vantage points by the tiny cameras. An oddity to film in total, but one take meant one take in La Rosa Negra, making each actor live his part throughout a wicked undertaking. The day's shoot was an outdoor location, and like all the days under the direction of Richard Carter, the weather changed to a dreary sky and a nipping, damp wind. The cold temperature deemed unnecessary to LaCoix, whose insistence, of waiting for a warmer day, was denied. Oblivious to all, Barrett bravely hung onto anything to keep him standing. Only one thought on his mind, he clasped his warm robe tighter, until someone rudely snatched it away.

David had spent the greater part of the night contemplating the inconvenient injury. With a sound plan, he received the Mistress' approval to change the position of Ted's hands, from tied to the saddle horn to behind his back. It secured both men's comfort, enabling Dusty to put his arm, holding the reins, between the thin torso and the broken arm. For the younger man, it relieved the tension of a potential mishap, falling to the ground, instead of dragged. With the new position working to the actors' advantage, it also gave the film crew a better view of the assault upon Jay.

With gentleness to Ted's arm demanded, David ensured wranglers, prop men, stunt experts, and outfitters tied the hands loosely. The horse behaved perfectly, allowing the blond actor to sit behind the saddle for the duration of the take. For Barrett, it was torture; for LaCoix, it was eternity. Ted again came through, choking in terror, the eyes saying everything, and the gag holding back more than screams and cries for help. Anticipating another triumph of filming, LaCoix saw the beauty of rising steam, off the warm horse and Ted's naked body, along with every breath and word iterated on a cloud of dissipating fog. Keeping his thoughts on a haunting and mysterious outcome, his last words drifted on a vapor of air, as he turned the glistening wet steed toward the next rise, loping at an easy pace to allow one angry man to hang onto a frighteningly cold one. LaCoix had sensed the pain endured by the body straining and shivering in his arms, until his ailing friend slowly drifted into semi-consciousness.

They reached their last mark, greeted by a wrangler who held the horse. Upon the gentle removal of the gag, David felt the body heave. Barrett immediately pitched over sideways, vomiting and choking, just missing the horse and his fellow rider who expediently saved him from falling off headfirst. Quiet hands undid the straps tethering Ted, and only David heard the few whimpers. Settling back, the naked actor leaned against the much-needed warmth of a chest, quickly bore of its jacket and wrapped around him. David remembered the death of a treasured butterfly within his hands, fluttering its wings in a last attempt to take flight. He felt the sensation again, with Ted stalwartly hiding his panic, remaining conscious, and controlling his stomach. His friend completed the scene with extraordinary self-will and a true actor's professionalism.

Helped off the horse by Carmichael and placed in strangers' arms, Barrett was sped away in a white van, attended by the Monk. LaCoix turned his mount to follow, but the wrangler's firm hold on his horse's reins stopped him. Forlorn and dejected, the hapless blond watched the vehicle pull away, only to be jarred by a honking horn; transportation for he and his fellow actors arrived. Clamoring on board, the journey back seemed agonizingly slow. David had not felt this badly about anyone for a very long time. He had grown fond of the younger man as a person, finally accepting the fact, and not thinking of him as an annoyance for stealing the picture, or a puzzle to unravel. With Ted, he wanted to be direct in their comfortable relationship, but he sensed the attentiveness could not be returned. Something in those eyes, seen on the screen the day before, held secrets. Tonight, with a friendship at stake, he would simply ask what the symbols meant.

After starting the morning in such a fashion, more misery lay in wait for two men in jeopardy. The day dragged on endlessly for David, who waited in full make-up and costume, to shoot the last scene. He had spent the afternoon biting his nails, foregoing his more favored cigarette for comfort. Listening to Ted's cries and pleas, while caged, tore LaCoix's insides apart. While these needed fill-ins were filmed, his young friend suffered with the nightmare of hours in the small prison; hysteria of confinement mounted. Jess' soothing voice filtered through occasionally, keeping the pitch of the screams down, and quieting the man during times Jay had to be still. An impossible task to endure, the dysfunctional young actor did listen to every direction softly ordered by the big man. The number of times David wanted to rush in to save Ted mounted astronomically. Finally, a call of his name and the last take of the day was made. A simple walk-on: enter the door, find Jay shivering in the cage, catch O'Reilly tormenting him, say his line, and this day would end. LaCoix added more physicality, but the reason for the speech remained.

"O'Reilly, stop! Jackson, Frank, pick up the cage and put it next to my bed by the fire. What's wrong with y'all? Don't want 'im dyin' on us, for Christ's sake. What the hell ya'll thinkin'?" Slade shoved O'Reilly hard enough to send the nasty man flying across the floor.

"Cut. Another great physical ad-lib, LaCoix. Great fall, Evans; it appeared very natural." A great deal of laughter came from both sides of the light filled studio, until the banshee shrieked.

"Get me out! Get me out!" Immediately delivered from his confines, in a near catatonic state, Ted dropped like a rock to the ground, crushing his bad arm against the floor to finish off his day. With little to eat for two days, his torturous body purging, in shock from his ordeal in the cage, and his outing in the cold drizzle, Ted started to cough and sneeze. David had not shied away, from whisking the sky-clad feather off the floor, with arms and legs dangling like a long-legged spider. With no hesitation and no one to stop the enraged star, he strode away, with his mouth clenched, and fire ablaze in his eyes. The elderly healer shuffled along to keep pace with the hostile actor, while the cast and crew watched in surprise and fascination. Very unlike LaCoix to care for anyone, except the occasional sexy vixen that captured his fancy, the intensity of the situation made this different. With a star's fury, David carried an unconscious, naked Barrett directly to the healer's room. Now, with fingernails in his mouth, he sat just outside the door, stewing with impatience.

The door opened slowly. Robed and stunned, Ted walked out alone to collapse in David's arms once more. A chair fell over in the waiting actor's haste to embrace and comfort his conscience. He pondered the thought, coming to realize the part Barrett played in his new life. The younger man kept him balanced, in what had to be done, and not what he alone needed.

A shaking hand brushed Ted's long hair off his exhausted face, while the other steadied his failing body. Without a word of belligerence from Barrett, David again swept him off the floor and carried him directly to his bed. Remaining silent and tensing his jaw, David held back a primal scream of pure ire in annoyance at the day. His only release came with fussing over the brunet-haired man-child who laid shaking and sneezing. With Sir Edmund in place and tightly grasped in one good arm, the injured limb was carefully elevated on several pillows. Covers heaped higher over the man needing warmth, and still no words came forth.

Satisfied that Ted lay comfortably, David dashed into his own confines to get out of costume and shower off the make-up. Back in minutes, still hastily tucking his shirt into his pants, he looked down at his quiet co-star and held back the anxiety created by the gray, dreary sky. A few, deep, noticeable breaths, he was ready. "Hey, Teddy Bear, how are you feeling? Still with me?"

"Been better. Are you mad at me?" Ted did not move, but for those tired blue eyes looking for an answer.

"No, of course not. Why would you think that?" The question caught David in the confusion his wrath created.

"You're not saying anything."

"Frustration and worry are better left in silence. My lightning strike temper could lash out at the person who could turn me into dust."

"Then I suggest we remain quiet." Ted gave him a faint smile, slightly calming the fire-breathing, green-eyed monster.

"Good idea. Bet you could do with a hot bath to take away the chill you're battling. How about some perfumed bubbles? Time for a little relaxation and a sober calm."

"I'm so cold; it would be welcome, but no bubbles."

"No bubbles? What fun is that?" David smiled paternally and swept away more of the hair growing longer every day. His mood lightened with the scratchy sound of a voice barely able to speak from screaming, and now becoming raspier with an oncoming cold.

"Water's hot, but the bubbles stay cold. Hate that."

"They do, don't they? Okay, one hot bath coming up. I think you should stay in bed and keep warm. You're exhausted, my friend."

"No, I need to get my strength back. Now that we know how to get around this place, let's walk over and get something to settle my stomach."

"If you're sure?" David gave him the questioning LaCoix look: hands on the hips, a tilt of the head, and a raised eyebrow for emphasis. With a nod, it was settled.

Ted heard the tub filling and smiled to himself. His idol seemed determined to contain him, like some tropical fish, in the warm waters of a Jacuzzi. Taking little time, his handsome knight, on a rescue mission, reappeared.

"You're still feeling unwell. Wish you'd change your mind and rest. You started heaving under the gag."

"The price of art sucks. Even last night wasn't that disgusting, tasting the grossness of puke, and holding it in my mouth until I got the nerve to swallow the putrid stuff. Man, it tasted ugly."

"I really needed to hear that, Barrett. You're making me sick as well. Can you manage on your own? I put some eucalyptus in the water to clear your head, and to aid your breathing."

"You are a wonderful human being, LaCoix, and all I need is company, if you don't mind?" Ted wobbled his way down the narrow corridor, ricocheting back and forth off either wall, until the only person, who seemed concerned about him, came to his aid. Submerging into the tumbling jet waters, Ted yipped once from the eucalyptus stinging a tender spot. Not serious enough to pass on the luxury of a hot bath and steaming vapors, he relaxed and closed his eyes, feeling comfortable for the first time that day. Chatting about all that lay between here and there, he wallowed happily with his hero close-by, sitting on the toilet lid, coffee in hand, acting like the protector of the weak and mortified.

"How's the arm? Maybe we better put some ice on it after you climb out of there."

"When did you become so practical, LaCoix?" A chuckle from Ted made David feel better than he had since the sun hit his face to find Ted sleeping on him.

"Since I met you, Barrett. About that arm, I can see it swelling with the heat. Did the healer say anything about binding it?"

"We have to make a stop and see him before dinner. I'd rather forego the ice. Told him I needed to warm up, and I knew you'd toss me in a bath. It's become a habit of yours."

"Guess it has. You conned me, you little shit, and I thought I was the master of the game." The two men participated in a real laugh together.

"Think the ancient is more than fragmented. He seems capable of concentrating on only one thing at a time. Sounds strange, but I can feel him sending me something, like a beam of light, straight into my arm--a blue one--and it makes my arm feel better."

"He looks older than Adam, so I would suspect a little senility. It's rather bizarre about the light, and the fact you sense and feel it. You even recognize the color as blue. He mentioned light last night."

"He did at that. Very scary." Ted joked at this new marvel, and for the first time, accepted something out of the ordinary, willingly without fear.

"Ready to get out?"

"Feel much better. It wasn't my best day."

"No shit. I think they kept you locked up unnecessarily at times. If yesterday's episode caused your nightmares last night, what will today's sojourn into hell create this evening?"

The rhetorical question went unanswered. Ted's shame of his night terrors still haunted him, unable to mask them. Not mentioned when he awoke, he sent prayers skyward for a small reprieve. Over the past few years, they had intensified, becoming clearer and more frightening. He knew LaCoix suspected his lies, but felt unprepared for the eventuality of the man's curiosity.

While they conversed, Ted climbed out of his comfort zone to dry off, while David searched through the new garments for something fashionable, yet warm. Both chilled from the morning's slight drizzle, if one man came down with a cold, the odds predicted the other would catch the incurable nuisance.

"Good choice, LaCoix--faded blue and bright yellow--my favorites. I can manage from here. Might have a saddle sore that the eucalyptus reminded me of, with a sharp bite to my ass."

"Got the hint; I'll go find something in my herbal medicine bag. Don't you dare move until we see the problem." David turned to give him a threatening look, before venturing toward his own suite.

"Yes, Daddy." Ted put on his best performance, unable to resist the remark to the blond who turned and rolled his eyes. Not the right nickname, the expression did not deter Ted from dwelling on a retaliatory name since dubbed with the moniker *Teddy Bear*. Unbeknownst to David, he actually enjoyed the affection evoked with its soft sound. Never having had a nickname, it bonded him closer to the infamous actor.

"Try again. My five-year-old won't be calling me that for much longer. Anything else you require?"

"Fix this burning sensation where I sit; and I'll be forever grateful."

"Before Susan stops talking to me forever, I'll have to get her to patent these concoctions, or give me the formulae." David returned to find Ted sprawled on his stomach, exposing a blistered sore, and much to his horror, a round, scarlet sun radiated from his arse, a consequence of the night before. LaCoix tensed, reluctant to touch the man. When Ted first told him of the painful area, it conjured up the medicinal. Now, he looked at something provocatively sexual, and he became instantly aroused. With a few deep breaths, he stood, staring at what his other head desired.

"Did you find a salve?" Ted lay quietly, staring at something on the far wall, not noticing

David willing himself to back away.

"It's a small saddle blister, but not in the best place. This lotion will take care of it. You're arse is extremely red from your purge last night, and looks sore as hell. Does it hurt?"

"It smarts. Can you put the salve on both? I've tried to find the blister, but can't locate it precisely. The pain extends further than the actual sore." Strangely nonplussed or shy, Ted remained relaxed; the situation had David extremely unnerved. Roles had somehow reversed.

"The sore blister has burst and is the size of your smallest fingernail. Appears inflamed, probably a result of infection from leaving it exposed to the dirt of the cage. The spot hides in the fold where your butt, thigh, and rocks rub together. I'm sure the eucalyptus hurt worse than one yelp." Reluctant to start, David had to subdue his erection before Ted noticed.

"If it stops the burning; I'm ready."

Definitively not ready, LaCoix sat on the bed. One hand lifted the little flesh Ted had in the area, while one finger quickly applied the ointment to the small sore. He controlled the shaking of his hands long enough to care for the most obvious problem. "How's that feel?"

"What's in that stuff? The pain disappeared!"

"Don't know. What about the inner part?"

"I can manage."

David swallowed hard, deciding what would be best, and knowing what he wished to do. "Your arm's a hindrance. It will just take a second." Placing enough salve on his finger, he set the jar down, and gingerly spread Ted's cheeks, to expose the reddened orifice, pulsating as cool air hit the spot. With his heart in his throat, he gently covered the puckered skin protecting the sphincter muscles, taking more time than he should. A tilt of a movement upward jolted him to retreat, but with enough patience, not to alarm the man into thinking that the feel was more than medicinal, LaCoix finished. "Done; you can get dressed." LaCoix could barely speak.

"Thanks, Dr. David. My jeans may be too tight." With no other reaction to the not-so-innocent touch, Ted turned and smiled.

"Since you lost weight, they'll be on the large size, so just slip into some soft underwear to keep your denims from rubbing." David diverted his attention to screwing the lid back on the jar, wondering about the reaction; but Ted lazily got off the bed and reached for the whitest of white briefs.

"Hate underwear."

"Too bad; they can be damn sexy. Maybe you should try a thong, or something more accessible." David chuckled at the shocked expression.

"Oh, please, you're talking sex again. What do you mean more accessible?" Before the answer came back to humiliate him further, Ted understood the innuendo and rolled his eyes.

"You sound like you're coming back to life, if you're bitching at me." A flash of white teeth brightened David's face. One of his gifts was a great imagination to come up with an instant visual.

"Men don't bitch, they complain. Do you think they'll show us anything tonight?" Ted slowly dressed, still showing signs of disguised fatigue.

"If they do, it would be the morning's scene. Strange how the weather changed so drastically, and then cleared immediately upon finishing. I guess we have to get use to these bizarre occurrences in this wonderland." David pondered on the day's events, and the mystery that continued to change their lives.

"Man, I felt cold. Thanks for wrapping me up."

"Unfortunately, you now have a cold. Lavender must have a steamer to keep in your room tonight. About this morning, did I hurt you when I grabbed..."

"...a little, but more unnerving than anything, although expected. Your hand was cold, giving me another surprise."

"Can't tell you how much it bothered me to touch you with that much force. Must admit, your privates warmed my frozen hand." David chuckled to himself, thinking how fear and temperature prevented a possible embarrassing situation for either man. On the other hand, perhaps, Ted did take a drug suppressant to stop an unwanted arousal. Pause for thought, David continued to muse to himself, while settling down without further discomfort.

"You've washed me down so often, I thought you wouldn't mind attacking that particular part of my anatomy. Well, I think I'm ready. A touch wobbly, but dressed and warm, I feel a lot better, unless a sneeze knocks me off my pins." Ted stopped any further mortifying discussion, wanting to forget the harsh handling of his genitalia in front of so many. David seemed to agree.

"You don't look much better, which might help in obtaining some food for you. With those black rings around your eyes, you look like a possum caught in the headlights of a passing car."

"Gee, thanks, but I thought you found me attractive." Ted joked, coyly fluttering his lashes.

"Everyone finds you attractive. Even more so, considering how frail and vulnerable you look." David triggered the wrong sentiments in his co-star's impressionable psyche; the comment would come back to haunt the older actor.

"Frail and vulnerable, hunh? Let's go. How about a steadying arm for this weary actor?"

With one arm around the toothpick, David easily supported Ted's weight. Together, they strolled leisurely out the door toward the aroma of a gourmet dinner. Making Barrett happy soothed LaCoix's trepidation of the potential impact that the cage may evoke, although the brunet bounced back like a racquetball, or masked the after-effects under a cloak of bashful charm.

No one reacted to another uncommon move by the one actor, but simply watched him assist his co-star into a soft seat. The cushioning helped protect the bony derriere, as well as the small blister and sore ass; both would take a few applications of the numbing salve to rectify. The wound would heal, before those dreaded close-up cameras drew too close to the unsuspecting man's behind; and David shuddered at his part in the drama to come. He could have ruined the scenario by giving into the temptation he touched: so hot, so red, and so inviting.

"You okay? It's not often your eyes go blank," Ted queried with a tilt of the head; a habit he picked up from LaCoix.

"Passing thoughts; now, let's see what I can do about food." David stood erect; covertly ensuring that his oversized pullover hung passed his crotch, which continued to misbehave.

Everyone was present, reminding the two men that many of their fellow actors would depart this night, making dinner a farewell party. With the last five remaining, time grew closer for Ted and David's intimate scenes. The blond actor was ready; the brunet appeared strangely oblivious.

Lavender walked in smiling, disguising an emotion David recognized from earlier. He caught her by the arm before she had a chance to sit down. Startled at the pressured grasp, she spun around violently to face him; her green eyes flashed a spark of dangerous red. LaCoix backed off quickly, but quietly whispered his urgency to speak with her. The two disappeared behind one of the many closed doors, with Lavender slowly turning, seething with mysterious rage. Sparkling ruby orbs, full of venom and hatred, dared David to make his request and to explain his nerve at touching her. No one set a hand on the Mistress, only she them, and always on her initiative. Barrett had been the exception, with a touch radiating directly to the center of her being. She scared David to his grave; but he was on a mission. His concern, however, now encompassed two people he liked and admired.

"What's happened, Lavender?" David settled his nerves, knowing too much of the irate woman's abilities.

"You first, as I may lash out inappropriately." Two sets of green eyes intensified with frightening emotion, daring the other to speak words of greater importance.

"It's Ted: no more weight loss. He's really sick and in pain."

"The healer told me about his arm and fever. I have been preoccupied with his mental state, forgetting the fragility of his body. I am sorry. How bad is he?" The bewitching eyes returned to normal, softening her timeless face to show deep concern for one of her stars.

"He'll put up with the inner turmoil and the physical pain you put him through last night, which by the way, has not fully subsided. Hell, he'll put up with anything you throw at him. I'll try to steam the heck out of his cold, if you have something we can borrow; but please, allow him to eat. He's as weak as a newborn. The healer manages to calm the swelling of his arm. Whatever magic he's using, also reduces the pain to some degree; at least he's good for something."

"Do not speak of the Monk in such a fashion. He is an old man who has immense power to heal. Unfortunately, his concentration is limited."

"That's what Ted thought."

"Our hapless Mr. Barrett will be better by morning. You are surrounded by healers who will focus on his physical problems."

"Thanks; now, why are your feathers in a flurry, your Ladyship?"

"I have handled this badly. I should have been informed. No excuses, it was my responsibility to find out. Damn his parents! Damn religious based societies! Damn the Fates for all eternity!" Lavender brought her arm down hard, hitting the closest table with her fist, and then swinging the arm up and out, creating a chaos of broken porcelain, and crushing anything made of crystal, including the delicate chandelier above their heads. Tiny fragments rained down upon them; the floor sparkled with rare gems and twinkling lights. The Mistress stood there, eyes raging red, and inhaling and exhaling breaths that came out in misty clouds of hot vapor.

"Whose parents? What Fates? Ted's?"

"His and half the parents of the men who come to take refuge here. Damn the lot of them for creating such devastation in the name of some holy deity, or worse yet, love."

"We all do stupid things for love, Lavender." David mellowed his tone, hiding his distress at her intentional damnation.

"It is not love, but brainwashing and abuse. I am sorry, condemning all parents, when the aforementioned are much less common than the ones who truly love and die for their children. I should have never made such a generalized statement. Considering the charges in my care, Theodore Barrett has me both puzzled and transfixed; I do not know why. He reminds me of another who returns continually, his life and pathway perpetually out of order."

"What do you mean, *out of order*, as in what? Destiny? Fate?"

"In a manner of speaking. A pathway, of set goals, must be followed by all sentient beings.

Sometimes they stumble, losing their way in the milieu of confusion that you call reality. We lend assistance, nudging them back on track to secure their future, whatever may lie in store."

"Good God, you call yourself a Caretaker, a Caretaker of people's destinies? Holy shit, it's true! You're not real!"

"I am very real, and, yes, I do tend to all living creatures. As for destinies, no one has a set destiny--a false assumption--a name given to an abstract concept unproved. Beings have malleable futures, which are not engraved in stone, thus our presence to secure a few, as it is easy for one to change the future of another unknowingly."

"What the hell does that mean? Some are better than others? Jesus, Lavender, that's fairly judgmental of you." David watched as the red flashes stopped and started, stopped then started again. The glittering room of broken prisms nearly blinded him.

"We see certain abilities in some, which are to be safeguarded; that is all. Your future derailed, when several usurpers pulled the proverbial rug from under you. Acting as living Fates, they stole pictures from you, resulting in your fall from your rightful path and future; and you did not attempt to correct it, although given several opportunities to do so."

"So I screwed up; figured that out a long time ago. You've just confessed to treating privileged people differently. A bit egocentric and discriminating of you, whoever you are."

"I am not in the mood, David. Just know this; fate is an improper term used for those who intentionally, or accidentally, take you for a flying spin away from your planned future, or the goals you set. Those goals are seldom taken to heart, or their importance realized by your species. Humanity tends to float through life, expecting the magic to happen naturally. If they fail, or succeed, destiny, or what you call fate (neither of which exists), is blamed. Humans form their own future by avoiding, or paradoxically, dancing with real Fates."

"Shit, that makes no sense at all."

"Neither of us are this evening. Let us leave this discussion for another day." Lavender turned to depart, but David persisted in his confusion.

"So who is off their path, Ted or I? Why? You're not real, and you're screwing around with only men's lives."

"Stop right there, LaCoix. You have seen very little of one place called La Rosa Negra. Do you believe we Caretakers ignore women, children, and other creatures? What do you take us for?" Her eyes glowed brighter red; David refused to back down.

"Of course; that would make perfect sense, but why me and Ted?"

"Take a good look at both of you; it should answer your question. You are progressing on your own, since vowing to change certain aspects of your life. Do not slip backward now. You have a long way to go, but you are having an easier time, of returning to your path, than Mr. Barrett, for which there is a reason. Listen and learn from everything that happens here, and the feelings they conjure up. Listen to your heart, LaCoix."

"You're scaring the hell out of me. I saw Ted's eyes: they held strange, frightening images, and then his nightmares. Is his future different from the current path, on which he staggers? He won't die by his own hand, as you suggested the other night. Please, at least give me that. Am I part of it? Is that why I'm here?" LaCoix's unraveling nerves knotted, in a ball, at the base of his brain.

"Leave it be, David. You will do what is right for you, and for the people who surround you.

Although having taken a while, you grew into a decent, caring human being. If you falter, remember what has transpired here, and pull yourself up, knowing I will appear when needed. You are a strong individual, diverted from the direction you chose years ago. The door is reopening for you. As for Theo, he is not yet ready. We shall feed him, of course. I did not realize how sensitive his system would be to a mild herbal mixture."

A curt ending, to a much-needed, deeper discussion, LaCoix had to let go for the moment. Without another word spoken, and thousands of questions left in his head, he followed the worried Mistress out the door, listening to the cracking of more crystal underfoot with each step. Aghast at her outburst and attack on a priceless collection of inanimate objects, he would remember this scene, and all she said. Their intense conversation threw him into a swirling eddy, positive the past few days were a dream he walked through; but then there was Ted. What had he gone through, and what were those eerie symbols that shone through his eyes? It jolted him back to his own horror of being an absentee parent, and a rather cold and austere one. He would change the disturbing flaw immediately.

Within those few minutes of absurdity, one thing David learned: the Mistress could hurt you badly, if she thought you messed up, and certainly if inclined to do so. She could control your entire future with a flick of a wrist, a flash of red eyes, or a thought. Ted had to be the reason they were there; but he puzzled over his own need to be present. David knew he had come a long way in a few days, becoming significantly kinder, more caring, and increasingly open to those who mattered to him. Those few changes tingled from his toes to his nose. Assuredly part of his new beginning, she confirmed he was doing the right thing, determined to meet the goals set when he first started acting. Thinking back, he always dreamed of a solid career as an actor, secure in his abilities, financially independent, with a happy, adventurous life. For the most part, he had achieved those ambitions; however, his dream future started here, in the present.

Barrett seemed intrinsically linked somehow. If not for the rewrites inserted, the cast would have dispersed weeks ago. His conscience, his friend, and, for some reason, his responsibility, helped him see the devastation he created over twenty-odd years. Payback lay at hand, by helping Ted through his strange entanglement, to ensure his young friend had a future. He suddenly had a strong sense that whatever happened, it would come through the necessity of these unorthodox scenes with Ted.

Through the door, with determined, floating strides, the Mistress headed in one direction; with equally long, deliberate steps, David strode into the dining room. Sitting down, he gazed into Ted's hopeful eyes and gave the man a wink and broad smile, while hiding his latest shock.

A sigh of relief came from across the table; the blue eyes danced and crinkled at the corners; Ted's dashing hero had rallied to his rescue. With another flash of a smile from Ted, David gave thanks for informing the Mistress. Apparently, a few things passed her by, never intending to hurt the young man, but quite the opposite. He could only hope that his own acting ability could veil the staggering assault filtering through his brain, attempting to put pieces of a puzzle together, with many of the key bits missing. The path he would travel included his usurper; he would do his part, whatever it might be. Helping the contradiction of a man, he vowed to stop Ted from stepping on another landmine. Theodore Barrett was only beginning.

Dinner turned into a delightful, boisterous affair, full of laughter and idle chitchat. Ted eagerly took part, although eating only a small portion of the meal set in front of him. He looked very pale and extremely tired. What he did eat seemed to satisfy him; and David received a happy thank-you grin, from the man who politely laid down his knife and fork, side-by-side on the plate, indicating he was finished. If this man had a horrendous upbringing, it included the teaching of impeccable manners.

A viewing of the Slade/Marshall/Jay scene reeled off, to amaze everyone further. Another technical masterpiece, Ted again set the pace in the lingering shots of a man in pain and terror. His perfect face, though gagged, disappeared into the rising steam and mist off the warm horse, his own skin, and David's breath against his cheek. The vapor enhanced the frightened feeling that symbolized Jay's inner turmoil and faltering mental state. Magnificent in every detail, the work appeared as a painting of the mystical--a vision of half-hidden terrors in the thickening fog--it was Ted's, not Jay's torment. Understanding the symbols in the blue eyes would uncover the truth and release the man's tortured Soul. They were one in the same; and the thought sent David spinning.

With no doubt in anyone's mind, Barrett stole the picture. With a flurry of congratulations, five waved good-bye to the rest of the cast, whirling away in Lavender's giant dragonflies, taking wing, and speeding them home. The Mistress rejoined the remaining group, sitting calmly, yet appearing nervous to speak. She looked at David who still vibrated from several shocks. Another pronouncement of equal magnitude may arise, as he watched the strange mauve tears glittering down her face. A questioning look, and a shake of her black curls, indicated a warning. Turning to Ted, she took his arm and led him a few feet away, close enough for David to hear and to be there for reasons unknown to him.

"Theo, I have bad news, Child." Her hands quickly grasped the trembling ones, and stopped the shuffling feet with a direct, sympathetic connection with her feline eyes.

"What's happened? Your eyes changed; they scare me."

"Listen closely, steady yourself, and do not think of me. The house, in which you were born, has burned to the ground. Nothing remains, but a pit of ashes and debris."

"My parents, are they okay? Was anyone hurt? My brothers?" Ted could not pull away from the intense stare and the consoling hands. Fixed in position, she forced him to pay attention.

"Your family is fine. Slow your breathing." Her Ladyship fussed over the man who started to hyperventilate. "Easy, my Child, as your parents were visiting your wife; and your brothers are handling the situation. They are not dismayed, and understand you cannot join them at this time."

"But I have to go." Extremely agitated, Ted struggled to move from his cemented position. He had to see the carnage left behind.

"Stop, Theo; you are not going anywhere. They do not need to see how ill you have become, and in this kind of pain. It would only make their situation worse."

"They've seen me hurt before. It won't bother them; but they won't forgive me for not being there. They need me." The whine in Barrett's voice became intolerable for David, but he understood and waited.

"No, and that is final, Mr. Barrett. I think it is time for our talk, but I will give you fifteen minutes to assure your family of your concern. Mr. Carmichael, could you escort Mr. Barrett over to the guide waiting at the door, and stay with him while he makes his call? Mr. Donaldson, Mr. Evans, please feel free to return to your quarters, or partake in a brandy in the study. Someone will meet you inside to take you wherever you wish to go. Good night, Gentlemen, I look forward to seeing you in the morning." Lavender stopped her tears the instant she looked at Ted, but now, with her man-child out of sight, they flowed down her exquisite, motionless face of white china. She turned in sorrow to meet LaCoix's uncertain gaze. Puzzled at the emotional display exuded by his fair Lady, he immediately remembered the floor of sparkling diamonds, and took a gasp of air. He understood completely and immediately.

"You know then, David; my temper and damnation of his parents caused the fire. Theo was correct; I am very dangerous when my emotions cloud my thoughts." The voice sounded empty and hollow, lacking the melody and tinkling chimes.

"How can it be your fault? Purely an accident, with no one hurt, only things are gone." David anxiously attempted to reassure one, wishing to comfort another, and needing to escape himself. He faced a situation of the paranormal; and even the most open-minded would be frightened of the truth.

"Memories remain, but when Theo finally sees the rubble, his nightmares will disappear, leaving him free to fly, and start to heal. They cannot hurt him again. I require time with our man-child tonight; you must comfort him afterward. I willfully caused the destruction of the house, David; and you know it. Precisely at the time I struck my hand on the table, fire swept through my mind; I unleashed it for the Barrett brothers, a necessity for their welfare."

"I don't understand. You have amazing gifts, but to burn a structure down at a thought; I just don't buy it." Putting on a good front, David played the dumb blond, hoping his assumptions to be absurd.

Lavender said nothing, but flicked her wrist like an aristocratic lady hailing a carriage. The empty chopper hangar ignited into a blazing pyre, to grow or diminish at the rise and fall of her hand. The final lowering of the virulent weapon stopped the devastation abruptly. Taking a deep breath, she closed her eyes in grim concentration, and blew softly toward the building, carrying away any telltale smoke into the still night air. Everything returned to normal, as if it never happened. "There will be a slight odor of charred wood in the morning, a small reminder of my capabilities."

"Jesus Christ, that's fucking amazing!" David stood stunned, allowing Lavender to bring herself into a balanced state. She had Barrett to worry about this night; the time had come to open his very closed, yet fragmented Spirit.

"I must go, David. Have a drink with your friends. Join them for some easy company, while you wait for Theo. I hope he will not need your assistance tonight." Lavender headed for the door, leaving the astounded actor alone under an ill-timed full moon. The place turned hauntingly still, not a breath of a breeze felt, not a sound heard from the desert creatures that serenaded them to sleep. Something unnatural had occurred; and the Cosmos seemed to hold its breath.

David stood in shock at what he had seen and now knew as true. The Mistress had immense powers, appeared human, but could not be real. Feeling blindsided with much missing, his thoughts churned to figure out his own version. He attempted to solve who she might be and what a Caretaker's job entailed: a living mystic, a ghostly Fey, an alien life form. A shudder ran up his spine with his last thought. He understood the Mistress' sorrow over her destructive actions and the ferocity of her temper. The vindictive intent remained; she admitted and demonstrated her wrath. Destruction of the house seemed of importance; whatever her grand scheme, David sensed her only concern was Ted. The game grew serious, and potentially deadly if anyone pushed her Ladyship.

Finding his way to the study, he shunned the bourbon offered and sat with the others. Jess joined them, to watch his long time friend bite his nails, until nothing remained to feast upon. Three men idly conversed about dealing with Barrett's arm in the upcoming foray. David only sat deep in his chair, legs stretched out, and his hands together. With raw fingertips tightly pressed against his clenched lips, he tried to make sense of what had transpired this night. It held him in a trance, whirling the possibilities between truisms and illusions, possibilities and improbabilities. The piece of the puzzle most terrifying, which ran through his frenzied mind, was the Mistress of Destiny. She had pointblank denied the existence of the one thing his beliefs understood, destroying it by giving him a future without a preordained destiny. With his only belief shattered, he had to replace it with stronger, higher goals, solid and correct, never to leave his thoughts. The message became imperative to manifest them into his newly awakened reality.

CHAPTER 17

Lavender walked into the small room occupied by an unhappy man and a concerned Jess Carmichael. Quivering in spite of the warm night, Ted listened to the closing story on the other end of the line. Tears of relief fell down his face, after bidding his father a *Go with Christ.*

"How is your family, Mr. Barrett?"

"Shocked, scared, lost, angry: they're praying to Jesus for deliverance. No one, not even the arson team, has found a cause for the fire."

"They will find no cause."

"What? How do you know?" Ted replaced his sorrow with annoyed curiosity, while the bright yellow sweater cuffs busily wiped the sad eyes of salty liquid.

A jeweled hand reached out, hesitantly taken by the man-child who wondered at his action to go willingly. Stumbling behind her, through a maze of halls and doors, he feared he would be lost forever and dared not let go of her powerful hand. His grip tightened, to his lifeline, in his time of duress, illness, physical pain, and exhaustion. He wished for a comforting conversation, considering his mind had scattered on the wind. New thoughts of guilt added to old ones, burdening those slight shoulders and thin neck that barely sustained the weight of his head. A wall opened; Ted pulled back against the powerful force lifting him off the floor. The feeling of floating, through a haze of soft mist, smelling of lilacs, seemed to confirm the identity of the Mistress. With no one to save him and no escape, Satan had him in her lair; he fainted from the crushing assault to his unstable senses.

Coming around had him in wonderland. He sat beside the ageless beauty, with her black curls trickling over his own face. Unseen but softly felt against his cheek, she wore velvet, and her arms held him securely, with his head resting on her shoulder. Tilting his chin upward, he gazed into green feline eyes, no longer disguising their unusual appearance. She peered deeply into his blue gems, straight into his being, and smiled knowingly, while rocking him to an unearthly chant. Her embrace felt right, necessary to ebb his fear of this loving She-Devil.

Lavender brushed away the loose strands of her hair, and those of Ted's, which fluttered across his sunken, ghostly face. Her chair seemed large enough for both; so high in the back, it ranked as a king's throne. Without moving, he scanned the area within his range. He first saw only candles, flickering and dancing from the slight breeze blowing through an enormous open window. The elaborate portal appeared to grow larger, only to see stars and too many moons, never witnessed while pondering the celestial orbs on a mountaintop. Breathtaking, the image conjured up visions of being forever safe in this woman's arms, coming to terms he belonged there. His fight blew away on a whisper, willing to remain within the mystical cloud and watching the millions of solar disks play and twinkle, fall and disappear. With no fear in such a dream, Ted remembered a rhyme heard as a child, from another not of his church. He murmured the words softly not realizing someone listened. "Twinkle, twinkle little star, how I wonder what you are. I wish I may, I wish I might, have this wish, I wish tonight."

"And what would that wish be, Child?"

Ted startled; but a hand, pressed against his overly warm brow, lulled him back to this invisible place of nowhere. "Oh! I don't know. I'm just remembering."

"How unfortunate, that a beautifully chanted spell has gone to waste, and so many falling stars to wish upon. When you cast even those innocent rhymes, visualize what you wish for, just as you called for the Monk." Lavender peered down at the head on her shoulder. A handsome man, many unanswered questions lay behind his mask. Perplexed by Ted, she tried to solve an unknown puzzle rarely encountered.

"That rhyme is a witch's spell?"

"Certainly a Pagan one, but I suppose its origin comes from a Wiccan ritual. For a poor orphan, a star became a focal point, while calling for a Spirit to make their needs known. The saying often worked, putting a crust of bread in their hand the following day. It has been recited for hundreds of years."

"It's that old?"

"There are many ideas, within your learned knowledge, translated from ancient languages, and passed down from person to person, place to place." Lavender smiled wistfully while gazing out the window. The man she held recovered quickly from his fright, to become interested in an ancient wisdom.

"Tell me another."

"A story perhaps, such as King Arthur whose roots, in legend, trace back to the Moors before they conquered Spain. A few name and location changes, additional embellishments from the original language, translated into Spanish, then to French, until the English claimed it as their own, long forgotten by those who started the tale. Apparently, researchers plan to spend vast sums of money to find the location of Camelot in England. Rather amusing, is it not?"

"Really? I like stories of knights in shining armor, coming to rescue all manner of men and women, while fighting off monsters of the imagination, including magical dragons."

"I like it as well. It holds great meaning for some of us; and dragons exist in other realms. Maybe we shall take you there one day. You sound better, Theo. Are you no longer afraid of me?"

"Can't fight what you don't know."

"Excellent answer, a lesson you must remember. Understand before you make up your mind, and always know with whom you are speaking."

A shy voice stated the obvious, "I don't know you."

Lavender chuckled softly in response to the timidity. "We sit here tonight, to rectify some of the mystery, my Child, since we need to know each other better, and now have the opportunity."

Ted looked up to a reassuring smile, only to pull away and sit erect next to her. His adult, masculine energy kicked in, suddenly having trouble with the coddling he received from both Lavender and David. The term *child* also unnerved him, yet it felt correct when spoken by the Mistress. "I'm not young, Lavender, but everyone treats me like a stupid kid; I don't understand why. My friends know how old I am."

An honest dilemma, the impact, of a youthful appearance, affected more than Barrett. "You look very young and sometimes sound it; therein lies the paradox. People want to stay youthful in looks, to the point of altering themselves surgically, but then they do not receive the respect their age and experience has taught them. It does make for a frustrating predicament."

"You even call me child."

"And I am the only one who has the right to do so. Everyone is my child, including your friend David."

"Why?"

"Age, my dear one: eternal, never-ending age."

"You don't look old. I could never guess your age, but the way you speak, and the things you know, say something else."

"Thank you. Now, shall we get back to you? What are your feelings toward the destruction of the home where you were born and raised?" Lavender abruptly changed the subject, leaving certain facts for Barrett and LaCoix to learn when ready.

"When you told me, my concern centered on my family's safety. To be honest, I'm glad the house burned to the ground, every last thing in it, and filled the pit." Ted's clenched fists, and the return of his head to her plush-covered shoulder, were all she needed to see and feel. His Spirit Guide proved correct; his cries for help were honest needs.

"You lived in a house built over a hole?" Lavender feigned surprise, waiting for a reaction.

"Let's talk about something else. You said, some time ago, that you had questions about Jesus?" This time Ted switched topics. More questions about his family, he could not abide.

"Yes, I did. Are you up to pondering new ideas? They may sound trite, silly, and somewhat fragmented, but do not laugh, Theo. Inquisitive by nature, I only ask to initiate a conversation as to what you have learned and what you have missed." Knowing all was a difficult matter, and this young man had nearly disappeared, from their scans, without a thought. Still uncertain of his importance, a strange feeling of loss, which he generated with a touch, grew stronger. His life was an ambiguity to those of the Cosmos.

"Think I'm ready, and I'd never laugh at you. If the questions are regarding Christ's teachings, there is nothing to think about, as I know the *Bible* backward."

"But there lies your paradigm, Theo." Lavender's smile turned into a faint scowl, not seen by the man on her shoulder.

"My what?"

"Sit straight and look at me. This requires your full attention, so listen carefully."

"Yes, ma'am," the quiet, hesitant voice returned.

"A paradigm is boundaries, your chronological list of everything in its place, never to be expanded or broken down. Set unconsciously, usually by others, your borders are about to shift, because you will answer from your heart only, without one word coming from your scriptures. Can you do that for me? Your responses cannot be forced into a square box, caged in as you were today. You told me of your prayer being answered, and how your positive thoughts manifested themselves into reality. Calling for the healer, with David, accomplished the correct result. As we discussed, neither of you prayed to a deity, but simply chanted your heartfelt desire for the Monk's presence. You both did an excellent job; I applaud you for remembering and trying what you thought impossible several days ago. Do you see there is no difference between a Pagan chant and a Christian prayer when it comes to the realization of one's needs? Visualization and honest feelings create the correct result." Feline eyes met mystified blue ones that paid close attention to the ageless face.

"In that respect, I guess I do, and I've witnessed your many capabilities. I bet you conjured up the cold, cloudy weather this morning." A tilt of the head, and a questioning look, gave Lavender pause for thought. This man replaced fear with curiosity far too quickly. She wondered if he would remain open to her questions, or fall into another abyss.

"If I said yes, what would you think of me?"

"Your powers seem limitless. Ordinary people can't change the weather on a whim."

"Yes they can, if shown how, or have the innate ancient wisdom in their subconscious mind. Perhaps, one day, you shall learn to change a dreary day into a sunny one." Lavender stroked his chin and held his head up to look at her comforting face. A relaxed hint of a smile returned.

"You're kidding me? At least baseball games wouldn't be rained out."

"Or shooting schedules pushed back." The Mistress laughed, teasing a face that brightly shone with amusement.

"If you're capable of such a miracle, how about curing my cold and arm?" Soft chuckling erupted.

"I may agree to help you, if your smile remains."

"Thanks. You're a handy person to know. Has anyone told you that?"

"Never, but thank you for the compliment."

"You're welcome, but we started talking about you. I suppose I don't think of you as a real person, Lavender, but what else could you be? Sometimes I think you're an angel, and then I wonder if you're the Devil." Ted turned away to contemplate a candle, while waiting for a truth he doubted he would ever hear.

"I am only what you see and believe me to be. We talked about this misconception of yours; and I have no other response. What else could I be?"

"A good Spirit or an evil one."

"I will tell you one thing, as you have the intelligence to surmise this. There are no evil Spirits, Theo; I guarantee the fact. Evil is a sentient-made force, an intellectual creation of a psyche gone astray, associated medically as a form of insanity. Evil is absent in nature. The term seems akin only to entities with abstract thought." Lavender attempted to ensure he listened to each of her words.

"Makes perfect sense, if the evil of insanity is eradicated when you die."

"An excellent, insightful response. Each Spirit has their own personality: some serious, some fun, some crazy in a good way, and some who do have evil identities while in your reality."

"So, there are evil ones?"

"No. Unfortunately, your soft heart makes this difficult, Child. Just know we nullified them, becoming an annoyance rather than a danger, and never released to wander the Cosmos. Such behavioral flaws will soon be terminated in your world, prior to becoming a problem in mine."

"So you kill them off, or banish them to hell?"

"Another misconception, as is heaven, but it is what they mean to you personally. If you believe in the abstract concepts of heaven and hell, can you conceive the possibility of many levels between, above, below, and all around said places? They are names that have taken on too powerful a meaning. Words do not necessarily make things real."

"You're telling me my faith is wrong. Why do I have to keep defending myself and what I believe in?"

Returning his gaze, Lavender dismayed at the slight annoyance shown. "When you can defend your beliefs, in the true light of your heart, you shall make the transition. How can I say this for you to understand? Your beliefs may, or may not, be your true faith; and faith is what matters, coming deep within your being, including your subconscious mind. Misconceptions of beliefs yield blind faith, which follows into precise, organized, administered thinking, resulting in law-based religions and all their factions. It is not a true path. When your Spirit is free of dogma, your heart, and mind, reinforces your faith with truths. You decide which beliefs deem fair, and which to discard. Question everything that does not feel right." Lavender hated discussions with someone not yet ready, never knowing if she helped or hindered. This man, of such innocence and so utterly brain controlled in his beliefs, required cautious thought, perhaps starting again with more childish-rhetoric. Barrett deemed too intellectual for frivolity; the idea may blow up in her face. She could only try, and may have only one chance.

"So, you're not attempting to change my faith in God and Christ, but making sure my beliefs are strong enough to support it? I'm confident about myself and my faith, Lavender, but you confuse me with terminology, and yet you won't let me use my own quotes." With Ted, thinking and asking questions, his conclusions gave her hope that another crack would open.

"Ah, yes--the cause of all the world's problems--terminology and not listening to what is truly being said. Your faith is strong; make sure your beliefs back them up. You said it quite correctly. Eventually, as your journey unfolds, you will begin to see, through some of your questions, and the answers found, your old truths will be renewed and strengthened, with many new ones added. Others will no longer be valid, and thus we exclude quoted scriptures; for each statement iterated would lead to years of translating the symbolism of each word, also adding the archeological, sociological, and different theological finds and acclamations as to which are true and which are false. Shall we make our conversation easier, by dealing with what we both feel correct?"

"Yes ma'am. So this discussion is about defending my beliefs and not my faith, using simple terms?"

"Exactly, but not defending them *per ce*, only analyzing them with explanations." Lavender muddled through her head, trying to find her way with Barrett.

"Do you want to start by telling me why you were so upset today?" Ted looked down at her hand that held one of his. Warm, white alabaster, adorned with gems, which caught the sparkle of candlelight, only the hand's firmness mattered; he would listen to what she said within the context of his understanding. A diversion into someone else's problems usually worked; something David often did with him, turning everything around with a question out of left field. He thought it a good ploy, to avoid discussing something he had to prove without the words that he knew so well.

"A quick change of subject, one I am unwilling to discuss at this time, but let us try. Do you remember a friendly animal or toy comforting you, or a voice speaking with you; anything that made you feel safe?" With Ted sounding resigned to respond without fear, Lavender vowed to keep the discussion at this level, without telling him the complete story.

He looked up at her, deep in thought, trying to remember something. "No, not really, although there was something, which sounds weird, which felt like it understood and wanted to help. A narrow beam of light, with a sense of being to it, distracted me from hurtful things. I thought it came from Christ. I'd forgotten about my ray of sunshine. Wonder if it's significant, considering what Jess and the others call me." While remembering, Ted shivered slightly; as if someone's cold hand rubbed itself along his spine. Lavender understood and continued her hold.

"It is not strange at all. At least one of them reached you. They tried very hard, which I must commend them for, but it was not Christ."

"One of them? Who are they?" The shiver returned, rattling the slight frame. A steadying arm, about his shoulders, settled the quiver.

"Every newborn is assigned a Spirit Keeper, to help them through troubled times. You and your brothers counted for three; but they were blocked, from every direction, by the constant repetition of erroneous words planted in your heads. None of you had a choice of religious philosophy when baptized in the name of the trinity, one of the cruelest forms of abuse a person can endure. An important choice is taken away immediately upon arriving on your planet."

"Never thought about it. I guess it should be a choice; but parents must inform God and Christ that the child arrived and is now in their care."

"Why would you have to tell gods of such a thing? They supposedly know all. Parents keep a child safe and teach them right from wrong. Unfortunately, there are those who have no right to bring a baby into the world, for many reasons; and then ones who believe they righteously teach their children a certain moral code, only to pass down false or old philosophies. Often a vicious circle of lies, and sometimes even hatred, is sent through those kinds of teachings, creating closed minds and impossible guilt for a growing child, becoming immensely destructive in adulthood."

"That's why christenings are needed, to offer the baby to God, for protection from such treachery."

"Did it help you, Child?"

Ted did not answer, turning his gaze to ponder the matter, and staring blindly at the array of sparkling lights displayed through the large open window. Her statement upset him, relying heavily on this one belief for his own reasons. "How would one know? Guilt is part of life, keeping you from repeating mistakes. Do Spirit Keepers talk to you? Should I have asked them for help, if I met one?"

"From guilt to Spirit Keepers, your mind is certainly hyperactive; the way it should be. Yes, they talk, they play, they keep you warm and safe. I do not think you even tried speaking to your ray of light."

"I recited scriptures to it; and it would touch me when I wriggled around to get its warmth."

"A Spirit would not understand your Christian philosophy, although it tried to help, knowing you needed guidance. You were certainly not a waste of its energy, I assure you. Unfortunately, it could only reach you during your trying situations, a very difficult place for understanding. You may have heard parents speak of their children's pretend friends; the ones adults cannot see. The child becomes confused when taught of the impossibility. They are told that their friend is only in their imagination, when they really do have invisible allies who are real and extremely important."

"So, a Spirit Keeper talks and plays with you like a real person?" Ted squinted up from under his lashes.

"Or thing. Let's step back and allow me to ask you questions." Lavender relaxed, releasing Ted to turn and face her. His nervousness was easily noticeable, along with the uncertain physical pain growing within; however, she did feel his interest. "You may be absolutely right in your faith; and it may be your eternal pathway through life. There may be, however, many other reasons for worshiping the god of your choice, besides your teachings. If you find it through vision and revelations, interpreted by your own heart and mind, without outside interference, then that is who and what you are. Your path is true."

"I believe it is, as the choice was made for me. It will always be my path."

"One of your problems, Child, the choice was made for you, instead of letting you choose. You still have choices, if strong enough to question things and rid yourself of unnecessary guilt.

Read scriptures, from the time you were in the womb, instead of nursery rhymes, you learned psalms. You have a child-like presence about you, because they never permitted you to be a sweet, natural innocent when it was your time. Unable to run free and explore, not even within your imagination, they allowed no questions, no answers, and no choices. Do you think a nurturing god-force would want such a life for you?"

"You believe I've been brainwashed, and my baptism made it more poignant?"

"Yes, Theo, very much so, as most humans are, in one religion or another; and the conundrum starts very young in all philosophies. There is a compulsion amongst sentient beings to protect their young through sacred rituals; and as humans are herding-type animals, they tend to be followers. However, unlike humans, other animal species, which group in families and have a social order, do not exhibit this birthing ritual. Animals have splendid ways to attract a mate, but they take full responsibility of their offspring, putting the baby's life first, fending off predators, particularly the mothers. You never see another mammal intentionally hurt its children, only in rare circumstances when the male becomes the stalker."

"But they are non-thinking beings."

"Of course they are. Humanity could learn a great deal from them, finally understanding man's place on the planet instead of destroying it. Animals do think, talk, and act, but in a different way. They are understood by others of different species, but not deciphered by the arrogance of the human mammal. To converse with animals is another ancient wisdom you are quite capable of learning, and a very necessary ability. Imagine understanding different forms of communication through telepathy. Thoughts, and the feelings behind them, would stop the misconceptions, the lies, and perhaps even an animal attack."

"It certainly would make life interesting, but telepathy? I guess it's how we met. It scared me then, and it scares me now, thinking of potential eavesdroppers. You'd create an entire race of paranoid people, afraid to have a thought." Ted started thinking rationally; the Mistress was pleased.

"It has the potential, but selected telepathy can be a trained mental function. We shall let you worry about it later." She chuckled, watching Ted's eyes widen in surprise.

"Me?"

"All things are possible." She laughed again and gave him a squeeze.

"So what do you want to ask me? What if I can't answer, without referring to a passage to back me up? Does it mean my beliefs are wrong, making my faith unwarranted? This is confusing, as I know Christ protects me, and I believe in him, with all my heart." Ted squinted straight at her, defending his God with those miraculous eyes, which did not charm the Mistress as they did on camera.

"I know this is hard, Theo. Just know I am not attempting to destroy your faith, only your Valkyrian attitudes toward your beliefs. We are here to help you become more Luciferian, to open your Spirit to dispel misconceptions, and possibly to reconfirm your faith at a higher level. Do you understand what I just said, and why I do not want to hear the words of the book of so and so, passage such and such?"

"You're trying to turn me into a Satanist! You want me to become Luciferian? I don't even know what the hell it means, or the other word you used." Ted tried pushing away and standing up, but the Mistress held fast. This was not the time for the innocent, who had started to become receptive, to take ten-paces backward.

"Hush, Child, for you must listen to all the words, and if one is unknown to you, ask for clarification before assuming anything. I shall explain and say this one more time. Opening your heart may reconfirm your faith at a higher level, it may change it drastically, or it may simply change a few of your beliefs, but not your faith. Do you understand that?"

"Yes, but what about Lucifer?"

"Again, those linguistics and terminology mix-ups arise. They are simple terms, and you have the wrong concept of one. You must give poor Lucifer a little credit, for he has been much maligned since Christian mythology rearranged his persona. You are currently Valkyrian, meaning you are a very staunch believer in your faith. There is nothing wrong with that. The first term comes from a Norse goddess: a warrior and defender of her faith. The *do or die* motto is Valkyrian. There is no judgment as to whether it be right or wrong, for you will always feel that way about many of your true beliefs. For instance, the commandment: *Thou shall not kill*. You would never murder another living being, would you?"

"No, of course not; although, in your words, I've murdered many a mosquito." Ted intently watched the eyes, which had added a flash of crimson to the green. With the warning taken seriously, he paid acute attention, but he had many questions. Everything said seemed wrong in his mind, and yet, he could not deny her words.

"It is a belief that properly justifies your faith, but said mosquitoes are predators. You have the right to kill hostiles if attacked. It is Natural Law." A questioning look and a gentle smile calmed the unstable figure sitting on the edge of the throne.

"It's also a moral code of civilized society." A retaliation of sorts from Ted, Lavender nodded her head in acknowledgment.

"Excellent, Child, for you are opening your mind and thinking. Unfortunately, there are many who would disagree, considering the use of guns all over the world, to shoot man and game, and usually for sport. Always remember that sport is between two opposing foes that know the rules. Animals only hunt for survival, and therefore, they do not know these rules; humans, who kill beautiful, wild creatures for sport, are murderers. Let us change subject, as the thought, of killing an elegant, endangered cheetah as a trophy, upsets me. Now tell me, who was Lucifer?"

"The fallen Archangel who rebelled against God, wanting to be the one Almighty. Banished to hell, he became Satan for his sacrilege."

"Go back further, Theo. According to Christian dogma, Lucifer was the bringer of light and awareness. Where do you think the words *lucid* and *lucidity* come from? These words mean clarity and enlightenment. They are a reminder of the bringer of light: a rebel who stood for the right of free speech, and yet, cast aside because of them. Your god seems tyrannical at times." Lavender mused to herself, wishing she could show Ted a glimpse of the truth. Time would present itself, if it were to be.

"But Lucifer wanted all the power." Ted's nervous stammer came back, in his bewilderment of a seemingly accurate statement on the Mistress' part, but his ingrained beliefs could not let go.

"According to some interpretations, but perhaps it was your god who desired full power for himself. Did the right one conquer?"

"It was truly a Holy War then; and Lucifer lost?"

"That it was, if the mythology is fact. We still have light, which makes one wonder. I would suggest, if you truly believe in the story, that Lucifer might not be the horrendous entity you call the devil, as he did not take the light with him when he fell. If he had, hell would glow brightly with enlightened spiritually; and heaven would be a cold, dark place. For those who believe in Lucifer, not Satan, he still shines brightly, doing what he believes is the right thing, making people aware of all their options, allowing them to be creative in their search for truths. He lights your way even in the dark. Being Luciferian is a wondrous title, until you have a complete understanding of your faith. It may be one belief to discard, if you find my point valid that Lucifer was set-up as a contrary to your god. Something else, which baffles me, is why do all gods have names but yours? Never mind, just a passing thought. It does seem, however, there has to be an opposite in almost all philosophies. I have never understood the reasoning."

"Duality, the trinity, things seem to come in pairs and threesomes in many religions. Even in your statement, you once spoke of the light and the dark; a duality you use. I've never questioned the rationale behind it either; nor the fact that God does not have a name to distinguish him from the general term, unless he is the one God that I have been trying to tell you."

"I believe the one god theory came after Pagans conjured up the name to be used for the many running around the planet. Getting off that strange oddity, remember my words did not infer an opposite, but rather a kinship. So neither of us knows the answer to either question; and we both use the terms for many things. We shall leave the number problem to a numerologist." Lavender chuckled lightly, affectively calming the young Spirit to a degree. Knowing, that some things would never be understood, was an important lesson for Ted, and a very necessary one.

"Now you sound like David and his women: tarot cards, the zodiac, essential oils, and candle burning." Wonderful to hear his gleeful laugh, the Lady Lavender hugged him for his insightful thoughts.

"When the time comes, you can be Valkyrian in your attitude, if you feel nothing has been left to learn. Be aware, however, that once you reach that point, you are no longer open to new discoveries, leaving your beliefs as targets, to come tumbling down like a barn-board building in an earthquake." Lavender held firm and hoped the young innocent listened, but she lost him, suddenly hearing him slip downward.

"I've never heard these terms. Both explanations are inadequate. I don't want to do this anymore. Please, Lavender." Ted's guilt came rushing to the fore, truly believing a lightning strike inevitable, if he even thought the Mistress' ideas valid of further investigation. He wanted to leave, without another word.

"I am sorry, Theo, but you appeared interested, opening to new ideas, and I have many other questions. This is only a discussion, to see which beliefs may be absolutes, and others that seem a little dubious. Your god is still your god, is he not?" She forcibly turned him to face the challenge.

"Yes, ma'am."

"I never meant to scare you, Child. There is nothing to fear in any of these new words. Tell me the truth: are you still frightened by that one possible change in a belief?"

"No, not if you explained the terms accurately." Ted backed down, his intellect ruling his deeply ingrained beliefs in the existence of Satan.

"As far as our limited discussion is concerned, I have. We will omit the many other myths of Satan's identity. Ready for those questions now?"

"No." After his long day, Ted was exhausted, and with each new puzzle, it became harder for him to focus. His head spun, and he doubted his ability to answer any question posed. He needed and wanted David: his protector, his mentor, his voice of reason. With another loving embrace, he backed into the warmth of someone or something he did not know, but needed. Unfathomable to him, the sensation offered bordered on affection, but only chaos ran through his head.

"In no particular order, let us see where they lead. Let us start with the easiest, and I ask this because I am curious, not degrading. This is from your heart, brain, and the deep subconscious recesses of that beautiful head of yours. Ready?" Lavender stroked the lustrous locks she created for such a purpose. It always brought the child out in a man when caressed.

"Guess so." Ted inched deeper into the lush warm velvet and the feel of the unearthly woman. His own mother never held him like this, not even a pat on the back or a peck to his cheek. This caring enticement made him feel like a needy child; and he wanted to remember the sensation of motherly love and compassion. Only her words frightened him; but he had to concentrate on the meanings, and not what he understood the words to represent in the past. He sensed a clue hid in her maze of ideology; he had to listen carefully.

"Why do Christians gather to worship their prophet, rather than their god? This is not just Christianity, but also a global affect. Do you see this trend, or is it my imagination?"

Ted turned to look at the stars, his comfort zone of contemplation. Had he deserted God to follow the son? It would appear as such, considering his affiliation and influence in a men's group that prided themselves on the teachings of Christ. "Not a prophet, Jesus is the Son of God."

"Excuse the profane meaning of the word I have chosen, thinking only of its true intellectual definition. Do not be offended by words, or think this a silly metaphor, but your Jesus was the bastard son of your god, just as Hercules was the bastard son of Zeus, a god with a name. Even worse than being illegitimate, in some people's bigoted minds, they were both of mixed blood: human and godly."

"Mary gave birth to Jesus, while Hercules is just a myth, a story, a fable of no merit or similar implication to the truth that is Christ." Ted hated this outrageous metaphor, and grew angry at the frivolous comparison.

"In defense of Hercules' mother, Alcemene did not hide who his father was, nor did Zeus. They spouted it openly, while Mary and your god said nothing, leaving Joseph and Christ to start the rumor. Interesting to wonder what Mary knew, if anything. Getting off that scandalous topic, this may sound trite, but let us use the comparison for now. Ancient deities are easier to deal with than disparaging other religions equally as controversial as Christianity. Remember your faith is new, only a few thousand years. The ancient societies, which man has records of, shared much of their philosophies and gods, standing by them for an equal or longer span of time. I am only using your religion; because that is all you know. So tell me, Theo, why Christ and not your god?"

"We learn about God's will through Christ's teachings."

"In other words, unable to speak directly to mankind, your god required an interpreter, thus impregnating an innocent girl to produce a son to teach the populace. Why did Jesus disappear until adulthood, before returning to pronounce whom he was, and then leave the storytelling to another to write your scriptures? It seems a drastic and inhumane measure on someone's part, not to mention a great folly. Who wrote the original manuscript, Theo?"

"I don't know; and God didn't rape her, if that's what you're inferring. Historically, Josephus chronicled part of his journey, and he was an accomplished historian. The Dead Sea scrolls, when found, revealed the Old Testament."

"Rape, a virgin birth, maybe an illicit affair: Mary has some explaining to do; and Joseph could only come up with a dream sequence turned into a vision. He did save Mary from being stoned to death, however."

"That's cruel and completely inaccurate," the mouse retaliated against a would-be predator.

"Back to Josephus then; the historical record of Christ and the New Testament is one man's recollection of stories told to him, mixed with what he may have witnessed. Whoever wrote the *Bible*, did they interpret your Christ's history correctly? I use the term *they,* as it has been acknowledged that anywhere from six to eight authors had a hand in it, one more reason to doubt its credibility. Therefore, did Josephus have his facts straight to begin with? He lived during the same period, but was it from personal experience of what he saw and heard, or an embellishment of others' stories? Did Homer recite the story of the Trojan War correctly, with each telling of his *Iliad* and *Odyssey*, and the trials of Hercules set upon him by the goddess Hera? Each work is a collection of interesting heroics and miracles. Some parts of the ancient writers' tales prove accurate; some have not; and so the debate goes on for eternity, if you allow it."

"You can't compare them. The *Iliad* is not Holy Scripture, because no one considered Hercules a god, not even a prophet. He hated his father. The only justification for such a comparison is the *Qur'an* and the written mysteries of the Far East." Again, too much for Ted, it sent him adrift amongst the stars. His intellect had to be convinced.

Lavender waited a moment, getting into a position to penetrate the tension and strain of Ted's neck with her massaging, therapeutic hands. He did not shy away and melted into her healing powers. "All are fascinating documents, Child, as well as the writings on the pyramid walls and Aztec temples. So many wonderful, creative stories, but where did they come from, and who wrote them down so meticulously? More importantly, who, in your contemporary world, has accurate knowledge of the ancient tongues and hieroglyphics to interpret these writings? The answer is no one. Egyptian hieroglyphics have been misconstrued, without anyone screaming to go back and rethink them. Now, the *Qur'an*, deciphered into modern language for the masses, is it truthful? Changes and misinterpretations plague both the *Qur'an* and the *Bible*. New versions, new ideas, and as Christians, you have almost eliminated the Old Testament from your studies. I rather enjoyed those particular stories: Noah and the Ark, Adam and Eve, and the poor forgotten Lilith, Adam's first mate."

"Lilith? Where did you hear Adam had a previous wife?"

"The Old Testament; and here is a rather interesting thought for you to consider. In your religion, Adam was the first man, the first to sexually couple without marriage, the first to commit adultery, and the first to divorce because of it, just to engage in a romp with a blatantly foolish younger woman who believed a smooth-talking snake. I wonder how the Roman Catholic Church deals with that one, when their Pope is adamantly against the breaking of such a bond, not to mention the number of commandments Adam broke. No wonder the couple was tossed out of paradise. The story of Lilith is hidden within the second telling of Eve being the removed rib of Adam. How strange that sounds, unless meant as an abstraction that humanity no longer understands. See what fun you missed, by not studying the older writings prior to Christ's coming, and destroying earth's historical calendar of events?"

"I never thought about Adam. It makes him sound like someone we know, but that was an unkind remark about Jesus' birth."

"It is one of our displeasures, this BC/AD paradigm in time and space. Changing the timeline of earth was of some concern for the Cosmos, although it will be set right again. The other tale, which I enjoy, is the telling of Moses and the parting of the Red Sea. An excellent, quite plausible story, if Moses remembered those innate ancient abilities similar to ours."

"You think Moses was like you! I don't even know who you are!" Surprise had Ted sitting upright, before settling back into the massaging fingers.

"He certainly remembered something of past wisdoms, to manifest the division of a large body of water. Now, what about the Old Testament? Why is it of less importance to Christians, if it is the book of your god?"

"Judaism is lived by the Hebrew."

"They are not Christian. They share your god, but they view Jesus as a misguided conjurer. Both groups are divided, debating religious dogma over prophets, still believing in the same god, as do the Sufi; but then they are considered Muslim, and things continue to become stranger and certainly more confusing as to who is who, your god or their Allah. At least he has a different name than yours, although meaning the same thing, but with a different personae. Meanwhile, even the Christian sects fight religious wars amongst themselves for unfathomable reasons. How difficult this is for us. Again, it lies in terminology. Perhaps you will be my guide through this maze of ideology."

"You make some sense, thinking of the many Holy Wars since recorded history. Most were strictly political, with religion thrown in to make each side feel like martyrs. It appears they have lost any kind of religious based morals and ethics."

"It certainly has me confused as to why these differences exist, and the incongruities of their similarities."

Lavender allowed Ted to turn, changing his sitting position to look at her directly. Squinting suspiciously, and now comfortable in a crossed legged position beside her, his contemplation grew stronger with his yet-to-be-asked questions. "You want me to help you make sense of this; but I keep telling you the one big difference: Christ is God's son!" Ted emphatically attempted to get the one point across, which he thought the Mistress kept missing. He abruptly stood up to challenge those peculiar emerald spheres with the black slit running down the middle of each. His ancient history studies, which his parents dismissed as sacrilegious, returned; and the Egyptian goddesses, Bast and Sekhmet, rose to loom over him.

"We are now back to those sons of gods. I am sure you are aware that the infamous *'they'* have found some of Jesus' own writings that state: *he is the son of man*, not your god. What kind of sense is that, Theo: *the son of man*?" Lavender shook her head, trying to figure out the conundrum. Even with her complete knowledge of all languages, this was a meaningless statement of folly. "Do you know what he meant?"

Ted shook his head defeated, not comprehending how it could be either.

"Good, something we both agree upon, adding to the drama. In the *Bible*, Jesus performed miracles of many good deeds, along with throwing major temper tantrums, patronizing his disciples with his own ego, and of course, the ultimate, sacrificing his life to become a martyr. I don't think we should discuss that event further, as it sends me into a depressed and irate mood. To the comparison then: the goddess Hera forced Hercules to battle horrendous trials of strength and heroics to save the world of symbolic or real demons, even being part of Jason's crew and their journey into a godly set-up. He succeeded through his own torment, going mad during one of his trials, along with his own self-sacrifice to prove himself worthy of being Zeus' supposed son. Now tell me, which is fact and which is fiction, or are they both true or both false. Perhaps a little of both."

"Hercules, Alcemene, Jason, and the rest are fictitious characters made up to tell a grand epic story. Christ's exploits were all written down."

"Theo, please listen. Josephus documented a very small part of the life of a man called Jesus, last name made up. Hercules' exploits had the likes of Homer as the teller of his tales. All I'm asking, is did these two men, out of many, get it factual? In years to come, will you be able to accurately tell your children of our discussion in the canyon when we first met? Do you remember everything precisely, word for word, without fear or judgment clouding what actually happened?"

"No."

Lavender lifted the downcast head to regain eye contact. Ted was a remarkable creature, brilliant mentally with the emotions of a child. How could she help him come to realize there were other opinions to consider, rather than his blind Valkyrian faith? "What about those missing years of Christ growing up and maturing into an adult. There are many imaginings of those times; yet there is no proof, including his supposed life in India. Is there any evidence of Jesus being on earth, besides Josephus, and the rare sightings of him in church towers, smoke signals, and wooden doors, even waterfalls?"

"You're being trite, and what of Hercules? Where's the proof?" Ted thought he found an opening in a conversation that had him frustrated.

"Only the stories and his name carved in stone in one of the athletes' preparation areas, outside of an arena in Greece, where they pursued various sporting events. It dates to the approximate time the tales were being told. It may be the Hercules we have read about, but that also may be speculation, like everything we have discussed tonight." Lavender watched Ted closely for reactions. The smugness on his face, from his last question, had been nullified quickly; and she could see him searching his mind for another comeback. He looked dismayed, but not defeated. She wanted neither emotion.

"I have no answer, but in my heart, I know Christ existed, and his teachings detailed in the New Testament. Maybe I can convince you, if you let me recite the passages of consequence to our discussion."

"Sorry, nothing but from your heart, Theo." She gazed thoughtfully at the man who could not utter a word without a testimonial scripture for support. "Okay, how about this? Can we agree that Jesus existed as a man, and an exceptional one, whether he be a true prophet, or the best con artist the world has known? Can we also agree that there may have been some poetic license within the writings?"

"I've studied them all my life. I can't just stop believing in him and his miracles. How can you even suggest he cheated? He has only brought good to mankind."

"Miracles or the innate abilities of Moses? Now, tell me one good thing he brought to your world?" Her eyes flickered crimson, under the long lashes, daring an answer.

"How can you even question it?" This Ted had no fear in answering; his voice wielded anger; the flashes of warning red ignored.

"Because that is what we are doing, Child, questioning everything; and you did not give me an answer. I can only assume you do not have one. What has been done in his name? How many wars? How many lives? How many sacrifices? How many nations, peoples of different races, and unique religions have been destroyed in his name? I am sorry, Theo, but I find it very disturbing."

"No, you're wrong. Why do people always use that as an argument?"

"As the saying goes: *where there is smoke, there is fire*. Do you send missionaries out from your church?"

"Yes. We aid underprivileged children in third world countries, bringing them medicine, food, and the teachings of Christ."

"Helping children in distress is always wonderful, no matter what you believe in; but you are inciting blackmail tactics: the teachings of Christ for much needed medicine and food. What about educating people to make them prosperous on their own? Charitable work, in foreign countries, is touted all over your television, always brought to you by the Christian foundation of such and such. I am sure you are cognizant of other world communities helping this endeavor, without the flagrant use of advertising. Has Christianity not destroyed enough indigenous faiths with devastating and murderous results? I would not exclude other religions from this act of aggression, so I am not singling out your faith. Helping children is a powerful thing to do; however, changing their gods and rituals to fit your own mythology, with blatant bribery of food and medicine, is ludicrous. Yes or no?"

"No, it's not, but it's a start." With one single word, Ted ignited the fire, turning the eyes scarlet.

"A start! A start of what? You keep them in the dark with the *Bible*, leaving nothing to live on but the sole belief your god will deliver them into a better situation, by getting on their knees and praying to a foreign deity, in a language they do not understand. It is a crime against Natural Law. You inoculate them with preventative drugs that your church does not believe in, and you leave them enough food for a few months. The heroes who save children do not carry *Bible*s or bring in high-tech equipment; they carry the gift of saving entire villages in their heads and bare hands. By teaching village women minor medical skills, instructing men how to use and maintain water pumps from the eighteenth century, building simple irrigation systems used by the ancients, and showing how to prevent contamination of their water supply, helps the poor flourish anew and with pride. The list of their successful accomplishments grows. Is this not a more lucrative and appropriate method of aid, than building a church and handing out *Bible*s and plastic toys that will break in a week, to become part of the debris and filth, never deteriorating into a useful earth supplement?"

"Stop, you're spewing blasphemy and hatred. I won't listen anymore. You're twisting and changing everything I am and hold dear. My life is guided by those beliefs. I'm a true Christian, and nothing you say can change my mind."

"Maybe I am trying to make them stronger, by making you think instead of following."

"Please, stop. Don't do this to me." Ted was too ill for such an intense conversation; but the Mistress wanted to use his vulnerability, to open the crack before it closed completely. No longer able to keep pace, his head reeled. His teachings disallowed explaining his beliefs in his own words. Everything he knew came from reiterating passages from his holy manuscript, where his truth lay.

"I am sorry, Theo. All life is joyous, even religion. You fear yours, instead of wallowing in the spirit of it. Tell me this. What if the *Bible* had never been written, Old or New Testaments? What would be your clue in believing in Christianity?" Her voice softened to bring him back, although her questions intensified.

Stunned with another hit, Ted could not come up with an answer. He searched his mind for a piece of scripture that covered the question. "I don't know what you want me to say, Lavender."

"You understand perfectly well, but let me use this as an example. Has your god or prophet spoken to you? Has their presence been felt deep inside your being, giving you visions and answers? Have you had any revelations outside the church, or what you might perceive as a newly found meaning in your life? If you meditate, has your god answered a question directly for you? What does he feel like when he is close by, or in your head?"

"He's always in my heart, telling me what is good and right. He keeps me at peace; and I do as is written." Ted started to hyperventilate, his mind whirling with what he thought as silly and bewildering questions unworthy of consideration. Wondering why he had not asked one of the elders, just out of curiosity, he shuddered at the disciplinary action they would invoke.

"At peace? Not since I met you, Theo, and written again. Oh, Child, your head is so full of these sanctified words that you cannot *feel* your own god. Only the words in your head, repeated continually, give you assurance. You have called for help all your life; that is why I am here. Only you can conquer your fears and manifest what you need in life. With all your requests for help, Christ has not been there for you. In fact, for the past 2000 years, he has been busy elsewhere. No heat or hot water in your trailer, your state of shock and bouts of dementia, it has been David coming to your rescue the last few weeks. I would venture to guess that he is one of those knights in shining armor from King Arthur's court."

"Christ made him do it."

"Nonsense and you know it. I cannot imagine anyone manipulating Mr. LaCoix for such a purpose. His beliefs lie elsewhere, deep in his subconscious mind, waiting to break loose; and they are not yours. What does that make David in your eyes, a heathen?"

"No, of course not. He's a kind, honest man."

"As is the Dalai Lama and the Pope. You believe in neither, yet they hold millions of people in the palms of their hands, and they are human, just as you. They differ only in their beliefs, one a little more enlightened than the other. Your David may be more aware than any religious head. Who knows, considering each travels a separate path to find his highest power. They shall all learn the truth."

"Are you saying there is no higher being than man himself? You have to be wrong."

"I am not saying that at all. It is up to you to put the pieces together. Perhaps it is not who is the higher being, but whom and how many, or is it all of us, each committing a part of ourselves for the greater good, or the downfall of humankind, even the Cosmos and beyond. The people involved, in your chaotic state, have saved you out of love and compassion, with only a handful believing in your god and less in your Christ."

"No; please stop." Overwhelmed, distraught, and unnerved by his strange debate with the Mistress, Ted's teachings deterred the questioning of anything. Now he had more than he wanted, and no one to ask. Lavender frightened him beyond imagining; he longed to be free from La Rosa Negra and its mysteries.

Lavender readily sensed his befuddled mental wanderings, and abruptly brought the session to a halt. "The world has not ended. Come with me to the window. Everything is still in its correct order in your world. Nothing has changed except a few new things to think about." Steadying the severely shaken man, she settled him gently on the wide sill of the huge open window, and sat behind him, clutching his arms that crossed his chest. He slowly settled against her, feeling the velvet, and smelling the lilac scent that always lingered in her hair. Intoxicating him, his sense of short-circuiting disappeared. He allowed the Mistress to support his weight unafraid, while beholding a sea of ghostly moons, cragged planets and sparkling stars in the blackness of night.

"Look, Theo, this is my realm, my home. You have never seen these stars before."

"They do look different; and the spheres are so close."

"And tomorrow, they will all look different."

"I hate to bring this up, Lavender, but there's nothing below us. How did the choppers get us here and how did they leave?" Ted became calm enough to change his confusion into curiosity with a little discreet, sedating, healing power from the Mistress.

"We are looking toward earth, and that is why time differs here. The helicopters returned your friends home safely to your world. We sit in a place where space has no boundaries, just as your mind should have no fences or locked gates. Eternity--boundless and endless--your imagination should be that free. You are special, Theo; that is why you sit here, viewing something few have seen. Your religion belongs to you alone, and you nestle within my arms to gain a better understanding that there is much more to learn before entering the *knowing*."

"So we all have gone wrong in some way? Why should I be singled out, and who are you really? What's the *knowing*?"

"As I told David, I am a Caretaker; and you are special because of your profound cries for assistance. You know something is amiss and you have to right the situation. You passed into what we call the *knowing*, by thinking of your faith in a new way, by believing in *mind over matter*, and by finally accepting your special self-healing powers. I believe you understand more than you let on, Mr. Barrett; and you will learn more in time."

"It's no big deal; I just heal quickly; that's all."

"You have already admitted to your growing power to David; although I do not believe he caught the enormity of what you said. It is a monumental gift. Since you have not sneezed once, I assume you cured your cold without my help. You must treasure your abilities; discover new ones that you can use for good."

"Yes, ma'am. Every faith has its faults and some have their truths; we just have to figure out which is which."

"Quite correct. Self-discovery and endless questions will teach you. Your Spirit is free to wonder and discover life's maze." A small shiver and the embrace tightened. He opened himself to thoughts of the *knowing*; her Ladyship's smile brightened the night.

"It feels like we're hanging in space. What happens if we fall out this window?" Back to the innocence of the fearless *Peter Pan*, Ted made Lavender chuckle. David picked up precisely what this young man was: a man with a child in his eyes.

"I would catch you, or another passing Spirit, Soul, or entity, just as we did when I dropped you. Nothing would happen to you, not here. It is the safest place you could possibly be."

"You have confused me beyond my reckoning tonight, Lavender. What other entities? You've said that before, talking about Souls and Spirits."

"Of course, but you are tired and ill; and I have taken much of your energy. One thing to remember, Theo, no one can be so naïve as to believe earth's beings are the only life-forms in the universe, let alone all the unknown dimensions, densities, or levels existing around you. You have heard this spouted by many generations of seers, but only recently taken into serious consideration. You will learn many new things through another. Believe in your ray of light, which shone upon you as a child. You may still require your Spirit Keeper to help you, remembering it is not human, but a simple sunbeam, trying to ease your pain, giving you warmth and hope."

"I have to believe we're unique or nothing else fits. I'm so wired, with everything that's happened, and now all this. My faith is dying; my hopes for a new life died days ago; my life is forfeited; I'm scared shitless; and there's no place to go or turn, only to continue on: empty."

"The baby?"

"Partly. I have to retain my beliefs in order to protect my child, but I don't know how. We're inbred with these ideas; and I don't want certain things recycled to frighten more people like my brothers, and me, but now I have to. We're believers, but many things we had to accept and perpetuate, just as you suggested. The baby--my baby--I have to change, yet here I am, arguing with you to retain years of indoctrination, which I must maintain. God will strike me dead for that statement alone."

"Not with me beside you. As I said before, you are in the safest place you'll ever be, Theodore Barrett."

"What can I do? I'm afraid of what lies ahead, if I don't hold fast to my church. It's driving me crazy, Lavender. It gives me the shivers, knowing what's going to happen. If I try to stop it, Karen will make it worse, making my life a living hell."

"I believe it already is. I can only support whatever decision you make. Only one bit of advice: before you can save the child, you must save yourself. I know what you were contemplating when you arrived. That is not your answer, only an option when your time comes. You have much to do before you depart this reality."

"How do I keep going when I don't want to?" His shoulders sagged, under the weight of what lay between here and there.

"Perhaps you should reconsider the decision you made, before hearing of the baby. Follow your dreams, Theo, and those important goals you set."

"It's impossible." He shook his head violently, whipping the long mane back and forth in exasperation. A slender hand caressed his forehead, absorbing the agitation into her tranquility.

"Admit your fears to someone who can help you in the real world. Your future is in jeopardy and may not be achievable, unless you firmly decide on stronger goals. Stay on your desired path, as I can only straighten it slightly, to keep you from falling."

"And what is my path, Lavender? I don't see one, except too much responsibility; and it hasn't even begun."

"You must decide, keeping your eyes on the prize, and visualizing winning, when you cast your spell upon a star. Manifest your hopes and wishes into reality. Trust in true beliefs of your faith; and I will send you a guide."

"It's an impossible situation. The fence or paradigm you spoke of is too high." Ted convulsed involuntarily; she held him tighter. A slow rocking movement returned his head to her shoulder.

"Hush, Theo; all will be well, if you give yourself a chance to learn and explore your innermost thoughts. Be still now, for I will not leave you to suffer alone." She held him firmly until his body relaxed.

"But I'm afraid of you."

"And yet here you sit, gathering strength in my arms. We must leave now. Take one more look at the beauty existing beyond all realities and dimensions. All things are possible, if you want them badly enough and your heart stays true. With so many alternatives, constant changes and choices, you feel death your only escape, but know I am a call away. Breathe in this air, Child; and we shall return you to Mr. LaCoix. He sits alone and waits nervously for you. I fear for his nails."

"He certainly does worry about me; his fingers are probably bleeding." Finally, a slight smile from Ted allowed Lavender to let go.

"Yes, he does; and I get to worry about you both."

"Why?"

"It is my job."

"Who are you? Will you ever tell me?"

"The Lady who scares the hell out of you."

"You're not kidding." A small grin again surfaced on the pale face of a very confused man.

"I am sorry you shall not learn more about me, until it is time."

"I still don't understand the significance of what we talked about, but thanks for inviting me into this beautiful space and showing me your stars. You are lucky to live here."

"And you are lucky as well, living in a world where you can ski on diamonds. The door will soon open for you, first through pain and torment, followed by great joy, and the two will overlap at times. You will fight the good causes, and conquer some manmade evil you already know exists. You will learn, Theodore Barrett."

"First joy, then sorrow, followed by confusion, and then the full moon is gone, leaving only a distant black sphere. I feel as if I'm being sucked into one of those black holes they talk about. I'm floating away, Lavender. Tell me this was all a dream."

"Remember the ones who support you, Theo, giving you sound advice and filling you with happiness. They will not desert you. Are you ready to begin life anew, with an open mind, even if the portal is only a speck of light, shining to caress your face in the still darkness?" Lavender kissed his cheek and gave him a last hug. She filled him immediately with renewed energy and hope. "You are so loved, my Child. Now, we must find David, as his concern is beyond measure."

After a bashful smile of hello to his handsome co-star, and a knowing look to the raven-haired Mistress, Ted's weak, unsteady frame was immediately grabbed around the waist and half carried to their cottage hide-away. Drowning in contradictions, Ted's mind sunk into the murky depths of unknown answers to impossible questions. He gasped at the thought: the unknown. A foregone conclusion, his life had been laid out in an orderly, chronological list at birth. She called it his paradigm; he need not be trapped within its boundaries. There were alternatives, and there could be change without guilt. The Mistress' words etched themselves deeply into his mind. His first revelation hit him with the ringing of a chime; he oozed with happiness and relief. Theodore Barrett came away understanding one important message: he had choices.

CHAPTER 18

"Why are you smiling, Ted?"

"I think I understood something she said. Lavender made me realize I could change things; I just have to figure out how. We didn't really discuss it; I was so scared of what she asked and said; yet I feel so free right now." Ted felt the rush of reaching the pinnacle, his toes hanging over the edge, ready to fly away. Joyous enthusiasm replaced his fear and trepidation. A high, only the Mistress could provide, kept his heart pounding, changing his direction and attitude.

"A true wonder your *Lady of the Rocks*." LaCoix smiled back.

"She seems real enough, until she nails you with something physically impossible."

"That's Lavender, all right." Not about to tell the man what he had witnessed that night, David troubled over his experience, debating on whether her skills were real or an elaborate hoax.

"She said I had choices." Ted exuded exhilaration upon confessing his confusing chat with the Mistress, making David question his own timing, to explain his visions seen in his co-star's eyes on the silver screen.

"You didn't believe me when I told you the same thing. She must have said something to ring a bell in your head, if you finally believe the fact. It's nice to see you're not backing away. Does she still scare you?"

"She sure does; as most of what we discussed I consider nonsense. I just know she won't hurt me. There's a difference. I'm acquainted with people who hurt me, but don't scare me. Weird, isn't it?" They reached David's quarters; and Ted readily accepted the invitation to continue their conversation. Barrett, though tired and pale, seemed too wound up to rest; and the blond appeared happy to watch over him. The day had been long for both men: one in fear and ailing, the other in panic and concern.

While David busily brewed coffee, Ted comfortably curled on the couch after finding Sir Edmund. A large unopened mailing tube sat on the table, demanding someone's attention, and it caught the youngest eyes first. "Looks like you've got mail, LaCoix. Maybe it's your house plans." Ted made the announcement; and his mentor looked up abruptly, having been caught contemplating much bigger issues.

"What?"

"Looks like a package from your architect." The lack of enthusiasm did not deter Ted from wanting a surprise.

"Good, but I wonder how they got here. I'll look later."

"But I thought..." Ted stopped, as David appeared disinterested in his cliffhanger. Flooded with disappointment, he longed to see the contents of the red tube, hoping a diversion would quell his surge of energy created by his conversation with the Mistress, and his unthinkable day. He needed mental stimulation, although physically drained.

"We need to focus on tomorrow, Ted. After today, I'm concerned how you'll react to more brutality, and whether you'll feel well enough."

"I'm fine, but I guess you don't want me to see the drawings. They're none of my business."

"What; the house plans?" David turned in time to catch a quick glimpse of *Peter Pan*. Preoccupied with what he deemed necessary to ask Ted, he had ignored the man's current needs.

"Yeah; after you described the details to me last night, I'm excited to see the layout."

"I'm sorry, it wasn't my intention to exclude you; but we're both tired. We can pick them apart another time, considering tomorrow's assault, on your already broken body, may affect you emotionally. I hope you have the strength to fight back."

"Another time then, but you seem worried about something besides tomorrow." Ted looked at him, out of the corner of his eye, suspicious of the deep frown and tense jaw.

"I'm very worried about you. You passed out on me twice today." David picked up the two mugs and headed over to his co-star who had miraculously recovered from his cold.

"Sensory overload, but I'm better." Ted blatantly lied, hiding his face behind the mug placed in his hands. "So what else is bothering you?"

"Damn, you're hard to figure out. Some things you take so lightly, while others hit you like a sledgehammer. Your moods change so fast that I can't keep up; and yes, there is something else. I have to talk to you about it, but don't know how or where to start. This is probably none of my business, but it's haunting me." David found a seat while attacking his nails. Leaning forward on the edge of the chair, his elbows were placed heavily on his spread knees to help him contemplate his next statement, and to prepare himself for any kind of reaction from Barrett. He hoped to maintain the young man's optimistic mood, but felt the time had come before losing his nerve.

"About you? Me? What?" Uncertain of this nervous side of his idol, Ted grew wary, wondering if he was the right person to answer LaCoix's questions.

"It's about you, Teddy Bear."

"Me? What have I done? Whatever I did, I'm sorry." The voice immediately choked in panic; the brunet actor seemed crushed at a statement hinting at a wrongdoing.

"You haven't done anything. Why would you even suggest it? Stop feeling guilty for everything. Maybe it's something good, did you ever think of that?"

"You're angry. I've wasted so much of your time; and you're always taking care of me. You'll probably be glad to see my back after this picture wraps." Ted's clench around Sir Edmund's neck tightened.

"You didn't hear a word I said. Would you settle down and listen. I don't intend to desert our new friendship, as I enjoy your company, although rather bewildering at times. I can't say that of many people. I'm very much a loner; and you bring refreshing thought to this neurotic recluse."

"I'd never consider you a recluse, LaCoix, considering..."

"...women again, damn. You still see me as a predator and a drunk. I thought we passed that." David looked down and shook his head in disgust, destroying the fragile ego across from him with a single gesture.

"No, what I meant to say, if there was a recluse in this room, it would be me." Ted eyed the man, praying for forgiveness; the return of a softened face answered his question.

"I suppose you are, considering the only time you're happy is when you're alone scaling cliffs or office towers. We're a pathetic pair. After our chat, I promise another surprise that I think you'll enjoy."

"A gift and a chat: so, what do you want to talk about? You look nervous, and that makes me nervous, quoting a famous blond-haired actor I'm acquainted with." Ted once again shone with a smile as bright as his yellow sweater.

"Very funny, as this is as hard to explain as the Mistress and her labyrinth. I've been having these revelations and visions, Ted, ever since we met Lavender. Some I can't explain; this is one of them. Remember the scene we watched last night?" Only the green eyes moved to look at his co-star through a blur of lashes.

"Yeah. By the way, this is her realm, which floats in space."

"How strange." David recognized the *Peter Pan* chatter, and wondered if Ted could handle something more mature in nature. Not surprised about the mysterious woman's home, he remembered the golden ocean, which he sat beside on his first night at La Rosa Negra. Perhaps the people, selling beachside property in Arizona, had been here, giving David a moment of mirth.

"Considering I felt like crap and couldn't answer her questions, it was an awesome experience. I wish my mother was like her. I can't describe the feeling when she held me."

"She certainly takes a maternal interest in you. Did she help you come to terms with this day?" David looked at him directly; his intense eyes searched for signs from Ted to say something. Barrett seemed enthralled with Lavender, but in a much different way than himself. He wondered at the difference. This man, of strength and will, made of the thinnest wires of titanium, with the sensitivity and emotions of a child, seemed to require a mother, or at least someone to hold and care for him. Another revelation struck the older actor, remembering when he first thought of it: Ted lay curled on the bed, dressed in an oversized sweat suit, waiting for someone to take control of his shocked state. A voice, with a raspy purr, whipped his thoughts back into the present.

"I guess. Since leaving her chambers, I feel relieved and happy, although she had me so confused. I've never lacked for words to defend my faith, but now I have to figure out what she meant by many things. Her words seemed simple enough, but now I see them as abstractions or metaphors. One thing I did learn was terminology means different things to different people."

"Makes sense, considering we all hurt each other with inappropriate comments that come out backward, or have alternate meanings to the other person."

"Never thought I could question things; now I can. Don't know what she wants of me, but I've never felt this whirling giddiness in my stomach before." Ted bit his lip, hugging the bear tighter.

"Sounds like you're finally experiencing the effects the rest of us felt that first day." David witnessed the secret hidden in the face, but he discarded the intrigue; other things on his mind ranked higher on his priority list. "What I want to talk about, before we get off track again, is the last image of you on the screen. Please listen, Ted. The last few seconds, the ones lingering on your eyes, showed me something I didn't understand."

"What?" Ted asked cautiously, not wanting his fear of small places revealed or questioned.

"Terror for one, certainly of being trapped, but it was so damn peculiar."

"Spit it out, man, you're beating that bush again. You drive me crazier than Lavender. Why don't you both just put me on the rack, and torture me with questions I can't answer, and statements that don't make sense." Ted's enthusiasm deteriorated instantly into angry mode.

"Okay, relax. This is going to sound very strange, so bear with me." David inhaled and rubbed his face, then dropped his hands between his knees to stare into those big blue eyes, so beautiful and yet disturbing. "I saw a jumble of blurred images. I could partially see them, certainly felt them, trembled sensing them, and I have no idea what any of them meant, except they scare the hell out of you. Something sinister hangs over you, my friend, and I want to help."

"You're nuts, you know that? We were acting remember? Jay was supposed to be terrified."

"Not what I saw in your eyes, man, and how the hell would I know if it's a crazy thought? I don't know you well enough. I'm just telling you what I saw, and it froze me to my bones. In case you didn't notice my tears after the showing, it wasn't the entire scene that upset me, but what I saw in your eyes."

"Okay, I admit, and only to you, that the tiny prison unnerves me. I don't know why."

"I think you do and won't face it. It's rare to suffer from claustrophobia for no reason, but then again, maybe you don't. I captured a sense of you, left alone repeatedly, somewhere cold, damp, and dirty; fuck, I could even smell it, and the whole thing made me shiver. For God's sake, Ted, the images in your eyes made me cry; and I sure as hell don't shed tears without a lot of directed motivation."

Barrett said nothing, burying his head into Sir Edmund, wrapping his arms around both the bear and his bent legs, while rocking back and forth on the couch. He hated the questioning and had sufficient with her Ladyship. Now his mentor, and supposed friend, became his interrogator, in a scene becoming hatefully familiar. Continuing to rock, he attempted to block out the thoughts coming at him faster than his *Peter Pan* psyche could assimilate.

"I heard something as well--voices crying--young, child-like voices. Worst of all, I kept seeing sticks, large ones, standing in a row, as if waiting for something."

"Stop: it means nothing, and if it did, it's none of your business, none of it. Leave me alone." Off the couch in a nanosecond, he tossed Sir Edmund viciously at David in his haste to retreat. With exhaustion tackling the frail body, he ran and fell, only to scramble up and fall a second time against the unforgiving tile floor. Desperate in his quest for the open connecting door, David's strength gave him aid.

"Okay, Ted, no more. Forget I mentioned it. I must have been dreaming." David had to retreat to rectify the drama he created.

"You had to be. Next time, keep your damn revelations to yourself." Ted knew his sudden flight would confirm, in David's mind, that what he saw was accurate. He made a stupid blunder by running, instead of laughing it off. His friend would not understand, and if up to the harried brunet, he never would.

"You okay? You probably re-injured your arm."

"I'm fine." Another lie, Ted's heart bled from the fresh wounds received. He thought they had mended.

"Good time for your surprise then." David reflected on the damp eyes, knowing he hit the source of the younger man's problems with his vision. He would not press further; but whatever happened to Ted, it had something to do with the house Lavender destroyed. She felt no remorse about the destruction, only her temper going off in an explosion of crystal and sparkling gemstones. Ted's holy upbringing had a very dark side.

"I'm tired and still don't feel well. Think I'll turn in. Can the surprise wait?"

"Of course, we both should retire, but promise you won't lock the door from your side, in case you're sick again." David hid his disappointment at the blatant refusal of his special gift for his co-star. The knife twisted too deep this time; but he sucked it back, hoping Ted would change his mind when he cooled off.

"Think I'll look over the scene, and then get an early night's sleep."

"As long as you're okay. Glad your cold didn't amount to anything. I'll bring your bear, and then leave you to read and sleep. I need to catch up on the script myself." With the blue eyes half closing, it gave David a respite in his disappointment. His co-star had to be fatigued after such a grueling day; and LaCoix disguised his lament by making his fellow actor comfortable with his dialogue sheets, the action set-ups, and the ever-present Sir Edmund. He should have kept his mouth shut, but it was too late for a retraction. At least he informed Ted of his concern, although now worried over his co-star's mental frailty. What he saw, in the blue crystal balls, had been acknowledged in his own mind. There lay something hidden, and now doubted the puzzle solvable.

"Good night, Ted. Call if you want to talk, or if you're not feeling well. By the way, how's your blister and ass?"

"Taken care of. Good night." The coldness of the voice snapped brittle as icicles off gables, forcing David to reluctantly step back into his own quarters and settle in. Tired and distraught, he imagined the worst of the younger man's past, and possibly his present. Tomorrow would be another long day, especially after a fitful night. Neither man had little chance of sleeping soundly through this argument; both were upset.

Close by, yet galaxies away, the Mistress sat silently, overlooking her many realms. She stared blankly through the mist that swirled about her open window and covered the stars, while she waited for an opening, a call, or a vision from unknown places, beings, and time. With revelations revealed, she understood some of her man-child's cries. His Spirit Keeper told her everything it could, which was very little; the information given, however, did fit the puzzle of Ted's closed heart and mind. A little crack opened this night; but the man, to pull him through into the full light of awareness, turned the soft heart back inside itself. She accepted part of the blame, rambling on incessantly with words so jumbled and confused, only to land like colorful tumbled gems scattered on a white background with no pattern visible. She had trouble speaking with humans regarding truths and lies; Ted missed her every point. Her misdoing, the only hope offered lay in his recognition of choice and change; and if not too late, he would make a wise one, necessary to continue along his rightful path. She had to get back on track before all was lost. David LaCoix experienced his first psychic breakthrough, but was not fully aware of what he saw. He would become more assured of his abilities as time passed; but for now, tomorrow had to be better. It had to be.

CHAPTER 19

"Damn, the sun's up!" David rolled over, for what seemed the hundredth time, immediately closing his eyes against the bright light of another annoying, sparkling, new day. Lying spread eagle, sky-clad to the world, he sprawled alone in the middle of the giant bed feeling miserable. He had not slept, and now physically tired, adding to his chronic mental fatigue, he took a deep sigh, rubbed his eyes, and flung out his arms in exasperation. The pillows softened the blow to his arms; he suddenly missed having someone next to him when he awoke. There seemed an urgent need for gratification; however, he laid the thought to rest, considering the open door to the sorrow, grief, and greater despair on the other side.

Theodore Barrett: had he slept, perhaps laying in the same state as David, or in a worse condition? The entire night was void of fitful cries and nightmares from his neighbor. Frustrated sexually and mentally, David's thoughts remained on his irate friend who probably remained motionless, holding fast to Sir Edmund, with unblinking eyes staring into space. They had their first real fight as friends; and David felt badly about upsetting the frightened man. One for making up after a domestic foray, he was left asea with a new situation: a male friend had shut him out.

"LaCoix, do you intend to play with that thing, or is it on display for the mortal world?"

"Ted!" David quickly grabbed the closest sheet and covered himself at his co-star's unexpected appearance. Mortification set in from the words, and from the view of his full erection, which stretched to its fullest, twitching sporadically for attention.

"I can be bare-assed, and you can't?" Ted's coldness in his snarl chilled the older man like the Arctic blizzard that blew in the night before. It had his teeth close to chattering.

"Hell, yes, in this particular position."

"Suppose I have to get used to the sight, squirming like some foaming-mouthed serpent." Ted did not divert his eyes from the object of his attention, now covered, ebbing, and behaving beneath the sheet.

"I'm sorry, is that what you want to hear? It's a natural occurrence for the male gender, at least for ninety-nine percent of us. You must be the one bringing the average down." The hostility of the man lying prone heightened; and David knew he had said too much.

"Is that another insult implying I'm asexual? Hell, I'm the one who's going to have that thing inside me."

"Hold it right there, Barrett. This is getting worse. I hate fighting, especially with you."

"Why me in particular? You think I'm such a wimp I can't fight back." Ted could not stop the flow of bitter words.

David choked, attempting to control his ire, as iterating more hurtful words would repeat the cycle. "Stop this. You're attacking for no fucking reason." With no immediate rebuttal, David did not give him the chance. "Now then, how are you feeling?"

"Like crap. Do you plan moving sometime today, so we can grab breakfast?" Ted slumped heavily into the closest chair, folded his arms in a defiant posture, and squinted as if looking down the site of a rifle barrel.

"Rather demanding of you this morning. Just because we share some sort of domicile arrangement, doesn't mean we're connected at the hip. I didn't sleep either; so don't take your bad mood out on me. I need a shower, and a few minutes to pull myself together."

"If you need time to jerk off, I'll leave you to your unholy temptations." Ted made a move to stand, initiating David to sit up and hurl verbal daggers at him.

"What's the matter with you? Shit, you can be a bastard when the mood strikes. Maybe you're the one who's frustrated and needs a release. Don't answer that; the question was rhetorical; and I don't want to continue this dialogue. Just let me get ready, and I'll be at your command, your Lordship. Christ, you're in a pigheaded, fucking, foul mood."

The green eyes scared Ted in their intensity. He regretfully lit a spark under an overwrought, overtired, raging Leo, and if the rumors were faintly correct, he would be sucked into the backlash of the explosion. Sitting quietly, Ted pulled back in anticipation for another assault, by attempting to recover what he had lost. "Sorry, David, no excuses for my rudeness. Guess I needed to vent, considering you really upset me last night with your erroneous assumptions, just after Lavender spun my head around, only to be calmed into some kind of esoteric trance. I short-circuited with all the information she handed out, and then you took a shot at me." Ted softened his tone considerably. His eyes looked tired, sunken further into his drawn face, and his lower lip quivered. Still upset but closeted, he released the anger and replaced it with a dark, brooding depression that shrouded the sorry face.

"You have plenty of excuses to be mad, and good ones. I don't, but I do regret what I've said to you this morning." David rolled out of bed, grabbed his robe, and headed for the bathroom.

With the fury unleashed, and now subsiding, Ted drew in a puff of air in relief. The figure remained transfixed, while waiting for his mentor that he had treated abominably. Only one thing left to do, he cooled his own temper, with deep breaths and wide eyes. Idly scanning the bed, he saw it torn apart from a bad night's sleep; Ted felt terrible for his unkind remarks.

LaCoix reappeared quickly, and with caution, looked down at Ted's splint. A sad nod gave him consent to remove it once more. Another brutal day awaited Ted's arm, which remained intensely painful, noticed with the grimace on the extrication of the limb.

"Man, this is the roughest, physical scene I have. I don't know how I'm going to stop from instinctively protecting my arm." Ted peered up into a woeful face equally concerned.

The famous jaw clenched, etching David's handsome features with exposed tendons and cartilage, enhancing the fine, yet masculine bone structure. His worry showed, over the assault that Ted prepared for, along with the others who had to deal with a stunt beyond their capabilities. "The boys will be careful, as we're an athletic bunch."

"Don't think so. I know they'll try; but with an attempted rape, of two men against one who's supposed to fight back, someone's going to get hurt. I'm too weak to fend off an attack, David. What am I going to do?" Ted slowly followed LaCoix to the door, his head downcast in contemplation.

The older actor turned around, sighed heavily, and held the bony shoulders in a tight grip to stabilize both men. Two exhausted actors, too tired for this action packed day, could barely keep their eyes open and their minds focused. David certainly knew it; flying off a galloping horse was not what he wanted to do that morning. "You'll be fine, Baby. You're supposed to be in a weakened condition anyway, and you look it. This scene requires a stunt crew, but filming so far has been reality based. We have to try what these characters may have never attempted themselves. Hell, Jess and I could be killed jumping off our horses, or hurt Ray and Kevin in the process. The speed and force, plus the perfect timing necessary, may be too much for us. Christ,

I'm getting too old for this."

"You mean you're doing the fight scene for real? You and Jess plan tackling Kev and Ray from the horses! Man, you're in trouble."

"You got it. Today, it's hit hard and fast. Can't remember the last time I did any street brawling, which usually meant falling down and shouting profanities, because I was too drunk to fight. Can't see myself giving a karate kick to Kevin's face, as the action wouldn't fit the part, besides breaking his jaw in the process. And you, my friend, who can barely stand, will be right in the middle of it."

"This should be shot bit-by-bit. Don't understand how it can be done in a studio, since it requires two locations." Ted looked down at his feet and kicked at the sharp edge of a tile, while he thought about the scene.

"Has me wondering as well. We'll talk to the stunt personnel, if there are any. They'll tell us what to do, or Lavender better include us all, under her protective umbrella. We'll all be black and blue, stiff and sore, by tonight." Feeling his own body parts that would suffer, David winced, turned, and opened the door.

"So, if your jumps are successful, you and Kevin get in a skirmish, while Jess beats the crap out of Ray. Evans doesn't stand a chance." Ted shook his head and said nothing of his sudden fright of two charging steeds flying directly toward him. LaCoix was right; he stood directly in the middle of the action.

"To be honest, I'm just too tired to participate. By the way, you realize your attempted rape won't be simulated either. Be prepared for a rude awakening, when they start manhandling you. Give it everything you have to slip out of Kevin's grasp to get out the door. He won't make it easy for you."

"Now you tell me. Gee, I get to see their dicks as well. How far will they go?" Apprehension took over when the answer came with a tilt of the blond head; the green eyes looked more disturbed. "Please, don't look at me that way."

"They'll let it run its course, like they've done every other scene. Jess and I have to rush in fast enough to save you, before it goes too far. They'll certainly be fondling you in places you won't be happy about, and they'll be exposed intimately themselves. We had better get there on cue. Ray and Kev have been told to really go after you."

Barrett suddenly stopped, not wanting to exit the door. He stood there breathing hard, grasping his situation, with David standing stalwartly beside him. The more experienced actor waited for the panic he saw brewing.

"Oh, God, I'm not ready. Why didn't I think about this scene and its consequences before?"

"You trust me, don't you?" David leaned down to look straight into eyes dragging him into the same nightmare. Whenever he gazed into them now, he could read Ted's emotions, which now showed consternation. He waited for a reply, still lost in the blue. A slight nod of the head made LaCoix inhale deeply. "Good, then trust the others." LaCoix dreaded this scene from the moment he read it. Besides the physical injuries they all could sustain, he did not want to see Ted molested by the others, and the consequences to the fragile ego. "We can do this, Ted. Good thing we've been shooting out of sequence. The interior and action shots, which we did before coming here, would be difficult to film if any of us get hurt today." David straightened and turned his attention to the garden that filled with sunlight, radiating a little tranquility to soothe his racing heart and throbbing head.

"You're right, considering my arm couldn't have endured the gunfights. Guess those scenes, after we become partners, will take on a new meaning, when they splice them with these new ones. I'm shaking again and going to heave." Ted pulled away, but two strong arms stopped his flight to nowhere.

"You're as scared as I am, and you're not going to be sick. This hostility, which you've been exhibiting, is it due to the scene today and the next few. Try to remember how good you felt after your visit with Lavender. You were scared then, but you came out enthusiastic and happy, having had a revelation."

"I suppose, but I can't think about that now. Maybe terror is a better word for how I'm feeling. I'm sorry about last night. I know you meant well, but I can't answer your questions, or the Mistress'. The fear and joy from one encounter, then your strange accusations, made me nuts. Thank heavens for Sir Edmund."

"If we survive the day, we'll spend the evening looking at the house plans and have some fun. I miss our little diversions of courting: the flowers, the bear, the roses, holding you through a movie, until the spell ended when the green goop went into overdrive." David subtly changed the subject. They needed to focus on the next few hours; a treat at the end of the day may get them through the trauma of one sadistic scene.

"I'm looking forward to your surprise as well."

"You remembered. Right then, take my arm, and we'll support each other through breakfast." David smiled at Barrett, who shook his head in amusement and grinned bashfully back, while peeking out from his lush lashes, and accepting the inviting arm gratefully.

"You're cute when you do that." The eldest chuckled, quieting fears with a little teasing.

"Cute? What did I do? Why do you keep embarrassing me? Oh, man, I blush so easy."

"And that's cute too. This flirting business is getting more entertaining all the time."

"Oh please, men don't talk to each other this way; I don't know how to respond. You treat me as if I'm twelve; and I don't know what to think of you."

David smiled mischievously at the pink face, when a finger poked him in the ribs. A special moment for him: Ted initiated physical playfulness for the first time. "Think of me as a devilishly handsome rogue bearing gifts."

"I hate to sound greedy, but I do love your surprises. They're so weird."

"My surprises aren't weird, just a little unorthodox, and a bit bewildering as to what we're doing."

"Flirting." Finally, a giddy response from Ted ensured this day might go off as planned. David encircled the slighter shoulders from behind in a wrestling gesture, ruffling the brunet head, until he heard thankful laughter. The two men gathered themselves and strolled under the wisteria-covered trellis; confidence returned in the one too weary to support his smaller accomplice in their secret game of strange mysteries.

They met a nervous threesome of actors, on their way to the dining area. Ray and Kevin subtly took over supporting Ted on their leisurely walk, discussing how they could perform the licentious act, without hurting the brittle body they saw deteriorating at a rapid rate. They could only helplessly watch what they had seen happen to others, not knowing what to do or say.

Jess and David hung back, planning their mad dash to the rescue. An extremely risky stunt for the older actors, their only mental compensation came from knowing they were in good shape and agile enough to attempt the feat. Unfortunately, jumping off a galloping horse, onto two men manhandling a third, required skilled choreography. Jess had the strength to hurt Ray physically; and David had no chance against his much bigger adversary; but there lay the story. They would act it out as written, and play the emotions felt during the ordeal. Staying in character deemed a stretch, but crucial. Their fingers and toes crossed for luck: to jump at the correct time, without landing in a broken heap onto the hard desert floor, or crashing into a breakable Mr. Barrett. The thought made them both cringe; they eyed each other in telepathic thought; this was lunacy.

Everyone ignored breakfast this intrepid morning, wishing to head directly for Wardrobe and Make-up. The call came; they hit their initial marks. Contrary to normal location filming, Ted, Kevin, and Ray were in the cabin, while David and Jess mounted up in the studio, out of lighting range, wondering how the horses would handle charging in from the dark into bright light, and whether their own eyes could adjust quickly enough to do the job. Only Lavender could answer this puzzle with her magic touch.

"Settle and action."

Jay trembled uncontrollably in his cage, covering himself with his hands, trying to hide from the lecherous ogling he received from Jim and Frank, the only two left at the hideout to take care of their priceless hostage. Slade and Jackson had ridden away to deliver a message to the Marshall, while the others poached fresh game belonging to nearby ranchers.

"Kinda pretty, ain't he, O'Reilly?"

"Thought I was your favorite?"

"Ya are, but just look at 'im, all pale and sickly like. He'd be easy."

"Yeah, real easy." O'Reilly smirked and licked his lips slowly. Jay forced himself further back into his tight prison, fearing something not understood. "You're always takin' me, Frank. Never get no chance to poke nobody. Whatta ya say? Ya get your pleasure from the other end, while I take him up the ass."

The sudden realization of the situation wreaked havoc and hysteria in the cage. Frantically, Jay pulled at the little pieces of frayed bedcovers that pressed tightly against the bars, as if they could save him. Screams became intolerable shrieks when Frank marched over and looked down at him like a giant, snarling grizzly. The boy continued to claw at the material in his manic frenzy, to grasp onto something impossible to save him. He had nothing; his cramped, emaciated body had grown too weak to attempt his own deliverance. Hysterical wailing unleashed from a sore, raspy throat.

Frank opened the prison and yanked Jay straight up by the arm. A torturous yell came from excruciating pain, along with a string of cries for help that created much laughter, as the two outlaws ignored his pleas for a reprieve. With one man nearly a foot taller and the other healthy and strong, Jay had no hope. The boy twisted and turned in desperation, attempting to get off the table, on which they attempted to pin him. Squirming frantically, his flying feet connected with the table, knocking it over, while one quick flex of his wrist, and a heel kick to Frank's shin, had him fleeing out the open door and onto the porch. Falling down the two forgotten steps, Jay landed face first in the packed dirt.

The stronger men had him up in less than a horror-filled second; and with screams of unabashed terror and humiliation, Jay froze at the rough fondling, front and back, to the point of losing what little sanity he maintained. Now bent forward, completely exposed and at their mercy, he heard O'Reilly snickering with lust. The revolting little man quickly stripped his own pants down to his boot tops, leaving his shirt to cover what modesty he had. Nothing could hide the emerging force, ready to take the kid in the cruelest manner. Frank laughed, watching his partner's glee, while holding the thin body in place for the first assault. Grabbing the naked hipbones harshly, O'Reilly sounded like a madman on fire. Hard and needy, he waited for Frank to drop his pants and pull out an equally menacing shaft. Jay's shrieks rose to a new level, coughing and choking, unable to catch his breath in his panic. Barely audible, the voice cracked and faded; his throat unable to withstand the strain. He did not hear the approaching thunder above the hysteria in his head.

Two riders came straight out of the sun at a full gallop. The one on the black steed ran over Frank, taking him down and freeing Jay to swing down from the waist, still incapable of defending himself from his other attacker. Jim O'Reilly leaned over his aching back, ready for his first lunge, ignoring the intrusion in his wanton delirium for satisfaction. From another horse, a rider's arm reached down and snatched the nasty, salivating fool with a firm clench around his neck. The would-be assailant reached up to the arm strangling him, wildly clawing and kicking to release himself from the chokehold. Unceremoniously dropped to the ground, he gasped for much needed air, not seeing Jackson dismount on the fly and head straight for him. A few hard punches to the face and several to the ribs, the smaller man writhed on the desert floor, blood spurting from his nose and mouth.

After being knocked to the ground, Frank bounced back up ready for a fight; Slade was his new target. Yanking the blond outlaw off his horse and smashing him hard to the ground, punch after punch flew, until both were wrestling in the sand. On his back, Dusty fended off each strike with his forearms to protect his face. Frank attacked the leader, of the infamous band of outlaws, with all the strength an unsatisfied sexual arousal created in the male animal. Only the cunning mind, of Dusty Slade, provided any defense.

Dazed, Jay wobbled to his feet, stumbled toward one of the loose horses, which had come to a stop, and pulled the rifle out from its sheath. With only willpower on his side, and double-barrels firmly in his grip, he hit Frank a power-laden blow with the gunstock to the side of the head. Blood gushed from behind the ear, rendering the man unconscious, lying dead weight on top of Slade. Wildly pushing the heavier man aside, Dusty stared up in disbelief, to see their hostage with a rifle in his hand. The blond desperado counted off the seconds in his head, as did Jackson, and now an upright and bleeding O'Reilly. Who would be the one to die, before someone had a gun in hand to cut down this now treacherous boy?

A long pause and breathing stopped, while they waited for Jacob Weaver and the shots never heard. The kid let the weapon slowly slip out of his shaking hands and turned back toward the cabin. Up instantly and grabbing the rifle, Slade trailed after the dazed figure, forgetting everyone else. He found the youngster standing in front of his little cell. Another startling move made, Jay climbed in on his own accord, submissively curling into a ball, closing his eyes, and pulling a tiny piece of the blanket from Slade's bed through the close fitting bars. The sad face had given up. The boy inhaled the scent of the blanket, and then rubbed his bruised cheek against the few threads of rough, gray wool. It was all he had.

"Ya coulda rode away, Weaver." Slade leaned down, quiet and pensive; his bright eyes darted about the naked body, trying to understand. He sensed no rage as he continued to study the boy, waiting for a word, besides the whimpers of anguish.

"Reckon so." The first calm phrase, which Jay had whispered since his capture, melted a stone-cold heart.

"So, why ya still here?" The crazed eyes softened in astonishment at the fragile creature that allowed himself to be imprisoned.

"Ain't got no place else to go." Quiet surrender settled in the voice barely able to scratch out a sound. His Spirit had finally died after months of torment. Jay was alive; his inner fire was dead. "Did I kill your friend?"

"Nope, he's still breathing. Why did ya do it, Jacob Weaver?"

"He was hurtin' ya; and you saved me."

Slade sat back on his haunches in sad bewilderment, intently staring at the scrawny kid. The outlaw, with the stoic mask that never changed, had tears spilling out of his eyes, turning them into sparkling green crystals of sorrow never felt in the outlaw's heart.

"Cut."

"God, Ted, you were amazing. Let's get you out of there." Back to frantic, David saw only Ted, not Jay in the cage, desperately clinging to sanity. The scene had him shaken, wondering what he would find outside the cabin. He quickly held out his hand for Ted or Jay to take.

"Can't move; help me."

"I've got you. Come on, Baby, we have to check the others. You're hurt, and my ribs are broken. I'm going to have one hell of a shiner in the morning." David's mind buzzed, not knowing whom to run to, forgetting he could barely breathe himself.

"I killed Kev." Disoriented and searching madly for help with his eyes, Ted croaked out his concern, while David hoisted him to his feet and out of the cage. One shaken actor whispered consoling words to another. Somewhere a robe appeared and handed to LaCoix, who covered Barrett's quivering nakedness and bleeding scratches. Without shame or thought, he held the smaller man for some time, rocking away the confusion and chaos. David had never been so frightened, pushing Kevin's lifeless body off him, without the opportunity to look at the devastation perpetrated on their friends. What if Kevin was dead! Aghast, the thought made him tremble violently. He could not take a deep breath, and each one that Ted took hurt his ribs. Five men lay wasted after a brutal, reality-based scene.

"I'm sure he's fine, Teddy. It's over, no more cruelty, only kindness. We better see how our friends are doing." Anxious to check on the condition of Donaldson and Evans, David remained cemented in place, impeded by the body attached to him.

"Why did I go berserk like that? I'm sorry, but I can't look." Barrett stayed locked around the painful ribs, with no intention of letting go, or understanding the agony he created.

"You had to retaliate in some fashion, and follow the essence of the script, even returning to the cage. Remember, Jay had no choice in his actions, neither did you. You're the gentlest Spirit I know, and that's why you can help Kevin and Ray right now, by going out there and proving to them you're still in one piece." Holding his breath, LaCoix continued to stroke the long, matted hair. Whom was he talking to: Jay, the victim; Ted, the sensitive one; Barrett, the intellectual one; or *Peter Pan*?

"I'm falling apart, but I have choices. She told me so, but they were going to do it. They were physically aroused, David. Did you see them? I can't believe it. They kept touching me; it hurt. I know they were supposed to try, but they went too far. I can't face them. And Ray, oh God, I could feel him." Ted stood firm, clutching David, making it impossible for either to move.

"I know; but we've all been paid handsomely for doing extraordinary things we wouldn't normally dare, or even consider. I won't let go. You're safe, and it's over. Just remember they're your friends, and we all agreed to take part. I'm sure they're as upset as you are." David eased out of the clench, and gently escorted a dazed actor out the open door, to view the carnage left after a horrid scene.

Real paramedics mingled with mystic healers. Donaldson lay on a stretcher, shouting orders. He had regained consciousness, but sounded slightly incoherent. Ray, on the other hand, was completely lucid, sitting on the side porch of the cabin, talking incessantly through the possible broken nose and bleeding mouth. David and Ted moved next to Jess for some input, before talking to the other two. Even the serene Mr. Carmichael appeared shaken.

"You two okay?" Jess asked, rubbing his arm and bleeding fist.

"Battered ribs for me. Can't get an answer from Ted; he's still stunned over the whole thing. Sounds like he did some damage to his vocal cords; but how about you?" David could barely say the words from lack of air, and the tight hold around his lower chest. "Ted, hang onto my arm, and I'll hold you. Good man, that's better." Taking a little deeper breath, the hurting blond-haired actor had done his job well, and paid the price. Now he had *Peter Pan*, who had suddenly grown up, to deal with. Without a flight of childish impishness left in the man, David only sensed unadulterated fright for doing his job, and doing it beyond perfection.

"How could I hit Ray so hard, and so many times? Could've broken his neck, I was so angry; it looked too real. I've never lost control while acting, David; and our ray of sunshine is suffering from the after effects as well." Jess looked down at the cowering Barrett, and for the first time realized what LaCoix had been dealing with since the fall. Ted was mentally incapable of handling the emotions of his character on his own.

"We all did, Jess. How's Ray doing?"

"They've got a collar on him just in case. At least he's still in good humor, considering the pain I caused. Told me how exhilarating the ordeal felt. The man's never been hit in his life, and as usual, he's about to write the entire experience in his memoirs. Truly an astonishing character."

"He's been lucky." A whisper from Ted left Jess and David exchanging perplexed glances.

"Well, it's a good thing he relishes new challenges." LaCoix reacted immediately to the deeper meaning behind Ted's unnerving statement, and tried bringing their reality back to just another day where a scene had gone right, but also terribly wrong.

Both men watched the thick fog of depression settle over Barrett, like a heavy blanket that could smother him. While listening to the double meaning, from the mumbling behind clenched lips, David's concern grew for everyone. His co-star was not the only actor traumatized by the attempted rape. One could only hope the older two had the strength to deal with their loss of control and help Ted in some manner. Was it real, or were they acting? LaCoix firmly believed it had turned into the former.

"Why don't you and David go talk to them, Ted; it will help all of you. Get yourselves checked out as well. They've brought a fully equipped ambulance into the studio."

"Take some of your own advice, Carmichael." David winked at him, and then lowered his eyes to the arm being rubbed. The knuckles, on Jess' left hand, appeared skinned raw, bleeding from plummeting them into Ray's teeth. Again, with very little oxygen getting into his painful lungs, David limped over, with Ted in tow, to witness the bandaging of Kevin's head.

"Well, Junior, never let me get into a fight with a rock climber. They may be skinny as hell, but they're wickedly strong. Did we hurt you? Things got a little out of hand, for reasons unknown to both Ray and me. We're sorry, kid, but I didn't see your actions in the script; and I think I yanked the wrong arm in the cabin."

"I thought I killed you, Kev. I'm so sorry." The words were said; the fright faded fractionally.

"Just a concussion. Blondie didn't put a scratch on me." Donaldson tried to smile, but scrunched up his face with the pain of a single movement.

"We'll see you later. Looks like they want to haul you away; and we need to check on Ray."

"It's a wonder the man's still standing, after what they told me Jess did to him. Good thing this is our last scene. I believe we've turned into these horrible characters." Donaldson's expression told LaCoix everything. Admitting politely that they had lost control, his actions scared the tallest actor more than he could say.

"Didn't see Ray get hurt, but I'm sure we'll hear about it tonight. You're right, Kevin; we've become these characters. Damn frightening, to think what we're capable of, under difficult and trying circumstances. Take it easy, man." David grew more distraught at the insatiable reactions of the assailants toward Ted. It looked as real to him as it did to Jess; and riding toward the foray, his one thought focused on taking out the Frank character to aid the boy. Was he saving Jay or Ted? His mind jumbled with anger, concern, and sympathy.

Leaving Kevin to the medics, they slowly made their way toward Evans. The laboring actor stopped in half-stride and bent over to catch his breath, after a stabbing pain hit his lower chest.

"David, you are hurt? This is my fault." A few hoarse words brought Ted out of his fog.

"Bullshit, you didn't lay a hand on me. Now, listen up, Ted, stop feeling guilty. We were acting; that's it." Convincing himself of the fact was difficult enough; never mind the man who had been sexually assaulted. Even the day before, he manhandled Ted in the most lecherous way, intentionally fondling his sore arse.

"No, we weren't. We all went crazy."

"Perhaps, but we followed the script, except for your use of the stock of the rifle. We threw real punches, instead of choreographed fights. We're all friends, and we'll survive to tell embellished stories of the event. Now, painkillers, which you don't believe in, will fix my ribs so I can walk upright. Forget about me, and concentrate on your own injuries. Your voice is toast; and you took a nasty fall when Jess grabbed Ray. They sure as hell weren't letting up on your broken arm. Man, this sucks." Another wince, LaCoix again assumed a bent over position to take in a few, short, rapid breaths.

The smaller man stood helplessly by, waiting and watching David scrunch up his face in pain, while slowly standing straight. Once done, the younger man gently put his good arm around the hips to aid his mentor. Gingerly and cautiously, they made their way to the side porch to listen to an excited Ray Evans.

The man was a marvel, talking through the blood, a broken nose, and a few missing teeth, all repairable on his return to Los Angeles. He would endure the pain, until reaching medical facilities a short chopper flight away. Both Donaldson and Evans would be fine. They even requested a delay in their departure, to watch the brutal action of the day. They expected miracles and had not yet been disappointed.

"Okay, Mr. LaCoix, Mr. Barrett, who's first?" The actors turned to face two paramedics.

"I'm okay." Ted maintained his grip on David, and hid behind the man ready to collapse from lack of oxygen.

"Let them check my ribs and face, while you watch. They won't hurt me and won't touch you. You're going to have to let go, Babe, but stay close and out of the way. Okay?" David increased his gentle behavior, considering the agony hindering his every move, which would normally have him screaming obscenities at someone. His main concern lingered on the spat the night before, with the very insecure man-child who could not let go. The repercussions of Ted's ravishment, along with his fierce blow to Kevin, had to be reconciled. Another revelation had him gasping for air--who was Jay or Ted saving--Slade or himself? The characters and the actors had merged, separated only by their speech patterns. They were becoming the film, hidden away in a mysterious realm instead of an outlaw's hideout. This was too much.

The medics checked LaCoix, within the confines of the white van with the villainous viper coiled around a sword against a blood stained cross. It terrified Ted to step into its waiting mouth, ready to swallow him in one gulp. Only his unnerved concern for David made it possible for him to enter. The longhaired actor sat close by, watching strangers in official uniforms undress his friend. They touched and poked the man, making him groan and cringe in pain. Little could be seen but cuts, bruises, and his left eye swelling and turning red. With the application of an ice pack on his eye, to subdue the swelling, the handsome features would return to normal under a make-up artist's wizardry for his close-ups the next day. Severe compression of two ribs caused his pain, therefore non-treatable, except painkillers that David volunteered to take.

While the older actor received help dressing in his everyday attire, Lavender entered the van and sat by a shivering Ted. An arm reached around his shoulders, and her familiar hand stroked his damp, distressed face. "My goodness, Child, you performed magnificently; and David, you were equally impressive, the way you knocked over Mr. Donaldson without falling."

"Tell my ribs that. I'm too damn old to be pulling stunts with a horse. I hope you weren't disappointed in my failure to attempt a flying tackle."

"Not in the slightest, but you had fun. Admit it, my friend; it gave you a rush not felt in years." Her eyes twinkled at him; he smiled broadly back to answer the rhetorical question. Painful, but certainly exhilarating, the fight had been fun, until he saw Ted heroically crawl into the cage on his own. The action broke the man's heart, to watch his co-star conquer his fear for the sake of his art, or had Ted turned into Jay when they entered the set?

"I know a little about healing, Theo. Do you wish me to correct any possible damage? I do not think you can feel anything, considering your mental state. Stand up, and let me look at you. I walk through doors, remember?" Her chuckle did not ease Barrett's tense face; she misjudged him again. His literal intellect would assume the remark meant she could see through his robe, right into his heart. He said nothing, however, and his thoughts seemed unreadable through his fear. Stroking the broken arm, she relieved the pain immediately, a welcoming act for Ted who looked timidly into the warmth of her face. His arm had further twisted, as well as hit by fighting humans, flying steeds, and one bone jarring shock upon bashing a man equally as hard as the rifle stock. It convinced him that his arm would never heal, not this time.

"Feels better, does it not? I am sorry, Theo, but the relief will only last while you remain in the confines of La Rosa Negra."

"That's okay." Ted continued to stand motionless, with trepidation etched on his face.

The Mistress scanned the man inside and out, cloaking her real power. Her man-child had sustained no major injuries, except severely strained vocal cords, and minor bumps and bruises. For now, she would relieve her actors' pain of fractures, scratches, and aches, including making David's face look normal. When they left, it would return to haunt them, but all five would mend. Like the Monk, she felt a strangeness happening within Ted's body; he endured excruciating agony from an unknown source. She had to find the cause, and his toleration of it. Not a normal human condition, she decided to speed up the evaluation using another. An introduction would soon be made.

All was still, as they had the afternoon to rest and recover from their ordeal. Ted became a leech, attached to his only friend, not wanting to let go, and no one paid the slightest regard. After much cajoling, David had him soaking in a tub of perfumed hot water, while LaCoix took a shower in the same bathroom. The action had become habitual, as the older actor had no intentions of letting the sorry figure out of his sight. After bathing, David rebound the arm, and a reprieve of a nap seemed in order. With the pain gone, thanks to Lavender, exertion and emotional strain took control.

With a bed freshly changed, fitting so tightly you could bounce a quarter off the striped bedspread; it beckoned David to find a large, soft blanket with which to hide. A little coaxing convinced an extremely tired and disturbed Ted to lie down with him for a comforting embrace. Silently accepted, under the watchful eye of Sir Edmund, two men settled in to catch up on lost sleep, and to forget the trauma they both experienced at different levels that morning. Too weary to object, Barrett contoured within the spooned position of the taller man who continued to whisper soft, endearing messages of Ted's brilliance, and the paternal pride David felt for conquering one fear. Sleep consumed them, lost in the limitless time they spent within her Ladyship's realm.

CHAPTER 20

A good and much-needed rest ended with a few yawns and a cautious stretch. Feeling their way very carefully, both men gingerly got up and expectantly waited for any stab of remembered pain. Ted lifted his arm, without a cringe or his stomach aching. David instinctively encased his ribs protectively, finding he could breathe deeply and easily. Inhaling a lung full of life-giving air, a grateful smile of delight crossed his now relaxed, injury-free face. A prayer of thanks drifted skyward for the temporary remission he wished would last forever. Only a fleeting thought, David remembered the Mistress' warning.

As early evening approached, both men wished to say good-bye to their friends. On reaching the screening room, they received a deliciously frothy drink, as they greeted the other three. Kevin sunk deep into a chair; his head secured with pillows. Nothing helped the man's dizziness, but he refused to miss the showing. Ray sat in a similar position, not moving his swollen face under the gauze that held his nose and jaw in position, and the broken tooth stuffed with an equal amount, or so it felt. A first for Mr. Evans--the total inability to verbalize in his excited babble--only his bright eyes moved, forgiving and reassuring Carmichael that he was not to blame.

Ted made his way to Kevin and apologized again for his unscripted actions. Through the veil of chaos and flying fists, LaCoix had caught a glimpse of Barrett removing the gun off the horse; and for the sake of cruel authenticity, he believed the harmless prop gun had never been intended as a substitute for a real one. In all truth, their youngest member could have killed Donaldson; David's knees quaked under him.

"May God forgive me, Kevin; I never thought I could be so vicious."

"It's okay, Junior; no harm done, just a headache. I must apologize for the behavior, of Ray and myself, toward you in the rape scene. It never occurred to us that the situation would provoke unspeakable urges. We scared ourselves and hurt you, Ted."

"Just happy we all made it through the day. I'm sorry for hitting you so hard." Ted reached out his hand to a powerfully larger one.

"No problem; I'm actually looking forward to seeing your wicked swing. You should take up baseball, Slugger." Kevin continued his cordial, humorous take on life.

"I don't think I can watch tonight." Ted smiled back, shaking his head, hiding the sudden fright of remembering how he truly felt striking the tall actor. Witnessing the intentional brutal assault, upon a friend, would not happen, if he could manage a disappearing act. The attempted rape was another matter; he made an effort to dismiss that it ever took place, and to forgive both men. Unfortunately, it felt too grotesque to forget.

"You have to witness me and Jess doing our crazy stunt, Ted." At his side from that point on, David remained vigilant over the demoralized victim.

Lavender walked in, making a resplendent entry, and smiled at them all. All five men took special notice of the black velvet gown clinging to her elegant body and floating around her ankles. She had them bewitched; David would bet his life her feet never touched ground. With several bottles of champagne cracked open and small edibles passed around (for those who could open their mouths or hold down food), a half dozen serious frowns turned upside down. Crystal goblets caught the light, sprinkling brightly colored prisms about the room, while toasts rang out to *Outlaw's Heart*. Bubbles popped softly; noses were tickled; and humor spread amongst the bruised and battered when useful straws appeared for some. Time for the showing, they settled in nervously.

Ted would not relinquish his clench on David's arm, looking like a half-starved parasite. The older man quietly sat him down, reaching around to contain his shoulders in readiness for a sudden flight. A shaking hand on his thigh made the blond smile; a one-armed hug reassured the anxiety of what they were to behold.

In a handful of minutes, it ended like the first. The intensity riveted them to their seats, with the pace of the action and every detail shown. Feeling and seeing the film enthralled them all, seeming to flow in slow motion; the small audience wanted a second viewing. The tearing green eyes, and the softening of the hardhearted outlaw's face, held them spellbound several seconds after the screen turned to black. They amazed themselves, and felt the resulting physical consequences worth the effort. Even Ted watched his agility in the sequences to free himself of his attackers, grabbing the gun, and striking the blow to the Frank character. It became an exciting, thrilling movie to him, without a cringe of acknowledgment to the nudity. He did not recognize himself as the victim of the horrendous deed, or the erotic showing of finely detailed body parts that made the entire ordeal more terrifying to watch. Only the characters came to the fore; but it chilled David to the bone. The rape, the rescue, the fights, and the final sorrow were all too real. The nail biting continued.

Time for good-byes, more congratulations, and wishes of luck, they shared hugs, including the usually untouchable LaCoix. Three departed; the brutality ended; and two men came into their moment. Both hid their fears; reluctance ran high. Returning to David's quarters, they stumbled into a Lavender surprise of a candlelit dinner, with soft music, and more champagne to tickle noses. It increased the tension immediately, and with quiet politeness, David pulled out a chair for Ted who bashfully accepted the gesture, while he turned bright pink. One handsome leading man sat across from the other, beaming happily at the results of their anxious day. He poured more of the dancing liquid into the long stemmed crystal to capture the candles reflections in the bubbles. Green eyes never left blue ones; Barrett was overwhelmed.

"Congratulations, Ted, a truly great performance on your part."

"Thanks, but I think I spent most of my time defending myself. But you, man, did a phenomenal job handling the horse; the knockdown was better than a tackle; and the fight was definitely high risk. As for Kevin, the man is way out of your weight class."

"He is rather large." The blond chuckled, delighted to hear Ted speak in a normal fashion, only raspier. With his throat eased slightly by Lavender's healing hands, the added crackle would give new meaning to their last three scenes.

"You were incredible with your sensitivity toward me; I mean Jay. I could see into your eyes today, David. They show your secrets as well."

"And what did you see? How transparent am I?" The famous face looked up with a serene grin, waiting for something to make him laugh, or make him think. He dismissed the corrected lie, or the attempt to figure out the true depth of its meaning.

"You've been lonely all your life, never feeling settled. Jay reminded you of that; you have no place to go either." Ted looked directly into the eyes that held the story of a life gone awry.

"I wonder if that's true. Having never felt particularly connected to anyone, with whom the union seemed complete, even with my children, I seem detached somehow. You are observant."

"Have you ever been really happy, David?"

"Have you? As you stated your first night here, and just now, you also have nowhere to go." With another of David's questions left unanswered, Ted stopped eating, pushed his plate aside, and stared into the nearest flickering candle. "It's okay, Ted; you've had quite a day. Time to think pleasant thoughts."

"Can't do that either, worrying about this baby I must protect."

"Protect? This is new."

"I shouldn't have said that. Please don't ask."

"The one wish I would have for you, Ted, is your happiness; the same feeling I've been indulging in, since we met the Mistress."

"That's odd, because you haven't had any fun. All you've done is hover over me, as I gag or go ballistic. At least tonight I'm feeling better; and you can now hover over your house plans instead." Ted brightened up immediately, rubbed his hands together, and his blue sparklers flickered in anticipation. From gloom to glee, David could only marvel at the mood changes, or incredible acting skills.

"That's right; a promise to be kept; and who says I haven't had fun. I want you in my bed tonight, Barrett."

"Excuse me?" Jolted almost out of his chair, the longhaired brunet gaped in shock with the straight out-of-the-beyond demand. This sounded more intense than just friends sharing a good night chat and a warm bed.

David laughed so hard, at the shocked face, that he doubled-over. "That certainly came out wrong. Sorry, just an innocent arrangement. I won't touch you, but I missed you and Sir Edmund last night, now realizing how good it feels to wake up next to someone. It seems I have to handle everything, like the control freak I am; but this place and these scenes have taken their toll. I'm tired, needing a little human contact to ease the strain. Although satisfied with what we have accomplished, we've been through one hell of an unnerving adventure. How are you at massages?"

"Terrible. I hurt people more than I help. It's my fault, and I'm sorry I've caused you so much trouble, David. Then today's attack, it scared me, man. To think of being in that position, knowing you could be walking down your own street, only to be dragged off and assaulted. Must admit, having you next to me would help calm the oncoming nightmare I apologize for now."

"No need. At least you understand that certain types of trauma induce those screams in the night. Would it be frightening to have a man beside you? It might."

"Between you and Sir Edmund, I'll feel a little less concerned about leaving the windows open." Ted feigned a smile, as a hand reached over the table to squeeze his own. Retracted quickly, the gesture surprised him, but it felt caring. His grin became real.

"You defended yourself admirably. I guess after coming close to experiencing it, rape has a new meaning for you. Molestation, without the penetration, is still a horrendous violation; and that's what happened to you today and yesterday."

"Hurting and hitting someone also took on a whole new meaning. Can't stop hiding my hands, in case they come out to strike again. I put all the force I had into the swing, to save you, and to retaliate for what Kevin tried to do to me. The latter increased my rage astronomically; I'll never forget that feeling. Every action felt real to me."

"You're still upset about the day, since you're confusing acting with reality. We've taken a chance on our mental stability with this picture, as if proving we can handle whatever her Ladyship throws at us. Can you do the next scenes, without feeling like I'm raping you?" David attempted ignorance of what may have been a slip; and yet, it was a gratifying thought his new friend would try to save him in a crisis. It showed a stronger side to Ted than he had seen before.

"I trust you, LaCoix, more than you know; and you're the only man I could actually kiss tomorrow. At least I know your scent and the feel of your hands. Being friends, I want it to be special, without flipping out. Sounds lame, but it's true. How much more idiotic can I get?" Ted downed a full glass of the French delicacy in a series of breathless gulps.

"Easy on the bubbly, Ted, since you're not saying anything to be ashamed of. It's precisely why I wanted to sleep with you tonight. I know how frightened you really are, and I'll be extremely gentle tomorrow. We must remain calm, yet build the desire to take the ultimate step. A simple touch makes me want you."

"No shit? You mean you're really attracted to me?" Barrett dropped his glass, to splinter into slivers across the tile floor.

"I seem to be opening my mouth just to change feet this evening. In some way we seem connected, whether it be this movie or the place we find ourselves. I don't understand what our relationship is, but I do know we'll stay close." David tried to make practical sense of his confession, knowing his attachment grew stronger to the striking man sitting stunned across from him. Their kinship gave him something unfelt before. Not just lust, passion, or power, he simply liked Barrett as a person, who required his presence as much as he needed Ted's. His respect for the young actor had no boundaries, his infatuation growing daily, delighting in the company of the starry-eyed, complex, and emotional train wreck.

"I... I..."

"Ted, it's okay; nothing needs to be said." David got up and found a handy broom to sweep up the sparkling powder. It took less than a minute, and gave Ted time to adjust to the startling admission. "Fill another glass and sip it this time. Let's look at the wonders my architect has created."

The pair settled in for a long evening of laughing and joking, both men enamored by the drawings. David penciled in one small change, and then circled another. Completely enthralled, Ted gave his mentor a number of things to think about, with many unique and gratefully accepted ideas. After several hours of detailed work, they looked up at each other and smiled the same wicked grin. The plans were perfect.

"This is going to be awesome, David. What about property?"

"Lavender told me that my offer was accepted. Many acres of steep rock formations shelter the canyon from dust storms, while the rest of the land is pretty much exposed. With beautiful vistas within the canyon, the house will lie under startling clear skies. Growing things may be a problem, although the realtor told me that underground springs are plentiful in and around the canyon. Might have to stick to cactus and the snakes they draw. I doubt if I can include roses for you."

"You'd plant a rose for me?"

"Maybe a white one." David winked at him and gave him a mischievous grin.

"Thanks, what a nice thought. Wow, a rose for me and the canyon sounds dramatic. There's a lot to do before you leave for London." Ted sat back, picked up his new glass, and marveled in wide-eyed wonder at a man who could accomplish anything.

"All will be in order before I'm gone. The problem I foresee, after completing major renovations on two large homes, is the instant crucial decisions required once building commences. Unfortunately, I'll have to rely on someone else's discretion."

"Do you want me to help? I'll be in San Diego, only a short flight away."

"If you want to, that would be great. You understand what I want and need for this house."

"This home and I'd love to." Ted bounced off his chair, with the prospect of seeing the wonder come to life. Experiencing a new art form, of architecture and landscaping, would never happen in his world; but he could live it through David's imaginings.

"It's nice to hear you laugh, Ted."

"Seems like forever for me as well. You're the only one who seems able to break through my moments of blue funk. Hey, what about a stable?" He sat back down, pointing at the location where horses could dwell.

"I knew I missed something. A small one, with room for a handful of horses, especially one with amber eyes. I'll need truckloads of feed and straw; that's the practical side of me, Barrett. The romantic side imagines long rides at sunset or sunrise. That certainly appeals to me more than pools or tennis courts; and you don't need a partner." David scribbled down the note on the exterior plans, and then lifted his head to see the bright smile and eyes closed in a dream.

"The solitary horseman riding into a deep purple sky full of stars, as dusk turns to blackness under a full moon."

"Arizona blood," David laughed. "Sounds like you have a touch of it yourself. You have a poetic nature I seldom hear. I like it."

Ted blushed, pushing back the romantic vision of a blond cowboy riding into the sunset. Shame filled him, believing his thoughts, of his mystical heroes, unmanly. He wished he could express them freely, without feeling the fool.

"You worry me, Ted. You're the proverbial fish out of water in your own environment."

"That's not a proverb, but probably should be."

"Planning to rewrite the *Bible*?" David chuckled.

"Not you too?" Another Lavender type attack, Ted could only throw back his head and groan.

"What?" David looked up, seeing his joke disappear in the blue funk Ted mentioned.

"Nothing; guess I'm just getting tired. I better locate Sir Edmund." Barrett left the table of perfectly rolled up architectural drawings, now penciled in with new lines and written remarks, and headed for the one bedroom that led to the other.

"Another nothing. Shit." Held to a whisper, the comment went unnoticed. Pleased with their effort, David placed his future dream home back into its mailing tube. He would check the plans once more with the architect and Ted, before venturing forth to England. Working with his co-star came easily, complimenting each other in their similarities and their differences. A colossal weight dropped from his shoulders, relying heavily on the young man to handle his new project. It dawned on him with an instant spark: his friend desperately needed something to take him away from what he called his austere surroundings. Helping David would keep him busy while he waited for his next script. Once his latest performance went public, there would be a steady clamor at Barrett's door, and then the longest wait, the baby, the strangest mystery of all. LaCoix puzzled at

Ted's distress on hearing the news one minute, and turning it into an obsession the next. The entire affair had him baffled.

"Are you coming?" Ted croaked from the closest bedroom. After an evening of nonstop chatter, and a morning of screaming until his vocal cords nearly snapped, even the healing hands did not sooth his sore throat.

Grabbing a few cough drops, picking up an attractively wrapped package, turning off the lights, and snuffing out the candles, David headed for a warm body to hold. He called out a casual request before entering his own bedroom. "I think there's a DVD player in there. Can you find it behind those cabinet doors?"

"You bet. Do you have something I can sleep through? If you chose a how-to, gay, porn tape, I'm out of here." Ted grinned up at the man, knowing LaCoix more tasteful.

"Never thought of it, but maybe next time."

"Or never." Ted heard David laugh aloud at his comment; and the sound made him feel better about the chaos he had piled on the man's shoulders. A remembrance of Lavender's words, he would repay the man with like kindness when given the opportunity.

"Here, suck on this a while; and I didn't mean anything by that. I should have thought of it sooner, but you have to get your voice back." David cautioned with the use of double-entendres, and carefully screened any other sexual connotations from his vocabulary. With Ted's naïveté proven, filthy language would not be part of the foreplay in the scenes to be filmed. Those words, in the script, would be rewritten through his own ad-libs. "Remember the promised gift? I have it, on the second best authority, that this is the most exciting action video of its kind. Only an hour long, you can be the narrator."

"What kind of action are we talking about?" Ted took the black and gold package in both hands, untied each ribbon, and carefully removed the paper. It drove LaCoix crazy, being a grabber and thrasher when it came to unwrapping presents; but Barrett savored the excitement of the surprise. "David, where did you find it? I've been waiting for its release. This guy's the foremost rock climber in the world. Do you know how exciting this is going to be? You'll think you're right up there with him. Thank you! Thank you! This is the most personal thing you could give me. Man, this is perfect! I'm so excited, I'll never sleep."

"You're welcome. I want full explanations of what he's doing, but in a much softer voice. Keep sucking on that cough drop." David watched as Ted jumped out of bed, placed the video in its proper slot, and leaped back under the covers on top of him, nearly knocking the wind out of the older man with his strengthening arm. Excitement lit up the dimmed boudoir.

"I will. In the promo, he constantly talks to himself when he climbs. He'll be saying what he's thinking as he goes, unfortunately in French. He's wearing two small mikes, with a small camera on his helmet. Man, that's tough going; it would throw your balance off, especially looking up for your next handhold. They covered his every move with cameras above, below, at many different levels. Even a helicopter shadowed him, far enough away as to not interfere with the extra wind factor. Oh, man, I've waited so long to see this. Hold on tight, this is going to be great." Ted's eyes grew wider than David had ever seen them; and he finally saw a speck of white in one of the corners. He chuckled at the younger man who wriggled his way into a half dozen pillows David had rearranged for their comfort.

"Hold on tight to what? You perhaps?"

"Maybe you better. I'm so thrilled to see this that every rock, which drops, will make me leap out of my skin. Be prepared to peel me off the ceiling after it's over. You'll see how dangerous this sport can be. Heard he had one mishap where he hung by one hand for a few minutes. Turn it on; I'm ready. Oh, man, this is so cool." Ted leaned against David's chest immediately, exactly like his daughter would do when sharing a fun evening with *Beauty and the Beast*. The nonchalance of the action caught the older man by surprise, as did the brunet's oblivion to the awkward position. Just like their first innocent evening of flirtation, David relaxed, content to hold the man and listen to his heart racing against his own. He tried to speed up his own beating rhythm to match the one against his chest. Unlike Ted, who had only recently learned of the sweet bliss of listening, this secret pleasure belonged to David. Once synchronized, it made him completely giddy. He tried it with everyone he came into close contact with, including his children when small, and certainly, with every woman he slept with. The feeling reminded him of Ted's enchantment on first hearing the heartbeat of another.

LaCoix smiled at his inner musing, happy at the exuberance he felt against him, and satisfied at another successful treasure he could give his mentally battered friend. Examining the image of the famed climber, on the cover of the video box, he saw Ted's body type. He had been right: a skinny spider, all eyes, arms, and legs. With the click of a button, the wildest adventure, David ever witnessed, commenced. The sore throat went through another torture test. Unable to remain quiet, Barrett groaned, gasped, and whispered helpful hints to the stranger scaling the sheer cliff face. A number of terrifying inhalations coincided with LaCoix's heart-stopping moments. David was transfixed with the man's successful attempt and hair-raising escapade, while Ted experienced it all, becoming one with the Frenchman. *Peter Pan* was in Neverland.

The climber reached his pinnacle, leaving two men exhausted. David had a new understanding of Barrett and his need for risks. It certainly confirmed for LaCoix, that he would not be participating in this sport, deeming it a little too death defying for him personally. The final scene and David saw Ted on the precipice, his toes clinging to the edge, and his arms reaching for the sun, ready to fly. With a shared glass of the remaining champagne, a toast rang out to freedom.

A sleepy yawn, the eyes still lit up like stars, Ted thanked David again. The older man could only smile at the delighted face, watching the lips form the words. They were so close and the eyes so innocent, he asked once more, "You sure about this? In case you weren't aware, we're both naked."

"Didn't notice; and it doesn't bother me, if you're okay with it? Preparation for tomorrow, right?"

David rearranged the pillows back to their normal state and slipped in closer, making contact with Ted and Sir Edmund. The taller body spooned around the smaller one, only feeling warm, smooth skin against his bare chest. "You do feel good to me, Ted; I don't know why."

"Probably because it seems forever since either of us has been gratified. Everyone needs to be touched and cared for. Isn't it one of my lines for tomorrow? It's pivotal to the story. Why should we be different?"

"You're being exceedingly cavalier about this; but yes, we all require closeness, even a bear. I've been behaving myself for once, with the lack of women in this picture. The only female influence, in our life, is our Lady Lavender who's unapproachable."

"She is rather unearthly. The Mistress believes we're all her children, and says La Rosa Negra floats in the heavens. It does when you look out her window."

"She certainly looked ethereal this evening, literally sailing into the room in the sexiest, soft, black velvet gown I've ever seen. Lavender certainly knows how to make an entrance, one we should take a lesson from, as it's important for our public image. You better close your eyes, Barrett, and rest your throat. I'm glad you're feeling better."

"So am I. It's been a rough couple of days and nights, but your gift took me to another place. Can't thank you enough for letting me feel the..."

"Not again, please, Ted, the what?" David pulled Ted closer, avoiding any contact, which may jab the innocent man in the wrong spot.

"The freedom felt, as he climbed, was a rush, even if it wasn't me climbing. I hope I can reach that level of expertise one day." Barrett suddenly rolled over; his head coming to rest on David's outstretched arm; and his eyes searching for the man in the quiet darkness.

"I enjoyed it myself, but I don't know if I'm happy about my friend dangling so far in the air without a rope." Going with the flow of the very disconcerting position change, David spontaneously raked his fingers through the mane of rich autumn brown, feeling the silky texture while he tenderly turned waves into curls, unthinkingly twisting one around a finger, to let it drop beside the remarkable face of gleaming wide-eyed enticement.

"It's not as scary as what we'll be doing tomorrow." Trepidation slowed the tide of exhilaration.

"Are you afraid now?"

"Yeah, aren't you? Makes me nervous whenever you're this close to me, but I can't resist human contact, like having Lavender hold me. I'm going to embarrass myself by telling you this; but there's something magical and comforting when either of you touch me. You sometimes feel and act like the same person."

"She is magical, and so are you. A night for admitting things, I'm rather embarrassed myself at the overpowering emotion you bring out in me. Starting to worry about you constantly, my friend, considering I'm usually consumed with my own ego. Let's get some rest; I'm exhausted physically from our adventure-filled day. It rattled me watching others molest you. Another good reason to be sleeping together; I want to make sure you're okay, and still here in the morning."

"You're a special kind of man, LaCoix. I'm sorry I ever misjudged you, but even with those notorious rumors, I still liked you. You really are a comfort behind those fire-filled eyes and quiet voice. Actually, you're not particularly quiet around me."

"I think I'm changing, in many ways; opening up is one of them."

"You're articulate and caring with your words, even when you're talking to me like I'm twelve. It's unusual for me to hear kind thoughts, especially outside this place of weirdness. Whatever you say continually resonates through my head, making me believe in Lavender's magic, which I'm actually beginning to enjoy, just like hearing your heart again. It pounded incredibly hard while watching the climb." Ted's eyes were never going to close, full of enthusiasm remembering his latest comforting discovery. His fright-filled day seemed to vanish while climbing a mountain with a Frenchman.

"In your excitement, I'm surprised you noticed. The movie gave me a hell of a rush as well. Told you this evening I'm attracted to you in some way. Wish I could protect you better. Just don't know how or why, and now I have to worry about you hanging by your nails from those heights. Good, God." David chuckled, laughing off the intimate confessions. His heart continued to race, but not from the movie. His inner Spirit whispered something he felt ill prepared to hear, but he deflected the words quickly.

"You're protecting me now. I feel really safe for once."

"For once? You're using a different type of cliffhanger."

"Strange, Lavender always finishes off my thoughts as if they were my own words. You don't; you just ask me outright; and I still can't answer."

"Sometimes I know where you're heading. Good night, Baby Bear."

"Night, David. I forgot to tell you; I've seen the stars from the other side of the galaxy."

"What?"

Ted dropped off in a dream, of far away suns playing in the night sky, leaving David alone to ponder the statement. It made no sense, but nothing did. He held, in his arms, a man who needed him; and in some strange intangible way, a man he was drawn toward. Whatever happened, he would remain a friend and guardian to this person of extreme emotions. He quietly succumbed to his own fatigue, under the heavy influence of scented jasmine, and the effects of mental and physical exhaustion. The brutal day disappeared with more thrills and a tighter bond.

Night passed slowly; and the Mistress felt revitalized with her charges overcoming their fears and exchanging their mystical revelations from looking into the eyes of the other. They were on their way; she could not be more gratified.

CHAPTER 21

Dawn painted the room a pale yellow, when Ted rolled over and opened his eyes to gaze into two smiling green ones. They shone soft and gentle, and appeared terribly amused. Almost nose-to-nose, it gave the younger man reason to gasp, much to the merriment of the older man.

"Morning, Ted."

"How long have you been watching me?"

"A while; you just turned over. Are you ready for two scenes today?"

"Two?"

"Heard about the change last night but forgot to tell you. Makes sense and gets this over with quicker. We're filming tough scenes in a blink of an eye. It will be the kiss, and then the seduction immediately after. We'll be done by lunch."

"No, I'm not ready. Shit, man, I really have to psyche myself up for something this big."

"No you don't. Look at us. I could reach over and kiss you right now, if I dared. Moreover, since you obviously hadn't noticed, while snarling at it the other day, I'm not that big. Relatively average I'd say." David laughed while the blue eyes grew larger and Ted's breathing shortened.

"No way, man, this is too weird; and sex isn't something I can joke about. It doesn't matter how big your dick is, it's going to hurt; and you're treating this like it's some ho-hum day at the office. Get up! I have to shower. How do I get clean enough? Tell me what to do, David, and stop laughing." Ted clamored out of bed, rushing for his own bathroom, with his co-star chuckling hilariously, over the nervous ranting and animated hands of a man with little knowledge of what came naturally through primal instinct.

Curbing his amusement, David followed the whirling dust devil, and sedately tried to calm him down. "You are a kick to wake up with, Barrett. There's nothing more to it than having sex with your wife: clean your teeth, relax the face, take a shower, and shave, although the latter seems unneeded. You wash behind your ears, don't you?"

"That wasn't funny. I must have to do something. Like you know..."

"You've been purging for days, and you're probably as clean as you're ever going to be. Do you think gay men stop to primp when they have a spontaneous rendezvous? I don't think so. Clean your scrawny derriere with a soapy finger, and rinse it off. Don't worry about it; I'm not. After the other night, you don't have anything left in your system, and a butt douche is definitely not in the cards for you. Even a bit of soap could start what the green goop didn't finish."

"Oh, brother, you're too eager, LaCoix. You're scaring me witless. God, help me."

"Explained it before; my only thoughts are my ability to rise to the occasion." David gave him a wicked grin and a wink to rattle Ted further. "I'm as nervous as you are. Now tell me honestly, how are you feeling and what about your arm?"

"How do you think? I'm scared, that's how I'm feeling. The only good thing is my arm doesn't hurt, and my throat feels better."

"My ribs are as well. I'll be eternally grateful to Lavender for our short reprieve from agony. I'd be hard pressed to make love to you with a rib problem." David cringed at the thought, knowing just how many muscles he used in sexual intercourse, not to mention the lifting, twisting, and turning of another human, adding to the exertion.

"Oh God, don't even say the words; life is getting too bizarre for me. What happened to simple and normal?"

"It's too early to discuss an abstract like normalcy, whatever that is. Now, get ready, and please, slow down. I'll see you in a bit. And here I thought you were starting to enjoy the magic of this place?"

With no response, except the rolling of blue eyes looking more anxious every second, David left Ted to his nervous toiletry issues, smiling and chuckling during his own shower. Bright-eyed and polished to the extreme, the famous face checked out the perfect features--not a hint of a bruise--and then he waited and waited. Another forty minutes of fussing over nothing, Ted finally appeared in his usual garb of a clean white robe. Together the two men headed out for an adventure that played guessing games in both heads. Could they do it? Could they do it in front of the many cameras and the people behind the consoles? Who would break the scene by giggling or crying out to stop? The questions were endless; and they had to get their intensity back.

"Good morning, Gentlemen." The Mistress bounced up behind them, causing the men to jump and spin around. "We are nervous today." She smiled with some measure of reassurance, attempting not to break out in laughter at the fearful expressions on their faces.

"Morning, Lavender. Just hope we can do this for you," David blurted, startled by her sudden presence, and now becoming quite unraveled at what they proposed to do.

"You can and will. The ambiance will be right; and Theo, you shall remain caged, until Slade becomes so sympathetic to your needs, getting you out and making love to you will be an emotional and realistic necessity. I need you to convince him, Mr. Barrett. This is the last time you will be trapped in your prison, so make it good; or we shall put you back in and leave you longer."

"No, please, I can deal with it one more time."

"But I do not want you to deal with it; that is the whole point. After eating, head for the studio. I shall be waiting anxiously to see the results."

"Again no direction? What if we have to start again, or can't get..."

"...an erection? I trust you will not have any problems in that regard. You are both professionals and extraordinarily gifted actors, with the benefit of a respectful friendship. Your performances will come naturally from the heart and your own feelings, as the sexually driven males you are. I believe you will feel more comfortable in the hands of my shadows, without me peering at you. Get into your roles, Gentlemen. There will be a fifteen-minute break between scenes, to change the lighting from a very cold night to a warm sunny morning, plus a change of wardrobe for you, David. I shall see you upon completion."

The Mistress left abruptly; but they heard her gasp and start to run down the flower-bordered path. A man ran toward her, calling out the name Morningstar, frantic in his search for this person. Ted and David remained frozen, watching one of the most recognizable faces in the world crumble into tears and hysterical sobs on reaching her Ladyship's embrace. He was soothed as one would a baby; and the woman, once again grew in stature, with the strength to sweep the handsome, six-foot actor off his feet, and carry him away, babbling into her neck.

"David... that... that was..."

"Yes, and we didn't see him." David's stern comment hinted at a warning. This had to be one of those guarded Hollywood secrets; and he wanted Ted out of it.

"Why? What's wrong with him? How did she pick him up like that?"

"I have no idea. She's shown such power before. As for seeing the man, I can only go by Jess' assessment. He suggested that people, who come here, learn to camouflage themselves in some manner, and that's why we seem to know them but don't. Occasionally, and this is just Carmichael's theory, when these men have to deal with something, which interferes with their meditative serenity, they drop the disguise and you can recognize them. I would imagine, someone as influential as Steven Kincaid is in trouble; and we're not to know about it."

"But I heard he just got engaged to... oh, what's her name? Besides, you can't pay the guy enough to do a picture unless he has all the say. He's not much older than me; and he has so much clout, it's nuts." Star-struck, Ted wanted to see and hear everything, not picking up the subtle warning.

"I know, but maybe he has a problem such as yours, considering this is a sanctuary of sorts. With the help of all these spiritual types, people are brought back from their despair, or whatever the dilemma. There must be many places to hide within the labyrinth for those in trouble, without their own energy spent to hide themselves, like us. I'm sure we can be seen; but we're here to work." Turning to his practical side, David attempted, to logically deduce, a way out of this illusion of incongruities.

"You're getting pretty philosophical, LaCoix. What problem of mine are you referring? I resent the implication." Barrett flared immediately, becoming angry and defensive, in the same manner when approached about David's vision.

"Don't go weird on me, Ted. You never wanted to marry Karen; and perhaps, Kincaid is only doing it for show. Your reasons may be different; but he doesn't appear to be a happily engaged man, like you're not the gleeful new father-to-be."

"Shut up, David, you don't know anything. For someone who's supposed to be quiet and reserved, unless you're blind drunk, you sure have a lot of erroneous opinions and a fearful imagination." Ted grew wilder and shoved the older actor aside.

"What did I say? Where did this come from? Besides, you've never seen me drunk; so whose opinions are accurate? Christ, now you're mad at me, a great way to start this particular day." David threw his arms in the air in confusion, not to mention frustration.

"You started it; and I've suddenly lost my appetite." With another whirlwind mood swing, Ted stomped off in a huff, with no apparent reason. Nerves were his problem; today he would sacrifice his temple for his art, with a rape he had to welcome. Ted was terrified.

One leading man stood quietly, with his mouth open, watching his friend disappear into the garden. Heard only by the purple wisteria hanging overhead, he mumbled in disgust over the reappearance of *Peter Pan*. He had no idea what he had implied to cause the misunderstanding. Waiting five minutes for Ted to disappear through the gates, and then with cautious deliberation, he slowly meandered through the fragrant flowers, taking in deep breaths to remain calm. The scenes would be over as quickly as the others; but it could take all morning to get his co-star back to fear and trepidation, instead of his sudden, misguided fury. It may be all day, just to get them both to want each other enough to perform. David felt like a circus bear, balancing on an unstable, bouncing ball.

Wardrobe and make-up complete, LaCoix readied himself, picking a few flowers while strolling about the wild, inside garden, allowing Ted a cooling off period. Blue and yellow dominated the small bouquet, which he tossed aside, remembering they were the man's favorite colors. They burned his fingers, thinking his co-star could sway him unconsciously. He began to doubt his reasoning to participate in this erotic and explicit endeavor. Sixty-million dollars worth of greed was one; and maybe, Carmichael's theory that he was a compulsive exhibitionist. Regretting signing the deal, he wondered at Ted's motivation to agree; that truly seemed an unsolvable mystery. David suddenly had the urge to run, except for one word, which whirled through his head, and the memory of the night before. *Lonely* kept coming to mind; he felt it the instant Ted walked away from his side. The notorious ladies' man wanted to make love to this high-strung paradox; it came from a revelation not of his mind, but of his body; he wanted Ted as his lover. David stumbled to find his mark in a blur of mind-altering confusion.

"Anytime you're ready, guys. Positions please: Dusty sleeping in the bed, Jay in the cage." A voice from the dark filled their heads. "Wait until he's ready, Mr. LaCoix, then go into your dialogue. We'll start rolling when you look comfortably asleep. It's your call when to finish. No hurry, and relax as best you can. There are only two of us here; so let the scene unfold."

The actors looked at each other in apprehension; and David saw the fear coming back along with the sorrow. Securing Ted in the cage, he hoped it would be the last time, and wondered how only two could handle so much equipment. The interior suddenly grew dark; the fire glowed only as an ember; and an autumn's night dropped to an unbearable temperature. The blond, in once red underwear now faded pink, sank deep into the covers of the small bed. Curling up in the position required, it became a necessity to keep warm rather than to hit the right mark. Someone made minor adjustments to their starting positions, including David's blanket, and Ted's first facial angle with a couple of words of advice to look at the fire.

David tried to relax, but with Ted so close, naked and frighteningly cold, his duress mounted. Easy to simulate, however, the scene required vapor rising from their bodies and from the words spoken between the two: another mystical take, making it feel surreal, yet true to life. He closed his eyes feeling a light hit his face; the cameras rolled, all of them.

Jay peered in dismay at the flickering of a dying flame, while he shivered uncontrollably. Mentally trying to figure out the months he had been imprisoned, trapped, and cramped in his doghouse of metal, he turned slightly to press his cheek against the few strands of woolen blanket he had pulled through the bars. Insufficient to soften the feel of the hard, cold iron, let alone keep him warm, silent tears fell. He learned to stifle any sound over the past months for safety. They still took pleasure in terrorizing him, smacking him across the mouth repeatedly, whenever he asked to go out. Relying on the last embers to keep him company, through the dark lonely night, sorrow was repressed, fear was repressed, and the ongoing mental torture was repressed, leaving him alone to cry from deep within. It would be a simple pleasure to let out the sobs and start screaming again, but such an act would unleash the fury. All was seen through the eyes and subtle movements of a rake of a body.

A quick turn of his head, he looked to see through the shadows at what had suddenly struck the cage and jarred his head: Slade's shin, covered in pink flannel. The blue eyes stared, mesmerized at something so near and yet so very far away. Two fingers reached through the narrow opening in a futile attempt to feel something warm, to touch someone, to sense a living presence, gently and kindly. He reached the warmth with a little struggle and poked the leg ever so slightly. The tears grew heavier and a sob opened his lips. It quickly disappeared, choked down with the abrupt awakening of the outlaw, who sat upright immediately and reached for his gun. It scared Jay to stone.

"What the hell ya doin' boy?" Slade snarled in an angry whisper.

"Nothin'." Jay had not spoken in days; and what came out was a puff of inaudible fog.

"Don't lie to me, boy. Go to sleep and stop sniveling."

"I'm cold. Fire's goin' out."

"Shit. I'll stoke it for ya, if that'll stop your cryin'." Slade got up, threw a few logs on the fire, and returned to kneel in front of his hostage. "Them tears are still running down your face? Sure got an endless supply. Know it ain't comfortable for ya, but got no other way of keeping ya."

"Didn't run when they tried... tried to..."

"No ya didn't, and I'm still puzzled by that. Damn, boy, ya really are cold. You're turning blue on me."

"Yes, sir, but your men won't give me no blanket."

"Might do yourself in with it; so Jacob Weaver, what choice do I have?" Slade smugly smiled at him, happy in how his plan had unfolded. It paid off in hundreds of dollars in paper money and gold, and trapped the Marshall as neatly as he imprisoned his son.

"Let me join your gang, or kill me now. Better than livin' like this forever." Jay moved closer, his hands on the bars, bringing his pleading face closer to the killer's warmth.

"Your right, it's been a summer. Reckon that's too long to keep ya caged like a snarlin' dog. Winter's coming on real quick. We might lose ya, if we can't keep ya warm."

"Be ever so grateful. Don't wanna die alone. Nobody's touched me in a kind way for as long as I can remember; and I ain't touched nobody neither. That's the worst of it."

Slade puzzled over the problem, returning the intent gaze of the sorrowful blue eyes. They were beautiful, but nothing remained of their sparkle and shine. Green eyes kept staring in puzzlement, thinking of what they had subjected the boy to for so long. Jacob Weaver had to remain alive and well. It would be beneficial to have the boy ride with them, exposing him to his father now and again. He rubbed the rough stubble of a day's growth, and softened his face slightly to look at the kid with more understanding. Tears started welling up in the cobalt orbs; the victorious outlaw watched his frightened hostage fall apart. Cameras caught every emotion and natural lip quiver.

"Reckon I best let ya out tonight. You'll sleep with me, where I can keep an eye on ya. One wrong move and you're back in the box. Ya understanding me, boy?"

"Yes sir." Jay was helped out and gently straightened into a standing position, while trying painfully not to awaken the others. Impossible to control, the kid burst into hysterical cries at the first gentle brush of the outlaw's hand against his skin, and his final release from his prison. He was free.

"Shush, boy, don't want nobody hearin' ya." Slade clamped his hand over the wailing mouth.

Young Weaver stopped the sobs, but the tears of relief and the pain of cramped muscles continued in silent crying. Helped into the warm, small bed, he felt and smelled Slade in the darkness, wrapping around him and covering them both with the gray, woolen blankets that he longed for. The flannel underwear next to his skin seduced the young man into a comfort he had never experienced. Jay won his battle for freedom; Slade won complete control. He had broken the Spirit of another living being.

"Go to sleep." The outlaw felt the shivering body, almost rattling the bed as the boy's temperature started to rise. It created a pincushion affect that would only go away by rubbing the extremities of the thin creature he held so close. Small sniffles and the strange crying stopped, replaced by chattering teeth.

"I'm scared, Mr. Slade, real scared."

"Reckon ya are, boy. Turn around and look at me." Slade rolled slightly to take in the slight twist of the head, allowing Jay to look into his glistening eyes. Sorrow and regret spoke volumes to the young man, and Jay again sobbed aloud, his thoughts only on the man who cared enough to help him after he had lost hope. Written in the firelight of those crazed green eyes smiling at him, they warmed his entire being.

"No more snifflin' or I'll stop ya myself." Slade knew he had Jay, any way he wanted. With the Spirit dead, all that remained was a submissive, frightened child. The empty look of the face told him as much.

Jay softly moaned, overcome with the comfort of another. The misty eyes opened wider, watching the clenched jaw and mouth relax on the face of the rugged desperado, and coming ever nearer to his own. Closer and closer, Jay found his own lips parting and softening, waiting for something to ease the ache in his heart. A single caress made him quiver from head to toe. The slip of a tongue moistened his cracked, swollen lips, showing off the burgundy shade of the bruising in the light of the fire's glow. Cries mellowed into a heated satisfied sigh, as lips melted together, and sealing them to form one. A delicious tongue slipped into the open sliver and danced into the inner lining of Jay's mouth.

The boy's first kiss grew out of need, so intense and so wanton, Slade continued his tender assault of the virgin mouth. Giving into the pleasure he never thought possible, Jacob Weaver fell into a deep rapture of lust, seduced by a gentle hand stroking his hair, and coming down to hold his quivering chin and mouth in a position to be taken in a long, silent caress. The embrace, between two lonely men, continued: one whose heart began to heal, and the other granting a kiss to last an eternity. Quiet, sensual, and purely selfless, Jay gave himself to the outlaw in gratitude for one passionate moment that made him swoon.

Slade pulled back and smiled endearingly at the boyish face. He watched Jay return from a place he had never been. The bruised lips looked like ripe berries, ready to be nibbled, similar to a woman's when aroused. Only sore and swollen, it had the same seductive effect on the outlaw. "Jacob Weaver, I want ya."

"Me too." The waiting desire came out, stuttered and hardly audible, but genuine in the plea for more attention, and the willingness to stay with the ruthless bandit. "Felt like ya needed me. It's important to be needed."

"Your right, boy; and I've spent a long time ignoring the fact. But what of you, Jacob Weaver, do ya need me, or is this a way to escape?"

"Near killed a man to protect ya. Didn't run then, 'cause I needed ya too."

"Least I know how to stop your constant cryin'. Now, roll over and get yourself settled in my arms. Ya belong there now."

"Night, Mr. Slade."

"It's Dusty, Jacob."

"Just Jay." The kid pressed himself into the warm body, fitting perfectly within another man's arms. Warm, comfortable, and slightly mystified by the wondrous kiss, he fell asleep with a smile on his face, protected by a mad outlaw, with whom he had become besotted.

Slade stroked the hair and face for some time, until his hostage's deep breaths signaled that the boy slept. With a remorseful smile, the older man also succumbed to weariness, dreaming of a young, handsome partner, with the daring of an outlaw, and the temperament of a sweet, obedient child. He knew he found one who could be trained; and two men drifted away, entwined in dreams.

"Cut. Great job guys."

David sat up and smiled happily. First scene completed, the experience felt right; in fact, it felt overpoweringly good. He had to get to Wardrobe and back in fifteen minutes, but first, a little time seemed a requirement to ease the pain of his erection created by a smoldering kiss to Ted's hesitant but receptive lips. Turning to his co-star, he noticed the heaving shoulders, and the head buried in the pillow. Crying or giggling, David assumed the positive.

"We did it, man, and it felt great. Just one more scene before we head home. Are you ready?" No answer and no attempt to acknowledge his presence, David became instantly annoyed. "Come on, Ted, look at me. What's wrong?"

Still nothing, the silence ignited the blond actor's frustration to an explosive level. He physically forced Barrett to face him. No mistaking the frightened, bewildered eyes, or the arms reaching up for consoling, *Peter Pan* returned in crying mode, planting the wet eyes into the closest neck. With his co-star out of control, David rolled his eyes and started again. "Hey, guys, can you give us some time here?"

"No problem, Mr. LaCoix. Keep up the intensity. Excellent work, just excellent."

"Thanks." David waited until the last shadow of another human disappeared out of viewing and hearing range. "Talk to me, Ted; what's happening? You heard the man. We did a great job."

"I... I can't... and you... you don't..."

"Catch your breath. You have to be relaxed, sleeping like a baby in the next scene. What can I do to help?" David donned his paternal role once more, stifling his aggravation. He stroked the hiding head and rubbed the bare back, hoping his actions might help Ted, but not his own problem under the blankets.

"God's never going to forgive me for this. I'll be sent straight to hell."

"What for: a kiss between friends? That's all it was, Ted. One take and we nailed it. It's amazing for any actor; and I'm thrilled. Shit, man, you should be proud of yourself. I enjoyed the entire act and felt like you wanted to continue. Was your swoon an ad-lib, or do I create such euphoria?" David tried to humor his way out of a rising attack of hysterical, religious ranting. Ted heard none of it.

"No. Yes. No, that's why I'm going..." The longhair even shook; Ted's mortification ran so deep. He had passed out from the pure pleasure of a real kiss never experienced, and now the man laughed at him.

"Stop, because you're not going anywhere without me; and hell isn't on my itinerary. Was it that disgusting for you?" His voice echoed with exasperation. The end of a perfect scene, Ted spoiled the moment of LaCoix's bliss.

"David, oh God."

"Enough. You're whining like a child; and so help me; I'll do exactly what Slade did to shut you up."

"No, don't kiss me again. I liked it. Don't you understand yet?" Frantic with thoughts of desperate action, Ted flushed brilliant crimson, and pulled at the faded underwear covering David's chest.

"Stop it. There's nothing wrong with that. Damn, Ted, would you settle down. Stop doing that; you're hurting me." The wrists were twisted and pulled harshly away.

"Sorry, I don't know what I'm doing." The head went down, not to rise to face the many lies. He cloaked his verbal error once more that day, and settled himself enough to face David's animosity.

"Okay, you, let's get a few things straight about kissing. It's a natural, affectionate exchange for all humans. It should be enjoyable. You like kissing your wife, don't you?" Only a single voice resounded through the empty studio; and David's mouth dropped and his mind went into overdrive. "You have kissed your wife?" Again, the impenetrable silence shocked the older actor. Ted spoke the truth; his religious moral code did not allow simple affection in any manner; and the child in his visions lacked physical nurturing. The puzzle started coming together, but still made no sense to him. "My God, I can't believe this of a thirty-year-old man, as attractive as you, in this business. You've been married for four years; you seldom have sex; you don't touch each other, not even in foreplay; you've never kissed your wife passionately; and you sleep alone. I can't believe it!"

"Stop! I can't do anything right for you."

"You stop it. We have to get through the next scene, and you haven't the slightest idea of what to do; that's why you asked me to coach you. Even in your love scenes with women, you're hopeless." Dumbfounded, and about to have sex with a sacrificial virgin, David doubted he could make it easy. No longer fun, he saw it as rape, and he could not be the perpetrator of such a deed. His only chance lay in Ted's needs, and he reconsidered why the man fainted over a kiss.

"You're right; I don't know what I'm supposed to do unless directed. I've watched certain movies, countless times, for the love and kissing scenes only, just to copy the actors. I don't know why you put your tongue in my mouth, but it gave me an instant..."

"You did it again! What were you going to say? You liked it enough to be aroused, giving you a hard-on! Is that it?" LaCoix shook the heaving shoulders, trying to get at the truth.

"Yes, now you know."

"Know what; that you got an erection? So did I, and usually do when kissed with such passion, and that was a hell of a lip sucker, Teddy Bear. You are an innocent. How did you ever get it up to make your wife pregnant? Listen to me; your body responded to a perfectly natural loving act. You can't control your pecker from expressing its desire to find satisfaction. It has a head of its own, if you remember. It may be an old joke, but a valid one. In the next scene, you have to become aroused, and don't get weird on me when it happens. We have to use it, or at least I do, which you probably don't understand. I'm going to be touching parts of your anatomy your wife hasn't even handled. Do you understand me?"

"Yes, and I'm not stupid. I know right from wrong, and this is wrong. Jesus, forgive me for the promise I must keep." Ted's guilt flicked the switch to a bolt of electricity that nearly threw him off the bed.

"Stop the crap; I'm sick of it. Sixty-million dollars is coming your way; and if you're so unhappy about it, give the entire amount to your church. Will that make you feel better? I'm sure your god will forgive you if you hand over some major cash. I bet the Almighty has his price. Just know this, Barrett; I will be back, coming through that door, to do exactly what we agreed to do. I refuse to feel guilty about making your first time feel great; and your god will have nothing to say about it. It's just the way of our world--strictly for greed, Baby--and my own pleasure of fucking you senseless. Are you listening, Barrett? I'm going to fuck you, and keep fucking you, like there's no end to this scene. Moreover, I promise you will enjoy every second of it. As for your little swoon, this time you'll end up in a dead faint of pure ecstasy. I'll have to carry you back to your quarters comatose." With his fury unleashed, he tossed the sobbing Ted backward onto the bed, rolling out of it himself, and stomping out the door to get his day clothes on for the next scene.

He left Ted in a pool of tears and regret, fearing the younger man unable to pull himself together and deal with the matter at hand. Kissing his co-star had been an unexpected delight, but he should have realized the younger man's inexperience at the lack of giving back what was given. Perfect for this scene, as well as the next, the character of Jay had no sexual expertise; but Barrett, the man, David could not believe it possible. Ten minutes later, he stood outside before entering the door. The lights blazed yellow over the cabin and filled the interior with morning sunshine. Becoming more agitated and impatient to start, he figured Ted had not yet settled into position. A familiar voice, from the dark, confirmed his suspicions.

"Deep breaths, Theo. Slow and steady. Curl into a small ball with an angel face. Soften the face, Child. Very good. Sound asleep, peaceful and warm. Hush now." Lavender's voice lulled both men into a comfort zone they could handle: Ted to appear sound asleep, and David to calm his anger and rattled nerves. Out of the corner of his eye, LaCoix saw the woman discreetly leave as *Action* was whispered. He inhaled a deep breath before stepping through the portal. This would be his greatest performance as an actor.

The blond outlaw quietly entered the cabin; the squeaky door barely made a sound, but allowed the full morning's light to spill across the barn board floor. Golden rays danced over the bed and across the young man who continued to sleep comfortably for the first time in months. Slade had sent his men on a variety of chores, just to have this time alone to satisfy his craving, and he smiled a crooked, lustful grin. The Marshall's son appeared to be warmer, his pale face regaining a little color. Too beautiful for a man, the boyish face made Slade chuckle; he gave thanks for his good fortune. Sex was sex where women were scarce; and a willing male partner could pleasure him as easily. He scanned the body in a heap under the blankets, exaggerating his quizzical look of hesitation, wondering if Jay remembered.

The guns and belt came off, along with the hat and jacket, left out of the reach of his hostage. Slowly, the rest of his clothes hit the floor, stripping completely without taking his eyes off the back of the beautiful head of flowing waves. Sky-clad, Slade was a magnificent specimen of manhood, with a handsome face, taut chest and flat stomach, perfectly carved buttocks, long sinewy legs and arms, and well hung, but not overly endowed. The cameras captured every inch of the man back and front.

Removal of the blankets, and sensing the presence of another, made the young man stir, while cool morning air hit his warm body and the one standing over him. "Wake up, Just Jay."

Two wondrous, sleepy eyes opened slightly, only to close against the light, and rubbed clear of nightly dreams. The younger man stretched out, exposing himself completely in his dazed state. Slade looked at the body before him, so very small, with thin arms and legs, lacking muscle tone since his capture. His skin gleamed white and smooth as cream; his face blessed with the look of an angel. Being hairless, the man looked even younger and more enticing; Dusty gazed licentiously at the pink, delicate crotch, soon to be under his control.

"You're a handsome little one, Just Jay."

"What? Where am I?" The hostage turned and shyly covered himself; a timid thing to do, considering he had remained bare for months, in front of the dozen men who entered and exited the cabin.

"In my bed. Don't ya remember last night?"

"Dusty! Yeah, I remember."

"We're all alone, and I've got ya to myself." Slade pulled the kid up slightly and wrapped his arms around the shoulders, supporting the sleepy head with his hands. Lips brushed back and forth across the mouth of the surprised, wide-eyed face. The gentle stroking continued, until a little moan came from the now relaxed, softened lips that separated slightly in expectation. A blush ran up the cheeks in natural shame, which would sadly change when the blood rushed to parts of more importance in the thin body. On a breath of warm, sweet air, a moan trailed off when the mouth was covered gently and another kiss took the kid far away. Hearing his soft whimpers of pleasure, Dusty slowly lowered him back to the pillow; as Jay's arms reached around to hold the neck and blond head from removing the taste he enjoyed. The boy struggled to return what he learned the night before, while Slade's calloused hands roamed over the small frame, causing the body to arch and tremble with each touch. As the outlaw lingered at intense pleasure points, Jay's instant arousal showed his lack of experience and created a sudden spurt of his life's essence to ooze pre-cum onto his stomach.

"Dusty, what… I'm sorry."

"That's what's s'posed to happen. Ya musta done that before. Even in your sleep it can happen." Slade pulled back, slipping between the two legs that did not want to separate.

"No, I never… I don't know… What are ya doin'?"

"Need a little more of your honey, Jay; give me more; and I'll show ya." Dusty played with his new toy, while the kid tried to fend off the assault. Jay quickly gave in to the sensual stimulation, and with a frenzied jerk upward, released a little more creamy liquid sporadically into his captor's hand. With one finger soon covered, the blond lifted a thin leg over his broad sculpted shoulder, while the prepared hand played with a body orifice never touched in such a fashion. A kiss quieted the small cries of rejection, while the taunting finger played and teased the extremely tight, craving, virgin orifice, allowing Dusty to penetrate and find the euphoric spot inside. With his thumb, he pressed another point of pleasure just outside and under the hairless, hardened sack. The action immediately had the virgin squirming in a frenzy of excitement, of which he had no understanding. The kid's entire world opened, to fly free with the touch of a finger and the feel of a naked body against his own. Panting in whispered breaths, Jay's desire mounted, as two glistening bodies created steaming vapors, to rise with the heat of their passion mixed with the cool morning air.

"Relax, Just Jay." Slade soothed, penetrating gently, barely invading the man who gave off a squeal and immediately bent his other leg, instinctively spreading his thighs for the outlaw's access. "Good, boy, that's it. Don't wanna take ya hard the first time." Every word became a hushed seduction, straight into the panting, gasping mouth of the angel face.

With his finger pushed in fully, Dusty rubbed the inner lining, discovering each place that created a response. Jay shrieked with an instant reaction, spreading his arse to accommodate more of the intruder, which created the wildly intoxicating sensation. He immediately delivered more of his honey into a waiting hand. Jay's wet essence covered the outlaw's hardening shaft, ready to replace the finger pulling out slowly, causing an unhappy look from the boy who misunderstood. Attempting to return the upturned lips on the wanton, dismayed face, Dusty pushed and poked, but the boy let out a whimper of frustration, unable to accept the larger organ. Sleek with sweat, the boy begged repeatedly for more, not knowing how to help or what to do with his hands, except to grasp frantically at the blankets on either side of his body.

With a quick thought, Dusty rose from his position and dipped his finger into the bacon drippings, still warm from their breakfast. Returning, he again massaged the opening and infiltrated with his fingers, long enough to lubricate the tight treasure and his own cock sticking out at right angles. The blond broke through the strong muscles with a grimace and cry from the body under him, but he continued to guide himself into the hot, tight interior, smoothly and slowly, allowing Jay to accept him at his own pace. Legs and arms would not stay still, while the mop of long hair tossed back and forth on the pillow, occasionally arching the neck and releasing a groan, or a squeal of pure ecstasy and approval. With every thrust of his outlaw, Jay released more tension from his aching cock, and would swoon in a moment of rapture. Slade kissed the closed eyes, waited those few seconds, until he heard the whimpers to lunge deeper. With the experience of the older man, they settled into a comfortable rhythm. Slipping back, almost disconnecting their union, the action caused a sudden rush of disappointment in Jay, but the smile returned when a deep, gouging thrust smacked the boy's butt on full entry with Dusty's hard rocks. The outlaw and his hostage became one in their frenzy, coming time after time, with unabated grunts, and the sweet sounds of purring and soft sighs. They squirmed and rubbed against the other within an embrace; another smoldering kiss ignited the ember to rebuild the fire. Euphoric over another stimulation lavished upon him, the youngster's body convulsed and shook violently. Jay swooned with each attack, to return to Dusty with a satisfied smile to melt the outlaw's heart.

The slow withdrawal had Jay panting and in tears. His sweat drenched hair hung in long strands, turning the waves into curls, which lay upon the pillow. Slade's own glistening body fell back limp, and his long arms pulled the younger one on top of him. His new conquest satisfied him completely, and he held Jacob Weaver tightly, stroking his weary head and smiling in his own exhaustion and gratification. "My God, boy, you're the best I've ever had. You're a wild little one, ain't ya? Reckon I best keep ya real close, wherever I go. Would ya like that?"

Jay lifted his head and tried to initiate a kiss in gratitude. Accepted and aided by Dusty, he rolled onto his back to try once more. One naked body rubbed up and down over the smaller one, sensually evoking another erection. The outlaw pulled away on cue with a satisfied, dreamy grin. Unlike his first sexual awakening with the kiss, Jay wanted more; the cameras caught every penetration, every squeal and caress. Even the sporadic white fluid caught in one man's hand was recorded for eternity.

"Love ya so much, Dusty." Jay's squeals of pleasure were undeniable, and he pulled up his knees, spread his own shivering thighs wide apart, stretched the puckering orifice with his hands, and exposed the bright red arse to entice his captor again. The eyes closed in total rapture of a man finally freed of a lifetime of torment, with a smile permanently etched on his face, and happiness glowing from within his awakened Spirit. He had won the heart of the ruthless outlaw.

"Cut. Great stuff, Gentlemen, wildly riveting. We'll leave you to relax. Thanks for the splendid effort. Congratulations."

"Ted, stop and put your legs down. Did I hurt you? Are you okay?"

"Don't stop. Please, don't stop." Ted had David in a firm grip, hands grasping at his hair, to bring him down to penetrate him again.

"What?" LaCoix tried to pull away, but a strangle hold of need locked him in place, with a mouth kissing his face, searching for the lips it craved. Already troubled over the unwarranted wanton display of Ted's cavern, the order to *Cut* came precisely at the right time.

"Please, you were ready to do it again. I want you to do it again."

"Steady, Teddy Bear. Do you know what you're asking?" Overcome by the desire in the teary blue eyes, pleading for love and more attention, David startled, wondering who lay beneath him: Ted or Jay. "I can't, Baby; I'm completely spent. I wish I could, but I haven't had a night, or day, of such passion in years. You made me come more times inside you than I can remember."

Ted came to his senses, trying to stay in control, but doing a terrible job. His eyes scanned everything in sight, seeing nothing, just trying to avoid the inevitable. Mortified by his need for this man, he immediately let go and hid his face in his hands.

"Don't you dare start calling for Christ; or so help me, I'll knock your damn head off."

"But I love you, David." All the tears in the Cosmos fell the instant of final admittance.

Hit by a stun gun, LaCoix held tight, incapable of leaving the devastation lying under him. Part of the secret came out of the closet: Ted was gay, and his whole life had been one colossal fight against his natural desire. The blond-haired actor had no words to say, or any knowledge of how to deal with the statement. He had heard the acclamation so often, it grew meaningless; but this truth came from the mentally unstable and highly emotional Theodore Barrett whom he lusted over the night before. Ted's needs could not be dismissed. The sex had been extremely gratifying and dangerously exciting for David; and he would do it again in a heartbeat. Could he love this young man without turning him into another charm never placed on the bracelet, but tucked secretly away in a delicately engraved jewelry box in his head? David liked Ted, very comfortable in his presence, but he could not return the words. Still in shock, he hung onto the sobbing creature, trying to piece the rest of the puzzle together.

Waiting several minutes for tranquility to return, LaCoix held on for those precious moments, listening to two heartbeats in rhythm. There was too much excitement, and far too much despair. The studio had emptied; peace prevailed. Pulling himself and Ted up slowly, David got off the bed to aid his wobbly co-star to stand. A quick check for damage or traces of blood, he returned his attention to comforting the younger actor trembling in his grip. "Shush, Ted, everything's okay. We need to talk. Let's find our robes and get the hell out of here."

David quickly ushered Ted back to his quarters. Once again, the only thing that came to mind, to restrain the emotions of the continuing roller-coaster ride called Theodore Barrett, was to get him relaxing in a warm bath, easing what looked like one sore and bruised derriere. The young actor said nothing, but stopped crying once on his feet. An experience that overpowered them both, neither man knew what to do next. They were at a turning point personally, and had one last love scene together. It would be the hardest to portray, for they had to act as if intimately involved for some time, accustomed to sexual intercourse, and enjoying every aspect of it. Slade and Jay had to be deeply involved for tomorrow's take, making David feel confused and in trouble. Ted went numb and silent.

CHAPTER 22

Pacing back and forth in his quarters, David waited for his co-star. Twenty minutes, and then forty-five minutes went by, while he traced his path across the hard tile floor. Every five minutes he stopped, believing he heard Ted unbolt his side of the adjoining door, but it was not to be. A soft tap on his main entry made him jump; and he rushed to open it. Lavender stood there, with the faintest of smiles, looking tired and unhappy.

"Hi, come in. I wasn't expecting you. How did we do today?"

"Marvelous from what I hear. Your concern is with our man-child, however, and so is mine. His world disintegrated under his feet today; and his fear is too great to bear alone. Truth can be a frightening concept when hidden in the reclusive part of one's heart. Unfortunately, he will continue to deny his words." Lavender sat down, pulling her hair off her face, twisting it at the back, just to let it fall naturally into place. A defeated sigh came with the melody of wind chimes; both her elbows leaned against the table; and her face rested in her beautiful, slender hands.

"Even the most powerful have off days, hunh?" His flirtatious grin did not help brighten her sorrowful face, nor his unbelievable surprise that required contemplation.

"Long days and nights in your time and space, David." The heaviest sigh, verbalized in words, broke the man's heart. Lavender showed the signs of being human in her melancholy, and dare he even think it: lonely.

"I realize now that we're not your only concern."

"You saw him then?"

"Couldn't miss a face plastered on every magazine cover in the world. Is he the man who reminds you of Ted?"

"Yes, and I hoped you missed his display of emotion. Even those who have everything call for us. You and Mr. Barrett did, why should he be any different?"

"And who's *us*? The last time I asked, you were rather vague, leading to all sorts of speculation. You leave people in wild imagination mode. Can you explain who or what you are? I've concluded you can't be real, or of our world, which is unnerving enough." His green eyes sparked their own hint of fire in reverence of the possibilities of the Mistress' identity.

"Just a Caretaker. What you see, and have seen, is enough knowledge."

"Are there more Caretakers?" David refused to lose his window of opportunity.

"Yes, and I seem to be the lucky one to have the more prestigious, or should I call you, the most infamous, neurotic group to contend with: wealth, fame, creative, eccentric, all mixed with self-doubt, drugs, alcohol, and sex. What fun."

"Destiny's servants!"

"No, Mr. LaCoix; remember destiny is only a word used to explain the unexplainable. Humans always need a word. They are incapable of just *feeling* the magic. It was a good guess; however, there is more. We are the foes of the Fates who dance with your destiny. How does that sound?" Another sigh and her hands dropped to the table, stretching out her arms.

It amused David, believing Kincaid too heavy for her, considering how thin and delicate this unearthly Fey looked, sitting so forlorn. "Poetic sarcasm; thought as much. Destiny doesn't exist, nor does fate, although the Fates exist; therefore, our only worry is the future. And, as you put it, what fun. Do I have it yet? Never mind; your lips are sealed. It's none of my business; but I hope

Kincaid feels better."

"Stevie is unwell. Just like you and Theo, he is not yet able to disguise himself, or understand who he is; therefore, you will see him on occasion. We should be finished by tomorrow, if our man-child can handle it. The film will be released December 1." Lavender ignored David's ramblings; her mind preoccupied with millions of other matters.

"December 1 of this year? Impossible! You can't properly edit and promote a picture in a month. It's almost the end of October. Who will be doing the promotional work? Not Ted!" David sat down at the table across from her and glared his most menacing stare, which had no effect on the Mistress, stripping away more of his ego.

"It is what we do. We promise miracles and produce them quickly. Since you will be in England within a week or two, Theo will do the talk-show circuit, and all the interviews. It will be good for him."

"Hell, it doesn't look promising he'll complete the last scene, let alone discuss a controversial movie in front of live audiences from here to Tuctoyaktuk. He'll be catatonic and in a straight jacket. You know him, Lavender; he's too shy for what could and will be asked about this film."

"We shall care for him. As for today, you both need a diversion. Hop into the red zinger you rented, and go for a drive. You will not get lost; and I will supply the picnic lunch. He needs to talk; you need to listen."

"He's already regretting saying too much." David turned to puzzle over the problem he faced. A change of venue would clear his head; his driving habits could shake Ted into telling him the truth. "Sounds perfect, Lavender, or is it Morningstar?"

"Everyone calls me something uniquely meaningful to them; and I rather enjoy the ambiguity, along with the ethereal value of each name that springs to mind. Titles I abhor, but for the official ones bestowed upon me. My nicknames, however, I treasure deeply. Give Theo a gentle push out of his self-imposed incarceration, and liberate his Spirit for the remainder of the day. He feels as defeated and empty as Jay. The movie has become a metaphor of your relationship."

"Whoa, is that a mind blowing thought, as if I had a grenade left to pull the pin." David reeled back, remembering his own thoughts on the matter. The film and the two actors' lives did mesh in startling ways.

"I must get back to my other man-child; the one behind the door is all yours. The car will be ready for you, at the wrought-iron gate leading to the studio. Good luck, David." She slowly raised herself from the chair, like a swan lifting its wings to take flight. Once on her feet, an elegant finger, with a large sparkling emerald of inconceivable value, pointed toward the adjoining door, magically releasing the bolt on the other side without a sound. "Do not startle him."

"Thanks. Sometimes your *mind over matter* trick comes in handy."

"That was simple electrical energy." She returned his wickedest smile and fluttered one eye with a wink that nearly knocked him over. He remembered a similar one that changed his life.

"That's all I needed to hear; you're an electrically charged conduit." The actor hid his surprise and laughed.

"You're getting closer, LaCoix." Tossing her hair back, the teasing glow dissipated, replaced by intense worry, etching lines in her pale face.

David walked her to the door, wishing her luck for something he knew nothing about, but only felt. With even more trepidation, than his abominable long wait at the cabin door, he turned the knob and entered Ted's bedroom, quietly and covertly.

With the shutters closed tightly, the room had become dark and insufferably hot. A small candle flickered, a tattered *Bible* lay open, and a crucifix looked saintly over a statue of the Virgin Mary. The little shrine had been ritualistically laid out on the small table next to the bed; and the young man piously knelt before it, head bowed, hands placed palm to palm, and prayers mumbled in whispers. A slow rocking movement appeared to maintain his pious countenance, while he begged for forgiveness. David's heart bled open wounds for hurting his friend in the worst possible way. A chosen path, desecrated by the sexual act of the drama, ripped away Ted's Soul. The blond actor thought his intrusion necessary, however, to stop the self-loathing presented before him. This would not be the man's future if invited into David's world. Another stunning thought, not considered an eventuality, nearly toppled him over; he took a step forward to regain his equilibrium. It brought him close enough to tower over the sacred little scene. With his hands secure on his hips, he let go of one wild thought to contemplate his next move. His decision took little time.

"Go away."

"No; I heard you say you loved me, and I want an explanation."

"A mistake ranted as an improv of the dialogue. You know how long it takes me to get out of character."

"Bullshit. If a mistake, on your part, why are you spilling your guts to God, Christ, Satan, or whomever else you feel you owe an apology, or to blame your feelings and actions? They had nothing to do with it. This involves you and me, and to hell with your handful of damned deities, Barrett. Stop letting them ruin your life. I know when I'm giving someone pleasure; and you enjoyed every second of it." David's anger overruled his plans A through Z. He reached down and harshly grabbed a handful of brown silk, pulling Ted up with the angry power of one hand. A yelp was heard, then a wail, when David swept the table clean of symbols with his other arm, and snuffed out the candle with the heel of an angry black boot. LaCoix had had enough.

"You're shouting blasphemy. What are you doing? You're hurting me." Ted clawed at the hand tugging at his long mane, while attempting to get his feet under him. Anger tensed his body, but he could do nothing about the hurtful hand jerking him around by the hair.

"Tough; we're going for a ride for a long chat."

"No, you don't understand."

"I understand more than you think. It's taken me a while, but the pieces to the Barrett mystery are finally coming together. Now move." David grabbed the good arm, and yanked Ted up to stand erect. He stopped towing the man forward, only to allow the struggling tornado to regain his balance, but not his composure. Without another word spoken, he strong-armed Ted to the wrought-iron gate, and seated him, not so gently, in the passenger side of the hot little car. The door slammed shut and remotely locked. David settled in on the other side, unsuccessful at calming his ire. With sunglasses firmly planted and adjusted on the strained face, and a pair thrust against Ted's chest, the fire breathing Leo grasped the leather wheel of the red menace. "Put them on and buckle up."

"Where are we going? You are an arrogant, obnoxious son-of-a-bitch, you know that?"

"Shut up, and don't call my mom a bitch. Hell if I know where we're heading, but it's straight into the sun until we fall off the edge of the earth. So hold on tight." The car spun its wheels on takeoff, twitching its tail like an angry rattler. Pushing the gear handle into second gear, David full-throttled the raging fireball into the open desert, redlining all the way. With nothing seen for miles, and only a dust cloud looking back, David was as hot and mad as his car; Ted shrunk down deep into his seat, white knuckling the safety harness.

An hour out, and David slammed on the breaks, spinning the car 180 degrees. After a wild ride, all his tension evaporated with the thrill, until he looked at the pale face of his passenger. "Thought you liked risk, Ted? This is mine: fast cars and open spaces."

"Fuck you."

"I think you have it backward, and mind your mouth. Damn, that was fun." David felt the rush he loved, and even with the angry bear cub beside him, could not help but smile the widest grin possible.

"Fun? What, screwing me, or racing this car? Now that you've done both, take me back." Crossing his arms in defiance, Barrett looked straight ahead, while David refrained from laughing aloud at the pout.

"Back to what, your doll and a stuffy room full of god-awful incense? No way, Baby Bear."

"Stop calling me names, including Teddy Bear, Teddy, and Baby."

"I'll call you anything I like while we're here. It puts me in the mood to like you; and we have one more scene to get through." Turning the ignition off, David closed his eyes to hear the subsiding of the Italian growl before the car slept in the blazing sun. Another *red boys' toy* day of adventure, he sat in joyful reverence, until his eyes flashed open at what he heard; and if looks could kill, Ted would be dying alone in an uninhabited stretch of desert.

"I won't do it. They don't need the last scene. It's overkill. End of conversation."

"Get out of the damn car, Ted! Do it!" The locks flipped open; and the infuriated blond leapt out, keys safely in hand. He reached behind the seats to pull out a basket and a large blanket, while Barrett reluctantly extricated himself from the steaming red demon. With nothing left to do, Ted had to deal with a man feeling just as hostile.

"Sit down and start talking or eating; your choice." David decided on a frontal attack. Everything debated in his head went asunder upon witnessing the pious figure, praying for his life's worth in front of an idol. Listening to Ted beg for unneeded forgiveness pushed the wrong button in the explosive actor. The younger man's guilt made LaCoix ill; he intended to reach the bottomless pit of questions he had for Mr. Barrett. His co-star responded too ecstatically to his first homosexual encounter; not to mention how readily his arse accepted the penetration; a tight entry, the muscles did open without a rip. David did not want his own enraptured experience to end with the frightened flight of an overly emotional, former virgin.

Ted sat quietly to ponder his next move; Chess was not his forte. Handed a crystal goblet of cool, well-aged white wine, he reluctantly accepted it without looking at the man who stared at him. He hated talking about his life and downed the liquid in a gulp. If he had to speak with LaCoix, he might as well be drunk.

The voice, so familiar to millions, reverted to softer and kinder. "You mean a great deal to me, Ted; and I still don't know why. You surprised me today; and I haven't been able to respond, not knowing how to react."

"It doesn't matter; just an out-of-control, stupid improv to fill dead air space. I didn't even hear them yell *Cut*." Ted looked at the still shiny Alpha Romeo, wondering how he could make his escape. He was trapped again.

"You called me David, not Dusty. You said you loved Dusty right on cue; then you said you loved me, minutes after the cameras stopped rolling. You weren't in character when you said David. So do you?"

Ted accepted a refill, of sun-filled wine, sipping this one slowly. He said nothing, acting out the long, lingering scene of someone admiring the beauty of desolation. David noticed the glass shaking, as well as the man trying to control his body from following.

"I'll take that as a yes then." Questions would be answered. LaCoix refused to back down until completely satisfied with a result to the puzzle sitting next to him.

"Didn't say that."

"Yes you did. You're gay, which terrifies you, and you're the best liar I've ever met." Sharp and right on target, David prepared himself for a test of his own path's fragility.

"I don't lie, and I'm straight, married with a kid on the way." Ted tried to laugh, but one was not forthcoming.

"That's a blatant falsehood, as it doesn't matter if you have a swarm of ankle biters. Being gay doesn't mean you can't reproduce, so there goes that piece of trash. Start telling me the truth, if you want our relationship to continue, and maybe even grow. I told you I'm bisexual and attracted to you. Recalling any of this, Barrett?"

"Yeah, I remember, and I don't care who you are or what you want. You mean nothing to me." Ted turned to glare back at the man beside him, seeing someone different from when they started playing this insane game with Lavender. It began with the bizarre illusion and the need for money, culminating in an unholy act generated by her Ladyship. The young man blamed everyone but himself, for the web he had created, within which he was now stuck.

Whirling the liquid in his glass, David refused to meet the ferocious stare, but watched the color change slightly within the small eddy forming. He had something to say; his words had to be correct. "Might mean a lot; might not mean anything; believe what you will. I've only had one consistent male lover, and I enjoyed his company and the pleasure, but I've stepped into the tempting waters with a few others. To be honest, Barrett, I felt more ecstasy, making love to you, than I have in years. I also said that I've never connected with anyone; however, you've managed to flip me upside-down. Do I love you? I don't know. If I ever said the word to you, I would mean it, and say it only once. Until I know and understand the feeling, it would have to do. One thing and this I am sure about, is I missed you the three days we were apart, and the night you ran from me. You surprised me with your sudden fit of anger early this morning, as well as upsetting me when you turned your back and walked away in a snit." David downed the expensive wine and poured another. The caviar and crackers no longer seemed appealing.

"A snit? You treat me like some stupid kid, and I get into a snit because of it? You don't think very highly of me, do you. As for you being hurt, nothing disgruntles the crazy, hedonistic LaCoix who lies in abundance, regarding his sexual appetite for the male gender. You used me; you've been using me all along. I'm not gay, and I don't need to hear the crap you're spouting, or whom you've slept with. Love you? Am I supposed to be licking your boots, thanking God you're able to return something I don't want? I've had enough. Take me back or give me the keys." A hand reached out for the getaway device, but received a hard slap instead. Ted's eyes widened in surprise, and he jerked back instantly with the stinging smack.

"Nope, and no matter what you say, you are not going to make me angry. You're afraid; I can sympathize with that. That decision you made, before hearing about the baby, was to divorce your wife and leave your church behind. You had to be what you are, exactly like Jay said to Dusty. I do apologize for not divulging the full quota of my male encounters, as I feared scaring you off into Neverland. I assure you, my intent was never to seduce you."

"Why not? Christ, just stop it. My life's in chaos and I've lost control." The glass dropped from his hand, which raced to join the other to cover a face cringing to stop an outburst of tears. It was too late.

Shocked at the short question, David moved closer to the smaller man and put an arm around the shaking shoulders, welcoming the head to rest in the crook of his neck. He had to say the right words, and hoped they came out correctly. "I know, Teddy; I do care about you. Would you like to come to London with me to get your head together?"

"Yes, I'd like to very much, but can't. I must stay to protect my baby."

"That's the second time you've said that. What's really going on, Ted?"

"I am a liar, and as you said, a damn good one. I love kids, but I'm desperately afraid for them in their screams of loneliness and pain. I can't take it; I can't." Ted shook uncontrollably ready to start convulsing. David secured him and tapped his face to quell the oncoming storm, stopping the blue irises from rolling to the top of his head in a seizure of panic.

"You're okay, Ted. Someone beat you as a child; your broken bones weren't accidents. That dark, filthy space, which I envisioned, is real. I'll listen with no judgment, but please talk to me." David whispered to soothe what pain he could, not realizing the extent of the hurt running rampant so close to the surface.

Ted pulled away and looked out over the desert, tears streaming silently down his face and breathing too shallow. He curled into a fetal position, with his knees embraced against his chest. Alone in his nightmare, he never needed anyone before, and never would.

"If it saves your child from a similar situation, someone needs to help you. Start at the beginning, and tell me the truth with no embellishment, only the facts." David inched closer with a gentle touch to his shoulder.

"You don't know what you're asking." The younger man turned his head to squint warningly at his idol. Sizing up the immediate dilemma, the dam he built, to protect himself from his emotions and fears, was about to burst.

"I feel and sense you so strongly, Ted, the pain is unbearable for me to handle. You've hidden your secrets long enough, and what a perfect place to speak the truth. Only the Spirits in the wind and I will ever know." David caressed the hair around the sorry face, leaned forward, and planted a gentle, fatherly kiss to a damp forehead. Hearing a hapless sigh, he encircled the younger man from behind and listened intently to the strange tale Ted began to unveil.

"In my church, you're read the scriptures from the moment of conception. Against natural law, for same sex partners to love each other in a carnal fashion, it didn't stop me from needing another man to want me physically. Even discovered a few sexual tricks, in case I had the opportunity to explore that part of me. I've been in need of you, David, since I first saw you. You're the only person to capture my heart; and I don't understand either. A kid, of about sixteen, when I first set eyes on you, I fell hard watching you in one of your bigger movies. From that moment, I would wait in agony for your next picture and figure out a way to see it. You became my obsession; even keeping a scrapbook of everything about you from that day forward. Don't laugh, but I keep it with me. I suppose I've needed you forever, dreaming you would ride up on your white charger to take me away from the horrors of living day-to-day."

Stunned at the confession, David went into automatic, continuing to caress the man who wriggled further into his arms. Smelling the soft hair, another kiss swept over the forehead, while urging Ted on with a rocking motion and nurturing touches of assurance. No words could be said over the shocking revelation.

"Children are disciplined in the same manner and it starts very young. The friends we had, in our age group, would discuss who could stay isolated the longest. A terrible, horrible game, it became our outlet to deal with something hidden, not knowing another way. They separated the sexes at functions, and even within some families, but the girls received the same retaliatory action if they disobeyed. My wife's true to our faith. What did the Mistress call it: Valkyrian? Karen's far stricter in our rituals than me, and she will discipline our child exactly as we were."

"How badly were you hurt?" David feared the answer, and released the unnerved Ted who compulsively wrung his hands, in a sorry attempt to regain his male façade of indifference.

Barrett looked back into horrified eyes, afraid to carry on. Only a warm hand rubbing his back gave him the will. "What you saw in my eyes was real. Those sticks stood neatly in a row, each of a different size, waiting to manipulate us mentally, with the fear they induced. The first time my parents struck me, I was four-years-old. It seems too severe for one so small; I'll never forget it. The attack started my nightmares."

"Your nightmares started at four? What happened?"

"I forgot a passage they had read to me the day before. They insisted I repeat it to my two-year-old brother, and the brother my mother carried at the time. Too young, I couldn't remember. They told me to put my hands on the table; one I could barely reach. They struck me once over both arms with one of those wooden sticks. The cracks, of those first breaks, still echo in my head, along with the excruciating pain. Being so little, they easily lifted me by both injured arms; and while screaming for them to help me, they lowered me into the pit under the house. Just dirt and rocks, the hole seemed so deep back then. They'd drop me in; and it felt like I kept falling forever until I hit the ground. There they left me, naked and freezing, with two broken arms I couldn't use, and only worms, insects, and slithering snakes for company. A single light, through a missing knothole in the floor above, kept me company. What you saw was accurate, David."

"Your Spirit Keeper tried to help you." The father of three could barely breath, sickened at such blatant cruelty, and he pulled the man back against his chest. He prayed to the sky for guidance, preventing his heart from bursting out of his chest.

"That's what Lavender called it." Ted leaned forward again, talking into open space, releasing his fear to the wilds and the warm hands massaging his shoulders. "In a way, I was lucky. With others, their punishment started at a much younger age. I can't tell you how often, or for how long, they kept me down there. One thing I learned, if you didn't scream, your release came quicker. When in the cage as Jay, although the script called for me to be silent, I couldn't. I had to scream, and once I started, I couldn't stop."

"Surely someone knew you kids were being abused?" David bit into his lip, not to explode in rage, keeping his demeanor relaxed with his stomach in his throat. It was an impossible task.

"Never thought of it as abuse, only discipline. Being home schooled, no one knew us except those in the church. As the eldest, I had to be strong for my younger brothers, to keep them from the fear, and to hold them for needed warmth. Sometimes all three of us would be down there. When they brought us back up, we promised strict obedience and not to deter from God's will; and after apologizing, making it sound sincere, we were fed, cleaned up, and rewarded with a scholarly book or a favor, like a movie they deemed appropriate, or the zoo. The healer would then come to bind our arms if necessary. Nothing else happened to us: no screaming or yelling, no hitting or beating with their hands, only cold silence and disappointment. I guess that's the guilt part. As for the breaks, they limited them to simple hairline fractures; they were very good at it. So, that's how I was brought up, David. I see it now as intimidation and pain; but unbeknownst to our parents and the church, all three of us became good actors and thus great liars. We didn't know any other way."

"They didn't feed you while confined? Could be the reason your bones are brittle: malnutrition. How long did this go on?"

"I can't say; you'll think so little of me. I started public school in my teens, even looked forward to college. My father has a Doctorate in Chemical Engineering, providing him with a lucrative job. School gave me the opportunity to act, taking me away from the terror of messing up, or saying the wrong thing. I acted my way out of many difficult situations, often taking the blame so my brothers weren't hurt. The chance to join the drama club was a favor granted, freeing me in some ways. My first audition, for a television series, landed me a job before I turned fifteen. Being able to pass for nine or ten, I was perfect for its two year run."

"You looked that young? Christ, you must have been tiny. Underfed, you probably didn't develop properly. You story's getting worse."

"A late developer, I didn't grow at the normal rate. My brothers did though. The food thing is a different matter, but it taught us to survive on scraps."

"And you still don't eat properly." Completely unraveled, LaCoix's stoic façade crumbled; his co-star felt it.

"It's okay, David; you've heard enough." Ted reached up to stroke the man's cheek, which felt wet and tasted of salt.

"Not yet. At least you found a way out."

"Sort of. On my fifteenth birthday, I started work with a broken arm and weak from hunger, but given the generous opportunity to do what I love. I became very good at masking the pain; the breaks always healed quickly. No one suspected I might be hurt, or older than what my biography stated. I fought the pain, so the director would keep me working. The more money I earned, which went to the church, the more important my parents became in their eyes. It went on forever, David; and you remain in the family unit until you marry, which is no escape at all."

"My God, Ted, you've described child abuse, unlawful imprisonment, and abandonment; and all church members treat their children in this hideous fashion, right into adulthood. You get married to escape one situation, to step into one that's worse. It turns into a vicious circle when you procreate. Your church is outrageous, barbaric, and archaic." David wrapped himself around the man, holding on in case he lost Ted to a hell in which he could not be found.

"As far as I know, and I want it to stop; but I foolishly sat there, with the Mistress the other night, arguing my faith and beliefs were right. How stupid is that? I didn't want to have this baby, because Karen will do exactly the same thing to it; I won't be able to stop her. I agreed to do these scenes for the money, David--strictly for the money--with sixty-million, I could escape with the baby. I'd be running forever, but it didn't matter; and much to my shame, I did it for one romantic, sexual encounter with you, just to remember how it felt. Now, I'm giving you grief over something I longed for."

"You did it for me?" David let go and leaned heavily on his outstretched arms. Breathing stopped; his head fell backward; and his eyes closed against the glare of the desert sun.

"I thought you'd never know; and the script would take us there; but it didn't, until the rewrite; and then I grew too scared. I'm sorry."

"I don't know what to say, Baby Bear. No wonder your nightmares are chronic. With this money, you believed you could raise the baby alone, in a hidden place, with the hope of stumbling upon a lover who wanted you both. A highly unlikely scenario, Ted, considering you have little experience sexually, and none caring for a baby. You may end up resenting the child for forcing you to maintain a low profile, away from your love of acting, while yearning for a long-term relationship with a man. We have to get you out of this mess. This is unbelievable." David shook his head, his mind whirling for answers for both he and Barrett.

"I didn't know what to do, but return to old habits. Whatever I have to do, keeping the baby safe is imperative. My brothers understand, and willing to back me up. We made a pact to stop the hurting, as did their wives, except for Karen. The five of us desperately attempted not to have children."

"You're all hiding; and you, in particular, need a male partner. My God, how did you manage?" The vision, of the horrendous lives of three young men and their spouses, broke the astute actor's stalwart façade, and without shame, David cried.

Ted turned and enveloped his mentor in his arms. Roles reversed; the smaller man became the healing force for so much misery. "I wanted you; please don't cry. When they told me you were the second lead, I almost went into cardiac arrest, and puked for weeks before we started. Felt like a damn fool meeting you the first time, not knowing how to act or what to say. I didn't want you to think I was gay, but I prayed you were. Isn't that stupid?"

"You've had this crush on me for a long time; and I'm sorry I wasn't there to save you. I hope I'm not too late."

Two timid, inexperienced hands erased the tears and eased the broken heart. "You are my hero, David. I need you even more, in every way imaginable, especially now, after being inside me, touching and caressing every part of me. I'll thank you forever for today's memory, but this responsibility is killing me. I feel so selfish."

"They've instilled such guilt in you; I now fully understand Lavender's point. Being a father, I'm torn apart. Come here and let me hold you." David pulled Ted down to lie on top of him; and together they cried, both knowing something had changed. Ted's White Knight rode up to save him; and the handsome blond found the purpose he wanted. Everything would be resolved for need of Theodore Barrett.

"I love you, David. Always will and I'll always remember." The two held each other in silence until the tears ebbed. Wide-open spaces of wild desert surrounded them when they finally pulled apart, but they saw only sorrow and caring in the eyes of the other. It was a point of time they would recall for eternity.

"Do you really want this child, Ted?" David peered into the revealing blue eyes. With new determination, he regained his control, vowing to correct every wrong in the world. Now on a mission, he started building the person who deserved to be loved. Ted was the one he asked for; he would not disappoint the man.

"Yes, very much."

"Then we have to find a solution." David sat up and helped Ted straighten to sit in front of him. They had plans to make and a puzzle to figure out.

"How can I stop it and who can I tell? They'll only see this gay guy, a flaky actor as well, who's making up this weird story." The eyes dulled in defeat before they had started. Those peculiar blue eyes, you could drown in, were the windows into the essence of this human being. If David could put him in the car and drive into the sunset, he would do it in a heartbeat.

"Not anymore, Ted; under California law fathers have a few rights."

"It still matters; you know it. Being queer will always matter. Leading men are never gay; they pay dearly to save themselves from an insinuation. You said it yourself when we saw Kincaid. He can never show his true colors, if that's what he is. They'd crucify his career. He's already a vulnerable-styled actor, and to be rumored as gay would destroy him."

"Unfortunately, you're right; considering those I know who remain hidden for the same reason. Dashing leading men and action heroes don't announce their sexual preference to the world, and still receive the money and respect they deserve with hard work and talent. Hollywood is a society of arranged marriages, covert or manipulated. We're mere puppets, Ted."

"At least you had a choice. I didn't, and I've never thought of myself as gay, certainly unlike the stereotypes on film. How they act doesn't fit me. I'm not like that and don't think I ever could be. What does that make me?"

David pulled Ted's worried face into his chest to cover his own expression of unknowing. The young man appeared as a straight male, but for those sudden fits of crying and flights of *Peter Pan*. The flighty side of Ted, witnessed only by LaCoix, seemed caused by the emotional turmoil Barrett dealt with daily. The dire situation was beyond any man or woman. "As you said, just stereotypes in comedic roles. You watch too much television and see too many movies. I sure can't tell who is and who isn't, or what *gaydar* is. You're a sweet, honest guy, lost in a cruel world; and I aim to get you out. Do you have the strength to maintain your faith, but fight your church? They're not one in the same, Ted."

"That's what the Lady's been trying to tell me. Yeah, I have the strength. With my child's life at stake, I sure do." Ted waited, praying a good idea would unfold, to help him out of a circle with no exit. He watched the wheels turn in the blond head, believing he saw sparks fly off each cog.

"Okay then, let's send some positive thoughts into the Cosmos." David came up with a plan, in a blink of an amber eye, to set them on course. Money came first; and Ted added some major relevant information of his business and financial minors to his degree in communications. He would set up Swiss accounts for both men and ensure they remained hidden. The original contract amounts would remain in California, dealt with according to two divorce cases, along with their other assets.

Legal Counsel, both Civil and Criminal, had to be found; someone willing to take on several high profile cases, involving a divorce, child custody, and a church's abuse toward its children. Of strong moral fiber and strict dedication to Ted's precarious needs, their lawyer needed a solid presentation, for the District Attorney to present to the Grand Jury, leaving his client's name out of it, until a judgment came down, either for a trial or a dismissal of the allegations against the church. Difficult to do, the D.A.'s investigation could justify the civil case to obtain sole custody. Ted had hard choices to make; and until they spoke to Legal Counsel, he could decide nothing. In Arizona, a few days a week, overseeing the construction of the house, gave him the opportunity to meet in neutral territory with whomever they hired. The Criminal case would be submitted to the District Attorney's office in San Diego, while Ted and his lawyer wrestled with all the paperwork required for the divorce and custody issue.

David's concern showed in his questions regarding his co-star's health to withstand the rigors of such battles, and the length of each undertaking. Encouragement came from Ted, promising to eat and grow stronger to fight. Unfortunately, he may have to stay in the closet until the settlements, particularly for the custody case, and he may have to remain there forever. Much depended on legal advice, and the arrival date of the baby, due mid-May. Lives would turn upside down and twisted in every direction, if they were to succeed. A list of reasons had to drawn up expeditiously, including the divorce (known very well by LaCoix), Ted's assets, and his desire for sole custody. With a few deep breaths, and the nod of agreement from the younger man, David got up to retrieve a pen and paper from the car. They would start with provable facts.

LaCoix tried to control the uprising in his stomach, reliving what he had seen in those beautiful eyes, and now knowing the truth. Overwhelmed with what had happened to the man, and the need for proof, he was deeply shaken. With an important cause to save an infant and its father, no matter how his relationship with Barrett unfolded, he would support him through every battle. Reaching the car, he stood for a few minutes, thankful for the return of his own parents into his life. They had been extraordinary advocates on his behalf until he discarded them. More thanks drifted skyward to all the gods for his wives. Holly had a good mother in Susan; his boys had a strict angel for one as well. The only problem, still unresolved, remained their misguided and absentee father who lavished them with expensive gifts, but little love. Things would change, if his children allowed him to become a real father who listened and nurtured. David grew up this insightful afternoon.

He returned from the car, pen and paper in hand; and the two men wrote a list in a sensible sequence. Ted would be extremely busy; David would be a nervous wreck filming in London. The long absence, although painful, would give them time to figure out how they really felt, and what to do about it. Finished, and the important reference paper tucked neatly into the tight back pocket of Barrett's jeans, they would speak with Lavender first.

"Thanks, David, I feel better knowing you're on my side; and there might be a way to fix this."

"I warn you, this will not be easy; joint custody may be all we get."

"No, it has to be sole custody. It has to be."

"No more worrying until we get sound advice. I'm on your side, Ted, or have you forgotten who kept you steady while you puked and purged from both ends one very long night."

"We? Do you promise? I can't do this alone." Ted looked down, only to have his face raised by a loving hand.

"I'm with you, Teddy Bear, and who could resist someone so cute."

"Are you flirting with me?"

"You're damn right, and probably have been all along. I can tease you for real, considering we may be heading for a more intimate relationship."

"Only if there's no one else in your life. I may be gay... God, I said it aloud... but I am monogamous. I'd be devastated if we did form a union, only for you to drop me with a fling with your next co-star. Love is a constant for me; and your pattern of ongoing courtships, marriages, and affairs is not reassuring. Besides, you need both men and women. How can you cope, LaCoix? How can I cope?"

"A long distance, slow courtship will be pleasant. I'm looking forward to it and promise to behave myself while away. We have a lot to do and think about, before we make advanced plans. After your reactions and excitement this morning, I think I prefer men, maybe always have. At least you don't get PMS." David chuckled and got a huge grin back from Ted.

"Guess it's one thing you won't miss. Did you add discarding Rebecca to our list? I never thought I'd say all this and admit my feelings toward you. Everything has changed, thanks to a hot little red car, and one crazy green-eyed monster I'm slightly attracted to."

"Glad you finally admitted to everything in that head of yours. My gut tells me, your *Lady of the Rocks* had something to do with our meeting. Now, what say we do a little practicing for tomorrow's scene?"

"Here? Right now?"

"Yeah, right here, right now, under the sunniest, brightest sky I've ever seen, fully exposed for miles in every direction. We'll start with this little button, then this one, until I get to this metal one, and a zipper hiding treasures. I'll be able to see every inch of you, and bring you back every time you swoon with the breath of life to those soft... yum... moist... hmm... delicious, oh yeah... lips..."

"David, stop!"

"Shut up, Teddy Bear."

CHAPTER 23

With screeching brakes, whooping and hollering, a red flash spun full circle; they stopped two inches from the wrought-iron gate that took them by surprise. David had Ted screaming in primal pleasure all the way back, laughing and giggling, doing exactly what an expensive *red boys' toy* was supposed to do: make a man a man, feeling it in his crotch until his toes curled in ecstasy, and the pressure in his pants bulged forth unashamedly. Pure passion, of taking it to the limit, doing wheelies, and kicking up dust, had them out of control with the freedom and erotic sensation it stirred within. Ted and David were hotter than a raging inferno and ready to start again. Their lovemaking, under the desert sun, turned into a wild, torrid experimental encounter, trying every position possible, and some they had only heard about. The outcome had been fun, and scandalously erotic; each discovery made their liaison more exhilarating. David's entire face gleamed, crinkling in lines of satisfaction, with giddiness long past due; and he still felt the need to reach over, throw his new partner over the seat, and indulge in the hot tunnel to paradise.

Jubilant, Ted could not stop laughing. With sexual frustration satisfied, the thrill of the act went beyond anything his imagination could conjure up. Patient and tender, his lover handled him with caring touches, seducing him with just a dreamy-eyed look. He came alive this day, with his knight beside him, on top of him, under him, and inside him. Making love felt joyous, gentle, sensual, and so intense, his head still spun, and his arousal refused to settle. Moonstruck over his hero in black denim, he could only gawk at the man with the broadest of smiles and a glittering of his own corrected Hollywood whites. Giggling like a foolish kid, he blushed at his thoughts. He wanted to play in an enormous bed with David forever, even though stiff and sore, particularly from the continual assault to his derriere. His own attempts to stimulate himself never resulted in the convulsive state another could induce in his ultimate sensitive area. The heart-jolting halt at the gates, the remembered responsibility, and all that lay before him, came crashing down on his guilty shoulders. With much to ponder, his sunshine smile turned downward into a severe pout.

"Was our little outing worth it?" David grinned, trying to maintain the enthusiasm of their recent union of body and Spirit. A tilt of his head questioned the sudden mood change of his partner; a comforting hand reached out for the younger man.

Ted turned and faintly smiled back, still with a hint of joy not easily forgotten. Both his arms extended to accept the invitation, to be swooped into the nest offered. Eager fingers entwined in the blond silk, to happily exchange a kiss of excited urgency and power. The gates opened; the embrace released. "What an understatement. You gave me the best day." His head fell on his lover's shoulder in satisfied exhaustion--his lover, David LaCoix--the man he had wished to capture.

"Happy?"

"Yeah, really happy! Fuck!"

"I think we did that a few times." Both men laughed harder at another old joke. With a little struggle disentangling limbs, they crawled out of the car: a little tired, a little unsteady, a little more relaxed, a little sore; and very grateful to Coppertone, which was used for many things. Hand-in-hand, they walked slowly back into the labyrinth, heading toward their cottage to create more fireworks.

"You disappeared for a minute, Teddy Bear. Where did you go?"

"Just thinking how long I've waited for this day. Once an impossible dream, you fulfilled everything I waited for; you made it better. It felt so good, David, I don't know how to describe it; but now, released from my prison, I have to face the consequences. They'll banish me from the church."

"That's a heavy statement, but you've decided to move forward. Besides, what they don't know won't hurt them, until you're ready. Banishment is one thing, but you haven't lost your faith. A church is just a building, a place, for like minds, to gather in worship of countless deities. You've outgrown being a follower. Lavender affirmed you could maintain your faith, by keeping only the beliefs that hold meaning to you. Your heart is open to new thoughts; and if you still believe in your god, he wouldn't want you to suffer and wallow in guilt. Your church can toss you out on your sore arse, but not a god or faith you believe in. Once you realize it, the guilt, for being who you are, will never raise its ugly head again."

"I suppose, if I believe God is loving and good; he would understand."

"Of course he would; any spiritually higher being would desire your happiness. I know, in my heart, that my beliefs, in the flow of life, are a mishmash of many ideologies; and they're all having a delightful day, knowing their black sheep is doing something right."

"I never did ask you what you believed in, LaCoix. I suppose, it can be construed as another lesson of the Mistress: keep your path to yourself. I sure got the message with her displeasure of our missionaries: take only education, simple technology and ideas, food and medicine, and leave the *Bible* at home. Build homes, hospitals, clean water systems, schools, and teach essential information, not useless church dogma to confuse them."

"I'm sure Lavender would be happy to hear your words. Now, let's remove the dust and find our gracious producer. She'll be pleased to know that you'll finish the picture."

"Now I'm really embarrassed to have sex on camera. It's personal now, too intimate for prying eyes. It's like having them in our bedroom."

"In *our* bedroom; like the sound of that. One more time, Ted, then it's our secret until we figure everything out. I can't be happier about you supervising the house construction. It may be your home as well."

"What? Are you asking me to live with you, or is it an idle thought to tease me, Goldilocks?"

"Goldilocks?"

"Since I've turned into Baby Bear, it seems appropriate."

"Nope, try again." David laughed at Ted's determination to find him a nickname, but he had to get this out before he lost his nerve. Continuing with his train of thought, he knew he had taken Barrett by surprise, not sinking further than the frontal lobe of the man's brain. "There's nothing to move into yet; and you have to stay with Karen, until you hand her divorce papers. You sure can't look suspicious, while meeting with lawyers and obtaining advice. I don't see why we shouldn't plan for a third party to join us. There's Holly and the boys to factor in as well."

"You aren't kidding! You are asking me! I don't know what to say; and it wouldn't bother you having a baby in the house? I'd sure like to get to know your kids. What will they think? My God, David, they may hate me and turn against you."

"We'll handle all the kids carefully. There's currently nothing to tell them. We have much to do, and a long stretch of time before our future is set. I do know, however, I want you in my life. Whatever happens, I'll fight to keep you and your baby. Actually, the thought of having another little cutie is a pleasant one. I like babies, and I've had three, all of whom were poster material. I get into trouble and out of touch when they start talking. Through all this, I hope my relationship with my own children will improve. Thanks to you, I plan to try. I love you, Theodore Barrett."

"David, I can't believe you said that! Do you mean it? Don't go yanking my chain." Ted spun around to face him. Those big sapphires grew wide with questions, needing the truth, and not knowing if what he heard was said. They stood beneath the secret-keeping purple wisteria; a sprig, of which, dangled against Ted's slightly sunburned cheek, and tangled in the brown waves. His face was the perfect look of innocence, in the perfect place for exchanging promises.

David smiled at the expectant, nervous expression, and gently pushed away the blossoms from the magical tresses. "Told you I would only say the word to only one. I love you, Ted; and you can take that to the bank along with your cash and the list. This may be the only time you'll hear the word; and it seems appropriate to tell you now." David drew the man closer, his hands on the small behind, and pressing Ted's manhood against his own.

"You better be sure; because I'm giving you my heart, and never want it back. It's yours and always has been. Keep it safe, and if you hurt me, know this, LaCoix; it will fragment into pieces of red crystal, sparkling and scattered under the sun, never to be put back together as it feels right now. I'm so happy that I can't stop saying it. I've never felt like this and can't bear the thought of being hurt. Man, I'm being gushy here, but I mean it. Men, and I doubt even gay men, don't say these things to each other, but I do. I've waited so long to say these things to you; it's the pathetic side of me. Knowing you'll be with me forever means everything, so don't even hint at something you can't honestly do." Ted rambled, afraid that if he shut up, his dreams would smash.

"Are you finished? Your poetic side is showing."

"It surprises Lavender too."

"I'm sure it does. These promises, you're asking, are certainly descriptive, touching me deeply. I can't pledge forever, Ted, but in my mind, I won't hurt you. It's a difficult thing to say and do. Eternity is for the likes of her Ladyship; but we're real and have a hell of a battle to win."

"I hate the idea of separating so soon."

"You'll be so busy, you won't even miss me."

"Yeah, right. Excuse me, but something is trying to get my attention. For an old geezer, you sure know how to put out. I think you need a cold shower." Ted's sad face perked up again; and he laughed at the man who let him go to look down between them.

"I haven't been this horny in a decade, and I'm not that much older than you. What you do to me, Barrett, and who else needs a bucket of water thrown over him? Damn, I'm going to miss you." David encircled Ted around the waist, and with a whisper of a kiss against the smooth, pink cheek, and a twist of his body, he directed his new lover toward their lodgings. They continued their stroll to their quarters, joined from the hip to the shoulder.

"You just suggested the Mistress might not be real. You've been hedging around it for sometime." With his head resting on a strong shoulder, Ted tilted it upward to question with a gaze, relying on David's eyes to guide him as they continued to walk.

"Well, it has me wondering, with so many mysteries in what she says and is capable of doing. She's very powerful in an unearthly way. I just don't know, and to tell you the truth, I'm a little leery about finding out. Let's go; I'll race you back." David tried the least frightening answer without giving anything away. Lavender's secret, one never promised, remained safe, too thought provoking for his new partner.

Ted dashed off like a born-again child, leaving David chuckling and following at a slower pace. It would be easy to catch the man in his weakened state, and the exertion placed upon the thin body that afternoon. The taller man leisurely jogged behind, enjoying the rear-end view of the man who had suddenly flipped his world. Barrett started breaking down fences rapidly; and experience hoped it would be with no remorse. One of the rails knocked over was David's heart, caught before it broke again, and captured without a second thought. The older actor now knew and accepted why his presence at La Rosa Negra deemed necessary. Back on his true path, he understood destiny to be a meaningless word, an abstraction to change on a whim, or steady a perfect future. The latter led him directly to Theodore Barrett.

Cleaned up and radiantly smiling, the new couple entered the double-doors to find the place empty. Even the screening room showed no signs of a shadow, and no delicious aroma came from the kitchen. Starting to know their way around a few of the rooms and corridors, they tried the study next.

"Sorry, didn't mean to interrupt." David apologized to the pair, idly keeping company in an oversized comfortable chair.

"You have returned! We have been waiting for you. I am anxious to hear about your afternoon, and I am sure Stevie would be delighted as well. Please join us. I trust something wonderful has occurred; you are both glowing from within." Lavender sat with Steven Kincaid who casually slouched against her. Long graceful arms dangled over the shoulders of the man, crossing his chest in a similar comforting fashion done with Ted in his time of need. With their feet up, both seemed to be enjoying a quiet chat over a glass of wine. The ambiance of the scene had a familiarity about it, as if played out many times before.

"We had a *red boys' toy* day." David laughed; Ted blushed.

Kincaid sat up immediately, bent over, holding his lower abdomen. He cracked up instantly. "Gets the juice pumping, doesn't it?"

"I am therefore confident it shall remain a guarded secret." Lavender smiled proudly at the pair; Kincaid continued to chuckle along with David. Barrett burned brighter scarlet, hiding behind his protector.

"Besides our little adventure in the desert, we uncovered Ted's problem; and it's a hell of a one. We need help, at least advice." LaCoix uncharacteristically blurted out the sensitive information, to have his arm unmercifully grabbed in a vise-like grip by an anxious Ted.

"This is private. I don't want anyone to know what happened to me." Barrett whispered in the man's ear, but was hushed immediately.

"It will come out anyway, Ted, considering this will involve the courts when it comes down to a church, babies, famous faces, who gets what, and how to prove the cruelty. What do you want to do? You can leave Karen and the church easily enough, but what about the baby. It's up to you."

"It is time we took a collective breath to ponder your predicament, Child. You have suffered in silence long enough, and now have much to do and a great deal to think about. It must start now, Theo." Lavender's tone grew serious; and Kincaid, hearing the change of cadence in her voice, sat up straight to take a position of interest and empathy. "Stevie, I am sure you recognize David LaCoix, and our rising star Theodore Barrett. Gentlemen, I would like to introduce Steven Kincaid, a friend and frequent visitor to La Rosa Negra."

"I've seen much of your work, David. You've racked up more hours of screen time than anyone I know, and fine work. You're an intense character actor. I've always wanted to make a film with you, but nothing has come forward. It will soon; I feel it." Kincaid got up and shook the older man's hand.

"I'll look forward to it."

"And Theo, a pleasure to meet you as well. I hear you're sensational in this latest venture of her Ladyship." His voice, renowned to millions, remained barely a whisper; a reminder he was an actor used to sensitive microphones. The famous lips always looked moist or glossed, opening only a sliver, except to occasionally flash a contagious smile, which drew gasps of sexual fantasy from all those whom watched the mega-star light up the silver-screen. In reality, it created instant ease and laughter.

"I don't know; but it's nice to meet you." Intimidated and embarrassingly star-struck, Ted faced the incredibly good-looking man, and shook his outstretched hand firmly. The intensity of the pastel blue eyes startled him; and Kincaid gazed equally in awe into the dark, sapphire ones.

"What you could do with his eyes on film." Steven finally let go of Ted's hand, much to David's relief, not understanding the overpowering connection between the two younger men. A hint of jealousy flickered red through his trademark wild eyes. Although unsettled, he continued to listen and wait.

"We used both Theo and David's eyes to great advantage in this film."

"So, what do you think, Morningstar? Is there enough resemblance? He's certainly thin enough, and certainly looks younger. Come on; tell me if it's possible." Steven gave up the hand, but not the stare that made Ted nervous. He felt like a poodle in a dog show, being scrutinized for conformation and the properly coiffed coat.

"Stand beside him, so we can get a side-by-side view. Come here, David, and give us your opinion." Lavender took the blond by the hand; and they both peered at the two men; David not knowing what he should be detailing; and Ted equally bewildered.

"On what; whether they look alike? Yes, they do." David saw the similarity immediately upon shaking Kincaid's hand. The two young men could easily pass for brothers.

"I believe they do as well. Both have high cheekbones; face and head shapes are similar; and they both have thick hair, boyish features, delicate bone structures, and dazzling eyes. Theo is about four inches shorter and much lighter than you, Stevie, but again a similar body structure. He is light enough for you to carry and throw around at his current weight. I would say it possible. Do you look like your brothers, Theo?"

"Not really. There's a certain way we all do things. Mannerisms I guess, but looking alike, only minimally. What are we doing, and who's getting thrown around?"

"Mannerisms: that's the key to all family members. We'll have to study each other, and come up with a few things that feel natural to us." Kincaid appeared delighted with something.

LaCoix could only smirk and question, "Can you shuffle your feet?"

"Not funny, David." Ted warned, perplexed by the conversation.

"This is great. Would either of you mind letting me see the dailies from the last few days?" The famous face looked at David for approval; the older actor nodded his head, understanding the enormity of what remained hidden.

Barrett, on the other hand, shook his head violently. The intimacy, of the last two scenes, had yet to be seen; and the youngest declined sharing something potentially scandalous, even with the likes of Steven Kincaid. If the Mistress had lied, their performance, of that morning, could be censored as explicit pornography; and these were not dailies.

David acknowledged the fear he saw with a quick return to Ted's side and a quiet word in his ear. "Not a problem is there, Baby?"

"Yes, there's a problem: we haven't had a viewing of them ourselves!

"It's been done tastefully so far."

"Yes, but this is different."

"I think we should ask him to join us. He has his reasons; and I bet they're good ones. Lavender hasn't let us down yet."

"Exactly; not yet! We're being blindsided."

"Say yes, Ted. Your life and career are changing; take the risk." David waited for the nod, and again dipped his head toward Kincaid.

Lavender clapped her hands in gleeful anticipation. "Good. We may have one of Stevie's problems solved, and something in return for you, Theo. Now, before we have any further excitement over the results of today's shoot, I think we should delve into your predicament, Child. Tell us what you need to face this formidable situation looming ahead of you. Perhaps Stevie can learn a lesson in matters of true importance."

"Thanks a lot, Morningstar. Sorry to be such a hindrance to you."

"You are always in our minds, knowing how often we have helped you. It is time you heard something far more serious in nature. It may make you think twice of your own behavior."

"Yes ma'am. I apologize to all of you."

"No need, Steven. You have no idea what will be revealed." David sympathized with the man who believed the Mistress belonged to him alone. Perhaps, the golden boy needed to feel that special.

"Sit with me, Theo, and remember there are always alternatives. Changes can be made, if your mind stays open." Lavender patted the enormous chair she sat upon, beckoning a very reluctant man to sit beside her. With some hesitation, he leaned into the welcoming arms, promising a motherly embrace. He immediately needed the others to depart, leaving him to his fanciful dreams. Not to be, two men and the Mistress began, stating every detail, every pitfall, and every feeling. Lavender already knew, but remained stoically silent, bleeding inside while one of her children confessed to his never-ending terror. Kincaid's face showed his horror; and David noticed a few tears drop. Even better looking in person, the superstar appeared overly sensitive; Steven Kincaid and Theodore Barrett were very much alike, besides their looks.

Upon hearing of the cruelty rendered on the innocent, silence filled the room. Everyone held back their emotions, waiting for someone to react. Lavender started, "All I can offer is a steadying hand and the name of a brilliant, discreet lawyer. They do exist. I am sorry Theo, but this will be a tremendous strain on you, physically and mentally. We shall be near whenever you call."

"Thanks." Ted looked down at his hands, stilled by the squeeze of gemmed fingers, making them ache with the pressure.

"Just promise me, Child, you will not be swayed from your goal, and only follow what you feel is right. You have taken a giant step, by keeping your faith while fighting the horrors of your church. You show great courage; I am very proud of you."

"I hope I can do it. The sensation of being a scarecrow in a tornado is giving me second thoughts, but I can't turn back."

"Not if you want to lead the life you desire, and to save your baby." David interjected, peering lovingly at the man who he saw sinking into another dark hollow.

Adrift with Ted's mood swing, changing this melancholy conversation was vital; Lavender seemed the impetus with a swift change in the conversation. "I have been remiss to congratulate David on his property purchase. You pined over that rock pile for days before you arrived here. With pure underground water, well protected, and grand vistas, it seems perfect."

"It holds memories for us, but Jess couldn't find remnants of the canyon you trapped us in?"

"He did not know where to look." Lavender gave him a Cheshire cat grin of the *knowing*.

"Now I'm unsure of what I actually purchased; however, Ted and I enjoyed figuring out the precise location for the house before my departure." David leaned forward, to grasp one of Lavender's hands and to peck his partner's cheek, continuing to wonder if his canyon looked like the one behind the rockslide; and unlike Jess, could he find this potentially magical sanctuary.

The youngest man's mood changed, and he nodded happily, trying not to explode with excitement at the use of the word *us*. "I'll take care of it, David. I think I know the spot."

"I hope it will not cause trouble for you, considering the site may bring back a rather menacing image of me?" Lavender looked straight at Ted, but his eyes sparkled like the gems they were. She need not worry.

"Finally, you admit it. I've wanted to ask why you dropped me."

"A learning experience, which flew over your head, as you chose not to see the pink light of uncompromising love given freely to save your life. Perhaps, you now travel a road to view such impossibilities as realities."

"I try to visualize our first experience in the way the others did, beautiful and serene; and I understand, sort of, why my words upset you. Hanging, a few hundred feet in the air, doesn't give a guy a chance to think straight and contemplate new theological beliefs. You scared me beyond anything I've experienced."

"It is self-discovery from whence you learn, Child."

With her final words and another *knowing* smile, the foursome retired to the screening room to watch the three scenes, including the upsetting ones from earlier in the day. Ted sat gaping, while the other two men could not believe their eyes and stopped breathing. The action was extraordinarily spellbinding, beautifully filmed in the fading watercolor of nature's pastel palette. Every touch, every feeling, every sound made, was felt, sensed, heard, and seen at such a deep level, you would have to realize these two individuals loved each other passionately, without the usual pornographic ramming and dubbing of grunts and groans in the wrong places. Breathtaking in its simplicity, the imagery blended into a moving work of art, with the careful manipulation of a dominant lover over his young conquest, amidst the rising steam of sweating bodies in the cool morning air. With the most delicate of touches and caresses to every part of the fragile figure, and the timid quiver and excited little moans of a virgin's first time, the film proved pure innocence in surrealistic eroticism; so intense and mesmerizing, you lost yourself in their pleasure, seeing only two people in ardor of each other.

The male body had never been filmed in such exquisite portraiture, detailed in every motion by two handsome actors. Living marble statues, perfectly carved in the most intricate of fashion, they moved to a symphony played in their minds. Two men, in euphoric bliss, were unmistakable: the subtle color changes of intimate body parts took on special hues; the soft whimpers of a virgin accompanied the deep moans of someone more experienced. The outlaw's intimate stimulation, of a younger man's genitalia, could titillate even the modest of individuals; the caresses held the small audience in rapture. The slow seduction played out in the exploration of a loving kiss, rather than the trained seal act, of one actor chewing the upper lip, as the other noisily sucked on the bottom one of the other. A silent act of passage, Jay's soft moans of pleasure purred as an enticement for more.

Aroused at the sensuality of what they had done, David finally took a breath, perspiring heavily, overcome by Ted's sexuality, just in the look of someone who could pass for seventeen. Close to being illegal to watch, the young actor increased the feeling of his vulnerability with a bashful blush of fever, running up his neck and cheeks, after the sexual act, and captured amazingly by one of the many invasive cameras. The scene could never be simulated, showing everything, yet exuding only sensuality. It would bring Ted the accolades promised him for his acting prowess, but created by his own excitement, fear, and pleasure, which only two people understood.

Also sighing in sweet arousal and enthralled by the magic, Kincaid wanted scenes replayed. He started on Ted immediately. Having scoured the Actors' Guild, for the perfect match he foresaw, he finally found his brother in a new acquaintance. David and Ted sat transfixed; Lavender approved enthusiastically; Steven excitedly explained the storyline of his next picture; and begged Ted to accept the role. It meant star billing opposite Kincaid, along with another famous, romantic, leading man, Ethan Peerce, who took an unusual supporting role. Peerce's name had become the lucky four-leaf clover for three men. In the confusion of more good news, Ted nervously sought out his security blanket, and clung to David's arm. The new film would be another emotional roller-coaster ride for the up-and-coming actor; and LaCoix knew Ted could do it; Kincaid knew Ted could do it; and the Mistress knew her man-child ready for the part.

The new partners in life hit the fast track with their careers, and would never look back or care, considering the amount of money earned for their name on the marquee. Steven Kincaid had one of his problems solved; and Lavender could finally settle herself for a moment's respite. With much work ahead of her, regarding all three men, she shivered, wondering which one would call for help first, or if they would. Wish upon wish, on every falling star, deemed necessary this night.

Practical business to take care of, she confirmed the Swiss accounts had been established, waiting only on their signatures. She agreed that their vast earnings be hidden from the pending divorce battles; they may need it to disappear, if not all went well. With the assurance that their salaries, from the next two films, would be deposited in a like manner, with no outside knowledge, she excused herself and entered her chambers. Candles and magic filled her space, and she gazed through the mist of her portal, waiting for it to open. Drifting down to sit, and her burgundy velvet gown keeping her warm, she touched the pewter goblet to her lips gently, to savor a small sip of rare wine. She settled a few things, while others remained in flux.

Her mind wandered back to Kincaid. The front-page face had more problems. One had been resolved with Ted's acceptance to be his co-star. By being close to the more troubled, younger man, Steven's life may turn around. He would have to expend energy and thought to help someone else; much like LaCoix had endured. Kincaid's self-destructive attitude needed another direction; holding Ted together, with the younger man's savior so far away, was the alternative. For the insecure mega-star, turnaround time arrived; and Lavender could not think of another way to take away the obsession ensnaring Steven so incredulously. While forced to face their own dilemmas, the two young men would have each other. The defining difference lay in Kincaid giving up his attraction to a sinister deviate trying to destroy him; but with the Mistress' will, something much more fitting his character waited on another coastline. He only had to stay on his corrected path. Hand-held his entire adult life, by those of La Rosa Negra, he would be allowed one slip, before he straightened out his life, or be destroyed by it. The thought filled her Ladyship with grief and despair. The horrendous consequences she saw, knowing she could shatter his mind with a mistake made, provoked caution warnings to grow more intense; she had to remain positive.

After another dainty sip, the emerald cat eyes caught the flickering light, making them sparkle in delight, thinking how far David had advanced in such a short time. Mr. LaCoix, the once selfish, self-absorbed, lecherous man, may still reach the pinnacle he craved; and the love of his life had been found and declared as such. Holding onto the dream depended on keeping his mind on Barrett, and supporting Ted on his dangerous path. All three men desperately yearned for a happy future; but her money backed LaCoix to be the first, and maybe the only one, to gain control of his personal life. He had started and seemed genuinely thrilled with each change of direction. His next step in spiritual growth would develop, along with Ted's, amidst the battle they declared against an unforgiving society and religion. They had no understanding their path led to a colossal undertaking, and one of importance to the Cosmos.

A delicate sigh, a melody of chimes, she said the name aloud, "Theodore Barrett." Whatever power she could use, in true conscientiousness, she would stretch to the limit to help this tortured Spirit. No one, not even the rich and famous, recovered from such a beginning. He too would reach levels in his career never expected, carrying some weight in the real world he had to deal with; there lay the problem. Would the real world, sitting on his shoulders, destroy the sensitive man before he grew in strength to overcome public notoriety? His sweet, innocent nature was similar to Kincaid's when they first met, but Barrett had David for now, and possibly forever. Highly probable that his legal battles would turn against him, and sole custody of his child not awarded, all his wishes--his career, his life with David, his faith, and his baby--would be gone in crushing mental agony. Nothing could save him, not even his love for the man who needed him equally. Unbearable to think about, she may lose him without drastic action. The gnawing feeling of Ted's missing Soul also continued to bother her, along with his increasing pain, of which he never complained. Physically and mentally, something else plagued her man-child; she had not yet fit him into her own puzzle. Battling his continuing Valkyrian philosophies, he seemed too submissive to be *The Start*. Distressing to feel something, yet unknowing of its importance, she also needed help, and assistance stood by her side.

The Mistress, in her magical world, would be waiting when her charges called. For now, she could release them to their new realities, while she floated in protective arms of one who gave her strength; and together they gazed out the portal to infinity. As the mist cleared, she leaned out to view billions of stars; her long black curls feathered and floated back off her face; and she listened to the whispers on the wind. A gentle, still night, many of her voices quieted for a few rare moments, particularly David and Ted in their cocoon, loving each touch learned and each word hushed in a melody. There was sorrow and there was happiness entwining the two men: a short good-bye and an eternal hello.

Her other man-child rested after a day of hysterics. Unable to sustain the peace given to him, tears dropped softly on the pillow he laid upon, only heard by the ears of the Mistress. Kincaid's path would abruptly hit a new junction, to deal with different matters. Which way would he turn, and how would it influence Theodore Barrett? It could strengthen or destroy them both.

A stronger gust of wind brought the scent of her favorite lilacs, curling her lips upward; serenity fell over her realm. With hair blowing straight back, her eyes closed, and with an *all-knowing* smile, she wished every voice a sweet good night and a straight path to follow. "Please care for them gently, and find my missing pieces."

"My honor, your Ladyship." Two arms wrapped around her; and she fell into the overpowering life force. Loving company would be attentive to her through the ever-changing watch they shared.

CHAPTER 24

Flying on British Airways Flight 282 direct to London, David blinked back every emotion felt. Everything sped past so quickly, in the last week, he barely remembered what had happened. Moment by moment, he reminisced back to the last scene; and the days and nights that followed.

Ted performed brilliantly during the last shoot, with Dusty taking Jay far away from the intrusive cameras. David remembered the sweet taste of each butterfly kiss he made up the inside of his co-star's ticklish thighs, reaching and engulfing something alive and succulent that finally exploded in his mouth. The flavor of candy canes, salt, and lemongrass tempted his palate; so tender and delectable, he thought his lover would melt in his mouth like candyfloss. Jay reacted to each sensation and stimulation received, with small sighs, a few squeals, and giggles of delight when his ticklish spot, above his right hip, was nibbled on. The scene went from a delicate, sensual tonguing of earlobes, nipples, and toes, to sucking and licking each other's genitalia and mouths, all within the confines of the small wooden bed, finally to end in a mad romp out the door and a frenzied ravishment in a paddock full of scratchy hay, with two horses looking on. An erotic series of images floated across the screen, of a handsome blond man loving a beautiful boy angel whom he sodomized continually, either bent over on his knees, or lying on his back. Jay lay fully exposed in the desert dust, with legs spread wide, hands widening the inviting opening, feet pointing toward the bright blue sky, and moaning with each thrusting penetration into his arse, which pulsated to the rhythm of his panting. Every detail of the loving, the fun, and the sexual desire, in both pairs of eyes, was filmed exquisitely. A paling evening sky became their canopy, until a purple haze engulfed the entwined, sexually connected men, capturing the final kiss of rapture and fading into the evening shadows. Another watercolor masterpiece ended; they barely heard the words, "It's a wrap, Gentlemen."

Lavender had kept her promise; and the two men watched her burn the footage too explicit for public viewing. David had seen the outtakes; Ted had not; for which the blond actor would be forever grateful, although unnerved at the very real possibility of duplicates. He had to remember the Mistress' promises and remain positive. She had been correct; the love scenes went beyond anything ever portrayed on film. Packed with power, the lovers looked, felt, and acted deliriously happy, making the act visionary and smoldering. All the eroticism and sensuality always seen in the rising mist of hot bodies reacting to the cold damp air, finally lost in the monochromatic haze of the purple dusk. How they captured each intimate moment, David could not imagine with his limited technical knowledge. Indescribable, this picture had to be seen and felt for the sexual impact, and the emotions evoked by the hapless victim. It was magic.

Saying good-bye to Lavender had been hard on David. Thinking about her grace and warmth, he was gently lulled into that tranquility, while enduring the long wait on the tarmac for their turn to take flight. His sad, weary face softened at the thought, but the nail biting continued. A remarkable woman, she taught them much, but not who she truly was, perhaps a secret to be learned in time. With Ted coming to terms with the impossibility of discovering her identity, David contented himself, knowing that she and Kincaid would be there for his partner. Their future lay within her hands; and if he felt the urge to stray, he would always remember to whisper a call on the wind.

Ted would start preparatory work with Steven within the month, after embarking on his two-week promotional tour, and then whisked away from his disastrous, dutiful life with Karen, to a location shoot in Mexico after Christmas. Much to David's sorrow, they required his partner to remain in his unhealthy state for his next role. He loved the man beyond reason, anyway he looked; but the strange eating habits had manifested into an obsessive desire to stay thin, even frailer for his next picture. The idea terrified the older actor of what might be the cause, afraid to believe or question the decision. Due to Ted's acute condition and at LaCoix's urging, Kincaid made an odd request of their director: they would film backward, with the last scene shot first, with Barrett's character dying. This would force the younger man to regain enough weight to look healthy at the start of the film. Ted would do anything for his art; it had to work.

After bidding farewell to Lavender, their magical Fey vanished into the darkness, leaving Ted and David to a long, sultry night of passion; a night neither man would forget. Morning had dawned too early; and they headed for Tucson in their favorite red toy. Looking behind them, La Rosa Negra wavered in a rising dust storm, whirling into a purple tornado of dirt and debris, lifting the mirage from the desert floor, to disappear as if it had never been. Everything they came to love was gone. Another mystery unsolved, both knew it would reappear on the sigh of a name. With the scent of lilacs as a constant reminder, and the rustle of wind chimes, now neatly packed in David's gear, they became his source of tranquility. Lavender remained in his mind, seeming to be an extension of himself, or more likely one of her appendages; he refused to guess over something that felt correct. Hoping Ted left with a memento of the peaceful place, he smiled, remembering the video and a very special bear.

A different spiritual world allowed them to open every door and window, to flutter freely with possibilities; it awakened the receptive mind of LaCoix, but played havoc on Barrett's mental state. Pondering incessantly upon the Mistress' words, Ted developed another obsession over her puzzle. LaCoix had asked Kincaid for another favor, to guide his unstable lover with these new thoughts, and if in doubt, to call for the *Lady of the Rocks*. A handshake deal, the older actor sighed in some relief. The two younger men had developed a friendship, two of a kind; and David felt confident Steven's interest lay elsewhere sexually. The famous face had someone else he cared for deeply, but a name never came up.

One day and two nights in Tucson, everything had been set in motion, with Ted now in overdrive, first checking the new Swiss accounts. Their money hidden, without a record of the transaction left behind. Feeling financially free, David had received a quick lesson on accessing his funds; and they eagerly sped to their next stop. Lavender's recommended lawyer agreed to take both cases, already primed to convince the District Attorney to investigate the dismantling of an abusive holy order, and to push forward civilly, for a baby in jeopardy and a father in mental anguish, all backed by a band of famous faces. Barrett immediately cut his ties with the men's group and resigned as Chairman of their children's welfare foundation, using work commitments as an excuse. He would remain within the church until informed otherwise. Promoting *Outlaw's Heart*, overseeing the house construction, and the preparatory work and filming in Mexico, would keep him clear of suspicion, away from the insurmountable stress. David feared it extended beyond the emotional capabilities of a Cancer who had defeated a stubborn Leo.

With his own pain returning, of bruised ribs and a black eye, David had them tended to at a clinic in Tucson, as well as medication for his ulcers. He also convinced his new partner to get his arm X-rayed and in a proper cast. It took some doing, but with a stern demand from his new producer, Ted relented. To all their horror, countless healed fracture lines, across both upper and lower arms, were clearly visible; and they received initial proof for their attorney's use. Although frightened of any medical procedure and the dreaded machines, Ted realized the need, knowing David insisted out of concern. The new lovers would spend the next month in discomfort; however, they had work to do; and as actors, they were obsessed with *bravado*.

Only the uncertainty of the custody battle rattled Ted, but with hope and happiness, he looked forward with positive thoughts of starting anew with David. They had spent a day at the new parcel of 160-acres, laughing over and planning every finite detail of the house. Easily finding the pastel rock formation, decisions came to fruition with the architect, landscaper, and contractor. Work commenced immediately, with a completion date of eight months. With everything in order and timed to the last placement of a hand-painted tile, Ted pledged his presence when the first bulldozer rolled in. No living plant or animal would become homeless or hurt, in the mayhem of the building process, only relocated.

Before LaCoix's departure for London, he heard that Steven called off his engagement. According to Barrett, the man appeared relieved; and David took solace in the ending of the would-be disaster. Strange to look at the familiar face on the front page of the tabloid he held, he studied the picture of the beautiful, once happy couple, along with all the lies and propaganda written and passed off as gospel. It was all trash. In typical Hollywood fashion, inexplicable reasons were given, as gossip did not start from within. No one spoke openly of such matters, each protecting themselves from slander, innuendo, and sometimes the truth. In this business of paranoia, it could be your ruination to talk about another actor's liabilities, particularly those wielding power. With only good wishes expressed publicly, it left the press to speculate on their own interpretations of harmless actions.

With one breakup splendidly announced in detailed form, David read of another, much further back in the scandal rag, from where two faces smiled at him. Out of his life officially, his attempt at letting Rebecca down gently had failed with a screaming tantrum heard for miles up and down Freeway 405. Waiting at the airport for him, on his return to Los Angeles, she confirmed nothing remained but showboating on both sides. The brunette vixen had met him in a fury, disparaging Lavender with jealousy rearing its twisted, two-horned head. She still misunderstood what the woman meant, which instantly enraged David. Stupidity, negativity, and intolerance no longer existed in his world. Without even the suggestion of remaining friends, the engagement dissolved before she dropped him in front of the Wilshire, his favorite getaway between arguments, separations, and marriages. Sighing with noticeable relief, he checked in with an expensive diamond ring in his pocket, to be returned to 'Harry Winston' in credit toward something more appropriate for another.

With Rebecca gone, and the townhouse sold the day it came on the market, due to the name of its previous owner, he shared a delightful two days with Holly and Susan. He loved his daughter, and he reflected on his detachment from his children. It changed, remembering Ted's needs; and David became consumed over the fate of his lover's unborn child. He envisioned the future of the poor creature, spending its life unhappy and hurt, with the best of intentions and the cruelest of torment. His children would never endure such atrocities, and his hugs and kisses grew more loving and caring, instead of the needed attention being forced. The aloof actor melted with one sweet baby kiss to his cheek from his youngest.

Holly never gave up on her father, loving him for who he was. She made him laugh when no one else could, one of the few people who understood his moods, even at the age of five. A little dynamo, imitating and looking like a female miniature of her handsome father, he had thrilled at his chance to take her knocking door-to-door, in her *Jane & the Dragon* outfit, on Halloween. He laughed along at each unexpected treat placed into her little jack-o'-lantern; it would be a happy memory to take with him.

Susan also came to understand the man, releasing him from the notion of getting back together, extremely gratified to get her own self-esteem back with the announcement of the broken engagement. A dagger viciously thrust into her back, she could not remove it readily. Forgiveness, however, came easily toward her former husband; a snake charmer and a dangerously wicked one that she still adored. The divorce would be finalized within the New Year, and to remain friends was all they wished. Life would go on normally for their only concern: Holly Jane.

David felt and looked more relaxed, than he had ever been, on his return to L.A.; and his friends and families saw it. Nothing was mentioned of Ted, but they had time, and with fingers crossed, his lover would be readily accepted when the day came. The first Mrs. LaCoix cheered him on; happy to hear the picture now grew directly from the book. One of her favorite novels, she had told David, long before the shoot, the script should be rewritten. His sons agreed, but were somewhat hesitant upon hearing their dad's subtle warnings of his scenes with another man. More laughter, embarrassed giggles, and a lot of teasing reverberated along the fiber optics between telephones. Promises made would be kept. With his two families no longer angry with him, he felt blessed with the lifting of the heavy guilt that lingered over both situations. To top it off, the call to his parents radiated with warmth; best wishes sent for his next endeavor. They looked forward to his return, back to a quieter lifestyle of his Arizona roots.

LaCoix's last day in town, he had his manuscript and a suitcase packed for a cold, damp winter in the English countryside. Only Ted remained; the call broke his heart. With one last torrid night of sex and sadness in Tucson, they separated unwillingly: LaCoix flew into LAX, and Barrett to San Diego. Trapped again, the youngest could not say the words aloud in his house, now full of unwanted family. Karen maintained her matriarchal status, assuming the role of the controlling, dominant partner. With the baby coming, and thus his presence unnecessary, until a second child deemed a requirement, she gave Ted little strife, and lived her life as one and a half. By the time the baby arrived, they would have secured proof and witnesses of his allegations; but the divorce and custody suits depended on many factors not yet in play.

With only a quiet, forlorn good-bye stated, the haunting sound of a disconnected line was all that remained of Theodore Barrett until Christmas. David pressed the inanimate object to his lips, caressing it, and yearning for one more touch, one more word, and one more lingering sigh. The sound, of his lifeline to his lover, had been reprogrammed to the magical tinkling of chimes; and he sadly finished packing the last remnant of his heart.

Eleven o'clock of a starless, lonely night, a surprise knock on his door made him put down his nightly bourbon. The portal opened; and Ted appeared out of nowhere, jumping into arms that needed him. David had wanted every inch of the man, the scent of him, the feel of him, the sight of him, and the sound of him, purring and whispering in pleasure and passion. Arm cast and all, LaCoix squeezed the thin body of a man who had his arms around his neck, his legs wrapped around his hips, and his mouth smothering him with frantic kisses. With his arms full of the most treasured of gifts, David had kicked the door shut, fumbled to lock it, and carried his lover to an inviting bed, where they both fell into their favorite position for the taking. Bruised ribs proved of no consequence this last night of promises, stripping off clothing, as the smaller man bit, chewed, and clawed to get at his knight. Full of unbridled passion, very unlike his passive Teddy Bear, David rolled off the bed, grabbed some left over lubricant, and gently smoothed it over the opening he remembered touching the first time. Steaming hot and deliciously plum-colored, Ted exposed himself by opening his thighs, raising the hungry orifice to pucker and twitch, and spreading the opening wider, allowing a finger easy access to press delicately on the erotic gland, while accompanied by a squeal of impatience. On the command to enter and push deep, David could not resist such temptation, and he lunged. Back and forth, hard and fast, Ted groaned for more and cried with every thrust. Through the tears and panting, they lost control; and the ravishment had them spent but unsatisfied, not to rekindle until one returned to fulfill them both for the rest of their years.

With but a few hours sleep, David had woken to feel the warm, smaller body. His arms wrapped tighter around his real live Teddy Bear, afraid to let go of the man, so strong and adventuresome one minute, and so dependent and needy the next. Never had he met anyone like him. With Barrett so shaken by David's leaving, the entire morning filled with whispers of tender, reassuring words, and touches and kisses to prove every one spoken.

After a tumultuous lunch in his suite, David had left the tear-stained face, to settle his bill and head out the door toward the taxi under the landmark canopy. He could not turn to face the window above, where Ted cried silently, abandoned with all the responsibility of building a life for the two of them. The two of them--the grim-faced blond actor took great comfort in the thought--a promised gift to carry halfway around the world. Reaching the airport, through afternoon traffic from hell, David hung over the precipice, trying to control his strained emotions. The sun bleached hair and deeply tanned face remained stoic, except for those ever-present nails between his teeth, and the wild, green eyes darting everywhere under the dark sunglasses. He craved a smoke and a shot of bourbon; he declined from indulging in either. Promises made would be kept.

Terminal B was jammed on his arrival. Two security attendants, informed of his arrival by Rod Morris, rushed to his rescue, and quietly and quickly ushered him into the VIP lounge. With his bags and ticket check-in taken care of by others, the advantages came with notoriety. They finally left him alone to walk the long, narrow corridor to the plane, but first running the gauntlet of metal detectors and dogs sniffing his carry-on bag.

A porter had tapped him on the shoulder. Being the last to go through and minutes late, the touch jump-started his sad heart. Walking in a dream, he believed himself completely alone, and he spun around to come face-to-face with someone he knew. "Sir Edmund, what are you doing here?"

"Sir, a young man asked me to give you this." The huge bear was placed in his arms. Dazed and slightly puzzled, unknowing the reasons for its return, he fumbled for a few dollars to tip the expressionless porter.

"Where is he?" David peered down the hallway, until his sorrowful, wet eyes came to rest on the small figure, to which the uniformed man pointed toward. A discreet wave, and Ted, with his magical mane still flowing down his back, disappeared into the crowd unnoticed. "Soon you will recognize that face, as well as you know Steven Kincaid's."

The porter nodded and thanked him for the tip.

"Well, Mr. LaCoix, what do we have here? We find these delightful passengers the least troublesome. Please hand me your lovely, big bear. I'm sorry, but I'm going to nuke you under the scanner, if I can stuff you through. You're so large; I may have to resort to poking the daylights out of you, before letting you pass."

"Not me, I hope." David had smiled in thanks for the needed chuckle and the lighthearted mood of the security guard. He looked down instantly, unable to hide his distress.

"That would be fun, and certainly something to tell my daughters; however, we must check your friend for illegal substances, or potentially lethal weapons, like ten claws; or do bears have twelve? You never know what these innocent, cuddly creatures may have in store. Is he a gift from a friend?" The cherubic woman in uniform, placing and scanning bags on the conveyor belt, happily enjoyed herself with Sir Edmund in an attempt to cheer up one of her favorite movie stars who appeared upset. She found most celebrities required coddling, either being standoffish or too nice. Mr. LaCoix seemed unable to hide behind either mask.

"Yes, a very thoughtful gift, from a dear friend."

"Please step through the metal detector, sir. I'm sure your friend is gone, as you are the last to go through, and no one seems to be around. Don't forget this letter attached to your traveling companion. He is a lovely present. Have a safe journey, Mr. LaCoix."

"Thanks." Once through, David had grabbed his carry-on bag, his warm coat, and a five-foot tall, fat bear. With a heavy sigh, he made his way stoically to face the torturous ten odd hour journey. *Lonely* hit his thoughts again; Ted had been right; it was exactly how he felt with empty arms. He knew his partner would be frantically driving back to San Diego in worse shape, with no rational explanation to give the Barrett family for his overnight disappearance, or the nasty bites and scratches all over his body, if any of them looked closely. A shudder raced up his spine at what lay in wait for such a deed.

A flight attendant had aided him to his seat with his items, while he clenched his jaw, fighting to stay in control. No one claimed the seat beside him in First Class; and he settled in, relieved to be in his own company to read the letter, and to buckle Sir Edmund into the position next to him. Doors locked, the plane vibrated to a low hum, and a flight check took place. He opened the tasteful card slowly, to see Ted's picture fall into his lap. His heart dropped right along with it. Quickly picking it up, those sad blue eyes gazed straight into him, and the contrasting bright smile inscribed itself deeply into his very being, allowing him to grin back as he always did. Shy and timid, the fake smile could and would break millions of hearts. Carefully storing the treasured image in his wallet, for future viewing, he knew he would have it worn out by the time he returned to receive another.

The card, with a teddy bear on the front, was opened slowly, one hand shielding his face from anyone's view, to read the sentiments within. Tumbling over in his head, David heard the sound of the words, begging him to keep the heart, given freely, in one piece, and to have only Sir Edmund in his arms. The reason behind the return of the bear burdened his shoulders with guilt of what he must not do; but in turn, Ted sacrificed his only source of security with little thought of his own needs. His loving partner had returned the gift selflessly to David, to keep him warm, to make him feel wanted, and to keep him on his path. Underlying the treasure and the words was trust.

Deeply hurt that Ted lacked confidence in him, LaCoix would prove him wrong when he returned Sir Edmund to the proper arms, and a half dozen just like him, at Christmas. Just over six weeks, they would be together again, if only for a short time. The handsome actor leaned sideways and pulled the head of the bear toward him. Inhaling deeply, he could smell the scent of Theodore Barrett. The bear would always remain close.

After safely stowing away his last memento, he picked up the trashy magazine with Kincaid's picture on the cover. Upon reading both absurd stories, he closed it along with a chapter on his former life. One last sigh, he regained control, only to startle at a female whisper. "We'll be departing immediately, Mr. LaCoix. Is there something I can bring you?"

"Something rare and black." Lost in thoughts of Ted and the Mistress, and when he would see them again, David eased into his seat, which would be home for exactly ten hours and fifteen minutes, not including the insurmountable time spent sitting on runways. He never slept on these long journeys, his way of fending off jetlag, and had already declined the use of the layout bed British Airways provided.

"Pardon me?"

"Sorry, just your best burgundy with all meals."

"And your friend?" The woman teased, her English accent reminding David of the peculiar, raven-haired gentleman, with the whimsical personality, whom he still could not place.

"Usually champagne to tickle his nose, but he won't be having any for six weeks. Thanks anyway." David gave her a slight smile, turned his head, and closed his eyes. The pressure of take-off pulled him into his plush seat; and he lingered a moment on his radical change in attitude and life, as he thanked the Mistress, and in return, felt her presence brush his cheek. She gave him the honest love promised; and he accepted Ted gratefully. The thought of what he asked for evoked a slight chuckle. Theodore Barrett was all those things and more; a man who made his toes curl; but he wondered why he had not specified a woman. From that day forward, an old saying imbedded itself in his mind: *be careful what you wish for*. David LaCoix was gone, flying into the next day, into a new beginning in the land of green, fog, and magic; and with the blink of an amber eye, into the *knowing*.

CHAPTER 25

December 19, and David LaCoix, once again, soared over a sea of clouds. They beckoned him to jump, appearing to be a more comfortable place to land than returning to a list of unknown factors. He had been in England over six weeks, and accomplished the necessary elements of the picture, before cameras started to roll. The character, of Lord Worthington-Smythe, came together under a strict, but ingenious director, along with David's own take on the macabre. Besides being one of the few actors who could play the part, he appeared a clone of the mysterious Lord. His intensity and sense of insanity had grown, not from the words written, but from his personal life.

It started when Theodore Barrett and David LaCoix became household names the day their erotic Western astonishingly released December 1, superseding the gross first weekend box-office draw of any movie made that year. No one believed editing would be completed in such a short span of time, with the pre-release promotions and preliminary screenings commencing the week after David's departure. The Lady Lavender swept the world with her magic, holding all spellbound with the controversial film, simply entitled *Outlaw's Heart.* LaCoix viewed his video copy weeks before the Premier, very pleased with the results. An artistic masterpiece, his mouth gaped from beginning to end; his arousal had him perspiring through the heavy woolen sweaters needed for English winter nights. The congratulatory call to Ted had been breathless and excited. Equally, in awe of what they helped create, his co-star fumbled for words in his enthusiasm, indicated by the return of his stutter.

Communication, between the two, had been frequent and extremely erotic in nature those first weeks in November, during which time Ted lived alone in luxury hotels while on the promotional parade. Difficult to stay in control, David listened to every raspy whisper of endearment, and what his young lover boldly dreamed of doing to the older man once reunited. Very unlike Barrett to be sexually blatant, David appreciated the effort, and in return, answered in equal passion for his lonely Teddy Bear. The conversations, hushed breathlessly, had both men's heads spinning, not to mention their free hands sliding up and down their aroused organs to come with an overwhelming sensation of relief, ending each good-bye with a groan of self-satisfaction. David did not look forward to the day their steamy calls would become *yes* or *no* answers on Ted's return home. With too many people in his house, watching him intently, they had him gagged.

Barrett spent most of November on the road promoting one film, while studying the script for his next. Watching the bashful man being forced to converse had David laughing in sympathy and delight. The shyness of the young actor became public knowledge, when barely able to make a full statement to the crack-up comedic-like hosts of every talk show. Overall, they could be very cruel, making their guests squirm, particularly one as vulnerable as Ted. Trying to get the real scoop on the sultry scenes, and what the young star thought of David LaCoix, seemed an innocent joke to all, except for the one who blushed through his actor's plastic smile, while coughing in fits until someone offered him water. He always answered the same way, "David is a patient and extraordinary actor who can make anyone look good." The next question would be answered with an uncharacteristic comment from Barrett, shocking the audience, and certainly the host, unsure of what he inferred.

"What was it like to be kissed so intensely, and in such close physical intimacy with another man, especially with the likes of the infamous lady-killer, David LaCoix? Those close-ups were extreme. If I didn't know better, I'd swear you both gave it your all, if you know what I mean?"

"I can certainly understand why women take great pleasure in his company." Embarrassed laughter from the audience turned to gasps with the teasing words, giving him a moment's reprieve from any host, only to be bombarded with more demands for further explanation. They received only a shake of a shaggy mane of hair and more snickering. If nothing else, Ted's innocent, sweet innuendoes would send droves of LaCoix fans to the theatres, along with making his own presence felt.

Pride had shone through David's smile, amused with each clip received by courier. Genuinely happy that his lover handled himself with great charm, the older actor's enjoyment also came from not having to participate. He hated this side of filmmaking; a dreadful ordeal to explain movies you hated, and even harder to endorse, enthusiastically, ones you liked. The Premier had to rank as the worst possible nightmare, with the shakes and an upset stomach the affair induced. David usually avoided these momentous occasions of insecurity over a potential disaster. Opening Night of *Outlaw's Heart*, however, remained permanently etched in his memory. Green eyes fixated on the video of the event, watching microphones coming very close to the boyish face and that of his escort for the night, Steven Kincaid.

Kincaid--he had become the enemy--one David had not foreseen. First stage, of preparatory work for *Brother Mine,* concluded near the end of November, when Ted returned to San Diego. The rigors of the promotional tour, the stress of returning home, the intensity of the next character portrayed, and the Arizona contractor making demands, took their toll mentally on Barrett. He started to decrease the length of their calls; the tone of his voice sounded polite, becoming frosty. The seduction of Ted by Kincaid appeared a possible consideration for the change; but a sexual liaison deemed unlikely, considering both were bottoms and extremely passive ones, as per gossip from Ted, and David's own inside sources. Answers became evident in their last phone call, shortly after the excited banter about the Premier. LaCoix remembered every detail.

"Hey, Teddy Bear, can you talk?" David continued to be cognizant when it came to Mrs. Barrett.

"Yeah, no one's home. How are you?" Cold, but civil, Ted gave the impression he had little interest in any kind of reply.

"What's going on? You're sounding very distant."

"Stevie's getting married."

"He's what?" David sprang from his chair at the single statement and started pacing. Kincaid was gay; there was no doubt. One of Lavender's lost Spirits, he had turned his back, blatantly ignoring her, and going against everything she so patiently gave, including an introduction to a new love interest: Ethan Peerce. Another famous hidden gay actor, this man had more box office appeal than Kincaid. Older than David, still incredibly sexy and a rare talent, Peerce's recommendation had won LaCoix his latest role. According to Ted, a bolt of love-at-first-sight scorched the two mega-stars, melding them into one. David could not believe Steven's abrupt turnaround to cast the man aside so readily and so soon. Warning bells went off in his head, shattering his consciousness, while the voice at the other end repeated the unwanted news.

"He's getting married to the woman he was engaged to. Stevie said they played the ruse to get the press off the scent of their wedding. It's this Saturday."

"And you believe him? Are you going?" Again, alarms rang loud enough to make his head implode. Visions of purple mist filled his room and surrounded him like a cocoon. He heard the Mistress' voice, unable to do anything but listen and repeat what he felt in his head. No longer in control, and not knowing if he wanted to be, he waited. Ted's voice snapped him back to the present.

"It's going to be a huge event."

"Why didn't he let me know? I thought we were friends; and he knows our situation, especially yours." Cruel silence reached across a continent and an ocean, except for the annoyed-sounding sigh from the California coast. David stopped breathing, sensing the answer. "Don't worry, Ted. He asked you and Karen; the show must go on. What about Peerce?"

"He wasn't invited either. After Steven told him, Ethan expressed his anger, by venting through the script written for today's fight scene. Like *Outlaw's Heart*, the acting became real. Ethan nearly beat the crap out of him; and no one came to his aid. I tried, but he's incredibly strong and just tossed me across the room. Stevie's bruised and pretty scraped up. At least someone had the sense to yell *Cut*; and Peerce just walked away. Ethan frightens me, David; and Stevie will be plastered with make-up the day of his wedding."

"Kincaid deserved it. Did Peerce hurt you? How are you handling all this?" David prepared himself for the next potential blow.

"That's a horrible thing to say, LaCoix. You told me no one deserved to be intentionally hurt or beaten. Things have changed; I've decided not to pursue the divorce. I'm staying with Karen."

The worst possible answer, the tonality of the voice did not ring true, sounding like rehearsed dialogue. The words spoken did not deter LaCoix from asking a string of questions in an angry snarl. His face turned crimson; the veins in his forehead and neck pulsated through skin stretched to the maximum; and his mouth clenched so tightly, only one corner of it curled up to growl out an attack to crush the Spirit on the other end of the line. "What in hell are you thinking? What about the baby and the criminal investigation? Have you forgotten the plan, or was it all lies?" His hand shook so hard, his grip could snap the communication device into splinters, if the pressure increased further.

"I know now; it's Christ's way. Stevie and I spent an entire evening talking with someone he admires. This man's into Scientology; and he made us see that our desires are deviant in the eyes of the Lord. I have to do this, David. This is my calling; my true path to what is right."

"That's just fucking great, Barrett; and the son-of-a-bitch promised to take care of you. He's dead for this; you can tell him that. I cannot believe, after what you've been through, you would give up everything because of a stranger's opinion. How did you get involved in the first place? Steven told him about us, didn't he? Have you lost your mind?" David hit the stonewall with his fist, swearing in excruciating agony, instilling more rage. Their secret could turn into blackmail with this insidious creature, and probably already in use to keep Kincaid in line. "If I'm right about this man's identity, that self-righteous bastard is Steven's obsession resurrected. He fucked the life out of your friend throughout the filming of the picture they made here in England. Do you understand what I'm saying, Ted? It's common knowledge, in the privacy act of Hollywood, that he treated Steven abominably. Every morning, in the inn where the cast lodged, they found traces of violence, including ropes, handcuffs, bloodstains--and not just a few drops--and then the son-of-a-bitch went home to his wife and kiddies. Now what do you think of him? I have an awful feeling about this, Ted. Steven's marrying to please this atrocity of a human being; an abusive lover who wants to entangle him in insidious games; and now he's involved you. Christ, I wish you could see through all this crap. Don't go, Ted. Please, do not attend the wedding." David could only think of reaching into the unseen optic fibers to grab Barrett by the throat, unable to squeeze it hard enough for his own satisfaction.

"Shut up, LaCoix. It's a marriage; and I want to see Stevie happy. He's had a rough time since we left the realm of Satan." The voice on the other end strained to stay calm; and David knew exactly how easy it would be to snap the strings.

"Stop right there, Mister; La Rosa Negra shone as a glorious oasis of mystery for both of us; and you dare call Lavender Satan? You know nothing, boy. She helped you recognize the potential of your life, explaining the truth, which finally reached your child-like brain. We both experienced the fun and euphoria. You're turning your back on us all. I suppose you'll be changing to Scientology along with Steven. Say good-bye to even more of your money, Baby, although, it puts you into the ranks to ascend higher professionally. It's the name of the game now in Hollywood. Like being a Mason's son, your chances of stealing a role, because of your religious affiliation, have grown astronomically."

"Christ has shown me the way back to what is right; and I have no intentions of joining the man's church. Give me a little credit. I have one of my own, so just leave us alone." Ted returned the anger; but David only saw the vision of the man back on his knees, praying to the Virgin Mary. He wanted to gag.

"Us, is it? If that's what you want, Barrett, but please, don't go to the wedding; take it as an intuitive warning. It's not a marriage, but a sacrifice. Christ didn't pull you back from forces of the unholy; your fear and guilt, along with Kincaid and company, accomplished that. You still don't see why he's doing this. It's all for a promise, from his obsession, of some sadistic sex on the side, to satisfy them both, while living within the confines of their marriages of convenience. It's sick, Ted, and sounds perfect for his abuser, but a disaster for Kincaid. You might as well tear his heart out now, and serve it as the main course at the grand gala."

"Stop it! You don't know anything. Lavender has you by the balls, squeezing them until they're ready to burst. What's the difference?" A sob stuck in Barrett's throat, but nary a tear fell.

"That's it then, Ted. Your wish is granted; I'll leave you alone. I thought, and still know, you will be my last love." His timbre justified the sad, yet angry sentiment. The water sign doused the fiery Leo; the resulting steam rose to leave a smoldering ember to die a slow death.

"Don't say that. I'm sorry, but you'll find someone else." The voice spluttered in panic, attempting to absolve himself in David's eyes and give his idol a choice.

"Go to hell, as you believe it to be. I assume you've called off the investigation, to accept full responsibility of protecting your child. You can exclude my house from your busy schedule as well. I don't want you within fifty miles of the border points. Understood! I'll take care of it myself. Any hint of you, having anything to do with it, will be remodeled and the old plan burned. There will be nothing left to remind me you were ever involved." David went very quiet with his threat. He seethed with hatred for everyone concerned; and tears fell throughout the Cosmos for the death of a love affair.

"No, David, please, I love working on the house; don't take it away from me; and stop your vindictive crusade; it will only hurt people. It's not necessary now. I'm begging you, man."

David ignored the plea, intensifying the hatred toward the dead, black, chunk of coal, which was once Ted's heart to keep safe. "Stay out of Arizona, and out of my way. Your church will pay for what it's done to you. I intend to vanquish it, boy, without you ever knowing what happened. If I have to take your baby away from you and Karen to protect it, or any other abused child from that sanctimonious institution of the misguided, I will. You can put money on the table with that promise." David stopped abruptly. The words coming out of his mouth were not his, but a strange echo of his own thoughts. They sounded like threats, capable of being said and accomplished only by the Mistress. She spoke to Barrett through him; and he could not stop her, nor did he want to.

"Don't do this. Please stop. I can protect my baby." Tears splashed against the small plastic phone in California. Devastated and trapped, Ted could say nothing to justify his actions in LaCoix's mind.

"No you can't, unless you leave Karen and kidnap your child. If that is your plan, I hope your money remains hidden. Is Kincaid's film your last? Look at the monumental surge of fame you recently acquired, only to increase when *Brother Mine* comes out. The notoriety you wanted, as a great actor, hell, it was all yours, Baby; and you're tossing it back into the wishing well. Who's the fool, Barrett?"

"I can't deal with you when you're angry. You can't see the whole picture." With no ammunition left to fight, Ted expected David to be upset, but not cruel. The ugly side of the notorious actor surfaced to stomp on *Peter Pan,* who helplessly flittered about to avoid being swatted like a gnat. Not listening to the words, or the sentiments, Ted was lost. The respect, of the only one who mattered, disintegrated into dust, along with his dreams.

"Better than you, boy, and I'm not stopping. You've never seen me when I'm steamed, ready to roll over anyone in my way. Go to the wedding with your domineering ice queen, and submissively confirm your vows in the front row. I'll make a wager, with Lavender, as to how long you can go without being ass-fucked. The sweet taste of real life's honey, Barrett, and you're craving it now. You can feel me, can't you, slowly sliding in and out, in and out, tickling and teasing. Your tiny hole is twitching. Better run to the nearest sex shop and buy yourself an anal vibrator--make it giant size--you'll be using it for a long time."

More attacks of vindictiveness chilled Ted into retaliatory snarls. "You're being hateful and disgusting; and stop calling me *boy*."

"Good-bye, *boy*, and grow up. *Go with Christ*, as you would say. Follow along like a good little lamb." Before a rebuttal could be iterated, the call, on the London end, disconnected in a crushing clap of cheap plastic, finally breaking the frame in his strong hand. Nauseous with grief, and frantic to throw a breakable object against the far wall, LaCoix held the bad-news object in his shaking hand, but could not let go of the demon machine. That was it; the end of his life as he thought it might be. Purple mist enveloped David; love and tenderness held him together that night; the man and the apparition cried holy tears.

After the final salty drops of grief had ebbed, the cloud disappeared, leaving David alone by the roaring fire. He shivered immediately upon the release of the warm embrace of the ghostly entity. The Mistress left him to his own misery; and the ancient stone fireplace seemed to permeate the rented manor house with shadows of doom and dark forces. Only one thing could release him from the nightmare of the hideously cruel call; and he headed directly to the workout room. He painted Barrett's face symbolically on one side, and Kincaid's on the other, of the kickboxing bag; and with every ounce of power, he pummeled them both with feet and fists until dead, forever buried but not forgotten. Oblivious to their first lesson, his thoughts of destruction manifested themselves, creating havoc on the other side of an earthly sea of tossing waves.

Even with the Morris family living in the same house, LaCoix became a recluse within the guarded gates of the manor, seldom seen except on the set. Every so often, someone spotted him walking in the meadow, or the thick woods, seeming in search of something. Lavender became his only light shining at the end of his dark tunnel. His life, turned upside down for the third time in a year, loneliness confronted him once again.

Lavender sent her presence to her cherished David LaCoix whenever he called. She could not tell him what she knew, or of her plans. Her duty lay in saving those who still had a chance; Barrett and Kincaid were another matter. Partially her mistake, for allowing them to meet, she violently threw her bottle of rare ambrosia into the darkness of the Cosmos that one hurtful night, only to watch it float aimlessly in the non-atmosphere of space. She made her decision. Steven had run out of chances; she could do no more; her wrath was fused. Only LaCoix could possibly bring Barrett back into the light of his now closed awakening. It would be a hard door to knock down a second time. Maybe a little Mistress mischief could bring some order into the Cosmos. She gloated and raised her bejeweled fingers, to cover a sinister smile never seen by others. With another candle lit--a black one--an idea brewed behind the fiendish eyes of a lethal feline.

Regret crossed her face, only for the loss of a bottle of her ambrosia. With a quiet sigh, she sat in her chair to gaze upon her many worlds. A point of her finger produced another full bottle, to sit on the rich colored tapestry covering the table next to her. A glance of those eyes flashed red; her goblet filled at a thought. On a day of cakes, flowers, and floating ribbons, she would deal with the situation between Barrett and LaCoix, Kincaid and Peerce, Mr. and Mrs. Barrett, and Kincaid and bride. Her other choice would be to leave them to the Fates, to fend for themselves. Unfortunately, such abandonment would interfere with the innocent bride's future. Lavender pulled back her hair, deciding another meeting deemed in order with the young woman's Caretaker. Having grown tired of one game, it would end on the next unholy Saturday afternoon.

CHAPTER 26

Melodic sounds of a string quartet floated through a clear California sky that early December afternoon. The shouting and screaming of young women around the globe could be heard as far away as the ghostly estate in the English countryside. Steven Kincaid was getting married. One nervous actor sat up late that night, thousands of miles away, with the hope he would see his lost love via television. Still unbelievable to him, confirmation came through loud and clear; the rich and famous were more important to the general populace than the many Civil Wars killing thousands of people and laying everything to waste over justice, culture, religion, humanity, and the environment. An appalling social dilemma, and yet there LaCoix sat, transfixed by a sacrificial wedding, only seen via the CNN helicopter and *Entertainment Tonight*.

Interviews conducted at the front gate drew his main interest. Good friends, with famous faces, expressed their best wishes before entering the private gardens. A chill went up David's spine; the serpent killer of love's death showed his fangs to the camera, along with his beautiful wife. The smug, smiling face had Steven whipped and cuffed for his own dispiteous pleasures, leaving LaCoix to growl at an enemy, to which he could not wage war.

With nails chewed to nothing, David waited for the clock to strike midnight at the manor house, and the late afternoon sun to bask down on his once-upon-a-time lover. It took some time, but Ted emerged alone, looking frail and distraught behind his flashing Hollywood whites. He wore his Born-Again-Christian mask, the one with dead eyes and hated plastic smile, but Karen Barrett seemed missing from his arm. David wondered why, after another sighting proved Ted attended the affair solo; and the darting blue eyes seemed to be scanning for an escape route from the attention his presence created. He appeared half past death and completely lost. David's heart sank, peering at the gaunt figure who stumbled over his answers to the many questions fired at him. Hitting the blond actor like a brick to the side of his head, he had manifested his vengeful attacks and hateful thoughts onto his only love. David could not feel worse, and tried to think of someone able to decode the mystery etched in Barrett's frown. With no mutual acquaintances, it left LaCoix to solve the riddle.

A telephoto lens, of amazing magnitude, scanned the mansion grounds of the beautifully terraced gardens. This particular Saturday, it sprang to life with red and white flowers, full of Christmas spirit and holy bliss. Enormous white awnings covered (what LaCoix knew to be) a lavish and expensive spread of rare delicacies and flowing champagne. He sipped his own bourbon, returning to gnaw on his nails until they bled, unable to forget the few celebrations he shared with Barrett. The bubbles tickled when they popped against Ted's fine nose, always making the young man giggle with as much effervescence as the liquid itself. Shaking away the memory, David remained vigilant, watching the sanctity of marriage crumble under another Hollywood illusion. Swept away by sadness, his concern veered toward the unknowing bride, triggering an instant need to find his hidden cigarette package stashed in his dresser. Having abstained from the habit since the day he entered the labyrinth, the present disturbing act weighed too heavy without a smoke in hand. On the strains of something other than *Here Comes the Bride*, he sat back down.

David shuddered when he saw an anomaly on the horizon, and held his breath beyond his limit. A misty, lavender funnel whirled angrily, growing larger as it drew nearer the shore, skimming the ocean's sparkling surface. It hovered indecisively, and then headed straight for the mainland, ripping off every piece of canvas covering, sending potted flowers flying, and causing havoc amongst the gathering with its force. People screamed while scrambling up the terraces to distance themselves from the cliff, which ended the property in a magnificent display of rocks, bushes, and weeds. Once breathtaking to look upon, it now became deadly if you drew too near. Even the unemotional broadcasting crew had trouble staying calm, babbling nonsense about something only David understood. The unearthly twister hurt no one, looking for something or someone in particular. Gasping in panic, he leaned toward the television, grabbing it on either side with both hands and yelling into it. "No, Lavender! No, please stop."

The color of the tornado changed to a deeper hue; a simple acknowledgment, to those of the *knowing*, that the Mistress was serious. Nothing or no one would stop her unknown plan. A terrified throng of guests tried to save themselves, but their shrieks appeared to be mimed gestures, inaudible with the roar of the whirlwind. Confused and frightened, the bride was scooped up by her father, along with yards of white satin, while she screamed in horror at her hapless groom. Singled out and pushed closer to the cliff's edge, as time became an eternity, the purple tornado took only a second. Steven Kincaid vanished with a scream, unheard and unseen by those above.

A well-placed shrub broke his fall; and he hung precariously with both hands around its base. With the chopper moving in dangerously close, the cameras on board caught the frightening event in every detail. The eerie phenomenon pounded him, blowing and twisting in its anger, trying to loosen his grip. David was aghast; Lavender wanted Kincaid dead. One false move, on Steven's part, would turn him into a shark canapé, first impaled by the sharp rocks below, then into the crashing white foam to wash them clean.

With a cigarette fired up and held within trembling fingers, David's lips quivered uncontrollably, unable to hold the much-needed tranquilizing weed. Finally inhaling, he choked on the drug. Coughing in fits from the toxic smoke and caught with an unwanted surprise, LaCoix spotted Ted making a break for the edge, running and stumbling to see what remained of his friend. Lying on his stomach, the man looked down cautiously, scanning the cliff visible to him; the only guest who knew Kincaid clung to life.

David yelled into the television to stop him. It was futile. Ted gently eased back, stood up, and frantically commenced stripping off his formal black jacket, the strangling tie, and the unstable black loafers and socks. Entirely focused on his next move, he did not hear the attempted telepathic alarm coming from a great distance. The funnel touched him gently, unsuccessful at warding him off. No one could stop Ted--no one tried--he was on his own. A million miles away, David screamed in unabashed anger and dire fear.

Barrett climbed halfway down to Kincaid with only his hands, one still in a removable plastic cast to his elbow, and his feet, expertly finding foot and handholds in the cliff's naturally textured surface. Steep, rocky, and treacherously unstable, the cliff had to be conquered. Ted inched his way closer to the hanging man; David saw only the Frenchman and held his breath. He also saw and knew why Ted could retain his fix, while Steven's position continued to disintegrate. The shrubbery slowly loosened enough to give way, just as a thin arm, with a white cast, reached down to grab a friend's hand only with his fingertips. One quick athletic maneuver on Kincaid's part had his other hand gripping Ted's plastic arm support, which incurred all the weight. Two men heard the crack, then another, and the accompanying groan. Another lifesaving reflex by Steven, he had his hands firmly digging into flesh and a leather belt, as the shrub and cast tumbled free, to end their existence violently on the rocks below, and swept out to sea. A hundred foot drop, the same peril awaited the look-alikes. The pain and terror on both faces increased, hearing the funnel roar its banshee-like scream of frustration, while it desperately tried to separate the fragile connection between the two.

David's eyes darted wildly over the screen, shouting instructions as if Ted could hear. He yelled again for help. "Lavender, please, it's not their time. What are you doing? Please, Mistress, don't do this. You're losing control, like the night you burned down the Barrett house. You'll regret this. Stop now, before you kill them. You're worse than the Fates." His voice trailed off, and he sank to his knees. With his eyes two inches from the screen, he gasped for air when the twister turned instantly into a soft lilac mist to embrace the two men in a safety net. His last pleading words worked, although Kincaid and Barrett remained in jeopardy. The smaller man clung by a firm handhold with his good arm, while the much taller one struggled to gain some solid footing. Both pressed themselves against the rock, with Steven holding Ted fast, appearing to protect him from flying dust and debris. Exhausted and injured from the first part of their ordeal, they glued themselves to the hard surface, while the softening cloud moved in closer to cover and support them.

Ted peered up, obviously figuring out a way to climb up the rugged face. He did not have to worry; the rescue team arrived and immediately started their descent on either side of the pair. With ropes and harnesses quickly fastened and secured, Ted expertly tested each to satisfy his own cautious nature. Adrenaline pumped furiously throughout a world watching in fear, or more likely, the strange magnetism that drew people to a disaster. The two super-stars defied humanities need for a death scene, using brute strength and terror-driven willpower, to clamor over the edge into waiting rescuers' hands.

Stricken into stunned silence, Kincaid understood what happened and who did it. Barrett went immediately into shock from the pain of his arm, and a claustrophobic attack caused by the circling throng of people, all reaching out to capture him. Ted felt himself being dragged into the darkness of the pit, by an ever-growing nest of serpents with unblinking eyes meant to blind. They were everywhere. With their hot breath felt behind him, beside him, leering at him, he had no place to hide and he dare not look. Phobic hysteria took over; and he could not hear the one familiar calming voice in his head above his own screams for people to retreat.

David grew quiet, drifting away to the day of the rockslide and their reception when they rode around the boulders. This time, both Barrett and Kincaid hid from view, surrounded by paramedics rushing them to a waiting ambulance. Ted attempted an escape in his panic, only to be wrestled onto a gurney, strapped down, and injected with a powerful sedative. He was out in seconds. Sirens pierced the air in warning of a tragedy; and they sped away. Once off the estate, they disappeared but for the helicopter following the flashing lights. Out of sight, an equally exhausted man, in a cold, damp castle, slumped to the floor to thank Ted's *Lady of the Rocks* for her mercy.

The Mistress fulfilled part of her plan; she stopped and indefinitely postponed the wedding. Her attempt to slay Kincaid, however, had David unnerved and perplexed. Suddenly, the same purple tornado appeared before him, and an ethereal image took form within the calm eye of the twister. She hovered within the quieting cloud of lilac smelling air, floating on a warm breeze that fluttered her gown and feathered her hair behind her. David fell under her spell, his corn-silk strands tossing in the aftermath, and his nostrils picking up the scent that took him away to another time, another place, another reality.

"You are also a hero, David LaCoix, although no one will ever know. I heard you, and you were correct; it was not Kincaid's time."

"Lavender, what were you thinking?"

"It is not your concern. I tried to keep Theo safe, but unfortunately his arm has been damaged further."

"You promised to be there for him, just as you promised Steven and me. What am I supposed to believe now," LaCoix lamented.

"Mr. Barrett made his choice; one of the few he braved on his own. I am tired, David; an eternity is crushing me. I do hope, when you cross the Chasm, you shall be appointed a more endearing job."

"Is there one? I thought saving Spirits, from the dreaded Fates, would be gratifying enough. Can't think of anything better than allowing people the chance to rectify their lives, whatever those lives are supposed to be. The act perpetrated on Kincaid did not seem appropriate for you. Direct interference is not your way, or so you say. You tried to kill a man today. Why? Why don't you focus on the truly evil side of the population? This is not a confusing issue, Lavender."

"You are becoming aware faster than anticipated, David; but then I have told you a great deal before your time. As to your ramblings of honest questions, we do not have to justify our actions to humankind. There is a reason for everything, and that is enough said; but to keep you from jumping to erroneous conclusions, other Caretakers attended to prevent possible disasters and maintain futures yet to be played out. One in particular was the bride's, to steady her path; the young woman shall succeed in her first goals chosen, before meeting Steven."

"Then what of Kincaid? Does he not have a future with strong enough goals, or are they of little importance? I don't know why I care, but I do."

"You are human; and I am glad to hear some compassion for a dastardly Fate of your own. He will be dealt with." A sigh from the cloud enlarged its field, surrounding David in a consoling circle of spring colors and warm breezes. The scent filled his senses and the chimes numbed his terror. Back into the gentle calm, she lulled him to sleep, unaware of being lifted and tenderly settled onto his bed. A voice on a wisp of air assured him of Ted's safety; and he slept.

Newspapers overflowed with images of the unexplainable occurrence the following day. Theodore Barrett had become an overnight sensation with the controversial picture, but like all enviable stars, he achieved his success after working his entire life at his craft. Now deemed a hero of cosmic proportions, his name remained forever linked with Kincaid. Rumors abounded and all were true: Steven remained isolated, healing from cuts and bruises; his fiancée stayed with her parents, trying to come to terms with the disaster and a lost love; and Barrett hid from everything and everybody.

Through it all, *Outlaw's Heart* remained a constant, growing bigger and packing in audiences nightly, with critics raving about old talents, bright shiny new ones, and a story so technically worked in script and cinematography, that it had to be a multiple Oscar contender and potential Motion Picture of the Year. David laughed aloud thinking about the unlikely possibility. Their little independent film was brilliant, although Lavender's magic had a hand in its promotion to become a winner. An intuitive thought hit him so hard he almost fell. This was Ted's picture, his time to be nominated and to win. The Mistress made promises and kept them.

The never-to-be-forgotten phone number and voice continued to leave messages on a cellular phone in England, with no pickups or replies. Most messages begged a blond-haired actor to answer the phone, or cried out in confusion with one question, "Why?" Two wild and tormented green eyes could only stare at the number displayed every five minutes. There was nothing to say; Ted had to find his own way. David's latest revelation assured him of Barrett's success as the great actor he wished to become. It had to be enough.

Watched intently by two lost men in the Kincaid Malibu mansion via satellite, LaCoix faced the one obligation forced upon him. The esteemed character actor had been requested politely, but emphatically, to attend the opening of *Outlaw's Heart* in London, December 15. Returning to L.A. for Christmas, production slowed to a stop in England, and the duty to do his part had to be accepted. With preparatory work for Morris' film completed, shooting could start on schedule January 1, exactly the day of Barrett's start in Mexico. Having turned down every show in Britain to discuss the film, David also remained secluded, working diligently on what he felt more important; but with a whisper from the Mistress, he relented and complied with her wishes.

The evening of the London Premier differed drastically from the usual ado about something insignificant. British filmmakers took these things a little more in stride, with a workable film, and far less glamour. The picture was important to him, but not earth-shattering news; he grew beyond tired of it. This particular evening, however, turned out to be pleasurable; and he felt comfortable in the presence of his beautiful companion, the radiant Mrs. Morris. The genius director insisted his two stars attend and have some fun, and fun they had. She was the perfect date: no threat, no expectations, and full of lust for taunting the press. Their appearance caused a flurry of rumor butterflies to flit their way across the Atlantic. Where was Rod Morris and was LaCoix having another affair? A private joke of their own making, Rod had graciously agreed to mind the children, while giving his extremely faithful, but mischievous spouse a night off to play games with someone as wickedly devious.

Both being the same age, David found that co-starring with a woman, of substance and talent, deemed a delightful surprise, and not just a pretty girl half his age. His roles, in his last few films, haunted him, finding them distasteful to the point of indecent, even in simulation, to make love to someone who should be dating his sons. The truth of the industry became disgustingly transparent to him, yet it made audiences believe it right and proper. In many cases, he saw it as a form of child molestation, with much older actors pretending to be younger, snuggling and simulating sex with youngsters who could be their grandchildren. A sick, perverted game of lies and soft focusing, he vowed to ignore the pressure of another insidious role. His choice of co-stars would be his choosing, or he would walk. Casting directors suddenly became his enemy: another cause to fight.

Not realizing the jealous hysteria the pair caused thousands of miles away, the two flirted and giggled for the cameras, indulging themselves happily in the game. For David, after too long in mourning, he reveled in the frivolity, the first time since his three-day red sports car outing. The second one lay hidden, tucked away as a memory not easily forgotten.

On the other side of the ocean, the Titanic sank, with a heart so heavy it could not stay buoyant in the black depths. Seeing the images crushed Theodore Barrett into fine talcum powder, and blown away on the winds of a California winter afternoon. Tears fell and work stopped for Barrett and Kincaid, both trying to define their characters, but neither able to cope with dialogue, which turned on the tears before lines were uttered. One saw the finale of his life's longing; the other had to face the former lover he discarded in hideous fashion. The last few days, before Christmas break, became a nightmare for three actors still in preparatory work. No one spoke but in dialogue. Tension threw their readings off schedule, but it made for brilliant acting when they could work. Time would tell when cameras rolled in the New Year. Two of the three shattered egos fell apart, but came together one lost afternoon, when Barrett reached out with a sad plea whispered to the other's solemn countenance. "Please take me to La Rosa Negra, Steven."

Lavender heard the words, thankful he made the request, but uncertain of the reason after forsaking everything they discussed. If nothing else, she would have a chance to talk to the tormented Spirit whose health weakened each day. The troubled Theodore Barrett wasted away from lack of food, lack of direction, lack of joy, lack of nurturing, and lack of David LaCoix.

CHAPTER 27

After ten hours of memories, between here and there, the plane landed in Los Angeles on schedule. The famous, blond actor put on his wickedest grin, which made his wild eyes wrinkle at the corners; and he confidently strode out of the transport area, carrying an armful of beautifully wrapped gifts, sure to delight the entire LaCoix menagerie. Sir Edmund was the only thing missing. The cherished bear had been tossed across a large, stone walled room weeks before, never to be found by anyone in the manor.

Taken aback by the mass of people who greeted his arrival, David closely followed the security personnel that ushered him through the crowd and protected him from hurting hands. An overwhelming and unexpected welcome, he hoped Lavender saved Ted from such a claustrophobic experience of chaotic adoration. Ludicrous in LaCoix's eyes, he honestly believed it should be saved for people of merit, and not actors. If there lay some crazy reason for the idiocy, perhaps it could be used with caution for recognizably acceptable purposes. His fight with Ted's church gave him such a goal, fighting to give children, of religious zealots, the freedom of choice. He already started the journey, with his rebirth into notoriety, secretly conferring and receiving sworn oaths, from a few notables of his acquaintance, to back an inspired, but difficult cause.

Maneuvered through the crowd with some dignity, he made it unscathed to the waiting limousine with not a package lost. His mind wandered off, while his body sank into the snug security of the luxury vehicle. Unknown faces peered in, changing faces like visual training cards, seen through the blackened windows of the car moving slowly through the throng. Everyone wanted a piece of the star of *Outlaw's Heart*; but he had nothing to give, not even his heart.

David remembered Lavender's words from a night an eternity ago, while gazing at her over black roses. *Read your fan mail personally. You may find someone of intellect and inner beauty who has nothing to gain from a relationship with you, except for the fact she adores you.* He experimented with the idea, corresponding with a couple of possibilities who caught his interest. These women proved the Mistress' theory, but he took it no further than exchanging a few letters via courier. It had been an interesting exercise but for Ted, and the unfortunate lack of time between the argument and Christmas. Still recovering from a third breakup within a year, he promised himself to resume writing, needing only a companion, a good friend, someone of merit to talk to; he hoped they would not be as rowdy as those encircling his only defense, a black, metal limousine.

Returning home, David finally warmed up from the perpetual chill of an English winter, ready to greet his two families. In less than ten days before his scheduled return, he had to deal with a list of unknown factors. Accepting Susan's gracious and welcoming invitation to stay in the guest room had been happily accepted. She knew how much he loved to see Holly's face Christmas morning; and her offer had immediately lightened the load of the dark shroud he hid beneath. Spending time with his daughter, the real joy in his life, became his primary goal over the holiday, and asked the Mistress to help sustain his enthusiasm. He would do better this time, proving to be a caring father to all three of his children.

A number of close friends had been invited to a Christmas soirée, arranged by his soon-to-be ex-wife. The party promised to be a pleasant one; and he looked forward to the day. Jess, Kevin, and Ray promised to attend with their wives and children. He could barely contain his curiosity, wondering if anything had transpired since the bizarre occurrence. According to the entertainment tabloids, and the rumor mill, it had.

Not forgetting the other three, Lavender bestowed her generous gifts upon them; ones they could have earned on their own. Donaldson reveled in happiness, serene and secure as per his wish; completely devoted to his expanding family and a new TV series he would star in for years: one future set. Jess Carmichael did retire on returning home, now joyously surrounded by his children, his grandchildren, and his forever wife, celebrating the start of a new life's adventure: second future set. As for the lively over-achiever, Ray Evans, he continued to be a work-in-progress. Constantly in motion, wheeling and delivering, his memoirs would turn into his success story. These three recipients of a great gift would never know their rewards came from helping two lost Spirits find each other; and there lay the unresolved wishes and uncertain futures.

Waiting was hard for David, but the day would come with no more nails to chew; in the meantime, he had things to do. He started in Arizona with the lawyer, appalled at what the District Attorney's investigators had learned, but pleased with proof of Barrett's story. It would not take long before enough evidence was presented to the Grand Jury, to make a decision on a trial. In the weeks, without the young man's presence and guidance, the construction of the house fell into shambles. A falling out with the contractor ensued, only to be rectified by the architect. The LaCoix boys thoroughly enjoyed themselves, watching their father rant. With that sorted out, they could tease their already irate parent about the success of his film. What was he doing with that other man? Old enough and smart enough to goad David, they almost had him convinced that they knew he committed the effrontery of having sex with Barrett and enjoying the affair. The senior LaCoix cringed and reddened with the taunting, wondering what they would think if they knew the entire sordid story. No longer a concern, that part of his life closed, with the slamming of a cellular phone against a stonewall. Only his heart remained open, bleeding a slow death.

His sons did lift his Spirit, however, with the rumors spreading of prospective Oscar nominations for the picture. The eldest offspring enjoyed the film, but both boys squirmed talking about the kissing scene, not to mention the familiar body parts exposed and touched. Even for his normally liberal children, the acts of lovemaking had been slightly radical. When asked about his obvious participation in the passionate first kiss, David seized his chance to get even. "A kiss is just a kiss, but when it's that intense, man, it doesn't matter who you're in a lip-lock with. To be honest with you boys, it wasn't bad, not bad at all. I think we shot the scene twenty or thirty times, and it just kept getting better and hotter." The mischievous glint in their father's eyes could not disguise his mirth; and they all laughed.

Coming home and listening to critics and public opinion, David finally realized the impact and extreme limits the picture had taken, an obvious choice for a number of technical awards. He doubted, however, a best picture contender would be in the cards; sexually driven films were as rare as Oscar-winning Westerns; *Outlaw's Heart* encompassed both. With so much at stake, LaCoix remained unavailable for comment, preferring anonymity. Hiding counted as his best defense, and his best publicity.

After two eventful, although entertaining days with his sons in Arizona, he returned for fun and frivolity with Holly. Born in December, her name came naturally to the little Sagittarius whose imminent birth came with little notice, while her mother hung the big green leaves with the bright red berries. A rally-winning drive for LaCoix, one special evening six years ago, he had roared his way through residential Beverly Hills to get to Sinai Hospital, taking the fastest route with the street racing savvy he knew. Susan swore she would never ride with him again, although it helped deliver a child on a gurney, rushing down a hospital corridor, while she shrieked a thank you for the high speed jostling. Not a long wait for this one, it made his little girl special with her anticipation to see the world. Having just turned six, her excitement on the appearance of her Dad, laden with pre-wrapped gifts, still came first, with Santa Claus' soon appearance a close second. Smiling broadly, he instinctively knew she no longer believed in the myth, only playing him for twice the presents.

The morning of the Christmas Eve affair, he smiled brightly, enthusiastically cheering her on, remarking on every outfit she demurely modeled for him, with a thumbs-up or a thumbs-down. Between father and daughter, the green velvet overalls were chosen, with a white stretch lace T-shirt. A definite two thumbs-up decision, the sophisticated little blonde ran to her mother to finish primping for an early-evening, semi-formal get-together. David remained in his chair, raising an eyebrow in surprise at her suggestion she needed lipstick. He snickered behind his hand, smiling in glee, fully aware of what Susan's reaction would be. Leaving such decisions to her mother, he gave no comment.

All was ready. His daughter's outfit complete; it turned her into an angelic Christmas sprite, with a hint of clear lip-balm. Dressed head to toe in green and white, the ensemble enhanced the color of her eyes inherited from her father, along with the long, white-blonde, straight hair, now tied up decoratively in ribbons and lace. A cute little Rockwell painting, she represented a treasure he missed. More weight of misspent time added to his mounting grief, and the chronic mental fatigue grew worse.

Susan looked resplendent in black satin, clinging to her beautiful silhouette. His first wife, also looked radiantly happy, donned in her favorite red for this holiday. Accompanied by their matching bookends, which she and David had created, the three arrived early for cocktails and more intriguing family updates. It gave Holly time to enjoy her half brothers' company and to exchange gifts. Bryce and Tyler had grown protective of their much younger half-sister, taking the promise given to their absentee father to heart. Even his two wives appeared on very friendly terms, laughing over and enjoying something that amused them both. The family portrait overwhelmingly gratified LaCoix. His first priority in altering his life came together without being forced, and in the happiest of fashion. The clever actor hid every other feeling under a handsome mask of Christmas joy and genuine laughter.

The house started to fill with friendly faces; and the remembered cold, damp air of London evaporated under a warm California sky. The adornment of the Tudor estate fit the decor, with candles and pinecones, crystal figurines and icicles, handmade baubles and ribbons. Each room smelled of fir and pine, frankincense and myrrh, with sounds of caroling floating through the hallways. More to the liking of a cold northern winter in the country, reminiscent of a Dickens' tale, Susan had done wonders, cleverly decorating the large home with trifling details. He beamed with pride at how she handled herself, and what she had accomplished, pulling her own life together. He regretted ever demeaning her. Even though she looked sensational for her new beau, and for David, she could not rekindle the glint in his eye. She did not try and would never know a man named Theodore Barrett was the real love David waited for.

With their romance over, LaCoix took in a deep breath of the heavenly scent of Christmas and attempted to rekindle his joyous smile, the one that wrinkled his entire face, fooling people into thinking it genuine. He stepped back to survey the crowd, for a couple of encouraging moments. Old friends gladdened his heart with some cheer; and he intended to make the most of the party. Kids scurried around, laughing and giggling, acting like the children they were. Happy to witness the chaotic situation, David wondered if he had ever been so young and laughed that hard. He called his folks earlier in the day, to wish them the best for the holidays. Another long chat about life, love, divorce, career, and children, he made promises of sharing them all on his next return. They received the news with loving thanks and excited approval; something David desperately needed to hear.

Enjoying his bourbon and the sound of tinkling ice in a glass, he watched the liquid sparkling with tree lights floating inside the cubes, while they danced a merry jig. He wondered why he seldom noticed such small, extraordinary things. Maybe love, then anger, then united family ties produced the enchantment, making everything appear differently. He thought of the Mistress, and whispered a happy holiday to her, although knowing she would be busy this time of year, holding people together, all those in desperation and loneliness. She would do it, even though acknowledging her dislike of Christ whom she knew. It seemed an odd thing to declare, but Lavender made it sound so commonplace, he had to believe her. Ted's son of his god would be in his glory this night, which would certainly irk her Ladyship. For David, the festivities were a time of celebrating a family gathering, and had nothing to do with the religious aspect. He wondered about Ted. Tomorrow would be a very special day for him, a very holy day, with no fun and laughter for his lost Teddy Bear, only *Silent Night* with no *Jingle Bell Rock*.

Bourbon in hand, the emotionally disguised actor turned to spot the Barretts coming through the door. It was a shock. They had been on the first list, but he had forgotten to inform Susan to scratch them after the quarrel. Too late, LaCoix's greatest performance awaited. Ignore them, he thought, hide amongst the other guests. With no escape from his own trap, he could not even mask the panic from his eyes and beating heart. The arrival of Theodore Barrett, who had fast become a known factor on the Hollywood Glitter Carousel, which Ted blatantly hated, created a great deal of attention. David's old friends clamored to meet the other brilliant star of *Outlaw's Heart*, while Jess, Kevin, and Ray showed their eagerness just to see him, and to talk about the buzz created by their picture. Like a mouse spotted by a cat, an unnerved but fiendishly quick LaCoix disappeared into the garden.

"That mad at him, are you? Your compromising scenes must have been a nightmare." Wise old Jess seemed to know everything, almost everything. He basked quietly alone in the late afternoon sun and cooler air blowing off the ocean a few miles away.

"Who, Barrett? Just a little disappointed. Guess I should do my host thing. Wish me luck. I'll try not to deck him."

"Good thinking. Wouldn't look good in front of the kiddies. Besides, he looks awful; a strong wind could carry him away. What's wrong with him? The buzz has it, he may have contracted AIDS." Jess' never-changing demeanor looked extremely concerned, certainly enough to frighten David to see for himself.

"Definitely not, he's been checked thoroughly, so please stop the rumor before it gets out of hand."

"I'll try, but something's wrong."

"Maybe it's this new picture. You remember what he went through for *Outlaw's Heart*. Besides, it's none of our business."

"Yeah, but this is different. He's sick, LaCoix; and he's lost again." Determined to change his friend's inner anger into compassion, Jess pressed harder.

"Glad you're here, Carmichael. Stick around; I may need your support." David moved back into the now overcrowded room and peered through a tree branch, twinkling with lights of Christmas joy, to peek at what he had to face. Ted did look terrible, even dressed in his new Kincaid influenced look, and shyly smiling. With an unseen leash around his neck, Karen had him under tight control, while vigilantly standing guard at his side. You could almost see him suffocating. Obvious in her body language, she did not approve of stepping into Sodom, or Gomorrah. Five months pregnant, it went unnoticed by everyone; the baby would be very small, and the thought upset David immediately.

Looking closer, he studied every aspect of his foe. Pleasant enough in appearance, she wore little make-up and sported a hair cut too short, lacking in imagination; her black locks and pale skin made her appear ten years older than Ted. She probably was. Tiny physically, compared to the statuesque beauties decorating the party, she did look fighting fit. Thin lips, set in a straight line of tension, mirrored her thoughts toward this degenerate group of heathens who surrounded her and her husband. He wondered how Ted convinced Karen to attend this gathering on such a holy occasion. Barrett had spoken of the austerity of his environment; and David saddened at the thought of Ted's penchant for the artistic in every form. He doubted the man would be allowed a single ornament to decorate his own home, but for a few devotional candles and a model of a manger, expertly crafted by the man's own talented hands. One quick glimpse at Barrett, and the innocent expression of wonderment, confirmed his theory. The blue eyes darted from one display to another, taking in the lavish adornment, the lights, and glitter of what Christmas meant to most people. Certainly not this lavish, but there would be a little tinsel strung from a lighted tree, a single pine branch, or even a small potted plant. With a deep breath, David stepped forward, crossing the room in determination not to break down.

"Mr. Barrett, good to see you again, and this must be the happy, expectant mother. Nice to meet you at last, Karen." His voice slightly choked; no eye contact made; and no hand extended in greeting; he could not will himself to follow the greeting. A touch from Ted would have him attacking the man violently in the foyer, or carrying him off to catch the first plane back to London. He pulled himself together, quickly finishing, before an utterance from either of the couple. "Please, make yourselves comfortable and enjoy." LaCoix retreated--retreated into the depths of his library--its portal hidden behind the enormous tree of flashing lights and tasteful display of silver and gold. He shut the door softly behind him, and slumped, a defeated man, into his private world of lost dreams and revelations he now had trouble believing. What had been a fun idea turned into a day-terror of holy proportions. A knock on the door and his heart gave out; he thought he had made a clean escape. "Take a number."

"David?"

"Not in the mood for heroes. Go save your wife from the Pagan savagery out there." The door opened without warning, and LaCoix jumped to his feet. Completely unexpected, not believing Ted so bold, David had no time to mask the distress overpowering him. If a man ever looked like a possum caught in the headlights of a car, it was David LaCoix at that moment.

Ted looked worse. Red, bloodshot eyes started to form, and the skeleton body shook uncontrollably. "Won't you even talk to me?"

"Nothing to say." LaCoix looked around for his drink. The habitual scanning of a room, for the nearest packet of cigarettes, gave him something else to do. He finally met the gaze and he snapped. "Don't you dare start crying, Barrett; I'm not letting you get away with that shit. You made your choice; I suggest you leave."

"You won't consider reconciling? Maybe those rumors are true about Mrs. Morris. You're back to an old habit of screwing your co-stars."

"Just like I fucked you. That's it. Get out." The remark ignited David's fury, but he eased back, remembering just how many of his co-stars he had made love to, including the one standing too close.

"I'm sorry. It made me crazy with jealousy the night of the London Premier, and I haven't thought of anything since."

"Well, you've been wasting your time. I suppose, since our last phone call, all I've been thinking about is you. We've both wasted precious time for nothing."

"I hope not. I wanted to tell you I called for Lavender, after Stevie's accident, and went back to La Rosa Negra." Ted sucked in his feelings, leaving only the blue eyes to mist over.

"Is that what you call it? A fucking accident? I imagined you and Kincaid would come up with a different notion regarding that particular near disaster. The Mistress would have set you straight, if you had actually spoken with her." David did not believe a word the man said, considering what he recently learned of Barrett. This particular Christian would never return to *Satan's den.*

"I did see her. I also know she tried to protect me from Stevie. He... we made the wrong decision, but he doesn't see it yet. Her essence turned from fury to forgiveness, and she held us against the cliff until they rescued us. No way could I have held on any longer; she gave him a boost to get him next to me. We were incapable of hanging there on our own. I just wanted to thank you for asking her to help us." Ted needed to say more, but his old childhood speech problems returned in his nervousness, and he choked back anything further, trying to regain his momentum.

"So, you realize that Lavender turned into your vindictive little tornado."

"Of course we did. We're not stupid. I just didn't know what she wanted from us, or understand the reasons you wanted to help, after what I said and did to you." The questioning expression looked hopeful, but David turned away from any chance of forgiving.

"Who knows what my reasons were. Couldn't give a damn if Kincaid fell to his death. You and Steven both took turns playing the Fates with whom Lavender wages war. You interfered with someone else's future." David's mind did a complete twist with what he had just said. This proved the Fates were real: other people blindsiding certain individuals before reaching their goals. Maybe he had been one with Ted, tempting him into something not possible for him.

"Stevie was supposed to die? I don't believe it." The information nearly knocked Ted off his feet. In his own mind, he thought Lavender was teaching them another lesson, not attempting to kill one of them for betraying her. His trembling increased severely, coming close to a seizure.

David recognized the potential danger of such an eventuality, and approached the skeleton before him. "I don't know. If he were, there would have been no way you could have saved him. We don't know what his goals are in life. Her Ladyship may help us along at times, but she never reveals the ending; it would take away her surprise. I certainly don't know where you're heading, Ted, or me either, for that matter."

"Yes you do; it's with me." Even with a quaking voice, Barrett spoke with determination.

"Thought it was, but I've been known to be wrong." David could not bear an excuse and started to turn away.

"I know you still want me. Why can't you forgive me? I can't keep going without you. The plan is back in play, as far as I'm concerned. It's only a question of timing." Ted reached out for an arm, only to be demoralized with David's lightning quick twist, to get away from his touch.

"Timing for what? Are you doing this to see what we have on your church? I suppose Karen's been told of our secret, at least one of them." David grew tired of the conversation, looking away to hunt for his drink. Found, he grabbed it and turned abruptly to face those bewildering eyes. "You're still here."

Incapable of handling the emotions flooding over him, Ted launched himself into the air with one leap, and flung himself into arms that needed to feel him, as much as he needed David's strength. The kiss was violent and savage; the glass dropped, to smash into a million sparkling diamonds, crushed to powder by frantically moving Gucci loafers. Heads and mouths moved back and forth, attempting to devour the other, while hands grappled frantically for familiar body parts, and fingers tangled in the long hair now crowning both men. Tasting Ted's tears created more excitement in the older man who had his hand down the back of his lover's pants, just to touch and push on the clenched, hot opening. An ear splitting shriek, and a bang on the door, jolted the two apart. A small bundle of green velvet rushed into the room in tears, screaming like a banshee.

Ted immediately turned away, straightened his clothes to hide his arousal, and covered his ears to muffle the raucous tantrum. David turned the other way, stepping forward several paces, and bracing himself for the bodily attack of emerald green. He knelt down to the level of the little blonde hurricane and embraced his distraught daughter, willing his own arousal to subside. Glancing over at a panicked Ted, he heard the oncoming hysterics in the slow mesmerizing chant whispered so quietly. "Make it stop. Don't hurt her. Make it stop."

Holly looked in the same direction as her Dad, and the infuriated little demon started to settle. Looking questioningly at Ted, then at her father, her curiosity peaked. David brushed the tears from her puzzled face; and tried to figure out just how much she saw if anything. "Be careful, Honey, there's broken glass on the floor. Now, what's the matter? You know screaming isn't allowed, unless you're in trouble."

"Justin Evans pulled the ribbons out of my hair, and he won't give them back." The voice whined, and the lips pouted and trembled in normal childish fashion.

"Is that any reason to scare your father half to death? We're all over excited today."

"Suppose. Sorry I scared you. Why's that man covering his ears?" Holly's fiery temper came and went in her usual volatile springboard way, exactly like her father. Tears immediately stopped.

"Ted, pay attention; you better get used to this. Now, sit and stop mumbling." A harshly toned order, one to be obeyed by a passive creature like Barrett, made the smaller man turn immediately, rubbing his face dry and taking a breath. Now steady, he sat down in the designated chair. With some embarrassment, he came face-to-face with a child whose eyes were as red, swollen, and surprised as his own.

"Listen up, Miss LaCoix. You remember our talks about abuse and what to do if someone touches you inappropriately, or hurts you." David stayed amazingly calm and gentle. The quiet voice of the consummate actor mesmerized the other two in the room, as easily as it did a paying audience.

"Yes. Has someone hurt Mr. Bar... Mr.?" The little girl tried to remember who was who, doing a very decent job, considering the number of people just outside the library door.

"Mr. Barrett: and he's fine. However, when he hears a child scream, he thinks something terrible is happening to them. Remembering that, there'll be no fussing over silly things. Deal?"

"Deal, but what about my ribbons?" The anger disappeared, replaced by an irritating whine, which made David shiver like the scratching of cat claws against a chalkboard.

"I'll tell you a secret about little boys, and even grown men, which you should always remember. First, never whine; it's unbecoming for a young lady, and a LaCoix never begs. Do not tell a boy the secret I'm about to reveal. Just use it to drive them crazy."

"A secret? Tell me! Tell me!"

"Don't react to the teasing; simply walk away and find another ribbon." David wondered if Ted grasped this metaphor to his own irritating behavior.

"But that's the one I want." More whining of dismay included a scrunched up face for emphasis.

"Then try this; it works better, and is a lot more fun. Go out and walk around like Daddy does, talking to people as if nothing happened. Wait patiently, and Justin will come to you, trying to get you to chase him for those not-so-important ribbons. When he starts acting silly, shaking your bows in your face, simply smile and suggest they would probably look better on him. If you get that far, then tell him you would be happy to tie them in his hair. I'll bet breakfast in bed that he'll drop the ribbons and run for his life."

Barrett smiled discreetly under the hands covering his mouth. He always knew David was devious in subtle matters; and his guidance showed in the strong-willed, bright, little girl who would be a handful for any man. The world had better beware in another ten or so years.

"Okay, I'll try. Thanks, Dad."

"Dad? What happened to Daddy?"

"I'm too old for that, now I'm six. See you later. Bye, Mr. Barrett." A green flash, with an undone stream of blonde hair, ran out the door to seek her revenge. The Christmas sprite had been defrocked of her hair adornments, and the game would go precisely as Miss LaCoix had been instructed, quietly and covertly. She was her father's daughter.

"Sorry, Ted, are you okay?"

"Not really. Old memories flooded back when I heard her scream. I'm still shaking."

"Children love to wail just for the fun of it, but don't let them get away with it. It's completely unnecessary, unless they're in trouble."

"We're changing the real subject, David. I shouldn't have lost control, but needed you so badly. Sorry for putting you in such an awkward position." Besotted with this man of quiet genius, Ted came close to bursting into tears at the loss of him.

"No we're not; and my little bet with Lavender turned out to be a draw, since we were cut short." David snickered at him, going from anger, then to a father's softness, and back to vengeance on what occurred just before. He should have stopped Ted with a smack across his mouth.

"You did make a wager?" Horrified at the callous behavior, Ted flinched, considering he came within a second of being ravished, by the man in the sanctity of the soundproof library.

David said nothing, smirking at him in retaliation for all the lies he thought he heard. It felt good to hurt the man.

"How could you? You're both cruel. Neither of you understand how much I wanted to kiss you and feel you rubbing against me, and you bet on that? One thing I have learned: I do have human desires, just like you, LaCoix, but unlike you, I wouldn't let someone fuck me just to get ahead. I want you in my life; I'm begging you; and you're acting like an asshole." Ted had learned, and stood up to gain some advantage, if it came to a face-to-face battle.

"You're talking nonsense, Barrett. Only a spontaneous reaction, it meant nothing to you, but a possible quick release of sexual tension you've been building since your last encounter. Was it with Kincaid or me? Maybe Peerce? Never mind, I don't want to know, but I hoped you used protection. Now, quit acting, and tell me the truth. Why did you come, and why should I believe anything you say? Let me guess. You're offering me your heart again. Hell, man, you gave it to me once to keep safe, and you ripped it out of me without a thought. You hurt me so badly, I can barely think. Why didn't you run me down with a fully loaded garbage truck, and back over me to make sure you did a proper job?" David once again tried Ted's favorite trick, the one he just taught his daughter, and headed for the door. The steamy kiss confused him; he too remained hard as stone. LaCoix buttoned his light tan blazer over the black T-shirt and matching pants, to cover the uncomfortable situation.

"I'm here because you invited us. How can you say those things about me? I'd never cheat on you. I'm going ahead with the divorce. After discussing it with my publicist and agent, they agreed, but I should wait." The new star held his ground with the aid of a heavy, leather chair.

"What a surprise; I've been waiting for this. For what, oh yeah, timing. Timing for what: a miracle from Christ? He's probably busy getting ready for his birthday." David turned and snarled. Like all arguments, this made little sense, and he had other matters to discuss with Barrett.

"I still have my faith, David, although modifying it with different answers to my many questions, so don't put me down for it. I'm learning; at least trying. Both you and Lavender said I could mold my God and Christ to what I believe them to be, and not what I've been told." The voice became steadier and more determined. Ted stared directly into the raging fire about to burst the veins in David's neck.

"Good, that's one thing in your favor. Now, the other side of you, the dark one with the thorn; tell me why you lied to me, and I'm still waiting for an answer as to what you're waiting for?" The squint and glare did not ease up.

"First the custody hearing: I need information from the D.A.'s office, and I'm having trouble obtaining it. Secondly, the lawyer doubts any chance of sole custody until the baby arrives and something happens to it. Christ, I can't even think about it, the one reason to stay with Karen as long as possible. I hate this. Then the third is for you, the Oscars; a divorce and scandal with a church could ruin the picture's possibility of being nominated, but the legal documents are ready to be handed to Karen the day after the awards."

"So it's all about you winning? I thought better ideals from you, Ted."

"Not me! You, the picture, the technicians, Lavender, not to mention something of major significance: my child's welfare. What's the matter with you? It's our livelihood, man, and my life!"

Ted could not believe David's accusations, or the illogical barrage of hateful thoughts.

LaCoix did not respond, but knelt on the floor to pick up the shards of glass with Ted's help, giving both an opportunity to cool down as they cleaned the stain. The first sound heard, came from the crashing of ice against another fragile vessel, and the gurgle of bourbon poured. Golden-brown liquid whirled around as David attempted to recapture the moment when lights danced in his glass. They appeared to glimmer slightly in the last of the sun's rays, filtering through the window. Not a word echoed through the strained silence.

"What lie, David? I've never lied to you." Barrett broke LaCoix's wanderings with a trembling voice. Maintaining their composure seemed impossible, and their only diversion focused on why the stain remained. For David, it would be a lasting reminder.

"Fine, where do we start? The first night in the labyrinth, if I recall, a pathetically sad face wanted to lie down and die in the gardens of La Rosa Negra."

"That wasn't a lie, not at first. That's exactly how I felt when I arrived. With everything looking so pristine and quiet, and having such a horrible time at home, it felt the right time."

"So, you wanted to commit suicide; it wasn't a trick? Since we last spoke, hero, I have this pain in my gut, telling me I was the prey and you the predator. The helpless victim of so many problems, and I fell for it. You played me like a pro, Barrett, agreeing to everything I suggested or wanted. Any other man would have succumbed to my sexual needs immediately, or beat the crap out of me for trying to seduce him. I guess I did pursue you to a degree, during our game of flirtation, not realizing what you really wanted. So, who was the seducer? Who became the real victim of everything that happened, you or me, Ted?" David felt the onslaught of a migraine from the tension, and knew he had to end the argument. He rubbed his temples, while he stared questioningly at the younger man unable to take his eyes off his fidgeting, shuffling feet.

"I admit to partially playing it out. Loving a famous actor, since becoming aware of the need of him physically, is not easy. Hell, I wanted you so much; I would have acted any way you wished." David noticed the near collapse of the thin body, but Ted quickly regained his balance and stood his ground. Ignored for the moment, the wide-eyed expression of surprise on Barrett's face did not hide the secret he kept. A firmer grip took hold of the chair.

"That's not love, Ted. It's puppy love. I gather from this, I don't know the real you. You're just an extremely talented actor, using his gifts to entrap. I feel like a fly caught in your web. Did you hear the last crack of my heart?" Again, David watched the fleeting movement Ted made to steady himself. He hated arguing with a sick man.

"At the first location, I did act in a way you responded favorably to, as if you might actually care; but the first evening at La Rosa Negra, it was me. The roses, both the white and the black, changed everything. Besides, who suggested snuggling on the couch, sleeping next to me, protecting me, agreeing to flirt, and calling me *Teddy Bear*?"

"All that is beautiful has its ugly side, and perhaps I did try to seduce you. Is that what I'm hearing?"

"One thorn on us both, I guess." Ted tried to smile, attempting in vain to curb David's ire. The next question had him sitting, no longer able to support his thinning body.

"Then here's the latest lie; your second thorn. Something from the D.A. that you should know, Ted, cannot be dismissed by your church, or you." He no longer sipped his bourbon, but swallowed it in one gulp. A hand brushed the remaining liquid off the famous lips, now on film forever kissing and taking the man whom he now faced down. Placing the glass on the nearest table, he leaned over Barrett, one hand on either arm of the chair.

"Why would I lie? I've told you everything I know. What does the District Attorney say?" Ted squirmed in his seat, wringing his hands, his frail body quivering in greater distress. He did not dare look at the disapproving and angry face invading his space.

"Your name, before the three of you changed it to Barrett, was Wagner; and there were five of you, not three. Two of your brothers died mysteriously. Only because of a bright coroner, doing two properly conducted and legal autopsies, has given us undeniable proof, although never acted upon. He performed them on both boys, since the deaths were only three months apart and in the same family. They exhumed the first body for comparison." David kept staring to catch any lies in the reaction.

Ted certainly appeared surprised, even in his voice. "Ryan and Roger? They died when I was two and never mentioned. I don't even remember them."

"I suppose that could be true. The man said he sent a social worker to check on the youngest child. They found a small, delicate, two-year-old male of extraordinary beauty. Sounds like you, Ted, or should I say Robert?"

"Of course it was me. I told you I had to change my name. What happened to them? Tell me." Tears finally burst the liquid bubbles of blue and ran down the pale face.

David wanted to wrap him up and carry him away from the awful truth. He had to tell Ted, but could not come up with the words until they surfaced out of anger and now regret. "Settle down, Barrett. Your brothers died of severe malnutrition and untreated injuries to their arms. Sound familiar? One was seven, the other four; the same age they started abusing you."

"No, they never hurt us that badly." The shoulders heaved; Ted was drowning in sorrow.

"Bad enough for you to tell me. After two deaths, maybe your folks eased up on the younger three." David pulled the head back by the hair and leaned down to stare menacingly into the scrunched face. These were not pretend sobs, or an actor's tears, which kept the face looking beautiful. Ted cried in heartbroken grief; but the older man refused to give in. They needed his testimony; Ted had to face the truth. "Stop it, Barrett, and answer me. Your eldest brother died, so emaciated and his arm so distorted that it shocked the coroner. Your folks convinced the police he suffered from a birth defect, and had always been a sickly child. That's not the case, is it?"

"I don't know. Around nine or ten, I found their names, births, and deaths in the family *Bible* of record. They told us they died in an epidemic of rheumatic fever; we were never to speak about them. My God, this man... this coroner can testify to it?"

"Yes, he's more than willing to reveal the truth. Although he's retired, he has access to the files and remembers the cases to this day. You had the right to know what happened to your elder brothers, before you heard it in court. I'm sorry, Ted, but you have to consider your parents killed your siblings, whether intentionally or not."

"It can't be, David. How did you find out?"

"Now you're digging. It's all you need to know; unless you can prove to me you're on board with righting this serious accusation." David stood erect, his hands firmly on his hips, staring down and daring Ted to push for more information.

"It can't be true. It can't."

"Yes it is, so you had better face the facts; something you've been avoiding all your life."

"I'm going to be sick. Where's the bathroom?" Ted put his hand over his mouth and dashed for the door. David quickly grabbed him; and the two men hurried through another exit, down the hall into the bathroom off the guest quarters. The man was ill--seriously ill--with something far worse than a nervous stomach.

CHAPTER 28

"Here we go again, hey, Ted?" David once again played nursemaid, but not as gently.

After Ted's vomiting stopped, his faced washed, and his mouth refreshed; strong, familiar arms gave in, to enfold him in a protective coating. His lover's shoulder supported his head; his favorite voice lulled his broken Spirit; his parents were murderers; his younger brothers could have been victims; and only he remained safe, by turning into a moneymaking machine for the church. The impending divorce and custody battle could make him a target. Nevertheless, for the moment he felt secure, rocked by his anchor that intuitively understood his need for a touch, while he poured his sorrow into the neck and corn-silk hair.

"Ted, you're very ill. What's wrong? You've lost more weight since I saw you scaling a cliff to save Kincaid. How did you have the strength?"

"Just did. David, my parents murdered my brothers. How do I face them knowing that?"

"They can no longer hurt you, but they'll put you through hell with your testimony. I'm sorry; but my investigators and attorneys have already started. The Grand Jury decided a court date, July 28; and you're on the witness list. It's unlikely your folks can be held accountable, considering the span of years, and the Statute of Limitations. Now, forget the horrible thought, and tell me what's wrong. Don't leave me guessing."

"July 28 is too far away! I can't wait that long for the custody suit!"

"Discuss it with the lawyers and go with your heart, Teddy."

"It's not going to work."

"Slow down; one thing at a time. Now, answer my question."

"I can't stop shaking. Okay, after Kincaid and I reached the top, they took us to the hospital and filled me with drugs to tranquilize me. I don't remember anything, except waking up in an old horror movie. They reset my arm and stole my blood. I was alone, David, with bloodsucking vampires in white coats. They couldn't be stopped; and I froze, scared to death."

"You astound me. It never enters your mind to be terrified of falling off a cliff, with a tornado blowing its wrath at you, but a little blood, taken from your arm, gives you a fit." David held his tongue, not divulging the probable reason for the precautionary procedure. Looking like a broomstick painted ashen gray, Ted had to be a candidate for a thorough examination.

"They didn't even ask me; they just took it. All I needed was a new cast; although, it should have come off permanently." Ted lifted the plastic covered arm high enough to touch David's hip.

"Means we have more X-rays of your old fractures. Did they say anything?"

"No, but they kept frowning at me, as if I'd done something wrong. Raymond and Richard's arms are like mine; and the D.A. forced them to get X-rays; but you already know that. We learned early how to heal ourselves."

"You've said that before."

"It's not important. You said Ryan and Roger were malnourished." Ted met the gaze; but the nod of a head indicated the reality. "That's what the doctors said about me."

"Damn, I should have seen it. Those half eaten chocolate bars, diet sodas, and cravings for hamburgers and fries; I kept seeing the same candy bar on your counter, didn't I?" With no answer, David could not see the face tucked into his neck. He had surmised the problem and had done nothing. The two stood in silence, except for their hurting heartbeats heard only as a hollow echo, within the confines of the porcelain white bathroom. "My God, you're anorexic."

The final admittance left David in disbelief and shock. His eyes flashed wildly, seeing himself in the large mirror, holding the thinnest creature he ever handled, and feeling a similar sensation of lapping his arms across his empty chest. Only the shivering confirmed he held the fragile man, slowly dying physically from a psychological illness. The embrace grew tighter, to his only hope for fulfillment, wondering how long he would have the man, before Ted succumbed to the inevitable. With no words to say, only tears fell, grieving the loss of so many, and ones in the throes of a society-induced disease. He needed answers, and he had another cause to fight, against the major manufacturers of the incredulous condition: Hollywood.

"I'm strong enough, but I just don't require food. Everything hurts inside, like it's whirling around and punching me from inside. I can't explain it; and nobody believes me. I've felt like this my whole life, thinking it normal; but they say it's in my head."

"Maybe part of it, but your inner pain doesn't sound right. Did your eating disorder start while in the labyrinth?"

"No, and I can't remember when I stopped eating, but the inability to eat grew worse after I started acting. My first drama coach insisted I try anything to make me look young, which meant small. Agents said the same thing; few child actors ever became recognizable adult actors. No one takes them seriously, just as you said, or allows them to grow up. Now, my facial and body hair won't grow because of it. Even sex, or want of it, may disappear. I can't let that happen. They don't understand how I've lived this long; but David, I know I'm not dying."

The words became more fearful; and LaCoix did not know what to say. Thinking this may be another game, it seemed a probability; but the look and feel of the man yelled *No,* with an earsplitting scream. "You're going to be fine, Baby. Now, how can I help? I've read that the disease can take the form of prepubescent regression. You remain looking young, until you become too thin and ill to carry it off; and it's starting to show. You look terrible. We have to get this under control. As for the sex part, I think you still have the desire after feeling you in the library." Crazy with worry, David continued to rub the back and support the body too weak to stand-alone. "Does Steven know? Did you tell Lavender?"

"The Mistress already suspected, although puzzled by it, as if there was something more."

"That's odd. If you're anorexic, she and the healer would have known when we were at La Rosa Negra. We should have all seen it."

"I thought you liked my looks? You told me being vulnerable turned you on." The tear-stained face looked up for an answer, only to see a stunned man close his eyes with droplets of salt water sprinkling down from the inside corners.

"Did I say that?" LaCoix's knees buckled. He remained standing, only because he held onto a broomstick. "It's my fault for reinforcing your illness." The older man lamented his words, although he had tried to stop Lavender from keeping Ted on a diet. His thoughts refocused with a knock on the door and a familiar voice.

"David? Is everything okay? Are you all right?" Susan's naturally cheerful voice sounded worried. It stopped the flow of tears inside the bathroom.

"Yes, thanks Darling. Could you ask Jess to come up; and please, take over my hosting duties for awhile?" Another great performance acted out by controlling the quiver in his voice.

"Of course, but you've been missing for some time. Have you seen Theo? His wife is becoming distraught, bordering on hostile."

"He's with me. Keep her occupied; tell her we're discussing business."

"In the bathroom? Good grief. You sure you don't need anything? You looked very pale upon your arrival, Theo."

"Thanks, Ma'am; I'm fine."

"Ma'am? You sure know how to make someone feel older than sin. I'll get Jess for you; and you should lie down for a while, Sonny." Susan's wit remained a constant; and it disturbed David she also used words to cement Ted's erroneous opinion about his looks. The entire world approved of his persona, doting continuously over their brightest new star.

"Sorry, Susan. Please stay close to Karen for me; as she's been ill since the second month."

"Okay, I'll take care of her, while you two do business in the unlikeliest of places. By the way, you're forgiven."

They heard the bedroom door close, and still Ted refused to move from his position, which helped him feel the warmth of another, never wishing to leave.

"Can you walk to the bed, Ted?"

"Yeah, and I'm sorry I ruined your day, playing the victim. You'll never believe me now."

"I believe you're very ill. It doesn't change anything; but we need to get you through this and on your feet. Come on, hero."

David slipped off Ted's navy blazer and loafers, helped him lay down on the peach and green flowered bed, and gently lowered the brunet head into the softness of a white encased pillow. He would sleep with his own head on the same cushion, from now until New Year's, breathing in the scent of what remained of his Teddy Bear. Raking his longer hair back, he looked like the crazed lord he portrayed, even beginning to think alike. The actions, on Ted's part, seemed too easy, as if another game unfolded; although the facts, counted in his head, could only come up with one positive truth: Ted lay near death.

Wanting to see how far the disease had manifested, and without hesitation or a refusal, David pulled out the silk shirt, then a white T-shirt, and another one, until he reached skin. He raised the bundle past the ribs and tried to hide the gasp stuck in his throat. Only skin stretched over bones, and everything else showed as empty hollows. One piece at a time, he tucked back each garment, counting five items, not including the jacket he had removed. He raised himself, from his leaning position, and wiped his face with his hand, changing the fear to a brighter smile. It was true; the layers of clothing justified keeping a body, with no insulation, warm; or building up his size to fill out his jacket. Aghast at the deterioration over six weeks, the sight spun David around, and he wondered how Ted really saw himself.

Jess entered to see one man lying prone on a fabricated field of flowers, and another staring down at the tearing face. Not discomforting for the retired actor, the scene had been played out many times since the miraculous rockslide, yet the astute gentleman detected a difference. David LaCoix looked paler than the pillowcase; and Barrett did not carry enough weight to make a dent in the bedding. A white piece of tissue paper came to mind, and no one had better open a window.

David pulled his old friend aside, sadly relaying the story of Ted's illness and the abuse. Questions and answers flew back and forth between the two older men, both attempting to find a way to aid their lost friend. Out of hearing range, Barrett drifted away into his own world of the silences, having over-expended his ability to cope mentally. Weeping softly under the closed eyes, his distress and humiliation could not be withheld. Ted's action proved Lavender's assumptions; any person, pushed to a certain point, could commit suicide. He knew Ted had his reasons; and they were many; his illness may be a way of committing the deed; and the beautiful man had planned to die since a child. David rubbed his face hard to cover his sorrow.

After some discussion, and with an agreement from Ted, they decided to call for Lavender. Her healing magicians may help; and they did. Within a second of their thoughts, both Carmichael and LaCoix heard the chimes. The next moment, the guest bedroom door opened; and in stepped the dark-haired Englishman, with the stately grace of a dancer and a happy go-lucky whistle. Finally recognizable, David's jaw dropped. He had watched the charming face countless times in a cult classic. In awe of this lanky actor, he had only seen him perform once and in an incredible film, which had made him an idol to millions. Brilliant seemed an understatement for this tall, elegant man, and his talent allowed him to steal every scene in which he appeared. He looked exactly like he did in the film, ageless and extraordinarily gifted, with amazing eyes that told you things without speaking. David acknowledged Jess' theory correct; the people from La Rosa Negra could be seen in this reality when required. They saw Kincaid because he was real, just as they were; but led astray assuming Steven knew more than he did. Ted's friend also remained in the dark, but being helped for some reason. The mystery became more intriguing, as David absorbed each new revelation into his awareness.

A surprise greeting, Quinlan Ambrose, with his hands in his pockets, strolled over to Ted. Pulling out his hands, he gave a quick flick of his wrists to each of the older men, forcing them away from the ailing party. Another Lavender, he easily moved inanimate and animate objects without a touch; and both men drew further away to watch what would transpire. Healing hands spread their fingers, a foot above the ailing body, and swept across Barrett. Blue light followed them, while darker blue eyes stopped tearing under the dark lashes. Ted quieted into a hypnotic state of tranquility.

Jess and David stared at each other in amazement: another illusion, a trick of the imagination, or the magic of the labyrinth. Whatever Ambrose did, he calmed Ted enough to talk. With few words exchanged, a decision was finalized. After the holiday, Quinlan would return with Barrett to his Mexican location, to become Ted's baby-sitter, until he regained the weight loss. Unfortunately, current damage could not be rectified, only the progression would stop. The Englishman said nothing directly about the disease, only insisting Ted would spend his free time under the sun, while in the desert hot spot. It seemed an oddity, when the young man really needed nourishment. Very persuasive, the raven-haired actor promised to collect Barrett on Boxing Day, not leaving his side even to go to the bathroom. The rules were set: no more vomiting, no more diuretics, no more purging, and no more pain.

Ted also placed where he had seen the smiling Brit with the enormous green eyes: La Rosa Negra. He inquired if he could make them look like a cat. Laughing with delight, Quinlan assured him he would refrain from turning into a panther. Another innocent question came from the ailing body, which seemed oblivious to the strange situation, in which they were. "Are Lavender's natural, or can anyone do that with their eyes?"

"Of course you can, Lad. People can do anything when they set their minds to it. You can all learn. Mr. Carmichael has studied for years and will soon be taught by the great masters, if he be so inclined. As for Mr. LaCoix, he learned to open his heart to all things new and wondrous, certainly enough to start rectifying his life for the better. Much has changed since we met during what you called *the rockslide*; a rather quaint expression for our Ladyship's dramatic entrance." The teasing smile forced a grin from all three men.

"Hell, yes, but why didn't we recognize you, Quinlan?" David wanted to know everything about this man and his relationship to the Mistress. From somewhere, he received a reminder of three horses and the two riders who accompanied Lavender at their first location. One of those raven-haired riders had to be Ambrose. It created an immediate memory of an amber eye, and the acknowledgment of the *knowing* from the Andalusian stallion. Feeling his heart skip a beat, David reached out and grabbed Jess' shirtsleeve for support. Quinlan and the horses were from Lavender's reality, and the strange moment of recognition, with the wondrous animal, changed his life. He had made a promise, with a wink, to what he now believed was the Cosmos, but wondered to whom he had pledged vows. Another quiet whisper in his head, and he heard, *'You promised them to yourself, David LaCoix. Stay on your path.'*

"Will this be interfering with your other projects?" Jess sensed the nervousness in his friend and continued the questioning of a known stranger. Estranged from the scene, he was unable to put the pieces together.

"Other projects: that is a laugh. I warn all of you; do not become known for one character; it can kill your career. I have not acted in years, but to answer your question, in a more positive fashion, it is my honor to care for and teach life's mysteries to Theo, including turning into a cat." Ambrose smiled at the man who began believing everyone thought him twelve. He had found an ally, however, in the next words spoken by his healer directly to David. "What Mr. Barrett confided in you today is the truth, LaCoix. Do not misjudge his intentions."

David pondered for a moment. In the back of his mind, it gladdened him someone knew of their delicate relationship, but it also struck him hard enough to know when to stop. Maybe Ted's new caregiver needed to know, but rumors spread quickly in their world. He returned his attention to the man sitting beside Barrett. Ambrose continued to stare directly into the young man's face, studying every angle, particularly the peculiar eyes. "Then he'll be all right?" David blurted out, stopping the interloping of Ted's mind. He felt lost in a science fiction plot.

"I did not say that, David. We can only help where we can. Now, we understand why the elixir, given to you, deemed too harsh for your degenerating system. The Mistress sends her humble regrets at being unaware of your situation. I am afraid that even her Ladyship does not catch everything in all her worlds. You slipped through the cracks, as they say."

"Who caught me, and why did Christ not help? He's the one who should have saved me, from falling through your so-called cracks." A hint of sarcastic bitterness from Ted, David remembered the same attacks he received eons ago.

"Oh, dear, we are into a theological scenario again. We will discuss your Mr. Christ, along with many other things, while you heal."

"Thanks, Mr. Ambrose, but..." Ted sat up, looking a little better and less antagonistic. Quinlan stood to let his patient stabilize from the treatment. Only temporary, the process would be repeated many times.

"...but what? You are afraid of no privacy, but you must get used to it, Lad, for I will be attending to you every second, whether I am in sight or not. I am not always the charming personage you see before you. Believe me, I can see through walls."

"Bet you can walk through them too." Ted muttered.

"His humor returns; we are off to a swift start. We will have some fun, you and I, while exploring life, death, and all that lies between here and there. Now, anything else you wish to know before I take my leave? I think you better ask it, Theo."

"Well, I wanted to ask a favor of you and David. Staying and rehearsing with Kincaid and Peerce has been a nightmare since the fall. His fall, not mine."

"We gathered that, Ted." David spoke in the same tone as if talking to Holly, wanting to help the younger man get the words over which he stumbled. "What do you need? If it helps you get better; we'll do it." Standing arms across his chest, the familiar tilt of the head and hips, indicated how serious David was over the yet stated request.

"Be careful, LaCoix, he may surprise you with something you do not wish to grant. Remember, *be careful what you wish for*?" Quinlan gave the blond actor a teasing smile.

"Are you two going to let me finish? Kincaid's terrified of everything and everybody, knowing his fall meant more than just a warning; and he's frightened of Morningstar, Lavender, the Mistress, whomever. He doesn't know what to do. I'm worried about him; he's so scared. He's on the edge and needs our help, especially your kind of help, Mr. Ambrose, since he knows you from the realm of the Lady."

"The realm is it? You are becoming a believer in her Ladyship's magic. So be it, if you do precisely what I ask of you. The Mistress will not be pleased, although she has moments of changing her mind. You had better not get me into trouble, or I can cause a few minor miracles myself. Now, what is the favor you wish of Mr. LaCoix?"

"I know you don't want me around, David, but if I'm to get through this; and you're in London, sorting your thoughts about..."

"What do you wish of me, Ted?"

"Please give me the house project back. I'll follow your new plans and add nothing of my own. You won't even know I supervised." The face, haunted by black circles around the eyes, begged for a life returned; and two men were concerned over how long a life it would be.

"Alright, and I haven't changed the plans. You can take charge, as I had a fit over the chaos created upon dismissing you, considering the fine job you had done."

"You kept the plans? Why?"

"I liked them." David finally gave him a genuine smile and received a timid one in return; the one from the picture he had burned.

"Right then, I shall pick you up Boxing Day, around noon; and you will disappear, for a few months, to shoot a great motion picture. We shall get you healthy and happy, with a lot of talking and learning thrown in, not to mention blue light, maybe even some pink. Cheerio, all." Ambrose vanished, only seen by the three bewildered men.

"What was that, Jess: a coincidence, a materialization of what we needed? What?"

"Have no idea, but there are no coincidences. He was sent; I'm sure of it, and for many reasons." Carmichael left to join the party, while David returned his look of astonishment back to a happier Barrett.

"Life's getting stranger and stranger." Weary mentally, David slumped down beside his last unknown factor. Turning to face the young man, his expression filled with forgiveness. With smiles exchanged, two shaggy heads twisted about, chuckling in merriment.

Feeling better, Ted managed to find his way back to his frantic wife. They would soon depart after saying farewell and thanking Susan. One thing left for Ted, it was paramount to wish Holly a Merry Christmas. He found her neatly replacing fallen tinsel onto the tree. With great amusement, Ted's ghastly day brightened, spotting Holly standing resplendent in the decorative lights, in her beautiful green ribbons and white lace, once again tied neatly into her blonde hair. She had succeeded in her quest.

"Congratulations, Holly, I see you got your bows back."

"Got them all by myself, just like Dad said. Guess I have to make him breakfast; and it's Christmas morning! I don't mind though, because it's Dad; and he showed me how to get my ribbons back." In a dither, the little sprite twirled for her new friend to show off her victory.

"Your Dad's a smart guy. You listen to him. He only speaks when he has something important to say. As for breakfast, probably just a good cup of black coffee would satisfy him."

"Yeah, and he taught me how to make it, just the way he likes. He never eats real breakfast."

"I brought you a Christmas present." Ted handed her a large, plainly wrapped box.

"For me? Can I open it?"

Ted knelt down and looked into those astonishingly familiar eyes. "Of course, I hope you like it." Holly graciously accepted the gift, while Ted watched with great mirth at the frenzy in which she opened it. A child's eyes lit up and smiled, letting out a little squeal.

"Oh, sorry, not supposed to scream. Did I scare you?" The extreme concern shown was so like her father's, it made Ted laugh.

"Tiny squeals of delight are perfectly okay."

"Good, because I love teddy bears. He's beautiful and soft. Got a whole bunch; but I like this one best." She hugged the stuffed toy with great enthusiasm and beamed radiantly at him.

"I have a much bigger bear exactly like him. I call him Sir Edmund. He's traveling right now."

"Bears don't travel."

"Sure they do." Ted gestured a surprised look of shock that Holly would not know of such a thing. Seldom seen, the young actor had an amazing gift of imagining things to be true; and watching from her window, Lavender laughed, wondering why he could not believe in other magic.

"Sir Edmund; I like that name. I know one." The voice became gleefully higher with excitement, and the sweet smile wrinkled up her eyes.

"Going to tell me?" Ted chuckled, gratified she approved of his gift. He knew nothing about interacting with children, although he had once been a spokesman for a Christian children's fund. He retreated from the post on the pretense of work commitments; but Lavender's comments, concerning the bribery of children to adopt a different religion and culture, for the sake of needed medicine and food, had turned him around. His smile came back, happy with his decision, and his ideas, of how to rectify the problem. An excited voice startled him from his thoughts.

"Sir Lancelot! We can pretend he's Sir Edmund's baby brother."

"Yes we can. You like the story of King Arthur?"

"Yeah, especially the way Dad reads the story."

"I bet. Merry Christmas, Holly, I have something for your Dad too."

"You can put it right there; he'll see it first thing. Thank you for Sir Lancelot, Mr. Barrett." Holly smiled brightly; and a man, starting on a new road, returned it with one that outshone the glitter of the room. He may still have a chance with David, staying his Teddy Bear forever, and perhaps Holly could love a live one.

David covertly watched and listened to the conversation from behind the sparkling lights and the shimmer of gold and silver. It brought tears, thinking about Ted's bear, and where it now lay, discarded like a piece of trash. Long chats with the giant bear might bring his life back into focus. The disturbed and worried host made his farewell wishes to the Barretts, but first pulled Ted aside, apologizing he had no gift for him, and had to leave again for reasons they both understood: work. The younger man bashfully smiled, his eyes transfixed on his shifting feet, while assuring David he received the best gift possible: the man's caring and the return of the house project.

The Lady breathed in a sigh of relief. Her promise of a guide for Ted seemed a perfect match with Ambrose. They would drive each other crazy and become fast friends in the process. New doors would open for her man-child with Quinlan's guidance, and the cult actor's true mission may yield the reasons for the man's strange illness. She hoped his thoughts might shed light on both Barrett and Kincaid. David also made a good decision, giving Ted an outlet for his anxieties and an escape from the ongoing saga of Kincaid and Peerce. Now experiencing revelations beyond his comprehension, she would start preparing David to receive the answers. Pleased with the unfolding of events, she could not help but giggle in her private quarters of candles and dreams.

As for Kincaid, he had been crying out apologies since the incident, and would soon come bounding through her garden to find her. She pondered on her choices, whether to close the gate permanently, to allow him entry for another last chance, or throw him a curve with one of her more powerful allies; someone presently as upset as Steven. She had not forgotten one of her oldest and most revered friends, Ethan Peerce. Lavender knew a slight nudge, from a silly, flighty Fate like Steven, would not interfere long with the stoic resolve of an entity of such enlightenment.

The Mistress wanted happy-endings. A black polished nail tapped the ever present pewter goblet, as her other hand held the stem. Two remarkable hands, so white and graceful, yet so powerful, they wielded destruction or rebirth with a simple flick of the wrist. Coming out of her mental wanderings, she caught herself gently fondling the cold metal stem of the vessel; she immediately stopped and laughed aloud. Thoughts of David poured into her head, dawning on her what she had been doing to him in his reality. Her hand covered her embarrassment. Of little matter, her habitual behavior made him feel like a man. A soft sigh and her worlds heard the approving sound of crystal chimes. Putting the container down, she rubbed her hands together in satisfaction; a few things worked this day; and the jeweled fingers sent prisms across her candle-lit room, sending an auroral display throughout the Cosmos.

"The stars are beautiful tonight, Quin."

"Yes, they are, my Lady. How did we do?"

"Very well, however, you must make him behave, if your soft heart is willing. Learn what you can about the body he has struggled with for years, and try to make him laugh. Theodore Barrett is to be cared for cautiously and gently, like the Teddy Bear he has been nicknamed."

"As will you, my dear."

CHAPTER 29

Two men, on separate journeys, were trying to meet at a junction. Theodore Barrett withdrew, protected within the understanding tenderness of Lavender's healer, Quinlan Ambrose. Genuinely battling something physical and psychological, both visible and unseen, he continued to diligently keep pace with his two mega-star co-stars. Master craftsmen, Kincaid and Peerce taught him a great deal about emoting as an actor. Watching them, as men sorting out their relationship, was something else; it played havoc with Ted's precarious mental state. Ethan behaved in a similar manner to that of LaCoix in the beginning, with subdued, uncommunicative ire. The serene, quiet-spoken man, besotted with Steven, said nothing, except his intense dialogue on the set, and then to vanish his secret refuge. Feeling badly about the torment of these two men, Ted came to understand how badly he had hurt his mentor who was so much more. Remorse added to his problems.

Quinlan did what he could for his main concern, succeeding to some degree, tending to the young man's needs, spiritually and physically. Although growing a little stronger, these two things greatly challenged Ted, but his all-encompassing problems overwhelmed him. At times, Ambrose could only hold him through the tumultuous nightmares and watch attentively whenever he took a hit, blindsided from another direction. Problems mounted: the decision of the divorce and ensuing custody hearing, turmoil between Peerce and Kincaid, construction of the Arizona house. The most devastating, however, was his yearning for LaCoix, telepathically picked up by Quinlan. Ted needed his lover's presence, an impossible situation for a man trying too hard at everything.

On another coastline, in a different landscape, David traveled a securer path. Long before leaving Los Angeles, he decided Barrett would be welcome in his life when ready. In the meantime, he left the younger man to sort out his issues under the necessary guidance, keeping him away from the suffocating coddling David felt disposed to do. Having the best help possible to heal, to grow, and to learn, Ted would succeed; and his steadfast lover had to be satisfied with that knowledge. They would be together soon enough, for whatever time remained.

One major hurdle impeded Ted's recovery; his overwhelming need for David physically, not for want of sex, but the mandatory support. In a secret talk with Quinlan, the blond-haired actor's heart broke, hearing that their private calls left Ted distraught and ten steps further back from whence he began. On the suggestion of a demanding Caregiver, David begrudgingly purchased a laptop computer to e-mail letters to Barrett. Apparently, Ted felt LaCoix cold and non-communicative over the phone. The feeling of rejection, after every conversation, left him in a puddle of tears, crying out he felt ill, and usually was. Ambrose handled the latter problem, but the sadness lingered.

David could not believe what he heard. His talks with Ted may not be of the intimate nature they once had been, but always amicable and caring. Ambrose assured him no blame was intended; but loving someone and trusting them were separate emotions. Guilt, on Barrett's part, made matters worse. LaCoix's feelings could not reach the young man until trust returned on both sides; neither man was ready. Ted's misinterpretation of each statement escalated the problem. Everything became accentuated whether said in jest, or without realizing the impact of a single word in the wrong place. Over-sensitivity seemed the common crux of most anorexic patients, taking every word literally and reacting to it inappropriately. An example, still remembered, was the mistaken but formative confirmation of David's approval of the man's appearance, when Ted had been too pale, too thin, too vulnerable, and too mentally unstable. The remark of finding him attractive, in those appalling conditions, embedded in the disturbed psyche to stay thin--very, very thin--and very, very needy.

The e-mail idea corrected the misunderstandings. David would reread every word, making sure nothing could be misconstrued for sarcasm, coldness, or worse yet, uncaring. With the *Send* button pushed, a heart raced until the happy receipt of a reply. Blossoming under this new rule, Ted thrilled with every letter transmitted. His knight still cared; the only thing he needed to know.

To keep himself from faltering, the more stalwart actor also buried himself in his work, plunging into the eerie depths of his character. The dailies returned to dreary dailies, and retakes followed retakes for the need of perfection. Evenings became his delight within the menacing manor, which he began to enjoy. Gothic and ghostly, his quarters had everything her Ladyship would enjoy. The huge, stone fireplace, hundreds of years old, kept his room warm and dry. Considering the last upgrade had been fifty years prior, the renovation allowed every pleasure an ancient house could offer, including electricity, telephones, flushing toilets, and hot water in an adjoining bathroom. Woe be it for anyone to neglect a LaCoix's need for the luxury of steaming showers and bubbling baths. The house easily had more than twenty bedrooms; and Morris allowed him the comfortable privacy of the west wing, second floor. He missed the sunsets of Arizona, but the mist, which veiled the evening gardens when this English sun fell behind the oaks, filled his imagination with friendly apparitions and strange visions. The estate offered him sanctuary; a place to piece together each new thought experienced, from the first touch of a slender, white hand.

Mid-January, with *Lord Worthington-Smythe* in full production, David reveled in the complexity of his character, more than any other he had portrayed. Three scenes with Ted had to count as his most joyous performance, although not acted. He laughed thinking about their Western, which continued to hit box office records, and masses of technical questions from insiders. The fans loved it, particularly women. He thought it odd, until he realized how erotic seeing two women together tantalized a straight male. Why would it not be the flipside for women? The flipside--he chuckled again--the terminology meant something quite different to Ted and himself.

Two weeks into shooting, Jenny Morris jabbered an incomprehensible line, and guffaws resounded around the set. In a particularly good mood, LaCoix joined the laughter upon the disgruntled word *Cut*. Out of the corner of his eye, behind the blinding lights, he spotted the producer handing an envelope to Morris; the contents turned Rod's face into undisguised grief. Muffled whispers passed between the two, and with consenting nods, Morris stood to gaze blankly into space. The cast and crew froze; who would receive the toxic piece of paper.

David's eyes grew. Green flashes of neon, under the strange eerie lighting, set alarms off in his head; and the purple mist suffocated him. Something was wrong. Morris spoke quietly to him, but he heard nothing, said nothing. Walking blindly forward with no idea of where they led him, he felt Rod support him around the waist, while the producer, on the other side, gripped his arm with two hands. His legs could not move in a straight line; his knees would not stay locked to keep him upright. He heard only Lavender's soothing voice. *'She is gone, David. Be still, my friend. I am with you.'*

"Who's gone?" David asked an unseen force, but received the horrible answer from Rod.

"A charter jet is waiting for us. We'll leave immediately for L.A."

"Why?" Understanding nothing, LaCoix felt numb, unable to think.

"Listen to me, David. Susan is gone; killed in a car accident. She did not suffer and never saw what hit her." Rod kept his voice low, repeating the awful truth to the shocked actor. Getting him off the set and into a waiting limousine took several men to handle. The tall, lean, unsteady body could not control its movements.

"It's impossible; I just talked to her last night."

With Morris on one side, and the producer on the other, they managed to wrap several heavy blankets around the shivering body. Dazed and in disbelief, he felt hands stroking and rubbing him to regain circulation; but it was Lavender who held him together; only the Mistress could help him through the horror.

"Holly! Where's Holly?" A deafening roar of panic came, precisely the moment the car lurched forward; and the motorcycle police turned on their sirens.

"It's mid-morning in L.A.; your daughter's still at school. The police contacted your agent who gave them our office number here. Your sons have been notified; both boys agreed to pick Holly up after school. Knowing her the best, they decided an expedition into the country would not alarm her, since the three of them go on these little excursions, since you started *Outlaw's Heart*. I gave them permission to use our cabin at the lake to keep her entertained, and away from any media coverage, although a tremendous responsibility for your boys. They came up with a story about her mother's new boyfriend treating her to an evening out; but both insisted her maternal grandfather would not come near Holly, for whatever reason. But you, David, are her father; you should be the one to tell her."

"Tell her what? How do I tell her something I don't believe? Susan!" David buried his face in his hands and broke down.

"There's a medic on board. He'll give you something once we're in the air. You'll find the words, man. You'll find the words."

"There are no words to say to a child, Rod. Hi, Holly, I'm home. Guess who died today? Jesus Christ, how do I tell her? Tell me first. Tell me again, and give me the whole story, every detail." David was lost, never experiencing a death of someone so close. His losses were of lovers and friends, but never from the grim reaper. A few colleagues had passed on, but this was family: the mother of his child.

"Susan dropped Holly off at school, and then headed out in her little yellow Mercedes she loved, to meet a friend for coffee and a little shopping on Rodeo Drive. She didn't make it, and she didn't see it, David. A semi lost control on one of the overhead bridges and flipped over the barricade, landing directly on the car. There wasn't time. Only a matter of seconds, she would have been under the bridge and safe. I'm so sorry, David." Morris could only give the man the facts in the gentlest of manner, with no other way to tell anyone of such a disaster.

"There's nothing left of her. She was beautiful, so beau..." Lavender had him pass out in Morris' arms. She could not help but for a small respite of sleep to stop the shock from overtaking him. Impossible to forewarn, she had denied him answers to his many questions for such a reason. He could not handle such a truth; no man, woman, or child need know of future tragedies. It was unthinkable to cause such fear in anyone. The end of Susan's journey, in this reality, the Mistress received confirmation from the late Mrs. LaCoix's Caretaker. It was her time and non-reversible; other lives needed corrected paths.

The unseen purple cloud surrounded David to the end. From the time they carried him from the car, strapped him to the bed on the plane, then the sedative, until he started to stir, Lavender kept him from the terror ready to greet him. His daughter and two stalwart sons waited, along with his first wife. David came around on touchdown, still stunned and confused, but quiet. With L.A.P.D. efficiency, they picked him up directly from the tarmac, by a waiting unmarked police car. He stumbled down the gangway, diving head first into the backseat of the car, away from the telephoto lenses Rod spotted. There would be no shots, of a wild, red-eyed actor in grief, for the press this day. Once safe from prying eyes, he leaned back in some control, and put his hands over his face to whisper one word, "Why?"

A worried Morris remained quiet, deep in his own sorrowful thoughts, unknowingly leaving an unearthly force to care for David. Her field of light enveloped him, felt only by the man she had come to respect, and in her way love. She had left him alone too long, and could only forgive herself, for the lost time, by bombarding him with revelations he may not yet be ready. He was a good man behind the mask presented to the world; the one that made him part of the gang of his generation's *bad boys* in the acting profession. The wild side of the man had changed. His future had always been to shine over Hollywood, along with her own desire of placing him amongst the brightest stars in one of her galaxies.

'David, there is no reason. Susan's journey was short but fulfilling. She met her goals by giving you a priceless treasure, and is now on a new path in another realm. Make her happy, my friend; become the father you promised to be. Holly needs your strength, and she will accept her mother's death in time, if you show her the way. Love her and keep her with you. Do not lose yourself in this pain; do not become a victim of the Fates. Your child will follow your example.'

Unheard, David asked what should be said and done. He could no longer conceive a future only through set goals; Susan had hopes for herself and Holly. A factor of less than a second, she would have escaped unscathed. This, the Mistress could not explain to his satisfaction, but assured him an unexpected loss never could. The late Mrs. LaCoix filled her days with grace and purpose; and although sounding harsh to David, his estranged wife had done everything right in her life, including fending off her own Fates to travel a true path, without the need of celestial interference. Nothing remained unfinished; she set goals for Holly, not herself; and there lay the end of a life.

Unacceptable to LaCoix, in his eyes Holly needed her mother, and an important goal was sacrificed. Once again, Lavender's calming voice made it clear that his daughter's future lay in his hands and his in hers. Nothing more could be said, but she promised to be there, surrounding them both when the time came for honesty; the time would come soon.

A small escort of motorcycle police guarded the speeding vehicle to expedite LaCoix's sad journey home. He examined every bridge they passed over, to see any telltale signs of a Herculean tragedy. There was nothing; they were not even on the same highway. Once in Beverly Hills, the sirens quieted, not to alarm the family who giggled over a silly video. Only one innocuous-looking car entered the relatively small estate, and remained vigilant, while two men stiffly dragged themselves out, stretched, and stood for a moment composing their thoughts. A darkening sky hung over them, and thankfully, people surrounding the estate kept quiet for the unknowing occupant within. A grieving man flew through a night to enter into the same day. Several deep breaths, a borrowed handkerchief to dry the swollen red eyes, David strode forth with his long legs. This was his changed future, to break a child's heart.

With only Lavender to keep him steady, it would be so easy to let his knees give way, screaming and crying in his sorrow. His only question was how to pour your heart out to a little girl and make her understand? As an actor, he could manage the short dialogue; only then could they fall apart together. He found Holly laughing with her two half-brothers and first wife, Angela; they all carried their emotions close to the surface. A glimpse of her father, Holly squealed with delight, flying through the air in one strong jump into his outstretched arms. Carried immediately into the library, he told his little blonde princess the truth, gently and honestly, without any silly rhetoric of reasons. As foreseen, father and daughter held each other in a waterfall of salty tears.

David looked around the room, through the sprinkling of wet lashes against his cheeks. How many liquid diamonds had fallen and vanished in this room? This place, once his sanctuary, had become his inner sanctum of tears. The place where Susan and he cried joyously on the arrival of their new Christmas baby; the place where he stood to discuss the divorce after being caught with Rebecca; the place where Holly ran to her Daddy when hurt or in sorrow; and the place where Ted's heart gushed out in his agony. Now he held his life's treasure in his arms, saying farewell to her mother; and the blood of broken hearts covered the floor once more. In his sanctuary of wounded Spirits, the stain grew darker crimson.

Holding Holly securely, David emerged from their *tête-à-tête* of life and death. Only simple explanations for a six-year-old, with no understanding of a tragedy, Holly now knew her mother would not return; it was enough knowledge. Everything had been said and shed, until he saw his sons. Nineteen-years-old, the twins spent a day and a night masking their sorrow to aid their sister. Now they could cry unashamedly with their parents. The LaCoix family clung together, washing their grief over each other, cleansing away the shock, and releasing emotions to share intimately. In a united force, they bonded; the healing of holy tears helped them recover from the initial shock. They sat down in the family room to silently mourn together, with Holly curled tightly in her father's arms, until emotional exhaustion won out. She slept in a cradle of Lavender's healing cloud. The little girl felt the love and heard the voice, which spoke to her father, while listening to the bewitching melodies sung only to her. Mommy sang with the angels, and the Mistress did not intend to destroy the image for the brave little being so much like her father.

Three days of agonizing trauma followed. Angela supported her boys, the boys supported their father, and the father supported his daughter through the long ordeal of a private memorial and a more public burial. For the gratification of the press, they captured shots of the infamous David LaCoix weeping, as he placed an extraordinary bouquet of exquisite white gardenias on the white casket. Susan's favorite flowers, they were strangely in full bloom this winter. The man stepped back; and a beautiful little girl, dressed in black with a perfect matching hat, bent down and placed a green velvet and lace bow next to the flowers. Unnerving hidden cameras could not capture the snip of long blonde hair attached to the special ribbon. Only a child's mind would think of such a wondrous memento; the daughter giving a part of herself to the mother; it made the circle complete. She stood up and gazed at her father who picked her up to bury their faces into the other's neck, and together they wept in disbelief and a beautiful goodbye. Tyler and Bryce immediately surrounded David in comforting arms, engulfing both the man and the small shaking body of the little girl, preventing them from falling into the abyss along with the casket.

To the press' good fortune and positioning, they caught many familiar faces on camera. One image, in particular, would earn someone a coveted payoff in the six-figure range. Three men stood a short distance from the rest of the mourners, barely visible to the family and invited guests. Ethan Peerce had one arm around a crying Steven Kincaid, while his other arm secured the man in front of them, Theodore Barrett. Strained sorrow showed visibly on all three faces, and only Peerce could hold back his tears, unable to console the two younger men. It was a freelancer's dream picture.

Finally over, the white casket lay in peace, the limousines departed, and the mourners made their way to the now austere-looking Tudor house, where father and daughter immediately retreated to the library; their sanctuary of broken dreams. Clutching Holly so tight, she could barely breathe, David sat down. The little girl became very still, satisfied to let her Dad get comfortable, and stretch out his long legs. She finally rested, protected within his arms, which loosened slightly, to fall into once-upon-a-time, with a few hushing whispers. David closed his swollen eyes to listen to the silence. Without a word uttered, he thanked the Mistress for caring for them all, during the destruction of one of his priorities. He did not hear her voice; only the feeling and smell of her presence gave him comfort, knowing she tended Holly. Peace at last, now what was he to do?

A light tap on the door had David tightening his eyelids. He did not want this intrusion, and kept quiet. The door opened and closed without his knowledge; nor did he hear the sound of shiny black loafers walk across the floor. One of the fallen, however, felt a blanket; LaCoix opened his eyes to stare straight into the salty waters of another's sorrow. Green eyes misted up to mime the cobalt blues; the stare grew intense; their grief exchanged without a word.

"Ted! Baby Bear, what are you doing here?"

"Rest. Holly seems to be comfortably sleeping. I'll leave you both. Just wanted to make sure you were both all right. Can I get you anything? Are you warm enough?"

"We're fine, but you shouldn't be here. Is Ambrose with you?"

"Yes, along with Ethan and Stevie. We won't bother you. I'll make sure no one else enters."

"Thanks, but why did you come? This is no place for you. You're not strong enough."

"I had to come. You've taken care of me since you first acknowledged my existence. Now it's my turn. Rest, David, sleep the sleep of the angels." Ted's hand swept the blond hair off the strained face, and the back of his hand caressed a cheek. LaCoix said nothing more, as father and daughter drifted into dreams created by an unearthly force and the touch of a lover's hand. Unbeknownst to the traumatized man, his unstable Teddy Bear took control outside. He would not have believed what Theodore Barrett accomplished that day, if his sons had not witnessed it.

While David and Holly slept, the house crowded with lawyers, agents, publicists, and accountants, to name only a handful. They demanded details and answers. The Judge continued to be belligerent at the obnoxious intrusion of his daughter's private funeral reception. Ted, on the other hand, remained calm. With Ambrose at his side, he ushered the unwelcome parasites into another room, while he invited Tyler and Bryce to stay. One at a time, the different parties presented their concerns, and one at a time, Barrett resolved them. With no authority to do so, or the practical experience, he threw himself into the task. His university degree returned to the frontal lobe of his brain; and he commenced the horrendous task of sorting through the data of the entire estate. Clearly defined thoughts and opinions, regarding each document, were written down and numbered in sequence for David's ease. Not yet time to bombard a man in mourning with this kind of turmoil, the LaCoix boys agreed and helped him were they could. The extremely astute Ambrose voiced his suggestions, particularly when it came to publicity and the press. The sadists lingered behind the locked gates, waiting like vultures to swoop down on any information: fact or fiction.

Only Susan's father objected, not knowing Barrett, except for calling him the filthy sodomite who exposed himself, with his former son-in-law, in a disgusting film that required banning. The comments hurt Ted more than anyone knew. Only Quinlan felt his pain and quickly stopped the flight to purge the horrible bile created by the fear of a father-like figure berating his sensitive ego.

After settling all factions and addressing the press at the gates, Barrett dismissed the unwanted crowd off the estate, and with an unsteady hand, turned over the neatly arranged folder to David's two sons with instructions. With Ambrose, Kincaid, and Peerce steadying his stance, Ted quickly departed the premises. Once in the black BMW 700 series luxury car, he broke down and cried himself into oblivion in lifesaving arms. He tried to help, and prayed he saved David from any unnecessary distress. His compulsion screamed at him to stay and hold the man until all his dreams returned. This he could not do, but he did thank Lavender for helping to shield his love from the nightmare he faced, and asked her to end David's sorrow, to bring light back into his life, and to hold him like the man held him during his moments of crisis. Through his own tears, he knew they were safe in her care; and Ambrose gave him that security, holding him paternally in the backseat. They would return to Mexico immediately, his three comrades assuring him he did the right thing.

CHAPTER 30

"Dad, wake up!" The urgent voice penetrated David's drugged-induced slumber; and his eyes blinked open against the harsh light of the lamp on the desk. He lay half-prone, with his daughter digging into every part of him; both snuggled warm under a blanket.

"Bryce! What? I feel ghastly."

"Come on, man, Ty will take Holly and get her ready. I need you up and moving. This is important." The eldest son, by 3 minutes, took immediate control, having vowed to carry out a plan laid out by a willful stranger they had met but once. Barrett felt like a friend, and a caring one of their father.

"What's so important that has to be done right now? I can hardly move."

"Get up and pay attention. Have you got her, Tyler?"

"Yeah, she's a feather, sleeping like an angel." The other son easily picked up his sister and exited through the wooden door without an objection raised.

"Listen up, Dad, because I have a lot to explain; and we don't have much time. Rod Morris has a jet waiting to take you and Holly back to England."

"We can't leave yet. Holly isn't ready. Arrangements have to be made." Still groggy from emotional exhaustion and a mild sedative, David wished to return to the comfort of dark obscurity.

"They've been made; and Holly and Maria are packed and set to go. Leave it too long; she may never be ready. Now, there's a short stack of papers for you to sign. Read them, and Tyler and I can take over from there. You need to move on with your life, Dad, and make one for our little sister. It's time you two grieved together privately, in that monolithic, Gothic manor you described. It's all settled."

"What's settled? What papers?" David finally hauled himself up from the embryonic-like confines of his favorite chair, rubbed his face to get some feeling back, and stretched out his long frame. His daughter was not a feather, after sleeping on him for some time; he looked at his watch; they had been blessed with a peaceful four hours. He felt like Rip Van Winkle, only to wake up with a smooth face.

"Bombarded by Hollywood fungi, we didn't want to disturb you. First, the Judge went berserk over custody of Holly, becoming a complete pain in the ass as usual; but your friend, Barrett, came through for us. He insisted Tyler and me help him; and we confronted every one of those scavenging dogs ready to rip you apart. Finding all sorts of discrepancies in his quick scan of your financial status, he had your accountants fleeing out the door with each red circle he made around a number. Your corporate lawyer immediately froze all your assets, only you can touch them. It might be just the start, so Barrett hired an independent auditor to take care of your money. Don't even ask how he managed to unravel the mess in such short order. All you have to do is sign the letter on top of the pile of papers on your desk, to give the auditor the authority to check for missing funds. Hate to say this, Dad, but your accountants were screwing you big time."

"You're kidding?"

"No way, man; the entire hoard, of leeches, was in panic; and then the two divorce lawyers went into action. Barrett went ballistic with the arguing, and realized their presence unnecessary. Since the divorce not yet finalized, and Susan hadn't changed her will, he tossed them out on their royal butts. Don't now how he accomplished that either."

"Ted?" David grew more lucid, yet disbelieving everything said to him. His claustrophobic, passive Teddy Bear could barely stand, let alone accomplish business dealings of such magnitude.

"He did everything, including the press release, which he conducted just outside the gates." Bryce reamed off the news faster than David could assimilate it, losing his father in another maze.

"What about my publicist?" David moved languidly toward the desk, finally sitting behind it, looking very out of place.

"Making plans with your new agent as to what to do. Barrett couldn't stand the arguing, so he just did the right thing. His words were magical, Dad. The man's a poet when it comes to wondrous imagery; and Susan will be remembered as the beauty he described."

"That's what he does best: make people cry. I can't believe Ted did all this." David carefully went through the papers, reading and following every instruction. His blue-eyed wonder astonished him. He readily signed the documents required, and in the back of his mind, he heard the words, *'Learn to handle it yourself, with the help of a true friend in the knowing of such details.'* The last item, sealed in an envelope, handwritten, and marked personal in Ted's signature style, had David's hands shaking with the power of the precious contents it secured. He would open it in flight, in private, and in silence. "Is this the last one?"

"Yeah, that's it. The Judge is snarling mad about you leaving with Holly, but the rest of us knew that you alone had the right to raise her. All has been taken care of. We'll be thinking of you both. We loved Susan, Dad, and Mom held us all together. She's waiting just outside to say good-bye." Bryce stood quietly, watching his father, whom he remembered as strong and determined, falter in his attempt to stand. They had become friends, once his boys came to terms with David's many misdemeanors publicly committed. The shaking of Bryce's hand confirmed his pride.

"Good, I wanted to thank her. You've grown into a smarter and more loving man than your old Dad, Bryce. You and Ty are the best." David clung to his son and exchanged a firm embrace. The father needed his boys this day, and they came through.

Tyler and Holly entered hand-in-hand. The little girl rubbed the sleep out of her eyes, while hugging Sir Lancelot and maintaining a grip on her brother.

"Thanks, Ty; you guys did a great job."

"Thank Barrett; he's so damn strong-willed, but looks like you could snap him like a toothpick. Is he sick?" Tyler did not understand the increased sadness in his father's slumped shoulders; perhaps the reason lay in not forgiving his father's many misdemeanors. Susan's death closed the chapter of mistrust; his baby sister, holding his hand trustingly, proved it.

"Yes he is. He should never have come; but I'm glad you all met and got along." The father finally smiled, realizing the boys' own grief needed nurturing.

"No problem with Theo; he acts like an older brother." Although shyer in showing affection, Tyler did not break away from David's rib-shattering clench, and obliged the obvious need.

"Yeah, I liked him. He did a hell of a job on this paperwork for an actor." Bryce quickly straightened up the papers, ready for filing the next day.

"What do you mean by that? We actors aren't complete idiots; at least not all the time." David's smile broadened, accompanying his objections. The two careers were oddities, one relying on the other completely, with the second being a parasitic monster preying on their naïve clients. To find out the truth, of her Ladyship's statement, had David in the throes of a nightmare, for allowing the mishandling of his estate. His ignorance could have been the ruination of both families who relied on him. "That's why you two will finish college. We need a business grad in the family."

"You could always adopt Barrett?" Bryce smiled at him with the twisted, wicked, LaCoix grin. "After all, Dad, you know him intimately."

"Maybe I'll marry him instead." David returned the chortle and devilish wink, musing at the thought. "You've both made me proud today; and I'm sorry I haven't said those words when you needed to hear them. Take care of your mom; I'll speak with her on the way out. We'll see you in a few months, and I'll keep in touch. Well, Holly, we better get moving if we want to catch the plane."

"What about Mommy? Is she coming?" After all the tears, three hearts crashed to the floor, adding more bloodstains to the carpet. Before another salty cascade started, David quickly knelt in front of her; green eyes mirrored the others with the same intensity and sadness.

"She'll be with us, Honey. You remember what we did today, saying good-bye to Mommy's body, but her Spirit flies all around us. She'll always be close by, never to be forgotten. We'll think only happy thoughts when we speak her name, and remember all the wonderful things she did for us. Okay?"

"Where are we going? Will she find us there?"

"Mommy will find us all right. We're off to England: the land of magic castles, Faeries in the moor, and gentle ponies to ride."

"Real Faeries?"

"Are there any other kind?" David chuckled softly; Holly smiled back; and their recovery started. Whisking her into his arms, and handshakes and sweet sister kisses all around, Mr. LaCoix and daughter departed for the land of fantasy and forgetting. Life had taken a strange turn; David became a full-time father.

On the plane, everyone settled in, quietly passing the time of a long return flight. While Holly played games with the flight attendant, David opened the letter. First, a glance at Maria who sat looking scared. Their nanny would make it, as he watched her conversing shyly with the steward. She had adapted more than once. Further to the front, Rod Morris sipped his Scotch quietly, never looking up from the liquid slightly shaking in his glass from the jet's vibration. Turning away, he read every treasured thought of Theodore Barrett: his hero.

> *Dear David, how much I want to say to you, but who knows where this letter may end up. Please forgive me if I overstepped my bounds in the handling of Susan's affairs. I thought it would ease your pain. Grief is best shed with love and family, not with bureaucracy.*
>
> *Settle in comfortably with Holly. We thought it best that one shock followed by another would be less difficult for her. A change of location, and adapting to life with her father, should be done quickly, away from outside interference. I feel and understand your fright and confusion, David. Remember La Rosa Negra, and the power of magic and visions materializing before your eyes. I'm becoming a believer, trying to make sense of Quinlan's words, and if there are other worlds and forms of life, then I did see the stars from the other side. Dreams, the Mistress, and other improbabilities do abound in everything. We all can get back to what we*

should have been; and I will be strong enough in Spirit to embrace this new reality.

Do not worry about me, for I am being well cared for with gentle hands and kind words. E-mails or calls are unnecessary, unless you need to speak with someone who is now capable of listening. You may never trust my motives, but please believe that I will testify in whatever capacity the D.A. asks of me.

Please direct your focus on the one who may be resting in your arms, while I strive to gain custody of my little miracle. Concerning your first priority, I will make the necessary modifications to the house for her. Let me know which rooms, and how to decorate them. The planning may take Holly's mind off things, and you will delight in her participation. It worked for me. So much to say and no words can be written. You already know them. T.B.

"Oh, Teddy Bear, I do." David leaned back in his seat and watched the clouds separate, allowing them entry into the dark, star-filled sky. "Is this part of your realm, Lavender? Help me one more time. Can I hold him to his oath in the criminal trial, and further trust him with this foolish heart?"

The word echoed like a lullaby with the answer, *'Yes'*. Ted had partially returned to the person he had first met. In control of his future, with some aid, David considered Theodore Barrett carefully. What Ted had gone through, to become what he was today, took courage and strength. The chronic illness did not reflect those qualities, but his power to face the disease did. To allow such abusive behavior, only to indulge in his love of acting, was incomprehensible. The majority would have succumbed, but not Barrett; he rose above it, like the jet rising to leave earth.

David had to allow Ted's lawyer to use information from the D.A. for the custody hearing. Out of their hands now, the time would come when Ted had to sit through an interrogation on the witness stand. Extremely risky for the fragile psyche to stand up and tell the world his parents were murderers; yet he had to believe Ambrose's words about regaining trust; this could be a way. The legal implications, however, could backfire, pushing his lover deeper into his problems, never to recover from his illness and die a young man. He turned the negative around, seeing Barrett succeed in reaching his goals. Unfortunately, the relevant question lingered; how far in his future did he see them? With that disturbing awareness, along with being a single father, David increased his own horizons to see Holly grown and on her own. He had to witness the growth and success of so many.

A glance up from the letter, his gaze blinked back wistful images, to finally rest on his innocent daughter. He had to set an example for her. Beads of perspiration immediately popped out on his forehead; worried he could disappoint her with his rediscovered sexuality. Sitting directly across from him, she looked intently at a newspaper. It appeared fresh, and the smell of ink confirmed it. The late night edition had been left for the adults' update on the world, but it had Holly caught in a puzzle. A little frown indicated an attempt to read words she did not know. After starting school the past September, she knew the alphabet and numbers; and watching Sesame Street, since she could sit in a highchair, taught her better than average academic skills. In his own mind, David knew Holly could read, at least convinced her capable of figuring out certain words in her impish head. She had a large vocabulary and did not speak in a particularly childish manner, except on those few whining occasions, which were stopped abruptly. It suddenly made him nervous as to what his daughter might be piecing together.

"Hey, Honey, what's new in the news?" He forced himself to remain nonchalant; hoping she would not announce the number of people killed in an unexplainable, unexpected, terrorist attack.

"Us." Holly did not look up, continuing her search for something.

"Those sons-of..." David knew it would be the funeral. His ire calmed; not Holly's fault, he had to stop the spontaneous profanity and jumping to fiery, erroneous conclusions, before discovering what she inferred, read, or watched.

"What?" She finally looked up with the sudden lurch forward of her father to grab the paper, but who had halted just as quickly and sat back in his seat.

"Come sit beside me, and let's look together." He had to learn patience and preparation for surprises. Some things he could handle; some things he could not, not yet anyway.

"Okay, but there's something wrong with this picture, Dad."

"Still Dad, hunh; miss being called Daddy. Show me what you're looking at."

Denim overalls pulled up against the plush, pale gray seating, as she awkwardly attempted to release herself from the Velcro grip, and off the seat that was too high for her feet to reach the floor. With little concern, she leisurely straightened herself out, while coming forward to scale the next chair beside her father. David had her under the arms and up before she knew it; and she expected the help. Carefully adjusting her position, Miss LaCoix nestled deep into the seat and stretched out her long legs, which ended with pink socks and white sneakers, the likes of which David had never seen. He wondered what a six-year-old needed with $200 shoes. High-tech footwear for growing feet, they made her a few inches taller, and actually looked quite comfortable.

"Now, let's see what this mystery's about." David saw the headlines first, aghast at the full page of pictures and text about the funeral on the front cover of the Entertainment page. Seeing the surprise and tension in his eyes, Holly understood the warning signal to remain still. Upset by something, her father would tell her when ready.

The first part of the article iterated Ted's words; he had made an eloquent statement. Although he never knew Susan, expressions of the heart lay heavily in every poetic word. The rest of the story indulged in lies and liable, tall-tales and trash, insinuating the LaCoix family a gaggle of spineless creatures, falling apart over the passing of a soon to be ex-wife. She had been discarded with no regard, only to be usurped, immediately upon separation, by a cruel engagement announcement. Once a fact, the one article made David feel like slum-sludge at what he had put Susan and Holly through; even his boys had stopped talking to him after he promised his hand to Rebecca, with a bigger, brighter diamond. The sordid affair now lay etched permanently in print, to regret for eternity.

More disturbing allegations, targeted by tabloid gossip, aimed at those alive and in his life. An insidious insinuation, about a picture he had not yet looked at, had him outraged. The closeness of three famous actors came under scrutiny. Why were they at the funeral? Was Barrett there just for LaCoix, confirming their film might have some truth behind the sex scenes? The press did acknowledge the filming of Kincaid's new picture, starring the three men. Could their entanglement have something to do with calling off Kincaid's wedding, turning to a man to comfort him in the likes of Ethan Peerce? The handsome, romantic lead had never married, and there in print lie the scandalous innuendo. David felt sick. This would put Ted in a downward tailspin; Steven into a hysterical pool of jelly; and lawyers, for Peerce, Kincaid, and now LaCoix, into a flurry of lawsuits.

David had not seen the men at the burial, with his entire focus on his daughter. He fought back the tears viewing the first picture, and his temper waned, seeing a still-shot of Holly and her ribbons, while he held her hand to prevent a fall. His own sorrow could be seen on his face and clenched jaw; the lines enhanced by a camera. Although a Pulitzer Prize winning picture, the invasion of privacy had gone too far. A second image caught father and daughter sobbing together in grief, and two handsome sons standing guard. The press had grabbed another personal moment for eternity. The third picture, which had Holly puzzled, included Barrett, Kincaid, and Peerce clinging together in a huddle of disbelief. Looking closely, the first thing that caught David by the throat was Ted's transformation for *Brother Mine*. While talking under the dim lighting of the library, he had not noticed the shock of white-blond hair, bleached out to match Kincaid's ever-changing locks. He had just sat there, worrying about the sad face, completely ignoring the wild color and the new shaggy spikes feathering around the forehead and tucked behind his ears to further float past his collar. Steven and Ted did look like brothers.

After the first shock of the blond, beautiful head, which made the man look sixteen going on twelve, David also puzzled over the picture. The first glance showed the three men as genuinely upset, particularly the younger two, and it pleased LaCoix that Ethan consoled them both. The words written, however, deemed outrageous with the context of the actual image; three saddened people, nothing more should have been read into it. Their lawyers could throw a parade, with brass bands and confetti, after feasting on press flesh for this libelous attack. Looking at the detail proved Holly correct; something was amiss. He noticed Ted's one hand held across his chest by Kincaid, but the other hand dangled in a position as if grasping onto something unseen. On further study, he spotted an indentation, a wrinkling of the left shoulder of Ethan's coat, as if a hand clutched it.

"Holly, what do you see in this picture?"

Astute enough to notice the slight tremor in her father's voice, the child pointed at the image. "He's not there, and he should be."

"Who?"

"The tall, skinny man, with the black coat, which touched the ground, and the really long, black hair; I saw him; and he stayed real close to Mr. Barrett, kind of holding him. He should be in the picture, Dad; I saw him. I really did."

"Thanks Honey. This is a peculiar picture. Maybe it's Mr. Barrett's new hair style, and the man in black may have moved away for a moment." With some doing, he regained his voice and thanked his daughter for showing him the puzzle. Satisfied with the answer her father gave, she jostled her way back to the steward, looking for something to do, while David smiled at her departure and covered his wonderment. Ambrose could hide himself in this reality, only exposing his human form to Holly and his three friends. Tyler and Bryce had not mentioned his presence, and they knew of his cult status. When Ted came into the library, to cover the two hardest hit by the death, he did mention Ambrose had accompanied him. Another hard knock hit him with Bryce's words; Ted literally threw unwanted people out of the house. It had to be Quin's doing. "It can't be," David murmured. "Is he alive or dead, real or unearthly?"

"What are you mumbling about, LaCoix? Hate to see my actors talking to themselves. It's a bad sign, unless there's a script under their nose." Rod refreshed his drink, and slumped into the seat across from him.

"Did you see Quinlan Ambrose at the funeral?"

"Hell, no; if I had, I'd have wrestled him to the ground, until he signed a picture deal with me. He's so elusive; the man can't be found. Only hints of sightings are rumored, like some UFO. Everyone's after him."

David wanted to jump to his feet and scream out Lavender's name for answers. Who was looking after Ted: a ghost, an apparition, or someone real in the same sense as Lavender? This mystery loomed as one of the biggest chunks left out of the game. Holly saw him; he let her see him for a reason; and he had shown himself to David, Jess, and Ted, while Peerce and Kincaid appeared accustomed to seeing him. The shrieking in his head gave him an instant migraine.

"Are you okay, David? What made you think of Ambrose? Do you know him?"

"Someone mentioned his presence. Another UFO sighting, I guess. Yeah, I'm feeling better, except for this headache. Still numb from the shock, a little sleep and getting Holly settled will fix things."

"You two have to get to know each other on a different plane."

"A different plane: shit, you have no idea." David slumped back into his seat, thinking about Ambrose, Lavender, and everything between here and there. In which plane did he exist at that moment? One heading for London he hoped; and he closed his eyes, said a sweet good-bye to Susan; and with a wistful smile on his softening face, fell asleep.

Lavender hovered close by, spreading herself too thin over the past several months of earth's time. The LaCoix family were on their way to establishing a new father/daughter relationship; and David had made a good start. Her happiness with Ted, and his new acceptance of the unwritten word, had her heart purring along with the jet she protected. One devastating day, however, created another concern; the man-child grew beyond worry for David's well-being, and nothing could console him. Three men watched over Barrett's every move. It would take Ted time to recover from a funeral, and to leave his lover suffering with no support. With the burden of a divorce weighing heavily on his bony shoulders, testifying against his family and church, would bury him. At the point, of not just sharing a room with Ambrose, Ted could not sleep unless cradled within the man's body. Tears and weariness had Barrett breaking down the moment the stars came out. He would remain in his dark, haunted hole, until things finalized on his life's docket, in the next three or four months. If not hanging onto earth by a fine, silver thread that could snap in a heartbeat, Ted would be gone. It took a great deal of the Mistress' power to hold him together. The quiet understanding of Quinlan's abilities, the hidden healing power of Peerce, and her own efforts, they would decimate the Fates hounding Barrett.

Another unexplainable circumstance dangled in front of David LaCoix. She had to explain Quinlan Ambrose. Of her realm, and her closest friend and ally, they had only found each other with uncommon luck in the vastness of the Cosmos. His talents and powers had Lavender bedazzled. Able to present himself as being very much of earth's reality, he had lived on the delicate planet for a short span of her time, and learned the emotional side of a straight human male. Ted felt and sensed him as such, with no reason to accept him as anything else. LaCoix's mind worked differently; he had discovered another incongruity.

Jumbled at the thoughts of the human mind's need to know, Lavender considered her dilemma. Ambrose could come out of seclusion for a year or two. With his talent intact, the admission to David that he missed acting, along with the sensitivity to offer a child something to puzzle over, to take Miss LaCoix's mind off her loss, had the Mistress wondering. A kind Spirit, gentle and harmoniously balanced with the Cosmos, it infused another thought; Ambrose would make the perfect Spirit Keeper for Holly, if what they believed her future real. Unseen by anyone else, he could speak to her directly and make sense. They had to do something about the inconsistencies, however, before LaCoix figured them out. Two alternatives for Quinlan, and he would probably delight in either one, or both. It would all take time; and the purple cloud lingered until all seemed quiet. Life would go on tomorrow, just not as usual.

CHAPTER 31

Within an English estate, with gardens and woods covered in winter shades of somber hues, the two LaCoix became acquainted at a deeper and an unusual level. Much to the amazement of her father, Holly's perceptiveness exuded far beyond a child of six, consciously taking everything for granted, yet seeing all. In her sprightly fashion, Miss LaCoix clamored every night for a new story; and without hesitation to accommodate her wish, a tired father looked forward to the enjoyable respite. Setting a grueling pace in front of the cameras, to regain lost production time, the cast and crew gladly followed his lead. The intensity grew stronger, as the plot unfolded at a faster rate. Although not always felt, with retake after retake, the British actors were repertory trained professionals in attitude and getting it done right, on time, and within budget. Strictly disciplined in their skill, brilliant in their interpretations, and deeply into their concentration levels, their presence humbled David. One of his goals reached: working with actors, and not celebrities who deserved little merit. Embraced by these extraordinary gifted men and women, he graciously accepted the honor, and his sorrow lifted.

On misty, eerie evenings of winter's cold nights, father and daughter took flight into the world of fantasy he had promised. The two bonded in front of the fire, or gazed out the large window into the foggy depths, a book always in hand or a tale in their heads. Although learning to read at an astounding rate, Holly preferred her father's incredible voice to make the stories enthralling. Every character had a different inflection and tonality; and he never forgot one. Scanning as he read, she would point out each piece missed. David would argue that an actor's sworn duty meant interpreting the dialogue in his own unique way; they would both laugh. In his fatherly mind, he took responsibility to protect her from the frightening parts, or those that would fly over his little girl's head. By adding the missing bits later, it would create a new story, as she grew more mature; at least until age thirty-five, when he may allow her to date.

Smiling, he pondered a future to follow, in handling his precious treasure. In his own world of fantasy, he visualized an image of himself, always in front of the fire, reading stories for an eternally enthusiastic Holly, and an equally captivated Ted who would be snuggled close beside him with his own baby. The ancient tales of magic and mayhem would also enthrall his man-child, experiencing them for the first time in his quiet innocence. The family portrait remained forever in David's mind.

Currently, father and daughter read something new to both: the original version of *Sleeping Beauty*. The horror of the tale captivated LaCoix, but carefully edited the ghastly parts for a child's Disney version. The governess suggested introducing Holly to the wonderland of old British myths and magical fables of queens and kings, princes and princesses, and particularly all those ghostly apparitions and beautiful creatures of the night. David happily agreed, and now, every new being had Holly's mind whirling. Each night, over dinner, which they shared privately in his quarters, she would present her father with a new interpretation of an old image, freshly painted that morning. LaCoix avidly endorsed her imagination, which made the words more enchanting than the original drawings of the misguided look of a troll. Understanding where the differences lay, he encouraged his daughter to see the world in her own way, with fresh eyes, truly believing these creatures existed, with their own dignity and charming uniqueness. Pride glowed within David, as he watched her abilities grow to change characters to her point of view, with the artistic talent to illustrate them, a perfect example for Ted to follow. With the reverence of a father, he meticulously hung each new painting on his stonewalls, to be saved for his lover to ponder. His daughter believed in magic, never to be changed; and he focused on keeping alive that part of her inner Spirit.

For their own pleasure, rare days off would be spent playing amongst the gardens in search of the unknown. Venturing into the forest on one side of the estate, they investigated all possible traces of the inhabitants that they read lay hidden. An occasional trek under the moonlight, just for the excitement of being amongst their enchanted trees, they laughed and played within the shadows that came alive, with branches dancing and swaying to a ghostly tune of an echoing wind. Holly shrieked; David gasped; and both laughed together as they sprinted for the safety of their pretend haunted house. Other days, they passed through the garden, squeezing through the unmoving, ancient turnstile, to reach an open field leading to the cliff. A spectacular, dramatic view overlooked the wild Atlantic waters, crashing against the rocks below. They sat together for hours, wrapped in woolen blankets, even when a skiff of snow covered the meadow. Sometimes they would talk, sometimes stories or word games were told or played, and sometimes the afternoon simply drifted away on a daydream, each in their own thoughts.

David became a stricter father as the days melted away. With no screaming, no whining, no signs of a snobbish brat allowed, Holly learned. She knew her boundaries in this reality space, the edge of the garden when alone. There were no limits, however, on her beliefs, imagination, and the stories she created for her father. They could not be lies, only fanciful tales of make-believe. Patiently, David emphasized the need for her to take credit when someone praised her for doing something right, with a simple gracious *thank you*, and to take responsibility for her misdeeds and admitting to them, with a sincere apology and an honest attempt to rectify the situation. David's hopes lay in raising an open-minded, well-behaved child, and one, of course, who adored her father. Their bond cemented and grieving dissipated over a few short weeks.

Due to a camera malfunction, David returned early one special day, in time for lunch. With a change of clothes into something extremely warm, to fend off the last blast of a cold winter's afternoon, he and Holly set out on another adventure. Early February, the frost nipped their California noses, and puffs of vapor floated from their mouths when they spoke, joining them in a new game of magic; the opening and closing, twisting and turning, of their lips created unique patterns in the small clouds they formed. With their warm breaths mixing with the cold damp air, David became the child long forgotten; and Holly reveled in her first flurry of snowflakes. The enticing fantasy reminded David of a day in October, and the movie scene too beautiful to forget: the vapors rising from a horse, a lover, and his own wishful, wanting, whispers into an anxious ear.

This day's pleasure did produce a sighting of the mystical; Holly found a Faery ring. Laughter echoed through the veil of gray fog, while she pirouetted in the middle of the enchanted circle of mushrooms. David's chuckling stopped short with a pronounced click of her tiny booted-heels, hands on her hips, and the tilt of the head in LaCoix defiance. She glared disapprovingly at her father; and he wondered what he had done wrong. A dreadful error, he had laughed at the ritual dance of the Faery Queen, Tatiana; sacred laws had been broken. With a sweeping gesture, bowing low from the waist, and his outstretched arm rising back and above his head, David apologized, in aristocratic eloquence, for his ill-mannered behavior, and begged her ladyship to continue. Holly looked at him out of the corner of her eye, gave a twinkling smile, and returned to the dance.

Turning 1:00 p.m. in the lingering English mist, David continued to watch it thicken behind the whirling, kicking feet. The cellular chimes suddenly went off. It seldom rang, except for Quinlan with another horror story to relay. He sent a wish into the dense forest, hoping one of those magical creatures would grant him a favor. The number, flashing on the new plastic instrument of bad news, was an unknown one, and he quickly answered. His head nearly spun off, listening to a happy, but authoritarian voice, informing him of his nomination, as one of the five nominees for Best Actor in a Motion Picture. The rest of the nominations must wait until told to the world in half-an-hour. Trying to stop himself from sounding like an idiot in his excitement, he graciously thanked the man and cut off the connection.

In his disguised jubilation, he dared hope a nomination went to the laid-to-waste Barrett. It would crush the man if passed-by. Too many things, over a very short period, enveloped the younger actor in a storm cloud, and another thunderclap would stop his soft heart. Good news was vital; considering Quinlan's miniscule updates reeked of foreboding. Forcefully throwing himself into every project undertaken, each made out of solid concrete, Ted grew more mentally battered and bruised. Packed with raw, unnerving emotion, even the love of his art severed his nerves. *Brother Mine* promised to be explosively brilliant, acted out by three overly emotional and taxed men. In Arizona, the house project gathered momentum with Barrett in charge; and he shouted orders like a man gone mad if something appeared amiss during his weekly inspection. Adding a few more sticks of dynamite into his grim reality, the divorce papers were ready for Karen when the time presented itself; and according to Quinlan's logic, it would be sooner than later. A sense of anger permeated everything Ted did, assimilating the character he portrayed into his own psyche. These new, uncharacteristic traits, of the passive Teddy Bear, frightened everyone. Only Ambrose saw Ted's problem as the unexplainable pain, secretly endured, which allowed the man to push forward ever harder.

Ted developed a *screw the Oscars* attitude, only wanting to escape his abominable situation. He yearned constantly for David, but his needs lay in the outcome of the custody hearing, heating up to boiling point in his mind; a decision had to be made regarding the divorce. Bordering on an obsession with the birth of his child, three odd months away, reality grew harder for one ailing man-child to juggle. His illness, which had been improving, took an unexpected turn for reasons unknown. Currently stabilized with force-feeding and intravenous drips through the night, Barrett appeared doomed for a breakdown or a coronary. The latter being the most probable, often the result of the disease he fought. David suggested that he fly to see him, but Quinlan jumped in with an emphatic *No*. It would be another tap on the shoulder to push the man into the depths of the black hole consuming him. They would be unable to pull Ted free, if he let himself succumb to the pressure.

Remembering the past deeply hurt LaCoix, along with a crisp inhale of air too cold for his nostrils to tolerate, but the freshness brought Lavender to mind immediately. Surrounded by the purple cloud, she gave him the peace he needed. Ted's nomination came through, along with Ethan Peerce. The other two possibilities did not matter; his Baby Bear made the ultimate short list; and he would win. LaCoix's heart told him this film belonged to Barrett, and not the voice in his head. At peace for the interim, he had something of his own to celebrate, a first-time nomination for anything; and a broad grin wrinkled up the handsome, very excited face.

"Dad, what are you doing?" A child's voice, somewhere in the distance, brought him back to the frosted meadow, too delicate to step on. "Dad!" Holly grabbed his coat, struggling to pull him into reality.

"Sorry, Honey, what was I doing?" Twinkling crystals stared into the puzzlement of his daughter's squint.

"Just standing there. Your eyes were closed and you frowned like your head ached, but then you smiled, softening your face, just the way I like it."

"Couldn't believe what I just heard. Dad has good news, Holly Jane." David's flashing eyes looked deliriously insane, as did the wicked, infamous smile, which could capture an audience in a tight infectious grip, waiting for the next action-packed plot twist.

"What? Tell! Tell!" His daughter recognized the look of excitement and eagerly joined in.

"You know what the Oscars are, don't you?"

"Of course; you hate them and always go out someplace. Mommy and I have a party when they come on, just the two of us. Guess we won't this year." The voice saddened at the mention of something special, which she and her mother would plan for days. Very much a mother/daughter event, David had to pick up the slack and quickly.

"No, not this year; however, you and I will stay up very, very late to watch them together. For the first time in my life, I'm nominated for Best Actor. What do you think of your old man now?" Green eyes lit up like Susan's Christmas tree, and he knew his late wife would be ecstatic for him and for Holly.

"You won! You won!" The little blonde sprite clapped her hands together, jumping up and down with joy. "Are we going? Will I see you dressed up?"

"No, no, and no. I probably won't win; but after all this time, Holly Jane, people noticed and approved of my work. You probably can't understand that, but it means a great deal to me." Being honest with his answer, David knew his time had not arrived, never expecting the nomination in the first place. The picture belonged to Ted, as well as the Oscar. "Guess who else is nominated, Honey?"

"You'll win, so it doesn't matter." She grasped her father's hand; and the two started toward the manor house.

"There won't be any fancy parties for us, but we'll have a mini one with the Morris family." David looked down and smiled at her disappointed face. "But we'll see a man we know, who might win. Who gave you Sir Lancelot?"

"Mr. Barrett?" She remembered the thin man she had met; and David nodded happily, until the high-tech sneaker dropped. "That's good, Dad; he's sick; maybe he should win."

"What makes you say that?" The father took a giant step back at his daughter's knowledge of things never spoken. It sounded like she knew there may be little time, and this would be Ted's only chance. His heart broke, understanding the truth behind the thoughts.

"You're so sad whenever you hear about him. I know the black-haired man is the one you talk to on the phone. He tells you about Mr. Barrett."

"My God, Holly, you are a constant surprise to me. How do you know these things? No one else does." David wondered just how much she knew.

"Sir Lancelot. Do you believe in magic, Dad, real magic?"

"Of course; I wish on falling stars; I know there are beautiful Faeries in our forest; and I talk to mystical, silver-black horses, with manes and tails that fall to sweep the ground, and amber eyes that change your life. I also know a young Fey whom is magical in the things she says and paints."

"Must be me. I believe in magic. Whenever I talk to my bear, he answers back."

"A male voice?"

"Yeah, and he's really nice."

"Does it help speaking with him?"

"Makes me feel happy, and I'm not scared and lonely anymore, like Sir Edmund does for you. That's Mr. Barrett's bear, isn't it?" Holly brought up the question; and David forgot the tale made up to explain the oversized fuzzy toy.

"Yes it is. He lets me keep it for luck. I'll return Sir Edmund to him when we get home."

"You really like him, don't you?"

"Sir Edmund? Yes, we share lots of secrets." David started getting nervous. All his thoughts were on Ted, and he had to focus on the bear.

"No, I meant Mr. Barrett."

Too late, he manifested his suffering onto his daughter; and her empathic awareness had him reeling. He never mentioned Barrett, so how could Holly know? The answer came from the purple cloud encasing them both. Almost unnoticed, he did hear the faint whisper in his head, *'She unconsciously heard you in the library speaking with your son, David; plus she has a child's keen intuition. Let it grow.'*

"Yes, I like him a great deal."

"Is he going to die and leave forever, like Mommy?" The voice returned to its melancholy state, indicating that his daughter understood Ted's illness.

"I hope not, Holly. I can't lose..." David almost blurted out what he could not say. His recent good news turned to headlines of the death of Theodore Barrett. He only saw the final closing of the sapphire gems, against a background of a deathly white face, white sheets, white curtains, with needles and tubes sticking into every orifice of his skeleton body. Ted would be so afraid to die without someone beside him. David suddenly stumbled and fell to the ground, pulling Holly along with him. The voice screamed in his head, ricocheting like rifle fire against the inside of his skull. *'LaCoix! Never think the negative! Never! We are close to losing him without your thoughts manifesting into reality. How dare you forget your first lesson? Now, think of Theo again; send him your wishes, and a strong message of good health and happiness. Do it, LaCoix! Do it now!'*

On cue, he immediately switched directions and a smile crossed his face. Ted stood beside him, standing in the rose garden. They both laughed and clapped, watching the Faery Queen dance. Soon Ted sprang into the melee, with David throwing rose petals over his two loves in honor of a May Day celebration around a colorfully decorated pole. Theodore Barrett glowed with good health, mentally happy, and full of the magic he had learned. The blond actor's smile turned into a chuckle, continuing to watch Holly and Ted light-step through his head. They played and romped their way amidst tall, spring-green grass, with a jubilant David at their heels.

"Dad, get up. You're squashing me." A complaint was issued breathlessly, from underneath one of his arms. "Why are you laughing?"

"Because your father's getting clumsy in his old age. Did I hurt you?" David pushed himself up, and helped Holly to her feet and brushed her off.

"I'm okay. That cloud did it. It pushed you over."

David snapped his head down in another surprise attack from below. He looked at the annoyed little face. "You can see the purple cloud?"

"It's mauve, not purple."

"Excuse me for being color-blind. You can see it?"

"Of course, it's your magic."

"My magic; I like that. Maybe it is." David closed the conversation by taking off at a run toward the manor house. His long-legged daughter eagerly chased him in full-flight, both laughing and giggling on reaching the huge wooden door. The butler heard them coming, and ushered the noisy pair in for hot drinks and dry clothes. With no further mention of Lavender or Ted, David would let his child delve into the fantasy this reality created, before entering other realms. He would join her in the adventure, which suddenly became real to him. Every drop of dew became a crystal ball in which to gaze. Every insect, flying past his ear, became a delicate Faery, winging a kiss against his cheek. Every bloom, sacrilegiously plucked, offered a velvet glove of welcome. Nothing would be touched; they were all creatures of the Cosmos, and not his place to damage such mysteries.

Holly started early on her path of awareness with her father beside her. He would not disrupt the flow with Christian church bells, Buddhist prayer wheels, or Islamic chanting, to name a few. Taught only the theory behind the beliefs, given time, she would decide on what felt right, wrong, or a piece of her own jigsaw puzzle of life. At this stage, she continued to learn magic, magic of this reality and all its exciting possibilities. Her father would make sure she always saw the mauve cloud, the sparkle of Christmas lights dancing in an icicle prism, the feel of champagne bubbles bursting against her nose, the sensation of greeting another creature with an amber eye, and the sound of the leaves whispering her name. She would come to respect the words on the wind, blowing through living monuments of the earth's elements, whether they bore fresh spring foliage, the darker, lush emerald of summer, or the autumn shades of Ted's hair, finally becoming the glittering diamonds covering the nakedness of winter. Both had much to learn, touch, see, taste, and smell; all the wonders of this planet would come first. A promise from his heart, David set higher goals for all his loves' futures, to experience life with Holly and Ted, and with good fortune, a baby Barrett. Eyes widened at the thought; he and Ted could be raising a family together. Having wondered about the possibility, the surprise now seemed extraordinary; he delighted in the eventuality. In a low whisper even Holly could not hear, a breathless voice urged the younger man on, "Stay well, Teddy Bear, we have much to do."

Lavender vanished to lend support to Ted. One continent west of the magic kingdom of green and fog, a man burst with jubilation, only to fall deathly ill, and then return with a radiant smile. Quinlan and Lavender watched Barrett wake up to the early morning call of good news, only to crater under David's imagined thoughts. LaCoix had lost him, finally to save him. With the ability to change reality confirmed, along with the Mistress' *knowing*, David collected more power, as did his capability of learning with one quick warning. Barrett would get stronger, if the man, thousands of miles away, maintained the wondrous images and messages of future happenings. Similar thoughts tumbled randomly into Ted's consciousness from his fans, friends, and colleagues. Unfortunately, the controversial film also created loathing, including the church followers who considered him a hedonistic sodomite, because of his participation in such a film; but paradoxically, they regarded him as their primary source of income. Their attitude turned ugly, hurting the man beyond anyone's control. What would their mind games do to him when his allegations became front-page news? Theodore Barrett felt both the rose and the thorn: one stroking him with velvet, the other leaving him to bleed.

CHAPTER 32

March blew in like a predator those first few weeks in the damp countryside, although the latter part of the month blessed the residents with fine weather and refreshing spring breezes. Holly and David enjoyed themselves thoroughly, back in sweaters and jeans, rather than the heavy coats, hats, and gloves of winter-forced wear. Now they could smell and feel what they had missed on their excursions. Amongst the newly discovered wild flowers, small animals skittered along their route, with the occasional deer in the thickets of the forest, or grazing peacefully in the long grasses of the meadow. Leisurely and respectfully, father and daughter first acknowledged the animal with the wonder of eye contact, only to stroll away, creating no fear.

Although reveling in these outings, with his sweet companion who listened to the wind whisper her name, David only heard the call of a broken Spirit a million-miles away. On that cold February day of nomination announcements, Ted had given the go ahead. Divorce papers were served; sole custody documents submitted; and a hearing date set for April 10 for the latter. Also coming to the fore, the press became aware of the allegations of child abuse against Ted's church and the court date set in July by the Grand Jury. When it came to California attitudes, children's welfare came first, along with famous names, particular those fighting unprecedented holy wars. Theodore Barrett stood unwillingly center stage, conducting a righteous crusade against a holy order, with the backing of such names as LaCoix, Kincaid, Peerce, Carmichael, and much to the world's surprise, Quinlan Ambrose. The man emerged from the unknown, without an explanation.

With a strategy set for the custody hearing, neither Ted's lawyer, nor David, could prepare Ted for only joint custody. With his mind unraveling, Barrett waited for his day in court. One man, far away, bit his nails until they bled, while the man in California uncontrollably purged, leaving him barely able to stand. Both men continually wrung their hands, sending prayers and wishes in a quiet chant. Lavender's concern for her man-child overshadowed the fourteen nominations for *Outlaw's Heart*, a miraculous number for this extraordinary film, which continued to shatter records. The outrageous investment in her actors continued to pay off; and the residuals of her Midas touch passed to her actors who received their own rewards. Financially secure for life, never to fall from the 'A' list pinnacle of achievement, LaCoix and Barrett, however, had forfeited their happiness.

Oscar night, and very early Oscar morning for others, instilled an excited buzz throughout the manor. The entire household gathered in front of a television the size of a small theatre, all becoming very nervous by 1:00 a.m. for the grand entrance and walk down the red carpet. Snuggled in blankets and pillows, everyone settled in for a long night into morning. Dark and stormy, a natural special effect, created a perfect atmosphere for ghost stories, while they waited the arrival of the glamorous and the fake to run the gauntlet. Since two nominees were involved with *Lord Worthington-Smythe*, the cast and crew had the following day off. This reprieve honored David LaCoix and Rod Morris, a Best Director nominee for his last film, and the instigator of Peerce's nominated performance. With much joking bias, wagers were placed on the Best Actor category, with only David's money placed on Barrett.

The arrival of the stars lighted the screen with their perfected, almost pliable, Botox smiles. Jenny Morris, the governess, Maria, Holly, and the two Morris girls were in awe of the dresses, and even the men's suits. Their approval came with one of two words: *marvelous* or *yuck*. Much to

David's amusement, he found it fun to see who liked what. The more he learned about the female sector of the species, the more confused he became. He would never have taken such advantage, or discarded them so readily, if he had understood the complexity of their thoughts. Holly had been proving it to him since her arrival in England. He concluded his daughter had impeccably good taste, along with Mrs. Morris. *Yuck* dresses amounted to the ones you could see more skin than material. For *marvelous*, they chose the simplest and most elegant of gowns, and the longest of black jackets for the men. David stored the bit of trivia in his memory for later reflection.

Kincaid and Peerce, both dateless, graced the screen with their presence first, being teased about Steven having to hold Ethan's hand through the excitement of being nominated as Best Actor. Peerce confidently smiled. Smooth as the petals of a black rose, he quietly stated they had just wrapped shooting of *Brother Mine* the day before, a good endorsement for Kincaid; and along with Theodore Barrett, they had flown in that morning, very lucky to have made the big event. Steven nervously stood back, saying nothing, playing the typical Hollywood consort or concubine, taking a backseat to the one nominated.

Again, to the public's surprise, the dashing Quinlan Ambrose came into view, wrestling Ted's arm away from a fan. Security rushed to the rescue before he unleashed a little unearthly force. Another interview started with a breathless and obviously frail Barrett. The white-blond hair made him paler, and only those eyes shone out from under the bleached lashes. He looked extraordinarily attractive, very young, and extremely breakable. Barely able to catch his breath after the small skirmish, Ted left the answering of stupid questions to Ambrose. The Entertainment Tonight crowd glowed radiantly, and demonstrated their politest behavior, asking only of the nomination, and excluding any mention of the impending divorce, or other unauthorized press releases.

Back to chewing his nails, David leaned forward with Holly's arm around his neck. "Take a breath, Ted. Come on, Baby." No one heard the whisper coming from under his hands. Barrett appeared extremely unstable, unable to hold it together, obviously in no condition to be there. Thankfully, his ghostly Spirit ran interference, lending a hand or an arm for support, protecting him from the inundation of well-wishers, or taking a crash to his bony knees.

"That's the man, Dad, the one with the long, black hair." Holly pointed at Ambrose, examining him closely.

"I thought so, Honey." The abrupt interruption of his worry did not veer his eyes away from the action. Behind the interview, and during Ted's zigzag march down the red carpet, the agonized actor in England heard the applause for his lover. Even the brightest names in Hollywood, within the walkway, appeared to be scrambling after the two men. Ambrose seemed a likely target of the producers and directors, but hordes stampeded after Barrett. Two opposing forces visibly pulled at the man. One faction received a shy smile and a handshake; the other startled the endangered butterfly, alerting Ambrose to shed discreetly the unwanted attention. Finally safe in their seats, Ted's biggest fan sat back and watched the curtain rise for the opening monologue.

The extravaganza began in fun for insiders and fans alike. David caught himself chuckling at the jokes aimed at *Outlaw's Heart*, while Ted shamefully turned shades of scarlet. Adrift in a world that he wanted no part of; he looked scared and agitated, held together with a one-handed grip by his Guardian Spirit. To Barrett and LaCoix's humiliation, what they portrayed on film became cannon fodder for incessant teasing, not stopping until the first category was announced.

Award presentations started; the torture ended. The four men in the audience, and the one chewing his nails in England, could sit back and relax. Ray Evans received the Oscar for Best Supporting Actor; and David clapped and laughed happily for him, glad to see no leftover disfiguration of his broken nose. Ritually, if the Best Supporting award went to an actor from the same production as the Best Actor nominee, the latter seldom received his own statuette. Another oddity, of significance, the Academy gave nods to two lead actors in the same film. The problem perceived remained the same: the votes would be split. David refused to care, knowing Ted would beat the odds; and he visualized the man standing center stage, Oscar in hand, throughout the next two and half hours, never letting go of the vision.

Technical awards came fast and furious for *Outlaw's Heart*, and yet not one face appeared to accept the Oscar. From lighting, to costume design, to its surrealistic musical score, each award announced brought cheers and whistles for the intense Western, which meant everything to the actors involved. They seemed the only representation for the film, and none of them had participated in a production earning such accolades in so many categories. Every movie had flaws; and David believed Lavender created the miracle. Nonetheless, it ranked as the hit of the year; and LaCoix slumped back in awe.

Finally, the introduction of the Best Actor nominees created enthusiastic wishes within the manor house. Holly squealed with joy to see her father's face on the screen, talking over Jay's bare shoulder to the Marshall. She clapped again when she saw her friend, Mr. Barrett, begging her father to set him free. The blue eyes cried in despair, lingering and looking straight into a full house of tearing faces. The image faded, returning to focus on the glamorous star holding the envelope. With breaths held, silence filled the auditorium; the envelope crackled as she opened it. Only the nominee in the manor house sat back to enjoy the announcement of his choice. In great excitement, last year's Best Female Actress, in the red *yuck* gown, announced the name; one that joyously resounded in David's head. He sprang to his feet, cheering and laughing along with Holly.

"But you didn't win, Dad?" She peered up at him, but his green eyes remained transfixed on the man who sat in shock.

"Yes, Holly, I did; I helped Mr. Barrett win. It was his turn." David watched carefully as Ted came into the realization of what had happened, and the thunderous ovation directed at him. People stood, attempting to get a glimpse of the young man who needed assistance to get out of his seat. Slowly, his legs stabilized under him, with Ambrose standing by and aiding every move made. Jumping into the aisle to camouflage his further support, Peerce picked up the frail body and swung him off the ground. An instant revelation and David came into the *knowing*: all three men, discreetly tending to Ted, had visualized the same thing. Peerce, Kincaid, and Ambrose wanted this award for their failing friend. LaCoix's heart shattered, believing they had been hiding a far more horrendous situation, but quickly changed his attitude to the positive, hearing a sharp clang of remembrance in his head.

Tears streamed down an unsteady man's face when set on his feet. Peerce's arms let go, replaced by a hug from Kincaid who twisted Ted around to face the stage. David slumped down in some relief, nearly crushing Holly who managed to get out of his way with her inherited quicksilver reflexes. Studying Quinlan carefully, he watched how tenderly he maneuvered the dazed Barrett toward his reward, which seemed miles away. Scarcely able to walk, let alone lift his arms to wipe his face dry, his chaperone escorted him to the first three stairs he had to negotiate. The mysterious, black-haired man let go tentatively, to watch each step taken toward the receiving podium. Two more stairs up, and Ambrose quickly walked around the sunken orchestra pit, in front of the first row of enthusiastic famous faces. He looked positively grim with fear. The man's actions shook LaCoix into a cold sweat; and a shiver ran up his spine. Positive thoughts, he kept repeating: positive thoughts.

With hands on the abstract form of the acrylic lectern, Ted steadied himself a few seconds before accepting the Oscar handed to him. It crashed to the floor, falling out of the shaking hand in one heart-stopping moment. The tall model bent down, picked it up, and placed it on the stand that braced the latest Oscar winner.

"Thank you. I didn't think it would be so heavy." Ted politely apologized to the confused plastic mannequin, usually ignored by all. She silently nodded and left the man to his audience. One nervous red-gowned actor, who presented the award, looked on in alarm at the man close to collapsing in front of her. She hovered nearby, ready for any possibility, returning to the old method of an acceptance, by walking back with the receiver of the award. The beautiful face glanced left and right, looking for help if required, and refusing to step too far away. The gesture upset David, now convinced Hollywood insiders knew their latest star was very ill. Wishes were sent skyward, truly believing their expressions indicated support over the divorce and the holy war to save children; but in his *knowing*, their peers stood and applauded in the belief it would keep Ted from succumbing to the ravages of his body.

A startled young actor waited nervously for quiet, with no acceptance speech prepared. In a hush, they continued to stand, and then the silence. Cameras scanned the room, in which tears flowed freely, and faces of both sorrow and joy seemed to be encouraging the man. They cared for this delicate human, facing a challenge greater than he could handle alone. David wished he had his arms around him, calming the shaking seen by millions.

"A very unique Spirit once told me to accept credit gracefully, and simply say *thank you*. I am truly thanking you from my grateful heart. Her advice has come to fruition tonight, considering the accolades received for all involved in *Outlaw's Heart*. Congratulations, my friends. Again, thank you all for this treasure and for acknowledging my performance. There are two, however, that I must share this with. Her Ladyship Lavender, the bringer of light and magic; I love you." Ted looked at the Oscar so wistfully; David thought he would break down right there. Holding fast, Barrett continued in a voice so low, only the high-tech microphone could pick it up. "The other, of course, is the man I voted for: David LaCoix. He is the finest, most generous actor I know, and he graciously gave me this picture, letting me act and stumble my way through, without judgment and a great deal of ad-libbing to cover my mistakes. Thank you all again; you are wonderful company to be amongst."

Surprisingly to David, Ted did not thank his God and the heavenly host. The man remembered one of the first lessons taught to them by the Mistress. Wildly proud of his young friend, he vigorously slapped his cupped palms together with the rest of the world. The woman, standing behind Ted and watching closely, made a sudden dash to encircle him with a strong arm around the nonexistent waist, and to catch the award before he dropped it again. Shock registered on her face at the feel of nothingness; and her bright red dress quivered and sparkled in the footlights, indicating her unexpected nervous shaking. With great deliberation, she gingerly supported Barrett, waiting for help. David saw the wobble and gasped. Quinlan appeared out of nowhere, and a pair of stronger arms lifted Ted slightly off his feet to prevent him from collapsing. The threesome walked off stage and disappeared behind the curtain, away from the countless star-struck eyes watching, and the uproar of adoration left standing in his wake.

For the moment, safe amongst friends, Ted could compose himself. The cameras would be on him again, just as they had done with the other winners. Post-win interviews came quickly, after a few words from the host; and those words, after Ted's exit, were simple and honestly spoken with concern and a quiver of a lower lip. People did know; they saw a man dying in front of them; Ambrose had lied to him. Horrified, David had no one to turn to for his own comfort. He bit hard into his lower lip to stop the tremble. Waiting for one last glimpse took his entire resolve. Quinlan had to get Ted out of there before he fell apart. While concentrating on every movement made, David noticed two shadows cross in front of one camera, suddenly switched to another. Peerce and Kincaid rushed to help.

In front of the world once more, Theodore Barrett, the toast of Hollywood this night, sat with the interviewer backstage. She bubbled with enthusiasm, strictly for the cameras, playing her part well and being delicate with her questions. Concern expressed itself in her body language, only masked to a degree by her wide-open eyes and pasted on smile. If the man beside her fainted or fell forward, she looked ready. Ted grinned sheepishly, appearing to have regained his composure to respond politely with few words, and taking the opportunity to wave hello. A kiss, blown at the camera, landed directly on David's lips.

LaCoix's hands immediately went to his mouth to capture the caress. He could have sworn he felt it; the taste of Theodore Barrett was unmistakable; a swipe of his tongue proved it. Magic, Ted had learned some mastery of it, while Quinlan supplied the power. David's disquietude diminished slightly with the soft voice in his head. *'He is all right, David. Do not let your concern manifest itself. He is thriving on your plans for the future. Please give him that. It is our only hope.'*

David stopped breathing: taking responsibility for your actions seemed hard enough, and now your thoughts. He had to; it seemed imperative to envision Ted alive, well, and happy. Nothing else must interfere with the materialization of their dream.

The manor house crowd all feigned frowns and smiles in sympathy for David who certainly did not show any sign of disappointment. Graciously accepting condolences, he chuckled for their benefit, and collected his winnings from the bet. A spark of happiness grew from the simple gesture; and he sent genuine laughter to Ted, hoping upon visionary hope that the new young heartthrob listened, and could giggle along with his three stalwart companions. In his heart, David knew Ted felt the adoration lavished upon him, and in his head, he called out, *'I love you, Oscar winner'*. The Cosmos heard.

The sleepy occupants of the manor continued to watch the final few categories, particularly Best Director, and again the nominee amongst them failed to gather more acclaim. There would be no Oscar win party at the Morris lodgings that morning. Rod shrugged, David returned it, and they both snickered for no reason. There was nothing else to do. Morris did ask why the director of their miraculous Western had not been acknowledged, or even listed in the credits. Without a believable answer, only the truth could explain it; there had not been one, but for the scenes that bore little resemblance to the final product. The amused actor, with the sardonic grin, reaped the accolades placed upon Ted and himself from Rod whom he respected. This time-honored director shook his head, not believing for an instant that actors could take material, improvise most of the lines and action, continue shooting through any miscue, and come out smelling like Oscar winners. Stunned, Morris immediately promised LaCoix more freedom to act and become *Lord Worthington-Smythe*.

The final bouquet sent David's way, and much to his astonishment, came with the announcement of Best Picture. *Outlaw's Heart* rang out over the very receptive crowd. Westerns did not win, but only once with Eastwood's picture. Another oddity, the reasoning seemed simple; the technical and acting quality were too profound to fail. Coming as no surprise to LaCoix, an individual did not pick up the most coveted award of the night. Lavender would have a world bedazzled by one of her grand entrances. With only the name of the production company mentioned, Black Rose Productions, David sat back, grinning ear-to-ear, to watch a happy purple cloud float over her Oscar. With rainbows sprinkling around the room for the audience's pleasure, he knew a spectacle of magical proportions prepared herself to light up the night.

Flashing sparks of purple and silver lit up the stage and kept the audience in their seats, entranced at the beautiful array of fireworks without the bang. A wondrous last minute special effect, they wanted to watch every second of its display. The legendary presenter, holding the twenty-four-carat, gold-dipped, Britannia metal statuette, could only stare at his hand, illuminated with light particles, radiating forth to blaze about the room at random. A feeling of well-being swept over the crowd, and the extravaganza grew in brilliance and size. They all heard the clear, sincere *thank you* in their heads, and felt the warm, inner glow. This would go down as an Oscar night phenomenon no one could explain, although someone would take the credit. *Outlaw's Heart* had been created through magic, and magic showed itself in the only way it could. David laughed along with the giggling he heard in his head. Up to her Mistress mischief, Lavender could only snicker, enjoying something that she alone manifested.

A soft whisper came through the astonished gasps. "Dad, your magic is holding the Oscar."

"It is, Honey; it most certainly is." David roared in his gaiety, squeezing and tickling his daughter, until she giggled just as hard. The entire Cosmos joined in the applause for one of their own, who won a special earthly prize. Delighted, Lavender wallowed in her few seconds of fun. Her man-child had reached one of his goals; nothing could make her happier. Another film would not be created in her realm; nor could another picture technically reach such a pinnacle of achievement for decades. Tonight, the Cosmos celebrated in peace and goodwill, but for one winner. The purple cloud vanished to assist less than a handful of men. The latest Oscar winning Best Actor lay safe but in jeopardy in the Malibu home of Ethan Peerce, with an intravenous needle in his arm and a tube down his throat, forcing lifesaving nutrients into his body. Steven clung to Ethan, fretting over his friend who fitfully slumbered between Ambrose and Lavender.

Out of her cloud, the Mistress gently stroked the back of a tired, frightened, and sick man. She rubbed his head gently; she sang her familiar chiming sounds; she kept him warm, surrounded with love; and she refused to give up on Barrett, in his up and coming walk through more of earth's hell. While Lavender soothed away the sobs in sleep, Quinlan picked him up and rocked the weary Spirit in his arms. There remained little to touch or hold. In his own way, Ted wept in happiness. He won a crazy, little, golden knight, and it meant nothing to him alone. Focused only on David behind the closed eyes, he saw his blond lover waving and smiling from a field of wild flowers, high on a cliff. He had heard the whispered call; he knew LaCoix cared.

"Quinlan?"

"Yes, Mistress?"

"When did we become magicians and not who we are? I am afraid I have led these men astray." A long pause and a sad expulsion of air came from soft lips that curled down wistfully at the corners. "The Fates are willing this one to end it all."

"I know. Kincaid's lack of forethought, the end of November, astounded me. I did not sense it coming. He pushed this man when most vulnerable, and then made a U-turn on him. No wonder Theo is confused. He tries too hard to please everyone." Ambrose slipped the sleeping figure back onto the bed, pulled up the blankets to stay the shivering, and checked the needle embedded and taped into a vein in the back of the left hand. The lines of magenta patterned their way up like a spider's web from the knuckles to the elbow. They had used them all.

"I feel the pain in his hand. It hurts terribly. Please ease it, Quin?" Lavender remained in human form for Ted's uncertain reality. With her curls pulled up and tied, and in jeans and a pullover, she would not startle him if he suddenly awoke. His response to her presence seemed more relaxed if she appeared of this world.

Blue light spread over the arm and penetrated deeply. Through the gentle sobs, a smile shone through, and the two unearthly beings looked at each other, wondering what or who created the hint of joy. "Must be something LaCoix is sending." Ambrose caressed the face gently with the back of his hand.

"It would be my guess. David has learned much, to give of himself so freely."

"He has; perhaps giving you the opportunity to take a night off. I enjoy this picture of you." Quinlan tried to charm another smile out of someone else's solemn countenance, without success.

"Thank you, but I cannot, for this one is important. I feel I am losing him, which does not happen often. How do we get him back? Kincaid certainly threw him into the deep end of the mire; and it drags him under like quicksand. We should have expected it, considering Stevie's unstable condition when they met. His obsession, over the demon Fate he calls a friend, should have been dealt with long ago. The man tortured him mentally, for the past four years, and unmercifully abused him physically, with his cold, demeaning sexual fantasies. Stevie would jump at every order issued, just to be near the fraudulent, insidious fool. We did not handle Kincaid properly and now this one." The slender yet powerful hand touched a pale cheek, and quieted the start of another bad dream.

"Theo needs LaCoix, no matter the cost." Ambrose's eyes turned into those of a cunning feline. "We know he cannot succeed in this state and needs more time. We have to expedite things in some manner, just as we recently unleashed drastic measures upon Kincaid. Perhaps a small push onto a relatively safe path from the Fates would help, if LaCoix can pull him back to be stronger and to try again." Ambrose placed more blankets on the body unable to retain heat. Spring breezes blew Oscar night, yet the room allocated to Barrett grew warmer, maintained at a high temperature by two apparitions. In the candlelit darkness, the stars shone through the open window, while the ocean sung its sweetest lullaby to the ailing figure under the fine linens. How much quieter and happier this ocean played, compared to the foaming breakers of the other, crashing on the rocks below the flowered fields of the old stone manor.

"His future is still unknown to us, and his Soul has yet to be found: a very unusual circumstance. We only sense the immense power within him; and yet he is lost in a labyrinth without an exit. Our man-child has fought the Fates his entire life, by interfering with a birth into the wrong family. Will he ever be able to protect his own child?" Lavender dusted away a strand of Ted's hair, blown into his eyes by the Pacific night wind.

"Alas, Mistress, it may not have been their first attack, but why this one to torture? They are using Barrett and Kincaid to juggle with, and they keep missing the catch. Only the third fiery club, LaCoix, seems to bounce back when dropped. I may have some clues as to what is happening, but until I spend more time with the troublesome two, I shall not speak of it." Ambrose puzzled, while continuing to hold the right hand, gripping even in slumber.

"Do you believe as I, that Barrett may be one of us? It would be a wonder if he was..."

"...was what?"

"I am sorry, Quin. Thinking aloud is something I rarely do. I had thought he might be the one to start the *awakening*. Our foes are devious and unmerciful, but they fear the *knowing*, which is unfolding with the possible emergence of the Black Rose. We must catch them, obliterating them from the Cosmos. Could Barrett be the one? It would seem unlikely, for he is pushing to reach a resting place, a peaceful spot where he need not worry about these oncoming battles. I believe that he understands more than he lets on, but decided, long before we entered his life, he did not have the will to perpetuate what he may foresee as his future. Fear is in his way." Lavender sat on the bed, stroking the damp, platinum spikes, turning into soft waves and growing longer. They continued to flutter in the softening breeze, brushing his cheeks and forehead with a thousand butterfly kisses. The only thing felt by Ted was drifting further and further away on a dance floor of dreams within the arms of David LaCoix.

"It is up to you, Mistress. Does he win or lose the game?" The Englishman looked forlornly into the face that held the answer. His enormous green eyes filled the hollow holes in the handsome thin face, distinctly marked with a black mustache and finely trimmed beard.

"With this one, I am unsure. His insistence, to take on so much, may be his undoing, particularly not waiting longer with his divorce; it could be his way to escape from what lies ahead. At least filming is complete, along with its underlying emotional savagery. We must take some kind of action to slow him down. Prepare Ethan for what may happen to Theo. I hope it does not interfere with his other problem, as he must keep up the attacks, without tipping this one off the tightrope he walks. Both Ethan and Stevie need to know how to care for our man-child. Teach them both, and make Kincaid listen, even in his duress. Remind him of his responsibility toward his friend's jeopardized condition, since his scandalous rendezvous with his own real-life Fate. I cannot believe Stevie agreed to copulate with the arrogant swine right before his scheduled marriage, only to have Theo walk in on the sick nightmare. It is beyond my reasoning why the world adores the sadist. One of the most charming, influential people in their reality, he--I cannot even say his name or what I think of him--but his glorious future will change. I will see to it myself." Lavender got up and encased herself in her comforting cloud.

"You are becoming a Fate yourself. Be careful, my Lady."

"I take your heed, Quin. A children's game to us, playing Fates, we shall tread cautiously."

"I will do as you ask. Shall I be notified as to what is to take place?" Ambrose grew suddenly anxious, wondering what the Mistress had in mind.

"You will know what to do; and I shall be close. Both Stevie and Theo are connected in some fashion. We must wait and watch what unfolds with our plans, although I loathe doing either. Let us hold these men together, and find out what you can. Maybe one of Ted's angels will appear."

"Sarcasm, my Lady? You are tired and discouraged."

"I suppose I am, Quin. Before I go, you have not told me of your plans, or the alternatives set before you. I don't even know how you feel about returning to this reality for a short respite." Lavender lingered, hovering over both men.

"I would enjoy the camaraderie of one more film, a fanciful epic of wild proportions. Sounds like I may need a diversion after this man's future has been won or lost. I am torn, as I do believe being a Spirit Keeper to Miss LaCoix may be of extreme importance. Both would be my preference. You carry too heavy a burden; one I would not care to tote on my shoulders, but willing to share. By the way, congratulations on your acceptance speech, I rather enjoyed it." A crooked smile finally broke the seriousness of the nightmare they had been watching, and Ambrose heard Lavender laugh. She vanished into the darkness, leaving only the candles to dance to the waters melody. "Oh, my dear Lad, what on earth is to become of you? I fear for you, Theodore Barrett. Hold on until the one whom loves you arrives. Safe night, sweet prince; you are a Shakespearean tragedy unto yourself."

CHAPTER 33

David heard the news moments after Barrett and company's notification. The awaited birth of Ted's child came two days after the awards gala, at home, and six weeks premature. Theodore Barrett had a little girl, but for how long?

The four men in Los Angeles had no means of dealing with the desperate situation. None had children, and they were understandably ignorant of the dangers the infant battled. Karen adamantly forbade Ted entry to see his daughter, immediately inducing a catatonic state in a man who took the blame. Unable to comprehend, the newest Oscar winner sank into oblivion: not hearing, not seeing, not feeling.

Quick with his response to Quinlan's call, David rifled off orders at a rate only a telepath could grasp. The only father, amongst the group, understood the insurmountable struggles to be waged by this child--Ted's child--their child. They had little time to rectify a complex condition. A premature baby could be saved; and David's total focus went into the survival of the innocent, underdeveloped little bundle. Instructions were laid out: get the baby into a hospital and incubated immediately. It may be this church's method of weeding out the weak, but certainly not the LaCoix way. Ted's elfin creature needed life-support urgently.

Three of the men heard the panic in the voice, and scrambled into action the instant the telephone went dead. In the submission, for the Order to Show Cause hearing, one of the father's requests included his child be delivered in a proper hospital. Too late, and with the situation critical, Quinlan contacted Barrett's attorney who hastened an urgent plea to a sympathetic judge for judicial intervention. Taking one look at the distraught first-time father, the court ordered the removal of the mother and child from their home, to be placed into the needed facilities in San Diego. Paramedics and two police officers escorted a belligerent Karen, and her baby, to a waiting medical staff. The church could do nothing in retaliation, and by nightfall, the one-day-old infant lay in the safest hands, along with its mother. Karen wanted and loved her daughter as much as Ted. Seeing so many children die in natural childbirth, for similar reasons, she nervously settled into her hospital room, surrounded by domineering wives of the elders, impeding the nursing staff.

The failing little girl remained secure, off limits to everyone except the mother, the father, and an unseen caregiver, Quinlan Ambrose. An early birth was Ted's first blow. For the next six days, donned in cap, mask, and gown, he and his shadow entered the frightening nursery of pink and blue bunnies, to helplessly hold his daughter, while rocking her to his beating heart's rhythm. His sadness echoed through his chest. She had arrived, now a mess of ugly tubes and wires hooked up to monster-size, humming machines. Close by, the nurses hovered, watching the famous new father carefully handling the disturbing, life-giving hoses with instinctive paternal delicacy. Those blue eyes, which bedazzled the world on film, rained down on his precious treasure. So tiny, he was afraid of her as well.

Quinlan waited painfully. Certainly not her Ladyship's doing, she stayed with them in her cloud. Ted wanted Ambrose's healing hands on his daughter, and when the staff turned their attention elsewhere, he came into being, to shine in healing blue light, directing his power to infiltrate both frail bodies. Within six days, her premature lungs, heart, and other underdeveloped organs struggled on their own. The doctors wondered in amazement at the progress of the little darling, and gave the credit to her loving father. Ted could only look up at Quinlan and thank him, in a mimed whisper, not realizing that he alone could see the man.

Worry over the child took Barrett away from his own disorder, and without thinking, he ate anything put in his mouth every thirty minutes. Much like baby food, he started to show some color in his pallid face. His strength in Spirit increased through the powerfully painted images David sent him in his head, passing through his mind to his daughter. She appeared a reflection of Ted's innate skills and stubborn character; and Quinlan looked skyward for a nod. Too soon to tell, Baby Barrett may be another part of the puzzle.

The seventh day, the day before the hearing, Ted collapsed with his second blow. He looked through the Intensive Care window into the nursery: his daughter was gone, discharged to her mother's care, and both had disappeared into the hands of the elders. Once more, Ted plummeted toward disaster, while three men and their half-dozen lawyers tried to rally him for the next day. Only reassuring words came from Quinlan; if Ted did not get sole custody, they would try again, depending on the results of the criminal trial. It seemed all they had, but Barrett refused to hear.

The Judge entered the courtroom, inflicting the third strike that snapped Ted's heart and mind. The entire universe, willing this single human Spirit to succeed, groaned at the crushing blow. Susan's tyrannical father would be presiding. Having become emotionally despondent since the birth, Ted did not recognize the name on the docket. Judge Matthews looked severe, determined to destroy the filthy beggar from that ghastly film. Immediately warned of the catastrophic circumstance, Barrett's lawyer drew in a breath and plunged quickly into his task. Matthews had secured all the submitted documents for his perusal beforehand, and had made up his mind the moment he saw Barrett's name. After listening to the reasoning of both parents to have sole custody, the Judge appeared adamantly disinterested and gave his supposedly unbiased decision.

Across the Atlantic, LaCoix finished dinner with Holly, who hustled away for an evening of painting. Ready for an early shutdown himself, to be fresh for a 5:00 a.m. call, David jolted to his senses as his fax machine started running off the reams of paper he had been nervously awaiting. Alone, he would bear whatever news another demon device threw at him. He began reading the judgment issued, and each word made his eyes grow wilder.

Ted's attorney made an excellent presentation, his witnesses sound, and the documentation fully prepared; unfortunately, a signed declaration by Karen Barrett, regarding Ted's mental health, rocked their case, and burned them immediately. Not amused, Matthews summed up his decision with what he referred to as facts. One redeeming compliment came from the bench to the man on the edge, noting the concern shown by the father over the safety of his child, and his quick action taken to save its life. It meant nothing when the ruling came down; Ted received only visitation rights, two hours per week under supervision.

Expecting at least joint custody, the decision threw Barrett into the mire; slumping back defeated; only to be asked to stand for the final blow, an unprecedented attack on his character. It shocked his entire entourage, including a stunned court staff. "Mr. Barrett, several disturbing items have come to my attention regarding you personally, and putting them together, I warn you, your rights to see your child will be withdrawn if these infractions reoccur. First, is your lurid act of a pornographic nature in a public domain. You may call it acting, but this court finds it an offense to moral decency, and is unacceptable behavior for a father. Next, the sworn statement of Mrs. Barrett, regarding your tendency to hallucinate strange occurrences, indicates an acute mental problem. If these outlandish accounts of the supernatural continue, you shall be committed for psychiatric evaluation. One last thing, Mr. Barrett, I understand, from my granddaughter, you have been gravely ill. How do you expect to care for an infant when you cannot take care of yourself? I leave you to ponder the question. Take what is given to you, and be thankful you proved yourself at least that worthy. This hearing is now closed." With the gavel smacking down hard on the nail into Ted's heart, he collapsed, carried out of the court by shocked friends.

LaCoix gagged at the atrocity of a supposed impartial Judge, and he frantically scanned the pages again. "That son-of-a-bitch, I'll kill him for this. He used Holly! He can't do that! My God, Ted, I'm so sorry the rockslide came back to haunt you. Karen blew a simple statement into wild accusations. Why did you tell her? I swear, to any god listening, he won't get away with such slander against you in a public forum." David cursed and gritted his teeth at his father-in-law's bias and sanctimonious stand. There proved enough evidence to gain joint custody, with some haggling over a religious upbringing, but the Judge simply hated Ted. Ideas of retribution whirled in the very angry actor's head; his only satisfaction would be the man's instant dismissal from his courtroom throne. Susan's father had always been a jackass, and now proved his insanity.

All the cellular numbers he tried were shut off, and understandably so. His only thought rested on Ted, and his need to be with him. Not his best idea, he found himself banging on Morris' bedroom door, and an invitation to enter gave him hope. He rapidly explained the situation regarding his involvement with Ted's legal and health battles, but Rod appeared less than sympathetic. Barrett was not immediate family, and having reached a point in filming where David's presence was crucial, Rod denied the man leave for an immediate departure. The director did relent, however, and allowed him to leave in a week, at which time they would shoot the few scenes in which his character would be absent. Graciously accepted, the man biting his nails could not divulge his true relationship with his former co-star, and personally did not know where he stood himself. He had to convince Ted to sacrifice his time with his sick child to accompany him back to England. David pondered on the unthinkable request; but if the disturbed young actor refused his help, and decided he had to be with his baby a few hours a week, it would be his choice; and two men would go their separate ways alone. LaCoix's sanity had to be kept intact for his own daughter; it seemed too harsh and cruel an ending.

On his last attempt, David reached Ted's lawyer, who remained in surprised disbelief at the libelous attack. He had heard rumors of Matthews before he knew the man would be presiding over their case, and agreed with LaCoix that they needed to stop this judge. David wanted to know the procedure to revoke a judge's position; and the man happily gave him the information and a plan to follow. Their attorney could only be a witness to testify in this particular case; and LaCoix would have to tread carefully when dealing with the bar. Just in the name itself, they bonded together with the sticky goop of a melting candy bar. It did not deter David's ire, only giving him more resolve to start immediate action of crushing his mentally abusive, senile father-in-law. The man would be kicked out on his legal ass, particularly after using his granddaughter's hearsay to rip Ted's fragile ego into bloody ribbons. Judge Matthews would pay.

The call from Quinlan arrived; and David prattled off his plan, with Ambrose agreeing. They had no recourse but the criminal case, proving the church guilty of abuse; and then they could try again. The divorce easily went their way, but final papers took six months to finalize, and by August, Ted would be free.

"How is he, Quin? Your fax said he collapsed."

Only silence and the faint sound of a sad sigh came over the line. Words had no meaning to describe the sorrow, which one long day had wrought on the unfortunate victim of the Fates.

"Oh, Christ, say something, man. Is he okay?" David wanted to slam his fist against a wall, but rethought his plan, looking at the two-foot thick, fortress wall looming before him. He nearly broke his hand the last time he tried.

"Sorry, LaCoix, but Theo is far from okay. He passed out when Matthews confronted him with his unmerciful ramblings. In a catatonic state, on returning to Ethan's estate, we believed the barrier could be broken once in familiar surroundings." A quiet hesitation, from Ambrose, made waiting worse. The need to know grew to astronomical proportions for the raging lion on the other end of the line.

"So, what happened?"

Ambrose heard the man's ire, and quickly spilled the story. "Without warning, Ted lunged for one of Ethan's prized samurai fighting swords, snatched it from the wall, and literally slashed the main sitting room into threads. One good flick of the wrist released the weapon; and Theo lay unconscious on the floor. I am truly sorry I didn't see it coming, the damage done before I had my senses intact. The little sprite surprised the hell out of me, with his sudden surge of strength. Kincaid endured a blade through his calf, a non-threatening injury. Ethan's unnerved with Steven's leg, and Theo's spontaneous reaction, as am I. The household will return to normal; and Peerce is unconcerned about his possessions. We are all upset with Theo's mental health and Steven's welfare. They have just returned, David. I see Steven is able to walk on his own with a slight limp. It will not take long to heal; I will see to it."

"I don't care! What about Ted?" A panicked yell stung Quilan, but nothing else mattered.

"What is normal, David? He has had a nervous breakdown and cannot be sedated due to his chronic condition. An antidepressant would stop his heart instantly. He said only one thing in his delirium; he could not leave California to be with you in Arizona. Right now, he is screaming his lungs out at nothing I can see. We had to tie him to the bed to keep him under control. I am considering a psyche facility, but wanted your opinion. The man needs both physical and mental care. We have tried everything."

"Everything but a telepathic link, that is your forte, isn't it, old chum? For Christ's sake, untie him; he'll stop struggling immediately. It's part of his problem, Quin, claustrophobia and terrified of being pinned down, especially in the dark. Lavender knows; where is she? You're scaring the hell out of him. Quickly, do it now. I'll see you in a week. Take care of him, man, get him settled without caging him; and make sure he knows he can be with me, without sacrificing his daughter. Do it now, Quin! Now!" David yelled into the phone, and then snapped it shut to get Ambrose to Ted faster. He visualized peace in his head. Over and over again, he saw a serene angelic smile on the face of his sleeping beauty.

"Haven't you been to bed yet, Dad?" Holly knocked, but David did not hear her, preoccupied over his ranting hysteria to save a frightened Spirit. He felt terrible for both his daughter and Ted, to have been used and abused in such a fashion by his sweet girl's cruel grandfather. The three letters he e-mailed that night would be the start in stopping any more of the ugly man's tyranny. Others would be saved by David's actions, the only thing to be thankful for this night. A sleepy little face calmed his headache slightly.

"Morning, Honey. Got a kiss for your old Dad?" A warm hug quieted his heart, and started a dialogue too serious for a little girl at such an early hour. He had no trouble convincing her to stop any correspondence with her grandparents in Los Angeles. The tilt of her head, and the expression of relief, indicated her dislike for them both. One horrendous situation agreed upon; another needed an explanation. The new day was now growing grimmer for the overwrought actor.

"It's okay not to like your relatives, Holly Jane, but you do have grandparents in Arizona, who very much want to meet you. It's time we all grouped together. I planned it as a surprise when we move to the new house." David received an instant smile; and life changed for one little miss, who clapped her hands while doing her favorite happy dance.

With more to say, he gently encased the excited, tiny hands to hold them still. "Now, about the Judge, I'm sorry if this is a problem for you. This is serious, Honey; he's done something terrible to Mr. Barrett; and I need to ask you a huge favor. Could you not talk about our dear friend to anyone, unless you ask his permission?"

"Sure, I can do that. I like Mr. Barrett. Is he feeling better?"

"No, Holly, he's worse. Would you mind if I fly to L.A. next week, and bring him back here to live with us? He'll stay in my room, where I can take care of him. Will you help me?" David looked intently at the little face for any signs of distress in sharing her father so soon.

"Sure, I'd like that, just need to know what to do."

"That's my girl. Be kind to him, that's all. One thing you have to remember, because Mr. Barrett is very shy: the knock rule. He'll need lots of hugging and handholding; and you can do both, just like Dad. Will it bother you to find Mr. Barrett in bed with me?" His eyes widened, penetrating the mirrors of his own, to get any kind of reaction of resentment or disgust.

"You hug Tyler and Bryce. It's the same thing, isn't it? I'm glad Mr. Barrett's coming." Lifted up and secured on her father's knee, she agreed to all, understanding little.

"There will be more affection displayed, like Mommy and I used to do. We need him with us, Holly Jane. Now, do you remember the rule?" David pulled her chin up to wink at her.

"Knock on the door, but don't enter unless invited." Happily, she reiterated a rule never to be broken.

"Perfect. Let's go have breakfast." David inhaled deeply, and mentally sent a Monet garden image of spring flowers and bright sunshine to a ravaged Spirit.

Lavender had hovered over the courtroom, struggling to hang onto Barrett. All her strength, everything she had, went into her healing powers to keep the man's heart pumping and his brain functioning through the hearing. After the disquieting ending, she entrusted Ted to the care of the other three, feeling the crisis over when the man fell limp. Her own strength had waned, and left alone, she absorbed the necessary power to continue. Coming back to life, she rested in her opulent chair to survey the Cosmos and beyond; but David's scream at Quinlan, to untie Ted, ricocheted off every star, reverberating throughout a universe. She dropped the forever-present goblet, and manifested instantly beside Barrett, ripping off his restraints with a flick of a sharp fingernail. Looking stressed and pale, Peerce and Kincaid burst into the room behind Ambrose. They caught the magic act in its final stages. Nothing of her Ladyship's skills surprised this group of men.

"I am sorry, Quin, I thought you knew. Easy, Theo, gentle and still, my Child. You are free now." Both her hands held the struggling figure, and little by little, Barrett started to calm. She let go as the strained muscles relaxed. The screaming softened to a whispered call for his Knight, while he curled into a tight fetal position on the oversized bed. Crying and drowning in despair, Ted fell into an abyss, incapable of saving himself, or his infant daughter. Nothing remained for him, nothing but David who now seemed only a wishful thought.

"Your Knight hears you, Theo. Hush, sweet Child."

"Let me try; I've seen how LaCoix handles him. This is entirely my fault. I'm so sorry for what I've done, and wish to apologize to everyone." Kincaid stepped forward, scanning the room for an appropriate place to sit and hold his best friend. He had destroyed Barrett, devastated Peerce, and infuriated the Mistress, but an opportunity opened to mend the chaos he created.

"You're forgiven for now, Stevie. Are you well enough to put weight on your leg?" An unexpected stern remark from Ethan, threatening in its cadence, created a shiver straight up Kincaid's back.

"I'm fine; but I need a footstool for the chair at the window, where I can hold Theo? I'll sit with him for as long as it takes." Steven limped over to the Bentwood rocker, sat down, and stretched out his damaged leg. Settled, he waited for his small look-alike to be placed in his care.

The white linen starched room fit the spiritual aspect of Ethan Peerce. Bordering on Oriental, with touches of the tropics, the guest bedroom gleamed with cleanliness; a precisely laid out space, belying how truly comfortable it made people feel. The sheer bleached curtains floated in the breeze of the open window Steven faced. His friend lay dying a slow death; nothing or no one seemed capable of stopping the accursed Fate hunting the man. His only honest friend, Ted saved his life; and Kincaid would hold him until he became lucid, or succumbed to his demons.

Barely breathing, when placed in Steven's secure arms, Ted began to chant, only understood by Lavender or David. Theodore Barrett attempted to stay the panic created by his imprisonment and his muddled head, while a familiar scent and arms encircled him. Someone neatly wrapped a straw-hued blanket around the two men; and both heads disappeared into the color. The ocean's lullaby, and the quieting sound of a friend's voice, breathed into his ear, blended the two into an earthly rhythm that eased Ted's terror from the black depths of the pit. "Hush, Scarecrow. Hush. Sleep now. Stay with us, Scarecrow. Stay with me."

The others departed, leaving a spoiled, emotionally unstable man to care for one who once shone in the brightest sun, thrilled in the climb of an impossible mountain, and dazzled you with eyes so wondrous, nothing worldly could compare. Lavender stepped away, agonizing over her failure. What had gone wrong in six months? She helped Theodore Barrett win an award of gold-plated Britannia, discovered his secrets he did not wish to share, and allowed him a quick taste of his sexuality, just to tear away his one honest pleasure. To finish the deed, she took his faith and screwed his head around so tightly, it reached its limit of endurance like a windup clock. The alarm rang loud, and no one could find the off-switch.

CHAPTER 34

A loud rattling at the gate, with a continual barrage of ringing, echoed through the Malibu mansion. Enough racket for Peerce and Kincaid to hear, in the furthest part of the house, they leapt out of bed and dashed for the monitor, inciting immediate attention and access. It interrupted a morning to share alone, particularly one for Ethan to enjoy the tasty enticements only Steven Kincaid provided willingly.

"What's going on? Stevie, look at this. It's LaCoix! I thought his plane arrived this afternoon." Kincaid peeked at the screen, while Peerce issued an order, to his gatekeeper, to allow the man entry. The two men quickly dressed, upon seeing the strain on David's face, and the nervous drumming of his hands on the leather-covered steering wheel he impatiently sat behind. They hustled down to greet him.

Wooden doors flung open in haste; the weight of them nearly knocking them off their wrought iron hinges. Out of the rented red Mercedes in a flurry, David slammed the door hard enough to make it bounce back open. He scaled the stairs in a stride. With no greeting or eye contact, he forcibly shoved his way past the couple waiting for him, yelling as he moved. "Where is he, Kincaid? What have you done with him? Ted, where are you?" David's old character returned in his distress, becoming obnoxious and rude. The tirade stopped with Ethan's firm clench on his shoulders.

"Slow down, LaCoix, Theo's better, even a little excited today. We expected you later in the day. Casey, bring coffee to the terrace." Peerce did not let go of the shoulders and directed the agitated actor out to view an ocean he had seen countless times and cared little for at that moment. David flew an eternity to find his lover; and all that mattered was the man's bags were packed; a room waited for them at the Wilshire for five days; and to screw love and life back into Ted until he could not walk a straight line.

"Got in late last night, and thought it best not to disturb you in the wee hours of the morning, or deal with another situation at the airport." Pacing the length of the terrace, of highly polished wooden planking, seemed the only way to diminish his aggravation.

"His brother picked him up early this morning. It's his first Saturday to visit his baby since her stay in the hospital." Steven's attempt failed to calm the man who did not want to settle. LaCoix took his coffee standing up, and drank it while making the same trek over the decked lookout.

"Where's Quinlan? Shit, something's wrong. I can feel it. Something is really wrong." Said with emphasize, and meant to his core, David sensed the onslaught of trouble, but could not pinpoint the cause. Overwhelmed with the feeling of disaster, the only one who could assure him would be the crazy Englishman or Lavender. Both ignored his call.

"Where is Mr. Ambrose, Casey?" Extremely polite, Peerce's staff enjoyed the rewards of working for the reclusive, famous man.

"If you'll excuse the expression, sir, Mr. Ambrose flew out of here, like a bat-out-of-hell, a couple of hours after the brothers left."

"Thank you, Casey. That's odd," Ethan muttered to himself.

"What's so strange about Quinlan suddenly vanishing without a trace? Aren't you used to that yet?" David snapped back, certainly not intimidated by the man who appeared to be a control freak in his quiet mannerisms and deadly eye contact. There seemed no doubt he had Kincaid in a dog collar, or so it led one to believe, by watching the interaction between them.

"You are in a foul mood, LaCoix. We know who and what Ambrose is: a fine, decent being, as frightened of losing Theo as you are. We're all nervous over your twitchy lover's every action and countermove. As per your request, we did not tell him of your temporary return to L.A."

"Sorry, Ethan; guess I'm just tired. It's nice to meet you finally; and I apologize for acting like an asshole; when I really wanted to thank you for suggesting me for the *Worthington-Smythe* role." Reaching out his hand, Peerce received it warmly, a little too warmly for David's comfort. He looked down at the firm, unnerving grip; Ethan immediately released it and smiled, again rather discomfortingly.

"My pleasure, as your skill and face seemed written all over the script. I couldn't imagine another actor attempting the complexity of the mysterious Lord. Stevie, as well as myself, cannot emote your insanity, which rages under the surface; and I mean that as a compliment."

"Thank you. I am doubly honored, I think." A slight smile softened the tense face.

"Can I help you with a neck rub, David?" Steven asked in an unusually childish manner. It caught David by surprise; but he allowed the younger man to get a chair under him. Ready to fall down, he appreciated the offer of the golden boy, who gave a great massage. Wild green eyes mellowed, nearly disappearing under the long, blond, upper lashes, on receiving the relaxing sensation. Ready to pass out from fatigue and worry, he now had to curb the insatiable desire to have the neck rub spread to the rest of his aching, needy body. First a hint of seduction initiated by Peerce, now a sensual message from Kincaid, he overcame his wonderment, with the feel of male hands easing his cramped muscles. He sighed and closed his eyes, finally to rub his face to wake up.

"Thanks, man. That felt great. How's the leg?"

"Okay, thanks. I've wanted to apolo..."

"...Not now, Stevie. Sit down and be quiet. How's your daughter, David?" Ethan appraised the man through the steam of coffee too hot to drink. The quieting actor had lost weight that he could not afford. His hair appeared blonder and much longer than he remembered at La Rosa Negra. They had not met while in his ghostly form in the labyrinth; nevertheless, Ethan had been quite engaged by this man, and his innocent man-child who reminded him so much of his secret live-in lover. The striking figure before him, however, was their complete opposite: wildly intense, prone to nervous habits, easily excitable behind the façade of a stone cold heart, and those eyes. As startling as Theo's, the green orbs were more frightening than the screen could ever capture. Presently, they darted about the sprawling deck and grounds, searching for a hint of Barrett. The older actor could feel the tension in the one true blond whom dropped into his solitary life, like the other two now residing in the house. All bombarded with problems never experienced, he felt quite exhilarated at their reactions to a single touch. LaCoix returned to his pacing, screaming silently; and Peerce could identify the panic terror. Something was wrong. It surprised him that an uninitiated Spirit had psychically matured so quickly. Returning from his human wanton yearnings, Ethan listened to the answer of his idle question.

"She's adapted very well. I enjoy her company; something I thought I would never say about my children, until six months ago. It's quite gratifying, considering it used to scare me senseless. Before Ted and..." Cut short by a yell, Casey dashed in with a cordless phone in hand.

"Mr. Peerce! Mr. Peerce! Urgent call from Mr. Ambrose."

Three coffee mugs crashed to the deck. Ethan grabbed the wireless phone and uttered a series of one-word responses and one-word questions. *Where* seemed the imperative one. "Let's go you two. Casey, ask Jonathan to bring the BMW around, the black one. He's driving, and tell him to move swiftly."

"What's happened?" Steven paled ashen gray at the annoyed look and unwarranted command. David could not believe the young man had reverted to being timidly cautious. Only two possible answers to the dilemma: either a habitual response to his former abusive lover or Peerce enjoyed the same sadistic pleasures. It made LaCoix think for a moment, but his concern focused on Ted; the news had to be about the man teetering on another breakdown.

"Hurry, both of you in the car!"

The two men raced after Peerce, down a hallway, through several rooms, to burst through the heavy exit. Once again, they tortured the exotic wood and its doorframe, and all three clamored into the safe luxury of expensive Recaro seating of a car ready to take off in flight. With the doors already open, before their arrival, the chauffeur did not assist any of them. No one was that delicate in this crowd, except the one limping and not complaining. Behind the wheel, Jonathan full throttled it on hearing three doors slam shut.

"It's Ted, isn't it? Tell me, Ethan. For God's sake, tell me now. Not a heart attack? No, not now! Say something!" Leaning half his body over the front seat, LaCoix wanted to see the expression on the face looking straight out the front window.

"Stay calm and listen. When we get to the hospital, the police will meet us, and probably the press. We have a long drive; and Jonathan will get us there. We're heading for San Diego."

"Which hospital, sir?"

"The Naval Hospital on the Base. It's the closest Richard Barrett could reach. Do you know it?" The chauffeur nodded his head; the centrifugal force, of the car, pulled them all back into their seats.

"The hospital! Christ, Ethan, tell me, before I strangle the man sitting beside me, and with the greatest of pleasure." Besides being upset, David's ire increased. He had never conquered his disappointment in Kincaid, and now Peerce issued the orders, giving no answers.

"I'm unsure of the facts." Stated sympathetically by Ethan; it ignited more concern in LaCoix.

"Why the police? What's happened? Please, not another car accident? No, that can't be, since you said Richard drove to the hospital. Tell me Peerce." Ready to lose his mind in frustration, and unable to move to douse the flame, David drove his fist into the upholstered door.

As Ambrose explained the problem over the phone, Peerce laid out the situation to the attentive listeners in the back. Ted had been picked up by his brother, to make the journey to San Diego. Upon reaching his former home, they walked into a gathering of church elders. Two innocent young men stood unprepared to face the half-dozen much larger, stronger men, including their father; a stunning blow for the brothers. The attack came quickly and unmercifully; and although Richard forcibly tried, his valiant effort could not save his older, smaller brother. Wielding two-by-fours, the weapon of choice for this god-fearing group, the attackers beat Theo close to death before Quinlan arrived in his special way. Barrett's first official visit with his little girl turned into a violent, vengeful retaliation by the church."

"Good, God! How long before Quin arrived?"

"Their salvation, he saved both boys. That's why he disappeared this morning; he saw it happening. From what he said, he took charge immediately, arriving to find Theo unconscious, but their attacks continued on his limp body. Richard kept moving, scrambling around to protect Theo and to topple whomever he could, only to receive the same beating. Quinlan sent men flying left and right when he came into his light. Once in full force, it did not take him long to end the ordeal."

"How bad are the boys hurt? You said Richard drove. Christ, I should have been with them. Why didn't I come directly from the airport; I could have stopped it." His mind in chaos, David tried to visualize the positive, but only the negative kept coming to the fore. Both hands entangled themselves in his hair, while he rocked back and forth, needing to run, needing to escape the confines of the car, and needing to race for the finish line: Theodore Barrett.

"Don't look back, David. It happened; accept it. After Hurricane Quinlan hit, he carried Theo and aided Richard to the car. Although not the main target, the brother sustained a fair amount of damage. Barely making it to the Base, and seeing the urgency, Gate Security generously allowed them admittance. Ambrose kept the concussed younger brother conscious, while trying to concentrate his healing light to keep Theo breathing. It's not good, David. Now, you two prepare for a press assault, as they've gotten wind of this." In control and agitated, Ethan brought both men, in the backseat, to quick attention. Their only hope lay in the hands of Quinlan and the Mistress. Too tired and in shock to argue, David would do whatever it took to get to Ted's side.

LaCoix felt numb by the time they stopped at the gates of the Naval Base. The few members of the press, blocking their way, turned back readily from the menacing force of the Military Police. Three handsome heads ducked to avoid unwanted eyes and curious cameras attempting the impossible, to see through the darkened windows of the black vehicle.

"So far, so good." Steven's voice shook; muffled in his attempt to comfort another man he had hurt. It came through the jacket both heads hid under, and a gentle hand caressed the younger one in a gesture of forgiveness. David's light wool navy blazer came in handy for at least one reason, considering the balmy day. Well past noon, they hustled through Emergency and quickly escorted into the Trauma Unit. Their pace doubled at the troubling sign. An officer of the Military Police stopped them, and ushered them into a room occupied by Quinlan, Richard, and members of the civilian police.

A quiet atmosphere pervaded the room. The presence of Ambrose, and now Peerce adding his own energies, created the tranquility; and David thanked them both in his head. Someone had to be the rock; these two men volunteered without question. Spotting a young man, with bloody bandages around his head and a cast on an arm, it had to be Richard. His ribs obviously hurt, and LaCoix winced, remembering how bad two bruised ones felt. The scarlet blanket around him masked any other damage, but indicated the staff's awareness the younger brother suffered from shock, and may need immediate attention. Everything stopped when three famous faces walked in on the intense conversation. Quinlan spotted them and excused himself from his meeting with the San Diego Police. Although a civilian matter, the Military obligingly added their support.

"Good to see you, LaCoix. Thought you would be arriving later today. No matter, this is a terrible thing to walk into. Theo is gaining consciousness. Unbeknownst to the staff, the Mistress is holding him in that state, waiting on your arrival; so please don't let the doctors frighten you by what they say. Now then, you should be the first person he sees. Authorities agreed to let you in immediately. They have not notified the family on his brother's request, since one of them tried to turn his sons into mincemeat this morning."

"Christ, their father was involved! Tell me straight out, Quin; how bad?" David gripped the tall Englishman by the shoulders, ready to shake it out of him.

The man, who also always wore black, retained his usual inscrutable demeanor. Removing the vise-like grip gently, he placed his own hands on the strained face, staring firmly into the startled green eyes. "We're all here to support you, David. You know that, and you know we can help Theo. Now, if you're a little settled, his doctor will update you on his condition. Steven and Ethan will come with me. We'll need all the power we can gather to help." Ambrose left him, gathering the others to tend to Richard, and allowing David to do whatever necessary with regard to Ted. The nervous actor watched the catering of everyone else, and wondered if anyone aided his lover. The chimes echoed; Lavender would be there. The powers mentioned would help, but which kind: healing or spiritual. Where were they, what happened, and who was this doctor? David lost himself in another maze.

In a small consulting room, a doctor, in Operating Room green, joined him to explain a serious situation to a man who only wanted to see, not hear. The quivering lips needed a cigarette between them to hold David together. Back in focus, his eyes came in contact with those of the green man who started from a point he could not remember the beginning of. Ted's arms were broken in a multitude of places, having used them to parry off the attacks like dueling swords. An unusual move on his part, according to the doctor, most individuals curl up to protect vital body parts. Barrett had not; and it saved him from a major blow to his skull, but the few, which hit their marks, fractured his cheek. The cuts to the famous face were handled meticulously by a plastic surgeon; and there would be no scarring or permanent disfiguration. Simply put, a battered Barrett looked like a sparrow that flew full speed into the glass of an unseen window. His ribs and lower back took a severe beating, yet left no broken bones. The doctor could not believe the viciousness of the attack, which the brothers eradicated, although the youngest man would certainly feel like a fully loaded cement truck had run over him. Then the dreaded phrase never said to a family member, *if he makes it*; David barely understood the words that followed.

Miracles unto themselves, the legs sustained no fractures, only crushed blood vessels, turning from red to black. One anomaly was his hip. A small chip off the right one was removed; and the skin stitched under a local anesthetic. It would not be missed; it would not be a deformity; and like the rest of his tortured body, it would be uncomfortable for a time. The doctor stood, and with some compassion, helped a shaken David to his feet.

"Any questions Mr. LaCoix?" The green man looked into the eyes his wife would swoon over, and received a shake of the head. He wondered if the silent, blond-haired man understood anything that he had said. David heard; comprehension was another matter. "Unconscious when we started this conversation, it will be a slow awakening."

"It has been so far." David contemplated an unearthly statement he could not explain.

"Excuse me?"

"Sorry, what were you saying?" An instant cover up, he suddenly realized he spoke the impossible aloud.

"He will need a familiar face to wake up to. Usually only family is permitted; but this is a rare and bewildering case for us. I understand you are the closest friend he has. Is that correct?"

"I guess we all are; I mean the five of us who are here. His youngest brother should be informed, as Richard will need him as well." His mouth spoke words, but did they make sense? David gave his head a shake and combed his hair with his fingers for the hundredth time.

"He's on his way, although Richard Barrett did not want him notified, because of problems with wives, police, lawyers, and someone impartial to keep an eye on Mr. Barrett's daughter."

"Of course, Raymond has to be protected from this. What a hell of a situation." David came to his senses, understanding there had to be an insider to take care of the baby.

The green man had been helpful, but it all seemed meaningless, standing exchanging words. Why was he not taking this in? He understood the problems; he heard the doctor mention Ted's father tried to murder his sons; he had to speak, but what had happened to his voice? Finally, a snarl came forth from the corner of a clenched curled lip, his voice filled with the resonance that scared people to their grave; the menacing Lord Worthington-Smythe asked, "Has Theo's lawyer been notified?" A public name, one he never used, David remembered even in his shocked state.

"Yes, he's on his way, but I don't think it's of immediate importance. We should be getting to Mr. Barrett. One thing, sir, Mr. Ambrose confirmed our suspicions; this talented young man is anorexic. He's in an extremely dangerous situation. We're monitoring his heart; he's on a drip; and a feeding tube inserted down this throat. It will be hard for him to talk when he comes around. The advanced stages of the disease are very pronounced. Please keep him calm."

"Listen, Doctor, all those tubes are going to scare him. His former beliefs did not condone contemporary medical assistance to treat their ill or injured. When he comes around, he may panic, not recognizing or understanding what's going on." A shaking hand pulled the doctor around, to reinforce the seriousness of Ted's fears.

"They are necessary; I am sorry. According to Mr. Ambrose, he has been using both for some time. I hate to suggest this scenario so early, but your friend may slip away before regaining consciousness; his anorexia inhibits him to fight his injuries. A possibility, sir, and one you and his brothers must consider. Are you of the same faith?" A direct look of concern stared into the startled famous face. Another incredulous statement to make at this stage, David nearly collapsed. Beyond his reasoning, he would not allow Ted to drift away alone.

"Christ, he's that bad? I'm certainly not of his faith; and Theo cut those chains some time ago. I simply meant to warn you his old habits and fears could return. He'll come around; he can't die. It's not his time. I can't believe you even suggested such a thing. He will make it; he's stronger than he looks. No *ifs*, Doc." David lost his composure completely. Shaking in anger, he grabbed the doctor violently, slamming him against the wall, his fists latching onto the green coat, unable to let go.

"I understand, Mr. LaCoix, as I'm only warning you. We'll do everything possible. Steady sir, let go and inhale. Okay, now let's get back to what you should expect, when he regains consciousness." The green man immediately retracted his first prognosis to something more hopeful, for a man who obviously had strong ties with the one who lay dying. "He will be in severe pain, since we are unable to come up with a sedative that won't stop his heart, not even a muscle relaxant. It will be torture to watch, and for him to endure. For your own update, Richard Barrett is pressing charges, as is Mr. Ambrose. Again, be careful what you say to the young man; he may not remember the assault in his shock, or his father's involvement. As for his protection and your privacy, two Naval Police Officers are posted to guard the room assigned to him. He'll be well taken care of; we have some of the finest doctors in the country working at this hospital. It's unusual for us to treat civilians, particularly famous ones."

"I'm sure, Doctor. I can't think of a more secure place for him to be. Can I see him now?" David stopped the urge to bolt past the two officers he saw on either side of a solid door at the far end of the hall. Ted's room, his Teddy Bear was nearly in his arms.

The doctor in surgical scrubs quickly led David down the busy corridor of nurses, interns, doctors, residents, all in trauma uniforms. Frightening to watch the activity, he had to get Ted out of this organized pandemonium. Shouting and screaming, accompanied by panicked voices straining to be heard, seemed the only form of communication in the Trauma Unit. Another doctor yelled for a crash cart, and a sudden influx of people appeared, only to disappear into the next urgently demanding room. Terrifying to the healthy, the commotion could be disastrous to the ill and dying. His attention snapped back like he had been rear-ended. On entering the door, which the M.P. held open for him, he came to a halt. A large, gentle hand gave him a little nudge forward; and the door closed behind him. He had been here before; he was too late.

A white tomb of intolerable silence, only the little beeps and twerps gave him a reprieve. Looking around, he grew as pale as the white bed, in a white room, with two white nurses, in white starched uniforms, hovering over a body, swathed head to toe in white gauze and white plastic. His thoughts had manifested into reality, but the blue eyes had already closed. David's heart stopped, and he snapped his knees into a locked position. Living the hell he had created in his own mind for Ted, the surrealistic vision vaporized in one of Lavender's clouds. She was there; he could hear her urging him on; and her familiar fragrance calmed his shock. Cold and sweating, he approached slowly, finally to stand beside what remained of Theodore Barrett.

On a little groan, David jolted into real time. He shook his head to clear the fog, and gazed at the torn, broken lips swollen to three times their size. Barely recognizable, the once boyish face had been beaten, until blood red in color, quickly turning to black. Tubes ran down his throat and up his nose, with more plastic and rubber streamers pumping fluids, and eliminating others. They all cascaded, like transparent snakes, over the side of the bed, from under the blankets, and what lie beneath: a body the size of a straw. David had never been so frightened.

His hand went down to make contact with the fingers of the least restricted hand. Cast in plastic to the elbow, the discoloration of the right arm continued to the neck. He felt the fingertips needing some reassuring warmth. Ice cold to the touch, as were the few exposed areas of flesh, David scanned frantically for the monitor, which would tell him Ted lived. Only the repetitious peaks and valleys of a heartbeat told him anything. Too slow, he counted them in his head; two beats followed another two; they at least retained a steady rhythm. A shiver of relief and the other arm came into focus. This cast went from the fingertips to a forty-five degree angle at the elbow, continuing up to cover Ted's shoulder, until it reached his neck, all fused to a brace encircling his upper torso. With his arms restricted in a torturous device, Ted's worst nightmare lay before him; David prepared himself for the reaction the entrapment would create.

The body shivered involuntarily, alerting LaCoix to ask one of the two nurses for help. They had left him alone. He made a quick search and found several more blankets; pink ones added some color to the deathly white room now in full focus. Another whispered groan brought him back to the man he carefully bundled up.

"There you are, Teddy Bear. Wake up; it's David. I'm right here." The ghostly form stirred to a familiar voice, but did not move. The pain came into play; the world stood still for the man waiting beside the bed.

"Dav..." Ted gagged on the tube, as he tried to figure out the constriction in his throat. Recognizing the device, Ted readjusted his swollen lips to accommodate the piece of plastic.

"I'm here, Baby. Just rest. You've been badly injured, but nothing permanent." David touched the only thing that might not hurt, the bleached blond hair gracing the man's head. A prayer of thanks winged skyward.

"Fath... Father..." A great imitation of David's low growl, muffled by the tube, the voice sounded sore and scared.

"Easy. They have something down your throat, so try not to move and don't talk. Can you feel my hand holding your fingers? Squeeze my fingers lightly for yes." David felt the slight movement. In his semi-conscious state, Ted knew and understood everything that had happened.

"My... my father..." Ted choked again, and David saw them coming. He had to stop any anxiety and fear. Impossible, he could not hold back his own tears.

"I know, Baby. I know; shush now."

"Help... help me." The fingers tried to grasp the warmer hand a little firmer, creating a tidal wave of tension up the arm and down through the entire helpless body.

"What do you want me to do? You know how to deal with pain. I know you do."

"My father... he wanted... wanted me dead." Barely understandable, Ted's statement confirmed the desired results of the church.

"You're safe. He'll never hurt you again. You told me once; you and your brothers could heal yourselves. Try it, Ted. I truly believe you can." David latched onto an outlandish claim he had ignored when mentioned after the broken arm incident. He had nothing else.

"Stop... stop the... pain..."

"I wish I could; I wish I could change places with you. You're bruised and bashed in I don't know how many places; and we can't stop the pain with drugs, even if you would take them. You're scaring me, Baby. Don't cry. Stay as quiet as you can, and open those beautiful eyes for me. Please look at me, Ted." On David's begging, the blue sapphires did appear through the swelling; and the salty tears made every facial wound sting.

"Pull... pull them out." Ted continued the downpour, and his entire body quivered with a tremor. David rang immediately for help.

"The tubes? I know they're against your beliefs, but they're helping you stay alive. Leave them in a while longer. Concentrate on sending the pain away. You have to try." The recognizable fear in David's voice did not help; and Ted's ability to concentrate on helping himself blew away with the anxiety heard.

"Can't... They hurt... they..." The hapless victim fought for air, and the sparkling droplets fell harder, splashing against the gauze. The panic grew in both men, until rescued by a nurse. On a snapped, nervous order, she scurried off to get the doctor.

"Okay, which tubes, Ted? Which ones hurt?" David brushed away his own fright with the sleeve of his navy blazer.

"The ones... the one in..." The blue pools looked directly down at his crotch. Nothing else moved; the eyes told David everything.

"The catheter? I can't remove it on my own."

"Can't heal... can't breathe..." Ted fought for whatever air he could get past the tube blocking his throat, while the oxygen into his nose became impeded by the mucous discharged by the sobbing. The doctor immediately crashed through the door to get to his patient. Between the green man and two nurses, they removed the plastic from the sore throat. After a great deal of spontaneous gagging, vomiting, and excruciating coughing, the nose tubes were extracted. A full oxygen mask over his nose and mouth came last, but Ted's agitation continued.

"Mr. Barrett, please remain calm. You're breathing pure oxygen, to make you feel better. Settle down, son." The doctor's bedside manner remained kind but forceful. Ted tolerated none of the coddling, and continued to plead for help. Whatever hurt grew harder to bear, turning the cries into continual childish sobbing.

"He won't calm down until you check the catheter. It's what started this tirade. Listen to him; that's not Theo. It obviously hurts like hell." David had stepped away during the removal of the tubes, but pushed between the nurses hustling to remove the first devices extricated.

With the blankets and sheets removed, it left Ted lying in a white hospital gown with a bloodstain spreading rapidly at the crotch. Lifting the fine cotton, the doctor said nothing, but looked up into wild green eyes on the other side of the bed. David saw and understood.

"Please do something. That's cruel and sadistic!" LaCoix could not verbalize his feelings of disgust and anguish. This had to be Ted's worst injury, but left unnoticed. Also aghast at what he saw, the doctor went straight to work on rectifying the horrific mess.

With the sound of a moan coming from under the mask, David felt fingers searching for his hand. "I've got you, man. Don't move. Shush, Theo. Think of white and black roses, the smell of jasmine, and Sir Edmund." The grim-looking actor blinked up at a startled doctor, and wondered what brought those particular items to mind. Lavender of course, and David saw the results slowly ease the strain on Ted's forehead. Visualization: he had to keep Ted thinking of the magical.

"I'm sure you two know what you're talking about. Since I'm the odd man out, and intend to stay that way, grip his fingers and get him breathing calmly under the mask. Stop him from crying."

"You heard the man, Theo, easy and slow. It will be over soon." David firmly held the cold fingers embedding their nails into his skin.

The green man never looked at the face, concentrating solely on the man's swollen, bleeding genitalia. "Don't pass out on me now, son. Ready? Deep breath and hold."

Ted sucked back during the single slow pull, as did David. Bleeding from the insertion and lacerations to the most delicate of parts, LaCoix had never seen his, or anyone else's penis and scrotum so tortured. He had received a few accidental kicks while training, but nothing like this. The pain, on removal of the obnoxious tube, was beyond any man's endurance, no matter how masochistic some men seemed drawn toward sexually. A high-pitched shriek came from the broken face under the plastic mask; Ted went limp before completion of the gruesome task.

Inspecting every inch of what appeared to be crushed genitals, the doctor implied the insertion took place before the abnormal swelling began. Possibly an allergic reaction to the plastic had started rupturing the tiny veins within the penis, not to mention the gouges to its exterior, and to the scrotum, which had been minimally checked in their haste. Cleaning off blood and tending to anything that would continue to bleed, the doctor assured David everything would return to normal. Just as any orifice of the body, bleeding tended to be profuse, only to heal quickly when treated. A horror-stricken face could not hide the fact that David did not believe a word said. Once complete, the doctor leaned over and yelled the public name repeatedly. "Theo! Theo! We're waiting for you, son. Good man, that's it. Open your eyes and look at me. It's out, and you should be feeling better. Now tell me calmly what else hurts, besides every bone in your body?" The doctor attempted to make light of a bad situation, while keeping Ted alert.

"Please... take... take out the other." Ted continued his begging; and David believed it might be an attempt to rid the body of all its tubing. The discomfort shown on the swollen face meant pain, as did the tears shed in front of a stranger who terrified the young man: a real doctor.

"Where else does it hurt Theo? You have to help me here." Undoing damage, partially created by his own staff, the doctor waited for his next unwanted surprise.

"My ass." The agony could not be denied, along with the muscle spasms cramping the thin body. It could lead to a seizure, not needed or wanted.

"It's another tube. Your anorexic condition only gives you a liquid stool, which you presently cannot control. It shouldn't be hurting." The doctor appeared puzzled at the request. The anal catheter seldom bothered anyone, except for the embarrassment factor.

"It hurts my back. Take it out." Ted came close to passing out again; his nose and mouth covering impeded further explanation; along with the shallow breathing from a chest unable to expand by an acrylic brace and sore ribs that screamed to remain still.

The green man went immediately to work, not understanding the connection, but willing to ease what discomfort he could, if only to stop a sudden fit. On completion, the doctor wrapped Ted up securely. It provided some relief for the agony of his genitalia and aching back. The lifting movement of his hips almost knocked Barrett out once more, but the young man sucked in the pain. Now settled and somewhat comfortable, the tears stopped. With David's assistance, the doctor scoured the room for pillows. Enough in hand, the two men raised Ted's calves, bending his knees, creating a softer cradle for the humiliating injury.

After a quick check of the rest of the equipment, monitoring the man's progress, and giving his organs assistance to operate, the surgeon stepped back, wondering how the man survived. The average person would live through such a beating, but this man's structural fragility, deteriorating internal organs, and suggested mental instability from Mr. Ambrose, could not take this kind of abuse. Barrett was a mess; and he could do no more but wish for more miracles. Satisfied that he would be notified of any further problems, he suggested that Ted be left to sleep. The doctor departed, leaving the two unhappy men to stare at each other. Eyes met; both pair misted over.

"Feeling better?"

"Cold."

"Think we can take care of that." David added more pastel-hued blankets, while repeating supportive words, quietly and steadily; belying his own terror of the emaciated body he bundled up. "Hey, man, congratulations on the birth of your little girl. Now we each have one."

"I don't."

"Yes you do. All I see is a beautiful picture of the four of us. Shush now, and do as the doctor instructed. We'll talk after your sleep. Close your eyes. Can you see the two of us, with our beautiful daughters, strolling through a field of wild flowers, laughing and playing? Keep watching the image, Teddy Bear. Sleep, as I'm here now." David sat down, no longer able to stand, but still playing with the few fingers and the yellow straw. One of the most well known voices, in movie making, continued to describe picture after picture for the once ray of sunshine. Ted did sleep, seeing every canvas painted for him; he would not forget one of them. What was seen through those green eyes, and thought in a great actor's imaginative mind, gave the younger man a window into a magical web, one woven by a master storyteller.

CHAPTER 35

Ted woke to the pain and did not move. The eyelashes fluttered; the fog of sleep lifted; and the ceiling came into focus. With thousands of little holes to count, he had little else to do. Concentrating, on something useless, helped when not knowing where you were. He tried to sigh, but the deep breath hurt. The consequences of his actions flooded his consciousness with all his dreams gone: no more films to make, no child to raise, no God to believe in, and no man to love him back. Having nothing left in his future but loneliness, he went back to the fascination of the ceiling tile, which briefly stopped the hurt plaguing him inside and out, and not caring why.

Counting each square, then the number of holes in one of them, multiplied by the number of tile, he would have the job done in minutes. Start with the twelve-inch units, he thought; and he moved his head slightly to see the upper corner of the right side wall. A movement: someone was with him. Moving his head a fraction further, the pain he fought returned. His head swam at the touch of his cheek against the pillow. Questions filled his head while it spun around in circles, even with his eyes closed. Being sick would hurt beyond his ability to cope; he tried settling his stomach. No crying, no vomiting, and no holding his breath, he had himself convinced, yet still wondered if he remained in one piece. Maybe he had fallen into hell; but the Mistress said there might be something below or above. Where was he? He opened his eyes again, remembering the motion caught in his peripheral vision. The important task of counting ceiling tile could wait.

"David!" The whisper hurt, sounding hoarse and raspy from under a mask, giving him another surprise. He could not move his arms to remove the object; but before panic struck, he had to make sure the man sat next to him. Remembering a similar scenario an eternity ago, his hero once again slept in a chair beside his bed. Looking haggard and pale, the Spirit, whom he loved, had etched lines running down the face instead of across. A creation of his broad, wicked smile gave the blond actor a look of authority and maturity; Ted loved every line. A feeling of safety lifted his woe, knowing LaCoix rested nearby. Further pondering on the figure in the uncomfortable chair, he wondered why the man looked half past dead. A shiver caught him off guard, with the recognition of a hospital room; and the weak heart started racing, pounding against bones unable to take another beating. A small groan came out in gut-wrenching pain. "David... please, be here."

The sleeping actor leapt forward, clamoring out of his chair before his legs were under him. He almost crashed to the floor in his attempt to get to the faltering voice. "Ted, you're awake! What is it?"

"Going... going to be sick." Ted started heaving, unable to move from his supine position. David had the mask off in seconds.

"Where are those tin things? Here we go. Don't move. Let me do the lifting. Easy, Ted." David placed the pan next to the battered head he turned slightly, allowing the patient to let loose the vile demons from his morning encounter. A damp cloth gently wiped clean the remains.

"Don't leave me alone... help me..." The mumble came from lips, which barely opened and bled when they did.

"I'm here, Baby, and we'll get you out as soon as we can."

"What... what happened? I... I hurt everywhere."

"For one thing, your cheek is broken, causing your face to swell, as well as your bruised lips.

That's why you're having trouble speaking. Anything else you need to do before I go down the list: shit, piss, vomit again?" David smiled at him, brushing back the damp, unnatural blond hair, turning the waves into curls.

"All those things or... or haven't you heard from Quin?"

"I know, Baby."

"You're really here? Are you staying?" Almost inaudible, the voice scratched uncomfortably at each sound formed and whispered.

"You bet I'm here. How long have you been awake?" Another cloth splattered its excess water into something ringing of tin, as David wrung out the cooling cloth.

"Don't know. Something covered my face?" Ted tried to lift an arm; and the eyes widened in fright at another unsuccessful attempt to raise the limb off the bed.

"An oxygen mask makes breathing easier for you. I suppose we should put it back on... or not." David foresaw the impending fit and immediately backed off. "What's wrong? There's nothing to fear in being able to breathe. A blast of pure oxygen is quite a relief. You should know how these contraptions feel, considering the high altitudes you've climbed."

"I can't move!" With Ted just warming up, the older man quickly snipped off the thorn.

"Of course you can't; you resemble a large paperweight. Your arms are broken and in casts, and right now, you're too weak to move them. You're going to be okay. They gave you back the blood they stole." David tried to be nonchalant and add some comic relief to a situation that could lead to almost anything. His fascination, with the new colored waves, kept him cooling the agitation with the damp cloth, creating the curling effect.

"Are you sure it's mine?"

"Not really, but it could be, considering you're a rare blood type. You're broken, bruised and battered, swollen, cut, and sore, in more places than we can count. You put up a hell of a fight this morning; you must be exhausted. Now, stop tensing and lay still."

Groaning softly at every breath taken, Ted scrunched up his sore eyes exactly like Holly would do for emphasis. Far more than a childish tactic, the action necessitated David to help him through the entire mess, but not knowing where to start. He leaned over the head, his fists firmly placed on the bed, either side of the body, and his eyes staring directly into blue orbs barely visible. "Okay, you, listen up. You fell asleep when we tried to stop the pain, by visualizing something wonderful. We'll try it again later. Healing friends surround you; and if I'm correct, you can add some sorcery of your own. You talked about healing yourself once before; and I reminded you of it an hour ago. Were you telling me the truth?"

"Did I talk to you before?"

"For a short while."

"Can't remember, but your question; small things I can heal not knowing how, but others are difficult. Man, this sucks; it hurts so badly."

"Maybe focusing and concentrating on the problem can speed up the healing. Try it on your ribs, so you can breathe properly. Lavender and Quin will add to your power later, so we can get you out of here quicker."

"I wish I knew how." Ted's eyes did look perplexed. A proven fact, people were capable of doing amazing things in a crisis, never knowing how they accomplished the feat. Spontaneous reaction to save oneself seemed a plausible explanation for performing impossible deeds.

"That's enough talking. How about some water?" David received a minimal nod with a groan held back; and Ted sipped on a straw between the swollen lips. "Do you recall what happened?" David kept stroking, and the tension eased.

"Do I have to?" The raspy voice came back, without the anguishing breaths breaking his thoughts.

"Sorry, Baby, but the police need to speak with you. It's a miserable thing to go through twice, but you have to tell them what you remember, carefully and cautiously. Be very precise in what you say. It's important." David raked his own hair back, straightened up, and waited for any answer. His courageous partner, in the final analysis, had sustained a slight concussion. Simply too sick to cope, Ted still had mental foes to vanquish.

"Not anymore. We had a good cause once. What they did won't give me my child, or stop other kids from being hurt." Defeat and despair added to the hurting; and David watched helplessly as Ted sank into the depression Ambrose described. Seeing it slowly overwhelm the man, it brought into perspective the seriousness of the problem.

"Maybe, considering Richard and Quinlan have already laid charges of attempted, premeditated murder. It may buy some children more time. Your church elders don't want social workers finding kids locked in holes with swollen limbs before the trial. We'll get your daughter. It will take some time, but we'll get her." David tried to feign a smile, but failed. Grim determination etched the lines deeper into his face; he rued the fright it instilled in Ted, but his cause escalated by this new travesty. He would not give up on dismantling this holy order, stone by sacred stone, in its behavior toward the innocent. Ted seemed to be one of their more naïve.

"No, we won't! We have to wait until Karen hurts her! Don't you understand?"

"They tried to kill you and your brother. It has to make a difference."

"Richard! He helped me. Is he okay? Then Quin appeared, I think. Ouch, it hurts to talk. There's blood!" Ted did not whine or wince, nor did he look at David's worried eyes.

"Lie still. Your brother's forearm is broken and a number of ribs. He incurred a beating, but not as severe as yours. The last time I checked, he sat just outside your door where the staff could watch over him. They're trying to convince him to stay overnight for his own protection, and to watch his mild concussion. He's terrified, but helping the police, with Quin standing guard. As for the blood, your lips keep breaking open; and you had a god-awful tube down your throat." The constant stroking of the hair kept the injured party calm and somewhat lucid.

"God-awful; isn't that the truth? I remember the tubes."

"That's one thing at least. Now, please stay quiet, and I'll get another cold cloth to stop the split from bleeding into your mouth. It's probably the reason you feel sick." David returned with a comforting yet woeful smile that everyone wore when worried, and gently dabbed at the lips swelling shut. It surprised him how Ted held back what must have been unbearable pain, and how alert he seemed, considering the doctor's foreboding prognosis. Lavender's presence would strengthen his confessed healing powers, and would until Quin laid hands of blue light upon the broken body. Quietly thanking her in his head, the voice coming back sounded tired and strained. He sensed her Ladyship draining of energy; she had done her share for this young man.

"I'll talk to them now."

"Pardon me? Oh, the police, are you sure? The Mistress is keeping you from experiencing your agony. She can't do it much longer." David's concern encompassed two beings he loved.

"They need to see what they did to me. You can let go now, Lavender."

Looking down at the unrecognizable face, David only saw a choirboy praying. A request of another spiritual kind, and not of a god, Ted believed in her. He marveled at the sweetness of the wish, and the concern the younger man expressed. A smile upturned LaCoix's lips, feeling Lavender's warmth and hearing the quiet message left in his head. *'Hold onto him, my friend. I shall return soon.'*

Ted groaned and tensed at the sudden influx of pure torture from his head to his toes. A single sob reverberated through the fragile creature straight into David's fractured heart. The tall blond grabbed the cold fingers and held them tightly, watching the brave man battle the wounds inscribed all over his body and etched within.

"My crotch hurts. They hit... hit me there on purpose." Growing more agitated and in the full throes of what had happened, the victim began to panic, hyperventilating under the mask. David pushed the red alarm button. Some rectification and comfort came with cool compresses gently placed over his genitalia, and ice packs against his cheek. Ted regained some control, although his speech pattern returned to stuttering out responses to the questions from the police. A breathless, hesitant voice accused and confirmed everything Richard and Quinlan had previously stated. His lawyer, filled with renewed enthusiasm, with a participatory, detached witness to the deed, followed at the heels of the detective in charge, wanting the paperwork immediately for the far-off abuse trial, not to mention this new case already in the hands of the District Attorney. In this instance, a trial date for the attempted murder upon the likes of the Oscar winning Theodore Barrett would come a great deal sooner; and with a lot of convincing, the two cases would become one, or at least follow the other. David privately discussed a personal issue with the attorney, before the man departed, whom agreed to LaCoix's request. This time they had no choice; and the ailing Mr. Barrett had to consent.

The room returned to quiet. Ted lay motionless with his toes and knees pointing skyward. Pillows supported his calves, and eased his painful hip and sore back. One blood-shot eye, underlined with a deep black semi-circle, from the attempt to destroy the famous face, and more so from the strain of the day, hid under the icepack covering the other eye, swollen shut from the gross bruising of his cheek problem. David watched him closely, from a tilted position against the door. The sturdy framework supported his own aching back, while his undaunted determination kept his knees locked in place. After another crisis, the actor standing was not beyond his own peril. Only a half-hour nap in the last forty-eight hours, David yearned for sleep beside a stable and happy Teddy Bear; but he had more work to do before he could close his weary eyes.

The room remained white, with a touch of pink and blue; the patient still lay in traumatic shock; and David just was, drained whiter than the victim. He pulled himself together and sat on the edge of the bed. With the icepack pulled away slightly, one sapphire blinked open to meet the exotic green jewels full of fire and the hell that came with them. Ted cowered fractionally, deciding whether the stare meant fury or fun. "Glad they took pictures of all the injuries, Ted, although I know how uncomfortable it must have felt. I've requested the lawyer not use some of them. As for you, Mr. Barrett, you described the occurrence very coherently. Great job, Ted."

"Of what? Charging my father... and his friends with attempted murder, getting my brother... getting him beaten and banished from his church, not being able to protect, or see my baby. Yeah, I did a hell... hell of a job, LaCoix." The words came out between each intake of a small breath.

"We'll get through all the work and trials; you must believe that. It's been hard for Richard, but he seems rather enthralled at starting anew, breaking free from his own dilemma. He and Raymond want to see you, if you're up to it, then we have to get your stubborn brother ensconced in the room across the hall, at least for tonight. M.P. will be watching his room as well, although I doubt anyone could get to you at a Base Hospital. He can't believe what happened either, and is showing all the signs of emotional shock, now the initial numbness has worn off. Both your brothers are badly shaken."

"Raymond's here? No, he can't be. He's my last hope. There's no one else to protect her." Ted's fears resurfaced; and maybe they had to after his unholy confessions to the police.

"Hey, slow down; we snuck him in on the sly. No one knows he's your brother, and as far as the family's concerned, he's busy attempting to get bail set. Considering the charges, it won't happen. It's all a pretense on his part; you, your baby, and Richard are his priorities. Do you understand, Ted? Raymond will be there for your daughter."

"I don't know, David. I can't fight anymore, I'm so tired." The voice faded off; and the man, sitting on the edge of the bed, leaned forward to hear. Defeat and surrender were not a mix for a feisty, exhausted Leo to ignore. It only made the man more resolute.

"Remember we discussed the stubborn side of a Cancer, which obviously runs in your family as well as your sun sign. Use it to get what you want. If you could, I'd let you stamp your feet and beat your hands against the wall, screaming a foul, demanding restitution. Fight for your life and baby. Come on, Ted; we have one to share for the long term." David rambled, desperate to rally the deepening melancholy into hope.

"The earth is falling out of the sky; and I seem to be the only one hanging onto a tree. What's the matter with you, spouting zodiac traits to me at a time like this? I thought you were the practical one, but your head's in the goddamn clouds, LaCoix; up Lavender's mist, most likely." It came out of pain, in one long string of meaningless, angry words, without the hint of a stutter.

"You deserve a smack on the derriere for that, considering she's held you together since the incident. I'm sorely disappointed in you."

"I'm sorry. How could I..." The voice faltered with regret, but in a fraction of a second, the Mistress' presence brought him forgiveness.

"After a difficult decision you and I have to make, I'll let your brothers in to visit. Raymond must leave soon; we can't have him looking suspicious regarding his activities." Awash, not knowing the words to use, David had to give this man a gentle nudge in a direction to heal himself, if true. Nothing would surprise the distraught actor now. He would not let Ted get away with playing the victim again. Resurrecting the sunshine personality and enduring everything ahead, his battle started that moment.

"What decision?" Nerves tangled Ted's tongue, and his childhood problem reappeared. The Fates had been playing games with a child, but now they battled a man. David would make sure he made it through another one of their attacks.

"Your baby girl." David spoke in a hushed tone, not to alarm the man for the third, or fourth, maybe the twelfth time that day.

"She's all right? They didn't hurt her?" A subject, paramount in Ted's mind, brought out a little more ire. The man refocused; and David hoped he would be willing to save his baby with drastic actions.

"The police checked on her, and she's fine; safe with Raymond's wife looking over Karen's shoulder. Annie offered to help care for the child, and watch for anything, which may lead to trouble."

"Raymond and Annie are the only ones in the inner circle I can trust. I think Richard will be onboard after today, and his wife is a good person."

"Raymond will ensure that they're not caught playing both sides. I'm going to pose a question to you, and I want you to keep still." The frightening eyes returned, and Ted gave a hesitant nod. "What if you are unable to see your daughter for a while?"

"What? I have to keep checking on her. Only in my arms for six days, they snatched her away. She won't know me." Panic shivered the voice.

David played with each exposed finger, contemplating his next move to stop the manic mumbling. He hated hearing Ted fall away into rambling, incoherent thought. Like playing a game of chess, the sanity of one pawn lay at risk, and so be the game. "I'm taking you to England with me, Ted; that's why I'm here. This gives me even more reason to do so."

"I can't leave now. That group of hideous, self-righteous, bombastic assholes will kill her." The plastic encased patient regained his strength quickly; a little water aided his voice.

"Not if the lawyer handles it properly. You're coming to England; there will be no argument. It's the right thing to do, to protect you both while you heal." Emphatic in his pronouncement, David refused to lose this match.

"Yeah, right, look at me, a broken scarecrow. That's what Stevie calls me. They broke more than bones, David. I can't leave; there's no place for me to go." More disheartening words fumbled out of the sore lips, but they were understandable reasons. David had few chances of getting the man back.

"That's nonsense. If you use the magical visualization trick, I know you can heal yourself and quickly. It's stopping your pain right now, isn't it? You felt Lavender surrounding you with healing power; when she returns, grab as much as you can. You'll have some time to try your powers, like the kiss you sent me."

"You felt it?"

"Almost knocked me over. Couldn't have asked for a more rewarding *sorry you lost* gift. What a kick, to be kissed without anyone knowing I tasted Theodore Barrett, Oscar winner."

"You said that too. I heard you say it that night. I did, didn't I?"

"Yes, and you heard it from thousands of miles away. See, you have the power to do this." David leaned over, kissed the puzzled frown away, and then slowly withdrew to flash his infamous teasing smile. A telepathic thought, transmitted to Ted, had been picked up through the air.

"You're kidding a sick man; you should be ashamed of yourself, LaCoix." Ted pulled back in surprise, with another door opening to his *knowing* path.

"A slight sense of humor. Good, now shut up and I'll explain. I spoke with your lawyer. Between the two of us, we thought it prudent to approach an impartial judge and a few police social workers to hear your case. They stated your condition will naturally heal within six weeks, and that's the time allotted before you can carry your precious bundle. The court will not consider it abandonment, since you're the one instigating the request on the recommendation of your doctors. You won't forfeit your visitation rights. It will be a selfless act of a sacrificing father, putting his daughter's safety first. Since Raymond is now head of the Wagner/Barrett Clan, he will undertake the protection of... what is her name, Ted? You've never mentioned it." David looked at the man, seeing the acceptance and contemplation in his face. With the facts presented, the eyes showed the wheels, in the bandaged head, caught each cog one at a time, but at a very slow pace. "Well, Ted?" David had him back and interested, preventing him from slipping into his hiding place. It grew more difficult to find, and harder to extricate the man unscathed.

"Six weeks and the casts come off. My face will look somewhat normal. I already miss her; they didn't give us a moment together." The man suffered from more than a beating. He had every right to feel shattered and betrayed.

David raked the waves carefully. Nurturing seemed so necessary; yet, uncharacteristically, the man did not lap it up. Try again, LaCoix, he thought to himself, try and keep trying. "Easy, Baby, the horror of today is over; and you, your brothers, and your daughter are going to be fine. Tomorrow, Richard and his wife, both of whom are scared, will be in protective custody until everything settles. They're staying with Quinlan in Steven's former abode. No one knows Kincaid is not living there; and it helps our two friends stay together."

"Quinlan won't be coming with us?"

"No, he'll be handling things from this end, but he'll always be with us. I believe the man is far more than what he lets on. Now, enough of everyone else; I'm going to become your enforcer to eat and endeavor to get you healthy, along with Holly's help." David managed a real smile. His magical daughter always made his eyes sparkle.

"Holly Jane: such a pretty name for a blonde-haired, little girl." Ted smiled sadly; and David received an agreement without a formal answer.

"I thought so, and still do. Born two weeks before Christmas, Holly seemed appropriate, and Jane is a family name on Susan's side. So what enchanting name have you given your tiny pixie?"

The small smile faded and heartbreak returned. This was becoming an emotional avalanche for even David. "I didn't. They called her something so unbecoming for such a small, beautiful little person. She has raven-black hair, and it's already thick and long for a baby. They say she looks like me, especially her eyes; no white can be seen."

"You still can't see the whites of your eyes. She will be beautiful then, a female version of her handsome father. So tell me this terrible name."

"They didn't even register her as a Barrett. Does that mean she doesn't belong to me? She'll never know who her father is. The court surprised them, allowing me visiting privileges, and it's probably the reason they tried to terminate me. It might have been a warning to stay away." The fingers held on tighter; and David leaned down and kissed the ever-increasing deep furrows forming under the waves of straw blond.

"Don't ever say those words again, Ted. They attempted to kill you; nothing else should be implied. Now, this name matter; they can't deny you the rights of being her father, even with Judge Matthews' ludicrous decisions. You were married when she came into this world. Divorce papers are finalized a year after the papers are served, so you still have legal time to get this name business straight. Your little one will have a beautiful name of your choosing. It can be done, just as yours was."

"Are you sure?"

"Of course. Scout's honor."

"Give me a break; you were never a Scout." Finally, a soft chuckle and hurting smile appeared from under the mask, which had been replaced.

"How did you guess?" David joined in the merriment, knowing even as a boy, he hated the discipline of a massive following, spouting ridiculous pledges, of which, none were carried into adulthood, when those incredibly outdated uniforms turned into Fortrel Indiana Jones attire. It certainly was not David LaCoix. "Now, what is this name to be changed?"

"Gretchen Ruth Swaggart: Karen's maiden name."

"Gretchen's rather interesting; but you're right; the full name certainly isn't pleasant on the ears. What do you wish to call her?"

Ted's eyes dropped, remembering the feel of his baby in his arms. She belonged there. "I kept whispering something to her in the nursery. Hope it doesn't sound silly, but I want to call her Willow. She's frail, but she's strong, like the expression: she bends with the breeze, unable to knock her down."

"It's lovely, very pretty, soft, and magical: Willow Barrett. No middle name?" David smiled wistfully out the window; the poetic side of Ted shone through for a second, with an acceptance of their mystical Fey. He felt a certain satisfaction and pride in the knowledge.

"Not yet."

"Something to think about while you recover. Baby Willow needs a healthy Daddy, starting now." Back to being jovial and a change in subject needed, Ted gave him the opportunity.

"Wishes and dreams, I try to believe in mine." Ted sighed; the one thing he could do without his lips cracking.

"Well, you are in luck today, Mr. Barrett. Holly and I believe in them; and we're going to introduce you to Faery tales and the real land of fantasy. You have to grant us our wishes as well."

"Oh, brother." Ted rolled his sore eyes in disgust. Being treated as if twelve again, Ted hoped no one would discover he actually liked it. A grin broke his lips, when he thought of the enticing wishes he would grant his lifesaving Knight.

"Guaranteed it will keep a smile on your face; one that won't keep bleeding. Holly and I have a wonderful time, discovering the magic in trees, ladybugs, and butterflies." Now, on a happier roll, David's captive audience seemed to enjoy his imaginings. Life became more fun with the thought of showing the younger man the enchanted world that he and Holly had discovered.

"Get real. You and ladybugs? Ouch!"

"Yes me, and stop moving. You might even receive an Elfin kiss, when passing through the woods, or in the open meadow. Now, stop talking and concentrate on fighting the pain."

"Is this how you speak to Holly? You sound like *the Beav's* father."

"I am a father; so are you. I rather delight in talking to you like this."

"Don't mind it myself, strangely enough. Maybe that's why I fell for an older man." Ted gave away his secret with a slight curl upward of his lips.

"I'm a father figure, am I? You did this to me once before. This time I'll find a cane, actually two trekking canes; one for each of us. We'll be walking the forests and meadows, while Holly does her normal running and dancing." David laughed again and lifted the mask. Two smiles collided with an *Ouch;* both men felt better after a day filled with horror.

One attempt made to raise the right arm an inch produced a groan, and the limb fell back onto the soft pillow. "I couldn't hold Willow like this. She could hear my voice though."

"You're not backing out on me. I don't break promises, and I made one to Holly to bring you back to the manor house." David laughed at him and smoothed the hair off the wet brow. "I really want you there, Ted. It will be more entertaining for you than this room."

"The place does sound mysterious." One blue eye twinkled. Fun was an incomprehensible feeling to Ted; and it hurt David. Only his mountain adventures remembered gave the man pleasure, other than acting and the taste of sexual satisfaction LaCoix had supplied.

"I told you it's a secret, magical place." David's wink created the glimmer of a future, of which, Ted had wished.

"Hope so. Hope it holds the power for Willow to remember me." On another sigh, a needed fact-based comeback deemed important.

"There should be a deep-seeded knowing from six straight days in your arms. For a baby, it's the warmth, the loving touches, and particularly the scent. Six weeks, and she'll feel and smell you again. She will remember, Ted. You can then let her hear you with your normal voice, whispering her name. She'll know she's in her Daddy's arms, calling her by an enchanted moniker."

"Thanks, David. I guess my voice is a bit rough to talk to a baby."

"Since early this morning, you've had a gross tube down your throat, you've been talking too much, and you've been sick countless times. You can't expect your voice to feel or sound good." David tucked him in again, and just for a little relief, tried raising the head of the bed ever so slightly. Okay with his first maneuver, he would try again later.

"There's one hitch to your plan. How do I get to England like this?" Completely lucid, Ted came back to him; and the taller actor inhaled deeply.

"We'll find a way. There's always a choice, Mr. Barrett. They're going to move your bed closer to the window, so you can get some sun. Seems odd, but Quinlan demanded it. Do you know anything about that?" David looked up from under his blond lashes, waiting for the lie. Ambrose had been insistent, and it made him wonder.

"Nope, haven't a clue. Must admit, he kept me outside much of the day while in Mexico, although slightly shaded, thank God. When we settled into Ethan's place, he constantly ushered me onto the deck, under the pretense of staying warm, and getting some color. I was lucky not to be sautéed in butter and flipped like a fish stick every couple of minutes."

"Wonder why? Never mind, it gives them more room to put a bed in here for me. They're breaking rules for us. I'll be sleeping right next to you; and you know I'm a light sleeper."

David raised the bed a little more, and with no complaints received, he secured the blankets for the hundredth time, along with the pillows supporting arms, legs, and head. The young man dealt with his pain in some fashion, without Lavender or Quinlan's aid. Extremely pleased with the strange phenomenon, he had to believe Barrett created the miracle. LaCoix's decision caused him concern, however, wondering if he planned the right thing for the wrong reason. It seemed life had come down to few, if any, choices. Ted would die a torturous death, left in a hospital surrounded by strangers; not to mention the long waits to see his daughter, wondering what lay in store for his little Willow in-between visits, too horrifying to consider.

"What will I do, incapacitated in a haunted castle while you're working, your Lordship? I guess it's back to twiddling my thumbs. Man, I can't do that either."

"You're already complaining. Someone has plans for you, Teddy. A miniature LaCoix plans to care for you, along with a Sherman tank of a nurse who comes with high credentials and recommendations. I haven't met him, but I hear he's built like Godzilla, out of the shrieking closet, a real-live flaming queen. He'll have you in shape in no time. Bodybuilder extraordinaire, and a very fine seamstress for his evening clothes, I'm sure Bernard will love giving you a bath and dressing you." The wicked smile came out, accompanied by a menacing laugh of the macabre variety. David loved switching into his latest sinister role.

"You're joking? Who would recommend someone like that for me? Tell me you're kidding." Ted's throat threatened to give out; but it did not stop him from calling for assurance.

"Nope, from what I hear, he is precisely the right man for the job. I'm rather looking forward to seeing what he buys you for nightwear." LaCoix walked out laughing, only to realize he would be coming back to a battle of wills and physical improbabilities. His first attempt at feeding had to succeed. Something sweet, warm, and delicious deemed in order for someone who did not give a damn.

While David disappeared, the three brothers met alone to discuss what each had to do. Anguish for Ted, to have his siblings entrapped in the same snare, Richard assured him all would be well, happy to end his own hostage situation, to live freely with his wife, Eleanor. Their future may be unknown, but it would be new and refreshingly alive. Raymond, being the youngest, had just been handed a responsibility he did not want. On first sighting of his beaten brothers, he caved in, imploding within himself. Besides the horrendous injuries to look at, he would be alone to face an explosive family situation, not to mention playing a pivotal role in a spy game. The youngest had to rekindle his lying abilities and quickly, sincerely backed by his wife Annie. Three young men bonded in their shock, yet scheming to keep Raymond and Annie in the warm, but sadistic arms of their church, if only for a while.

Lavender could only smile sadly. Too ill and in trauma to master his own healing, the eldest Barrett attempted the formidable job of easing and disguising his pain, consoling his brothers, and wondering how to rebuild something already lost. LaCoix, meanwhile, helped him through every woe. She sat quietly, regaining her power slowly. An endless earth day, Ted was not her only concern; there were so many; and ones very close to the couple she loved. They also scrambled with an unpleasant nudge to make Kincaid understand his own type of mental disorder. The ground lay infirm beneath his feet; and the Mistress created tremors to shake him into sanity. For now, they would gather to help their fallen recover. Seven humans would not drain her. On the morrow, their battles would start again.

CHAPTER 36

The healing began: the slow, painstaking consumption of food by a body straining and gagging at every swallow. Vomiting seemed to preoccupy most of Ted's evening, and cleaning up the results kept David busy. Two mouthfuls of hot, steaming oatmeal, laced with sweet brown sugar and skim milk, went down, two came back up. By late evening, three went down and only one came up. The drip of an IV remained constant, but the feeding tube vanished from sight; no need to scare the perpetually frightened.

Later that evening, their three friends joined them. They had not faltered in their vigilance of the two men behind the heavily guarded door. With the help of the fair Lady, they had Ted dreaming and visualizing his own recovery, in an imaginary world of fireflies and moonlight wanderings. The torturous day ended, when eyelids closed over two precious sapphires, and shallow breaths inhaled pure oxygen under a mask. Theodore fell into slumber.

Lavender lingered in her cloud, making sure he would remain asleep for hours. A man, back in her good graces, along with her two healers, disappeared for the night. The lovers headed home, emotionally tired, unable to take up where they had left off that bright shining morning an eternity ago, while the unearthly man in black remained vigilant over Richard: the forgotten one. If Ted feared hospitals, at least he had dealt with them on occasion. For Richard, however, his first experience into the ungodly had him scared to death. Ambrose stood resolutely beside him, comforting the inconsolable. Meanwhile, David crawled into some scrubs thrown to him by a nurse, and slowly slumped into a military cot, closely placed next to Ted. After forty odd hours of sleeplessness, with a half-hour respite, LaCoix came close to falling comatose when he hit the pillow. Exhausted, anxious, terrified, all combined with a good case of shock, the day had been too long; and the Mistress left them all to their dreams.

The next four nights and days became a ritual of Ted sleeping a few hours, moaning with another fitful nightmare, and waking up with a gasp of pain. A little more food, every fifteen minutes when awake, he finally retained the little fed to him on the third and fourth days. Not sufficient for a man, he continued to try, and chewed on a piece of dry toast and tasted a spoonful of scrambled eggs with Ketchup.

News of the retaliatory occurrence spread rapidly through the film industry. Famous names wished Theodore Barrett a quick recovery, and publicly demanded an even faster trial for the men whom assaulted him. The sordid business, of his father being one of several men arrested for the attempted murder of his two sons, was headline news. Sympathy filled the many cards with tears; Barrett's holy war was accepted by his peers; and his backers grew. Each note expressed grandiose gestures of giving to, helping with, or supporting his cause with their name and money. A few scripts also passed his way, to while away his time during his recovery. Ted lay quietly, happily listening to the mesmerizing voice of David LaCoix reading the mail, fascinating him with the possibilities of different roles, while trying to hold them both together. The chance to watch the hand, of such erotic pleasure, carefully handwriting *Thank You* notes and forging his signature, made the ghastly mess less disturbing. His gallant, blond knight smiled into his eyes every moment he turned and found him awake.

David readily accepted one generous offer of a flight back to England on a private jet. A friend of Kincaid's expressed a sincere willingness to fly them to Britain, where the young star could recover in peace and quiet. Barrett had joined their ranks, becoming their latest martyr to conquer injustice. LaCoix laughed silently, considering what one had to go through to be accepted; but Ted breached the ultimate barrier with tremendous grace and innocence.

With the flight back to England arranged, specifically to get LaCoix back in time for his shooting schedule, David performed his last task, greeting each staff member of the Naval Hospital with heartfelt thanks for their favors so generously offered. The court also came through, allowing Ted to forfeit visitation rights until out of his casts, able to handle and protect his baby, as a loving new father should. Another gift, from the San Diego Police Department, enabled Ted to leave the country until required to testify, another favor from people with nothing to gain.

On the fifth day, Ted could sit up at an angle, with a great deal of support from the raised back of the bed. Always cold and never hungry, the patient made every effort to please. David could ask no more. The man improved remarkably, but more miracles would have to wait. On a happier note, a little strength showed itself, able to lift the right arm cast, and stretching his legs, without the banshee-like scream. Cries while urinating diminished; his frightfully battered organ returned quickly to normal; and its utilitarian function drew only a whimper. Leaving only the breaks protected, the expression, *don't touch anything,* relayed its way to everyone.

With the jet prepared for a patient in Ted's condition, and a departure time set, David received an unexpected invitation from Ethan Peerce, to dine with him and his partner his last evening in L.A. A good night's sleep in a real bed, rocked to an ocean's lullaby, coyly dangled before him. Poignant nudges from Ambrose, with an offer from the black-haired mystic to watch Ted through the night, convinced LaCoix to accept. Upon Richard's release after the first night, he and his wife moved into the safety of the Kincaid estate, along with the new tenant, Ambrose. The estate and staff allowed the middle brother, all the care and pampering never received in his life, and left alone to discuss openly, his new responsibilities with Eleanor. David laughed at the brothers, formerly known as Wagner, believing, that the niceties of life would be a treat for the awakening Richard. All three men were gentle, sweet Spirits, as were their wives, stumbling in bewilderment, putting their lives into perspective with the real world.

David finally pushed Ted into accepting, if the blond would pack his gear for the morrow's departure. This needed service LaCoix could do. An unusual request from Quinlan seemed rather foolish, but he agreed to watch over Steven for one night. With a kiss good-bye for his Teddy Bear, and a twinkling of approval in those black-rimmed eyes, David set off for his favorite kind of entertainment; an intimate gathering of friends, for a little laughter and some diversified adult conversation. Arriving at Peerce's estate, David entered the wooden portal; the doors still amazingly intact from their speedy get away. Escorted to the terrace, this time he could appreciate the view; and he stretched out in the late afternoon sun to gaze upon the foaming waves until reaching the horizon, where he could slip off the edge into nothingness. David thought about it for a second, remembering Ted's words of falling out of the sky, demonstrating the odd poetic side of the man. Tonight felt proper to wish upon stars, to relax, and to fall into solitude.

No one seemed at home, and no one scrambled out to greet him, the exception being Casey who looked hesitant and uncomfortable. Handing a glass of bourbon to David, the little man scurried away, vanishing for the night. Fresh salty air, the squawking of seagulls, the sun growing heavier in the sky, and the soft sounds of breaking surf, soothed away guilt and pain better than any manmade sedative. Peerce and Kincaid would be happy in such a tranquil sanctuary. The house appealed to David in its simplicity and informality, with touches of Asian mystique. Ted's attack would have devastated the intricate, delicate objects, if they were anything like the few replacements he saw. Appearing to be exquisite collectors' items, expensive and certainly rare to find, David wondered what kind of havoc Barrett had wielded upon like masterpieces. Considering their value, he felt obliged to pay for damages, but doubted even his recently acquired millions could cover the tab. The thought vanished on hearing the impact of a far away wooden door. Those imposing monuments of redwood had taken a kicking since his initial arrival. Who dared break his contemplation of white waves mixed with soft sand, to transform the patterns left behind every quarter minute? He emerged into the main salon off the terrace, only to collide into Kincaid, nearly toppling them both.

"I'm sorry, Steven. Are you okay? You seem to be in a rush." Only a statement of fact, but David noticed the hesitance of his nemesis who stepped one-way, and then another, all the while looking at his feet: the Barrett shuffle. The older actor shook his head and chuckled. He did like Kincaid, and accepted him as Ted's friend who cared enough to believe he had done the right thing. A tragic misdemeanor of long ago, all parties involved tried bravely to forget and forgive; or were they to remember, or another lesson to learn?

Amusing, charming, talented, and certainly wonderful to look at, the only description David had for Steven was magical, watching him flow off a screen of silver until he infiltrated every DNA molecule in your body. David respected him for his rare gift, but there seemed something vulnerable and flighty about him, which made David nervous. To the rest of the world, he played the role of the astute, actor/business man; to the seasoned older actor, he exhibited fearful bashfulness, underlying a submissive yet manipulative mind, always courting disaster in his personal relationships. Highly confused seemed the appropriate term LaCoix could label him.

"David, you're here!" Steven looked at his watch, retracting his statement. "No, I'm late. How's Scarecrow today?" The man took a step sideways, walked straight past LaCoix, to rattle through the many bottles behind the bar. Finding one to his liking, he poured the clear liquid into an Austrian crystal glass filled with glittering ice, only to douse it with a diet cola. A strange mix for one who did not partake in the libations of the common man; the contradiction amused David for some reason he could not explain.

"Worried about his daughter, but he's doing very well. Managed to sit up, using his one arm to get into position. Took a bit of doing, but he hid the pain. He ate a piece of bologna and some mashed potatoes before I left." The older actor kept the conversation trivial, putting down his drink to watch the man's back. Something had occurred, and he watched Kincaid act his way out of some situation. People with the rare talents of Steven and Ted, with the emotions of children, could deal with their secrets, for a certain length of time, before crumbling under the lies. Patience was the key. He remembered Quin's request, and wished he had stopped for more information. "What are you drinking, Steven? Looks like diluted shit." David peeked at the drink from under long lashes, thinking how sickly sweet and chemical the beverage would taste.

"Vodka."

"Half vodka and half cola? Sounds revolting."

"It's good. Really." Kincaid seemed unwilling to make eye contact; and David took another sip of bourbon.

"Considering vodka has no taste, all you're drinking is chemicals with a kick. Are you and

Ethan joining me on your terrace, or should I leave?" David inquired, edging for more detail than a *yes* or *no* answer.

"No, of course not, but it looks like just me and you for dinner. Do you mind?" Kincaid became the shy man David saw when with Peerce. His lips were back on the glass of sweet, brown liquid with a brutal punch, to hide a noticeable nervous quiver of the perfect mouth.

"Just Me sounds fine. Where's Ethan, or should I ask after the slamming of the door?" David hated beating around the bush, although he often did with Ted and Holly to ensure they thoroughly understand what he meant. It tended to create more chaos than understanding; and he could not get out of the habit. With Kincaid, there seemed no necessity for holding back, due to possible hurt feelings.

"Ethan apologizes for suddenly being called away; and he's annoyed about missing dinner with you." The lips still had not moved from the glass, or the slow sipping of the sickening drink.

"Of course, but I still intend to enjoy the end of the afternoon on your terrace. Care to watch the sunset with me?"

"Yeah, I'd like that. I hope you've forgiven me, David?" The pale blue eyes darted quickly for confirmation and just as quickly turned away.

"You thought it best at the time; can't blame you for that. Thankfully, you both survived the wrath of a tornado." David smiled reassuringly, but it went unnoticed.

"Definitely a wild moment I'll never forget; and I couldn't believe seeing Theo's plastic arm reach for me. I owe him my life; I won't forget that either. Besides my life, I owe him for the best performance, I can ever recall, in *Brother Mine*. He's brilliant, LaCoix. Ethan and I looked like amateurs in comparison."

"It would help his confidence if you reinforced the extraordinary compliment directly."

"I have, many times, but he's too humble to accept any credit. Let's finish our drinks while viewing the sunset; and then I'll help you pack his gear before dinner. Might as well get one job out of the way, then we can relax."

The natural blond head nodded, as Steven led the way to the terrace, his guest a few paces behind. From the rear, LaCoix noticed the unsteady way the man moved. His fingertips, against the wall, appeared as support to walk a straight line, while the other hand, which could not be seen, appeared to be pressing the cold glass against his abdomen. With the observant eye of a meticulous artist, or an ardent jewel thief, LaCoix could wait no longer. "Something wrong, kid?"

"No, of course not."

"Good, I'm just pleased to be basking in California sun. Springtime is beautiful in England, but still too cold for these old bones." Uncomfortable with idle chitchat, as was his companion, David felt the strain in pauses of awkward silence.

"You're not old, LaCoix, far from it."

"Thanks; and I'm sorry for calling you *kid*."

On that note, both men sat to uneasily ponder the spectacular view in front of them. Orange light turned the two blond heads into halos of golden fleece, and the paparazzi missed the moment. An hour passed with the only movement being David, who rose leisurely and poured each another drink. There were no words spoken, while the oncoming darkness lay heavily on both shoulders. Always a delight to watch the moonrise, and the stars burst forth, LaCoix hoped for some familiar company to share them. A very nervous young friend would be welcome, but Steven seemed oblivious to the Cosmic display. The older man's voice broke through the hidden, strangled screams of the first fall of night. "Time to pack up Ted's things. Does he have much?" David's question startled Kincaid who shivered at the unexpected anticipation of something.

"Sorry, I'm being terrible company this evening. Theo has a backpack and his laptop in a briefcase. Let's go. I'll show you where we put his stuff when he moved in. You can stay in his bed if you like. The sheets haven't been changed."

A strange thing to say, but David understood and shot a smile back at Kincaid. The scent of Theodore Barrett, on 800-thread count, Egyptian cotton sheets, would certainly make his night comforting. "Appreciate your help and the thought. Where's all your staff? This house echoes with the sound of the missing." David grew weary of the wait. Something was awry; and he wanted an answer.

"I don't know, but I think Ethan forgot he invited you to dinner and gave the staff the night off." Kincaid finally fell into his own lie with a blatant contradiction. David let it pass, while watching the mega-star meticulously fold clothes, and fill the backpack with Ted's belongings: the tight denims that no longer fit, the bright yellow sweater David loved, a little of this and that, all fit snugly into the bag. A man's lifetime carried on his back; it was a sad, disturbing thought.

"You better tell me now, Steven. You can't hold it back any longer." The green eyes continued to scrutinize Kincaid, while the golden boy secured the zips and buckles.

"What are you talking about, LaCoix? We're done. Let's see what's on for dinner." End of conversation for now, David followed the stiffening body. Once in the kitchen, so sterile without a crumb for a cockroach, certainly indicated no lavish dinner awaited an invited guest. David suspected something; but whatever the conundrum, it hurled Steven into an outburst of panicked agitation; and he started to roll. "Shit, he left us nothing. Damn him. What does he want of me?" The voice vented through a tirade of profanity and the banging of cupboard doors. Slowing down, Kincaid slumped against the counter, looking at David in confused despair.

"What did he do, Stevie? You really pick them, don't you?" David hit the tear switch; and they fell without a movement of the face. Walking slowly over to his nemesis, with his paternal instincts growing more naturally within him, he surrounded the crumbling shoulders in fatherly arms. One of his children, even his own partner, required nurturing during rough episodes of real life, and now, another young friend, although not that much younger than himself. LaCoix had become a father and a caring man. He liked this role better than any other played.

"I'm sorry, I can't cook, and we invited you, and then he walks out. He dismissed the staff to embarrass me." Kincaid rambled on in humiliation.

The only cure David knew, for babblers and mumblers, included a strong-armed embrace, some consoling words, and an unhappy face buried in his neck. The mega-star fell into the hug offered, but winced at the touch. David withdrew, adjusting his hands to steady the heaving shoulders. "Where did he hurt you? Show me."

"It's nothing." Tears fell faster than the hands could wipe them away; the oversized sweater sleeves saturated in seconds.

"Probably, but let's look anyway. Damn, you and Ted are so much alike; you could be brothers. Lift your pullover; better yet, take it off." David intently watched the struggle to pull the garment over the bleach-blond head and the tight-faced grimace accompanying the action taken. Kincaid took an order right on cue, appearing to expect retaliation if he resisted. The red marks remained visible, particularly where the knuckles drove hard into the pit below the ribs. "Arms are bruised, and he really nailed you in the stomach. Do your ribs hurt?"

"No. He didn't mean to. I say the wrong thing sometimes."

"It's not your fault. I seem to be repeating myself. Perhaps I'll have it printed on both sides of a T-shirt, so I can stop lecturing Ted, and now you. Turn around." A harsh, blistering color crept above the low-slung waistband of the white denims. "Slip your pants off."

"Excuse me?"

"I'm not asking you to bend over, for God's sake. I've seen my share of bare butts in our line of work. Just pull them down to your knees, and maybe we can ease the discomfort you're in." David's eyes scrutinized the enticingly hard, little derriere, but much to his dismay, his assumptions were correct. Peerce had paddled Steven, until his entire behind radiated burning scarlet and stung to a touch. The assault left no lacerations; but had certainly meant to hurt. On bending from the waist to reach his knees, and hearing the quiet whimper, another injury ignited LaCoix's fury over the wanton behavior of an abuser who ripped into Kincaid without preparation. He had clearly been forced, and likely raped, leaving him devastated, hurt, alone, and unattended. Not only a brilliant actor; Kincaid was a great one. "Jesus Christ, why didn't you stop him; or is this a game you like to play?" David's anger smoldered under clenched teeth, while he helped pull up the pants with a certain amount of grimacing from the victim.

"It's not a game, not for me anyway. If I don't give in to some things, worse shit happens."

"Come here, Stevie. Let's sit and talk. Does the Mistress know about this?" David reached out a hand, but a step backward indicated a refusal.

"She knows some things, but not this. He can hide his actions from her. Ethan has a great deal of power; and I don't think she's aware he uses it for other purposes besides the betterment of man. That's what we're learning to do, isn't it?" The sad pastel blues held a question, to which LaCoix had no answer.

"To be honest with you, I haven't figured out the puzzle myself. Good things happen, then bad, and I don't know who's pulling the strings. All I can say is she wants each of us to walk our chosen path with set goals. You, my friend, just like Ted, are being annihilated in your attempts just to crawl. It's time to get a better grip on your path." Turning away, David sat down on the love seat in the guest sitting area of the kitchen; his hand offered a second time.

"Maybe she's forgiven me, but is she listening? She forgot me for a while, after I broke her heart for what I did to you and Theo, and to myself. Morningstar thinks Ethan is something else. Quinlan, and a handful of others, she trusts completely and never watches." Unsure of what to do, Kincaid slowly walked over to the man waiting and accepted the outstretched hand. He could only stand there, looking down at the kindest men he had ever met, who wanted nothing from him.

"Sit down gently. I think she's hearing you right now. Listen; what is she telling you?" David nestled the younger one beside him, his arms surrounding the shoulders. An affectionate cuddle and a soft kiss to the bleached-hair had the tears rolling again. This time the face emphasized the sorrow of an unconquerable emotional battle. With the fight lost, David held the remains. An ocean of salty brine splashed against his black shirt, like the soft motion of the water they could hear from below. Soft whispers of comfort, wave upon foaming wave, were all the older blond had to offer.

"She's telling me to leave; but I have no place to go. Theo's lucky to have someone who cares so much."

A hand held the quivering chin, and the normally terrifying green eyes softened in sympathy. "I'm lucky to have him. Now then, what are your choices? You can go back to your own home, and let Quinlan protect you. You'd be safe; and I'm sure he knows about this. You're possibly one of his non-interference orders." More stroking and LaCoix wiped away the watermarks cleansing the sadness from swollen eyes.

"No, as it's only a few minutes drive from here. I hate the strange game we seem to be playing. Can you feel it, David?"

"At times it feels like a chess tournament amongst a number of us; and we're here to figure it out. Maybe we're the pawn pieces for some higher being's amusement."

"Shit, I didn't need to hear that. I have to disappear from all this."

"And I don't want to hear that; Ted says the same damn thing. Although unaware of it, he's guarded every moment of every day, so he doesn't. Now, there are two of you threatening to end your lives. It's not your answer, Stevie. Come to England with us, for a short time. Give yourself a break, to decide what you need to do, and what you want from life, love, and everything that lies between here and there. You have a lot of work ahead of you, supervising the editing of *Brother Mine*, Mr. Producer, but perhaps a few weeks, or a month's holiday, will give you fresh eyes to see the final results."

"I don't know, David. One thing I'm sure of: Ethan won't be spreading our affair around, but he may hunt me down. I can't think of anything else to do."

"Sounds perfect to me, and Ted needs company while I'm working. Pack your things, and we'll be out of here tonight, in case Ethan returns." A light sparked in the pale blues for a moment; and the two blond heads were too close. David's tempter blinked his misty eyes, while looking at his mouth and slowly moving in to capture the taste a world hungered for. The kiss lingered long, sweet and gentle, something Steven had obviously not experienced. A little moan, and a tantalizing tremble of the younger body, had David pulling away. "You need to be kissed like that more often." Kincaid leaned closer, wanting more of the same, plus a little extra. "A very pleasurable kiss, my friend, but that's all we are. Remember, we can't hurt Ted in this way."

"Yeah, I'm sorry. Got a little carried away." Kincaid raked his fingers through his hair; and a hand washed over his face.

"It can happen, and it felt special. Thank you."

"I thank you as well, David, and promise never to mention it. I will remember, however."

"As will I. Now, these men you get tangled up with; what do they do to you, and why do you like it, or put up with it?"

"I don't know. Sometimes it's gentle, but..."

"...rarely. They ram the hell out of you, and expect you to enjoy it. Instead of making love, they ravage you, rolling over when they're satisfied with the demoralization of Steven Kincaid, and leaving you to bleed with a hell of a hard-on to take care of yourself, if they allow it. When that no longer thrills them, they force you into things you don't want to do. Damn, Stevie, I've heard all the reasoning behind such abuse from a few unfortunate women I know; not to mention Ted's idiosyncratic behavior; and it still doesn't make a handful of sense." With another quick embrace and fatherly kiss to the forehead, an understanding agreement solidified; another wayward Spirit would be safe.

"I don't know anything else. Scarecrow used to tell me how you and he... well, he told me some things. I've never had anyone be that kind." Steven looked away, now embarrassed he and Barrett shared such intimate conversations about their bed partners.

"How do we stop your need for such punishment? This is a need, man, believing you deserve it. You seem to force yourself into relationships you know will end this way, until the day comes when they carry you out in a body bag. I'm not going to let it happen to you. Tell me honestly; do you like being hurt? Is it part of the sexual pleasure? It is for some; masochistic kinky sex is exactly what it is. It sure as hell isn't making love, and loving every inch of the person so much, even a hangnail's snipped off like an unwanted thorn, before a touch considered."

"No, I hate it. I fall for powerful, strong men who eventually want to control me because of who I am; and they take advantage of me. Then I'm imprisoned, not knowing what to do, in case they go screaming to the press. I thought Ethan would be different, but he even wanted a piece of you when you arrived from London, with me included in the game."

"The handshake?"

"To test you, and then he signaled me to seduce you with a massage. I'm so sorry, but Ted's misfortune saved us both. I seem to mess up whatever I do. Maybe I should go back to..." A sigh and a pause, Steven regained his composure, but gazed about the kitchen as if seeing it for the first time.

"Over my dead body, Mister. Christ, you're as innocent as Ted, and yet you're both so damn strong in the things you accomplish. Two of a kind, you both amaze me, willing to take a beating for what you love to do, or for whom you love. You, my friend, are definitely coming to England. It's getting late, so we had better decide on our next move. You don't expect Ethan back; but what if you read him wrong, and he suddenly pops up unannounced?" Time to get the man thinking, David pulled him back from returning to his last obsessive abuser. With quick decisions needed, he must get the disturbed mega-star out of his habitual, disastrous behavior.

"Not tonight, if the staff is gone. It's a form of punishing me."

"Yeah, and he might have given them the night off, so they couldn't hear you screaming through his next fantasy."

"Don't even think it. No, he wouldn't with you here, would he?" The voice trembled and the eyes grew wider. David stopped Kincaid's dash for an escape route.

"I think it may be the reason Quinlan insisted I come. Don't be too hard on our Gothic-looking friend. He did ask me to watch over you tonight."

"No shit? You have a lot of power yourself, LaCoix, and a way of making things sound possible. After meeting you, after your *red boys' toy* afternoon, I never thought of you as the mystical type."

"I'm not. Just like these new thoughts, and the complexity of the mind to figure out the unexplainable puzzle we talked about. Enough of the spiritual and into the physical, we have to make some decisions. I'm starving; and one thing I do know how to make is scrambled eggs and toast. You game?" David stopped the shaking and the tears of another untimely ward of the misbegotten; a man handed to him for safekeeping without a choice. While Steven quickly left to pack, LaCoix thanked Lavender for sending him to this place at the right time. The man began to enjoy taking responsibilities, aiding people in duress. With more work, the selfish bastard, he once had been, would never return. David felt the Mistress' warmth and gratitude when her purple cloud appeared to linger by the table. She suddenly appeared.

"Good god, you freak me out when you materialize, or whatever you and Ambrose do."

"Sorry, I am tired tonight. Ethan Peerce, playing the good, the bad, and the ugly, teaches you lessons after an eternity of learning."

"You look paler than usual, if that's possible. Are you okay?" He rushed over and pulled out a chair for her.

"Thank you, David. You are concerned about everyone, my friend; and I am worried about you. What happened to my arrogant son-of-a-bitch I tossed across the trailer? I rather enjoyed playing with him." With a sigh of resignation, she sat down with her minimalist's movements.

"No need to worry about me; still trying to make up for being a jackass all my life. I refuse to fall backward; it's too easy." David stepped away and took the seat across from her at the table. Two pair of elbows settled there, while two faces rested in their hands. Tired and frustrated, both had things on their minds.

"Yes, it is. Now, how do we get you all back on track? Be careful here tonight; I noticed your temptation with Stevie. That is why I am here. He will take advantage of you because of his own vulnerability. Capable of seducing a rattlesnake, he usually does. The major flaw in his character has been proven numerous times. It would kill Theo if he found out, which you know, so why am I telling you? Disappointment does not sit well with me, neither does mistrust." Ethereally she sat and gazed at him, looking like an elongated angel without wings; and he loved her. "Do not even think it, David. You are perceiving things you should not. Be careful with your thoughts and do not eavesdrop on others. Listen only to those who call. I will admit that I do love you, and our man-child. Even this flighty one, you just caught in a butterfly net, is dear to me."

"I do love you in my way; I can't say that about many people."

"Oh, David, you have families to rebuild, and new ones to create. Winning your battles regularly, you keep fighting the Fates who also grow tired of the game, of which you are not buying. You have frustrated them; and I applaud you for it. You are a good man, LaCoix. Do not forget it, or who made this judgment call of your character."

"I'm grateful. Things are certainly going my way. Ted still has his battles, but he appears happier. Only the well-being, of his child, is the one constant blade in his heart." David reached for the slender hand, which did not pull away. "You're overloaded with more than holding Ted together. If I'm even remotely correct, you're juggling worlds and lives far more important than the handful of us. We'll be okay, if you wish to let go." David never wanted her to leave; yet, in whatever reality she came from, she should also have choices.

"Yes, there are; more than you can put your mind around. Thank you for offering to help, but who ranks as more important? I just may accept your proposal, when you are in more control of what you know, and how to use it." The power-laden hand grasped the larger one, and the strange connection rekindled. Another startling revelation, David could feel her hand as if it was his own. More than a few shivers ran up his back.

"What of you, Lavender? I thought perhaps you were lonely."

"Life is lonely, David, for everyone and everything. I once witnessed something extraordinary on your world, which remains forever with me. An alpha male wolf idly wandered off, leaving the alpha female to her new pups. By happenstance, a young female trotted down the same path coming toward him. Frightened by his powerful presence, she coward, not knowing what to do. So young and so beneath him in the pack, she should have avoided him. Shaking in fear, she waited, rolling submissively on her back. He did not attack to reprimand her insolence, but started to play; perhaps remembering she was one of his own offspring. They spent an earth's hour romping joyously through the fresh snow; he gave her equal footing that special day, nuzzling her ears and letting her return the favor; and then he left. She remained quiet and still, watching him walk away, but you could sense the joy radiating from her heart for being noticed. Truly a wonder of the wild, David; a reminder everyone and everything is important, no matter whom or what they are. I loved that male wolf, and have found his strong, kind heart in Quinlan, as Theo has found it in yours."

"I hope I can live up to that; and as for Ambrose, he is a wonder and will bring fun into your existence. Did the young female live a happy life?"

"I follow her progress, growing in confidence, rising higher in the pack. He gave her the gift of courage and unconditional love; the only gift he could share."

"Does Quin offer you such a present? I assumed you as alpha in your realm."

"You cannot trick me in my weary state, LaCoix. You do amuse me with your attempts to discover who I am." Lavender straightened her back; and those wondrous hands rested quietly on her lap. She looked beautiful in her informal attire, and her curls bouncing out of the strange gizmo holding it all precariously on top of her head.

"I'm glad it's Ambrose. He's an endearing Spirit; one I like. Leave Ted and Steven to me; I promise to care for them. It's nice to be loved by your Ladyship and by the man whom you gave me. I've missed so much time with him." The sadness lingered in the whisper; the Mistress raised her head to catch the fleeting glimpse of remorse. LaCoix's grief, caused by the death cloud hanging over his lover, she could not console.

"Theo will be fine, David; I am sure of it. Missing someone makes time drag, and you have not shared his life's most monumental moments. There are no barriers or boundaries to time; however, you still must make every second the best it can be. Although time does not exist for me, there seems a little space or gap when you feel those human emotions of longing to see, to reach out, just to touch. Stay this sincere man, LaCoix. Those Faery rings will show up wherever you trek. Take the time to dance the steps of their King Oberon. Good night, my friend, and beware." Gone with a blink, she left behind the scent of lilacs and twinkling chimes. Magic, it was always magic; and he smiled.

CHAPTER 37

David had the makings for dinner, and it took little effort to throw a meal together. Steven walked in just in time. "Hungry?"

"Not really. A punch to the gut makes eating unappealing." The excuse did not stop him from pulling up a stool to the counter and gingerly slipping onto it.

"Sorry, Stevie, but you're not pulling a Ted on me. I don't cook, so this is special. Be thankful." Bolstered by his evening visitor, David reveled in the knowledge the Mistress thought highly of him. They both felt a strong emotional bond, sex seeming irrelevant, just as it had with the male wolf. Only an unearthly Spirit like Ambrose could truly win her heart.

The two men sat at the high lunch counter and eagerly ate what David set before them. One of the few things LaCoix could prepare, culinary wise, the scrambled eggs tasted surprisingly good, much to Kincaid's delight. Sitting close together, only a few tempting inches away from the other, and exchanging nervous glances, David understood Lavender's concern; this beautiful man had the innate talents to charm the most ardently faithful.

Steven felt better; a certain sense of freedom pulled him from the dregs; and he officially accepted David's offer to fly to England for a few weeks. With the Cannes Film Festival coming up, his presence would be required to promote *Brother Mine*, although incomplete. Being the producer, one of the actors, as well as taking the unusual risk of using his own money, this picture could make or break him. The two men enjoyed their debate of the tumultuous position; David insisting he would never put his money, other people's money, or his faith into a production company, although it had made many an actor much wealthier. A *real job* was not his forte. Both men chuckled, but their laughter stopped abruptly at the swishing sound of the opening kitchen door. The entrance chilled at least one of them into silence. Kincaid started to shiver, tensing up, only looking down at the leftovers on his plate.

LaCoix stayed his instant anger, turning to smile at the stern expression. "It's about time, man. We started without you. Care for some dinner, such as it is?"

"I've eaten. Sorry, David, I forgot you were staying tonight." Ethan's voice remained too steady, too serene; and the faint smile too well posed with the lie.

"Well, we made the best of it. Finished, Stevie? I'll take your plate." David immediately sensed he had stepped out of bounds and turned to accept his fate, his destiny, and certainly his immediate future; at this point, it mattered little. In the now, he had to think fast. Trouble loomed a few steps away.

"Stevie? When did you become so familiar?" A searing fire hissed the words; they burned. David needed an escape plan.

"After two bourbons, and a week with little food or sleep, one cuts out the formality crap. Shall we retire to the terrace for another glass? I found this great bottle of burgundy in your cellar, to share under a star-filled sky." David wondered when he had become the host.

"I think it's time Stevie went to bed, don't you, baby boy? Off you go, and get ready. I'll join you presently."

"Help me, David." On Steven's plea of terror, whispered into the leftover scrambled mush, David had to get them both out of there. Honesty seemed the only way, and the odds favored them, two against one. A glimpse at Kincaid narrowed it down to one against one. He could not back down, to leave his nemesis to a sadistic game forced upon him. The term, *baby boy,* made him cringe, thinking of the sexual antics it conjured up, and the spanking already received. Swept with emotion seldom felt, he now hated Ethan Peerce.

"Steven's leaving with me; his bags are packed; and we'll be departing immediately." David helped a frozen Kincaid off the stool and escorted him, without incident, passed Ethan and out the door. "Hustle, man, grab your things, bring them with Ted's and mine, and leave them out front. Here are the keys to my rental, and be careful with it. Bring the car around, stow the bags, and wait for me." The young man scurried away with an unnerving flicker of fear on his face.

"You plan on a threesome, LaCoix? I know Stevie makes a good filling for a sandwich. I'm sure you would enjoy his sweet arse, while your ailing baby lay there, getting the best blowjob he'll ever experience. My boy is quite adept when prodded."

"Shut your mouth, Peerce. These men aren't like that. They do need satisfaction in the blatant physical sense, but with the mental knowing that they're loved, gently and kindly. You're an abuser, Peerce; and I'm sure the Mistress knows." David's ire flared, but the menacing stare he received had him wary of how sadistic this recluse may be.

"Her Ladyship does not frighten me, or her crazy minion Ambrose." Peerce slowly edged sideways along the counter. Green eyes caught every movement; and hundreds of hours of training gave LaCoix the advantage. He saw the pointed carving knife stealthily picked up and hidden behind the man's back. He waited for the attack; it came. A racing heart jolted David into action.

Wielded with extraordinary dexterity, the knife missed its first slicing swing: advantage Peerce. Ethan, however, being a romantic and dramatic lead, had never learned the skills of an action hero: advantage LaCoix. A snatch of a towel off the counter, quickly wrapped around the left arm, gave David something to parry off a lunging attack. With his amazing reflexes, spinning him around, he landed a high karate kick to his opponent's chest, allowing the blond a chance to gather his wits and energy. He could do this; and it was real. The knife terrified him; lives were at stake: mental advantage Peerce. Long arms reached up and grabbed the hand holding death. David's street smarts came back instinctively to defend himself: physical advantage LaCoix. This had to be the reason Ted did not curl into a ball: attack and not submit. A double maneuver, at heart stopping speed, had a knee planted into Ethan's crotch, followed by a head-butt against an equally hard skull, all the while holding the knife at bay. David's head spun at the jolting crack. He had the upper hand, however, slowly gaining control. With a quick twist of the man's arm, and Peerce already in a crouched position gasping for air, David took his opportunity. The knife dropped with a sickening thud, digging itself into the finely polished wooden floor; a horrific reminder of its treachery. Another sharp turn with a leg-hook had the famous recluse on the ground; and LaCoix's knee finished him off with a second crushing blow to the abuser's masculinity. One hand grasped the throat to squeeze the neck unmercifully, while David's other hand grabbed the handle of the knife, taking some effort to pull it out of the floor, and tossing it across the room, leaving two men to battle without the blade: advantage LaCoix.

Muscles strained, burning to the bone. Peerce fought back, but one more nut-cracking crunch to his genitals had him unconscious. David kept his hold on the neck, his own face forming a growl, showing every tooth in his mouth, like a wildcat ready to take the first ripping bite out of the creature he had vanquished. A yell stopped him when Kincaid rushed in. For an unexplainable moment in his life, LaCoix lost control; his strangle hold grew stronger, turning Peerce's face blue. He could not let go.

"David, stop! Is he dead?" The eyes could not hold back the horror, but showed little concern for the body.

"No, he's alive, but he'll wish he wasn't for a few days." The hiss came through clenched teeth. He won his first battle with a deadly weapon, and he could not stop shaking. His face muscles locked; each one told him so.

"Come on! Let him go, David! We have to get out of here! Hurry!"

David willed each hand to relax and release, difficult but done. Two men headed out the front door in a flat-out race to win. The equally fiery red Mercedes awaited. Steven jumped into the driver's seat, as David dove into the passenger side, panting in his awakened fear. They roared off around the estate driveway, only to be stopped by the locked wrought-iron gates. With no gatekeeper, they were trapped; what protected also held you prisoner.

"Know the code?"

"No. Never tells me shit."

"Quick, change positions." David leapt out of his side before Kincaid could react. Adrenaline kept pumping from the rush of a death risk. Steven opened his door, to be unceremoniously hoisted out of his seat, and rushed at a limp around to the passenger side, which remained closed. After a quick game of Chinese fire drill, David regained control. Now behind the wheel of the expensive red menace, he jammed the car into reverse, screeched backward one hundred feet, and came to a body jarring halt. Wild eyes scanned the gate; lips pressed so tightly they formed a circle of white. The look he gave Steven nearly had the man jumping out of the car. "Buckle up, and hold on."

"They're impenetrable! You can't get through!"

"Maybe not; but we'll try to loosen the lock. Brace yourself against the dash, and for God's sake, keep your head down. Do it. We're about to test the toast of German engineering."

"And you told me to be careful with it!" Kincaid clutched the solid frame of the open convertible, to be immediately forced back into his seat when the car lurched forward and took off from zero to eighty in a matter of seconds, leaving half the tread of the tires on the neatly patterned brick driveway. Steven saw the gate rushing toward him, and he forced his head down to touch his knees. LaCoix had lost his mind; and Kincaid was not prepared to die beside him.

Hitting the imposing gates at full throttle, the metal bars severed the windshield, pulling off the built-in roll bar. The lock gave way, but the impact killed the car. After the neck snapping front-end collision, David tried the engine. Once--twice--a couple of sputters, and the quiet hum sang to him. The gate opened gingerly with a push from the new nose job of the red demon, and they turned left, checking out the car's stability. It required a wheel alignment, but still handled very well, considering the bits and pieces hanging from it. With no lights to betray them, the tires spun, catching hold of the pavement to fishtail a few feet, finally to scream off into the night. They were free.

David drove like a man possessed, seeing only by streetlights and the blessed full moon. Coming to his favorite desert road, leading to nowhere, he slammed on the brakes, miraculously still working. Sweat dripped down his face, along with the blood from a cut to his head. "Still with me, Stevie? Move slowly, and don't brush against anything." LaCoix looked down, unable to release the grip on the wheel. "Damn, I can't move my hands." A few deep breaths, his grip released.

Kincaid lifted his head in slow motion, eyes wild with fear. He had not moved from the braced position he held when they first hit the gate. "Wow, you did it! Look at the car! There's precious little left of it!" The eyes caught everything, inspecting the damage, too afraid to move, considering both men sparkled in fine glass fragments. No longer recognizable as a Mercedes, the purr of the engine remained. He heard David laughing; laughing so hard his entire face glowed under the brightest of moons, with diamonds of glass sparkling in his hair. Even his eyebrows glittered like fireflies in the dark.

"What a kick. Hell, we're in trouble." LaCoix giggled even harder.

"You're bleeding from the head. Are you hurt anywhere else? I can't believe you thought that was fun. Count me out of any action films. Shit, you scared the hell out of me; I might have to change my clothes." Kincaid certainly saw nothing to laugh about, until David turned to him with a devilish look of excitement in his wicked eyes.

"Scared me as well, but ducked in time. Think it's a metal graze." A touch to the side of his head reassured him no major damage had occurred. "Some cold water and a few stitches will fix it. Get out of the car very slowly and shake yourself off." David's door opened, but Steven's stuck tight. The wild risk-taker got out with the grace of a cougar, and shook before taking a stride. Confident nothing lurked in hiding to gouge him, he managed to loosen the passenger door on pure adrenaline. Kincaid gently extricated himself, and shook off the glass chips. A handy little brush, in the glove compartment, had the car swept clean, aided by the brightly lit night sky, dulling even the lights of the Los Angeles area on the horizon. Stars glittered in two pairs of eyes; smiles radiated unabashed joy with the realization of what they had done. Both were now creatures of the wild, outlaws to the end, and they laughed until they could not stand erect.

"Well, what do you say, Thelma?"

"Dump the car and steal another, Louise. Man, do I need to take a piss, and badly."

The driver cracked up again, covering his face, while his passenger dashed to the nearest bush. Another *red boys' toy* adventure, of death-defying thrills, their laughter filled the night air; they were free and unafraid of consequences. Peerce would survive; the Mistress would handle that inconvenience in her way; and the police would not be informed of their escapade. Quietly covered up by the security company protecting Peerce's safety, the bizarre event would be kept secret, or their hideously expensive reputations would be at stake. Upon the first ramming of the gate, security personnel would have been dispatched; and the pair on the videotapes easily recognized--drunken friends of Ethan Peerce--LaCoix and Kincaid. Their famous faces saved them.

Having turned itself off, David gently ignited the car's fire. With the touch of a lover, it sparked to life; and the broken red toy headed into the darkness with two howling blond heads, glowing purple under the moon. Lavender giggled at the pair. Her plan worked; Kincaid escaped and would learn from David and Ted. LaCoix's tension disappeared, and now full of invigoration, he could stabilize his look-alikes with ease and enjoyment. Everything fell into place, with a night of savagery and breathtaking risk; the Cosmos again paused in relief.

"Well, Ethan, have you pieced yourself together?" The Mistress laughed heartily at the pained expression of the man sitting on her window ledge. She fingered her glass gently, lounging in her throne-sized chair, while the constant candles flickered and danced joyously around her.

"You failed to mention his skill level, or the fact he plays dirty." Peerce smiled slyly, still in discomfort. "I have lived in this human body so long; it now feels things; and that tussle hurt. I wonder how long it will take David to figure it out."

"We shall wait and see. However, your treatment of Mr. Kincaid, well, if that does not kick him into a change, nothing will. Thank you for your sacrifice, my dear friend. I did not expect it to be this painful for you." Lavender saluted the man, of salt and pepper hair, who appeared a little frazzled. The winds of change were churning, and his position at the window allowed those new breezes to whip the slight curls around his handsome face. He turned to stare at the Mistress; and they both burst into giggles.

"Your fans in the outer Cosmos truly enjoyed this evening. We all needed some comic relief. I can hear Quinlan laughing in the most regrettable way for the damage sustained to your person, but you did call him a minion. He may desire restitution." Her amusement rang out again. More chimes on the wind brought a certain peace within her realms.

"Oh, you can laugh. LaCoix beats the crap out of me, and you think it funny." Peerce played the miffed victim like the star he was.

"You performed your job splendidly, and you did volunteer."

"Kincaid is an enchanting young man. I did not think I had signed on to be an undercover Fate, to administer those incredulous deeds upon him. To be honest, I did enjoy Stevie's company, until you and Quin hatched your devious plan." Peerce grinned in a grimace.

"He is a sweet man; one who may return to you in his distant future."

"I truly hope he is capable of forgiving when told."

"Thank you again, Mr. Peerce. You can return to earth's reality and mend more than your gate. It was stronger than I anticipated."

"Good night, Mistress of the Devious." Ethan teased and gave her a wink. "I shall soon depart earth, once I have things settled, at which time I can vanish without consequence, and return to my duties here. My last fling at being mortal, although disturbing, I believe the action justifiable and should put your charge back on a corrected path. You do realize I love him, and to have brutalized him in such a fashion did not come easily. It offended my senses and desires."

"I believe you will get him back, Ethan, once they awaken. He will be frightened, but you are the kindest of Spirits who can make it up to him in the gentlest of manner." Lavender nodded her head and smiled. The results of her plans delighted her, believing Kincaid now safe with her student of the *Power-That-May-Be:* David LaCoix. Kindness and commonsense may not completely intercede the ravages of the real Fates for them all, but a little blonde lady might. The world would come to know her as Holly Jane; and she would weave a magic circle around them in her innocence and *knowing* power.

CHAPTER 38

Two very recognizable men dropped off the unrecognizable red vehicle at the rental agency before the sun rose to see the entire disaster. LAX officials could only stare with mouths gaping. Nothing could be said to the giggling pair who laid down a cheque to cover the replacement cost sufficiently. Around the corner, at another rental company, the pair obtained a small, unassuming, domestic, economy car, and their mood changed. The little gray car turned them into exhausted, anxious men. From high risk to no risk made them average, and they had no understanding of it. The fiery night, full of fear, sadism, violence, and adventure, turned sluggishly into a new dawn, suffocating them in a heavy haze of smog.

David LaCoix and Steven Kincaid crawled onto the freeway heading for San Diego, with bags and bodies still intact. Deep in thought of what had occurred, under a secret full moon, they drove unheard and unseen. Unlike the night before, they felt no magic in this day, no wind blowing through their hair and in their faces, no breathtaking views to stop and ponder their lives, and no silence. Only the roar, of millions of cars, was heard, all making their way to their various work destinations at a sloth's pace. How different it felt from their daring run of passionate beating hearts, wild and free, primal screaming with the coyotes under a cloak of black, glittering with spangles. Caught wanting, it never came to fruition; rules had been set. No matter how they felt, lips did not touch, hands not held, and eyes veered away from fleeting glances. It was close, far too close, but one night meant only one long night of self-sacrifice, temptation, and aching need. They fought the burning urges created by the Fates of fire and did not succumb. They had won, or had they? Emptiness filled the youngest; mental exhaustion depressed the other.

David's minor laceration required three stitches. Neatly sutured by the green man, the cut would go unnoticed under his fine, straight hair. With an ointment, to help stinging raw skin, requested and received, allowed Steven to slip discretely into a restroom with the substance and to emerge feeling more comfortable. A quick lie, for the small bandage, appeased Ted's worry, as did Steven's gifted storytelling. Amusement spread across the youngest face, rather than mistrust, and only a hint of jealousy showed in having missed the excitement. No mention of Ethan's brutality came up, keeping things at a less emotional level. Reasons, however, were required; and Kincaid quietly informed his look-alike that his love for Peerce vanished in the smoke of a quarrel. Irreconcilable, life together had not been their future: the end of a love story. Simplicity made the tale more palatable.

If not meant to be, at least Ted could look forward to Steven's company for a few weeks in England. With that confirmed, a wheelchair appeared, along with a pile of brightly colored, woolen blankets. A new, gray sweat suit, of the proper size, would keep the frail body warm and eliminate any embarrassment. Ted hated the gawking; and carried out, only in a hospital gown, would have him hiding his head under the new covers in mortification. David understood the deep shyness of the man who could also step in front of a live audience sky clad, if scripted. This was different; this was real life; and it was time to leave.

Ted's mouth dropped open at his promised caregiver. Through the door pranced Bernard, taking over his duties immediately, insisting he would prepare Mr. Barrett for the journey. All neatly planned by the hospital and Military Police, their escape resembled only another ambulance run, to pick up an injured or ailing sailor. Once on their way, they would turn off the sirens, slow to a comfortable speed for their main concern, and head for Orange County Airport where the jet waited.

An unusual gathering assembled on the tarmac. On first seeing the twenty-passenger jet, David could only compare it to a flying cigar. Today it would carry twelve, with one prone. LaCoix smiled on entering; Kincaid's friend had done his best to make the trip comfortable, including Ted, with a hospital-style bed installed and bolted firmly into position. Bernard had his patient strapped in, warmly wrapped, and hushing the whimpers of pain each movement created. A tiny butterfly, with Goliath hovering over it, was the picture David saw; and he unleashed his most devious smile. Kind and gentle described the muscle-bound man, only to learn later in flight, a little champagne encouraged the giant drag queen to wiggle out, bellowing a Broadway number for his captive audience. Outrageously fun for the others, it greatly disturbed Ted, viewing the stereotype of everything he wished not to be. David rushed to his rescue, with a severe warning, followed by a deadly sneer and a dangerous growl, sobering the caregiver to resume his tender care of a very nervous patient.

LaCoix sat beside the bed, scanning each person aboard; he would have to be careful how he handled Ted and Steven. This was not the group to display affectionate coddling, whispering sweet intimacies to a male lover, or trying to comfort another in misery and shock. He watched Kincaid intently; learning the man never changed his public decorum, whether in the midst of a group of straight couples, or with the flamboyant queen of hearts. In high spirits or despair, Steven proved to be an excellent example for Ted to follow. The mega-star hid his sorrow better than David, as roles reversed. Kincaid would make it through the trip; LaCoix would be there for the crash.

The owner of the jet brought his airhead mistress instead of his wife and family; and it set the tone for the long sojourn. His co-pilot also picked up someone off a very expensive street. David mused at the thought of the many mistresses, of wealthy men, who shopped the elegant stores on Rodeo Drive. Sexy young kittens also clung to the arms of their new friends. The young women played their parts well, giggling and acting stupidly for their middle-aged male barracudas, and glowed more brightly in their blatant attempts to hustle the three famous blonds. Kincaid went along with it, laughing happily at the raven-haired beauty ruffling his hair. It took a fine actor to take such harassment, and that is exactly what David saw.

The sexual advances scared Ted speechless. When two women approached his bed, with their hands coming close to places they should not, David stood up and snarled at them. His technique was simple: don the frightening death mask of Lord Worthington-Smythe, turn his tonality to seriously lethal, and suggest the women open the hatch and jump. Not subtle for the notorious lady's man, the act deemed effective. Between LaCoix and Kincaid, who also witnessed the uncomfortable position of Barrett, they interceded on his behalf several times; but Ted quickly learned how to discourage the unwanted. Air sick, nothing could stop his vomiting into the bag that his nurse held for him. The steady vibration of the plane had his head reeling; and no position, sitting or lying, could stop the man from heaving. David and Bernard hid the pathetic, apologetic face from view, with a divider of blue drapery installed for such an emergency.

Three men tried everything to settle the whirling head and the sweeping nausea. Nothing helped. With instructions given, regarding which drugs to use, Bernard chose only those meticulously packed in a medical case of supplies. Checking through the many prescription drugs brought instant hope; the simplest of solutions, a dose of Gravol injected directly into the body that gagged on a tablet. Worn out and embarrassed, Ted endured his suffering, considering he should be in a hospital. The drug worked, but not fast enough or that well. Another solution quickly came to the mind of Kincaid, although the man lying prone disagreed adamantly. A sound idea of putting a better shock absorber under Ted's head; three men agreed, inviting Goliath to lift his hapless patient into his arms, accompanied by a series of whispered profane complaints. Ignoring Ted's wishes, the strong man came out from behind the curtain, to find the most comfortable chair for two men to lounge in. He found one: the seat occupied by the more obese barracuda, swigging down champagne with the voluptuous redhead sitting on his knee or lap dancing. Difficult to discern, the action warranted flushed faces to veer attention to something less scandalous. With a request made, Bernard stood his ground with a few words to the man, but again Ted ended the argument. On cue, he pitched up more yellowy-green bile onto the minuscule, pale-pink dress. No further need for discussion, the seat vacated with much drunken profanity, and squeals of disgust from the pink person.

David had enough of the public fondling, and scowled at the other man who took many liberties with the brunette. He thought back, remembering the times he had been involved in the same scenario. Women, barely of age, had been used for his own pleasure and sense of masculinity. He had married young, and thought himself more of a stud during his sexual liaison with the director. Several decades later, he saw it as a reconciliatory reaction, to make up for being emasculated, as the passive recipient of another man's adoration. What he now witnessed was not manly, but insidious behavior for anyone. Ted's words, from long ago, echoed through his head; and they churned in his stomach like a milkshake maker. Like these men, he also had been proud and arrogant; now he disgusted himself at the thought. The gurgling organ below his ribs felt like spewing his rage over the other couple; but sadness filled his heart, reflected in the woeful eyes of Kincaid and Barrett, realizing they could never play such games with their partners of choice in view of strangers. A handful of friends may see the innocent, intimate gestures of any infatuated couple, but no one else. All three were slightly jealous; and there loomed their truthful reality.

The remainder of the trip, Ted sprawled on or over someone, head braced, leaning against one of three strong shoulders. Bernard, Steven, and David each took turns. This arrangement allowed the men some intimacy with a patient, a friend, and a lover. Ted came to accept it, after discovering how much better he felt. Once securely in place, he never moved, and the spinning stopped, thanks to three different shock absorbers and several more shots of Gravol, with the thankful after-effect of sleepiness. Kincaid's idea worked, compensating for the up and down motion of the small jet to refuel. Jiggling inside a vibrator would have been more fun, or even sitting in a spin dryer. Preventing Barrett's head from spiraling into orbit kept the threesome busy and away from the antics played out around them. Only sleep gave them a respite.

With a great deal of gratitude bestowed upon the pilot, four men escaped into the waiting Bentley. Ted rested semi-prone, comfortable against David's shoulder, sleeping most of the long drive. He did catch a few glimpses of the overcast day, which made the flowers contrast more brilliantly against the bright, summer-green background speeding passed the window. One of the many colorful images David had painted; unfortunately, blurring the scenery increased the dizziness, forcing his eyes to close. The conversation was equally foggy, yet he loved the voices, each different, all softly low, creating a lullaby with the steady hum of the Bentley. The car gently stopped at a large set of iron gates; Kincaid and LaCoix exchanged silly grins, and shrugged in unison. The sapphire eyes missed the mischievous gesture, but opened to a visual feast of flowers, gardens, fountains, trees, and a magic palace. Theodore Barrett finally arrived at the manor house. David's verbal paintings had detailed the haunting glory of the fortified, rock castle, making Ted smile at the man. "Thanks LaCoix, it's awesome."

"I've waited a long time to show you this place. Heal quickly, Teddy Bear." A sweet kiss flickered lightly over a pale cheek, as the black hearse-like vehicle came to a slow halt. Knowing the condition of one man, the driver drove carefully, making the road trip comfortable; and David thanked him for his courtesy. Rod Morris and family first appeared, and from out of the menagerie, a little blonde LaCoix came running down the stairs, hitting the cobbled driveway at top speed. The long legs tried to keep stride with the even longer ones racing toward her. David caught her in full flight, swinging her high into the air, and around three or four times. Both laughed and smiled the identical look of excitement.

Bernard came around, and with help from Kincaid and the driver, they hoisted the cast figure out of the car and into the giant's arms. With greetings and introductions quickly made, they hurried the shivering patient inside, and out of the cold dampness. Freshened up and changed into a burgundy, fleece-lined sweat suit, which stretched admirably over his plastic armor, they placed Ted in bed without argument. Now settled and quiet, yet still encumbered and exhausted, he snuggled deeper into the massively high bed within the confines of the room he had dreamed about: David's room, David's bed, and David's scent lingering throughout the ghostly dwelling. Ted pulled himself further into the quilt that smelled of his heroic Knight who rushed to his rescue and succeeded.

While Barrett closed his eyes, wallowing in the dream of the man who would soon be lying next to him, Bernard unpacked his few things, and then disappeared at a knock. Opening his eyes, Ted happily witnessed the grand entrance of Mr. LaCoix and daughter, Miss Holly Jane, who clutched Sir Lancelot. "Hey, Ted, can we come in?"

"Yeah, I've been waiting for you. Hi Holly, you still have your bear."

"I'd never lose Sir Lancelot, Mr. Barrett. He talks to me." She came around to look closer, and stood on the riser, which ran around the entire bed. Stepping up the one-foot stair, and another effort of grabbling bedding as a handle to scale the height, seemed the only way to immerse oneself in its softness, unless one could fly, or jump tall buildings. It meant trouble for Ted. "Dad told me you've been sick. Now you're hurt. Do you feel better?" Holly did a little tapping on the plastic, sensing the difficulties of her father's friend.

"It looks worse than it is, Sweetheart." Ted looked into those familiar green eyes, a reflection of her father in every way.

Reaching out, she touched his swollen cheek with the softest of caresses. "What happened to you? Heard Mr. Morris tell someone that your father tried to kill you." Holly had no notion of what the words conveyed, or the sudden downcast look of Ted's face.

"That's enough, Honey. We don't want to tire our patient out. Why don't you go downstairs and play a while. The two of us can go for one of our special walks. Sound good to you?" Father and daughter saved the day and brought back the cheery atmosphere.

"Yeah, I found more Faery rings. Think they like summer better than winter."

"Quite possibly, my fair lady; now run along. I want to talk to Ted alone for a few minutes. Don't forget the knock rule."

"I'll remember, but I found something for Mr. Barrett." She jumped off the step and scampered over to one of the chairs in front of the fireplace. From Ted's vantage point, he could enjoy the large, crackling blaze framed between two monster throne chairs.

"What could this possibly be?" David looked puzzled, wondering if Holly had made Ted a welcoming gift; it would certainly be like her. Both men laughed when the little girl reappeared, carrying something priceless.

"I think Dad's finished talking to Sir Edmund. Now I know where your bear has been traveling." Miss LaCoix had the stuffed toy around the neck, trying to be careful in her struggle to drag the monster bear along the floor. They had forgotten just how large this particular brown snuggly was.

"Thanks, Holly, this is great. I've missed Sir Edmund." Ted laughed and eagerly accepted the bear with his least restricted arm. The cherished listener of sad tales found itself in rightful and grateful arms.

"I'm going to take care of you, Mr. Barrett, if you promise not to make Dad cry."

"I made him cry? When? I didn't mean to."

Too easy to hit Ted's panic button, David had to ease the man into these sudden shots, although just as baffled over this one. "Holly?" LaCoix frowned at his daughter.

"They were happy, sad tears. Remember, at Christmas?" Confused as well, her tiny hands went directly to her denim-clad hips, followed by the famous LaCoix stance, and a sneaker tapping against the wooden step. "The present, Dad." She returned David's frown with the same look and tilt of the head. If Ted had not been so unnerved, he would have laughed, watching the two mimic each other.

"Oh, my present from Mr. Barrett; I guess it did bring tears to my eyes."

"It's so pretty. Soon as Dad opened it, I saw him wiping his face, but then he smiled. It's sitting right there, with his worry chimes. See, on the table, beside Dad's side of the bed?" Ted's eyes misted while looking at it, rousing David into quick action.

"Okay you, out. Go and play, and be dressed warm in one hour." He caught his daughter, squeezed her tight, set her on solid ground, and tapped her little behind to start the race. Gone in a scamper, she giggled and closed the door with a thud. David watched her, and then turned his attention to the man who could not even rub his face.

"Sorry David; must be the long trip." Tired of his pain, and now tears of emotion, this day continued to drain more out of the injured party. David had liked his gift; and Holly approved of their sleeping arrangements, accepting it as perfectly normal. Ted could not ask for a better welcome.

"It is beautiful; and I never thanked you. The sentiment behind it overwhelms me whenever I look at it." David picked up the sterling silver frame, tracing his thumb over the delicate blooms pressed firmly between two sheets of glass; a white rose with a thorn crossed over a black one with a smooth stem. "Which one of us has the barb; I've never figured it out?"

"Since white means innocence, I assumed you thought it would represent me. The first thing you ever gave me, with its treacherous thorn, you surprised me that night with your seductive behavior. I would have given in, if you had asked; at least I think I would have. What a strange world we had entered." Ted relaxed deep into his coverings, feeling safer than he had since leaving La Rosa Negra.

"Indeed, and I needed you in my life the moment you pricked your finger, but I couldn't admit it, even to myself. You were the start of everything, Ted. Now, you must explain why I'm the black one."

"The light, hidden in the shadows of the night, and understanding not everything is as it appears. I need to apologize for not understanding the concept. The dark and the light, they exist side-by-side, sometimes overlapping, one explaining the other. The darkened path is as illuminated as the lightened, only the fear of the dark keeps us from seeing our way." Blue eyes looked up through dark lashes, seducing a man who wanted to be, and who drifted into the entrancement of the verse, the voice, and the eyes.

David blinked several times, hiding his need for physical contact with the body in the bed. "You remember the inscription precisely. I think I cried over the words more than the roses. Can I make the assumption you understand, that between the light and the dark, there are many veils of gray we must learn to see?"

"I'm beginning to. The words came from Lavender, in some context of whether she was good, bad, or evil. She told me that evil did not exist except in the human mind, and she could be good or bad. I'll never forget, and it's something I've pondered since we left the place. After my stupidity, listening to Kincaid's obsession, I knew the time had come to act on my feelings. One of my first thoughts: Lavender could be both, as are we all. She tried to kill Stevie, yet she saved us. Weird, isn't it?"

"One of the thicker gray veils, I'd say."

"Guess so. I learned a great deal from the Mistress and Quinlan between Christmas and now, and even more from you. It still confuses me, but different pieces, unexpected pieces, are beginning to fit."

"You're becoming a philosopher and a poet about your own theological teachings. I'm glad you're trying to solve your own life's puzzle into an order you can truly believe. This place should help you assimilate all you're pondering. Are you up to talking, or do you need to rest? I'd like to speak with you about something of major relevance." David sat beside him and stroked away the stricken look of dismay. "It's nothing to be upset about; in fact, I hoped you'd be pleased about what I have to say. Shit, I don't even know how to ask this." The older actor's eyes went to the bear, and nervously tried to fix its position against the thin body under the covers. Something to do, he pulled the quilt over the plastic protective coating, to rest under a smooth, hairless jaw, and a teddy bear's chin: two teddy bear chins. He settled back into a sitting position and tried to find something else to do with his hands. A smoke would be gratifying at this point, as would nail biting. Unfortunately, both would inhibit his speech, a narrow escape on all counts.

"As long as it's not about hiding our lives away; I couldn't deal with that, while sleeping next to you every night, LaCoix. Once I'm better, and even tonight, I want you near me, or this arrangement won't work." Emphatic in his own needs, Ted oozed with renewed confidence. Tired of his inability to touch David, he needed to feel cared for and stroked in some loving, definitive manner, besides the ruffle of his hair and a paternal hug he could not feel. Having conquered his physical pain, now his mental torment fell under siege, but Barrett came back fighting.

"Something like that." David could not look into the peculiar eyes that reminded him of a child, making him feel criminal with his thoughts. Nothing could stop him from chewing his nails either, while he stared out the window, silence filling the Gothic chamber full of possible promises.

"Come on, man, spit it out. You drive me nuts. Stop gnawing at what's left of those overly stimulating fingers, and start talking; or better yet, do something more pleasurable with them." If Ted could sit on his own, he would smack the man in his utter annoyance. A large bush was something he could no longer run around.

"Just let me get this out. You can be so unnerving at times."

"Me? Okay, I'm sorry. I'm listening. Go ahead."

David continued to fondle Sir Edmund's ears, avoiding the sapphires forcing him to look anywhere but at those eyes. One of the rare times the quiet-spoken, articulate LaCoix could not utter one sensible word; he stumbled incoherently through his entire monologue. "I spoke to your lawyer and mine, while you were in the hospital; and they both agreed. Now, it may be a risk, but it could be done. Maybe it would give you some respectability. Sorry, bad choice of words, anyway, it may give us a better chance of getting your daughter. I completely agree; I guess I had to, being my idea. What they did to you and Richard, while Karen stood by... and watched... she did, didn't she?" A question gave him a chance to breathe. His quest assuredly grew more difficult than he thought.

"Yes, but they couldn't charge her with anything." Ted looked completely bewildered, only understanding the last question.

"True, but she didn't help either; like calling the police, which makes her look bad, if used properly. Now, with your father possibly being convicted of attempted murder, plus the D.A.'s findings, your chances are getting better to gain full custody."

"I've heard some of this before, LaCoix, but I can't see how it helps. Why are you jumping all over the place?" With his face almost normal, except the swollen cheek, the fading bruises, and a few bandages, it certainly did not prevent Ted from frowning.

"I talked to Tyler and Bryce as well. Bryce is okay with it, but a little confused; unfortunately, Ty took it badly. My sons will come around; I think; I hope so." David lost his thought line, leaving him dangling in the confusion of what to say next. Ted's furrowed brow and bewildered expression said it all; LaCoix had to get this out.

"What are you raving about? What's the *it*? The house?"

David's eyes darted around the room. Any object to concentrate on would work, before he choked. Coming to a natural diversion, through the huge double window to his room, gave him an intake of air. "It's raining!"

"What? *It* is raining? What does that have to do with anything? Where's your head, LaCoix, still in those clouds?"

The natural blond went to the window and peered out. A perfect enticement lay before him: better than candles in the sand, ringed around two lovers, under a black-velvet, no-moon night. Gothic, morbid rain, graying the sky and washing every tree and flower clean, would do the same for his lover. He turned with a laughing smile, making the young man squirm. "Have you been on your feet yet?"

"Where are we going now? This better be good. Ouch, watch it!" At Ted's side in a stride, David stripped off the layers, tossed Sir Edmund off the bed, and wrapped the man, casts and all, in a cocoon of wool. Carrying the featherweight did not come easy with the cumbersome plastic, but he made it to the window and sat the perplexed man on the cushioned window seat.

"Can you stand? How about kneeling?"

"I don't believe this. I've been dizzy for days; I'm so tired I could drop like a rock; and you plunk me down on a window seat to fend for myself. If you have the need to know, I've stood to piss, and only twice. Someone had his arms secured around me to do it. Do you know how embarrassing that is? Puked my guts out at the same time, and now you want me standing or on my knees, when it hurts to sit. I'm about to heave now. Don't think I'm ready for what you may have in mind, LaCoix, if you get my drift; although it has been on my mind." Asea by the conversation and the actions taken, Ted shivered with nervousness, and from the cold draft coming through the rain-splashed window. Even the room added to his puzzlement, as it moved in a concentric, whirling spiral.

"Stop fussing. I didn't mean that. It's the magic, Ted. It's starting."

"You're nuts, and I'm dizzy. Your mind has rusted in this damp air. Return me to California."

"Lost your sense of hanging by your toes to feel the freedom? How about a little fresh air to bring it back? I want to open this window, and let you feel it."

"Okay, I'll play the game. What am I going to feel, David? Sometimes you are so weird; and I thought you were the practical one."

"Hush and listen. Fresh moist air will make you feel better. I'm going to get you on your knees so you can look out." David helped Ted into a kneeling position, resting his butt on his feet. "Comfy?"

"Oh yeah, this is a fun way to finish me off. My leg hurts like hell where they had the needle."

"Forgot about that; do you want me to move you?"

"No, I can tolerate it for a few minutes to feel whatever *it* is. You are becoming way too abstract for me, LaCoix." A sideways squint, and a scowl on Ted's part, had David giddy with the expression he hoped would appear, if he could get the question out.

"I like that: abstract." David pushed open the massive windows to view the increasing drizzle of opaque rain nourishing a field of thirsty flowers. They seemed to breathe with new life, springing into brighter colors in thanks. "Mr. Barrett, I don't want to continue this relationship as it stands. I have thought about this until close to losing my mind; and why this is of such relevance, I have no idea; but if Holly agrees, and you accept, I want to announce it to the public."

"Announce *it*? What, the rain? The weather channel does that. Man, you have me so confused. Don't you want me anymore?" Perplexed by every word spoken, nothing made sense to Ted. The ghostly manor house had to be playing tricks with David's mind; and it terrified him as to what the answer to his last question might be.

"Don't be ridiculous. If you want a permanent partnership, we can sign any legal papers you like. I want you forever in my life, Theodore Barrett."

"Excuse me?" Ted lost the frown, and those eyes enlarged to the point one could see into both the Pacific and Atlantic Oceans.

"This is illegal except for a few European countries, some of our states, and I think Canada; but we can make it work with legal documents to bind us. I want you on my arm at Cannes; letting the world know, before we arrive, that we're *engaged*; a formidable couple who will conquer and vanquish anything in our way. This will put everyone off-stride because of our current notoriety, but even the New York Times will have to put this announcement in their rag. If nothing else, Teddy Bear, we'll stir up some fun." David's eyes glowed neon green and a hell-raising, supercilious grin stretched from ear-to-ear, wrinkling up the incredibly handsome face.

Ted was lost. This would be coming out of his non-satisfying but safe closet at the height of his career; and LaCoix, being bisexual, had never been in a closet, unless it had an open door. All very mystifying, but David said it might help him gain custody; it could go either way. Perhaps he could prove himself a good, caring, family man with David and Holly. Miss LaCoix may be the key. Tears poured from the blue orbs, and his proposed partner laughed, hugging and kissing whatever part did not hurt.

"Like a real marriage; real swear-to-God marriage? Do men do that? Would you adopt Willow? If we get her, and something happens to me; I can't leave her to suffer with my family." Tears streamed at a rapid rate, as Ted made his demands without a stutter.

"As close to one as we can make it. It won't be legal, but we'll fine-tune partner agreements to look like a *marriage* contract. Whatever you want, we'll include, except you have to swear to me and not to your god, that's for monks and nuns. Which makes me wonder why priests are servants of your god, and nuns are married to him; sounds rather homophobic? Sorry, I'm rambling. Holly would have to agree, since she still remembers her mother, and will be a little confusing for her. I have only my parents to take her in, if something happens to me, and I'd rather have you care for her, Ted. She doesn't know them, like she'll come to know you." Excited at their possibilities, David prattled on and on.

David had stewed over the matter the entire flight, soaring over clouds into his fantasy come true. The question lay on the table with no turning back; rejection scared him to death. If accepted, however, the proposal could ruin his career; it could ruin Barrett's star status; it could ruin Ted's chances of ever getting child custody; and it could ruin the pictures in production. The royalties from *Outlaw's Heart,* however, would go on forever, and the two men had sufficient funds, in offshore accounts, to secure them for many lifetimes. Why was he thinking careers and money, when sharing and making the last of Ted's time memorable took priority; he had to ensure the happiness of the love of his life; although it came with a twist of the Fates. There had to be a good one amongst them--Lavender--and he chuckled to himself. Still a provoking thought, Ted had been given to him from a wishful thought to a beautiful lady, with glorious raven hair and floating garments of celestial making. She had transformed him into a man he liked, one who could take responsibility of such an exquisite, delicate gift. He could sense her presence in the purple cloud, hiding outside in the gray, wet sky. She was both good and bad; and he laughed.

"Will you marry me, Theodore Barrett?" With the windows wide open, his head soaked by the cold blessing, David yelled his desires for anyone who could hear above the crack of a lightning strike. Perfectly timed, it resounded in each falling raindrop as a congratulatory tear from the universe. He had done it.

"I... I... yes, I..."

"Stick your head out the window, and shout it for the world to hear. Please marry me." Still supporting Ted, David forced the dizzy head out the window to feel the magic against his face, and to turn the salty tears into fresh water fountains.

"Yes, I'll marry you, David LaCoix." A smile lit up the gray day; the sparkle of silver rain washed away a lifetime of sadness, while their laughter buried the sorrow. The cold, crystal droplets permanently froze the ecstatic smile, and stopped the physical torment, if only for the flash of an adorned moment in time.

David pulled him away from the blast of cold, to nuzzle the wet face softly; their excitement tempered by one slightly sore cheek; but the simple lip-to-lip touch promised a future not planned. Romantic: yes. Gentle: yes. Comfortable and warm: no. Two hearts did not care or feel anything, although the same excited rhythm echoed in unison within their chests. Smitten entirely by the other, the long gaze confirmed it. Precious gems, of emeralds and sapphires, smiled at each other, and could not be forced apart.

"Thank you, Ted. What would I do without you?"

"You'd be lost too. In a biographical movie I saw, this gay guy said no man ever told him he was loved. Men just don't say it. I think women claim the same thing about their male partners. We just don't say the word enough. I wonder why it's so hard." Now Ted rambled senselessly. If he stopped talking, he would have to face the strange decision. The deal was sealed; and he quivered from fright, or from the cold. He had no idea which; but if he could keep his mouth moving, it would all go away. Another caress of his lips stopped the chatter, and softened his lips into a pleasurable sigh.

"What were you saying, Teddy?"

"Nothing important." The younger man reached up with his right arm and pulled the wet blond head down. He had missed the taste of his Knight, and he wanted more. A lick of his lips, by a warm tongue, sent another shiver down his back, straight into that strange aching pit that ran from his bellybutton down, while simultaneously curling up his toes.

David pulled away and smiled serenely, filled with those other worldly eyes, twinkling and dancing. Christmas again, he could see tree lights shining in the blue crystal balls. "You are a wonder, Mr. Barrett. It only happens in sad and gay movies. Maybe we have an advantage over the average male."

"How? You told me, long ago, you would only say it once."

"Loving you is so easy; we made love without a word spoken, Ted, by experiencing the wonder of rainfall together. Nothing binds two people more than the intimate exchanges of knowing each is there for the other. Women need to hear the word and see physical actions of the romantic variety. Perhaps, men only need to be there, to feel it in their own way, without all the finery. Our reassurance is more like a child's, with touches and nurturing. I wonder who feels it the deepest."

"We'll never know, but *It* was perfect; now I'm the biggest fan of rain. Thanks LaCoix."

"Thank you; I enjoyed it myself, although unsettling. I can't believe I asked, and you accepted. So, when do we announce our engagement?"

"Engagement, does that sound weird."

"Too gushy? We'll think of something not so..." David laughed, trying to say what he meant, without sounding the fool.

"...feminine?" The entire idea had Ted sweating, wondering how to react to something so easily understood by women. It had him lost in ruffles and lace; and he almost gagged.

"Let me start with Holly. I promised her a walk, and a shower has never stopped us before. An outing with her old Dad will help persuade her. Besides, my amazing Teddy Bear, you need sleep. It's already been a grueling few days for you." David winked and had him in his arms, carrying him back to his bed, their bed. With his promised partner safely tucked in, he had some talking to do, and much convincing. With a sweeping kiss to those enticing lips, he readied himself for his next conquest, reassured by the glow of renewed vigor on his lover's face. "Get some rest until dinner. The three of us will spend the evening together. You will eat, Ted; and that's an order." David laughed and opened the monster-sized door, which Ted figured was beyond his own capabilities to try.

"Will she want to, after you tell her?"

"She's part of the magic. Shush, go to sleep. I'll get Bernard."

"Not yet; I want to savor this, LaCoix. You talk about magic all the time. I'm becoming a believer; and this place is full of it. Let me just lie here, remembering the feel of the rain. I want to be swallowed up by this room; it has to stay with me forever."

"I adore you, Mr. Barrett. You make me crazy."

Ted laughed, his eyes watching the heavy old door close, and wishing he could tag along. For now, he had to relive the past half-hour, and everything that went with it. A whisper in his head told him it was real; he found a safe haven; and when needed, she would come. After sweet congratulations, her kiss blew across his forehead, to flutter his hair; and the warm embrace of a purple cloud made him smile. The Mistress was the first to know, and properly so. Ted heard nothing more; his pain faded, to fall asleep and dream of visions filled with a happy future. Everything else floated away, if only for a moment's rest.

Lavender lingered until he slept comfortably. Theodore Barrett won his prize, and he could face his future with intent. The Fates would not find him here, not for a while. *'Sleep safe, Theo. You shall make it, conquering everything in your path; and if a Fate tries, it will only make you stronger.'*

Her Ladyship disappeared to catch up with another of her charges who cried out in masked sorrow. She arrived to see LaCoix knocking on Kincaid's door. On a mission to correct every life he felt in danger, David's quests were many, and his learning curve surprised them all. If anyone could portray a chivalrous knight, it had to be David LaCoix. Forging ahead at an unearthly rate, he would join them soon.

CHAPTER 39

Calming himself, with a few deep breaths, David stood in front of the carved rosewood door. He had to talk to Kincaid whose guilt, hurt, and hostility remained disguised. Two raps on the door and an echoed yell invited him in.

"Am I interrupting?" The voice remained cheerful, still thinking of the acceptance of his difficult proposal. David bit down on his lower lip to contain his excitement over the secret.

"Hey, come in. Great place Morris found. Thanks for inviting me. How's Scarecrow? Feeling better with his feet on the ground?"

"A bit perplexed for now, but definitely happier. How are you doing?"

"In comparison to what? Guess I'm fine, if I'm spouting old one-liners. Escaping a sadistic madman, whom I thought loved me, certainly makes up for missing him. He was kind once." Kincaid slumped heavily into one of the giant chairs, looking down at the fine pattern of the Persian carpet between his shoes. After many undetermined hours, since their crazed dash to freedom, Steven Kincaid had much on his mind and his life to sort out. It came unmasked in his voice and on the incredible face no longer able to hold onto the pretense. "Guess we're really all we have; one person--all alone--in every thought and action."

"Do you want to talk about it?"

"No... Maybe... Where do I go wrong, David?" Kincaid blinked up into eyes full of kindness and no judgment.

"Hell if I know. You tell me." David settled in the throne chair, with a view of the man's actions and reactions. Eyes filled in the feelings the voice could not say. Sinking deeper into the plush cushioning, he did not wish to comfort this man physically, a temptation even after making an honest proposal to another.

"I got scared and turned to the one person who hurt me the worst, even insisting Theo listen to his sermon over a speakerphone. He convinced Scarecrow that our desires were ungodly; but I, like a damn fool, just wanted to please him. Screw his religion; I just wanted him to screw me. A stupid contradiction, that I didn't pay attention to, until I looked at Theo's face on hanging up. His entire world crumbled around him in one giant rockslide."

"You have no idea, Stevie. Certainly a rockslide, it happened long before your telephone call." The remembered event struck David hard; any misunderstanding of a simple lecture on good and evil, right or wrong, could crush Ted. Religion was not in his lover's way; only those around him, acting as Fates of godliness, threw him into the dank mire. No matter how hard Barrett tried to fit his own puzzle together, an opinion obstacle would send him hurtling out of control. His mind twisted to another, wondering if the reason Quinlan mysteriously appeared was to help one ailing Spirit, by becoming Ted's guardian. It jolted David back to listening.

"It's my fault he's so confused and ill. Man, this is hard. Theo walked in and saw the son-of-a-bitch, who called us unholy, rape me twenty minutes before the wedding; and I don't mean Ethan. God, what I let the man do to me; and Scarecrow saw it all. The room was a mess; I was a mess; and then came Theo. I'll never forget the look on his face. Before my unholy friend left, he laughed at us, smacked me across my torn arse, promised a more fulfilling rendezvous the next weekend, and then delivered a bruising kiss to Theo's lips; probably the only male lip sucker he's received, besides yours. The sadistic, married, egotistical, superstar devastated him; but Scarecrow saved me twice that day, although bewildered over my actions and that son-of-a-bitch that the world adores. After untying me and helping me without a word, Theo put everything back in order, and then hastened to find my brothers at the gate. You may have seen his frantic search on the News. Then the ceremony, man, I could barely walk, let alone climb a cliff. Theo shouldn't have tried with his broken arm; and I really took good care of that, breaking it a second time. It makes me a perverted whore and the worst friend imaginable." A streaming fountain washed down the saddest face, unable to find enough dry clothing to wipe his eyes and dripping nose, which continued to sniff between statements and sobs.

"It's not your fault Ted's ill. You added to his spiritual and moral dilemma; but his disease perpetuated itself long before we met. We all should have been more aware, but we let it slide. Now we have to wait and prepare for what may happen. I can't come to terms with it myself; it scares me, Stevie; and I have no one to turn to when it happens. His every second has to be special now."

"I'm sorry. Here I am, complaining about my stupidity, when there are greater concerns. Listen to me, David. I may be a prick, but I refuse to believe Theo's dying. I'll never give up on him. Whatever I can do to help you both, I'll do. I'll support you all the way, LaCoix. So many lives I've messed up, male and female, this is one promise I won't flee from." The tears stopped for his own mistakes, replaced by grim determination for David's benefit.

"Thanks, Stevie. I'm glad you're here; but I still have to say this. You have truly done some hideous things with your life, out of disrespect for yourself, for whatever reason. It's time to end it--no more--a lesson learned. Promise?" The direct eye contact continued, while admitting honest statements of the worst possible actions taken by them all.

"I vow never to be used again. If I must, I'll stay a hermit the rest of my life, devoting my energies to keep you and Scarecrow happy, until the... God, we are going to lose him. You're the rock for so many; how do you stand it?" Holding tears and fears in abeyance, Kincaid sucked in his breath with the sudden dose of bitter reality.

Concern for someone else, and anger for what deemed unfair, indicated positive; the beautiful man would not tolerate further violence to befall him. David saw the rising ire and wanted it to continue; Kincaid had been passive long enough; and the promise of support gladdened a faltering heart. The older actor needed someone to share the terror he felt over Ted's condition, one who would be there to hold him together when the time came. "It's okay, man. We still have him, and we'll need you at the end. I'll need you."

"I'll be there, LaCoix." The weight of admittance took its emotional toll on the younger man. This talk continued the one interrupted before their wild ride, hinting at Steven's understanding of his life gone dangerously awry.

David listened to a stream of confessions, of a man who could no longer cope with hiding his need for sexual abuse. The rambling took one anxious actor's mind off the unknown, to help bear the weight of another's agonizing torture of his inadequacies exposed in spoken words. "Thanks Stevie, your admissions explain a lot about Theo's mood swings."

"Guess it would. After Morningstar tried to kill me, both Theo and I changed. We threw ourselves into the film, leaning only on each other and Quin. Scarecrow just pined away for you, becoming more difficult to reach after seeing you at Christmas. I offered little help, acting the jackass, only desperately thinking of how to make amends with Ethan and to get back into his bed.

Needing him so badly, in every sense, I tried everything to be forgiven for what I did." Steven shook his head in disgust and leaned back into his chair. The eyes were red, and a shaking hand again wiped away the continually running nose.

"He hurt you first in rage. You believed it to be a retaliatory beating, not imagining there would be more." David filled in the short pause, and kept the admissions coming of a lost love.

"After the cancellation of the wedding, it took time, but he did forgive me, understanding what we do for our public image. What a way to run your life. The day Theo ordered the issuance of the divorce papers marked the change in Ethan from tender to tyrannical. It was so odd. Nearly the end of shooting in Mexico, two weeks before the awards, and with three of you nominated, we decided a small party seemed appropriate. I don't know his reasons, but Ethan turned violent the night of our celebration, and continued until you saved me. I can't believe we all made it intact to the awards."

"What happened?" David's mind wandered back to his life and death struggle with Peerce. Something felt wrong, something forgotten. He pricked his ears, hoping Kincaid's words would help him remember.

"I don't know if you can call it rape when it's your partner. He grabbed my hair, hauled me back into his suite, and literally ripped off my clothes. Yelling and hoping for a savior, I guess that's what it was. Sick from heatstroke, I couldn't fight him off; and he forced himself on me like some wild animal. Once over, he went into his bedroom, closed the door, and left me naked on the table. He hurt me so badly; I passed out, only to wake up in his bed, washed clean, with fresh clothes left at the foot of the bed. Talk about *deja vu*. He said nothing, but greeted me with a smile and breakfast. It continued from there. That's when I first felt his power, and knew he'd never allow me to leave. With the twist of his finger, I'd be in agony, with distorted positions he forced upon my body, and then to..."

"Please, Stevie, let's leave it to my imagination. It seems he has the powers of the Mistress, and now remembering back, he said as much." Horrified at the thought of Lavender's abilities unleashed for insidious purposes, David's arm-hair bristled and a shiver ran up his back.

"Exactly; she's another you don't want to mess with; although I do love her. She has given me more chances than I deserve." Drained and unsettled, Steven neared the end of his sad tale.

"She loves you, Stevie. You just frustrate her, but Ethan... Holy shit, I missed it! I missed the whole damn thing! How did I win the fight? We were set up, Stevie, but why?" David's head nearly imploded at the thought; Peerce let him win.

"You're right. He could have annihilated us with a thought. What's going on?" Equally rattled, Kincaid stared unblinking in his surprise.

"It had to be a lesson we both missed, but for what and for whom, unless a message from the Mistress to stop your masochistic behavior and a test of my fidelity? Your abuse started with the divorce papers. What's the connection?" Revelation after revelation rocked his understanding of the *knowing*, and again, the question of the Mistress' identity came to the fore. Was she bad or good? David leaned forward to see if terror also filled the pale blue eyes. Only nervous sadness lingered under the long, wet lashes; and another hit nearly knocked him over; Lavender directed her suggestion to Kincaid, not to him. He had been appointed mentor to a man who could not concentrate on anything but making great motion pictures and submitting to abusive lovers. As the Mistress' courier, David became the guide to Kincaid's new future. The scream in his head could topple their stone fortification. He waited for a sign, receiving a whisper of acknowledgment; LaCoix drew in a breath and waited reluctantly for his opportunity.

"What can you do but laugh. And now the latest, Ethan's gate has been repaired with an addition." Steven sighed, his eyes cleared, and he took a last sniff.

David forced himself out of temptation by the seductive man who did not recognize the effect he had on people, much like Ted. Maybe their close resemblance, in mannerisms and looks, kept tearing at his defenses. Stopping himself from the deep contemplation of the two men, LaCoix mentally changed course to face his new challenge. "That was fast. What did he add: a stronger steel barrier, a moat with alligators, a drawbridge? How wide and at what speed can we trash this one? Maybe a change in cars, like a Hummer, can knock it down or jump over it."

"It's not funny, David. It's a *For Sale* sign. I just heard from Morris; Ethan Peerce officially announced his retirement from the industry, and immediately headed out on a vision quest, wherever it leads him. He's gone, with all the grace and that soft smile of the star he became. He gave me an enormous gift; my movie will be his last; and there won't be a person who'll miss seeing it. It's my fault the world has lost one of its finest actors." Steven hid his face in his hands and broke down from within his deepest sorrow. His lost heart spread itself across the Persian carpet, adding glittering rubies of red to the intense burgundy background.

David reached out and laid a hand on the bleached hair, not knowing how to explain what he knew had happened. With no proof but his inner *knowing*, he had figured it out.

"Wherever he goes, he will be missed by millions. What are you thinking, LaCoix?" Kincaid finished grieving, shrugged off the comforting touch, and sat back staring at his thrill-seeker whose eyes wildly darted about. The older actor was back to chewing his nails, at a rabbit's rate. "Please, what is it?"

"We were set up; and I know why, Stevie. It's probably too soon to know, but you have learned your lesson, correct? Can you swear to me, you will stop being used?"

"I'll say. I promise; the first smack and I'm out of there. You'll have me pounding on your door to stop me from ever submitting again." Kincaid crossed his heart in a gesture of an oath.

"Good man. Now listen up. I think she meant this for you, and don't snicker or laugh. What kind of man are you looking for? Honesty, my friend, nothing but the truth." David prepared himself for a tough task, like a pit bull ready for the kill.

"No one has ever asked me that, but I can tell you the most important part of my dream guy: someone kind and gentle for a start, a man of intellect and a survivor, who just loves me for me, a straight gay, if that makes any sense. Do those qualifications come in a combo pack?" With a false smile, Kincaid eased out of his depression into another type of hopelessness.

"Maybe, and it makes perfect sense. You want a natural, free flowing partnership of trust and kindness, without the hurting kinky side, or the humiliating bizarre games. A slow, innocent courtship of discovery, beyond the physical need, in search of a partner you respect, and one who adores you with all your flaws. You want a gay lover, strong enough to take care of you, and as much a man as yourself. You're *enfant perdus*, you and Ted." David stood up, walked over to Steven, and braced his hands on either arm of the giant chair. His wicked stare and smile lit up his face, and in turn had Kincaid pressed tight against his back support in trepidation.

"What does that mean?"

"Lost children for one. Now, for your combo pack; ready to order? You can find the right person, when you know where to look. I just happen to know the secret, whispered to me by a very good friend. Amazingly, it's easier for us than the rest of the population." The intensity of the eyes disturbed the beautiful one enough to pay attention.

"How? We're hidden creatures, David, isolated from what's real, and protected from anyone who might fit our needs."

"No we're not. That's a load of crap. We have the world to choose from, but we're too scared to try. Do you ever read your fan mail?" David gave him a twisted grin as a dare; but the man did not take the bait.

"I pay someone to go through that catastrophic waste of good trees, with only a few read; just one of a thousand glossies mailed out with my signature. I don't even sign them. Just one scrawl digitally transposed onto the picture. Why?"

David returned to his chair, made himself comfortable, ready to test the bubbling waters with the idea given to him by Lavender and had actually tried. "Dining with a friend some time ago, and as is my custom, I began complaining of my inability to attract women of substance; someone I could love, who only wanted me with the same list of wishes and dreams; a normal, caring, extremely bright individual with no Hollywood lights in her eyes. My friend's thoughts and suggestions were too simple for me to comprehend at the time. She told me to read my fan mail, believing much of what we receive are simply letters from people who write once or twice only to talk. They feel more reclusive and afraid of exposure than we do. Who better to write out your thoughts on life, than to a person you know will never see your letter, or respond to it; a foolish, famous face that makes you want to trust them for unknown reasons. It seemed to make sense, so I tried it during the short period you split me and Ted apart." David winked at him; Steven flushed with embarrassment.

"You won't let me forget that, will you?"

"No, it will keep you to your vow; and I'm not letting you forget this."

"Right, LaCoix, just throw me to the wolves. Are you crazy? Did you find a person who could become your ultimate love match? I don't see anyone here I don't already know." Kincaid sneered at the thought, playing the snobbish, spoiled, sarcastic, Hollywood star brat. It did not surprise David, or change his mind.

"In that miniscule space of time, I corresponded with two women who proved the theory correct. Thank heavens for overnight couriers." David's green eyes squinted slightly, watching Steven for a reaction.

"Guaranteed they were gorgeous, or you wouldn't have written." Kincaid remained rigid in his demeaning attitude, not paying attention.

"You're not listening, Stevie. Why am I bothering to help you?" David started to get up, waiting for the curiosity factor to kick-in.

"Sorry, please finish your story."

"That's better. I hate talking to brats who can't concentrate for less than two seconds, and who rudely yawn in my face. Now, listen up. I didn't know what they looked like at first. One of them was an exceptional beauty, but more importantly, mentally. She had a dream-like Spirit, believing the whole world was a passing phase in one's life, to gather strength to venture forth into the next reality. The woman reached out into no-man's land, because she never left her house. Can you imagine being terrified of your own looks? She would have been captivating on screen, but the idea held no interest for her. Both women wrote articulately, with each letter received full of powerfully moving vignettes of their lives, where they lived, what was happening there--a treasure trove of real life--I loved it. They had strong personalities, yet protected themselves far more than we do. Both would have made excellent grounding partners for this flaky actor, and would have never taken advantage of who I was, if I am somebody at all."

"Why did they write to you? If they were so smart and attractive, they would have been snared." The callous insult, of two women he admired, upset David. It was not Steven's place to berate his new friends.

"Don't ever be cruel with your words, Kincaid, when you know nothing. You're definitely not one to talk." LaCoix's stern command brought back the man's sensitive side. Steven retracted his first statement, to reiterate the question without the undue verbiage, while David continued, "For the same reason strangely enough. Having seen several of my films, enjoying the performances, they thought it only polite to tell me. They wanted nothing more than an ear to listen, for they had no one else. My reply surprised them both, never believing they would or wanted to receive a reply. Rather comical in a way."

"You're pulling my leg, LaCoix."

"Nope. As for why they hadn't hooked-up, as you so crudely put it, I think their intellect scared men off; and they weren't the type to take second best. Do you now understand this very important concept, Mr. Kincaid? We *Glitter Town* folk are trapped in arranged marriages, often caught by the repetitiously seductive love scenes. Few relationships last, because they are not true of heart; and the saddest part, we do it to ourselves without a second thought." The natural blond saw the puzzled look: he was winning. David sparked some intrigue in Kincaid, to help him out of his self-absorbed and self-destructive path. "Once I started weeding out the letters of substance, and eliminating the outrageous, I discovered a lot of very nice people out there. Many of them are loners, expressing their thoughts in written form. It's become a habit of mine to write a few simple notes after a day's shoot. All I'm saying, Stevie, is your so-called *public*, which we snarl at with distaste, are individuals who seem more beautiful and far more refreshing than the many false faces with whom we work. You remember real life and how exciting it was. Our world is of the pretend. I'm not saying our entire industry is shallow minded, but I do see it as a general impression. Out of the hundreds I know, I could count less than a handful of people who I could rely on or consider a close friend."

"So you're suggesting I try this? I find my ultimate lover in my fan mail?" Steven shook his head and laughed.

"Why not, it wouldn't hurt? I wouldn't count on a lover, but at least a friend who just happens to like you for you. What else are you going to do, besides mope around and wonder why Ethan turned into a mad dog after his first taste of blood?" With a quick reminder of his past, LaCoix had him. If nothing else, it would keep the man occupied.

"That's gross."

"That's exactly what happened. Now, get on the telephone to your assistant, and have her or him send you all the latest mail you received from men. That should cut down the quantity by millions. Even the gushy ones can be pure delight for a deflated ego, and you are losing air by the minute, Kincaid." David got up and started for the door.

"You really think this could work? How do I write them and not sign my name? They could lead me down some sordid path, and then publish the letters. My notes could be worth millions of dollars with an authenticated signature." Captured in David's maze, Kincaid's eyes twinkled at the thought, and his mind started working overtime.

David turned back and shook his head. "Hollywood paranoia strikes again. You have to trust yourself before you can a stranger. Even within your circle of dimwitted friends, I bet you can't put your faith in any of them. You haven't found one close friend in Hollywood, have you?" David hit a sore point, and thought he might have pushed the man backward.

"I have you and Scarecrow, I hope."

"Of course you do, and always will. We consider you family, but we can't be all you have. In each letter, the person writing will reveal something identifying you to them, and vice versa. It's a puzzle, but you'll find a way if interested. As my friend said, you have the biggest dating service coming to your studio door with countless letters per day; a sure guarantee someone will intrigue you. Now, I have a date with my daughter, and we're then dining with Ted. See you in the morning. Don't let the ghosts get you." David laughed and departed with the scent of lilacs drifting passed.

He heard her giggling merrily. The message had been for Kincaid, delivered by a trusted human Fate. Maybe Steven would find someone outside his close circle of trendy friends. They were a group of silly people who did not even know him, or really care. As stars, or rising ones, they clutched the famous tuxedo tails, hoping their image would forever grace the front of a magazine, standing beside Steven Kincaid. David knew the fact well, as he counted the starlets he had slept with, and who now donned only celebrity status.

Remembering the scent of lilacs, David called for Lavender, while walking down the long hallway of rosewood doors. The chuckling in his head stopped; and he mentally asked her of Peerce. He heard a soft sigh, then the silence of a long pause.

'You are awakening to a new world order, LaCoix. Do not concern yourself with Peerce. You know my powers are strong, used in many ways. Let us say, you need not worry of saving Stevie from him again. Now on his own journey, he left the young man to carry on with his own life, with the advice I passed to you. I am very proud of you for remembering, and trying it yourself. As you guessed, you did not win the fight per ce, but most certainly the battle. Enjoy your walk. I will be there if you need me.'

Without any confirmation of what had become of Peerce, or that it had been her plan to get Kincaid back to following his desired goals, David could only assume he had won the first round of something. He laughed to himself, and through the silent halls, a whisper floated from his mouth at the revelation. "You never lie to me, Lavender, but you do tend to omit the entire truth. I'm going to assume you let me win to save Kincaid. I'll take your silence as a confirmation; and you may be overloading me with too much responsibility. Does the term *flaky actor* ring a bell? See you outside, your Ladyship." He heard her laugh; and the feel and scent of her presence vanished.

CHAPTER 40

David seemed to be starting a pattern of standing outside large doors, taking in much needed air to maintain his stoic façade. His chronic mental exhaustion worsened with every worry. He knocked; a small, excited voice invited him to enter. Another emotional task awaited; but he could count on Holly's optimism to level his mood. Before opening the portal, he wished upon wish she would take this well. A monsoon seemed to be washing him away, with tears from all corners, even his own. His mind remained on Barrett whose heart had been given freely; and that knowledge elevated his own Spirit to grow in strength, believing he could handle whatever came. He opened the door to achieve his ultimate goal.

Maria completed adjusting the last bit of rain paraphernalia on a happy little head. With a yellow sou'wester, neatly tied in a bow, under Holly's pretty chin and glowing smile, LaCoix grew more proud of his daughter. Brilliantly open-minded, she absorbed everything, and understood in her special way; innocent to all that surrounded her, she took whatever occurred in her life as a symbol, or a need of something greater. Never able to explain her ability in the words of a six-year-old, she just did it. Between Susan and himself, their genes produced an exquisitely attractive child, physically and mentally, and not a dull lusterless Barbie doll with little to say. Miss LaCoix would grow gracefully, each year becoming more striking. It made his heart set sail with the winds of an oncoming change.

Ready to depart, they set off to find new Faery rings. David guessed they would be in the garden; with boundaries set, his daughter would not slip in her excitement by showing him something outside her borders. Entering the rose garden, there they grew: two perfect circles of mushrooms, one slightly smaller than the other, entwined in a symbol of unity on a small patch of grass. It delighted them both, and the identical smiles shone through the softening rain.

Holly stood there, pinwheels whirling in her head, and her expression changed to one of mischief. With something up, accompanied by a request of her Dad for the clippers he carried, he became increasingly intrigued. On these excursions, they would often snip the flowers, in need of plucking, to help speed the creation of new blossoms. Never touched were the wildflowers, only occasionally disturbed when carefully walked through; for the homes of Faeries and Elfin creatures lay amidst their bright array of yellows, purples, pinks, blues, oranges, and reds, and their favorite greens.

"Be careful, Holly. Do you need help?"

"I can do it. Got my gloves on." She disappeared amongst the bushes, leaving David vigilantly standing guard over the rings. According to his daughter, they could easily disappear. It gladdened his heart that the fanciful winged-ones left them until his return.

"Are you okay in there, or have you run away with Oberon?" David chuckled, hearing the giggle on recognition of the name.

"Oh Dad, Oberon's the King, and Titania is the Queen. Remember? I'm the Princess." The small voice precisely pronounced the ancient names somewhat breathlessly, while struggling with something a bit difficult for her to handle.

"Are you sure, your highness?" Only gone a week, David had missed the enchantment of Holly's flights of imagination; and the stories she wove around the mystical beings.

"Got them; I'm coming." She hustled out of the bushes, scraping her rubber and plastic attire, rustling like the flight of a thousand butterflies. The familiar sound reminded David of a time past, when his new life began; he closed his eyes to remember. The green sparklers flickered open when the large sunflower emerged from the foliage. In her bright yellow rain gear, he could never lose sight of his daughter, not even in the dark. "Pretty, aren't they, Dad; a present for the Faeries' kindness."

"Sorry, I didn't know we were to leave gifts. I don't have anything for them." David apologized to his daughter and nature's circles.

"They accept wishes, dreams, and always a dance or song. You have to show them you're grateful. You always have a gift in your head." She had that look of not understanding why her father, the knower of all things, would miss something of such great importance.

"Of course, so what are we giving them?"

"Our wishes." Holly showed her father two roses she had clipped; a perfect white one and the darkest red bloom she could find.

David smiled in wonderment, while accepting the clippers and watching his daughter delicately handle the easily bruised petals. "What made you think of roses?"

"Sir Lancelot. I asked him what they meant in the picture."

"What did he say?" David grew very tense. Obviously, this Spirit Keeper, hiding inside a bear, never held back from answering any kind of question, no matter how personal.

"Mr. Barrett and you are good friends; and I have to get to know him. He's going to be with us for a long time." She looked directly at him; and he wished he could veer his eyes away from the trusting look.

"I hope so, Holly, if you agree."

"Do you love him, like you loved Mommy?" At the mention of her late mother, the voice quivered slightly. It had not been that long.

"I miss her too, but I know your mom liked Mr. Barrett. I love him, Holly. Can you understand that I need an adult to stand beside me; and he needs me just as much?" David knelt in front of her, deep in the damp grass, soaking his knees through his pants.

"Are you going to marry him?" The chin tilted to look straight into her own likeness, not knowing if she wanted this or not.

"It's different between men. I can't explain it, but will it bother you to see me kissing him, or holding his hand, making him part of our family? It will just be the three of us, like the Musketeers."

"I sure like him better than that Rebecca person. He needs us more; that's important."

"Yes, he does, and it's very important." David chuckled a little wistfully, but received a happy grin from his daughter.

"That's what the roses are for. Sir Lancelot told me it would keep you together forever. By tomorrow morning, they'll be gone; and our wish will be granted." Holly delicately laid the perfect blossoms; one to a center of each enchanted circle of mushrooms, firmly believing her spell would work. Holding back tears of monumental joy, David unleashed his broadest grin.

"Thank you, Honey, for a beautiful wish." LaCoix picked her up and held on for his life's worth, and for Ted's happiness as well. "I need you to understand something. People may say terrible things about me and Mr. Barrett." He squeezed his magical creature tighter, never wanting to release her to the cruelty of the real world.

She leaned back and looked at the wet eyes. Pulling off her glove, a tiny hand wiped the streaks away from her father's face. "Then they're not very nice people. I want a family, Dad, a big one. Are those happy tears?"

"Very happy tears; and we will have a big family, just a different kind, like the addition of your new Uncle Steven. You're a wise little girl, and you're mine, mine, mine." David kissed her face three times, until she giggled merrily along with him. Finally done, the one person, who could destroy two men's lives, gave them her blessing.

"And you're mine, and so is Granddad and Grandma. We phone each other now. I didn't tell you because you left to get Mr. Barrett. I think they like me."

"I bet they do. You'll be your Granddad's favorite Morning Glory." Suddenly attacked with a new terror, he had spent the last six months making up with his estranged parents; and this new scandal could ravage the rekindled relationship. They had to hear the news before the announcement, and the consequences dealt with appropriately. After he shattered their world again, Holly may be his only link to his parents. The blow nearly crushed him.

"Can I tell them we're having a wedding?" A child, beyond her years, who understood everything in its literal and simplistic form, pledged to help in her excitement. She made her father smile, and he believed that his daughter could handle an alternative family better than either he or Ted.

"Your old man has to tell them first; and we had better leave the idea of a *wedding* for later. I don't think the *bride* would appreciate it just yet."

"That's funny; men aren't brides; they're grooms."

"You're right. We'll think of another word before Mr. Barrett jumps ship. Listen, Honey, because something else needs explaining. You know he is very sick; and we lost your mother suddenly. It will be very hard on us both, if..."

"...if Mr. Barrett goes to live with Mommy in the Spirit World?"

"Can we pretend he's getting better to help him out, by always thinking in our heads that he is healthy and safe?" This gray day had David finally admitting his fears about Ted, expecting little time. Shattered within, he stayed strong for his daughter, preparing her for whatever may occur. Ill equipped to handle what he perceived through his fright, he focused on a sunny future for them all. Juggling the impossible, he felt Lavender warn him, but this time with extreme gentleness. She comprehended his reasoning and misgivings. "No tears now. We have to make the best of everything we do, and always think happy thoughts. Agreed?"

"I promise, Dad, and promise to love Mr. Barrett."

"And I love you, Holly Jane. Let's put on our happiest smiles and return to the house. We have to leave the Faeries and Elves to their important task of wish granting." He put her down and took his daughter's hand. The melancholy disappeared with a little more coaxing of the fun the three would have. She began dancing and skipping along beside him, no longer a care in the world, if David could be as lucky.

He entered his room quietly. Sleeping soundly, Ted appeared enveloped in a halo. LaCoix quietly checked the exhausted figure who twitched slightly at the touch to his cheek. Drawing in a deep breath, he had to make the call while he still had the spine. Picking up the dreaded phone, which allowed him access to the far corners of the room, he could converse unheard. A window, to view special memories reflected back, or one to transport him into the misty world beyond, seemed the perfect place to say the right words. The telephone rang once--twice--trepidation willed him to hang up before someone answered. Too late, his mother answered and commenced doting on her granddaughter, while calling for his father. They could now speak over each other, with a clear line and no static to deliver him from something he could retract.

David heard the delight in his parents' voices over Holly Jane. Being their only son, they could not help but love her, the one grandchild who contacted them on her own fruition. The day would be happy, when they saw her for the first time, and then hopefully the introduction of Bryce and Tyler. Ted's inclusion depended on their acceptance of his next words; but the lavish praise of his ability to help his child, with her grievous loss, had him in indecisive turmoil. Acclamation to disappointment would be over in an instant. Carefully and cautiously, he took over the conversation. There seemed no way to prepare them for such news; and he blurted out the announcement. He found a partner for life, a partner who happened to be male. The silence and long pause nearly killed him, waiting for the slam of a receiver. It never came. Now what was he supposed to say?

His mother started first. Hesitantly, and with a definite waver in her voice, she congratulated him, and asked if he was the man Holly mentioned. David quietly acknowledged the fact; and she started to cry. His father's turn had his son gnawing his fingernails. With no anger, no disgust, only a simple question came forth: would it make him happy? Adamantly confirming he never felt better, and with the assurance that Holly fully agreed, he received their awkward consent without a spoken word. Further hesitant conversation turned to the question of Theodore Barrett and the courts. Shocked at the devastation the man had gone through, the concern of both his parents gave David a reason they accepted the arrangement; they felt badly for his lover, truly wishing him well. If it had been any other man, they may not have accepted the strange twist in his life. Sadly, Ted's problems became David's key to fulfillment. A thoughtful surprise caught him off stride, when his father wished for two granddaughters to meet. After another long pause, the stalwart David LaCoix burst into tears.

No matter the age, family support meant everything; and he received all the nurturing his parents could send through an electronic device. He cried all his life's sorrows and joys into the phone. First stunned by their son taking a gay partner, the news gave them the chance to share his family, and to accept their wayward child for who he was and had always been. He needed them more than he ever had. Time came, for Mr. and Mrs. LaCoix, to accept something immensely important in their son's unsettled life; they would not dismiss his needs and dreams again.

Expressed in a sobbing stutter, he thanked them. A tearful farewell left three LaCoix emotionally unraveled. David laid down the phone quietly and sank into one of the high-backed chairs in front of the fire. Barely able to support himself, David's one arm came in handy to rest his head on the still clenched fist, while the other hand returned to his mouth to rip into his nails. David heard and sensed nothing, not even his shivering, from the wet pants he still wore. Alone, he struggled to gather himself from so many emotional events. Numb from his toes to his nose, only his brain functioned fractionally. A future required planning for a new family, with a new baby added to the mix of two emotional wrecks, and one little girl holding them together. An unexpected touch to his shoulder startled him, and he knocked his head against the hard cast upon jolting upright. "Ouch! Ted! You scared the... You're walking!"

"Sort of, this chair is doing most of the work. I think I better sit down." Ted looked like the ghost of the manor house, swaying slightly on his weakened, bruised legs.

"Can you walk around, or should I help you?"

"Help." A comical plea, from a man who had reached his limit of endurance, gave David reason to chuckle.

"Okay, take this chair, just a few steps to go." The nearly vanquished blond relinquished his seat for the man he carefully supported. Ready for any necessary action, he watched closely. With tremendous caution and a heavy lean to one side, Ted inched his way around the chair, and with assistance, came to rest on the throne big enough for a giant. Once settled, a heavy sigh, a thank you, and his head resting against the tapestry of green, the young man smiled up at his sworn Knight in wet pants.

"You're voice is sounding normal, just a little raspy."

"I always talk like this."

"Bad set of lungs and a throat constriction from bronchitis, I expect." Trivial, but enjoyable conversation deemed necessary for David; a small dose of family intimacy of life's day-to-day goings-on.

"Someone described it as the inside of a hushed Rolls Royce going over gravel."

"Maybe an octave higher purr than a Rolls." LaCoix chortled while he delicately cushioned Ted in the oversized chair.

"You look tired, LaCoix; have I given you a bad day?"

"Quite the contrary, although it's been one of the longest stretches in days I've put in for some time. We survived the flight; Holly's happy at our news; my parents gave us their blessing; and you brighten my world just looking at you."

"So, plastic turns you on. Did you kiss me? Don't remember anything of this past day." Putting on his best poker face, Ted baited his hero, one with a long list of quests. He heard the man's tears and the beautiful good-bye, ending a torturous deed successfully. Shaking off his lightheadedness, Ted braved the short, unstable journey to bring his caring to his protector, who held up his end too long. Time for laughter and a much-needed release of tension, Ted wanted to please and lift the weight off the man's shoulders, if he could just keep his stomach in place and his head from spinning off.

"So, you don't remember anything? Too bad, I don't feel like telling you anything now." David shrugged and smiled at the pretense of disappointment. At the sound of the weary sigh, and seeing the involuntary shiver, it took but a minute for the healthy man to snatch a couple of blankets and tuck them around the ailing one.

"Okay, let's just say I forgot the kiss and need a refresher." The sadly missed ray of sunshine once again blazed throughout the room with his quiet charm, changing even the dreary day to blue skies. With all his possible demons defeated for now, David eagerly yearned to give his partner more than a kiss. The refresher intensified, with Ted parting his mouth at a breath, allowing the expertise of a damp tongue to tantalize and penetrate him. A little groaning on both men's parts started a heightened ravishment of each other's lips. Two very needy men had to stop. They wanted to go on forever, but a broken cheek and hip were in the way, not to mention two restricted arms, useless for the art of making love.

Ted disagreed, not wanting to stop, and gasped for air when his favorite taste moved away. Insufficiently appeased with a caress to his forehead, the younger man begged, "Touch me, David.

It doesn't hurt, I swear; I need you inside me. I know you want me too. I need you so much, but I don't know how to tell you what I want. It's a different kind of ache." One arm reached up, and the tips of a few fingers latched onto the black turtleneck sweater. Ted wanted it off, to touch the skin beneath, to feel its warmth, and to smell the heady scent of David LaCoix.

"You're still bruised, Baby. You have to be uncomfortable, tired, and certainly dizzy. I don't want to hurt another part of you."

"Please, it's been so long." Ted's pleading continued, until the older man lifted him off the chair and back onto their bed.

"You really do want me out of these saturated pants. How do I make you feel good, plastic-man, and not hurt you?" David tapped the protective coating, knowing what he needed, but concerned if Ted could handle it. His skittish, young lover could easily regress several paces.

"Do whatever you want. I can't even play with myself." Ted's exposed fingers grappled at the man's clothing, panting in his haste to give of himself, without a thought of the possible pain. He only wanted to feel his promised partner fondle his most delicate of organs, nearly healed but ready to play, and his chipped hip unnoticed while lying down. Gazing up through his dark lashes, he trembled slightly at the recognition of desire in his lover's green eyes. Ted watched, as one layer at a time slowly came off, and his heart raced. With the wet denims unzipped, his lover peeled them off in a tease, inch-by-inch from the hips, exposing the bulge entrapped by a spandex thong of black, to continue down the muscled but slim legs. They went on forever, and every body movement rippled under the skin, like the surface of a fast running river, then to harden at a blast of frozen air. Beyond handsome, no one compared to David in looks, right down to his feet, where the pants ended their journey, but neatly tossed aside with a kick. Over the head and tortuously slow, the sweater came off, ruffling the straight blond hair and spiking it upward with electrical sparks. David loved to play seductive games with wanton victims of his charms. Ted was no exception, tingling at the sight of the flat abdomen, well-chiseled chest, and swelling crotch.

"Guess I better lock the door, Teddy Bear. Looks like you're ready under those sweats?"

Nodding, Ted's eyes followed the man turning toward the only exit, and intently focused on the smooth, carved buttocks, while his mobile fingers scratched unsuccessfully to seize the sheet on which he lay. The object of his attention flexed with each step, creating a pulsating reaction of the younger man's sphincter muscles; and he ached deep within. David's body belied his forty-three years, and the sight, smell, and touch of it held Ted captive. He heard the thud of the ancient bolt; and the long, lean frame walked stealthily toward him. With the lion ready to pounce, the cub lay still, panting heavily, waiting.

David climbed onto the bed, made for the king of beasts, and straddled the man whose forehead glistened with beads of salty liquid. Gasping, Ted needed more air; he inhaled deeply. The blandishment of fingers slid under the elastic waistband of the overly warm sweat pants, and sensually pulled them down an inch at a time. A kiss to his lower abdomen ignited his erection further, catching it in the confines of fleece. Whimpering enough for his lover's satisfaction, a little gentle manipulation exposed Ted's purple veined, agitated cock.

"You're beautiful, Baby. You still have a few scabs that could break. Does it hurt?"

A shake of the head, Ted's bright eyes gazed up into the green laughing stars. With his head swimming, he concentrated on every feature and line of the remarkable face. It stopped him from passing out, as had become his custom when aroused. A soft tickle ran down his legs when the flannel slipped off and over his socked feet. Skinny limbs trembled in anticipation when talented fingers ran up the inside, from bottom to top, and then spread them apart. Sliding in between, David leaned over and kissed him. Two men exchanged breath for breath, moan for moan, and taste for taste. Rock-hard and sweating profusely, they playfully touched foreheads, then noses, and another soft brush of lips. David sat back on his feet, to watch Ted's organ dance and twitch on the sunken stomach, waiting impatiently for help, in its urgency to come to full life. With the grin of the Cheshire cat and his slightly closed bedroom eyes, David's concern became the gratification of his forever partner, putting a genuine smile back on his pale face.

Releasing the thong at the back, David's manhood tumbled lose, ready and searching for a nesting place, like a hound on the scent. Ted squealed in excitement, pulling his battered knees up and spreading his thighs. Hands were under his cheeks, lifting them up, and forcing them further apart. He willed his muscles to relax, as the silky ball, wet with pre-cum, hit the crease, and slid to the entry of the relaxed opening. A mouth engulfed the scream, and with a little push, David entered. A little further in, Ted's eyes widened in pain. He pulled away from the kiss, and bit his lip, suddenly straining against his lover's advances. Breathing heavily, David readied himself to take his first full lunge, perspiring with his heaving chest slick for the tasting.

"No. Stop." Ted's face cringed in agony, and his only desire withdrew immediately.

"It's okay, Baby. Shush. It's okay." David rested his chest on the plastic cast and swept the hair back off the wet brow. The grimace on the boyish face remained, and the blue eyes clenched tightly.

"It's not okay. It's not; but it hurt."

"My fault; I should have used a lubricant."

"No, it's not that. I'm sorry. I thought my back and hip were better, but they're not. Why should it hurt my back?" Ted wanted to sink into a hole, never to peek out at the world again. Having taunted his lover into making love, he had to reject him, leaving them both unsatisfied.

"Settle down, Ted; you're tired and it hasn't been a week. Now let me try something. Tell me if it hurts." David eased backward and crouched between the trembling thighs, never taking his eyes off what he could see of the dismayed face, now covered with a plastic arm. Slipping the straining, twitching organ between his tightening lips, and with all due care, began a long seductive suck and tongue licking to his unhappy lover. It took only minutes for his relatively inexperienced partner to gush sporadically into his mouth, and the tasty treat swallowed. After a long withdrawal, and no need to clean up any residual mess, the sensitive blond actor lifted the left thigh, to flutter butterfly kisses from the inside knee to beneath the scrotum. Laying it down gently, the right thigh received the same tender gesture, accompanied by a soft purr from the recipient.

"Feeling better?"

"Much. Thanks. You're too good to me."

"My pleasure. I think I felt something, which may have caused your pain." Weary and bursting with his own need, David played doctor, reaching for a tube of lubricant inside the bedside table drawer. With a little on his finger, he penetrated the willing orifice. A feel forward, specifically to the prostate, a touch left, then right, and finally, the one to the back yielded a yelp and a tightening of muscles. It stopped any further investigation. He withdrew and looked at his finger: no blood. The pain resulted from rubbing against the end of the spine.

"I'm only guessing, Ted, but it appears you may have broken your tailbone. Let's roll you over." With some maneuvering, and not a sound from a grim-faced Mr. Barrett, Ted lay uncomfortably on his stomach, until David placed a pillow under him to ease the stretch of his body created by his cast. Relieved of his one frustration, now another filled his mind. It passed with a sensitive hand on his lower back, rubbing it gently from his waist to beyond the crease of his arse. The light up and down strokes of one finger, along his lower spine, relaxed him, until it reached between his cheeks and touched the tip of his last five fused vertebrae. David confirmed the problem; and Ted burst into tears.

Distraught as his lover, LaCoix lay beside him, stroking the hair until the disappointment and tears subsided. "We'll take it very slow, Ted. No bouncing around, but now we know the problem. I can still finger play inside you, if you like. It would certainly be a pleasure for me."

"Yeah, but what about you? I can't believe this. Has anything gone right?"

"I'm pretty respectable at taking care of myself, and a few things have gone my way." David combed his fingers through the bleached waves and smiled at the forlorn man.

"I guess, but it's not fair. How can I..."

"You can't, until your casts are off, which leaves sufficient time for all your breaks to heal. I fear this new discovery will remain in that position. Feels rather erotic rubbing against it; at least the one time I managed to touch it. I can wait; and we can still make love in some fashion. You okay with that?" With the same reassuring grin, he tried to cheer up his lover. David chuckled lightly, hearing the tone of his voice: his inflections and softening voice sounded paternal, and Ted was twelve again.

"I'm so sorry. Are you angry?" With his he last sniff, Ted pushed himself up with one cast, to roll with aid onto his side.

"Of course not, since we found the problem. The injury will heal. It's not a rarity; ask any woman who had trouble in childbirth. I bet that's why the tube, up your arse, hurt so much; it rubbed against the painful point, and no one checked it."

"Let's e-mail the green man and give him hell."

"He did seem perplexed as to the problem, but nothing would have helped."

"So what have you been doing without me? Can I be of assistance?"

"You, Mr. Barrett, can only watch if that is to your liking. Actually, it turns me on thinking about it; I've never masturbated for an audience. It's a rather private thing." The action hero received a wide-eyed look and a nod of a shaggy head. With the simple approval, he leaned over and gave his lover a lip peck. Whatever his Teddy Bear wanted to witness would be his privilege to supply the pleasure. David pushed his pillow away to lie flat on his back, his erection bobbing for a controlling influence. Green eyes turned to stare into the wells of blue filled with sweet bliss, while he masturbated himself into oblivion. With delicate kisses delivered to the straining face and neck, his nipples pinched and tickled by a moist, hesitant tongue, he splashed out his life's essence, bucking with each jerk through his own firm hands. This was the essence that created Bryce and Tyler; the essence that produced Holly; and now the essence that would fill his sworn partner until he had no more to give. Breathing hard, his hand came up, and urgently licked clean, by the man whose head rested on his shoulder. As satisfied as the first time he entered Ted's silken delights, he needed nothing else but this creature beside him.

After a short uncomfortable cuddle for the feel, a few sweet caresses for the taste, some nuzzling of the hair for the scent, and a little purring of contentment from Ted, this encounter ended the long wait for their senses to be filled and enjoyed. David slowly got up. One more kiss to the morose face, he disappeared to shower and change. Returning to Ted's side, he lavished his troubled partner with a sensual sponge down, to titillate the man further; and with a smirk, ended the cleaning with a sudden cold towel over a hardening response to his kindness. It brought on an outburst of squeals, giggles, and curses, but Ted came out of the ordeal cleaner, fresher, and jovial.

Now dressed in pale blue sweats, socks, and white sneakers, to warm the shivering goose bumps, Ted sat in his Gothic throne, warming under a few blankets by the fire. David found himself wanting a cigarette, while his lover yearned for liberation to make things right. A tap on the locked door brought a diversion. Since he felt incapacitated to do anything, Ted waited for the latch to be unbolted for the butler, who would prepare the table for dinner. In the perfect seat to witness the trivial, he eased back into the cushioning comfort provided by his hero. Time to forget his problems, he watched with interest as an artist elaborately decorated a round table. More akin to a royal dinner than a high tea, he grinned in appreciation at the regal butler, who gave him a knowing, friendly wink. It flustered him, but it increased his smile. His first family evening, he looked forward to something special. The final touches and candles sparked to life, and the fire stoked to blaze brilliantly, the expected rap on the door was answered. The butler discreetly departed, allowing the diminutive guest entry. The third member of their party arrived, dressed head to toe in Ted's pale blue, including the ribbons, probably stamped with the seal of approval from Sir Lancelot. Ready for a welcoming party for Mr. Barrett, Holly giggled eagerly for the fun.

"Good evening, Miss LaCoix. You look nice; and we match. I don't have those amazing blue sneakers though." Ted breathed in deeply, relieved to see the excitement in her entrance, with no hesitation in approaching him. He spoke first, attempting to ingratiate himself with his greatest surprise; he had, or would soon have, a six-year-old daughter.

"I have them in every color, even purple. I'll show them to you tomorrow, Mr... what should I call you?"

"Whatever you like, Sweetheart." Amazed at how easily she accepted a startling new situation, Ted wondered if she understood that her world would turn asunder after the public announcement. She radiated more confidence than he did.

"We came up with something, but your daughter's not yet with us, Ted, or even old enough to call you anything." The words came out before he thought. David immediately recognized his error, when the blue eyes fell to study the shuffling feet, which could not touch the floor. LaCoix wanted to kick himself around the manor house, with boots fitted with climbing irons.

"You have a little girl?"

"Mr. Barrett has a daughter whom we're attempting to gain custody. Will you be okay sharing us with a baby?" David took two strides to stand at Ted's side, enabling him to watch over both the sullen man and the little girl dancing in front of him.

"A baby! Will she be my sister? I always wanted one." Jumping with exuberance in her blue sneakers, she could not control the little shriek.

"She's just a tiny little thing, Holly." Ted tried to look happy; but David heard the sadness, as did his daughter. The younger LaCoix reacted first.

"A baby will call you Daddy, Mr. Barrett. I can call you that too, if you like?" She skipped over in a rush of excitement, to brush a kiss over Ted's cheek. It had two men close to babbling and crying like a pair of proud parents over their child's first word.

"That's perfect, Honey; Dad for me, and Daddy for Mr. Barrett."

"I accept the name gratefully, Holly." Ted choked at the overwhelming surge of happiness and sadness combined. Both could create the same response in the emotional water sign.

"What's her name?"

"I haven't decided, and she may not..." Talking about his daughter hurt deeply within the new father. With battle lines drawn, miles away, nervous trepidation settled on frail shoulders.

"Okay, you two. Let's get to the table and ring for the man to bring dinner. I'm starving. We'll talk while we eat, just like grown-ups. What do you say, Holly? You sit in your normal chair, and I'll help Ted." David immediately took charge, hoping a lighter conversation could disperse the black cloud shrouding his promised partner, and unveil a bit of the mystery for his daughter.

"It sure looks pretty tonight, doesn't it, Daddy?"

The use of his new name and status caught Ted off guard, unsure whether to answer. David eased him to his feet, but the question spun his head around and he lost his balance. Now completely unraveled, he felt his tall partner lean over him, rubbing his one shoulder for reconciliatory comfort. "Everything's fine, Ted, just answer the question. You have to get used to the name and unexpected surprises."

"Easy for you to say." The lips whispered into the closest ear, and then he turned to call across the large room. "It sure does, Holly. Is it like this every night?" Ted managed to stand semi-erect, his nerves settling, and hoping he made sense.

"Good job, Daddy." Another hidden whisper came from David, as he wiped the perspiration off the panicked face.

"Not every night. They usually don't give me a glass like Dad's."

"It's a wine goblet. I think you'll see milk in yours." The biological father continued to keep the dialogue going, while lending a supporting arm to his partner.

"What are you doing, Dad?"

"Me? Nothing." David looked up startled; maybe he should not be touching Ted. He immediately jerked his arm away, causing Barrett's body to lurch forward. Those quick LaCoix reflexes snapped into action, only to hit the sore hip. Cringing in pain, the younger man continued to fall, until another rapid movement secured him without further mishap.

"Pick him up. He hurts; he's dizzy; and Daddy can't walk by himself." Holly slipped off her chair to help Ted stay upright. Using both her arms, she locked them around his thigh. A look of terror was shot at David, who shook his head and gave him a wink. Having never been touched by a child, not even to hold a hand, Ted froze to stone by this intimate gesture. LaCoix almost laughed aloud when he thought of Ted learning about squirming, unknowing, little girls who could knock you senseless with an accidental knee or heel to the crotch. An exciting new world was opening for his innocent; and he and Holly had to teach him.

"It's okay, Honey; let go and sit down. I've got him." Physically and mentally worn out, David had to get through this with his faculties intact. He felt Ted shaking, but it seemed inappropriate for quiet whisperings in front of his daughter. She let go, but remained standing too close. "Please, Holly, go sit down." David begged her once more to move, while picking up and carrying the featherweight, in full upper body armor, over to the table. "How's this, Ted? Still feeling dizzy?"

"I'm fine, thanks." Not what was said, but how it was said, had the failing older actor stuck for a solution as to how to get his lover to act normally around his daughter.

With a sharp command, she gave him one. "Do something, Dad. Daddy's upset." The exasperated plea, for her father to respond quicker, demanded more orders. "Just hug him to make him feel better. He's really sad."

Ted's few mobile fingers, and part of his cast, immediately covered his face. His first meal with his new family turned deadly; he fell apart. As Holly had iterated, he needed a hug, and felt David enfolding him within caring arms and offering a neck to hide his shame.

"Okay, Teddy Bear, I've pushed you beyond your capacity to cope in two days. I'm sorry." David released his inhibitions, with his daughter's unorthodox permission, caressing the hair and kissing the wet face. Flipping out one of the intricately folded napkins, he dabbed at the swollen eyes. Barrett looked like a train-wreck, completely knocked off the tracks.

"I'm so sorry. I feel like shit. You didn't hear that word, Holly." Barrett barked a stern command while crying his eyes out. Not to throw off the man's innate paternal instincts, David continued to laugh in his head at the strange mix of sorrow, humor, and discipline.

"Dad says it all the time."

"I do? You'll have to start correcting us both." Back to light and trivial, family life commenced, taking a new shape, uniquely LaCoix.

Holly nodded, contemplating her father and her new one, unable to figure out their nervousness. She watched her daddy intently, wondering why her real father did not help him settle properly in the chair. Ted grimaced when he tried to get himself comfortable; and she felt badly that he felt so ill. They both turned solemn, as she did not know how to help.

David read her mind and returned to Ted's side, sitting on his haunches, gazing up into frightened eyes. "You're not feeling well, are you? Need another cushion? I'll have Bernard buy you one of those doughnut things. Can you manage sitting a little longer? You've got to eat, Ted."

"A cushion will help, and I'll try. I will. It's just... What if I don't get Willow?" The new father had become upset, when the attention shifted to his baby.

"We'll get her; just keep thinking of the picture of us all together. I'll get you something soft to sit on. Now, let's just relax and enjoy dinner when it arrives." In a quandary as to how to rectify a complex situation, David stood erect, grabbed a flat but soft cushion, helped Ted adjust to it, and sat down in his own chair still thinking. He immediately took a set of fingers on either side of him and squeezed them both. "Listen up, you two. Holly, we only have a small chance of getting Willow, and it's very upsetting for Daddy to think about losing her. Now, Ted, you have to get used to discussing your baby. We have a great deal of work to do, in the next few months, to try again. Do we all agree?"

"Sorry, Sweetheart. It's not your fault." Ted pulled himself together, relying heavily on the reassuring hand applying pressure to his fingertips.

"I'm sorry too. I'll be even sorrier if I don't get a sister." Holly peered dejectedly down at her plate. It shocked David to recognize himself, seeing the loneliness of being an only child. His daughter needed other childrens' companionship; and he remembered why, as a boy, he sought out any activity that gave him interaction with others. It struck hard; and Ted felt no better. Both sets of fingers received an increase in pressure, to match the strengthening hold placed upon his own hands. Saved by a rap on the door, the butler entered with their evening meal. Without shying away, David stayed his hands; and Holly reached over to touch the plastic shell of her

Daddy, completing the family circle. The three were left to themselves, all under duress.

"Can I ask a question?" Holly's melancholy permeated through two men, and her little face had trouble controlling the tears too close to the surface.

"Of course." David immediately took on the responsibility of head of the household to get them both smiling. His cadence changed to interest, with a touch of excitement. Not an actor for his face alone, his voice controlled a situation as a flute entranced a serpent.

Holly recognized the tone, immediately brightening; she had done nothing wrong, allowing her to continue. "Our baby's name is Willow, an Elfin name; I like it. What's her other one?"

"I haven't thought of one as pretty as yours." Once spoken, Ted's mouth clenched, forming a trace of a white line around his lips. With emotions bubbling underneath like hot lava pools, David prepared himself for the man's heart to give out.

"I can think of lots."

"I bet you can; and let me guess: Titania!" David laughed and saw a twinkle in her eye, and a small grin from the other side of the table. "Queen of the Faeries, Ted, the real Faeries; it's an ancient, mystical name." His green eyes filled with fun; and a game began to find Willow a name.

"I've never heard of it. Sounds unusual, but very pretty." It sparked Ted's fascination, a joy in itself for the other two.

"Dad's so silly sometimes, but I think I know a good one. It's best, because it's special to both of you."

"Something meaningful to us: any ideas, Ted?" David's eyes darted back and forth, watching his family to see who would falter first. The pair appeared to be recovering, showing interest in a game of creative thought, and certainly of relevance.

"I'm clueless. Having looked at, and pondered over, every name in every baby book, I'm completely confused. There are so many choices." Ted regained a hint of enthusiasm, the shaking stopped, and his face beamed radiantly at the little girl across from him. Another fine actor put on the happy theatrical mask.

Holly leaned over the table, avoiding smearing food on her clothes, and delicately plucked one of the yellow flowers from its nest. She handed it carefully to Ted whose mouth fell open; the blue sapphires were once again awash. He looked at David, then back at the child of wonder.

"Rose. Willow Rose." Holly whispered the name, while looking into the unusual eyes, which glittered like stars when wet; and her new Daddy smiled a real one.

"Perfect." Ted and David chimed in unison. They both laughed to brighten a little girl's face.

"Why didn't I think of it? So, Willow is a yellow rose, I'm a white one, your Dad's the black one, and just which one are you, Sweetheart?"

"All colors." This time, the other two voices rang out in unison, father and daughter laughed together in silliness. Two men and a six-year-old shared smiles, as a new family came together in harmony, giggling and chatting through the rest of the meal. The start had been unnerving, with the emotional day experienced by each in their respective way; and yet David wallowed in the essence of his own Utopia. Holly approved of the match; his parents blessed the controversial partnership; and Ted accepted his outrageous proposal, all understanding the ramifications. David LaCoix vowed to marry and sign his life away to the last love of his life; this script would end with *happily-ever-after*.

Lavender smiled and took in a deep breath, watching the new family squeeze together in a chair in front of the fire. Her handsome, blond-haired, leading man read a story neither daughter nor lover had heard. For the one who could not keep his eyes open, his life's fantasy came true, capturing the man he desired since his youth; loyalty of such devotion would last a lifetime. For David, his dream manifested itself, nestled comfortably around him. He had struggled so long for happiness, not knowing how to find it; his tumultuous lifestyle indicated that confusion, bringing him nothing he required. Now, in his hands, he would not give it back. With his forever partner surrounded by his arm, and his daughter, so much like him, leaning against his chest, David's rewards would come soon enough, and of a magnitude he could not conceive. With Ted's promise to remain at his side, he would take a giant step that the entire world would witness. Holly gained a second guardian, who would love and take care of her; with tiny fingers crossed, she may have a sister. The LaCoix family represented the start of an *awakening* to change earthly reality. Quiet for now, undisturbed by what lay ahead in the next months, only a few Fates stood in their way. This tiny group would handle the fiery demons, with grace and power, achieved under diversity. Convinced of their safety, the Mistress closed her veil of clouds.

CHAPTER 41

David opened his eyes, only to clench them tight with a grimace, in response to the jabbing pain in his armpit. His face came down to brush his chin against soft hair, and to catch the familiar enticing scent of candy-canes, lemongrass, and sex. The culprit, digging into his arm, was a plastic encased shoulder. Any kind of pain would be insignificant compared to the rapture of the gentle taking at midnight.

Although not a wildly ravishing romp in the ancient bed, with Ted too weak to handle any more than he had the previous afternoon, the passion still simmered on low. David played with the sensuality of a velvet rose to entice, and moist lips to kiss everything, from a ticklish bellybutton to his lover's toes. Ted tried to participate, hindered by the annoying casts and the newly found dilemma. Frustration won out, bringing on a melancholy mood for the young actor. A night of experimenting with their five senses changed into one of just being together, holding onto the moment.

David could not be happier; and yet there persistently loomed that *but*. Should they keep their affair silent, under the covers of satin and cotton, or bring it out to enjoy under the sun and moon? Disguising his nervousness behind the happy theatrical mask, he knew any hesitation on his part would send his butterfly flying in the opposite direction. Waking before the alarm, David still startled when it went off. Although antiquated, the method brought the actor to an immediate racing start. Morning at the manor began very early, but barely disturbed his partner. Ted snuggled back in, struggling for needed sleep after enduring an emotional week beyond any man's stoic abilities. Only seven days, David thought, and the battered, near-death Theodore Barrett lay comfortably where he should be, curled up next to him, protected within his arms and the cold, hard casts. Whether Ted's current fragility, both physically and mentally, could withstand an instant family situation and a controversial public announcement, after an ego-shattering hearing, had LaCoix biting his nails. A tap on the door, a little girl's voice made him smile. Forgetting all the insurmountable problems, he invited her in.

"Morning, Dad. Is Daddy still sleeping?" She rushed in, climbing like a monkey onto the high bed. Lying prone on top of her father's chest, she barely missed Ted's nose in her attempt to wriggle into her father's neck and one arm. Bursting with enthusiasm, at such an early hour, she kissed her Dad and the day began. "Are you ready? I've been waiting for you."

An unfamiliar peck on Ted's sore cheek surprised him into the English dawning. "What? Shit!" Fully awake, mortification set in swiftly, with the nose-to-nose intrusion of a bright, young female face.

"Not supposed to say that word."

"Oh, no, David, I'm... and so are..."

"Relax, everything's fine. Good morning; did you sleep well?" David kissed the furrowed scowl.

"Relax, are you nuts?" Ted's head poked out like a turtle coming out of its shell, pulling his thin neck higher out of the plastic casing.

"What's wrong, Daddy? Today's the day we tell everyone. I've wanted to tell since yesterday." She put her tiny hand on his cheek and gave him a baby kiss to his lips.

Ted's embarrassment ran up his surprised face, wondering if it the appropriate behavior for his new daughter; and even more frightening, was he covered. He glanced down, feeling his bare leg resting over David, and rubbing against the unfortunately referred to nuts. The heavy covers hid the infraction, but a little girl's torso sandwiched his smaller cast against the bare chest he had bitten and sucked on most of the night. More color flushed his cheeks, looking cross-eyed at one red mark directly in front of him. He closed his eyes in a cringe, afraid to move.

"Say good morning, Daddy." David lay within the confines of two bodies, thoroughly bemused with the squirming between the sheets.

"Hi, Holly, is this a habit of yours?" Ted slowly opened one eye and squinted at her.

"Get used to it, Ted. She's excited about announcing our betrothal." David laughed at the two stunned faces.

"Betrothal?" The word came out in unison: Ted shocked by the remembrance, and Holly not knowing its meaning.

"Without a large diamond on my finger? Never." The blond head, with the dark roots, tried to hide a little further into the larger body shaking with a chuckle.

"And spoil my surprise? Have some patience. When did you start liking glitz?" David's mirth made him laugh aloud at the sarcastic, but meaningful remark. "Go get ready, Honey. We need to shower and dress. We won't keep you waiting." David had his daughter off the bed and out the door in a flash. "Scared, hunh?"

"Shitless."

"Why?" David spoke softly and with caution. Everything had to be perfect this day.

"What do you think? We could have been lying here stark naked." Ted peered up to see the green eyes twinkling. This father business may be more difficult than he thought.

"We are naked. Feels good, especially where your knee and crotch are situated. How did we get you into this position? I like it."

"You think this is funny? What if she catches us..." Ted was annoyed; at what, he did not know; but his partner delighted in making it worse.

"...doing the dirty? You are fun to wake up with. My daughter knows what a man looks like, so if she catches you in the shower, or in a compromising position, carry on with what you're doing. It should be as natural as breathing."

"Easy for you to say. Simply carry on, while I'm kneeling in front of you, or my feet are reaching for the sky. It is true; you are an exhibitionist. I'll buy you a T-shirt."

"There are limits, Ted, just like any married couple. Just enjoy the freedom, like your preference of not wearing underwear."

"I'm starting today."

"Which reminds me: you might try some I've seen, which are extremely sexy. I'll ask Bernard to buy you a few pair when he's in London, something dazzling in color. I'm sure he'll know what size you are." The wildest grin taunted the man who scowled at him.

"He would, but sequined thongs and teat tassels? Is that your surprise? Still think I deserve a diamond." A pretend shudder, and a pout, warranted a morning ruffle of the disheveled hair.

David continued to smirk at the charmer attached to him like a bloodsucker. He completely understood the trepidation behind the dry humor and the need for reassurance. "We were safe, Baby. She knocked; we were covered; and I invited her in. It's crucial she sees her parents comfortable in the arms of the other; after all, that's who we'll be. She needs to feel love, not dissension; learned that over the past year or so. And, just so that cute pout disappears; it will be more spectacular than a diamond." David smiled at the eyes searching for his, from a very difficult position. "Roll over. How's your hip and back?"

"Feels best like this. Better than a diamond, hunh?"

"If you don't stop, you won't get anything. Now, if you'll excuse me, work awaits."

"Oh yeah, work; too bad." The operable fingers tickled the hard chest the world recognized in color, and in black and white. Too close to bite one nipple, Ted quickly swiped it with his tongue, earning him a growl of pleasure, along with a slap across the exposed digits ready to pinch.

"Oh, no you don't. I'm off to shower and call Bernard to help you." David could not stop chuckling, fully enjoying the morning, although difficult to pull away from someone so adorable.

"Bernard, great: he enjoys it too much."

"Five weeks and you can do it yourself. Besides, our friendly giant handles you like his prized poodle. I've watched him. Slightly unorthodox, not even stereotypical, but he's a good man: one unto himself."

"Now I'm a lap dog. You're all against me." Ted rolled onto his back, with little control, to ponder his predicament. A little girl, maybe two, running into their private chambers, just when Dad is busy rimming Daddy. He conceded to being a nervous wreck until their children left home. Now, Goliath sashayed into their room, ready to molest him. With one cast resting over his eyes, Ted lay there and moaned while stripped of his warm covers. "Morning, Bernard."

"And what a lovely sight to see this bright day."

"Oh brother." Ted sighed, closed his eyes, and waited for the inevitable.

Breakfast at the manor house went from normal disorder to sober silence. No one knew how to respond to Holly's theatrical proclamation. Bernard clapped with enthusiasm, appearing to be the only one genuinely overjoyed at the news. Tension hung over the rest of the table, as the newly acclaimed couple sat quietly, waiting for something: anything. David felt Ted controlling his need to purge the demons who stared at them. Only a mini announcement, what would happen when they opened the gates of hell and screamed it to an unforgiving world?

Steven Kincaid made the next move, standing up with a smile bursting across his face. He proposed a toast; and Ted had one ally who winked at him through a short congratulatory speech. David saw the eye exchange; and his sullen lover lit up briefly. Before Steven sat down, however, the two Morris boys, fifteen and thirteen, started snickering. The oldest one taunted Holly with a rude rhyme about her father being a fag who made love to fairies. His daughter had no understanding of the words but one, and only used in a positive context. The remarks grew more insidious; and she could do nothing but sit there in confusion. She recognized the nasty smirks, however, and they hurt worse than the words. David squinted at Rod and his wife. Neither moved nor helped, deep in thought, oblivious to their children's rudeness. With Holly in tears, and Ted close to breaking down, initiating further incredulous sneering, LaCoix slammed his fist down hard on the table. Everyone jumped. Not a Justin Evans thing of a simplistic game of children teasing each other, this was cruel.

A quick look at Bernard insured Ted's swift deliverance from the toxic room. You could hear him gagging on exiting the door. Another wild-eyed glance at Steven, and a few words to Holly about a day off from school, had Kincaid whisking the little girl into his arms and up the stairs, followed by a stunned Maria. David heard their friend endearing himself to Holly, enticing her sad little face into a smile, with the thought of exploring the woods together.

With his loved ones out of hearing range, he ripped into the two boys, displaying his displeasure with a voice that boomed and echoed through the dining room built for Dukes. Calling them every derogatory name, which came to mind, he scanned the room, hoping for some gesture of compensation from Rod. With the eldest son about to retaliate, his fist hit the table a second time, knocking a glass across the expanse, dumping its sticky contents over the youngest. The children sat motionless at the ferocity oozing from David LaCoix when ignited. This time his ire flared directly at the parents; and it was not kind. While the Morris' remained in shock from a profane verbal lashing, he growled venom at the boys, squinted menacingly at the innocent daughters, straightened his shoulders with due deliberation, and left the scene.

Breathing fire, he sprinted up the stairs to check on his own child. She did not understand what went wrong, or why they could be so hateful. Her father's rage, defending her, himself, and her Daddy, was easier to comprehend. Kincaid retrieved her from David's arms, and assured a harried father that he and Holly had wonderful plans of strolling through the forest, to talk about fairies and Faeries, nasty little boys, and the upcoming announcement. After a quick kiss and hug good-bye for his daughter, a grateful caress to Steven's cheek, a reassuring hug for Maria, David scrambled down one flight of stairs, stumbling along the hall to reach his own quarters: their quarters.

Bernard's distress glowered in a very showy display for the gentle man, and yet he caringly eased Ted into a semi-prone position against a stack of pillows, while wiping the perspiration off the face as white as the linen itself. With a firm nod and a determined angry expression, the brawny nurse readily agreed to tend them all. He rallied and flexed his muscles to defend the LaCoix team to the end.

"You okay, man?" David rushed to sit beside his partner, and squeezed the exposed fingers of one hand.

"That went well, as the expression goes." The tears never surfaced, but lay behind the wistful smile. Ted's second shock of the new morning, he maintained control.

"I thought you'd be more upset?" A helpful hand swept away the few strands of hair that clung to the long lashes.

"I am. Seems I'll have to develop the hide of an elephant, if we're going to do this." Ted kept his eyes downcast. One glance at David would have him drowning in the backwash, rushing his body out to sea.

"Regrets?"

"No, I'll deal with it. I want to, more than ever. Another cause to fight and a battle to win, making it four now, or is it five. It's okay, David, go to work. Bernard and Stevie will be here." Ted raised the hand holding his and kissed it.

"You, my forever one, continue to amaze me. I'll see you later. Guess our family of six will band together after this little foray." Another hug had David on the move. Rage could not describe how he felt over the behavior toward his daughter. Perhaps inappropriately timed to make the regrettable announcement, he could only blame himself. Irreversible words spoken, Holly and Ted bore the consequences. A great deal more wrath would scar his director. Too late to fire him, he knew he had the upper hand. This would not be an enactment of a spoiled actor, but one of an angry father and soon-to-be husband.

Seething, he clamored into one of the four cars rented with the manor; and it was not red. The dark-green, twelve-cylinder Jaguar spun its wheels less than a second, and surprisingly jumped into gear as quickly as the smaller, fiery, red ones. The car flashed in anger down the drive, like the green eyes behind the wheel; and they made the twisting, turning trip to the location in an explosion of animalistic fury. A screeching halt, amidst the equipment trailers, forced the onsite crew to jump aside, away from the steaming anger created by the cool morning mist and two fire-breathing dragons, one who stomped his way to Make-up, while the other waited for another getaway. With nothing said to anyone, not even a thank you for the copious amounts of coffee handed to him, David continued his silent rampage with each stride taken down his warpath. Make-up done, wardrobe complete, the leading man stormed onto the set, scanning his lines, ignoring all those in his way. The dramatic scene would play out, in front of the cameras, with everything he felt burning inside; venting his wrath at Rod would come privately. Morris' direction stopped for a single-take of one man's insanity that day. The entire cast and crew watched a master in action, catching every detail of the performance. With another brilliant piece of acting, David evoked the torment of the character, with a continual close-up of *Lord Worthington-Smythe*. Nothing more could be asked of the drained actor.

Back in the green machine, which disguised its underlying power under a mask of sedate luxury, the blond-haired demon, behind the wheel, pondered its potential for knocking down gates. One in particular, he did not feel like stopping for. Calming down, he drove the winding road like a slalom course, to return to the manor unscathed, ready to relax in the comforting confines of his family. In the blink of an amber eye, it officially grew to include Steven, Bernard, and Maria. They dined together for a special night to celebrate their futures. Happily settled, the group of six remained intact in their wing of the house, far away from the Morris clan. It would remain that way, until David deemed a sincere apology came forth.

With other arrangements for Holly's schooling decided, each adult volunteered to teach something attuned to him or her; and even Kincaid threw himself into the endeavor while he remained in England. The horrific incident provided a fortuitous opportunity for Ted and Holly to spend time together. David's partner and his daughter needed the chance to bond, without his interference, and what better way than educational discoveries they could share. Ted agreed hesitantly, thinking about the morning's fiasco and their dinner the night before; but his new daughter smiled happily at the entire scenario.

The next morning, from his dressing room, LaCoix aggressively made the important calls to both his and Barrett's publicists and agents, confirming how to handle the media. Aghast at the notion, they tried to convince him otherwise. Refusing to be deterred, he demanded a press conference be held the coming Sunday, six days away. With wheels in motion, he hung up the phone, leaned back, and raked his hair. Life would never be normal at this rate; and he choked at the thought. A knock on his unlocked door proclaimed the uninvited entrance of Morris.

"What is it? Are we starting early?" LaCoix snapped at the short, chubby man who dabbed nervous perspiration off his forehead, and then cleaned his bizarre-looking spectacles.

"I've been trying to apologize since you stormed out yesterday morning. You won't give me the chance."

"If you have the spine, Morris, ask forgiveness from the two people you hurt the most; and make damn sure your wife and boys do likewise. If you don't muzzle that kind of talk from your eldest, and teach them some manners, I'll arrange to leave immediately."

"David, you can't run out on me!"

"From this picture; hell no; whatever gave you that idea?"

"You said you were leaving."

"From the house, yes, not the picture; I'd never do that. What's the matter with you? Oh, I forgot; my being bisexual is a detriment to the film. I pondered on the situation, and wanted your opinion, just as Theo planned to discuss it with Kincaid. I should apologize for Holly jumping the gun, but she wanted to express her happiness with her friends, not the entire bloody world! The only consequence, of the incident, is my loss of respect for you and your family. Hurting my daughter and my partner hurt me; and believe this, Morris; forgiveness will not be forthcoming anytime soon. I owe you a great deal after Susan's death, but Ted; just keep your family away from mine. You had a chance to delay the inevitable; but your attitude, and lack of quick disciplinary action, leaves you without a choice. The official announcement, of my *engagement* to Theodore Barrett, is scheduled for Sunday, outside the manor gates."

"Are you finished?"

"Not by a long shot, but I'm tired of being angry."

"Good, because I'm sorry about everything, except for your ire, which makes for excellent drama on film. The scene from yesterday is outstanding; and I'll fire anyone in Editing that cuts a single second. Now, if you would give me a personal time out, I would like to congratulate you, Theodore, and Miss Holly, every success in creating a happy family unit. You're all strong and smart enough to face the rigors of the scandal you know your outing will create. I also hope Mr. Barrett gains custody of his daughter. Mrs. Morris and I are mindful of his hellish nightmare."

"That's a few points in your favor. Well done, Rod." David's sarcasm honed in, wanting to hurt someone.

"As for the picture, I only see disadvantages to the announcement of your sexual liaison. You hold this entire picture in your hands, keeping every scene together with your constant presence. You've been brilliant; and I expect you'll continue to be. I set my sights for this film to interest an audience of adults, from the youngest male adventurer, intrigued with Gothic horror, to the oldest lover of classic, mystery thrillers, and to those women who come only to see David LaCoix."

"Thanks for the boost to my aging ego. With everything that's happened, I think we did a damn good job, staying on schedule and keeping you on budget. Your cast and crew require a hell of a thank you. They did it for you." David turned away, to brush off a fleck of make-up from his velvet coat.

"And you rallied with them. I certainly have no complaints about your work ethics, your talent, or your professionalism..."

"...just my personal life, sexual orientation, and morals. Maybe I do it with dogs." The blond sniped back spewing fire; while the black, made-up eyes enhanced the molten fury within.

"Now you're being revolting, LaCoix. You're making this hard. We've become friends; I want you to be happy, but I must appease my backers. I'm so at odds over this, I can't even gauge if it will hurt the picture. Maybe the curiosity factor..."

"...Curiosity factor? Is that what I've become in your eyes? A freak sideshow attraction; not the fine actor you labeled me? Maybe recasting would be best." David's outrage exploded, and he jumped out of his chair, sending it hurtling backward. Another intense scene loomed in front of him; this verbal attack primed him to ravish it vengefully.

"David wait, I didn't mean that."

"Shut up, and let's get this movie finished, if you're still game. Jesus Christ, this day's just getting better and better. I never thought yesterday could be topped." LaCoix reached for the door handle, but halted by a clasp of his upper arm. He spun around, only to see a softening, remorseful face.

"Please reconsider staying at the manor. Sincere apologies will be forthcoming. Your new partner is still a stranger to us; and we'd like to get to know him." Morris made a pitiful last effort to keep his star from fleeing, not only from the manor house, but also from the picture.

"I hope as a talented actor as well."

"Of course; okay then, let's move. I think I've raised your ire enough, by the fire in your eyes." Morris looked wasted. His had dealt with temperamental actors his entire career, but he created this catastrophe. LaCoix had every right to walk out on him; and he endeavored to undo the damage cautiously. An expensive production hung in possible limbo; and he shuddered as he scurried behind the long strides of an irate lion with a thorn in his paw.

The next week turned into a whirlwind of hurricane proportions for all. Strain and tension abounded, leaving Holly the one redeeming bright light. Early morning walks with Kincaid infused her with fresh air, sunshine, exercise, and the proper name of each flower and tree found in their guidebook. In return, she taught him folklore, and filled his head with ideas for scripts. From late morning to mid-afternoon, she sat with Bernard learning the sciences. Her afternoons became special times with her Daddy, playing games and discovering the world, from Ancient Egypt to the current situation in the Brazilian rainforest, while Ted ventured down his own learning path of little girls and their fanciful notions. The two grew inseparable; and a work weary David often caught them waiting for him, snuggled up napping on the bed, or peacefully snoozing together in a giant chair in front of the fire; Holly's head inevitably lay on Ted's good shoulder, with a tiny hand holding his fingertips. Evenings belonged to David, making up for reading lessons and the pleasures of English literature. Father and daughter would settle in to read together, warmed by a freshly stoked flame. Unable to sit for long periods, Ted listened from the bed, transfixed by a great actor's gift for storytelling. Family living started to fall into a routine.

Feeling stronger and ready to return to normal, Ted's facial stitches came out painlessly; and his hair returned to its beautiful rich colors of brown, thanks to Bernard who used twenty different shades to create the illusion of a brilliantly-hued, autumn day. On David's return from work that evening, he stopped himself from cringing at the pallid color it made Ted's face, reminding him of a nine-year-old street urchin who just lost his puppy. Stepping forward with a fun smile, his fingers raked the silken hair, and a kiss of approval took away his lover's doubts. LaCoix, however, continued to trouble over the degenerate illness of the body and now the mind. It had taken away an adventuresome young man, who reveled in hanging by his toes from the edge of a cliff, full of energy to try anything dangerous, into a woeful, misbegotten caricature of a hapless kid. Fragile, sensitive, and extraordinarily handsome, Ted had changed; and David still adored him.

On a glorious, spring Sunday--a good omen according to Holly--two men, hiding their fears and insecurities behind the happy actors' masks, stepped out of the car, along with Bernard and several bodyguards, who scanned for trouble amongst the unexpectedly large crowd. They exited the estate gates to stand above the cheering throng of unknowns, a noisy press of mostly familiar faces, and too many unnecessary flash bulbs. The constant clicking of cameras had Ted's head spinning; and he nearly fell with a bright glint that stunned his eyes. He had remained indoors since they drove onto the grounds, under a cloud-filled, gray sky; their remembered day of rain-washed faces, pledging promises with holy tears.

Barrett blinked at the mass, stumbling along, but secured by his partner who settled the bewilderment, of what they were doing, with a few endearing whispers. While searching for the end of his long, dark tunnel, he listened to David's words. They created an uneasy silence. Coming out was one thing; but two of the proclaimed Sexiest Men in the World, one with an Oscar and the other a last year's nominee, proclaiming an illegal marriage, to raise a family, was a very distinctive twist. After the initial shock, explosions of questions fired off at machine gun speed; each shot penetrated the youngest Spirit. His blond Knight smiled and laughed through the entire event, yet maintained his quiet, mysterious demeanor. He answered polite questions and ignored those he refused to discuss. Unfortunately, Barrett heard them all; it scared him not knowing who was winning or losing, or what game they played. Keeping quiet, he wore his famous glued-on smile as his defense.

Fifteen minutes, and they rocked a world. Back in the car, they returned to the house with Ted still unsure of what actually happened. He would witness their coming out on video tape, once safely back in their room, where he could then die of shame, unseen by the scrutinizing eyes staring at him in disbelief. Instead of a safe haven, Morris herded them into the audio-visual room for the instant replay of CNN's full coverage. The sordid after-comments hit hard and below the belt. Ted's eyes never left the book beside him--*The Agony and the Ecstasy*—a metaphor for the bitter truth. The young man settled back, relieving his sore tailbone, and closing his anxious eyes.

David watched the tape closely, particularly the images of Ted clinging tightly to his arm. Looking so young and frightened, he came to believe he should not have forced such a staging. *Peter Pan* had been caught by an entire horde of Captains Hooks. Cellular phones rang in everyone's pockets; but while Ted turned his off, David greeted every message with excitement and expectation. He was not disappointed. The calls continued the entire afternoon, until a pair of blue eyes pleaded for mercy to cease. With a finger gesture to take one very important call, David rubbed the back of Ted's neck while he spoke. His parents wished to speak with their soon-to-be new son. With his head shaking and pushing the dreaded device away, Barrett finally answered. Nervously, he said his first words, while his lover urged him on. The LaCoix seemed to be caring people, wishing them the best, and to visit immediately upon returning to the States. Ted thanked them, and pulled away from the cellular held to his ear. David wrapped up the conversation, clicked off the device, and turned around. *Peter Pan* had fled the scene.

Excusing himself from the gathering, all now forgiven, LaCoix hustled to follow any trail left behind. The heavy thud of the front door closing gave him his answer; and he quietly pursued his prey. He found Ted standing at the top of a long drop of stone stairs, looking down as if to fly. David held back, unwilling to startle him in such a precarious position.

With a mind whirling with emotion, Ted could not comprehend; and confronted by one contradiction after another, he withdrew from reality. His sexuality had been thrust upon a shocked world, and no one needed to know. Feeling very lightheaded, he swayed slightly, unable to focus on the next step, to somewhere between the toes of his highly polished loafers. How high was he? Somebody had asked him once before; were they asking now? A hundred feet--two hundred--it had to be high enough to kill him if dropped. Leaning forward, a chasm of soft pastel rocks beckoned, and they came ever closer. The pink light would break his fall, as the image faded to black.

"Come on, Ted, open your eyes."

He smelled lilacs; she saved him, wrapping him in something warm. The blue eyes flickered open, to smile at a deeply etched frown. "Where are we, David? Is Lavender with you?"

"The Mistress has been with us since early this morning. We're both worried about you." The frown disappeared, but not the distress on seeing a befuddled nod. "Stand up straighter and look out in front of you. You haven't seen this view. It's late afternoon; all the shadows are chasing away the colors across the garden. Look at the water playing in the fountain. It's creating sunbows; little prisms of light captured in drops of water, flickering through the air, to be reflected back by the sun." David rambled on, shivering in fright at the near fatal disaster. With his quick actions, he had lunged for Ted in time. Not believing the happenstance to be premeditated, it would have been a freak, cruel accident, if his lover plunged off the upper stair, to crash headfirst onto the cobblestones below.

"It's beautiful. I remember walking out here. I needed the sun, but then..." Ted's mouth barely opened to speak. Discomforting in the tone, David's concern heightened to a new level.

"...then you fainted."

"I did? It felt like one of those days I told you about, standing on a precipice, knowing you had conquered your fears and an intimidating mountain alone, to finally reach the moment when you could stretch your arms to fly. I'm free, man, finally free." The exuberance clouded; the voice trailed off to nothing; and the face strained to remember. "But I've never fallen or blacked out before. I don't think I have... maybe once."

Confusion mounted, and the fear of what this horrific disease could do to the mind hit David with the smack of a bat. "Sorry, Baby Bear, but it might be a little matter of your wings being clipped." David feigned a laugh, while knocking on the chest part of the bulky cast.

"Balance, hunh?"

"Probably; not to mention overtired, overexcited, overemotional, and overanxious. You're scared to death, because of what we did today. I'm happy to hear, however, that you feel free. It means we did the right thing." Enthusiastic over Ted's easy acceptance of their new arrangement, David also came to understand his lover's need for freedom. He would give him the space whenever required.

"Great excuses for stupidity, LaCoix. Let's sit here for a while. Thanks, Lavender; we did it. Man, did we do it." Ted looked through the softening light and felt the kiss on his cheek. She left him with a lingering song of sweet chimes and angelic voices.

"That was nice of you. It felt complete to have her with us today. Are you warm enough; does this hard stone hurt your back? These steps aren't exactly butt friendly." David's first panic attack dissipated at the words of thanks expressed to their ethereal friend.

"Yeah, I'm okay. I'd like to catch the last rays and look at this spectacular vista. Seems forever, since I sat under the sun, or walked in the grass. Now that I'm partially mobile; it's time to set out and help Holly find more Faery rings." Ted rested his head under David's chin and glowed in the radiance of the solar disk, which lowered itself within the arms of the ancient oak forest.

"As long as Stevie or Bernard goes with you, as it seems sunshine gives you more energy. I think our place is going to suit us even better."

"Our desert is full of magic. We just have to find it, and get Holly to tell us who is who. Should be fun." Ted's mind grew more lucid the longer he spoke. Perhaps, he needed the solitude, to contemplate his former life and where it had led him.

The taller man also received some peace taking in the view, and smiled down at the top of the luxurious hair. "Holly's eager to show you the special places we've found, interpreted through her drawings."

"I've studied her paintings closely. They're excellent. She has a gift for storytelling as well. I love her tales of elves and fairies..." The head went down, although carefully tilted back up to see his favorite vista of green crystals. "I'm sorry, David."

"Don't think about it. In our world, a Faery is a Faery, a special creature with translucent wings. Even the spelling is different from the accursed word used to humiliate gay men. People are afraid to use it in the proper context; and it springs to mind such enchantment. It should mean what it means, nothing more. Holly continues her search in every wildflower, to coax one out."

"You two are clones." Ted chuckled at him, shivering slightly.

"She's the creative one. I'm only the actor who brings a character to life. I wish you would let your poetic nature come through more often. You, my superstar, have a unique way of seeing the world, much like our daughter. Hey, you're really getting cold; we should go in." David touched the good cheek with a brush of his lips.

"In a minute. Did you know I can conjure up every picture you've ever created in your words and mind, like those sunbows? I never noticed them before, and yet you and Holly see all these miniature things. I guess I only observe larger pictures." Ted wanted to be like David, and he pulled himself out of the doldrums with a silent promise to try.

"You're sounding better. Lavender once told me you ski on diamonds, which sounds very observant to me. I adore you, and every second I'm away, I miss you. It truly scares me, Ted, not knowing what is happening to you, or what you're thinking while I'm working. At least Bernard and Stevie are here; and through Holly, you'll experience what you missed as a child Sometimes I think she's wiser than all of us."

"You raised a smart little girl; one we'll have trouble keeping up with, as she grows older. I'm sorry I worry you, David. I try to get back on track and seem to get a good start; but sudden unseen barriers push me backward. Something odd is going on, besides what everyone says. I'm sure of it, but I can't explain it. No one believes me, and just says it's because I don't eat. It's damn frustrating for me as well."

"Maybe we should take you to a few specialists. In our chaotic lives since Christmas, I forgot that hidden pain of yours. I dismissed it so lightly, thinking more of your talents to heal yourself, which still blows me away. Is it really bad?"

"Sometimes more than I can withstand; but I've learned to live with it. There will be no more doctors, thanks. The only thing that helps is the sun, which seems to be disappearing on us."

"Answer me honestly: can you handle Cannes in a week? I'm serious, Ted, particularly after reminding me of this obscure condition."

"I intend to conquer the festival, and I shall be ready, Mr. LaCoix." Determined to deal with whatever came their way, he chuckled away the last of his melancholy, as David got him to his feet and turned him around. Face to face, they both smiled, and only the flowers saw the illumination surrounding the couple.

"You've had quite a year, Mr. Barrett. Cannes will eat you alive if we're not careful. You'll be representing *Outlaw's Heart*; and I'm not letting you jump into a school of piranha on your own."

"Man, do I get excited watching you fight man-eating fish." The contented, upturned mouth came from within; Ted shone as LaCoix's beloved ray of light.

"Then I'll do it more often. I don't know about you, but I'm getting cold, and my butt feels numb." David grimaced in mock discomfort, while trying to rub some circulation into his derriere.

"Hope you'll be doing that to mine tonight."

"One good turn deserves another."

"By the way, Stevie said he had something to show us. If you don't mind, I'd like you to myself this evening. I need you, LaCoix, just to hold onto something tangible."

The slightly worried face, and the plea, blandished David into agreeing. The beautiful, strange eyes looked up, filling David with so much passion and caring that he almost passed out. Thinking as a man, love had been a word used to appease the insecure; now it meant something too deep for David to understand. Jess Carmichael said it best--*go with the flow*--and the river he floated down felt unbelievable. He could not see himself without Barrett. Every word said had to be correct and mean everything spoken. His world had changed dramatically within a year; he intended to keep it a happy, healthy environment for anyone who chose to enter his kingdom. With that promise to himself, David watched the sapphires drift away, closing slightly. The face tilted up to expose a pair of lips requiring a feather light touch to awaken their beauty.

"Don't ever leave me, Ted. You might as well cut me open and leave me to bleed." The blond actor received a kiss, as he buried his head into the bare section of neck. The scent filled the need for the feel.

"You are a dramatic actor." A tease lightened the morbid thought. "Give me that diamond and I'll think about it."

"You just can't wait for the surprise. Why is it so important to you?"

"Don't know; maybe the symbol of vows. Sounds stupid to make a fuss about something that legally doesn't bind us."

"If a symbol is required, we'll make it special; and as far as I'm concerned, it will bind us. Let's get rid of family business, and then lock our door on the world. What say thee, Sir Theodore?" The clench released; and they strolled through the ancient portal arm-in-arm.

"I say we hurry, your Lordship." Ted snickered at David's groan on picking him up, when they arrived at the bottom of a long set of winding stairs. Walking he could do for a short distance, but climbing had not yet been conquered. Toting Barrett, two flights up, deemed more than LaCoix could handle. He surprised himself with his newfound strength, acquired by lifting a six-year-old regularly, and a fully-grown man. Not man-size, not even skinny man-size, his partner weighed less, including his casts, than the tiny female actors he had starred with. He set Ted down on the last riser and caught his breath. While hanging onto the railing for his own support, he watched Barrett's balancing act, using the mobile arm to brace himself against the wall. Exhaling sighs of weariness, they both managed a smile for each other's benefit.

With kisses and love lavished on Holly who had a glint in her eye, their daughter, her nanny, and Ted's nurse bid them sweet dreams. No argument from any of them, and no story requested, gave one cause to puzzle. One left to go; David took a deep breath at the top of the stairs, and hoisted Barrett up and over his shoulder. With a curse, a complaint of being dizzy, and much giggling, the technique gave him a handhold on the railing, while going down the one flight to their quarters and further along the hallway to reach Kincaid. It would be a relief when the plastic man could climb without fainting. A knock on the door, and it opened to an excited face.

"What's up, Stevie?" David leaned against the doorframe, sweating and out of breath. His leg muscles needed work if this continued.

"I'll just grab it, and bring it to your room. It'll only take a second, but I want your gut response. I'll be right behind you, and then out of your life for the evening."

"Fine, you have five minutes." David laughed, knowing Kincaid understood exactly the peace and quiet the newly uncloseted couple desired.

"Perfect. By the way, you both spoke very well. You are a godsend of eloquence for gay rights."

"Did I speak?" Attempting to joke his way out of a serious problem, it did not nullify the fact that Barrett spent a good part of the day in a complete daze, and honestly did not remember.

"I think you mumbled a few words." David lied, turned him around, and nudged him forward.

"Did I make sense?"

"Always." LaCoix chuckled, masking his worry over the continuing memory loss. With the thought lingering heavily on his mind, he nearly toppled over when Steven rushed passed to open the door.

"Stevie!" Ted stopped to take in the dozens of bright red roses, a blazing fire, soft Celtic music, flickering candles, and a bed pulled down sprinkled with velvet petals, creating an ambiance of the Gothic Romance novel in which they lived. A white rose rested on one pillow, and a rare black one on the other. For two men's indulgence, a table of elegance laid before them, lavishly decorated with fine china, crystal goblets, chilled champagne, fancy delicacies of everything imaginable, and dozens of opened telegrams placed beside the high-back chairs. A gift to be looked at, and probably cried over, David's enthusiasm grew, knowing Kincaid censored each note, to rid them of undue harassment. Beautiful in every way, and embarrassingly romantic for the two men, it hinted at the doings of a few mystical creatures of their acquaintance.

"What a surprise. This is great, Stevie. Join us for one glass." David insisted, and Kincaid accepted. The pop of the cork went unheard. Very adept at handling the explosive devices, LaCoix wondered if he had celebrated too much in his life, not waiting for the perfect moment of this day of sacred tears. He spilled half a lifetime's worth, before anyone awoke that morning, refreshing his Spirit and cleansing the fear from his heart.

Kincaid made a far more erotic toast than his first, turning Ted a shade to match the roses. While sipping from their fluted glasses, full of dancing bubbles, Steven handed a letter to David. With a questioning exchange of glances, he urged his rescuer to read the one page letter, handwritten in an eloquent masculine style. As David silently read the text, a helping hand positioned Ted by the fire. The youngest wondered what this secret letter contained, and he gazed up at his lover who seemed to be rereading the message, looking for something hidden. It was all very mysterious.

"So what do you think? I trust your instincts, LaCoix, but this feels right, and I don't know why." Pacing with nervous excitement, Steven could not stop smiling. Ted had not seen Kincaid deliriously happy, since they first met at La Rosa Negra.

"A professor at a prestigious university: interesting. A twenty-year age gap but has a youthful outlook toward life. Certainly is articulate, yet laughs at his writing skills. A historian of linguistics, languages, and dialects, plus a few other Doctorates in a variety of unique subjects, he also has a great sense of wit. I like his approach: telling you he's looking forward to your next picture, praising your dialect in another, but not over-stroking you by mentioning a problem with one of your other accents. If he is what he says, and there seems no reason to doubt him with this impressive letterhead, you've received high praise from a man who should know of what he speaks. Here, Ted, check it out." David handed the letter to Barrett who sat completely baffled by the conversation.

"So that's my plan for tonight. Try to figure out how to respond, and get it to him quickly. If he's leaving for Africa, in a couple of weeks for more research, I don't have much time."

"Has to have tenure by now, with only graduate students under his wing, but don't get your imagination boiling over yet, Stevie. You're already thinking he's some grand adventurer; yet in his own words, he just likes to read, enjoys fine music, and would like to get to know you over a quiet cognac. Don't disappoint him with your favorite beverage. He also has you pegged, Kincaid, seeing the vulnerability in your eyes in every picture you've made." David hoped this man lived up to his well-written note, and the expectations seen in moon-filled eyes. Kincaid did not need to be disappointed this soon; this was far too soon.

"I'll do it then. Why am I shaking?" Steven rubbed his hands together nervously, after setting his empty glass on the very high mantle. He had not tasted the liquid gold, or felt its magic bubbles bursting in his mouth, so rare and playful. One gulp and the expensive treasure disappeared.

"Because you're afraid of disappointment. Stick with the dialect part; ask him where you went wrong. He'll then know it's from you, without your signature. Now, say good night, Stevie." David retrieved the letter from Ted, and returned it to the man who he ushered out the door. "It's just you and me, Teddy Bear: a little romance, a little dinner, and more champagne. Perhaps a story by the fire can seduce you into some pleasant memories and dreams in our bed of rose petals. Man, I do lust over you, and maybe tonight, we can try a few more things to get you giggling." He leaned over Ted, his hands grasping the arms of the chair on either side of his *fiancé.* It felt a strange thing to call Ted, but there seemed no other word to use. The green eyes danced with mischief and started to half-close, growing nearer to smell the essence of his favorite treat. The scent of roses added to the heady mix, reminding him of a particular white bouquet.

"Lust sounds partially right." Ted hummed.

"Love: is that romantic enough for you?"

"You don't have to seduce me; it's my constant mental state. Man, I've wanted you for more than a tickle. Can we try again? I've been trying to heal my most annoying injury." The rare blue eyes filled his partner's heart with wild imaginings; and a cast lifted to pull down the blond head. The lips were so close.

"Easy enough to check, but I don't want you going into a funk if we can't. We're alone and have plenty of time to play. Here's to us, Ted; this evening is the start of forever. I'm going to touch and kiss every part of you, not made of plastic." David helped the man to his feet, hungering for only Ted's mouth.

"I could never live without you either, David."

"You won't have to. I'm here, Baby, and I intend to stay. I promise."

"I'll keep you to it, and hold onto it with my promise."

"Poet."

"Don't you have something better to do with that mouth besides talk, David?"

A soft purple mist left unnoticed, to the echo of tinkling glasses touching as delicately as two pair of lips. This kind of adoration and tenderness belonged to David and Ted alone.

CHAPTER 42

As predicted by LaCoix, the *New York Times* did run the controversial announcement; and with Ted's proclamation, they conquered Cannes with charisma and charm. Every person, in attendance, wanted to see them, touch them, talk to them, and photographed with them, against a background of continual screaming. It appeared, to two of the Sexiest Men in the World, their appeal to women had not diminished. Quite the contrary, it seemed to be thriving. Accolades and bouquets bombarded them from every direction. Interviews were requested; few were granted. Producers, directors, and casting agents clamored for future meetings, with one or the other, of the infamous couple. Their peers provided some fun, wishing them well, and congratulating them with no judgment, provided they clung to a wife, a husband, or an extraneous member of the opposite sex.

For Ted and David, they survived the grueling week of genuine smiles and gentle shoving into theaters, restaurants, limousines, and even into their hotel. David, in his Leoistic glory, wallowed in the adoration graciously, while endeavoring to deliver himself and his partner from the manhandling. His paradoxical nature, however, told him such praise belonged to important people--those who made a difference--he was not one of them. LaCoix became all business, donning his guise: *I am only an actor*. His main concern focused on his nervous companion who he firmly supported. Steadfast a few feet away, David never missed a quiver of the voice or a wobble of the unsteady body.

To everyone's amazement, Ted withstood the rigors of all the events and the interviews previously arranged. He even enjoyed the few films they managed to slip into, without the couple being too recognizable. Unfortunately, white plastic stood alone amongst the multi-colored, shape-revealing sequins. Impeded by a deluge of difficulties, the newest star held his head high, although terrified the tightrope would break, hurtling down amidst a circus with only red-nosed clowns.

Two weeks since their victorious trip to France, they returned to a stack of work, but without Kincaid whose preoccupation turned to another. The mail, placed in their hands upon entering the massive portal to safety, destroyed their glory, and life stopped. A summons had arrived, requesting Ted return for the trial of his father and accomplices. With his presence unnecessary for the Grand Jury decision, the court set an early trial date for attempted murder, with a statement issued that the abuse allegations against the church would follow immediately in a separate trial. The emotionally charged event involved many high profile variables; and the Judge presiding went into action the moment of her appointment, prepared for emergencies of any kind. Any happy remembrances of Cannes disappeared quicker than Holly's Faery rings. They gave him three weeks to return; the date, marked on the calendar, meant only three days to walk with David and Holly through a field of wildflowers.

Ted strolled along quietly, looking across the meadow, taking in every image he could. He recalled the first day he emerged, out of the darkness of the black Bentley, into this place of wishing; and he hoped to find a tangible souvenir of the once-in-a-lifetime day. He needed to remember, to visualize the beauty and serenity, before falling alone into Dante's inescapable pit of fire. As his family busily caught ladybugs to let them fly away to an old rhyme, Ted slowly set adrift with flashback pictures of other good days. He found and picked a blue flower, a perfect shade to match his eyes. One more in yellow, and another in white, each enchanted him with their variety of color and shape, their contrasts of light and dark, cool and smooth, to warm and fuzzy. The teachings of Miss LaCoix could not compare to the feel and smell of each in their reality. Trembling fingertips of one hand, along with his teeth, successfully wove the flowers together, while carefully adding grasses and leaves to the intricate chain. In his depression, Ted forgot the rule not to disrupt the harmony of the meadow; however, in his scattered mind, he felt obliged to be swallowed up by it.

The young man smiled wistfully, delighting in the sound of light, dainty hooves behind him. He turned to look at three female deer, one with a fawn, perfectly blending amongst the taller reeds. Quiet company he longed for; they gave him that tranquility. Far away from the wilds of his mountain hideouts, where the deer were skittish with many predators, Ted felt the same way, hiding from talons ready to swoop down and snatch him by the throat until they squeezed the life out of him. He returned his gaze to David and Holly, both standing motionlessly, also watching the wonder.

Ted returned to his idle weaving, attempting to control his trembling lower lip. The perfect Hollywood whites clamped down hard, wanting the lip to stay calm for his companions. Gathering himself, the only way he knew, to overcome the constant, devastating pain, running through him like the trickling stream in the nearby forest, he breathed in a surge of freedom, which had become a rarity. The faint smile never changed from a wistful hope; and he continued to entwine his chain of wild beauty into a fragile circle, finally tying the two ends together. A surprised chuckle, he felt better, seeing the dexterity of his right fingers had returned to achieve the feat. Imperfect like all of nature, it symbolized his future. The wheel of life became a closed circle, to continue flawlessly or snap with a toss of a baby. For now, he took time to merge into the gentler landscape of England. The wreath of blue and yellow flowers fit haphazardly on his head, covering his brow, hanging down to just above his ears, and holding back the shaggy hair at the nape of his neck. A little big, it mattered little when the blossoms smelled like paradise. Ted sank further into the tall grass, disappearing amongst the spring flowers.

The deer ignored him, as they slowly grazed by, but the fawn became curious, cautiously approaching the still human creature. Two soft brown eyes peered into two misty blue ones, making a quiet connection; and the little one reached out to nibble the man's headband. Ted grinned, trying not to laugh, but drawing strength from the sweetest, purest experience he ever shared in the wild, until the baby heard the mother call. With a deep sigh from the man, the fawn skittered away, with high kicks just for the joy of a beautiful day, leaving Ted to his solitude and a treasured memory.

David had warily watched since his partner commenced plucking the delicate blossoms, one by one, tenderly loving each bloom chosen. He sympathized with the sad figure draped in flower chains; his own heart burst for lack of what to do. Depression deepened for the young man since the summons; and yet there he knelt, smiling pensively as a butterfly rested on his good shoulder. Although adrift in his own world of the silences, Ted startled, feeling his lover scrutinizing him. With a whisper, he asked his sole support for help to sit more comfortably, allowing father and daughter to venture further afield.

LaCoix had seen the man through his triumphs, yet now, he sensed Ted's demise. Nothing seemed to help his promised partner, except hold him when asked, or when swept with need.

Days of work lingered long; and David reached for his cellular on every break. Ted responded, although sounding unaware of the words spoken. His lover, lost in his mental pain and fear, faced a possible two-month ordeal without his Knight. A torturous nightmare for more than one, many eyes wept for the man who stumbled through his food, attempted to regain his strength by walking, and continued to keep a body moving; one that desired to lie down and succumb to the never-ending black. The dark melancholy now confronted David, holding his own sadness in check, while looking down at a man decked in a crown of blue and yellow flowers. Ted focused on a watercolor of innocence, against an impressionist's interpretation of a peace-filled countryside. Two hearts were breaking in a field of magic and dreams.

"You okay, Ted? Appears you found a new friend?"

"Nice, isn't it? They're not afraid. I haven't felt like this for a long time, David."

"You need nature's tranquility and time for yourself. We'll be close by."

"Thanks, I'm fine. Go do your ladybug thing." The butterfly on his shoulder suddenly flew by his ear and whispered something. Ted clasped the black-clad leg in alarm before David turned to leave. Hushed without raising a finger, the startled blond stopped and quizzically asked with a raised eyebrow. Holly also came out from behind her dad; and the winged creature, of translucent blues, turquoise, turning subtly into chartreuse, flew into the little girl's hair. Their daughter giggled and took no offense. A wondrous sight, the butterfly teased her nose and bewitched them all with its exquisite beauty of shimmering color and graceful motion.

In the quietest of moments, David looked at the shocked expression on Ted's face. What was this tiny creature with no fear, which could so easily startle a man into accidentally swatting it, leaving nothing but leftover wings? The taller man became its next attraction, flittering around his longer hair, whisking it up and around his face. The small insect seemed to delight in its softness, happy to play amongst the corn-silk threads. He heard it; and it was not Lavender. A high, soft, twittering sound, the rustle of rapidly flapping wings, murmured on a sigh, "Willow Rose."

David stepped back a pace in surprise and exchanged quick glances with Ted. The blue-green, whispering creature returned to Holly who giggled and danced with the flight of fantasy, as she moved to Titania's dance. She suddenly stopped and grinned at the butterfly, hovering a foot away from her eyes. A soft breath created enough force to push the tiny being backward. "I love you too, my Lady," Holly whispered.

An excited little girl stepped away to watch the flutter of wings land on Ted's broken cheek. The man did not move, while lowering and crossing his eyes in an attempt to focus on such a diminutive entrancement. It stood for a moment with a full wingspread, and then went back to a crouch, touching the fractured face. Seeming to be busy with things to do, it flew down to his hip. More twittering sounds came from the flowers at their feet, and dozens of winged beings merged into the dream. Although each unique and distinctive in appearance, they carried one voice as a breeze through the long grass. David and Holly stood silent: one in glee and in the *knowing,* the other in awe, remembering the flapping of black fringe. A flurry of flying creatures attempted to pull at Ted's shirt, near the chipped hipbone. Impossible for them to remove, the friendly one, of blue-green, flew around David's head. "Help us."

Without question or hesitation, the stunned actor bent down and loosened Ted's clothing, slipping the man's pants down his thighs. Having no idea why he did it, particularly in front of Holly, he felt it the appropriate action to expose the healing hip, displaying the sexy new undergarment of royal blue. The multitude of diaphanous beings disappeared, leaving only one to caress the bare hip, with its wings in constant motion. Finished the task or the taste, the talking butterfly fluttered down to the base of Ted's spine and caressed the touchy area. Surprising both men, the glimmer of blue-green flew straight up to the hard plastic to find an opening. Flitting about in exasperation, it finally came to rest once more on Ted's cheek. It stood erect to peer into one huge blue iris, which could barely focus on the exquisite being of long, flowing, green hair. It had two arms, coming out of its translucent covering, which was shed to form a diaphanous gown, exposing two legs, which separated in a stance reminiscent of the LaCoix tilt. Deep blue filled its eyes, very much like Ted's; and it held him spellbound within a comfort never felt. A moment's connection with another realm, and it was at his ear again.

Ted heard correctly the first time; the creature repeated the same words. "Willow Rose, the *Beginning*." Abruptly it vanished into the pale sky, after a sweep of the blue and yellow crown. Putting his fingers to his face, Ted needed Lavender to explain, and tried to call for her. She did not come, leaving him to solve the riddle with David.

Holly, in her own world of the *knowing*, skipped happily along the path she and her Dad had forged over several months of trekking. Completely enthralled, she had met her first Faery; and that Faery loved her. From the fragile, chartreuse body you could see through, to the translucent wings of royal blue to turquoise, glittering in the sun, she glimpsed into an unknown world and introduced to a new friend. The unique face of a Faery had been duplicated in Holly's paintings, with luxurious hair in all the shades of the blue-green palette. Carried away with the feeling, one little girl became empowered by the visitor, as did her fathers who remained staring at each other. David did not notice his daughter's departure.

"I heard it say something." Completely bedazzled, the lanky blond remembered the peace once felt in a pastel rock canyon. It overwhelmed him then, as it did now.

"I know; and that was no butterfly. It kept whispering my daughter's name, and something like *the beginning again*. What does it mean?" Ted's mouth gaped open in bewildered surprise.

"Christ, I heard *Willow Rose* repeated twice. What did she do to you, Ted? She, it, he, whatever, asked me to help them; the reason I undid your pants."

Fingertips prodded to figure it out, pushing harder and harder on the bone fracture in his face. "It doesn't hurt! You can't even feel the bump! I should have thanked it, but I didn't know."

David knelt down and brushed against the soft cheek. For the first time, Ted did not flinch, bringing hope for more miracles; his hand swept over the hip and again no pain. Cautiously, he ran his finger down the crease of the arse and touched the tailbone, receiving no reaction but a gloriously brilliant smile.

"What just happened?" Ted reached up for David to hoist him to his feet, and to get his pants back into a respectable position.

"I think we just met our first Faery." LaCoix startled himself saying it aloud. Although coming to believe in their existence, with a great deal of persuasion by his daughter, the extraordinary insight had him dumbfounded. Another world existed in their reality; and they had been stepping on it. A realm, with tremendous healing power, revealed itself to mortal man without calamity. How many like creatures were there, never seen or written about? When faced with the truth, David stood stunned, feeling blessed with a great gift, with no one to tell. For now, it would remain a secret, until the fragile creatures desired to meet their world. David's puzzlement struck another revelation: Willow Rose and Holly Jane must be their connection.

All thoughts of wonder vanished with a child's fading scream; and two men immediately scanned the meadow. The eldest bolted down the path leading to the cliff, scrambling and falling, getting back up and running ever faster with his long legs, calling his daughter's name in his mad dash through the tall grass. He received no answer. A father's panicked voice filled the meadow, with an echoing scream for his daughter.

Ted followed; his legs had regained their strength; and with his mended hip, he could run with some agility. Only his upper cast hindered his stability. He caught up with his partner near the ridge, and heard the chilling crash of waves below. Turning toward the sea, he saw it; part of the ridge had recently given way. While David yelled out wildly, scanning the open field for the color purple, Ted stepped closer to the hazard, his old skills returning instinctively. With a light press of his booted toe, he felt the unsteady ground. Swaying in terror, he had to look, holding back the scream of loss. Bending down slowly, he awkwardly attempted and succeeded to get on his stomach and crawl gingerly to the edge.

"Where is she? We'll never find her. She was right beside me. Ted?" David's frenzy ceased, spotting the man inching his way toward the ledge. His world crumbled with a gasp. A stern voice, he barely recognized, halted any further progress.

"Stop, make a move we both die. Get down on your stomach and inch over to the right a few feet. Distribute your weight evenly." All business, Barrett recognized the signs; he prayed to his God, Christ, Lavender, and the Faery that Holly had not fallen. Hindered by plastic, he still managed to get to the lip before David. His heart skipped a few beats, only to start up at a rate too rapid.

"Do you see her? Is she down there?" David battled against unknown hysteria. His little girl could be dead; he yelled out for Lavender in his head.

"I can see her just below us. I can't do it, David, but there may be a way, if you do what I say. Don't panic and think; Holly's about twenty-odd feet down and appears unconscious." In his own fright, Ted carefully chose his words to maintain calm for two.

"I need to get to her!" David started scrambling, moving too fast for their dangerous position, and another warning came swift and harsh.

"Shut up, and listen, David. Stop shifting around. Have you got your cellular?"

"Yeah." David consented and lay still, needing to see his daughter, but his attempt to move closer stopped with new instructions.

"Call 999 or 911, I don't know which number. Ask for the Chopper Rescue Unit, tell them precisely where we are, then hand me the phone carefully." He had no time for any nonsense from a man ready to dive off a cliff to save his daughter. David followed his instructions, and those received from the coordinator on the other end of the line. Taking responsibility from there, Ted reached for the phone with his barely capable fingers. He could not afford to drop it, and with great care, secured it without incident. "Is there a way down, David?"

"A path about a hundred feet over, can you still see her?" The stricken father lay motionless, his fingers grasping the small flowers beneath his hands, waiting for something to do, or confirmation of anything.

Busy with three people, Ted's mind shifted into a higher gear to save them all. With David ready to get them all killed, Holly drawing closer to her mother, and now, the coordinator rattling off questions, he settled his short-circuited nerves and began. "Yes, ma'am. A little girl has fallen approximately twenty-feet... She's just below us, lying on her back, on what seems to be a relatively sturdy ledge... She appears unconscious... Keep the chopper well back from the cliff-face. It's unstable; do you copy? He took the phone away from his ear to see if he could see the path. It had a gentle incline, not far from Holly, but enough to make it a serious climb.

"Dad's here, Honey. We'll get you." David finally could look down, with frightened hysteria etching the lined, handsome face. His little girl looked so tiny; he had lost her. Someone kept talking when a handful of earth fell away from him. He froze.

"If she comes to, she'll fall. We have to do something. You have to get down there. Are you following me, David? Someone has to be with her."

"What do I do? We can't climb down without the cliff disintegrating." Gasping for needed air, LaCoix listened closely.

"I know, but you can sidestep your way from the path, then up a little ways to get beside her. Every handhold and foothold you make, you check first. Got it?" Ted yelled at him, bringing the man's attention to righting a treacherous situation. Knowing he could do it himself, if able, made the frustration come out in anger.

"Got it." David could not take his eyes off his daughter; and they grew wider at every fearful thought.

"Okay, listen. Crawl backward on your stomach, until it's safe to stand. Go down the path until I tell you to stop. Repeat it, David."

"Backward, and then down the path until you yell stop."

"Good. Now remember, this is not a race. If you hurry, you'll slip; and I'll lose you both. When you get to where I yell stop, take off your shoes and socks. You'll have more feel, and you can grip with your toes if necessary. Move slowly sideways and upward. Check your weight each time you change position, making sure it can hold you firmly. Don't move her, until I tell you what to do next. I'll be up here, giving you instructions, talking to Holly, and speaking to the rescue team. Be careful, David."

LaCoix eased his way back; he would get to his daughter if he had to fly. Once standing, he did not hesitate to run the length to the three-foot wide incline to the rocks below. As promised, he cautiously made his way down the slippery route. There had been a lot of rain that winter, making the ground damp to the touch. With a sharp order to stop, he completed the first leg of his trek. Looking across and up, he saw one tiny leg dangling from the knee, about thirty-feet over and ten-feet above his head. Shoes came off; socks were tossed; and a sweater removed. Pushing up the sleeves of his shirt, he readied himself with no time to spare. He paused, searching wildly for his first handhold. His daughter lay still, while his own body shuddered and tensed. He had done this a thousand times in simulation, training on a movie set. This was different; this was real and extremely dangerous. With one deep breath, he remembered the techniques, and he started.

"Holly, it's Daddy. Don't move, Sweetheart. Your dad is coming." Ted soothed deaf ears, not knowing if she would move or follow instructions. Fearing the worst, he wanted to hear at least a moan to keep from crumbling in his fear. At the same time, he watched David's progress. The man began his ordeal, methodically securing handhold, then foothold, each one tested for safety. Back to Holly, and the same repetitive voice tried to stir her gently. He heard it; a soft whimper of *Dad*, and he softly issued more calming directions. "Lay still, Holly. Your dad is almost there. Very still,

Sweetheart, don't move a finger."

"It hurts."

"What does?"

"My arm."

"You'll probably have a small cast just like mine, Holly Jane. What about your toes? Don't move your legs, but scrunch up those little toes of yours. Can you do it?"

"Yeah."

"Does it hurt?"

"No."

"Good girl; your dad's almost there. Stay still. David, she's awake and she feels things. You'll be able to move her closer to the rock-face." Ted could not believe the small body remained intact, not to mention the very lucid mind. He deduced she landed on her side, and with the ensuing force, ended face upward. His relief gave him hope of a miracle on David's part.

The older man, breathing hard with the exertion, listened to every word his two loves uttered. With a heart pounding out of his chest, he made it. Calming slowly, he rested next to her, with one hand on her thigh and one on the ledge; it held firm.

"Dad, is that you? Where's Daddy?" Holly lay motionless, except her mouth. Sounding coherent, nothing else mattered.

"I'm here, Holly Jane. Daddy's above you. Can you see him?"

"Told me not to move, so I haven't opened my eyes."

David smiled with relief at a child's innocence and lack of fear. "Probably a very wise choice, Honey; are you hurt?"

"Daddy thinks my arm's broken. I do too. My head aches." Holly attempted to roll over, but a hand stopped further progress.

"Not yet. Hey, you've lost one of your purple sneakers. Guess we'll have to find more. Can you feel my hand on your toes?" David inched his way around, staying his terror.

"Your hand feels warm. What happened? Where are we?"

"Hard to explain. Do you remember the Faery?" David wanted those eyes to stay closed and her mind on other things. She may panic if she knew the real situation; they were not yet safe. He gathered his wits to obey the instructions from overhead. First task: make his position stable. The firmer ledge allowed more maneuverability; and he found a strong platform to brace his feet, leaving his hands relatively free.

"She talked to me, just like Sir Lancelot and your purple magic."

"The Lady Faery sure was pretty." Nerves settled just in touching her. Second task, he secured her small body and ensured her physical condition; she felt his every touch. Her neck was not broken nor her back. With gentleness and the lightest of a single-handed push, he moved her closer against the rock-wall. A smile of gratitude filled his face, feeling the safety net of Lavender's mauve cloud. With his daughter secured from falling further, and firming his own grip, he waited for help, while conversing with his daughter about Faeries, flowers, and Dad's purple cloud. A wreath of yellow and blue blossoms fluttered down to land gracefully on her chest. A present from her Daddy took the little girl away with magical thoughts.

David could finally breathe with his hands on his daughter, and hearing Ted, safely above, directing the approaching helicopter. Another glance, three choppers honed in on them. Cursing under his breath, he braced himself and Holly against the wind created by the two unnecessary ones that drew ever closer. It wreaked havoc with their unsteady position, and weakened the cliff above, showering them with hurting particles of dirt and stones. He tried waving them off, now fearing for Ted's safety. If the ground gave under him, they would all plummet onto the boulders washed by the resounding breakers.

Chaos ruled the upper ridge. The larger, emergency chopper landed far enough back for Ted's satisfaction. It appeared an army of people jumped out, stomping to the edge with all manner of equipment. Only a fraction of the count emerged, but in Barrett's eyes, he only saw too much weight. He yelled for them to stay back, and to secure their lines and ropes further from the edge. In a hurry, they accepted any advice offered. Two men went down one side safely, swinging over to David and Holly's perch. The rescuer, on the other side, felt the terrifying rush of adrenaline as the earth gave way, flinging him through the air, only to smash his body into the bone crushing rock as he swung back. The man, unhurt, caught his breath and repelled down to join the others. All secured, Ted breathed in a little calming air, watching tentatively as the experts did their jobs, amidst the whirling wind of two unwanted tornados. Very efficiently, the rescuers strapped Holly in a basket, while the third man took seconds to harness and start the ascent with David.

Ted started to inch his way back, suddenly jarring himself, caught on a jagged rock by his cast. A certain amount of profanity brought another member of the team rushing to his aid. In instant panic, Ted yelled in a voice hoarse from the strain. "Stop, get back, it's ready to give!"

"Easy sir, we'll get you."

"Stay back. We'll all..." A sound of cracking thunder, Ted fell head first over the precipice. David came over the lip to witness the earth give way; he could do nothing. Ted's life hung by a silver chain; held by the hands of his god. With no scream, a limp torso, encased in acrylic, dangled freely in the air. A quick rescuer had grabbed his ankles, before Theodore Barrett disappeared into the purple mist coming to meet him. Lavender--she would save him--and with that comfort, Ted slipped into darkness.

Three British climbing experts frantically held the man firmly by the legs, attaching clips and ropes around his ankles and knees. A fourth, lighter man scurried on his stomach to release the piece of obstinate acrylic from an equally treacherous rock. Keeping movements to a minimum, they were secure if another piece broke away. Ted remained silent.

LaCoix jolted to life, shouting above the horrible sound of chopper blades and fighting his rescuer to get out of his ropes. Pandemonium ensued; and Holly started to cry, hearing the hysteria in David's voice. Now strapped in a safe place within the chopper, unable to run to her traumatized father, fear swept over the child, while a busy doctor tried to calm her, simultaneously watching four men struggle to save her daddy, dragging his limp body to safety.

"He has a weak heart!" David screamed over the roar, as he scrambled after the stretcher jostling Ted unmercifully over the rough terrain, and heading directly for the dragonfly's mouth. They would revive him, if possible, en route. The chopper took off minutes from landing. Holly was broken and bruised; Ted was in cardiac arrest; and David was catatonic with terror.

With precious little time, no one could be heard above the racket. A steep turn toward a major medical facility gave them a heart-racing moment, as they slipped between the two menacing choppers. In their attempt to get coverage of the famous family, two news teams put them in greater jeopardy, along with their heroic rescuers. David never overlooked details in a crisis; and he would remember, on his deathbed, the call letters of both helicopters; they would pay for their folly. On just that thought, one lost control and headed for the cliff. A push from a purple cloud helped it land safely in the meadow. The horror-stricken blond manifested an out-of-control thought; he stiffened with another shock. The shivering started, and a red blanket appeared, encasing the catatonic Spirit.

Dressed in a flimsy hospital gown, David sat on the edge of a hospital bed refusing to lie down. Rod Morris rushed in to find his leading actor sitting deathly still, staring at a blank wall. Nothing more could happen to this stern, but feisty Leo. Chalk white, sweating, and shivering, David did not acknowledge his friend's arrival, until a hand came up to touch his scratched face. An instant, involuntary reaction swatted it away.

"Scratches aren't bad; and you're a hero, David. How's Holly?"

"Broken arm, ribs, slight concussion, and bruising. Nothing major, not even fear." Looking through glazed eyes, he gave Morris a recitation without emotion.

"Saw your escapade on TV when they interrupted a program the children were watching. We all ran like hell to help, but the chopper was already in the air. Quite a dramatic ending after seeing the footage."

"Ending? What ending? He's not dead! He can't be!" David leapt off the bed, and scrambled out into the chaotic corridor. Who were all these people? Where was Ted? Only hearing a cacophony of voices, and too many people blocking his way, he could not find any hospital staff; while in his head, he viewed only the skinny, limp body, hanging by an attached thread in space, surrounded by a purple cloud.

"David, stop. Let's ask. It's too crowded with reporters." Rod pulled him back against the wall, and a flash bulb went off, then another.

"Please remain in your room, Mr. LaCoix. Come now. Your daughter is fine, and telling a nurse about her encounter with a faery princess. You there, get that camera out of our way, before I beat you over the head with something made of tin, or better yet, with the expensive camera you're flashing at us." The nurse exuded an authoritarian exterior when it came to her job and the care of her patients, and yet turned to marshmallow with those who no longer had control of their lives. "Miss Holly Jane spins a good story. Now you relax and get back into bed. We want to make sure you've recovered from the shock."

David's mind spun and his headache grew worse, along with his paranoia. Being overly nice, Rod and the nurse hid secrets about Ted. His shallow breaths and shivering caused the nurse enough concern to start pulling out more blankets. "Where's Ted?" For the first time in his life, he called his partner a name never mentioned in public.

"Who?"

"Theodore Barrett, my partner, where is he?"

"Ah, Mr. Barrett, of course, such a sweet man. Now I know where I've seen you both, in *Outlaw's Heart*. Extraordinary film, sir. I cried for days over it. Yes, well... I guess you are family. They're just giving him the once over, nothing to be alarmed about. He will be up within the day."

"There were so many people, Rod, I couldn't get to him. He looked like a rag-doll swinging in the wind. God, he looked dead."

"Now, now, Mr. LaCoix, please; Mr. Barrett is fine, but worried about you and your daughter.

What you may be recalling is the rescue team's removal of the casts; and not very gently, I might add. We changed his casts to lighter ones and freshly cleaned him up. He's feeling much better just for that. According to the X-rays, he does not need the supports; but it hasn't been six weeks, so we'll leave it to his own doctor. I believe our medics said he experienced a fainting spell, which they couldn't be sure of at the time. His heartbeat could barely be detected in his neck; thus the quick extrication from all that ghastly plastic. His weakened state caused unconsciousness, which is common for trauma victims. Let him rest, leave your daughter to her dreams, and you stay warm in bed. I will ensure your partner knows you are both well and thinking of him."

"Thanks." David's knees shook hard enough to rattle every bone he had, including his teeth. He felt Rod and the nurse help him into the high bed; but his mind fragmented with thoughts of Ted, fitting together what he saw and what they said. A fright induced black out; his weak heart pulsated through it all; they just gave him a push. Curling up to stop shivering, he forced himself to relax, knowing his family survived a horrendous accident. With reassurances from Rod to take care of his family, David fell asleep from shock, exertion, and fear.

Very shaken, Ted left with the others under the black cloak of night. The drive seemed painstakingly slow for David who wanted his injured babies home and tucked in bed. Holly's hugs and kisses settled some nerves, but the biting of nails continued when Ted slipped into preoccupied oblivion. After another heroic day, they faced the world once more, exposed in another terrifying family moment.

On hearing the news, Tyler and Bryce boarded the first flight out of L.A. Notified immediately, David would meet them on the morrow, giving him some comfort in a magic kingdom gone mad. He sat leaning against the headboard of their bed, watching the quarter-moon shine through the window. Asleep with a painkiller, Holly hurt all over and came to understand what her daddy went through. Her first initiation of every child's folly, to break an appendage, manifested itself; the physical and emotional scars would mend in time. David had no doubt she would bounce back, but his lover may not recover. Ted fitfully dozed beside him, only at rest with the constant stroking of his hair. Outstanding in his handling of a situation, which could have killed them all; his traumatized body seemed to remember every detail in sleep. The late news applauded both men for executing a daring plan to save their shared child. Necessity called for action; his lover carried them through; LaCoix could not thank the man enough.

David smirked slyly while watching the rebroadcast of the drama. The flying licenses and press passes, of those on board the other choppers, had been revoked; the offending news personnel were grounded for a year, paying heavy fines to the British equivalent of the FDA. Their disreputable conduct could not be denied, considering their recorded tapes stood as proof. Satisfied with the compensation, a telegram arrived with good news: the announcement of Judge Matthews' retirement. David laughed aloud, cheering him up immediately.

He relaxed deeper into the pillows and tapestry headboard, pulled the covers higher over Ted, rested his hand on the brunet head, and smiled down at his brightest star. Acting his way out of another dilemma, his lover went into shock once released from the hospital. David's pride gushed over the man who took control that day, but now lay shivering and mumbling of blue-green Faeries and Willow Rose. David wondered what frightened him the most: the near tragedy, or the introduction to a new world. His thoughts turned to his own phenomenon: coincidence, or a visualization gone berserk. The smell of lilacs, a reassuring touch, and Lavender filled the room with light. She confirmed he had manifested the near tragedy, and warned him again to keep positive thoughts. Realizing the Mistress' frustrations, and the power one emotion could unleash, David sat aghast that he could create the same force and willful destruction. A whimper from Ted, and a calming cloud, brought it into a more enlightened perspective--the magic of such potential--it opened a door to meet a special entity of healing power. Two realities, inhabiting the same planet, came together in a compassionate moment; proof lay in Ted's healed breaks. The beautiful, flying creature may disappear forever, but she would always be the start of their *knowing*. Lavender caressed David's cheek; a true action hero fell asleep with the touch.

The Mistress inhaled deeply; it had begun with the Faeries' acknowledgement of Ted's presence, identifying him as the father of Willow Rose, by the simple wreath he made for his head, and the reflection of their own eyes in the mysterious sapphires. The crown of yellow and blue then passed to Holly, as they brushed over his head, carrying the adornment to the one who would understand and pass the truth onto others. The belief in the *Beginning Again,* the chosen word of earth's many realms, and the *knowing*, a term of the Mistress' worlds, came into the subconscious understanding of two men and a little girl. They were the start.

The Fates had not contrived the accident. An earth element's decision to test them all, they were hazardous rites of passage. Earth approved, as did the wind and water, which created the unstable conditions. Fire already acknowledged three of the four coming into play, all born under its distinctive symbols. They could control the burning heat and use it when called upon. The one water child would come into his own power to devastate and to create, but the Fates continued to chase Theodore Barrett. He could easily be destroyed; and the Cosmos inhaled a breath. The change drew closer: preparation, certainty, and action became the priority. Lavender stirred with hope.

CHAPTER 43

David sat in the V.I.P. lounge, waiting for his sons and biting his nails to the quick. Although good of them to rush to his aid in their concern, the bitter distaste lingered of his lifestyle change. The man, with nerves of well-strung titanium, felt himself unraveling spring by wired spring. Already on his second hand for accounting purposes, his two arriving problems could derail him completely.

A familiar voice called out. Steven Kincaid rushed through the door, ordering their favorite beverages, and settling himself next to his own hero. Surprised to find LaCoix waiting for his sons, it proved fortuitous he arrived from Paris in time to be of assistance, and to catch a ride back to the manor. Kincaid's concern proved sincere, sacrificing time with his new love interest, immediately upon hearing of the accident. His questions illustrated his anxiety, including Holly's condition and the affects of the fall on Ted. David did need his nemesis to pass the long wait. He related the story of Holly's first breaks; his own panic climb; the collected authority of Ted during the rescue; and subsequently, the man's ensuing decline into a severe depression. It reminded Steven of his own grisly incident; and Barrett's ability to rise above the calamity of a desperate situation; only to descend into that strange abyss only his look-alike saw. He understood David's feelings ran deeper than gratitude.

LaCoix admitted fearing his sons' impending arrival, along with their disapproval of Ted, not to mention the continuing worries of the upcoming trials. With Barrett's departure the following day, it left little time to spend with Bryce and Tyler, or to mend the rift. A little reassurance bolstered the creaking shoulders of a would-be-Atlas, with Steven's reminder that Ted would be staying with him in Los Angeles, along with Quinlan Ambrose, Richard Barrett, and Eleanor. He would watch over his Scarecrow, and make the return trip to the States with Ted. With some practical coaxing from his new amour, Kincaid decided to keep his Malibu residence, since Peerce's disappearance. Always his refuge from a hurtful world, he felt restless to get back to his luxurious safe haven.

David, who looked like he had not slept since the accident, worried Steven. Urging the man to open up, regarding his well-being, received a shrug. With that door closed decisively, it would remain so with the announcement of the flight from LAX. Do or die, Kincaid stuck to LaCoix like a tack in the older man's awesome, new, high-tech sneakers. If a cliff required scaling again, he looked ready.

Escorted to the private lounge by airport officials, David's sons sped to embrace him with hugs of sincerity. They almost lost their sister and their father, but failed to inquire after Barrett. It would require work to convince the boys his partner saved them from a double disaster. For now, he had them for twenty-four hours, and their little sister would recover from her boredom of being careful.

In one day, plans and schedules changed to accommodate Steven, Tyler, and Bryce to accompany Ted and Bernard on their trek back to California. Spending time with his father's lover, Bryce created some laughter in the deeply troubled man. Warned of Barrett's mood swings, the son finally convinced his over-encumbered wreck of a father that he approved. Difficult to say, he still approved, displaying it with a hardy clasp around the plastic man. The second son barely acknowledged Ted's presence, backing off from any discussion with the pervert who stole their father in a sordid, public scandal, shaming them all. What he saw on film, he now knew to be real; but he granted David's wish to stand behind the new superstar every day of the trial. His sons' promises were enough for LaCoix Senior.

The day of good-byes turned gray and dreary, much like Ted's arrival in England. Different from the comfort felt in the first part of summer, this day forebode a very different and dark emotion for the couple. The black cloud, filled with rain, hung over heads lost in the unseen shadows. In the back of the Bentley, graciously allowed to sit on the tarmac for security purposes, two lovers held each other for the briefest of time. David clutched Ted in a death grip; and his Teddy Bear returned it tenfold with what he could; neither man wished to let go. With Bernard and Steven's assistance, they pried off the one arm of the smaller man and removed him bodily from the car. The unsteady figure waved farewell to the black hearse carrying away his partner. He had no further time to think, escorted at a walking run, up the stairs, through the staff doors, into the covered gangway, where they settled him expeditiously in the humming jet.

Ted remained silent through the long trip, holding onto his composure and Sir Edmund. Ensconced securely in the window seat, with his casts supported by dozens of small airplane pillows, Kincaid and the bear protected him from star-struck passersby and flight attendants. Steven interceded admirably, entertaining first-class eavesdroppers, while conversing directly across the aisle with Tyler and Bryce. Being big fans of the famous face, a gabfest ensued; and the bleach-blond actor put on his happy public persona to tease them with his answers about the starlets he dated, the many beautiful women he made love to on film, and those rumored to be his next interest. Kincaid showed off his wide smile and soft laugh; one that enticed a world when displayed. If they only knew, Ted thought, listening to the banter from his safe, hidden corner.

Landing in L.A., the boys went their separate ways, promising Ted they would not let him down. Barrett saw the earnest concern in Bryce's eyes, but had to rely on Tyler's word, knowing it to be a promise kept. With a wave good-bye, they slowly vanished from view. A sniffle in the back of the limo, Steven quickly raised the privacy window to envelop his look-alike in a bear hug, while Bernard watched in concern. The sordid mess restarted; and Kincaid vowed to stand beside the man through his trials of the real and those of the mundane. He owed both LaCoix and Barrett for his new life, vowing his friendship for all eternity and beyond.

After three days of preparation, Barrett once again became the focus of world attention and media hysteria. He started to believe that true reality meant living in a tiny aquarium, the size for one small guppy like himself. Whatever happened, his face would be spread across the globe, perhaps throughout the other realms of the Mistress. With only a thought, her familiar warmth swept through him, uplifting energy carried him through a humiliating and dispiteous undertaking. The meetings with the prosecuting attorneys took the first toll on his mental fragility, stumbling over what had to be said, asked, inferred, with everything rehearsed in a complex pattern of variations, twists and turns, which the defense would throw at him. Jogging the young man's memory to that terrible day upset everyone. Ted slipped further backward, barely able to utter the truth to convict his father, along with those he promised to follow into hell if ordered. He choked on every word and vomited every half-hour. What strength and weight he had gained dropped rapidly.

Stoically, Richard and his wife also prepared for the battle, along with Raymond and Annie. The latter two had kept busy with a plan of their own, concerning their niece. One of them visited

Karen and the baby daily, keeping up a good front of support; but while conversing amicably with the former Mrs. Barrett, they secretly recorded everything talked about, nailing her with a confession. Two days before the trial, Karen informed Annie she could not see her niece and explained the reasons in detail. Unable to believe the disciplinary action levied upon an infant, and the insanity behind it, Annie retained her composure throughout. Given a few minutes opportunity, she telephoned Raymond, whispering the time had come.

With the younger brother's call to Ted's lawyer, action commenced immediately. Annie invited the police into the Barrett home, ignoring a shocked Karen, and showing the uniformed men the locked closet. They found Ted's baby on the floor, lying naked beside an oddity: a dead rat. With the child's arms black and blue, and a nasty bite to her little face, they immediately arrested Karen Barrett for child abuse. The Officers removed the infant to a secured facility, to await the father. Accompanied by his attorney, a member of the D.A.'s office, and his friend Ambrose, Ted rushed to his child's side, where the Barrett brothers anxiously awaited. The safest baby in the hospital, undercover police acted as vigilant nursery staff. Shattering an already defeated heart on hearing the tape, the new father blamed himself for being too late to save his daughter, relying heavily on Quinlan to provide the needed shoulder and words of commonsense. No longer able to function rationally, Ted asked Ambrose to inform David. The man in England had no words, but his knuckles connected a crushing blow against his stonewall.

The piece of controversial evidence deemed the custody case would become a criminal action. With an unprecedented emergency meeting of the Grand Jury, a quick decision was made. The D.A.'s office turned over their findings of this latest situation, along with other relevant evidence against the Barrett's church, to the Judge presiding over the attempted murder case. With legal arguments made, the tape became official evidence for possibly three trials. An unorthodox maneuver under California law, the Grand Jury, which had pushed up the trial date against the church, arranged Karen Barrett's trial to follow. The three separate cases had merged, with one directly following the verdict of the preceding one. Although a San Diego court matter, Raymond, Annie, Richard, and Eleanor, all became protected witnesses, within the fortified mansion of Steven Kincaid. The three Barrett brothers remained as Steven's private guests. All nervous, including a distraught Annie, their key witness, they could not be safer; an unearthly entity of immense power lived amongst them: Quinlan Ambrose.

Seeing his baby those two days before the first trial, and knowing experienced, loving people kept her safe and healthy, Ted stayed resolutely on his path. His skepticism of science's interference with the injured and dying changed dramatically since her untimely birth. On a happier note, a diversion came via Kincaid's new man-friend. For Ted's amusement, Steven explicitly detailed his new love affair, and excitedly admitted being hopelessly smitten with the Professor. Their meeting in Paris, after Cannes, and before the man's departure for Africa, had him doing cartwheels, never imagining the letters would play second best to the man himself. Kincaid radiated with uncontrollable lust and love, but his heart bled openly for his look-alike. At best, he could make his Scarecrow smile with every memory of his Love Professor, and their slow courtship, taking four days and nights of nonstop talking, and a dozen ticket exchanges, before he invited Steven into his bed. A new experience for Kincaid, he learned lovemaking could be gentle and kind, perfect for the passive man who desperately needed affection. Every second spent with Dr. Thurgood made him feel brand new, never viewed as a punching bag, or a tight hole for torturously jagged games. Intoxicated by every light touch, he came to understand fulfillment and the pleasure of drowning in it.

His admission, that he envied Barrett's relationship with a doting man like David LaCoix, came as no surprise to his look-alike. The only exemption to the younger man's strife turned out to be Kincaid's joyous affair. Someone loved Stevie for himself, one who cared enough to be forgiving and kind. Ted wanted to meet the miracle man, of many academic achievements, on his return from Tanzania. Time would drag for Kincaid, but he had to learn patience, which appeared more difficult to endure than sexual abuse. Ted shook his head in amused puzzlement, considering his own long wait for the notorious LaCoix. Ted missed the man desperately.

The attempted murder trial took ten days, involving all six defendants. Tried as a group, it granted the court a short and concise trial, with each assailant accepting whatever the verdict. With the defense over-confident, the prosecuting attorney did everything right, even ingratiating the Judge with his sharp, direct statements of fact, and no harassment of individuals, leaving that folly to the defense. Overpowering his adversary, with lightning strikes ricocheting around the courtroom, he created overwhelming hatred for the six men. The idea of two brothers intentionally beating themselves close to death, in retaliation for abusive parents and a cruel religious dogma, smashed into dust by the final, flamboyant, spellbinding testimony of Quinlan Ambrose, who held the jury in his magical hands. As the Barrett team's main witness, not party to the church but involved in the skirmish, his dramatic skills remained unflustered. He compensated for the emotional tidal wave washing away the Barretts.

Both brothers passively testified, and when cross-examined, came close to falling apart. The Judge scrutinized the two young men, particularly the one who appeared very ill and wearing the remnants of the beating. Any libelous accusations, against the brothers, were immediately stricken from the record. The Barrett team stopped the defense at every juncture. On the final day, the jury made their decision within a few hours. *Guilty* rang out repeatedly against the six defendants. Much to the three brothers' horror, never dwelling on the results of their actions, the Judge sentenced their father and the others to a maximum of ten years, up for parole in seven. The full penalty seemed harsh to the Wagner family, and certainly, to an outraged church membership, which filled half the public seating area.

Anger increased, with the announcement, by the Grand Jury, that the trial against the church would start in three days, agreed to by the defense and the D.A., to be held without a jury. Another five days of battling, a court decision shut the uproar down with a state authorized investigation into the church, particularly an account of the children and their medical conditions, to commence immediately. Records of members, money received and spent, were confiscated for auditing; a situation in progress by law enforcement officers as the Judge made his ruling. One last blow came with the loud smack of a gavel for order, deeming this particular group no longer a religious order; culminating in its ruination with a demand to pay State and Federal taxes retroactive to its conception.

The stunned silence turned to riotous shouting and physical violence by church members, until police, wielding batons, hustled the sniping mob out of the Court House. The pronouncement remained rhetoric, however, considering the eventuality of an appeal, the years to sort everything out, not to mention a Judge who overstepped his judicial boundaries. Nonetheless, the heavy ball of destruction started to roll; and Theodore Barrett became an instant hero to many and the devil incarnate to others. If it happened to one small sect of Christianity, it set a precedent for others to fall. The Cosmos and the fair Mistress laughed, while chaos filled the courtroom. A blur to Ted, his brothers, and their wives, they listened unbelievingly to the decisions of this very angry Judge, thumping a gavel so hard, its head nearly snapped.

Although Karen was out on bail, the baby remained under hospital security. Ted had one last devastating case to hear, and if the results came in as *guilty*, he would have Willow. Another abuse trial, with a female Judge in charge, took only a few days, since the church was busy with other legal problems. Karen Barrett received a full twelve-vote count of guilty, thanks to Annie's shy testimony. Taken away without a glance back, she vanished from sight. With a nod from the Judge, Annie slipped through the door behind the bench, to bring and place the bruised baby into judicial arms for her own eyes to witness. Cradling Willow gently, the woman gazed up from the dazzling blue eyes, to fixate on those of her crying father, who reached out tentatively with his cast-covered arm to touch his child. The room instantly quieted. Holding the real proof in her arms, the woman struck her gavel softly, like the ringing of a chime. Custody belonged solely to Theodore Barrett, with no visitation rights for the mother upon her release, and another gift was graciously bestowed --the baby officially became a Barrett--given names to be determined.

Life started anew, with one request to come around the bench and claim his daughter. Aided by his attorney, Ted made the walk toward the tiny bundle, in a pale yellow blanket, placed judiciously upon his good shoulder and snuggled into his neck. Everyone stopped to watch the emotional father falter, as Willow contently smiled for the first time. Stillness reigned to hear only one sound: a baby breathing and remembering her father's scent. She knew him instinctively, and that was not all this little creature knew.

Lavender smiled at the tears of joy filling the room, watching a father struggle to stroke his child's dark mass of hair with his free fingers, while she slept safely on his shoulder. In her rightful place, this infant would blossom into the spiritual leader of the *Beginning Again*. The Mistress relaxed in her realm of mist and magic, pondering on what may come.

Six weeks of hard-hitting, hurting evidence, all Ted's burdens fell from his shoulders. Knowing the decision non-retractable, he had his daughter forever. No longer having to face the church or his parents, he had a bigger, happier family with David and their daughters, his brothers and their wives, Steven and Dr. Thurgood, and always to be included, Bernard and Maria, plus an industry of friends cheering him on. For the first time, he did not feel alone, and one call to his partner had two men sobbing over their new baby. From the quiet of the Judge's chambers, Ted babbled incoherently, as David heard and understood the emotion of the words, and the tears of happiness and sorrow that fell. As a father of three, now four, his heart could not stand the strain, and he urged Ted to let him hear Willow coo or cry. Only a few sweet breaths, thousands of miles away, came through. Enough for now, he whispered her magic name into the receiver, sending messages of love to a baby so small, yet hearing every word.

Miraculously, Willow Barrett's bruises, scratches, and bites disappeared the day she was placed on her father's good shoulder. His armor also came off within the week of returning to the safety of the Kincaid residence, and his daughter never left his warm, loving arms. Only Bernard's strength forced Ted to relinquish Miss Barrett for changing and bathing, while insisting the father rest, one who wanted nothing more than to hold his daughter and cry in thanks, waiting for his Knight to join them. With their new home complete, Ted and Willow moved in mid-July. Delayed by technical and weather problems, David would return mid-August, giving Ted a chance to ensure every picture hung straight, and each fence post held firm. More importantly, he became a father to his little girl.

On David's insistence, Ted checked into the hospital with Willow for full examinations as a precaution. Through all the shuffling back and forth, she remained beautiful, happy, and very alert. No one could deny the extraordinary looks of the petite innocent; perfectly shaped for one so small; and she had her father's remarkable eyes. Almost frightening when fully open, they glistened as two sapphire gems flickering with fire; oceans of deep blue drew you in, drowning you with emotions never experienced. Ted recognized his own eyes, remembering nickname, devil-child, because of them. His most lucrative asset, they also would be for Willow.

With the drag queen in tow, to teach the new father everything needed to raise a premature baby, and a female one at that, the three departed the Kincaid mansion to begin anew. The world saw hundreds of different images, of the man now capable of holding his child properly; and in a Gothic manor house in the English countryside, a steady hand cut and pasted each picture of father and daughter into LaCoix's own scrapbook.

CHAPTER 44

As predicted for mid-August, David, Holly, and Maria packed up and flew away in a dream. The moment the words, *'that's a wrap',* echoed across the set, the curtain came down on their adventures in the land of magic and mystery. They would remember it all. A change of planes in L.A., with a short flight to Tucson, would wing them to a new house never seen, a new baby never met, grandparents never shared, a *wedding* not yet planned, and a partner, father, and friend to lavish their love. Life thrived abundantly with the promising merger of two families, currently scattered and bewildered at how to react within the central core of the whirling vortex.

His new life pleased David who thrilled over a beginning with Ted and their daughters. He smiled contentedly throughout the long trip. Adding his parents, sons, and a consenting first wife to the milieu, along with Ted's brothers and a sister-in-laws, many special occasions of their own creation waited celebrating. They were unto themselves, a small band of independent thinkers and imaginative minds, open to all the possibilities presented. He looked forward to the wild ride, and reflected upon the loneliness he felt when *Outlaw's Heart* commenced. With Rebecca strangling him into submission, he sensed missing something inexplicable. By finding the lost piece, and inserting that one integral part into his jigsaw puzzle, his life fell into place. It had not been easy; and he had been warned; but he would never stop thanking the Mistress for her gift of Theodore Barrett: his most important wish.

Ted arranged to pick them up directly on the tarmac, away from the crowds. Airport officials complied with the request, happy to avoid unwanted screaming or jeering created by an appearance of the infamous pair. Any rumor of their presence drew riotous attention. A unique feeling for David, he hid his face and paranoia behind the London Times on landing, while business and economy class marched through first-class. Once the aircraft emptied, lightning speed took over, with Holly running the distance to the rear of the plane. With her injuries now only reminder twinges, she dashed down the gangway in a sprint to the outstretched invitation of her daddy. Immediately tossed into the air, she felt his loving arms for the first time. He did not flinch in pain, but squeezed her sore ribs until she could barely breathe. Upon receiving the hug and kisses she had waited for, Ted popped her into the back of the new BMW 700 series chariot of gold.

Ted turned to catch a striking man watching from the hatch: his Knight, with platinum blond hair dazzling in the afternoon sun, and a laughing smile recognizable to millions. His heart leapt across the blackened tarseal, bounced to the backdoor of the plane, where David plucked it out of the air to keep forever. The man, who saved him from the fringe of madness so many times, stood frozen waiting, as he did himself. Suddenly, as if jabbed by an electrical charge, two men took off at a run, the tall blond clasping his smaller partner around the hips, hoisting him up into a full body press. Ted encircled the handsome head and held on tight when whirled around, coming to a gentle landing and a sensual rub all the way down. Feeling and smelling the other, they cared little of whom might be watching.

David could only grin devilishly at the boyish face. Ted looked healthier and happier, with a slight tan bringing out the freckles on his nose, and those shining sun streaks in the whimsically styled, longish hair. His young partner walked with the agility and stealth of an Asian cat, while his arms moved freely, growing stronger. To prove it, Barrett lifted a heavier bag without a grimace. Luminous and alive, he radiantly glowed for the adoring gaze of his lover. Excited on seeing him, after too many months, David grabbed him again, and squeezed hard, until giggles filled this special day. After a little tussling and much laughter, they approached their new vehicle, where Maria prepared herself to climb into the back with her charge. Stopped for a hug from Ted, it was a moment, considering Theodore Barrett never touched a woman unless in front of a camera. Their nanny received a treasured welcoming gift; she could not be more delighted. Life started anew for Maria who chuckled, patted his cheek, and comfortably made herself at home in the luxury sedan. Ted insisted on driving; and David relented, happy just to sit beside him, staring and grinning. Their lives unfolded to the *happily-ever-after* page.

Everyone comfortably settled in for the long drive, ready to hear Ted speak. They had made wagers on the plane; but he fooled them all. He did not start with Willow, the house, or events in England, but forced them to wait expectantly for something besides the welcoming words. Driving at a respectable family speed, Ted only smiled brightly, while playing seductively with the hand squeezing his thigh. His quiet signal of a come-on, David held his aching groin in check, prepared for an uncomfortable journey.

Silence came as an unwanted surprise. Holly tried first, with a question about her room, receiving a one-statement answer that he hoped she liked it. David's turn, he inquired about Willow, only to receive a two-statement reply that she grew stronger, and the one night in hospital had been worthwhile. LaCoix took it no further and turned to look back at Maria for help. She only shrugged, knowing the man would speak when ready.

An hour into the drive, they passed through the most spectacular desolation, known only to a few venturesome types. Acres of dried parched earth and shrub cactus spread in wonder before them, and David remembered the magic Ted promised. A dramatic change of environment, he already loved it. The passengers, however, could not stand the silence another second; with thousands of questions, they refused to wait. Holly opened the floodgates with her further understanding of mystical creatures, through her meetings with the Lady Faery who gave, to the very grown-up six-year-old, new ideas of the *Beginning Again*. She even understood when Willow spoke to her. The revelation received a look of acknowledgment, which made David ponder on the easy acceptance, considering it derailed him when Holly told him a month earlier.

LaCoix used another tactic, with one of their favorite subjects: moviemaking. He rattled off the comings and goings of *Lord Worthington-Smythe*. Editing would make it a great picture. A very pleased and proud look came from the one-sided discussion, along with a hard squeeze of his hand. He kept quiet, pleading for help a second time from the backseat. Again, Maria said little, only expressing her relief at coming home to her country, her territory, and her climate. She wistfully whispered a wish, to see the desert in full bloom come spring; and with that thought, the slow, rambling monologue by Barrett began. The man could speak; they quieted to listen.

With the dramatic landscape of wilderness surrounding the estate, perfect for riding, trekking, and exploring the legends of long ago, it waited for Holly to discover. Ted had honed his knowledge on the folklore; the mystery lay hidden within the tales of Native Americans and those south of the border. Together, they would venture forth to uncover the reality of such phenomenon as shape shifting and speaking with animals. Although, the land was sparse and sandy, the few varieties of cacti held a sense of mysticism within their spiked arms, reaching for the sun during the day, becoming eerie, haunting silhouettes at sunset. Every night and early morning, since moving in, Ted watched the drama of the slow dance of light and shadow with

Willow, introducing his daughter to the moody sky's ever-changing palette. Nature's displays of thunder, lightning, rain, rainbows, and brilliant sunshine would be a backdrop for their adventures. He had washed away Willow's first tears under a soft, warm rain.

The house, not yet in view, appeared to merge into colorful gardens; and Ted surmised the underground springs created the luxurious foliage they had planted. With the entire estate too large for them to handle, even with Bernard's help, he took the liberty of hiring additional staff. Ted engaged a middle-aged couple, both of Mexican-Cherokee descent. Another woman seemed a necessity in raising two little girls, and someone for Maria to converse with, thrilling their nanny, considering the isolation. A wonderful cook, Carmen even enticed Ted to try anything placed before him. Her husband, Paulo, a gardener and builder of things, also marveled at the plants already established, making it his job to raise their own vegetables and fruit. He suggested they choose a name to put on the main gate, which he would engrave in wood. The idea started wheels turning, but the passengers remained silent to hear more.

After his first success, Barrett forged ahead to employ another pairing, rather more unusual, to take on the responsibilities of housekeeping, to care for the needs of the family and guests, to aid the cook when necessary, to tend to small children, and to care for the stables currently vacant. A gay couple in their fifties, they had lived together for some thirty-years. Quiet, polite, and very hard working, they had remained secluded on their own small working ranch for three decades. Away from prying eyes, they grew accustomed to peace and quiet, yet their loneliness drove them to respond to the small advertisement in the local paper. A hidden oasis and a gay family, with special children, appealed to them immediately. Jamie and Craig had Bernard's approval, happy to have some male company to talk with, over a glass of Chablis. Both David and Ted laughed over the scene: a flamboyant drag queen, with expensive tastes and bizarre clothing, befriending two older ranch hermits of beer and beans; they would fascinate each other if nothing else. David's smile grew wider, enthralled by the choice of employees. Having never made such decisions, Ted had little criteria to choose the proper people, initiating more amusement in the older man, wondering how this mix would work. He said nothing and allowed Ted to continue.

Maria and Bernard had quarters both private and within the main house, depending on the situation of Ted or the girls. With the constant fear of the baby's health, someone needed to stay close. Holly required female guidance, along with an escort for the ritual shopping, school, and transportation. Willing to participate, the newest father hesitantly volunteered for numerous activities, from dumping them into a bath, to teaching them desert survival techniques. Accompanying them to shop sputtered out of his mouth, including entering the dreaded department men refused to go through, the exception of Bernard. David chuckled over the announcement, but heard the fear in the voice. Ted took a giant step as a father to take on responsibility of caring for girls he knew nothing about. It would open his eyes to new wonders; and a picture filled David's head of their teenage daughters tossing flimsy lingerie at him, while they buried themselves in the business of buying. The amusing thought gave him a reason to look out the side window to stop from laughing aloud.

David agreed the girls came first on their list of priorities. The lessons Holly learned, in the meadows and forests of England, were not be interfered with, by a discriminating remark by any member of the staff or her teachers. School had become a major problem for the older father. He attempted to find suitable arrangements for his daughter, but with her extraordinary abilities surfacing, few facilities could provide sufficient understanding of such a gifted and enlightened child. She challenged everything intellectually and spiritually. Not wanting falsehoods dictated to her, David opted to continue her home schooling for the present. With fatherly reasoning coming to the fore, he did not want his baby in a boarding school far from home. His search stopped, to concentrate on finding possible playmates for her. Another brick wall rose before him, realizing Holly Jane incapable of communicating with her own age group, as she was far beyond them in many ways, boring easily. It had become apparent with the Morris children, even after the forgiveness, that Holly's peers were adults and smart ones: a major dilemma.

His concerns swept away with other pertinent matters, as the car turned past a weathered, wooden pole, with a pink rose bush growing over it. They came to a stop, blocked by a charming, old-fashioned entry. The posts, from which the simple gate hung, and part of the barbed wire fencing, were covered with the same shrub roses of yellow and pink. Beautiful in a simplistic, quaint fashion, it appeared too easy to knock over by the smallest domestic. David again chuckled to himself; a far more efficient form of security required installation; for now, he waited for more of Ted's innocent view of life. Much to his surprise, his partner pointed to six locations hiding security cameras, randomly scanning the length of the fence on either side. Located in the thorny bush, enveloping the post marking their property, one clicked pictures of the rear license plate, while another two, covertly placed, pointed at the driver and eyed the passenger side. Pushing the remote, the gates gently opened without a mouse's squeak. Ted leaned through his open window to talk to the last camouflaged camera and monitor. You could actually see and speak to a face, one that laughed and smiled. An outside company tracked all arrivals and departures.

Another surprise, more cameras viewed the length of the estate along the main road, and along the electrical towers, stretching toward the hidden dwelling amongst the pastel rocks. Once through the gate, their road turned into a treacherous track of dust and rocks, bumps and jarring attacks. Rough and primitive, it appeared as a simple decorative little gate, leading down a terrible road, to a possible small ranch house, dispelling many intruders by just looking normal. David liked the warm entry into their private world, without the visual impact of formality, which usually accompanied such secured premises. For his own paranoia, he certainly wanted more. The conversation would never come up.

Nearing the rock formation, the car took a sweeping turn, to confront a more imposing entrance. It hung from twenty-foot adobe walls, blocking off the horseshoe canyon. Almost impenetrable on their own, along with the non-scalable rocks on either side, this camouflaged entry satisfied LaCoix's need for protection. The austere fortification softened with a purple-blossomed vine, climbing up the pastel-hued stucco that blended into the protective boulders. Blooms filled the air with a sweet fragrance, hiding the innocent looking but hot-wired blockade. Only the most skilled of thieves and criminals could scale the walls, only to be fried at the top, if they made it through the entanglement of prickly, poisonous foliage. David's smirk changed to wonder, while scouring the entire structure for imperfections, and then smiling in disbelief at its indestructible beauty. In awe, he turned to Ted, who cocked his head, as if to question any other color could protect them better than lavender.

Barrett hit the remote again and drove on. Red earth cinders leveled the road within, stopping the jostling and their teeth from rattling. They entered a wide expanse of greener desert, which included meandering rows of columnar cypress, to stop the ravages of dust storms from hitting the staff quarters on their right, and hid what may be the main house. The smell intoxicated David, while it freshened the stifling desert air. Amazement grew, spotting the very private oasis of seven cottages with their own gardens, shade trees, carports, and an even greater surprise, a camouflaged green vehicle for each, in a variety of models. Maria squealed over the cottage given to her; her first real house had the charm of a perfectly cared for home of undetermined age. A small green station wagon sat idly undercover, and their nanny had her own car, just for her and the girls. She could not stop giggling, clapping, and chattering to herself in Spanish, with Holly equally as excited.

David considered the expense, but the cars were domestic and extremely road worthy. Another good idea, considering they would be traveling to pick up supplies, kids, horses, and the list went on. No need to run down the bright golden chariot, another choice of Barrett's for his continuing need of sunshine. LaCoix immediately thought of Peerce's black one, rocketing them to San Diego that dreadful morning. He shook himself from the horrific memory, and jumped back into this afternoon of wonderment.

Driving further, along another winding road, with tall cypresses obstructing and guarding further viewing, a similar vine-covered wall loomed before them. A monolithic, wooden gate opened by remote, and the immense doors slowly unveiled their new residence. Three mouths dropped. The house lay as if it had been there since Mexican territory. Magnificent, it captured their Spirits and imaginations, hearing fountains splash, feeling the faint warm breeze through the newly planted eucalyptus, and smelling the myriad of different flowers and foliage covering everything. The car halted at a splendid staircase, leading to a dark wood, deeply engraved doorway, which suddenly flung open, as Bernard charged out in an exuberant greeting with kisses planted on each cheek, including David's, much to his surprise and merriment. A day for smiling, life flowed around them, waiting for the next wonder beyond the threshold. The portal to their sanctuary from the world, LaCoix stood quietly, gazing upon what he had imagined for so long; his vision had materialized. He was home, and felt it the moment he stepped over the threshold.

The biggest grin crossed his face to see the two signs hanging overhead, *Welcome Home,* and *Happy Birthday, David*. He had forgotten; he had forgotten Ted's as well. It did not deter his lover from pulling him around to give him the smoldering kiss he wished for at the airport. Nearly collapsing from the erotic lip meltdown, he held and squeezed the younger man tightly, knowing he could no longer hurt the frail figure physically. The slip of a body, he wanted to play with forever, made him ache for the need of what the man's scent conjured up. Everything from love to lust luridly tempted David to ravish his favorite Teddy Bear amongst the heavenly bouquet of sweet roses decorating the foyer.

Reluctantly pushing away, Ted shifted David, to return his gaze to the driveway. Bernard drove up in a bright crimson Ferrari, sans top, fluttering with black ribbons and white roses; the only birthday gift needed for a feisty Leo. Wildly excited eyes, and the happiest grin of thanks, brought on more embraces, increasing the ecstasy within his young lover. A past memory filled the two men, but this *red boys' toy* belonged to both, as Ted considered it his birthday present as well, since a diamond had not appeared to adorn his finger. With a great deal of laughter and many apologies, LaCoix promised many birthday gifts, whenever the mood struck his heart; and Barrett still had to wait for his surprise. Another hug and a spin off the ground, Ted beamed and enticed them into more magic.

One wonder led to another. They walked around the expansive gardens; shown the many, large, guest quarters, placed away from the house to secure their own privacy; and the stables hidden neatly and sheltered in the shade of a little outcropping. Even the horses would breathe cool, fresh air, scented by the eucalyptus shade trees and hanging roses dangling off the roof. Everything fit neatly into its rightful place, within what David thought to be only a small canyon. Somehow, it had grown larger when he looked past the last row of green windbreaks into the pastureland, running for miles to the end of the boxed-in rock enclosure. He had made the right choice; and Ted brought him home.

Introduced to the new staff, they seemed very amicable, almost cute in their first meeting with the famous LaCoix. His bright smile and sparkling excited eyes eased their nerves; and everyone went back to work. After the long drive, David and Maria headed for the nearest bathrooms, allowing a nervous Ted to show Holly her room. She clasped her arms around him in approval, while excitedly dragging him about, giggling and squealing at every treasure found; he passed her test of good taste. His daughter seemed older than the ages, in the guise of a six-year-old; and he wondered at her newfound abilities. She acted like a contented little girl; but the overwhelming revelations, which sprang from her mouth, were incomprehensible to him. On cue, David walked in and his slow whistle gave Ted approval for the decor of his daughter's room. Adult in a dainty, feminine form, it had a hint of rustic charm, inviting enough for her fathers who could be easily intimidated with ruffles and lace. White, pink, with touches of English country green, the room oozed of British East India charm; and it had the fair young miss dancing in new purple sneakers. Last seen in a state of broken bones and bruises, Ted thrilled to see her back to *Tigger* bouncing. Picked up and squeezed harder than their meeting at the airport, she knew her daddy loved her, and sensed that whatever she said, he would believe in his own way.

Nearing the finale, the elder LaCoix could not wait a moment longer, requesting Ted and he be left alone for a few moments, giving Maria and Holly a chance to investigate their quarters. After a private cuddle between fathers, the blond one made a move to find his new daughter. He caught the sad tear in Ted's eye and a hapless smile, but a soft kiss melted the tension he felt run through the skeleton. Something seemed awry, underlying the excitement of their return, and a shiver ran up David's spine. Not the time to ask, he followed Ted toward their own quarters. Hand in hand, they entered.

"I'm speechless, Ted. This is exactly how I imagined the house in my head. It looks like it's been here forever." Everything felt like Barrett, yet wherever he looked, amazingly he saw himself as well. This sanctuary fit them, and probably had always meant to.

"It took on a life of its own when we moved in. I tried to make it light, with lots of open, airy spaces in the house, and certainly outside for the girls to play in the gardens. Can you imagine Holly in the labyrinth? We'd never find her."

"You certainly succeeded in softening the look of stucco and rocks. The gardens flow into the house and vice versa. You did a hell of a job; it's perfect; and I like these colors, better than the samples you sent me: all natural earthy hues, dusky in tone, like the canyon itself. The entire venue is extraordinary, much like the man who supervised and added his own magic."

"I hoped the interior would meld into the exterior, like you wanted. That's my last surprise for later tonight, when everyone's asleep, and I have you to myself." Ted's bashful grin shone for a moment, only to look down to watch his feet shuffle.

"Definitely looking forward to that, but there's something I haven't done. Congratulations on your Oscar. Where have you hidden it?"

"I feel embarrassed when I look at that freaky statuette; so for now, Oscar is standing solo in a niche of the Library."

"You earned the award, Ted; and I'm extremely proud of you." David gave *Peter Pan* his overdue hug.

"Thanks, but it won't be fully displayed until you receive one."

"So, we have to wait until hell freezes over. Since you've placed everything else appropriately, I'll find it and situate your first award in the proper manner. Now you, Mr. Barrett, impressed me today, handling the long drive on your own." David turned the conversation around and did a quick scrutiny of the man, assuring himself that Ted looked and felt as well as he acted.

"What a blast. Always surrounded by babysitters, an open road, a CD blaring, it was awesome. You have no idea how I looked forward to picking you up on my own, even stopping for a Big Mac, if you can believe that." A beaming look vanquished his partner's fears.

"And now you're exhausted. You look so much better, Ted, but you appear ready to fall over. Are you feeling okay?"

"I'm feeling great, David, and really happy to see you. Right now, the Princess Willow Rose awaits." Ted sheepishly grinned, still unable to express himself, unless in private. He opened the nursery door, connected to their room for the meantime. Filled with prisms of crystal, creating rainbows in the sun-filled room, the effect of so much light, and sparkling reflected color, dazzled the older man. Used to fewer windows and much cooler rooms in a desert dwelling, this shone as an incubator for their baby. Both father and daughter needed the warmth to maintain their intolerance to cold: one because of his illness, and the other to regain what she had lost with her premature arrival on the planet. In reality, she should only be three-months-old, not nearing five.

David watched impatiently, allowing Ted the time to introduce their daughter to him. Feelings of being a new father washed over him; he wanted to snatch her away and bury his nose in the smell of a fresh, clean baby. The remembered scent made him smile, thinking he may borrow Willow's talcum powder to sprinkle over Ted. Saving the mischief for later, he delighted in seeing his young partner gently handle the extraordinarily small package in her brightly flowered sleepers. He wondered if Ted purchased them, and further mused, imagining Bernard and his lover fussing over baby attire in a department store full of pregnant women.

The young father cuddled the tiny bundle within his bony arms, and their baby wallowed in his warmth, not missing the comfort of a full chest of plump softness. David heard not a coo or a sound, but only the breaths of a baby's sigh and her father's soft whisper. "Hey, Willow Rose. I'm home, and Dad has finally arrived. I know you've been waiting; but sometimes Daddy can't be here. We're together now, all of us."

David thought it an odd way to talk to an infant; and yet Ted seemed to wait for answers in his head. The proud man walked over, trustfully placing his treasure into the outstretched arms of her other parent.

"Goodness, Willow, you're the size of a button. Look at those beautiful eyes; you are an Elfin princess. Your Daddy mentioned your long, curly, black hair, but I never imagined you'd have so much of it, just like a friend of ours." David could not help the gushing tone coming out of his mouth, to the great surprise of Barrett. The austere façade melted away at the smell of baby powder, and he cradled her close, blowing on her stomach, prompting smiles about the room, visible and invisible. The volatile actor was a pushover with babies. "Ted, she's so tiny, barely fitting from my hand to my elbow. She certainly has your eyes and contagious grin. How did your Daddy get so lucky to have such a happy baby? Your sister also smiled a lot at your age. Do you both have a secret to share?" Kicking in her joy, David nearly dropped the excited little bundle.

"She likes you."

"I sincerely hope so, because I've waited a long time to hold you, Willow; ever since you breathed into my ear over the phone. Do you remember that? We're all starting a big adventure today." David laughed, gently raising her in both hands, to stare directly into those miraculous eyes. It hit him instantly; she spoke to him in Lavender fashion, but without a voice. A silent giggling filled his head, and thoughts flowed into him at rocketing speed, while gazing into those sapphire crystals that filled the entire eye sockets. Bewitching and mesmerizing, they revealed pure loving thoughts for her Dad. "I love you too, my little one."

"You heard her? Guess I should say: sensed her."

"Yes I did, and very distinctly. She's awesome. Holly's starting to do the same thing. It's damn eerie sometimes, to be told what you're thinking before you've said it."

"Get used to it, David. You have to feel her in your mind all the time, and be aware of..."

The blond-haired father looked right, to see Ted wiping his face dry with his hands. "What is it? Remember those cliffhangers? Let's not start that again." Instantly concerned, this was not just a happy reunion; something more drastic loomed before him; and it appeared Ted could not understand its full meaning, or how to tell him.

"I'm glad you can feel her thoughts. It's important because my... our daughter is mute."

The word reverberated in David's skull, with the real sound said by Ted, and the thought from Willow. Their baby would never be heard; no little angelic voice, only the thoughts she sent, and the ancient wisdom shining from the dark pools of the bluest blue. The smile on her face beamed brighter, comforting the older man in his shock. He thought they would have some difficulties, but this represented a massive hurdle.

"Are you sure nothing can be done?"

"Yes, and she doesn't want anything done. Look at her and listen. She's telling you everything is as it should be." With another sniff, Ted swept away the liquid welling in the matching set of blues.

"You honestly can't believe that? What did they say at the hospital? Is everything else okay?" David's new concern, over their baby, had him cuddling her paternally, playing gently with her little hands. She had a powerful grip for one so small.

"She's extremely healthy and fit for being premature; her internal organs developed as they should. She's only missing vocal cords, and will always be on the small side."

"So, little one, we're going to have a quiet household, unless you take up drumming and join a rock band. I don't think your Daddy could tolerate such a scenario, but would probably let you get away with it." David directed his blackened spirit to more important matters. Willow appeared content, and another baby giggle tingled in his head. Ted chuckled, and the gloom of bad news dissipated. Other than being mute, Willow radiated well-being, with eyes glistening killer gorgeous.

"You'll know she needs you from a great distance. I have to apologize for talking so little on the drive home. Our first time apart, since the trial, I could hear her calling, until she fell asleep.

My depression in England came from her sad cries, but I didn't understand then. She needed my help, David, and I couldn't hear her thoughts." Tears suddenly splashed down the remorseful face; and LaCoix reached out his empty arm to capture each droplet on his black-clad shoulder.

"How could you know, Ted?" David nearly collapsed himself, but a baby's thoughts soothed away the grief.

"I'm sorry, Willow, but I tried to send you messages today. Did you hear me singing to you while I drove? I guess I'm just not very good at it yet. She does cry, David, but only through tears of sadness or joy. You're such a clever, beautiful, little girl; I just wish I could keep up with you."

The blond actor felt a few tears bubbling in the corner of his eyes, as he held his newest baby against his chest with one arm, and his bigger baby with the other. The proud, young father took it all for granted, as if normal. How would he know otherwise? Unable to receive comfort from Lavender, he felt Willow's overwhelming mystical power blocking their Fey. The baby became his soothing consolation, while she grinned at her Daddy who stared across David's chest into the bewitching little face. Blue eyes were two inches from the identical ones, as a slim finger touched the diminutive hand reaching for the elusive object in play. Right on the mark, the little one had it in her grasp and held on with a big smile. David's heart broke, his head spinning with the love transmitted between the two he held so tightly.

"Sit down, David; I'll get Holly. Willow's worried you might drop her." Ted laughed at the surprised look on the man's face, and scooted out of the room, leaving him alone to converse with his uniquely special daughter, another magical being that filled his thoughts with beauty.

"Now listen up, soon-to-be Miss Willow Rose Barrett-LaCoix. Your Dad will never let you fall. I've never dropped your sister, or your brothers. That's right, you have two grown brothers to meet, once they get used to us. You are a wondrous child; and it feels so good to hold a baby again. Maybe you could stay like this for a while longer, since I missed your first months on the planet. I sense you have the power to do almost anything." David received another baby grin when he looked down at the impish face. This extraordinary child understood everything said; with an attitude he could understand and deal with; a little spitfire, and if she had been a car, she would glow bright red.

Holly arrived, happily attached to Ted's hand. Extremely quiet, almost in reverence of something greater, David saw the understanding in her eyes. She knew; and it amazed him. Holly Jane made herself comfortable in the large rocker, custom-built with a little girl in mind, who would be holding a smaller, more fragile one comfortably, without the chance of a mishap. Ted thought of everything, or was it Willow? Intrigue grew by the second, watching his own daughter, sitting calmly, waiting patiently to take the baby away from his arms, which did not want to be empty. Placing Willow securely within her sister's embrace, Ted stepped away, while David encircled him from behind, feeling the heart beating overly fast. Two men stood, watching their daughters with pride. A close study of the girls brought instant recognition of a deep level of communication between them, and not in words. Holly would smile and nod, occasionally wrinkling up her face and shaking the long blonde locks in a gesture of *no*. Enjoying her telepathic conversation, she giggled, while Willow happily squirmed and kicked with each reaction she received from this very important person in her life.

The two men heard only the gaiety in their heads and smiled in wonderment. How many conversations would they hear? David grew more entranced; Ted only felt jealousy. His daughter accepted the two people he loved; he never felt so bad. A paradox he did not understand, until his daughter's thoughts rushed at him, vowing she would always remain beside him. With the joyous confirmation, Ted sank back into his lover's arms; he now understood happiness for the first time.

CHAPTER 45

Weariness filled the evening with yawns and sleepy eyes. It had been a long trip from England for three of them, with a two-hour drive to their new home. Although they tried to rest on the plane, excitement caused fitful naps and anticipation headaches. Ted's first day out alone, and the drive to and from Tucson, also took its toll. Physically and emotionally wrecked from manic panic, at what his family would think of the home he helped create, Ted felt the desperation to please everyone, spurring the household to make everything perfect. With the important enthusiastic approval received, it gave the young man a little energy to fulfill a promise.

A quiet, family dinner, graciously including the staff members, enticed them all to eat. With the excellence of the food, along with the fine Beaujolais Ted had chosen, the anxious band of fatigued humanity dined in family fashion, with steaming bowls placed on the table to serve themselves. Enjoying the company of his new employees, David kept grinning, waiting for the proverbial pin to burst his enchanted bubble. Holly happily consumed something new and delicious; but her eyes told him she could not wait to put her weary head on her new pillows. Already fed and prepared for bed, Willow rested in her baby seat, her eyes never leaving her father until she dozed off. Once they had their little darlings tucked in, and if his partner could keep his eyes open, David looked forward to holding his lover, while whispering words he longed to say in private.

Ted ate slowly, Carmen reminding him to chew every mouthful to keep it down. He did very well; and David beamed at him, meeting his shy gaze across the table. Each sip of wine toasted a secret; the charming tinkle of crystal against crystal celebrated the faint chimes of *once-upon-a-time*. Exhausted from their year of tribulations, they now felt secure in a place of their own, finalized in a grand surprise of a sparkling fireworks cake, covered with white and black roses, and two names written on top. With the traditional song sung, birthdays forgotten commemorated, life began anew.

Willow had fallen asleep with a kiss from her sister and doting fathers. Holly's turn, she clamored to get undressed, oblivious of the two men scrambling after the little desert mouse to accommodate her every wish, from the right bubble bath, the heart-shaped soap, to the strawberry shampoo, until she splashed happily in her own luxury tub. The spray jets created more fun of floating bubbles, which drifted from the bathroom into the bedroom, where the couple sat laughing. They enjoyed the angelic little voice singing English lullabies; but Ted's head drooped, for he would never hear Willow in this sweet manner. Reaching over, LaCoix lifted the chin, stroking it gently, with his thumb, to bring the smile back. The melancholy lifted as their mouse scampered in, donned only in a towel. David did not hesitate to rub her down, reminding her not to run on slippery tile floors, as he threw her favorite nightie over her head to cover her shivering nudity.

Ted intently studied each move made, learning the appropriate manner of handling such a whimsical creature. It appeared so natural and easy for LaCoix; necessity and adaptability became his gentle Knight. With a brush tossed at him, he hesitantly accepted the honor of untangling the white-gold silk. Afraid he would hurt her, it was a start; and he finished polishing her shiny new, before she took a flying leap into the soft pillows and slip under the feathered, wildflower comforter. Contented with their fatherly kisses and the feeling they would always be there, she drifted off with Sir Lancelot in her arms, to a place only Willow understood. Someday it would make sense to Holly; but for now, she had a sister; and dreamtime awaited.

David and Ted walked hand-in-hand to their own quarters, where the new arrival took the opportunity to better scrutinize his surroundings, finding them very much to his liking. He had been concerned, unaware of Ted's tastes, considering his inability to express them in his former world. Cozy and comfortable, in tan leather and patterned native blankets, it provided everything two men required. Some of David's mementos, from his various film locations, some of Ted's, the eclectic collection of paintings on the walls, all complimented the light shades of a dusty desert sunset. There were quaint little touches of white roses in heavy terracotta pots and Medieval, day-counting candles, the decor also mixed with a few broken relics found on one of Ted's adventure trips. David's Christmas present, taken from his luggage, added to the menagerie that made up two men's lives, not to mention the large bear staring at them from the rocking chair. The two men did fit together: their similarities and their differences. Flickering firelight shadowed the room, making lights unnecessary to appreciate the comfort of the seductive setting. His favorite heady fragrances of leather and silver fir merged with the candy-cane and lemongrass scent of Ted. Masculine in every respect, for David's male psyche, the room also paled with the duskier hues of evening for a softer heart. His lover had made it theirs.

A hidden door mysteriously opened on the opposite wall. He would have never noticed it, if Ted had not released the lock with a flick of an unseen switch. The mysterious portal led to a private courtyard for two to share and converse. Something never discussed, having no knowledge at the time, two men needed a special place to play; it afforded them an ingenious sunken garden, tunneled into the rock for hot summer days, and trees and shrubs of white flowers to sparkle silver under the night's bright moon.

David lunged for the suddenly fleeing Ted; he missed the attempt. With a breathless laugh, thoughts of his lover willed his weary body to play any game to please an equally tired, but teasing partner.

Chuckling happily, Ted proved his prowess for climbing, scampering up the Hopi-styled ladder, to get to the very high roof of the hacienda. Right behind him, David chased the man up the rungs, to something he hoped would be his last surprise for the day. It was much more; they had their own personal lookout. Even in the dark shadow of nightfall, a panorama spread to the craggy escarpment at the end of their canyon, to the surrounding protective rocks on either side, only to turn to face the vastness of a desert with no fences, and the sky gently touching down to earth. They could view the sunset and the sunrise, from this ethereal piece of paradise: a sanctuary for forbidden desires and actions.

David LaCoix surveyed his kingdom, when Lavender suddenly brushed his cheek. *'Welcome home, my friend. Be happy.'* Her presence disappeared, as the flicker of a match caught his eye. With candle after candle lit, the roof glowed in every detail. Four-foot walls protected them from falling; different night-blossoming flowers of white glowed lantern bright to cover the pastel stucco; and a black velvet curtain, full of pinprick holes of twinkling light, provided a shroud to hide their secret sins. A night garden of silver and shadows left David moonstruck. A magical place for two very special people, he laughed like a kid winning his first stuffed toy at the circus.

Closing his eyes, he took in the fragrance of the desert air, filling his being with hope, until he stood frozen, sensing the aura of what Ted would describe as heaven. He opened them to catch the slender body silhouetted by the falling sun. Sky-clad and pale, his lover had never been so bold with his flirtations. A futon lay at the younger man's feet, covered with blankets and satin sheets, while two glasses dangled between the slim fingers of the hand holding a frosted champagne bottle. The other hand held a long-stemmed black rose; the velvet head stroked across a silken chest, arousing nipples into burgundy garnets. David's heart soared at the birthday gift he desired--Theodore Barrett--free of all his misfortunes.

The leading man slipped out of his clothes, never diverting his eyes from the erotic statue before him. In two strides, he accepted the bottle, uncorking it without a sound. The splash of bubbling liquid, as it filled the glasses, echoed across their land; and the coyotes joined in the song. One glass David maintained; the other he handed to Ted. His partner peered up at him, his blue eyes shining from under the black lashes, beckoning him to come closer. With due deliberation, the rare blossom and its one thorn were shown to the older actor. Pricking a finger, Ted offered it to his lover in a ritualistic sacrifice. Sucking gently to stop the bleeding of the index, in all its sensuality, David then kissed it and smiled into a teasing grin. A remembered gesture, of an attempted seduction of long ago, became their first toast; a sip of champagne, shared between two loving mouths, grew into a delicious, devouring kiss. The caress started the moment; the rest of their lives unfolded to the tempo of earth's heartbeat.

Picked up without a word and gently placed in the soft cushioning, Ted felt the coolness of the sheets. He shivered slightly at the feel. Love and lust intermingled with every romantic gesture. The growing pain of his crotch, the twitching of his rectum, and the giddy feeling reaching into parts unknown, necessitated the slow exposure of his treasures, to seduce the only one to satisfy all, just with a touch. Pulsating uncontrollably, the craving orifice puckered and released, igniting every nerve in Ted's arse, aching for fulfillment. The thin legs parted and pulled forward, opening in the fluid motion of a peacock's tail feathers, displaying the waiting hunger to be satisfied. Glistening with oil, and smelling of an intoxicating fragrance, the offering bewitched his handsome hero into a temptation never seen or felt. David gasped at the erotic sight, a spectacle for his own delight, not to be seen by another. His forever partner reached between his legs to tantalize him further with the black rose, stroking the blossom over the entry to his delights, and twirling it around his swelling pink arousal, to firm the wrinkled sac with his life's essence. Up the abdomen and chest, caressing raisin-ripe nipples that protruded for suckling, the rose came to rest with a feather light touch against the boyish cheek. A final kiss to the black petals, with a sultry lick of his lips, had David throbbing in his torment to ravage the man. The blond moistened his own mouth, with a sip of champagne, on hearing the raspy whisper from Ted to enter.

David needed no further blandishment, than the sight of an ethereal figure playing the sacrificial virgin, with a seductive smile on an impish face and a little fear in the eyes. He slipped down onto the frail creature and penetrated, gently moving in so slowly, the man holding the black rose passed out from need. The green eyes rolled upward, feeling the hot interior, gaining pleasure from a tiny bone fragment, exciting his cock at the rough touch. Nothing compared to the initial entry, and knowing he could take this young man until their hearts stopped. Making the hair on his arms and legs stand up, the goose bumps created made David shudder at the intense sensation. He waited, for Ted to open his eyes, and LaCoix smiled, knowing he contributed to this ultimate reaction of his young lover.

Coming around with a soft purr, Ted arched his neck, shifting positions to allow the magnificent intruder to reach its full extent and breadth. He could feel his penetrator grow, setting off explosions along every nerve in his rectum. With tendons straining, he tucked his chin to his chest; and the thin torso curled forward. The wanton affection of his craving, slipped in that much further; and David growled deep in his euphoria. Inexperienced as he was, the younger man knew how to gain the greatest pleasure from a man whose cock tipped slightly upward. A front entry exuded more euphoria for them both, far more than the hands and knees position. Intensity of their passion rose like the steam off their sweating bodies, straining to maintain the titillating sensuality of such a torturously slow pace. The bigger man, with hair sparkling platinum in the moonlight, placed his arms in the crook of the bended knees; his fingers laced themselves into the unruly perfumed hair, pressing his palms against those perfect cheekbones. Kissing Ted without a sound, and feeling only each other's vibrations deep within, David spewed into the scorching orifice, before he had given a thrust. Ted returned the ejaculation; and two bodies lay connected, relieved of the initial need of pure lust.

Time to enjoy the pleasures of the other, after a long separation; David reveled in the feel of skin against sweaty skin. He chuckled aloud at Ted's dancing blue eyes, which watched the stars fall between his feet. The smile, of the face lying on the pillow, looking through bent knees, was real and endearing, allowing the other famous lips to come ever closer for a taste of a happy Barrett. Nibbling and kissing every part of the other became all, while the Universe watched the dance of spring and summer.

Tracing and tickling every nip and curve of a muscle, tender caresses screamed for more, reaching their lips to crave the passion of the erotic. An indulgent mouth nibbled on sweet, moist lips, intentionally protruding for a wanton attacker. Entwining tongues were hungrily accepted; mouths sealed to retain the ravishment between them. Heavy groans of needed air exchanged with open short gasps, as two men panted and sweated in the urgency of taking more and returning it tenfold. David pulled away, inducing a sensual sigh, which begged to re-ignite them with a raging fire. Ablaze with the rapture, the blond head disappeared between the outstretched thighs, lifting the smaller behind, to rim the hidden succulent morsel of the two sphincter muscles becoming more flaccid with every touch. The puckering of the sensitive orifice inflamed the need of the original offering, turning the brunet into a lightheaded frenzy of rapid in and out breaths. Experienced with only the dream of desire, David's first distasteful fears dissipated, not to return; and he gratified himself with the flavor of moistening, and then penetrating, the younger man's arse with his tongue, until Ted's whimpers initiated a convulsive jerk of his slight body.

After delighting in the wondrous remembered taste of what could only be Theodore Barrett, David pressed his tongue against the salty flavor of that one-inch hot spot under the younger man's scrotum, feeling the rising bump of the inner end of the penis hardening. The sublime pressure created a deep groan from the raspy throat and a couple of expected hip spasms. Suckling the hard, treasured stones, in their tight velvet sac, David started Ted's squirming of excited agitation, finally bringing two strong hands around to hold the frenzied action of the bony pelvis. David went down hard, engulfing the twitchy, pink shaft in need of affection and torturous foreplay; and with a long, slow sucking motion of the hard organ, he had Ted writhing, but holding back the temptation to lunge upward. An inspiring shriek of instant stimulation taunted the older man to continue his manipulations more dramatically. Taking extreme pleasure in controlling the enlivened mouthful, David attempted to maneuver his tongue around the slippery, plump snake, to tickle the slit until he heard the gasp, readying himself to swallow what would come, including the sudden attack on his head by fingers that scratched and pulled his hair.

Squeezing the bottom of the shaft a little tighter, increasing the pressure of his lips, sucking frantically while continuously taunting with his tongue, he moved his head rhythmically up and down over the straining object of his desire. It had both men in an attack of delirium. Ted let out the expected shriek, puffing instructions of harder and faster between breaths. With a simple delicate press on the sensitive magic spot with his thumb, David slipped a finger up and in, to tickle that inner fancy, turning his lover into quivering jelly with the gyrating hips of the king. Again, the younger man came, and he delivered wave after wave of sporadic gushing cum into his lover's accepting mouth. Pure nectar to David, he withdrew, licking his lips, and sharing the wonders of the taste with the provider of such a delicacy. A long kiss, without the sound of a smack, only a low growl and a softer purr merged them into one, rolling over and over amidst the rumpled sheets, only to break free, gasping for air, but still struggling for position and control. In a frenzy of two wildcats, Ted emerged the victor, landing in a position for his own playfulness, to tempt his partner's puppet back to life.

In a sixty-nine position, with David lying supine, Ted's open mouth took Knight's hardening sword deep into his throat, without the teasing or foreplay of a gentle tongue. The blond's veined, silky organ slipped easily along the natural channel, while Ted expertly accommodated the avarice snake directly into the open throat that had no end. A gasp escaped from the man losing control; David felt the hot dampness, as he slid ever further into the relaxed, dark tunnel, fearful of being swallowed by his young innocent. Ted's greatest joy to perform, the difficult action allowed David to lunge and withdraw, back and forth, into the moist cavern, so unlike the feeling of the tight, steaming excitement he looked up at and studied in amazement at its involuntary actions. Ted's enticing derriere continued to open and close, matching his frantic breathing. David pulled it down to his mouth where he eagerly rimmed it again, licking the puckering hole in unison with the uncontrollable thrusting of his deep-throated lance. Allowing both, Ted strained to stay still, taking advantage of each rapturous motion. A squeeze of his own needy shaft surprised him; and he withdrew to close his throat and suck the steaming rod in his mouth. Rolled onto his back, Ted allowed his lover to empty his essence, spurt by spurt, into his mouth, filling it rapidly to swallow and suck for more. Once again, his Knight's amazing organ grew larger in his mouth, while his own cock never ebbed for the adoration of this man. David's life essence exploded again in small ruptures for Ted to drink his fill, as his own euphoric ejaculation bounced off David's throat, to trickle its cooling essence over his own pleasure. Ted was spent. He turned, and they were both back in each other's arms, exhausted and gratified. Barrett had not yet finished with his lover, however, and he pushed himself up to lie on top of the sweating chest and heated crotch. Smiling down at the closed eyes, he gave a quick peck to the weary face and received a mischievous snicker back. Those Hollywood whites glowed in the dark; and Ted could not help laughing.

"You are a wonder, Baby. My head is reeling; I didn't think it possible. I've never felt this good or welcomed home with such bravado."

"Bravado, hunh? Man, you did all the work; and I've been waiting too damn long. Want something else from you, LaCoix."

"You're killing an old man on his birthday."

"Never, sex keeps you young and strong." Ted straddled the taut chest, his hands pinching the nipples to become hard again. He gingerly reached between his legs to capture his prize, which remained semi-erect, but with a little encouragement, created by a ring of a thumb and fingers, it rose fully, to find Ted's waiting orifice stretched wide apart by David's own willing hands. Cautiously and slowly, Ted impaled himself, groaning long and deep with a sultry gasp of success. Connected in the most physical union two men could contrive, the youngest near fainted again in his rapture.

Arching his back, he contracted his inner muscles, increasing the sensitivity for the life-giving organ that lunged in harder. Ted securely engaged LaCoix in the perfect place to satisfy his last need: an explosion inside his most sensitive erogenous zone. He wanted this blond-haired man more than riches and notoriety, desiring only this kind of adoration inside him; and he grunted and strained in pleasure, grinding the shaft in deeper, rubbing against nerves with every motion. He quivered at every stroke, sporadically spewing his own essence over David's chest; and as a finale, the rare sensation that made him swoon after an orgasmic frenzy of bucking hips.

The older man kept up his long thrusts to meet Ted's own tiring movements. Two hands were on the slight hips to help lift the smaller man, then to slam him down hard onto the full length of the penetrating intruder. Ted deeply inhaled at each smack of his butt against David's hard stones, continuing in a wilder frenzy, with David's lunges increasing in speed and shorter strokes growing more urgent. Two forceful, grunting male animals climaxed, fulfilling all expectations. Hanging on for his life, trying not to pass out and miss the moment, Ted received the most sexually induced experience a man could endure, electrified by the sensation.

Hot and sweating, the younger man fell limp, his head coming to rest on the sticky chest, panting in rhythm to the racing heart under his ear. Drained and satisfied, every inch of his sensitive rectum had been stimulated beyond imagining; he could ask for nothing more but the comforting hug. Left impaled, until the softening spear slithered out on its own, created another sudden burst inside. The phenomenon felt only once before, this night it happened twice, shooting him directly forward with its force, almost knocking his head into David's chin. The older man chuckled and gave him a squeeze, knowing what the man experienced, but wondering what it felt like. Cool desert air, mixing with the steaming bodies, surrounded them in a soft mist, easing the weariness, and entrancing the two men in its mystical, hovering motion, letting them disappear into a cloud for a few moments to finalize their ultimate bonding.

"I've missed you, David. Happy Birthday."

"You felt extraordinary tonight, Baby; and your new tailbone protrusion is an adrenaline rush."

"It didn't hurt you?"

"Hell no, makes you even sexier, knowing the satisfaction I get from rubbing it and your prostate, which gets you so excited, I can barely hang on. You're a squirmy demon, and have more strength and endurance. I couldn't keep up when you were ailing. What am I going to do now?"

"You do more than keep up, LaCoix. I lost count."

"Teddy Bear, you're a wonder, and you're mine."

"Wish I could find an endearing name for you. In the throes of passion, it would be nice to breath out something that turns you on."

"Nicknames come from tenderness, or an easy friendship. Yours came from a moment of confused affection, although you thought I was teasing."

"A secret to share. To be honest, the name turns me on. I have Sir Edmund, Holly has Sir

Lancelot, and you'll always have Sir Theodore, a.k.a. Teddy Bear."

"Think I got the best bear of the bunch, or should that be bare? You know, Mr. Barrett, you very seldom say anything when we make love. Perhaps we're busy using our mouths for something more important, and we can only groan in pleasure, or squeal like mating stallions."

"What a thing to say! Mating stallions? You may be a stud, but I can't say that about myself. That's hilarious. My Knight has changed into my stud. Gross."

"Now, that's a nickname I like; and you've inferred it unknowingly."

"What? Stud? No way." Ted laughed and nuzzled his snickering into the sweaty chest that needed a quick lick of his tongue.

"How about *Knight*. If I remember correctly, you've whispered it once or twice. The way you say it, with the word *my*, seduces me to my knees. It makes me feel protective."

"So, you really are my Knight, my Knight with his sword always ready? It's very suggestive."

"Does have those connotations; and yes, I'm always ready for you." David tickled the healed hip, until he had Ted giggling aloud. The smaller body slipped off his Knight to cuddle close.

"Think it's time we got some sleep, Baby. You've had an exhausting day. Which reminds me, I forgot to ask about your overnight stay at the hospital. How did you make out? You never said."

"Yes I did. Told you it was a good idea, considering Willow's potential problems, although it scared me."

"It's important to me, Ted. Is your health improving? I feel like I'm living on that weak precipice back in England." David held on a little tighter to a body starting to tense. Barrett had been standing in line for the Grim Reaper too long; it plagued David, wondering how much longer he would have this man next to him.

"Didn't really want to talk about it, but I guess you have to know, if you plan on spending the rest of your life with me." Ted pulled away to lie on his back and gaze at the stars. The instant feel of cold air made him shiver, as it dried off the remaining sweat.

"Let's get these blankets over us; and you tell me exactly what's happening." David bundled them together, and let Ted rest his head in the crook of his elbow. The stars sparkled gloriously in the blackness of the Mistress' Cosmos. It had been a long time since the older man had slept outside under the velvet of night. The distant songs of coyotes lulled the two men this night; and the haunting whispers of ghostly Spirits blew through the cypress trees, sending a sweet fragrance mixed with roses to surround them, lighting the last candle on David's cake. Ted's smell, and their lustful reunion, made it an extravaganza; and a fleeting idea, to bottle it as an aphrodisiac, had him smiling, knowing the aroma only belonged to his lover.

"They told me again the difficulty of correcting the damage already caused by my disease, as if I had to be told. Some things are still serious, like my stupid heart and my bones being brittle. Good thing I'm so relaxed when we make love. You could snap me like a dry twig."

"Is that what you call relaxed? Only one part of your entire body was easy to penetrate tonight; and you've trained yourself to release those muscles, as well as your throat. Man, you drive me crazy with your tongue. Now, let's hear the rest. You're stalling."

"Well, for the heart problem, I have these stupid little pills old men take. And for my bones, I'm taking enough calcium and Vitamin D to kill an elephant."

"I'm glad about the pills. They're to start your heart, right?"

"Guess so."

"Didn't you listen to the doctors, or is there something else you're having trouble iterating, like Willow being mute? I must admit that caught me in an ugly, unwanted surprise; and yet, between you and our baby, it seems strangely right. Stronger messages come from silence, listening to the inner voice of reason." David suddenly went numb; Willow was mute to teach them telepathy. Preparation for something, Ted and Holly had already begun.

"I wasn't sure how you would react. You tried to mask your duress, but Willow saw through it. Looking into her eyes, you knew, and your attitude instantly changed."

"Discussion for tomorrow. Now, tell me what the doctors told you. No more diversions." Recovering from this new revelation, David refused to place the thought into an innocent head this night. Matters of more importance needed addressing.

"It's just hard to say, let alone what it means to me. I can never climb again." Ted wiped away an onslaught of melancholy, attempting to avoid David's question. There would be no more consoling, until he uttered the truth from a mouth needing more love.

"Why not? You climbed the ladder like a monkey. Is it because of the pain you told me about in England? Did they figure it out?"

"No, they still don't believe me, but they gave it a name--idiopathy--a disease they can't identify. Can you believe it? Sounds like they're calling me crazy to my face. Maybe I am. Remember Quinlan telling you how ill I became in Mexico; and everyone thought my chronic disease of the brain, which happens to be connected to my stomach, caused the problem?"

"You're confusing me; just say it, Ted."

"Let me finish this tale of incredible stupidity. I felt like I had food poisoning, but it was something they should have known. They ignored every possibility because of my so-called anorexia. Apparently, I'm allowed only one chronic condition, never to get another. They looked no further at what could cause me to heave every five minutes for three straight days. It still makes me mad. I was so dizzy; they gave me nothing to stop it. Even after two more unwanted visits to the hospital, one after the wedding fiasco and then the beating, at least Bernard came up with the Gravol on the plane, recognizing a spinning head from purging. The aircraft accentuated the problem, which had existed for months. They could have diagnosed it in its first stages and corrected it, if they had opened their eyes. Promise me, David, if I'm ever seriously ill; make sure they check for other reasons. I bet every chronically ill person has the same problem."

"Yes, but I didn't realize the medical profession had tunnel-vision."

"You have no idea. Ask a diabetic or an epileptic who just broke a leg. Their disease caused the problem, not the treacherous tree they ran into while skiing in Aspen."

"I didn't know. I'm sorry, Ted. Your acceptance of allowing them to treat you, however, certainly makes me feel better." David's concern grew with the ramblings of one who had received another disappointment in life. Secretly hiding his strange physical pain of idiopathy, now something new drew LaCoix even closer to the brave man.

"It's an inner ear virus that causes dizziness, thus losing my balance. Remember the stairs at the manor house, and the fainting spell over the cliff? It was my inner ear; and no, it can't be rectified; it's too late. That's why this wall's so high. Looking over this vista, I get the same sensation as I do looking straight down. If I do faint, I'll only land on the roof, not a far drop."

"Why didn't you tell me when you first found out?"

"Oh, man, so much was happening."

"You've been fighting battle after battle, with little support except from Ambrose. I can't thank the man enough for taking care of you since Christmas." A cooling hand came up and brushed away the damp hair from a sad face.

"He's a good friend, David; I couldn't have made it without him. He's taught me a lot." The hand gesture closed Ted's eyes, allowing his lover to soothe away some of his disappointment.

"Good, as I think I've seen his influence in the way you handled today and Willow. So, we have to regain your equilibrium. Did the doctors give you any indication as to how to cope?"

"Of course not, but Quin suggested I start slowly, with something I like to do, and see how it goes. Uncertain of the covert problem as well, neither of us knew where to concentrate our powers. We've been trying to heal it, since this last diagnosis, but it doesn't want to go away." The frustration and hurt in the voice refused to abate.

"Let's try Quin's idea, starting with some easy hikes with the girls, going slowly at first, and gradually building up." David's tonality changed to enthusiasm; but a teasing squeeze did nothing for Ted.

"The girls, there was so much I wanted to teach and show them." Ted faltered as his dreams fell away, and he slipped into his silences.

Someone's voice broke through in determination of the cheerful variety, "Never fear, Teddy Bear, your White Knight is here. We shall vanquish this problem, one-step at a time. An inner ear problem we can deal with." A kiss to the forehead, and another attempt at a light-hearted jostle, sparked a little life into Ted.

"Now when I faint, pop a heart pill into my mouth, bring me around, and make sure I didn't break anything important."

"You are fun, Mr. Barrett. Do I check you out when you swoon making love?"

"I don't faint!" A little ire popped up; and David retracted quickly.

"Sorry, Baby Bear, but you do. I wouldn't think it terribly uncommon, since men's blood rushes to other parts of their body during sex. Maybe that's why we lose our minds and continually think of sex. Now I have three little darlings to worry about. It certainly has been an eye-opening day and an intoxicating night. Almost time for a *red boys' toy* outing."

"It's always parked, waiting to roll." Back to chuckling, Ted returned to his position on a shoulder he had grown accustomed to, confident he alone created the indentation, which precisely fit his head. "Did you know your lips are coming closer? Care for a taste, my Knight?"

Granted sincerely, the intensity burned deep into their groins. Passion consumed them with the scent of the other; and Ted felt another smooth penetration into the sensitive fleshy part of his lower body, as David turned to embrace him. He pleaded softly for more, with little whimpers and sighs. His big blue eyes closed in a grimace of euphoria, unexpectedly taken again.

David sweated and growled, penetrating into the curled body, which afforded him the greatest access. With arms around his neck, the shoulders pulled up, the avarice orifice thrust upward to take in another deep lunge. The younger man came again in little streams of ecstasy, enjoying the constant rubbing against his inner gland of erotic treasures. It would make him lose all sense of time, space, and reality. David, again, released his life's essence into the fragile creature and breathed in the haunting, panting smell of a man fully satisfied; the sweet breath that sent David reeling with their first *hello*; and the soft, shy greeting whispered back, to only realize it now. Breathing heavily, it took no further conversation to snuggle under warm blankets, inhaling the scent of cypress and roses, and falling into an exhausted stupor.

Beyond nature's magic, their passion exuded superhuman male ability, thanks to some kindly mischief from the Mistress. She toasted the loving couple with a goblet of ambrosia, and a wishful smile on her face that they would remain so deliriously happy. Disappearing from the tender moment, she had other matters to ponder, now coming into play. Willow Rose and Holly Jane were safe in the hands of their fathers. The Fates settled, unable to harm them in their desert oasis. Not actually there, unless they wanted to be seen, she manifested it only for them, from their visualizations, which grew strong enough to create their own magical space. The property, however, remained her fantasy, from the first time she showed herself to them. She hid the entrance into their lives, and allowed them to come and go through her portal into real time, whenever they chose. The smiling face on the monitor was not of this earth, but an Aegis, a Guardian Spirit for the home and its inhabitants. They lived in a safe haven of another realm, but bound to earth in its roots. It would protect them from the reality of the outside world, and grow to be a sanctuary, much like La Rosa Negra. The Black Rose had come into being; the *Beginning Again* would soon commence. Sipping her wine slowly, she watched the purple clouds, just outside her window, opening to view the future. She contemplated on whether it would be a mistake.

CHAPTER 46

On a wisp of hot air against his chest, David welcomed the sleeping, contented Spirit within his embrace. Something was changing. He opened his eyes to see a sky losing its stars, and the watercolor light of dawn creeping over them. His first sunrise at home, he wanted to see it.

"Wake up, Teddy Bear."

"Hunh? It's you, my Knight. You ready, already?"

"You really are a kick. Whom did you expect? Don't answer that. I might have to file for divorce before I'm married."

"You already did that." Ted snuggled into the man, wishing to remain in his cozy position, never considering his words hurt deeply.

"Thanks for reminding me. Good thing you're still half-asleep or I'd deck you. Come on, sun's almost up."

"It is something to wake up to, after two hours of sleep. What did I say?"

"Never mind." David let Ted roll off him with a groan, and he laughed to himself. He still awoke partially aroused, as did his young partner. For the average male, it seemed a valid reason to take cold, brisk showers, or a dash to a close-by river, all the while pretending to be macho. Men seemed contrived to be ruled by the wrong head, no matter the sexual orientation. He snickered at how it controlled his life and at the oddest times.

He leaned over the thick wall, waiting for the final spectacle. His trim muscled body, of finely sculpted marble, felt the first rays of the sun caress his face and torso, while the morning air fluttered his fine hair. A moment of feeling alive, after such a wickedly erotic night, he smiled recalling every touch. The view may be grand, but his thoughts, and the warm parasite latched to him, tempted him to return to bed. Only Ted's presence ignited the ember burning within him.

"Everything you've done is magnificent, Baby; and the house blends right into the shadows, the rocks, the trees, absolutely amazing. By the way, will you be adding my name to yours, or will you leave it?" The question came straight out of the sunrise to surprise the sleepy heart. Having no understanding why he felt compelled to claim Ted as his, considering he hated the idea of possessing someone, and yet there he stood, demanding it, wanting to etch his name on everything he loved. "I'm very thankful you're allowing me to adopt Willow and you taking the same responsibility with Holly, who thinks that our surnames should become one of those double-barreled monikers. She thinks it sounds like her few aristocratic friends in England. I rather like the idea myself. No matter what happens to either of us, they'll have a father without suffering the different name stigma."

"I don't know. I'll have to tell Stevie to change the marquee and posters. That's a stupid thought for such an important question. Sorry, I'm rambling. You've thrown me a curve; and I don't know what to say."

"*Yes* would be good." David smiled the paternal grin he could not hide when speaking with *Peter Pan*. He had to admit the oddity of his request, and his partner's inability to rationalize such a monumental decision when still drowsy.

"I'd rather keep my name, and change it for the girls. It makes them sound like ours. Then again, it gives me a middle name for my professional one. What's your second name, LaCoix?"

The smugness of David's expression promised something fun; and Ted's smile lit up the rest of the brightening sky when he heard, "Jacob."

"No shit? You're Just Jay?" Ted laughed hysterically, in tune with his dashing Knight's soft chuckle. "What a coincidence. Okay, let's do it, since a double-barrel name has become the norm for actors of the female persuasion, not to mention trying not to replicate names within the Actors Guild. Does that make a person twice as famous?" The silly question came with an overdue yawn, and a rub of sleep-filled eyes.

"In your case, it makes you twice as infamous. Besides, I don't see how you could gain more notoriety." The older man beamed at the whimsical character he now would always wake beside.

"What a strange topic while watching a sunrise. You're fun to wake up with too." A little turn of Ted's head captured David's kiss, which was as soft as a swipe of a brushstroke.

"Just thinking about a lot of things, Barrett. It's the middle of August; your divorce papers are finalized; let's get married the first Saturday in October. We'll fly in one of our many lawyers to make sure we have all the documentation required to make us sealed for life, including adoption papers, name changes, wills, and then arrange a celebration with friends. Too bad the large majority of the world refuses to condone mixed marriages of the gay variety, except in a few states and countries."

"We're not mixed. Everyone else is."

"Damn, you actually do think when you first wake up, or do these quaint ideas unexpectedly pop into your head?" David continued to laugh, as he straightened and pulled his partner closer.

"Sounds like common-sense to me."

"Six weeks gives us enough time to meet with lawyers, before you can run, and also to warn the guests to disrupt their schedules. Whoever shows, shows, and probably in the most grandiose of fashion. I'd like my parents to join us the week before the festivities, as my mother wants to help. So, what do you think?"

"You want me to plan a real wedding... and your mom wants to help! Good God, I thought we would just have a party. I don't know, David, I just might run. It might look stupid and feel too effeminate for us." The controversial act suddenly sank into Ted's befuddled head: even an illegal marriage meant a ceremony, with cake, presents, and ribbons. Aghast at the thought, he pushed away from the man, who surmised he could mastermind a ceremony, of which he knew nothing.

"Don't be foolish; it's only vows, and a get together of friends and family. Mom missed two of my marriages. I won't have her forfeiting a third, although a little unorthodox. Besides, my folks are anxious to meet you and their grandchildren."

"Interesting: my parents want me dead, and yours are so loving. Can't believe you wasted time fighting with them." Ted ensconced himself within the strong arms, after the first initial shiver ran through him. Any mention of his parents brought on a chill of fear.

"I can't either. My coming out has been a tremendous adjustment for them at their age; and I can hear how hard they're trying. Have to give them credit for getting over the shock so quickly and accepting it."

"They've missed you. As you said before, where have you been all their lives?" Another shiver tensed Ted's body.

"I've upset you. Sorry, I shouldn't..."

"...It's okay, I'm getting over the sentencing, sort of. I'm just nervous about meeting your folks, which is probably normal; but this marriage thing, I think it was one of those ideas that seemed a good idea at the time, but now sounds weird, LaCoix."

"You can't run out on me now, particularly when you're babbling. You promised to marry me. What did you expect?"

"Guess I did. Can we make it small?"

"Whoever is important to us."

"Good, because there's only five, maybe six, on my list. We can fly them in with small aircraft over there. It's also lit for night flights." Turning David's head slightly, Ted pointed toward the open desert, where the new sun directed its first rays.

"You built a landing field! I can see the windsock. I'll be damned." David received his first surprise of the morning, along with a few confirmations from his lover. Theodore Barrett-LaCoix would be his.

"Thought it a good safety measure, particularly now, in case one of us has a coronary exchanging vows in front of people. I won't have to wear lace, or do something stupid?"

Hands went to work immediately on the bony hips, tickling Ted unmercifully. His giggling echoed through the canyon, as he ran for the ladder, where David helped him down. Able to scamper up, coming down required ropes and harnesses.

With everyone up, showered, and dressed, their first day of real exploration commenced. Domestic rituals first: Ted fed Willow, Holly crunched down her corn flakes, and David watched over the group with a cup of coffee in hand. The main gate phone rang; he answered, not knowing the routine of the household. Jamie appeared on the monitor, looking rather puzzled.

"Morning, Mr. LaCoix, I believe you'll want to see this. I don't know if I should let them in."

"Who?" Another sip of coffee, and the green eyes grew wider, waiting for some oddity with the ominous words.

"I don't know, sir; they're not saying anything. Can you and Mr. Barrett grab an all-terrain, and speed down to the front gate?" David saw Jamie turn his head to look at someone, to come back into full view with a slight grin and shake of his head.

"Let me talk to them? How do I change the monitor to see them?" Habitually on guard, David set his morning beverage aside, to study any change in the man's expression, while scanning the console for buttons to switch camera angles. Fingernails immediately went to his teeth, not having a clue as to how things worked.

"Don't think so, sir, as I'm unsure of the cameras as well." The monitor switched off. Utterly bewildered, David turned, expecting some information from his partner. Ted continued to smile down at their daughter, nodding his head in some kind of response to Willow's thoughts. Getting up, Ted set the baby in Maria's happy arms to finish the chore.

"Let's go. Willow and Holly seem to agree they are non-threatening. Right girls?" A nod from the petite blonde confirmed it, as she handed the bowl of gruel to their nanny.

"Oh, good, we're leaving our entire security to our daughters' Vulcan mind-melding abilities. Ted, you have lost your sanity completely. I know what they're capable of, to a certain degree; but we have to protect them." Surprised at his lover's contentment to abide by the wishes of a five-month-old telepath, and a-six year-old becoming one; life took an eerie turn, and his Hollywood paranoia set in.

"Both of them know more than we do, LaCoix. Why are you snarling at me? Willow seemed very pleased at their arrival; and Holly senses they are peaceful. Don't be such a grouch. To the

Hummer, my Knight." Ted pressed forward, arm raised in an onward and upward motion.

"We have a Hummer?" Right behind him, wondering about Ted's newly-arrived-at-revelations and his blasé nature toward them, David nearly tripped over him when his partner spun around to face him.

"Do we have the worst road on the planet?" Even looking up from under the dark lashes, dark blue was only seen, and certainly mirth.

"Good thinking. After you, Tonto, a surprise waits at the gate; I hope Jamie isn't being held at gunpoint."

"Didn't notice a quiver in his voice, Kemosabe, but sounded rather enthusiastic." Ted laughed at the man with the deep frown and strained jaw.

"Between you and our little darlings, we'll all be murdered in our beds, with smiles on our faces. What have I let myself in for?" The two men clamored into the olive green, very expensive, practical status symbol, along with Craig who had also been summoned. Over the rocky road of horror, and no broken caps in the perfect smiles, they came to an abrupt halt. Both David and Ted gasped, one in awe, one in delight. On their feet and looking over the windshield of the open-air vehicle, they could only stare at what awaited them behind their rustic little gate. Three majestic Andalusian horses stood quietly. An overly inquisitive one had nipped off a few rose blossoms, covering her nose with sticky-sweet, pink petals; and although she persevered to sneeze them away, they refused to budge from her sensitive, ticklish nostrils. Lavender's three horses waited patiently for an invitation to enter, while four men stared entranced by their beauty, but baffled at the lack of ropes or halters, leaving them wildly free to come and go as they pleased.

"Let them in, Jamie." Out from behind the wheel of the Hummer, David strode toward the steed coming toward him. The magnificent beast, with amber eyes, twisted his head to one side to see and smell the blond human. Their strong connection cemented with a touch to the curly forelock by a human hand, and a stroke to smooth it evenly between the *knowing* eyes. A piece of paper, braided into the mane of black curls, shook loose. David caught it, before it fell to earth.

Barrett recognized the horses immediately, and happily greeted the other two. The pink-petal nose gently touched fingers willing to remove the annoying blooms. Ted chuckled softly and talked sweetly to the grateful creature. Gentle and mannerly, these exquisite animals expressed affection.

"The blue-eyed mare belongs to Mr. Barrett. The other two are stallions. I've never seen the likes of the eye coloration, and the stallion with green ones is a complete mystery. What do you think, Craig?"

"I don't believe it, but they're beautiful; true wonders of nature." The former rancher had not moved or blinked since they drove up.

At his remark, the mare whinnied her pleasure at the compliment, making Ted laugh upon hearing her thank the man. "She thinks you're cute too; she likes you both."

"You can hear her?" Craig could not take his eyes off the creature. Both ranch hands stood in awe, starting to understand the magic of their charges, and the world in which they now lived.

"I can feel it, if that makes sense. It's part of what we call the *knowing*, right my beauty?" After Ted relieved her ticklish nose with a gentle scratch, the blue-eyed mare teased him back with a little nibble to his fingers.

"I'd be more careful, Mr. Barrett; horses tend to see fingers and carrots as the same thing."

"Oh, she knows the difference and a whole lot more. They're very special, Craig." Ted continued to enjoy the company of the affectionate mare, nuzzling him softly, reminding him of the loving fawn that had been so brave to taste his flowered headband.

David came over to join the others, with the amber-eyed stallion vigilantly following behind, and stopping to stand guard over the man. "Listen to this, Ted."

"They're from Lavender. I hope she lets us keep them." Whispered into the bright blue, morning sky, the Mistress answered with a flutter of a dozen butterflies, kissing Ted's cheeks and playing in his hair. Butterflies or Faeries, he graciously accepted the priceless gift, secretly understanding Lavender's expression of the *knowing*. He smiled complaisantly, watching them return to the protection of the rose bushes. Another profundity went unperturbed by the young man, who kept his wonderment hidden, away from others' thoughts, including David and the Mistress. Quinlan had taught him well.

"Your right, listen to what she says. The stallion of golden eyes, and strength of will, is Ra, and will always be for David. Theo's mare, with the brilliant star-filled eyes, known as Bastet, will shower him with affection and loving thoughts. Shu has green eyes; a stallion of immense wisdom to protect and nurture Holly; he will never let her fall and will grant her every wish. Awaiting Willow's pleasure is a young filly with violet eyes, known to us as Isis. These unearthly beings shall protect you, transport you to La Rosa Negra and beyond, and teach you lessons of the Cosmos. Listen to their thoughts and heed their advice. No one else may ride your chosen entity. They are yours, but must remain free, to come and go as they please, and to take you places yet unknown. Let them guide your Spirits, and they will do your bidding with a thought. My love protects you in your new home. Congratulations for eternity, The Mistress."

"Wow." Ted breathed in the scent of familiar lilacs in the mane of his new horse Bastet. Her name sounded mysterious, and when said softly, lingering on the pronunciation, it had power behind the sweetness.

"Wow, indeed." David turned to lay his head against the dark, warm neck, and breathed in the same essence. They were real, but they were not; his joy abounded with the emotions they stirred. He could ride forever on the back of this enchanted animal.

Returning to their vehicles, the slow parade commenced to the stables, with the horses walking calmly beside the Hummer. They took no notice of the excitement they aroused in four men, for they had jobs to do, and would not wander far from their designated charges. Jamie and Craig easily placed them in shaded stalls, which allowed them to wander freely outside, through the back entrance, and to return to their cooler adobe dwellings, where they could look out onto the gardens. David received their first thoughts, approving of their flower-laden new homes, and he could do nothing but stand and stare at the spectacle.

Ted rushed in to retrieve Holly, sharing her enthusiasm when presented with her new steed. She had a mystical horse with a strange name and a strange spelling. Leaning over and nuzzling his new responsibility, Shu would care for this tiny human, and he would let her fly if she so desired, while holding onto his mane and chanting his name. They would be off on a wisp of air, to soar into realms never imagined.

David continued to stand quietly, overwhelmed by the gift. He needed time to contemplate the letter received. Listen to their thoughts it said, and he heard Ra laugh. With a horse chortling at him, he urged Holly and Ted to find the meanings of the names, and he would soon join them.

On that command, and right at their heels, Craig followed.

Smiling up at a horse, unlike anything the others could understand, David wondered if Ra had been Ra, or if the famous Isis prepared herself, in her godly way, for the likes of Willow. They could be older than the famed deities themselves. Another crooked grin crossed his face; he shook his head at another *awakening*; Ted spoke of the *knowing*. The man slipped, acknowledging he had scaled the gates of his hell, to believe in himself and the Mistress, with all he had experienced and now knew as true.

Looking down at his boots, still in wondering mode, David spotted a rather sharp object protruding from the heavy wooden gate of the stall. No injury must befall these particular guests, and he gave a yell for Jamie. "Hey, I need a hammer out here."

"You called." Jamie paled, coming around the corner to meet Mr. LaCoix's shocked face. "Oops, sorry sir; thought you were Craig. How embarrassing; I do apologize."

"One of those strange nicknames whispered only in private?" David laughed and waited for the rangy ranch hand, with the slight beer belly, to fix the nail he had found.

"Yup, one of those. Extraordinary animals you have here. Seen pictures of them, but never one to touch and care for."

"They're priceless treasures; treat them gently and with great respect, Jamie. Do whatever pleases them, except giving them chocolate, which is here in the letter. I wonder what it does to them." David heard the thought coming from Ra, with an answer as equally confusing; it destabilized them in flight. Stunned at what he heard in his head, he stepped back a pace to catch the same glint of amber.

"You can count on that. Excuse me, Mr. LaCoix, but your voice doesn't sound as happy as it did. Is something wrong?"

"No, of course not. I guess I'm still tired and have a lot of work ahead of me. Can I ask you something personal? How have you and Craig stayed together so long? You don't have to answer that; it's none of my business." David sat down on the rock wall a dozen feet from the gate to Ra's stall. Looking and feeling mentally exhausted, he did not react when the ranch hand took the liberty of sitting next to him.

"I don't mind. Instant attraction that never diminishes; he still takes my breath away after all these years. Picked him out of the dust after he tangled himself up with a bull. Being one of the bullfighters, I released his hand from the rigging to get him out; and I guess I've never let go."

"Love at first sight, but sounds like you two lived a dangerous lifestyle."

"Guess we did, but we got out young and relatively intact to start up the ranch. I think our relationship is slightly different than yours."

"How so?" David turned to look at a pleasant profile of a weathered face. This kind man would bring stability into their lives.

"We hid from necessity in those early days. You announced your engagement to the world, an extraordinary feat, plus the responsibility to succeed. Considering your fame, you've put yourselves in a serious and potentially dangerous position; however, you have given hope to people like me and Craig; a hope that our relationship will become legal one day."

"Now you have me terrified, but that's not all you wanted to say." David could relax with this cowboy, and he had no one else to confide in, not even Kincaid. Steven was Ted's friend.

"Well sir, Craig and I are equal in every way; neither of us controls the other, even sexually.

Mr. Barrett seems to depend on you entirely. I assume you're the dominant lover."

"Shoot from the hip, don't you? I hate the word dominance, but you're right. We met when I had lost control of everything in my life. He gave me a reason to become strong again, and to use my head. Being a selfish prick, to everyone and everything, I looked up one day into a mirror; and there he was, staring at me. I pulled him out of a rockslide; and in exchange, he changed my life. A wish fulfilled, and when I think about it, I did ask for someone who relied on me completely. I guess that describes him. Such an innocent baby, and the tortures he went through, I couldn't help care about him. He craves nurturing and love; yet he's stubbornly independent in a crisis, unable to say what he feels, just trying to do the right thing in his own way."

"Heard tell of his heroics; and he surprised me when we met, since he looks too delicate for such dangerous stunts that few men would risk. Even you, sir, came to the daring rescue of your daughter. I'm sure the average father would have panicked. Hell of a climb for any cowboy."

"I did panic, but a parent does extraordinary things when it comes to their children. At least, I had Ted yelling instructions to me, saving us all. I can't thank him enough for what he did. As for our relationship, I guess I am the dominant factor, although Ted is growing stronger, which I'm happy about."

"Nothing wrong with your arrangement, just different than ours. At our first interview, we understood how high-strung Mr. Barrett is, like a wild horse. You come up to them quietly, even able to stroke their neck, then they fly off at a gallop for no reason, and no one can catch them. It puts more of a burden on your shoulders. With this wedding, are you beginning to doubt yourself, and in return, hurt the young man beyond his ability to cope?" The horse handler leaned forward, elbows on his knees, habitually chewing a piece of straw that dangled from between his teeth.

"You are perceptive, Jamie. I certainly believe the relationship will last, but did I move too quickly? There's much riding on what we do and say, including the raising of two daughters. It appears that we've taken off on the wildest ride at Disney World, and there's no way to jump off." Raking his hand through his hair, David matched the man's motion, but with his nails in his mouth.

"Lurking inside your frail partner is a proven tornado. Since our first interview, he appears mellower and in a way I can't explain."

"He's not my only tornado. I have two more ready to blow your mind one day. It's the magic."

"Magic, hunh? Your daughter certainly exudes it with animals. I'd swear she was speaking with her stallion, which might prove a handful for a child."

"She was, just as Ted heard Bastet. Holly has an uncanny ability to adapt to any change, and understand it at a level I can't reach. It scares the hell out of me."

"You all seem to be fitting right in; and the devotion between you is strong. Have to thank you for allowing us in, to work on the estate, and sharing your thoughts with us. You'll manage just fine, Mr. LaCoix. There is no doubt, in this old cowboy's mind, that you and Mr. Barrett will succeed in this very public world you live in. At least you have a safe place to get away, and such a place it is."

"You used the word devotion; a subject that comes up often between me and Ted. Do you love Craig, and can you say it easily?"

"We just feel it, so there's no need for words. What does it mean anyway?"

"You're right. Thanks, Jamie, I needed a pep talk today from a new perspective. We're a paranoid couple of actors, with equally paranoid Hollywood friends. Be gentle with us, for it's a hell of a way to live. Glad you're both with us, to keep our feet on the ground. Take care of our new family members. By the way, where are your horses?" David finally stood up, with the cowboy respectfully rising beside him.

"We weren't sure about stabling arrangements, and sold all but our best two. They're an hour's drive away; and I promise they won't shame the estate."

"A rangy, baby burro wouldn't shame us. We'll buy a few gentle steeds for guests to ride as well. Sounds like your job for today. Pick up your horses, some feed, settle them in with these three gracious beings, and start hunting for a few more. If I'm not around to ride with Holly, I'd be a lot happier if you or Craig would take her out, and subliminally give her some ideas about horsemanship. Even with Ted, someone should go with him. He's a fine horseman, but prone to dizzy spells. I know Bastet will not let him fall, but if he looks down, she may have to scramble to keep him in position."

"Will do, sir; you have made my day. Don't tell Craig where I'm heading. This will make him crazy happy. Could see his disappointment when he heard only you could ride these animals, which is right and proper. He just needs his horse to race across the desert. It's his first love; he's missed it, as do I."

"Happy we can give joy back to him. Wish I could do the same for Ted. It's all about freedom for them. One more thing, you won't be working the gala event." David caught the flash of disappointment spread across the face of a man who had suddenly become a friend and confidante.

"If that's what you wish, we'll certainly stay clear."

"Like hell you will; you're invited, as we can't have any family members miss partying with the likes of Steven Kincaid."

"Thank you, sir. Both Pretzel and I are honored to be included."

"That's a good one; I don't even want to know where it comes from."

"Bull riding." Jamie teased and put his employer into a fit of laughter. It felt good to both.

David wondered at the nicknames, making his and Ted's sound terribly mundane in comparison. He turned and waved his hand in a gesture to stop chuckling, and caught the glint of an amber eye. A subconscious knowledge: he felt it. He had also seen it in Barrett's eyes. Feeling a little lighter, he left after one look back into the eyes of the *knowing*. "Later, Ra."

CHAPTER 47

Arrangements were made and documents executed within a few weeks. Perhaps not legally married, they signed their lives to each other with secret promises on paper. With the clock ticking, plans took their proper and expeditious course. Expecting further surprises, before their friends arrived on their doorstep, LaCoix learned the outcome of the exhaustive audit of lost funds. With much of his and Susan's money retrieved, and their former accountants charged with embezzlement, Holly Jane's inheritance grew substantially. Along with David's assets, the many facets of financial responsibility were entrusted to Ted; and the young man forged ahead immediately, setting down rules, and requesting statements on a monthly basis from their lawyers to their tailors. The rest of their money remained hidden in a Zurich bank, while Ted started teaching David about real-life business.

Weeks passed in a flurry, with every invitation accepted. With David's parents arriving on the morrow, the entire household dithered about, preparing for another exciting day. A long evening ride into the desert seemed a necessity, and under the darkening sky, the couple took time for a gentle walk, to quell their hearts from bordering on the dysfunctional. Two frazzled men rode bareback, to the far end of their unnamed canyon, hand-in-hand, horse touching horse. The magical beings protected these humans, no matter what the barriers; Bastet and Ra willingly carried them over anything.

"It's so quiet out here. Would be great to stay and camp out for the next twenty years." A wistful sigh escaped from Ted's lips, while slipping off his mare. He gazed up and wished aloud on the first falling star, as a deep melancholy swept over him.

"You can't run, Ted. Don't you feel the sense of being where you're supposed to be, or is tomorrow going to have you tiptoeing around, hiding from my folks?" David's constant concern of the lingering mood swings had him pursuing any outlet to keep his lover on a high note.

"I'm excited and frightened at the same time: a strange paradox."

"Well, Baby Bear, one exceptionally pleasant surprise will be meeting the Love Professor. When will they be arriving?" David knew Ted needed Kincaid's support and looked forward to his arrival. The thought of his friend put a happier look on the boyish face.

"Flying in celebration morning and staying the week. It's great he received word of Dr. Thurgood's early return. Richard tells me that Stevie's worn a hole in the carpet from pacing. I hope this guy's the one, never hurting him, or you and Kincaid will end up trashing our Ferrari."

"Very funny, so you have one week to find out more about his new amour." David continued to keep his partner from slipping away with so much coming toward him. The possibility of one long week of nightmares and silence loomed disturbingly before them: one experiencing them, the other holding fast. "You're tired, Ted; let's get you home. Do you want a sleeping pill? Stupid question, because I don't want to kill you off before you meet Mom." A morbid attempt at humor partially succeeded, but the two weary eyes, drifting off into the limitless beyond, veered David onto a course to get his forever partner to bed.

"Appreciate that. I'd prefer a *Sleeping Beauty* sleep, and her special wake up call." Ted accepted a lift onto Bastet, but even a moon-enamored kiss did not help the body stay calm. Back on the patient mare, his nerves dissipated to some degree; and two men silently rode home, through the stillness of shifting shadows.

A four-hour drive from one LaCoix home to another, their eagerly awaited guests rang the main gate monitor at precisely twelve o'clock. Ted was a car crash waiting to happen; Holly played the puppet, continuously jumping, attached to a sightless bungee cord; and with no sleep for three people, David wondered who would snap first. He ventured a guess it would be him, but at the sound of a car coming to a halt, he flung open the doors, and bolted down the steps. Eyes peered from within, to watch him bear hug an elegant, tall woman, frosted with snow, and big green eyes. A striking woman, David had forgotten how attractive his mother was. People always commented on how much he looked like Daphne LaCoix; and staring into those copycat eyes, he suddenly saw the resemblance. His dad came around the car, grabbing his boy's hand in a firm shake, and pulling him into a fatherly embrace too tight to breathe. Both smiling broadly, the male-to-male hug had to be a bone-crushing, back-hammering experience that could kill. David accepted it happily, and could have held onto his father forever, but for the three impatiently waiting inside for a signal. It came with the linking of arms; the three oldest LaCoix stared up at the inviting portal. Time for introductions, and with his father, Jake, on one side, and his mother on the other, David escorted them arm-in-arm up the few stairs into the entry courtyard.

A frail figure in the shadows could no longer hold back an exuberant little blonde-haired whirlwind. With a shriek of excitement, a takeoff of a sprinter, Holly ran to her grandfather, who caught his Morning Glory in full flight. Both laughing and giggling, they chattered in a way David had not heard since childhood. Beautiful to witness, and to remember the feeling, David gushed with pride to see the laughter in his daughter's face, while being passed to her grandmother. A little heavy for the statuesque woman, Daphne LaCoix held on, covering the pretty head with soft kisses and whispering happy words. His little girl radiated with the love showered upon her, and she returned all she had.

Ted unsuccessfully attempted to disappear behind the biggest plant he could find. Spotted by Jake and yanked out by his right hand into a fatherly tussling of his slender body, it rocked him to his bones at the genuine squeeze of affection. Pushed back by the shoulders, LaCoix Senior looked at the young man from his loafers to the top of his head. Ted felt smaller than a desert mouse, with this six-foot four-inch handsome figure towering over him. He looked younger than Ted expected, and certainly a lot fitter and leaner. The thought of his own father made him tremble.

"My God, Theo, it's good to finally meet you. We've been worried sick about you; but you're looking good, son." The voice sounded like David's, but more excited, and never raised beyond the same quiet pitch, even with a lie.

"Thank you, sir." Ted had no idea how to react to such enthusiasm. With his thoughts jumbled, his weak knees deprived him from running. Panic-stricken, he looked to David for help, only to receive a mischievous smile. He was on his own.

"My son calls me Dad. I hope my new one could call me that as well."

"I'll try, sir... Dad... we certainly have enough dad's around here, don't we, Holly?" Ted tried another escape to get out of the tight grip of two large hands pumping his own.

"No, I have a Dad, a Daddy, and a Granddad, and so does Willow."

With no help from his blond daughter, another female voice came to his aid, "Davie, would you introduce me to this handsome man your father is shaking to death?" A smiling face beamed at her cherished son who had broken her heart along with his father. Waiting years for this reunion, she never gave up or dwelled on the injustice of missing his entire adult life, for which she took partial blame, by not interfering sooner over something neither man could remember. Of little matter now, her handsome, blond-haired boy filled her eyes and his hand warmed her heart, all grievances forgiven. Her life, even with Jake, changed that day so long ago, destroyed by her two stubborn men. Nevertheless, the present, now enveloped her, invited for the first time into David's beautiful home, to share his growing family, including a very pretty granddaughter who looked exactly like her son when he approached seven. She would have cried, if not surrounded by those to whom she wished to bring joy. The strangest greeting awaited; she truly wanted to meet the man who had turned David's world onto an unexpected path. All her trepidation vanished, looking at the frightened, bewildered man-child her husband continued to terrorize. She recognized the gentle lamb, intuitively feeling his need for affection, and conversely, his fear of it.

"Mom, this is my partner, Theodore Barrett-LaCoix. Ted, this is my mother, Daphne." David hung over her shoulders, gently escorting her forward.

"And what shall we call you, son? It seems you have a myriad of names." Her face may be a little austere in its elegance, but a sense of warmth filled her eyes. More formal than her husband, it made Ted's trembling worse.

"Call him Ted, an intimate family name only. Okay with you, Baby?" David peered at the tension mounting in the boyish face, and tried to soften it with a smile of his own. He received a nod.

"Ted it shall be. Do I get a hug, and I hope you can call me Mom?" Daphne reached out her arms; but Ted hesitantly took a pace toward her only to stop mid-stride, not understanding how to react. His Knight, in black denim and a sand-colored pullover, came to his rescue.

"You have to show him, Mom."

Mrs. LaCoix walked the two paces toward the wary man, and pulled him gently toward her. A delicate kiss to his cheek, and an endearing hug, eased his fright. Smelling of his favorite fragrance of roses and jasmine, she held him with a light touch; and he melted into the warmth of what a mother should feel like--gentle and kind--like Lavender. A tall woman, and in her high shoes, she seemed to soar to her son's height; his partner's tall, lean body came from both gene pools. A steadying hand pressed his head against her shoulder, to caress his hair, until released to meet a smile: a reflection of David and Holly's.

"It's fine, Ted; you'll get used to us after a few days. We won't push, and we don't bite, just get a little testy sometimes in our old age. We're immensely proud of you: for your triumphant Oscar win and speech, and your courage during the trials. Congratulations to you and Davie on your baby. Both of us wanted to be there to help, but understood the overwhelming pressure placed upon you. So what will it be, my dear--Mom, Mother, Daphne--hey, you, with the white hair?" The woman stoically hid her panic at the feel of the man, coming to the full realization of what her son had spoken of over the telephone. David's acting talent came from his mother; she disguised her own fears.

Ted succumbed to her charms, relieved to hear the soft chuckle, hinting at a crazier sense of fun than he imagined from David's description of his mother. "Can I interchange between Mom and Daphne? Mom isn't quite comfortable yet; and Daphne is a beautiful name. It floats off the tongue and whispers at you."

"Certainly and thank you; what a lovely thing to say. I'm rather partial to it myself. Now, I demand to see my other granddaughter before we go any further. Also an enchanting name,

Willow sounds like a sigh on a soft breeze through an ancient forest."

Ted recalled his partner's reaction to his daughter's name, as well as Holly's, and they had been as meaningful. He flushed with embarrassment. David's mother accepted him, as did Jake, and his worries dissipated with their excitement and eagerness to adopt both he and his daughter. He had a family: a complete family. Daphne took his arm, insisting he escort her to the nursery immediately. From that moment, Ted decided to don his boots with riding heels, to gain a few inches on the stately LaCoix. His imagination raced wildly into the future, looking up at Holly while she patted the top of his head.

The entire group made the trip to see Willow Rose, with Daphne refusing to let go of Ted's arm, and Jake playing, all the way, with a skipping, chatty Holly. David could not stop smiling; time misspent no longer mattered, leaving it as a colossal miracle to enjoy in the present. Thanks went up to a mauve cloud hovering protectively above the roof.

Leaning over the crib, Ted winked at those beguiling eyes and whispered endearing words to his baby girl. Kissing her several times, as he lifted her, female hands immediately forced him to give her up, quickly teaching him that grandmothers were extremely impatient creatures. Willow smiled joyously at the beautiful face, the female version of her Dad. This woman seemed a contradiction: poised yet gentle, cool but warm of heart, aloof yet all loving. With much tummy tickling, gushing, and baby gestures of contentment, two grandparents played and laughed with their first met grandchildren. Without a thought of disapproving consequences, Ted leaned back into David who encircled him from behind. They stood together, cheek against cheek, beaming at the scene so perfectly set before them. Nail biting stopped for one; the shuffling of feet and small fits of jealousy halted for the other. The moment passed with a necessary change, and again his new mom pushed Ted away in his attempt to take care of his daughter. With little effort, but a firm hand to hold the young man back, Daphne disappeared further into the nursery with two happy little hearts.

"Come on, Dad, I'll buy you a drink. She's in safe hands, Ted. Let them get to know each other. It's a girl thing; our daughters need that in their lives." David took Ted's hand and half dragged him, stumbling backward, until they were out of the nursery.

Jake stopped them both, on the closing of the door, and wiped away one coursing tear. "I want to thank you, Davie, for coming back to us. I've never told you how proud of you I am: such a remarkable actor and wonderful father. After the surprise of bringing Ted into your life; believing him the one who brought you home, we can't be happier. A hero, an inspiration, and a person who can hold my son together, what more can I ask. I guess there is something: two delightful little girls, two grandsons yet to meet, and your two brothers and sister-in-laws, Ted. Our little family will grow tremendously. Thank you, my sons." An approving hug, given to each of the two younger men, brought smiles, with a few embarrassing tears brushed away.

Three men leaned against the bar; drinks splashed merrily into crystal; and toasts clinked to family and new beginnings. They discussed work, children, the house, children, Ted's Oscar, children, and each enjoyed every minute of it. Without an eyebrow lifted, LaCoix Senior contented himself in the company of his shy new son, even accepting the handholding and occasional shoulder hug. It was a start, a very good start; and the protective purple cloud vanished, her work complete for now.

CHAPTER 48

On a special Saturday morning, the rising sun painted another watercolor masterpiece. The white solar disk brightened every pastel bloom in the garden, to open up and hunger for the first warming rays. A spectacular day for a wedding, Ted waited through an entire night. Not once had he shut those pools of unblinking blue, showing both fear and excitement. The courtyard would fill with famous guests, which he had met only in passing down a red carpet, and a few at the trial. Steven Kincaid, his only friend, would stand beside him; but the majority of the invited guests were David's acquaintances and old comrades who approved of the pairing. It intimidated Ted into silence.

Although bound by documents, concerning children, money, property, wills, and royalties, the awkwardness of a celebration hung heavily over the youngest partner, like a threatening storm from his hell. David's worry over Ted started twenty-four hours earlier. Refusing to eat, his lover had been violently ill throughout the day before, continuing to release his demons, which returned to haunt him. The pale face, so strained throughout the night, forced David to sit up with him, watching *Ben Hur* and a few other classics, while he held the man who shivered in the heat of a warm night. David believed it a symbol of their first innocent flirtation in a platonic bed. The morning would prove disastrous, if Ted did not pull himself out of the muddled mire in his head. He only had to remember the words.

For LaCoix, this day meant his honest commitment, in front of family and friends, to the long awaited love of his life--Theodore Barrett--the one thing he had asked for from deep within himself; someone who only wanted David for himself, without the unreliable strings of a want-to-be. The older man shifted under his young love, to find those startling eyes still open, blindly watching *Fantasia*. How appropriate, he thought, for a man from Wonderland. Having slept on and off, David had at least rested. Ted, on the other hand, had not blinked since the chariot race started; and now broomsticks marched menacingly after Mickey Mouse. Neither a word nor a sigh came forth, from the firmly clenched mouth with the determined white line around it. David gazed up at the ceiling, raked his stringy mop of unruly hair, and debated on what to do with a zombie. The day was meant to be perfect and magical; but *Peter Pan* had returned in his most formidable form. All could disappear with a flick of Tinkerbelle's wand.

"Morning Ted, did you sleep?" The disheveled blond received only a shake of the brunet head. "Do you think you can hold something down this morning? Maybe your ear decided to play tricks yesterday. Is that inner pain thing happening?" Again, an agitated shake of the head; David cursed himself for posing three questions, with three potentially different answers. He tried again. "Are you dizzy?" The *No* gesture grew more agitated. Another tactic would perhaps receive a *Yes* answer. "Will you still marry me?"

A definitive nod did not eradicate David's own blackened mood over the rapid, static motion. The expression on Ted's face did not change; only those blue eyes became larger in their terror. LaCoix tried again. "Do you remember what you're going to say?" The distraught blond tried desperately to be gentle, when he truly desired to slap the younger man silly. He did receive another minimal nod, but by 1:00 p.m., Mr. Barrett-LaCoix had to have his mouth operational and speaking articulately.

"Okay, it's seven o'clock; I'm getting up. People will start arriving by nine. Stevie and the Doc are flying in early; it's his turn to get you ready. Please, Baby Bear, close your eyes and nap, while I get ready. Just try for me. I'm turning off the video, or you'll never get through the day if you can't get it together. I don't know what to do or say to help, when I don't know what's wrong. Do you still want this day to happen?" No sign of what Ted needed, however, a single blink of the eyes did accept what lay before him.

The older man wriggled from under the warm body, which refused to move. Hitting the cool tiles with his feet, David stretched weary muscles. His own capacity to get through the day hinged entirely on Ted's happiness; but his partner's current behavior reminded him of those strange silences his partner slipped into while in England. There were unhappy reasons for those moods. Sighing heavily, David gazed out the bedroom window, taking in the splendor of the awakening garden; another beautiful Arizona day blessed them. A cloudless sky slowly turned from lilac to turquoise; a white sun shone down to illuminate a joyous occasion; and his greatest joy lie silently still and scared. He took a moment to visualize the calming colors of nature, fitting the one remaining piece into his Monet jigsaw puzzle: his lover. All would take care of itself, if he kept the picture in his head.

LaCoix emerged, looking like the dashing leading man he was, with honey-blond hair and a deepening tan. He sparkled as bright as the day, a sight beyond anyone's dream come true. Perhaps, a touch old for competitive beach volleyball, he had the build and agility to handle the game.

A subtle glimpse, Ted's *Peter Pan* personae flew in, making his head whirl, wondering how he had caught this fleeting man who no one had tamed for more than a few years at a time. Could he keep him? A tremor ran through him from his toes to the top of an exploding head. If he moved or closed his eyes, all would be gone in a puff of purple smoke.

After a quick kiss to the lips of the supine, overly warm, stone still body, David left to meet Kincaid and Dr. Thurgood. An excited hug from Stevie nearly toppled him over, but a firm handshake, from a ruggedly handsome man, with the gentlest of bearded faces, kept him on his feet. LaCoix smiled with pleasure to see their happy friend, without a bruise or painful walk. The wide smile, of perfect teeth, no longer disguised hidden pain, but genuinely beamed with giddiness. The bearded man, holding Kincaid's hand, did that for him: David could not be more pleased. With a quick explanation of the situation brewing in the boudoir, Kincaid raced off to see what remained mentally of his screen-brother. With only four hours remaining, Steven hustled to get through the strange wall of depression where Ted hid.

"Hey, Scarecrow, it's me. Can I come in?" It took time, but the door opened. Ted looked like he had regressed ten paces. Kincaid walked into the room and shut the door behind him. Turning back, he looked sadly at the catastrophe in need of repair. There it stood, the perfect skeleton for an anatomy class, swimming in an oversized T-shirt, which had to be one of Bernard's castoffs. "At least you're on your feet, but it's nod and shake time again. You did this to me after your breakup with David, then at your first hearing, both ending with broken, priceless objects. Come on, man, talk to me. What's the matter? You drive me crazy when you do this." Steven eyed the man, whose mouth appeared permanently locked. A movement made, however, eased his foreboding, as Ted slumped down on the enormous bed, looking down at his toes, fruitlessly attempting to grab the rough edges of the tile with his toes.

"All right, then, guess I'll make the decisions. First, food; maybe yogurt and fresh strawberries, and to top it off, we'll each have a glass of champagne." Kincaid put in the order through the telephone intercom. Five minutes later, Craig arrived, laden with the requested items. Steven's cunning mind came up with a devious plan, and wondered why David had not thought of it. In Ted's condition, with no food, a glass of anything alcoholic would let him sleep for a couple of hours. On the first sip of the sparkling liquid, a firm finger tipped the fluted glass upward, forcing the expensive nectar to be swallowed in two gasping gulps. It worked immediately, hitting Ted like a stone to the temple; and the exhausted Spirit fell adrift. By 9:45 a.m., Ted slumbered.

Steven quietly dressed in the casual outfit ordered specifically for the ceremony. Concerned about Ted, his idea had to work. If the man slept until noon, he would have him showered, polished, and coherently conversing at the timeless moment that came only once. His plan failed; Barrett awoke within minutes of Kincaid finishing off his last touches to the perfect male specimen.

"Sit up, Scarecrow; this is ridiculous. You should be helping David entertain your friends. Are you keeping your mouth shut, to control your tears of fear? If that's the case, little brother, you better do it now, or do you want to spill them in front of a hundred people when you make your vows?" Kincaid hit his mark, straight into the soft heart. Ted lunged for him, to be held until every tear dried and each fear evaporated: the notorious friends of David's never met, the family members only recently welcomed and those missing, the pressure of looking good for cameras, words long forgotten, and the concerns over Willow's health. The continuing drama of an entire year permeated through the slip of a body and soaked into the neck of his friend. The climax came after a self-purging of despair, until Steven pushed him away and shook the failing shoulders firmly. "You can do this, Scarecrow. Remember, you're an artist, one of the best actors I know. Let's start again. Morning, Scarecrow."

"Hi, Stevie."

"Good start. How's your stomach?"

"So so." Ted emphasized the response with a hand gesture.

"In that case, lie back down. You still have time for a little sleep. Do you still want to do this?" Kincaid peered at him questioningly, while pulling a sheet over the bare legs.

"Yeah, but will you stay with me?"

"What a baby. I'll be here; now sleep."

After the emotionally cathartic cry, Ted relaxed and slipped into a light sleep, with Steven patiently sitting next to him, rubbing the scrawny arm for extra comfort. Kincaid, however, required further instruction. The mega-star slowly stood, adjusted his own attire, and peeked out the door; left then right, he spotted someone who looked familiar. A small wave and a request for assistant, Daphne happily obliged the man, with the extraordinary face that greeted her whenever she went for groceries. In person, Steven Kincaid had a striking resemblance to her new son.

"Mrs. LaCoix, I presume?"

"Mr. Kincaid, I presume?" She smiled back at the precocious twinkle; and his grin grew more beguiling. Even an older woman, with years of experience, would grant this man anything he desired, so charming without saying a word. Watching over Ted, for half-hour, would be her own comfort, while Kincaid caught up with David and Jake. Steven took off at a run, leaving Daphne to slip into the sanctuary of her son and his lover. Ted looked years younger than his true age. She felt the tears welling in her green eyes as she affectionately looked down at him. His boyish features looked more pronounced in sleep: soft, sweet, a man with a child's heart. She sat down on the nearby chair, wanting to hug him until he felt alive and at peace. For now, she sat on guard duty, happy he had emerged from his silence, if only briefly.

Left to ponder the previous day, she also felt shrouded, despondent in disappointment with her grandsons she had yet to meet. Bryce telephoned the day before, informing them he had a second interview for a job he sincerely wanted. The father understood his excitement, pleased his son might have found his niche. After exchanges of luck between father and son, Daphne caught Ted's face drop. The telephone call started his spiral into a black hole of darkness, from which he refused to claw out of, although Bryce wished them the best, and promised a visit in a few weeks with a gift in hand.

The second shoe fell for the couple, when Tyler admitted he just did not want to come. The publicity, the sordid affair, and his father prepared to rupture the sanctity of marriage with another man, continued to humiliate the conservative second son. He liked Barrett as a person and a man he respected, but the sex aspect had traumatized the kid. Reluctantly understood by David; the contempt devastated Ted.

Two more calls put the last shovel of dirt over the man's coffin. Heading for Italy on the next flight, Richard Barrett had just received his first break, winning a small part in a movie filming in Venice, but had to leave that day. His wife, Eleanor, conveyed good wishes of luck and love, and again, Ted grew grimmer in his determination not to fall apart. The only good news received came from Quinlan, who would be there, giving Ted hope of having two friends he trusted.

The final call flattened Barrett into pulverized dust. Raymond and his wife could not make it; Annie was pregnant. Both frightened of old habits returning, they feared missing one class of counseling. This baby would be treated with the greatest love they could bestow; and they had Theo to thank for being a role model with Willow. Their plans to attend the wedding had to be cancelled, due to Annie's fainting spells and severe morning sickness. A despondent man thanked them, blessed them in his way; and without another word, Ted shoved the receiver into David's unsuspecting abdomen and left the room. Raymond apologized again to LaCoix, hoping they understood how much he wanted to stand up for his older brother. David accepted the sincerity behind the words, and congratulated the youngest Barrett and his wife on their new beginning.

A man, drowning in rejection, could not be consoled. Four fatal blows to his heart, another he could not tolerate and closed down all thought. Daphne rallied a rescue attempt by adopting his two brothers and their wives into the LaCoix Clan, sealed with a toast of champagne. Accepting the gracious offer with barely a hug, Ted silently vanished from them all.

Remembering the disappointments, Daphne wistfully watched the tossing and turning body, and softly sighed at the sight of a full-grown man, wriggling and squirming in his sleep, very much like his baby daughter. Rolling onto his stomach, the covering sheet twisted off, leaving a sight reminiscent of days long past. Ted's shirt pulled up, exposing his derriere to the warm sun shining through the window. His sexy new briefs left him fully exposed from the rear, but for the straps pushing up each cheek. Adding to the elderly woman's delight, she chuckled lightly when the tight fist went to his mouth and remained there. She tried to help with their special day, making the event simpler for the man before her; but simple seemed unheard of for the likes of the guests coming. It seemed a matter where her two sons differed, but it hurt this one. A sudden fluttering of eyes brought her back from yesterday's memories. Very groggy, Ted twisted his shoulders and head around, having no clue as to his whereabouts, or why David's mother sat where her son normally positioned himself when being protective.

"How are you feeling, son?"

"All right, I guess. Where's Stevie?"

Ted did not move; and Daphne had to get him moving. With this shy creature, a simple trick sufficed. "You are more scattered than any nervous bride I've ever seen. Mr. Kincaid required further instructions, leaving me to assist. Now then, there will be no more fussing. Get that cute, naked behind out of bed, and into the shower. Hurry, before the temptation to swat it overcomes me." Daphne laughed, looking directly at the probable object of her son's desire. Embarrassment should get the young man on his feet, and it did.

"Okay, I'm moving; and why am I the bride?"

"Because you're cuter; now hurry, Ted."

"I'm hurrying, Mom, but I'm not the bride."

"Thank you, Ted; I'm happy to be called Mom," Daphne called out, to a man fleeing into his dressing area. He would be ready in minutes from her week's observations of him. Fifteen minutes later, a new man emerged in perfect order. The whimsical hair suited him, washed, dried, and shining in colors of an October's day in Vermont. His eyes grew wider with anticipation; even after his long night, they shone clear as crystal and rare as dark sapphires. Only the dark circles, under those peculiar nickel-sized, blue orbs, refused to disappear. They never let one forget Ted was ill.

"Do I look okay? Have I forgotten anything? These clothes make me look like a hippo."

Back to bad habits and attitude, Daphne interceded before he unconsciously downed an entire package of purgatives. "Listen to me, Ted; you're far too thin now. Look at me in this full-length mirror. Do I look fat to you?" Daphne took his arm and dragged him over to stand beside her, to look at their reflections.

"God, no, you're just like David, tall and thin, as is Dad." Ted stunned himself with another word that came out so easily.

"Now look at yourself. You're half my size, and certainly your thighs are no bigger than my arm." She lifted her long flowing sleeve of pale blue for comparison. "Can't you see your bones sticking out, from under that sweater, and your hipbones? Well?"

"No! I can't see it! I can't!" Now in a panic over his size, Daphne shook her head, unable to fight the back and forth condition. His mind continued to play the game the disease manifested. The entrance of Kincaid interrupted the dash to the bathroom.

"Stop right there, Scarecrow. What's going on?"

"He's too fat."

"No you're not, Ted. Get your scrawny ass over here. We're almost ready for you; and this is going to be a hell of a bash. Everyone's asking for you, so we don't have time for purging. I don't think David wants to kiss someone who's been puking yogurt and strawberries. Let's see if everything's in place." A sheepish Ted stood still while Kincaid circled him, looking for those actor's details from habit. The younger man flushed with anxiety, ashamedly looking like a misbehaved child caught in the act.

"He looks wonderful." Daphne beamed.

"He certainly does, with a natural blush to top it off. Very cute, Scarecrow." Kincaid grinned wickedly as he stepped back, folded his arms, and appraised the figure before him.

"Shut up; it's not funny." Ted pushed passed them and stopped; his mind still adrift, wondering where to go and when.

"That underwear does give him a perky little tush." Mrs. LaCoix laughed along with Steven, sweeping away the dire symptoms they were witnessing.

"Shit. I was... I..."

"...yes, you were semi-naked while sleeping, and a tiny, naked behind happens to be my favorite part of the male anatomy, particularly when the cheeks are lifted with bright yellow spandex straps. Small derrieres are something one has to pinch or smack; it's natural law. It broke my heart when Davie stopped walking around the house with just a jock strap. A mother's baby is always her baby, even when he grows to be an incredibly good-looking man." More chuckling and bright smiles, from Daphne and Kincaid, brought a rush of embarrassing pink, up a hidden neck into the cheeks. As the color heightened, he almost looked healthy.

"So, your son has always been an exhibitionist? Now our Scarecrow is turning into one."

"Davie certainly had no qualms of parading around the house half-dressed, until he left for college. Now, Steven, what news of the ceremony, and can I leave to join the others?"

"Of course, we can't start without you, and we're on schedule. Fifteen minutes left, so we had better hustle. Thanks for getting Theo up and looking delicious."

"He is delectable. Do you think we added enough pink to his face?"

"Go away, Mom; you're a bigger tease than your son."

"Someone had to teach him. Good luck, Ted." Daphne smiled, gave him a kiss of encouragement, and hurried out the door in the most elegant of manner. Her dress floated behind her when she walked away; and Ted remembered another flowing gown of flesh tones. He hoped Lavender's arms supported him this day. At the thought, the scent of lilacs filled the room and a wisp of air brushed his cheek. *'Speak what is in your heart, Child. It will lead you on the proper course.'*

Steven checked over his look-alike and nodded in approval. Taking his hand, he escorted the rattled sack of shaking bones back into the bathroom. With the skill of an experienced theatrical actor, a little concealer patted under the eyes would go unnoticed. The black circles vanished; and a perfect face shone through. With the last minute touch-up, they were out the door, covertly slipping behind rose bushes and cypress trees, to get to the left side of the vine-covered pergola.

In awe of the crowd, Ted nearly passed out from the large number. He dared not look at a face, in case his knees gave way. Taking a few breaths, his attention suddenly diverted to the trellised stage whence a soft drumming sound drifted. A Cherokee love ballad, sung in harmony by Carmen and Holly's angelic voice, filled his head, haunting him with mystical words, piecing two lives together in song and tears, and hitting his *knowing* heart at its tender-most junction.

David also listened, hearing and visualizing Ted in every word, and everything the two had accomplished. Uplifting and heartbreaking, chills ran through him. He sent a prayer to the Cosmos that salty droplets would not fall on the other side of the garden. Jake put a fatherly hand on his son's shoulder, squeezing it with the pride that had been building all week, coming to know the man and not the troubled boy. David felt the strong support; he was ready.

The charismatic, blond-haired Knight strode out confidently from behind the protective tree, followed stride-for-stride by LaCoix Senior. Like father, like son, they were all smiles, tanned with glittering white teeth. Both men looked comfortable and casual, attired from head to tan toe in denim and cotton pullovers. The best man wore navy, while his equally lanky son sported the palest of blue, with his jeans skin-tight. The two-inch riding heels on their boots made them that much taller and leaner. While nervously pulling the annoying sweater sleeves up past his elbows, David never took his eyes off the man approaching from the other side. His mother was right; the image soared beyond handsome. He had won the grand prize; and his smile broadened, thinking of magic and mystery, and Ted the integral link. With no idea where the thought came from, he left it as another revelation to sort out after this special day.

With a little shove, a very nervous Ted stepped forward, his best man steadying him up the few risers. Holding his breath, he contemplated a mad dash to the stables, to leap on Bastet, and to fly away with her. Lavender said she could. It might be a good time for a test flight, but the toss of a coin, in his head, would not land to make a decision. Another push and quiet whisper, to get his perky butt in gear, had him walking toward the man who beamed at him. Following Kincaid's advice, he looked at nothing but David, his beacon at the end of the tunnel, and he returned his approaching lover's smile.

Dressed immaculately, Kincaid wore similar navy threads as Jake. To match his partner, Ted donned the same colored pale blue denims without an inch to squirm, and a warmer, white cashmere turtleneck. The look of this pale creature could deem the ceremony illegal. Steven wore the required tan boots, but Ted forgot, shoving his bare feet into expensive Italian tan loafers instead. At least six inches shorter than the other three, the remembrance of a minuscule desert mouse came back to stick its tongue out at him. Thin could not describe the man; and when he stepped to clasp David's hands, a few gasps filtered from the crowd. The new star, amongst their prestigious ranks, looked healthier to some, but to most, his jeans showed LaCoix's worst nightmare. The murmur stopped when the couple pulled together for a sweet kiss of greeting and a whisper of encouragement from the taller of the two.

Holly approached and stood just in front of them, one-step down, dressed in light denim coveralls and a white lace blouse underneath. Her fathers' choice of wedding attire dismayed her frivolous side, believing she required something far fancier. She convinced them a few white and blue flowers, poked into her coiffed tresses, would be appropriate, since she was a girl; and the tilt and toe tapping emphasized her point. Willow sat on their grandmother's lap in the front row, the eldest in soft blue chiffon, and the youngest in a white jumpsuit sprinkled with primroses. The wedding party took their places, with Jake behind his son, and Steven standing close-by to grab Ted if he fainted, or made a dash for the open desert. The picture represented a Rockwell painting of a new form of domesticity, set against a cloudless blue sky, contrasting with the freshly painted white pergola, dripping with deep purple blossoms. A timeless, theatrical setting created a soft-hued illusion for the gathering of people who wanted the best for the much loved and admired actors. They were groundbreakers for freedom of the heart. A hush swept the courtyard to hear the first vows; someone had to start; David took the initiative.

"Theodore, you are a promised wish come true; and I need nothing more than you by my side." David stopped and reached for the white rose Holly handed him with great delicacy. "I, David Jacob LaCoix, take you, my lover, partner, and friend, in all your sweetness, softness, and tremendous courage, like the touch of this rose." The taller man slid the cool petals of the long-stemmed symbol gently down either side of Ted's face. A larger hand manipulated a smaller one, and drew it up for them both to see. A prick of a finger, the thorn had done its damage, but mended with a seductive lick and a slow suck, ending with a kiss to make it better. "And like its thorn, I accept all your barbs and faults with no judgment. This ring symbolizes that we are truly one, united in body and Spirit." David slipped the better-than-a-diamond, masculine ring, of a solitary, rare, intense-blue sapphire, set in platinum, onto the bleeding finger.

There was silence. Another soft kiss to the cheek, the younger man awoke from his beautiful dream of a sworn oath by his Knight. With his simple speech long forgotten, Ted's heart exploded with confessions of adoration. "David, you are my life. You gave me your heart, which I'll keep forever. You stole mine years ago and will forever belong to you. Care for it gently, my Knight. We have seen eternity and the other side of the stars; and I will love you beyond even those distant borders." Ted paused, but did not take his eyes away from the green ones misting up. Holly did her duty, handing him a black rose, and stepped back. "I need your velvet touch to keep me happy and fulfilled. Your softness and tenderness have no bounds, and you only share them with our daughters and me. I will take that loving side of you, and..." The same ritual commenced; and David stood bleeding. A sensual sucking grew more intense for the blond actor, but a delicate kiss eased the sharp prick. "...and I accept your thorns, understanding all of them as you understand mine. With this ring, promise me you won't ever break..." Overcome with emotion, Ted faltered.

"I could not deny you anything, Ted." The actor holding his hands gave him his cue.

"I return that promise tenfold. Love is not a strong enough word to express the intangible bond between us. The essence of my being is eternally woven within yours. And... and I can't stop talking. David, I..." A ring, of a single, even rarer, yellow-green sapphire, with the same ritualistic symbols engraved in platinum, slipped onto a slightly shaking hand by another who almost dropped it while trying to place it correctly. The two ringed, bleeding fingers met, stopping the nervous rambling to swear silently on a vow not to be forgotten.

"I know, Teddy. What we have is beyond words, and only found in the limitless depths I see in your eyes. You are my perfect wish come true."

The ad-libs and unstructured sentiments had their audience spellbound, allowing a pause for Ted to throw his arms around David's neck, exhibiting a full body press and kiss to his partner. Not the usual sweet gesture of a shy bride and groom, the intensity was seen and felt by the sensitive crowd watching. A fluttering of dozens of butterflies, all translucent and every color of nature's grace, danced and swarmed around the handsome heads, creating two interlocking halos to bind them. Only five people knew of the wonderment. David whispered a *thank you,* as the winged creatures disappeared into the roses; the most elusive confetti that money could not buy. The taller actor gently subdued the heated passion, pulling away and embracing the autumn silk into his neck, only to feel the droplets drizzling under the neck of his sweater.

Kincaid stepped forward and addressed the tearful crowd with his teasing, bewitching smile. "Ladies and Gentlemen, I'd like to introduce Mr. David LaCoix and his handsome partner, Mr. Theodore Barrett-LaCoix."

David turned Ted around, holding him from behind, with arms crossed over the racing heart; and two bright smiles faced their friends who stood to applaud and cry. Two men conquered hell, and stood laughing at the world, as they floated in their serenity.

"Everyone, please raise your glasses to our friends, David and Theo." Steven stepped away, and dozens of non-threatening cameras and cell phones clicked to capture the famous couple.

It had all been said; and David continued to hold the quaking body. He extended his thanks to those in attendance, from supporting Ted at the trial, accepting them as a couple, to his parents for teaching his forever partner what love and forgiveness meant. Laughing happily and hugging Ted, he raised his own glass in a salute. The new couple never left each other's side, as they started to mingle through the throng, with Holly firmly clasping Ted's newly ringed hand, and Willow settled happily on David's hip. Their girls enjoyed the spectacle of swirling ribbons of colorful dresses, smiling faces that enticed giggles, and large hands that gently grasped theirs in greeting and love. The family portrait delighted all.

A day of socializing, merriment, and sincere wishes overwhelmed both men. David could do nothing but show off his new family, in grand Leo style, with Ted shyly in tow. With much enthusiasm, Steven introduced his look-alike to the Love Professor; and the younger man's day became more relaxed with close friends nearby. The sounds of an ancient lyre and Celtic flute drifted on the air, well into evening; and David never left Ted's side. A hidden rendezvous, in a cloud unseen, they met with Lavender and Quinlan. With touches of healing hands and breathless kisses, tranquility calmed both racing hearts. The Mistress had been the start, becoming their guardian; Quinlan remained as Ted's teacher and healer; and the unearthly couple vanished as quickly as the Faery rings, leaving this special day for David and Ted.

CHAPTER 49

The beginning of their life as a unit started with the fading light of a desert evening, enveloping the pair for a promised lifetime. Ending the few days of drama, their celebration turned into a happy, comfortable sharing. They had much to be grateful for, and with the predicted difficulties of understanding, they would conquer the upcoming eventualities David foresaw; and he saw many. Besides his worry over Ted's mental and physical difficulties, his girls troubled him deeply. Overly brilliant in their perception of all things, their daughters needed guidance. Always a statement of fact for Holly, and the profound thoughts of Willow, common sense and controversial ideology belonged to their girls. David felt alone, comprehending little of their concepts. Ted never let on, one way or another, seemingly frightened to discuss the *knowing*.

Their good friend Kincaid restarted his spiritual journey on firmer ground; gentleness of a hand created the empowering sensation. Dr. Thurgood accepted his ideas, helping him fit the missing puzzle pieces together, by asking the simplest of questions. David wished he could do the same for Ted, but an opportunity never opened, as his partner appeared to absorb things without a word. Barrett seemed to fit the theories together, although he remained shrouded in fragments of two ideologies.

Exhilarating, fun, and informative, the week with Kincaid and his Love Doctor sped past, leaving them to their last night and David's needed call for help. He had watched their closest friend and his new lover carefully; he had made his decision. Looking for other role models, he found them. Neither couple blatantly flaunted their sexuality, only confirming a nurturing bond of the very masculine variety. The two youngest appeared somewhat flighty within close ranks, but no more than any young male exuding an innate shyness and emotions ranging from blasé to off the scale. Only a camera turned them into a character; a disguise they hid behind, only to remove the masks for their lovers. The foursome became close quickly; friends to take cover behind when bullets commenced firing.

The Professor genuinely appeared a modest man of worldly knowledge and tastes. Medium build, slightly shorter than Kincaid, he had a fine graying beard that blended into his silver-streaked, dark-brown hair, making him handsome in a leathered way. A contradiction of sophistication, academia, and the rugged outdoors, plus the glasses and how he wore them, gave him away as a possible man of letters; and intellectual conversations manifested themselves around the beehive fireplace in the Library. Besides an Oscar now sitting center stage, the room held every picture Holly had drawn of her unique world, each one framed and meticulously displayed by her daddy. Fond memories for two men, the images held the other two spellbound and examined thoroughly: a constant source of entertainment.

Conversations filled LaCoix and Thurgood's week--serious, intense, and humorous--reflecting new facets of each man's knowledge, unbeknownst to their partners and friends. David craved the stimulation, drawing him closer to Joseph Thurgood who promised to care for Kincaid for the long term, and with divine intervention of some variety, to take on an important role for LaCoix. Subject matter turned to the *knowing*: spiritually, artistically, theatrically, intellectually, to the comical. Everything, from the existence of the devil to the Three Stooges, was discussed; and Ted awakened with something David could not define. The younger man had no trouble in participating in these lively discussions with his own changing ideology. Only his fatigue blocked his way; and concern, for the winsome creature, was seen on the other three faces, particularly when he faded off in the arms of his lover, or stumbled over what he wanted to say.

David remembered his conversation with Jamie, whenever Ted cuddled closer. Over the past two weeks, it became evident that Barrett would have problems coping on his own, if anything befell a member of the family. It worried the older actor, whose nightmares returned, of Ted alone, unable to understand where he ought to be, or what needed doing. The vision remained unclear; it frightened LaCoix, until a whisper from Lavender harshly repeated to think only of positive thoughts.

Their last evening together, and on David's suggestion, Barrett and Kincaid disappeared for a ride under the stars and a private chat. Snickering mischievously, they waved good-bye and rode away at a gallop. They had been inseparable filming *Brother Mine*, when things turned so terribly wrong. Secrets still shared, they now had happy ones. Their late night ride left LaCoix with Thurgood, finally giving him his chance. "Doc, I know this is very early, but I have a question; no, a hard favor to ask of you."

"Anything, David; I think all our boundaries have been broken and the paradigm has shifted to expand further." Thurgood had a way with the metaphysical, studying it from an outside perspective. Surprising to the actor, the man understood the complex theories, held as truths by his daughters. Doc resounded of Luciferianism, making him perfect for the job.

"Thanks. Stevie's one of Willow and Holly's godfathers, along with Ted's two brothers who, although very fine people, remain under the scrutiny of the remaining members of their defunct, sanctimonious church. I'd like to add you to the top of the list, considering the reaction the girls have toward the delicate theological problems within the Barrett households. You have already alluded to the fact that our daughters are unique compared with other children; and I hope I'm not boasting as an overly proud father."

"They are extraordinary; and if you desire that Steve and I care for them, we'd certainly accept the responsibility." With no hesitation in the voice, Thurgood accepted a difficult undertaking, as if prepared for the question.

"Thanks, I'll have the changes drawn up legally tomorrow. You have no idea how relieved I feel." With David's first request granted, he could let out the breath he held.

Pulling out two cigars to seal the deal, the Professor offered one to LaCoix. It had become an evening ritual between them, whereas Ted and Steven always declined to partake in the extravagant, strong-smelling trend. "Holly is far more learned than her age would indicate. She could probably qualify for a Doctorate in Philosophy right now. In some ways and thoughts, however, she remains a little girl, learning at an extraordinary rate. I do hope you have a one-on-one teacher for her."

"She is home-schooled in a fashion, since we can't find a place or teacher capable of instructing her without being antagonistic. She's beyond their knowledge in many things; and they will not allow her to progress in her natural state. Bernard continues with her studies in mathematics and the sciences, which she picks up quickly. Unfortunately, she insists these subjects are irrelevant and a waste of time. According to both my daughters, they are useless in the world that is coming. Holly won't look at a computer and seldom turns on a television. Occasionally, you catch her listening to some odd, mysterious doctrine, which she'll most often shake her head in disgust. On a sudden whim, however, something clicks in her head, and she'll listen intently to a complex scenario of the metaphysical, which I certainly don't comprehend, let alone discuss with her. She scares me, Doc; so damn sure of herself, and what needs to be said and done. I feel badly that her social situation and attitude do not require children of her age." David shook his head, perplexed over the change in his daughter, from a silly little girl, fighting over ribbons, into a spiritual guru. Unsure of how to deal with his own biological daughter, Willow, still a baby, was completely beyond human reasoning.

"Certainly unnerving, I grant you that. In all my travels, no child has impressed me to such an extent, besides her sister. Willow Rose is unto herself; and whether she be truly human, it does make one wonder. That little bundle's thoughts, when ready to be heard, are unbelievably important to humanity. If her visions, interpreted into words by Holly, remain undisturbed, to nurture and grow, she will be a spiritual mentor for an entire generation. Between your daughters, they could annihilate established global ideas, causing untold mayhem. At six-months, Willow already has much to teach the world; and this planet had better bloody well listen. She also has the uncanny opposite side, one to destroy anything in her way. Have you felt it?"

"You're scaring me, Joseph, and you're damn perceptive. Willow is human; but her thoughts have affected us all, experiencing her power. I've only known her for six weeks; but in that time, some *thing* happens; and you never know what will result."

"Such as?" Thurgood leaned forward and studied his new friend, who strangely bit his nails nervously, between calming puffs of the fat cigar. More to this man's concerns, the Professor sensed they reached beyond taking parental care of his daughters.

"Shit, this is hard to believe, let alone witness. Objects soar through the air, crashing into fragments, always turning mysteriously red. The jagged shards will then burst into flame, only to have everything revert to its normal state, just as quickly. Another example: a person, who intentionally attacks either Ted or me verbally, is burned; and I do mean that literally and over vast distances. Capable of destruction, as you said, with the experience of a pre-toddler, she's too immature to wield such power. You see the proof in the news; yet you can't believe it. Holly's developing the same talents, but a destructive thought never crosses her mind. It may be the result of their different initial upbringing, Holly's so unlike Willow's first few months of torment." David came forward to rest his face in his hands, disappearing into the gray haze, which thickened with each nervous exhale of a Cuban cloud.

"It may be true, but both children need some harnessing of their abilities. I have no idea who could handle such a pair. Even his Holiness, the Dalai Lama, would have trouble with your two. One of them appears to be a delicate white rose with no thorns; the other has a black velvet touch, with a piercing barb that could cut you to ribbons. So what do you wish of me, David?" The Professor leaned back into the plush chair, waiting for something his promise may not fulfill.

"My God, how did you know about the roses?" Choking on smoke and surprise, LaCoix could barely say the words.

"A simple metaphor, as seen in your ceremony."

"A metaphor! Man, I need to think about that one. Why didn't you tell me, Lavender?" David's eyes nearly rolled to the top of his head. La Rosa Negra was Willow. Ted created an uncanny image of their daughters, only missing which rose kept its thorn. All their meaningful gestures, from the first white roses given to tease, led to the sisterhood of Willow and Holly. His head spun; the cigar smoke made it worse; and he hastened to butt out the pacifier.

"You okay, David?"

"Yeah, just another wild, mind-blowing thought. Back to business then, with something drastically more important. You understand the dilemma of our daughters. With your intellect and self-awareness, you perceive a little of what is going on. If something happens to me, Ted will be lost. He takes it for granted that all little girls are capable of these powers, since he only knows Willow and Holly. He tries, and is succeeding to some degree; but like his brothers, his f deeply imprinted background impedes his subconscious mind from looking further, and though he won't admit it, so does the abuse. It terrifies him, and he continues to have nightmares to this day. Stevie comes from the spiritual world we literally fell into; and it certainly can't be called a religion. Perhaps, the only appropriate verbiage is *our truth*. Has he said anything to you?" Green eyes asked for recognition of what they had been talking about for days. David needed Thurgood's affirmation that he understood. He felt the fool, but had no other way to ask, except beating that infernal bush to death.

"This and that. I understand a little of his philosophy of life, and accept it honestly, believing a great many of his ideologies are true. Not just the fanciful tales of an neurotic actor, he intrigues me, watching him piece a strange puzzle together in his head, with clear definitions of wordings like *the knowing*, *the awakening*, and *the beginning again*. The three of you, and your daughters, use these terms in place of religious godlike titles. These terms are part of our mythological history, but not our theological one. You, Ted, Stevie, and your girls are all fascinating."

"I like that analogy. For Ted, it's a theological war, and yet, he has witnessed and does believe in the phantasmal. What else has Stevie revealed?"

"He has a clever mind when talking business. With his industry shrewdness and his spirituality, I can't fathom his former personal life, allowing someone to batter and belittle him as if deserved. Occasionally he reverts, trying to bait me into beating or taking advantage of him, for unknown reasons. I refuse to respond, which confuses him, making him feel rejected. In our short, but intense acquaintance, we have spent many hours talking about his needs, but I flatly decline his requests. Only soothing words and gentle touches make him happy again. Old habits, as they say."

"He needs to mend his mental dependency on the abuse. Such a sweet Spirit, I still wonder what or who put him on such a kinky path of adoration."

"I can see his response to kindness grows greater; although I wonder if being hurt physically disguises some other kind of pain."

"We'll never know, unless he eventually confides in you. So, a few favors, Doc, besides helping Stevie: whatever happens, would you oversee the education of our daughters, letting them find their own way for the most part? Teach them this world's knowledge in its natural sense, to interpret it for themselves. Your travels and fields of study interest them, and you enthrall them with your historical adventure stories. I sense they agree with many of your theories, while others they question more dubiously."

Again, the Professor broke the nervousness of the moment, with a soft chuckle and shake of the head. "I'd be delighted. I'm sure they will teach me far more than I can teach them. We will certainly be there for your girls, David, and particularly for Theo, if that horrid consequence should arise. He's a loving man whose only joy seems to be you and your daughters. I do hope he continues to brighten with some happy news from Steve tonight."

"Thanks for accepting, Thurgood; I needed to ensure all my bases were covered when it comes to my three babies." David picked up the cigar, still smoldering slightly, and took a couple of puffs to rekindle it. Still missing his cigarettes, which aided his thinking, by giving him something to fiddle with; these few Cubans satisfied some of the loss. With promises made, he indulged himself to taste the flavor circling around his tongue.

"Babies they are, and all three hide wisdom not yet shared. You're very insightful yourself, David. You know it, and like Theo, do not let on to anyone. If I were you, I would only think the positive and the beautiful; for I believe any negative tendencies could lead to one of your so called occurrences, a danger to you all."

"You're right. Came close to terminating a chopper with a thought, can you believe it? I try to control that part of me; and we're teaching the girls to think, looking at things from both sides, before reacting. So, another request of both you and Stevie: would you mind moving here for the girls? We can enlarge one of the guesthouses for you, as we are doing for Mom and Dad. Stevie can fly in and out, when he occupied with business."

"I need to discuss this with Stevie, but I don't see a problem, as he's always in the air. He's turned down numerous scripts, as I'm sure you and Ted have. Besides, being here would get us out of Malibu and into a simpler life. I rather like the idea of communal-style living. I'm sure that Ted's brothers and their wives would also enjoy moving in, away from the threats of those still within their former church."

"Thanks, Joseph, and it would be a good idea for the other two Barrett families. A baby must be born first, and who knows what that child will inherit." David leaned back, thinking of a huge family surrounding them, but with different homes to maintain privacy. It could be done with a thought.

"You and Ted need to discuss it, as will I and Stevie. Having tenure and the ability to choose whatever project I desire, the teaching of brilliant children would have merit."

"Fantastic; I'll make arrangements as soon as I get a definitive answer. Now tell me, what are these surprises Stevie has for Ted?" The wicked grin returned and nerves settled. Hard requests had been made; all had been accepted.

"First off, David, I owe you a colossal amount of gratitude, which I can now repay by taking care of your family. You conjured up a way for Steve to find me, by convincing the elusive, too-famous Kincaid, to reply to my letter. Such a delightfully shy introduction, his nervousness showed in every word, and each word carefully chosen. I thank you from this enraptured heart."

"You're welcome, but I promise you; if you ever hurt him, you'll have to contend with me."

Thurgood smiled a gesture of understanding. "I'm incapable of swatting a mosquito, and my exotic creature was difficult enough to capture."

"Ted will be pleased; he fears for the safety of our Ferrari." The two men laughed, having divulged their adventure during a week of honest talks.

"If *Brother Mine* is successful, David, and the snippets I have seen are brilliant, it will decide our next move. Stevie tires of the hiding game, and admires the two of you, in what you've accomplished. A few days ago, after hearing you exchange those endearing words, we decided to come out of our vault-like closets, very secretly for the meantime, to make our union legal; at least as legal as yours. If the sky falls on us, when we announce our marriage, I have money, along with a somewhat exciting lifestyle, but no glory. I don't believe, for a second, Steve's popularity will wane. He may grow weary of it instead, being very much a homebody who needs nurturing more than stardom. I think it actually frightens him in many ways."

"Congratulations! Man, what great news! The decision is a little quick, but if you both feel it's right, I'm very excited for you. I do need a promise, however; you'll protect his fragile ego and sad, sorry Spirit, so much like Ted. Mend him for us, Doc, and we'll be happy. You have me convinced you're the right man, just from your faith in his abilities, and your willingness to bare the financial burden, which I doubt will ever be a problem. It's good to hear you're happy to take responsibility for him. He's a man of the world, but like Ted, a child at heart."

"Being older than my love-starved pup, I'd appreciate the same of you."

"Wouldn't have it any other way." David stuck out his hand; and silhouetted by the golden fire, two strong hands came together in a firm handshake of agreement. Several of David's concerns dissipated into the hovering cloud above them. An honest, caring person, Thurgood would nurture Steven Kincaid to become the confident, happy man represented by his public persona. The nervousness would fade into gleeful chatter, and his wires, so tightly strung, would loosen his Spirit into tranquility: very good news. His daughters' educations would be handled delicately, by a man who understood their needs: even better news. Theodore Barrett-LaCoix, the passive little imp who could conquer mountains, now had an intelligent, comforting shoulder to support him when lost: the best news. All David's babies would be cared for and loved; he leaned back and relaxed for the first time since arriving home.

"I keep losing you tonight, LaCoix. Are you getting tired?" Thurgood's observations registered every emotion expressed in body language.

"No, just thankful we have you and Stevie as friends. Let's get this fire stoked before the boys crash in here with their happy tidings." David got up, placed a few more cedar logs on top of a dying flame, which burst forth with a little jabbing of a poker and the breath of life blown over it.

"I do have one more problem, Doc. Don't know why I agreed to it; but it's a signed deal. Coming up, we have a round of interviews for a two-hour television special. I respect the woman; and she attended the wedding, but to spend two days followed by a camera; what was I thinking? Christ, I can't believe Ted agreed." David sat back down, realizing he had returned to the obnoxious character who wanted a spotlight for his own opinions, not once considering how his family felt.

"Last Saturday, you caught him unaware of what you asked. Perhaps ill timed, you should have concentrated solely on the ceremony. He'll get through it. As for requests, I have one to ask on Steve's behalf. He wishes Holly's help, if you will allow her to participate."

"Holly? What is it? Something to do with your upcoming nuptials?"

"No, this would be work; and she would be given credit for her part in any manner you deem appropriate. Remember the short spell Steve cared for her, while in England? It left a deep impression on him, climaxing as co-writer of a screenplay about the folklore she taught him. It's a beautiful adventure story, full of magic, wonder, and a thrill a minute. Steve would like Holly to detail every character in looks, colors, and oddities, from Faeries to Trolls, like her paintings that surround us. I can't tell you how many times I've found him carefully scrutinizing them. If you're willing, he wants you to play the part of the villain, and Ted, hopefully, is currently agreeing to play King Oberon."

"Oh, man; what a trip, if it all comes together! I'd love to do a film I could take the girls to see. I've done nothing but heavy dramas and action thrillers. A Faery Tale villain: I love it! This is too good to be true. Ted would be the perfect Oberon, having met a few real Faeries." David chortled sinisterly, rubbing his hands together, smiling his ear-to-ear infectious grin, and his eyes non-stop dancing about the room.

"You don't say!"

"They showed themselves Saturday, and it's not what you're thinking, Thurgood; shame on you. Those mysterious butterflies that encircled us for a moment--like a living wreath or halo--were Faeries."

"Not butterflies and you have not been recently certified?"

"Not yet. Even Stevie knows about them; but hadn't seen one until last Saturday. He recognized them immediately."

"I'll be damned. Your world becomes more intriguing every second. No one would believe it." The man of letters did not shake his head, but only smiled in wonder. This intellectually astute actor, who he had come to respect, confirmed all Kincaid's stories; and Joseph Thurgood sat back, peacefully, joyously flabbergasted at all the possibilities, which his lover and this extraordinary family believed in.

CHAPTER 50

Two days turned into three. If thought about, it should have been expected, considering the amount of equipment flown in, to interview the family. David felt it important to express an alternate, healthy lifestyle, still waiting on legalization, and to introduce a different perspective on another outrageous topic: spirituality. Time grew nearer to allude to the *knowing*. Proud of their family situation, and while in the spotlight, an opportunity opened to shed light on those of the homophobic variety, and perhaps, open a few Valkyrian minds to a new awareness. A quiet interview appealed to LaCoix. Challenging past assumptions, now thought to be truths, became his cause; and although having nothing to prove, he felt obligated to offer another choice to the world. The question of how seemed imperative.

His *knowing* lay in what he had experienced and seen: the abilities of his girls growing stronger, the unlimited powers of the mysterious Fey, the healing hands and flights through time of a ghostly Spirit, the potential of his own visualizations, and of course, the knowledge of a Faery who welcomed him into her world. With these revelations, LaCoix positioned himself for the impossible, to introduce the *Beginning Again*, already his family's enlightened path.

The host, of this intensive look at a family in its glory and its disarray, had supported Ted through his court battles, and rallied behind them when they announced their intentions to defy a world's abhorrence with an illegal union. Considered a good friend, with a heart that broke at a melancholy whisper, David had granted her request. Both men admired and trusted this lovely person, a major mogul of the industry, now semi-retired, and consented to present themselves in an open forum. The masks would be dropped; eyebrows would raise. David's mischievous nature, of the macabre, waited for a door to open and a few secrets unveiled. Ted's quaint, shy remarks would be his grounding force, while Holly supplied the mystery. Who knew what topics she promised to unfold in her innocence; now iterating ideology of catastrophic consequences that both men scrambled to grasp their meaning. Growing aware of so many possibilities, David believed everything transmitted between his daughters. Frightening and exhilarating, the Mistress had bestowed a great gift upon him; he sensed her passing secrets onto two unlikely little girls. He would never express this insight to his partner, whose fear intensified with each new revelation uttered, although masking his feelings with loving thoughts.

Day 1--the photo shoot--a room emptied to accommodate a few props and dozens of lights, for a series of still photographs taken in a myriad of poses and combinations. David and Ted understood the grueling effort of capturing the perfect portrait: hundreds of clicks of a camera, never looking like you were twisted in knots, while touching places one should not, to stay in position, and straining every muscle to accentuate them in finite definition. From flexing arms to sucking in cheeks, you never forgot to keep your lips relaxed and slightly open. An artistic portraiture came through pain and aching muscles: a contortionist's nightmare. While contemplating an easier method, David groaned with the placement of his wrong arm around the front of another who tried to twist a leg over someone's appendage too high, just to capture an elusive group facial close-up.

Happily, the girls came through like professionals, for their first formal shoot. Quiet and uncomplaining, whatever the request, Holly would do. She remained relaxed, intrigued by it all, as did Willow who also remained composed, with no wriggling or squirming of a normal toddler.

Their fathers could not be prouder. Even the Polaroids, taken for lighting purposes, captured private little vignettes of their feelings toward each other. The final prints would be extraordinary, whether in the nude or clothed; and the artistically elegant portraits, both serious and joyous, would be an unprecedented success story for an interviewer's magazine, to become a collector's item over many decades.

Day 2 included a nervous private talk with Ted in the gardens, and a more animated conversation with David in the stables. They proudly showed off their home, wandering through the grounds, each speaking separately on life and death, love and hate, fantasy and spirituality, not to mention their competition for the same award, and the resulting rise to super-stardom. The two-hour special would be a statement of everything they had been through, between here and there, between La Rosa Negra and the newly named realm of Awakening Canyon.

Holly became a little sullen and more serious Day 3; however, a ride into the depths of the Canyon brightened her mood, with the young miss on Shu, David on Ra, and Bastet keeping a very good rider from passing out. The mare learned to give a little rear, and a high-flying dance of her dainty front hooves, to remind him not to look down. The action jolted Ted back to life, laughing and looking straight ahead: a lesson learned. Due to the medical problem, David held his beloved Willow between his thighs, pushed tightly against him. He would never let his treasure fall; the only living remembrance of his lover's genes, it made her beyond priceless. With their mental capabilities increasing, David instantly understood her every whim and need; and he relayed a message back without a sound. A charming, quiet time with the family, they laughed along with their good friend, who bounced like a basketball on a very gentle horse, while still asking questions. Although the day passed pleasantly, the scenery spectacular, their guest did have trouble moving on their return to the stable. Giggling merrily, the video cameras caught her every groan and followed her, as far as the Jacuzzi in the guest quarters. After a rest, all would be happy.

An interview, over dinner with children, pointed toward entertaining, or disastrous. Excited about the potential revelations that may occur to any family member, David hoped an opportunity would reveal something wickedly controversial. This evening, family fare became a theatrical production. Easy to converse, and every angle covered, the *Beginning Again* started early, perhaps too early.

"Well, Miss Holly Jane, I have been talking to your fathers the last two days. They told me how proud they are of you and your sister. So what do you think of having two men as your parents?"

"It's better than having only one." Sadness fell over the adults, thinking of the loss less than a year ago.

"Yes, it would. Do they treat you the same way, or is one stricter?"

"They're just different. Dad gets all serious and cranky if any of us do something wrong." Holly looked at David, already knowing the comeback.

"I'm not cranky," he protested, looking terribly surprised at the notion.

"Yes you are." Ted and Holly rang out in unison, having fun teasing the appointed head of the household.

"Only when something bad happens, like last week. Daddy fainted again, and you got all weird. Didn't he?" Holly eyed Ted who nodded and chuckled at the surprised father, while the blonde sprite continued her story. "We knew you were just worried. Remember when I played that game with Shu; you thought I'd get hurt? You yelled at everyone, but you scared Daddy the most. You forgot he hates loud noises."

"You nearly gave me a coronary, attempting a dangerous stunt like that, even with Shu."

"I know; you worry about all of us. I didn't cry though." Both father and daughter did the LaCoix tilt, and broke out with identical smiles.

"No, but your Daddy did."

"And thank you both, so much, for telling the world that piece of nobody-needs-to-know news." Feeling antsy about his emotional status during a private moment, Ted's raw edges frayed rapidly, while battling the unknown inner pain alone. Growing worse, he and Quin could do nothing, increasing his frustration. Even his Knight could only take his mind off it for a short while. Self-loathing began to manifest itself, now increasing rapidly, looking at the quantity of food spread before him. Nausea could not help but reach into his throat, which he tightened to stop an onset of spewing his first sip of wine across the table. The interviewer came to his rescue, with another question for Holly.

"Tell me more about your dad."

"Let's see... He's a Leo; I'm a Sagit... a Sag... Anyway, Willow's an Aries. We're all fire signs, except Daddy. Dad needs stroking and admiration to keep him happy; and Daddy does a good job of that, keeping him strong and courageous like the lion. That's his symbol. He's fun to play with, because he likes to show off, especially when he acts out the stories we read every night."

"Reading is very important, and with two actors in the family, I bet it makes for interesting storytelling. I'm jealous. Now, what were you going to say about you three fire signs? I didn't think one so young would know of such things." The woman leaned forward, placing an elbow on the table to rest her curious face. David smiled, waiting for Holly to be the start.

"If you know the ancient truth of the *Zodiac*, you know how to treat a person. Since we're fire signs, and are more violent... no... vol..."

"...Volatile." Ted slipped in, knowing exactly what all three were.

"Yeah, volatile. That's why it's important to know to who you're speaking with, because we have to be careful not to hurt Daddy's feelings. He's a water sign; and they're very emot... anyway, it's easy to make him cry, because we just open our mouths and say what we think." Holly contemplated her next bite of food, looking at the flowery green object on her fork, while Ted sank lower in his chair.

"Like now?" David cut in, not to stop the conversation, but to remind his daughter of what she had just said and done.

"I thought your daddy was happy with the family together. He has Willow and you, and of course your dad loves him very much." The interviewer instinctively knew this little girl would reveal many things this night, relaxed and sitting between two men who grew more wary.

"He is, most of the time. I think he's the bravest man in the whole world, because he's so deter... he doesn't give up. He saved me once, and our friend Mr. Kincaid. Daddy's just..."

"...Just what, Holly? Find another word, like you did with determined." David prayed, to anyone listening, that Ted could withstand whatever came out of her mouth. He continued helping her with her language skills, no matter where they led. Both her vocabulary and understanding eluded her age and, in ways, her maturity. Clearly visible to anyone, both men allowed their eldest daughter to speak freely, to be heard and understood, to converse appropriately, particularly when to be quiet and when to intervene. One learned the art of conversion early in this household. David refused to stop anyone halfway through a thought; it hindered acknowledging the *knowing*.

"Okay, he's happy, but he's sad. He's always thinking, and he's really shy."

"Maybe I've grown up, Holly." Ted refused to divulge the dynamite of his secret schooling by Ambrose. It made him a more reflective person, pondering continually about everything. David often asked him where his annoying ray of sunshine had disappeared; and he had no response for the change. His depression grew, but his mask remained fixed.

"No, Daddy, you still blame yourself for Willow's early birthday. She's not sick you know; she just talks in her head and not her mouth. It's not your fault; and it was her choice, deciding to come when the planets aligned correctly. She told me, but I don't understand that part yet." An awesome speculation on the part of a child, plus a willful stripping down of one of her fathers, David looked over at Willow to receive a smile of agreement. They were hearing Willow. The calmer, older man reached over to give Ted an appeasing arm rub. The simple, yet complex discussion may prove a fascinating start, but not for his young partner.

"Are you sure you're only six, Missy?"

"Almost seven."

"So you believe in the zodiac, tarot cards, and the magic of a nomadic gypsy. Who taught you these things?" Becoming more intrigued, the woman pressed gently for something more telling.

"The Lady Faery in England. We have to relearn what we forgot, like the tarot. People don't understand they're not the right symbols anymore, and they don't know how to read them anyway. When the ways of long ago return, we won't need fortune-tellers or tarot, math or science, as life will be easier in the *knowing*; and we'll only need to think it. My sister and I talk about it a lot. We have to correct what's wrong." The statement of such profound belief amazed the woman with the Baptist background; but she ignored the teacher as just one of those odd English names. Fanciful stories were one thing; but this child had notions to shake you into Post-Concussion Syndrome. The responsibility pronouncement also startled her fathers with something new, but neither spoke.

"You said a few minutes ago, Willow speaks through her thoughts and not her mouth. I don't understand." The interviewer looked away from the child, who took another mouthful of something, to catch the nervous glance between fathers. One looked disturbed; the other shrugged. Something seemed amiss between the two.

"I'm sorry; we should have told you; our girls speak telepathically. Willow is mute." David had no idea what to say but the truth. He sounded like an idiot, and could not read how Ted received his candor: whether embarrassed by his daughter's disability, or unnerved at what he had come to view as normal.

"Good heavens, is that why I feel a sense of her? It certainly has not hurt her power to communicate at some level. Nothing can be done?" The woman turned her attention to the distraught father.

Ted said nothing; he had not eaten a bite; and a churning stomach, created by the unexpected conversation, made him nauseous. He shook his head in response, too static in motion for David's liking.

"Eat, Theo. Are you feeling all right? You're growing pale." Genuine concern by the older partner added to the natural caring displayed for each other.

"I'm sorry I upset you, Theo." The worried interviewer watched the color literally drain from the boyish face.

"I'm fine, thanks, but it's such a part of us now. We take telepathy for granted, although all humankind can mentally converse if they tap into their innate powers. I think I'll pass on any more food, David." Ted pushed his plate away, after saying something he hoped LaCoix would address.

"Something later then." The look between David and the interviewer said it all. Something that the older actor had to deal with every day needed addressing by one or the other: the vowed crusader against Hollywood's worst disease, or the outspoken woman being herself. The latter started.

"How is your health, Theo? The strains of the past year, and your illness, continue to concern our industry. We have brainwashed a world with this travesty; and it will take many years before they start hiring actors of normal size. Through my own production company, I attempt to impress upon the casting directors not to hire someone who is obviously ill from the disease. You have done much good in bringing it forward, proving it happens to men as well, but your anorexia has taken its toll."

"Guess so, and now you're convincing directors not to hire me. I don't know if I like that idea. Besides, isn't Hollywood known as the Land of Little People? There's few as tall as David." Ted smiled and feigned a laugh, only to quietly continue. "I don't understand why people are so curious about us. David wonders why we actors become the focus of attention, when so many terrible tragedies occur daily, throughout the world, to far braver people. It's nice to know, however, one has supportive friends and fans." Ted wanted to run for Bastet, his only comfort when confronted with things he hated about himself. The beautiful black and silver horse understood him, forcing him to deal with his problems, to face life again with an open heart.

"You've admitted to a lifetime of misfortune that very few people would have the courage to bring into the light. You've helped a great number of people, my friend. Personally, I'm tired of seeing very sick people walk onto my set, and the accolades received, reinforcing them to stay that way. Western culture, the arts in particular, perpetuate this false ideal in everything we do. You know my philosophy behind this tragedy, having fought a weight battle all my life."

David listened. Having someone beside him to fight the losing battle, against Hollywood's biggest obsession of unnatural perfection, he nodded to her and smiled gratefully.

"I don't know if I've helped anyone, like you have with your campaign, but it has to be worth something. Some good things emerged from the problems of this past year." Ted wanted off the subject; and Holly graced him with a cheerful out.

"Yeah, we got Willow!" The excited voice indicated another sudden change, from her sullen, serious mood, into joy beaming from within. It only lasted a second. Something troubled her; the cameras again captured the fathers' exchange of worried looks.

"Yes, we did, Holly, but it's hard not to blame myself for Willow's..."

"...but I told you. You weren't listening." With a little ire in Holly's tone, the solemn expression turned into exasperation. Ted eyed David haplessly, looking for needed rescuing.

"Holly, please; remember what you said about fire and water signs?" David scolded her for the insensitive remark to an already teetering Barrett.

"Sorry, Daddy, Willow and I just want you to be happy." She hung her head in regret.

"I know, Sweetheart." Ted bit his lip, composed himself, and tilted her little chin upward to receive his smile of forgiveness.

David interjected, to avoid someone falling apart. "Listen girls; it's hard for grown-ups not to feel guilty about certain things. With your telepathic and metaphysical knowledge, not to mention your physical age, you don't understand guilt. Having lived eons longer than you, Holly, I'm afraid the concept creates havoc in the adult mind, and so it should for many reasons." The older father spoke to a six-year-old, but he focused his words and attention toward Willow.

"Does that mean you don't believe us?"

Needing to snip Holly's ego damaging thought swiftly, LaCoix had to explain. "We believe all right; but you and your sister are miles ahead of us; we're scrambling to catch up. Remember, we talked about Daddy's christening, immediately embedding guilt into his persona. You have a fresh start to think and study anything you please. Daddy didn't have a choice." David attempted to take command of an adult discussion, and out of the hands of two growing Spirits.

"What are you saying, David, that children should not be protected by God; and yet baptismal rites are that power?" Gaping in disbelief, the expression, on the woman's face, turned into a disapproving frown. The LaCoix family understood the concept, but it blew up in David's face. A miscue on his part, the world heard. Too late to retract, lesson one of the *knowing* unfolded.

"Oh, boy, here we go. It's our belief that any type of sacrificial rite of birth takes away a child's first right of choice. Until all religions and philosophies are studied, whether it be Wicca, Christian, Buddhist, Islamic, *et al,* a child cannot decide. We have left our world divided into fragments because of it. I find it an appalling situation and an intolerable ritual of passage, leading to falsehoods. Let's not take this further, before I drown myself in a sea of hate mail." David leaned back, waiting for someone to say something, wishing he had a cigarette and the wine had a stronger kick.

"Guilt is something really hard to understand, isn't it, Dad?"

"Sure is, Honey, until you experience it yourself, and there are times we should feel it. You've been taught that when we've done something wrong, it's necessary to take responsibility and correct the mess created. Forgiveness, especially of oneself, eliminates the guilt and teaches you not to repeat the error." David leaned down to peck the contemplative little face. He returned to look at a distressed interviewer.

"I don't know what to say. One question for you then: who protects the child from the evil to which they are vulnerable?"

"A higher being, if there is one, would never leave the innocent defenseless. No evil exists in nature; it's manmade, like plastic cups, and just as destructive and non-biodegradable. Evil fills the hearts of sadistic lunatics, usually created by religion, politics, and misguided social perceptions of decorum. As for children and babies, Spirit Keepers care for them. Holly has one who's very verbose. Theo certainly had one, but could not help him in his trying situation." David did not know how to shut this conversation down, without dragging his failing partner into the melee. Ted took over without a stop; he had become a believer.

"I remember now, that something tried to reach me. I tried, in my way, to absorb the heat of a tiny beam of light: my only friend in the darkness. With my upbringing, only Christ could save me, I had no comprehension of something better. I'm sorry I didn't know how to listen, as an open-minded child should. Guilt, created by my church, hurt me badly, both physically and mentally."

"Whew, I think we should switch topics here." The confused woman leaned back in her chair, while David poured her a second glass of Shiraz, to calm the *awakening* he could sense in her head. Her mind twisted and turned with a new possibility; exactly what he wanted her to do, whether she believed or not. "Thank you, David; it's a very good wine. Let's get back to Holly, and how her daddy is different from her dad."

"Daddy's sometimes sad, but he's really fun too. We giggle a lot over silly things, like cheering for the good guys in the cartoons. Our favorite is the X-Men: he's Wolverine, and I'm Jubilee. He teaches me all the time, like Dad, but different things. Dad talks about life and the difference between boys and girls as we grow. He also helps me study. Daddy teaches me the secrets of the wilderness, how to build shelters, and survival if I get lost. We have fun playing in the rain and mud, until the lightning gets close. He knows lots about animals, crawly things, and plants, especially roses. They're his favorite. We have a high wall in the exercise room, and he's teaching me to freehand climb. I'm going to be a mountain climber and visit Shambala."

"Shambala?" David and Ted questioned in unison, one nearly choking on his food, and the other spluttering into his glass. Being extremely well read, the interviewer also gasped at the known mythological land, but not a child of six.

"Ultimate, that's the word, I think, the ultimate climb. Daddy calls them the Hima... Hima..."

"The Himalayans." Ted gave the correct Tibetan pronunciation, and looked at David completely baffled. The blond father could only shrug at his daughter's knowledge of a sacred place never mentioned.

"Willow and I are going. It's just beyond the clouds of those mountains Daddy said." Holly grew more excited again; and it pleased both men to see the change. These mood swings from happy to sad in seconds perplexed them both. Too young to have hit puberty, there had to be some reason.

"When did you take up with a Shaolin priest?" David teased.

"Doctor Thurgood."

"Of course." Ted and David exchanged smiles, as the interviewer nodded for Holly to continue.

"Daddy loves to cuddle. He, Willow, and me..."

"...Willow, Daddy, and I." David automatically corrected.

"Well, the three of us squeeze together in the big chair and cuddle by the fire, while Dad reads to us. He loves hugging, and we give him lots, especially Dad." The little face perked up into a wider, loving smile; her eyes closed with a look of bliss; and her arms wrapped around her small torso, rocking back and forth in an expression of how it made her feel.

"You give him just as many. We've become a bunch of huggers and kissers. Ted missed thirty years of affection, which I stupidly dismissed, believing it unmanly. We're making up for it."

"You and Daddy are touchy, tickly people. I feel you at night, kissing each other all over."

"Holly!" Again, in unison, the scandalous statement shocked the two men, justifiably mortified and uncomfortably horror-stricken. Her biological father took over the discussion, with a little discipline.

"You know the rules, young lady. No reading of thoughts not meant for you, particularly those of your fathers' when they're alone. It's like the knock rule. Now, no more eavesdropping when you're not invited, our chambers remain forever off limits to your mind. That goes for both of you." David looked back and forth between his daughters, while gesturing with the butter knife in his hand. A serious rule had been broken.

The interviewer did not know whether to be shocked by the embarrassing revelation, or laugh at the thought of a grown man, shaking a blunt butter-knife at a seven-month-old baby, in a highchair, and a young child, both giggling at him.

"Oh brother. David..." Ted implored, his hands cupping his face.

"It just makes us feel happy when you're happy. Your thoughts are so strong, it's hard not to sense how much Daddy loves you; and you love him." Unable to see her error, she did understand that she had upset her fathers.

"Are you saying your daughters know what you do? Oh, Lordy." The woman came into the full realization of what the child may have witnessed between two gay men and their sexual activity. Aghast at the notion, the big brown eyes nearly popped out of her head.

"No, she only feels the loving thoughts. Right, Holly?" David appealed to every possible being or god he could imagine, that she would not speak of an explicit action on his part or Ted's. He had to regain control over a conversation gone awry. His partner confirmed it with an anxious look of wide-eyed shock, seen through his spread fingers covered his face.

"That's all they better be receiving, David." Ted's body rattled so hard, he thought he would end up in a heap of unidentifiable bones.

"Grown-ups are so weird. Is there something else? Oh yeah, I forgot the knock rule once." Nonplussed by the situation, Holly remained relaxed, looking up with eyes twinkling mischievously.

"Yes you did, and now you know why we have it. Adults need privacy; and we're not just studying scripts. You interrupted a very intense moment for us." Not a conversation for the dinner table, in front of millions of people, it was a scandalous topic. David noticed Ted faltering, a man taking the blow, vanquished in shame, and no way to stop it. A quick look at the stunned woman, his green eyes sent a warning signal of a time to come. "You've just heard one of the difficulties of raising telepathic children."

"Why? You were just wrestling on the bed."

"New topic, Holly Jane," Ted insisted, not wanting his favorite sexual position conveyed to the world from the mouth of his daughter.

"Good idea." The woman laughed nervously; and Ted wanted to run for the hills. The subject remained in the frontal lobes of the adults' brains, however, but with kindness, it was cut short. "So, Holly, you were telling me about magic. You even live in a Fairy Tale realm. No offense, Gentlemen."

"None taken." The three adults chuckled nervously, and then returned their attention to the little blonde who planned to set them straight. Mr. Kincaid had explained to her why people laughed when she said that word.

"Faeries aren't those dreadful, hateful names they call my fathers. They're real, like Elves, Nymphs, Sprites, and Pixies. We also have to make friends again with Ogres, Trolls, even the Fates and Furies. All their realms exist and some are returning, while others have been gone for a very long time, waiting for us. They will show themselves when ready." Obviously getting a little bored, constantly correcting this adult, Holly wondered why all the questions came directly at her.

"Do you really believe in these ancient Pagan stories and fanciful tales of Merlin and

Morgana?"

"Like the *Zodiac* and the tarot, some are made up, while others remain true. Fortune-tellers and wizards, like Merlin, are empathic: people who can read minds, but can't return messages. That's how they know some of your secrets. You tell them with your thoughts, not the other way around. They are starting on the journey, and that's good. You have to believe in the unknown, or you miss all that's gone before, and what's coming up. Even Dad has a magic cloud that helps him and Daddy. I can see her."

"Magic clouds and fairies, it sounds like you know for sure. You must be a very old Soul."

"A what?" Holly's head snapped around, not having heard the terminology.

"The word is used inappropriately, Holly. It's contrived wording that refers to a person who has many past lives. Reincarnation, Sweetheart, when the Soul and Higher Self goes from one Spirit to the next." Ted managed to iterate something he knew, which would not hint of Quinlan's teachings.

"Oh, that. Dad has an old Soul, guiding his Spirit, and a Higher Self who sometimes has trouble controlling his sub... you know? It's more than this life they care for. Willow and I are brand new Souls, and we'll only have these Spirits, like Daddy. There aren't many of us yet, but we're the start of the *Beginning Again*."

And so it began, the ancient wisdom never recorded manifested itself in a new language, in a new medium, by a new Soul, with the aid of another. Proud fathers responded in agreement when asked, but allowed their children to explain, to someone not yet of the *knowing*, new thoughts to ponder.

"Let me get this straight. Your father is an old Soul, and carries the knowledge, good and bad, of his past lives."

"Things are only passed on from one life to another by listening to your Higher Self and Soul. They reincarnate together, to experience new things within a new Spirit; and it's not learning to be better. Dad is in his final life; but we're not sure about Daddy. We know they'll be joined eternally after a space of separation." Holly played with her dessert, looking distressed and considering what she had just said. It had certainly shocked three adults, along with a film crew, into a silent holding of breaths.

"What do you mean, Honey?" David's concern raced through his body; etching lines so deep in his forehead, they cast dark and serious shadows. A separation from his lover could happen any time; and although he concentrated positively on a long future with Ted, the words of his daughter crushed those thoughts, creating a far worse rockslide. Holly's dejection also threw him into the same vortex. She hid something; David sensed it, increasing the anxiety of his despairing heart.

"Because you're the Soul's last life, it sets your Spirit free, along with the other Spirits of your past lives. It will be a happy celebration when it happens. Your Higher Self will go on to other things, no longer needed to guide and protect all your kindred Spirits, and so will your Soul that already has many things to do. Some are so busy that they forget the earthly Spirit they tend."

"What were you referring to; when you said Daddy and I would be separated?" David hid his distress, while Ted's face expressed his fear.

"Just like Mommy, one of you will leave before the other." The little girl looked at no one, only contemplating the dessert placed before her. Every adult in the room held tears in check, from TV mogul to gaffer. The emotional evening grew more intense, as a little girl spoke the truth.

Life did end, and lovers parted to drift away alone. A simple statement and an accurate one, it upset the interviewer. The nonchalant statement of fact, from such a tiny human, jarred and bashed every belief she had been taught and taken to heart. Childish meandering this was not, but a rare insight into a new attitude fast approaching. She did understand that, but not knowing where it led. The woman's thoughts vanished at the interruption of the calming voice of LaCoix.

"Are you seeing the future, Holly? It's not wise to predict anything of such dangerous consequence. You know thinking about it will only manifest it." David warned her from his own erroneous mind wanderings, but he needed to know. The terror of an unfulfilled future blinded his reasoning, struggling to maintain his actor's guise to keep from screaming.

"It's just a feeling, Dad."

Ted eyed his blonde daughter suspiciously. "Is that why you've been so sad the last while? Do you think something will happen to one of us?" A believer in his daughters' intuition, only his faith in one god-like force remained, which could no longer sustain him, as the bricks fell one-by-one from his final barricade. Death had occurred to him, knowing it would come eventually, possibly by his own hand, and his latest thoughts found peace in that respect. The revelation of spending many years without his new partner, however, had him reeling. David's possible early death had never occurred to him.

"I guess, but you have to remember when your Spirits are both free, you'll be together forever. You both have to promise that whoever goes first, the one left behind can't kill themselves; that would ruin everything. You'd never be together in the same realm you want for your future; but I really don't understand that part, Willow." Holly positioned herself on her knees in the chair she occupied to look at her sister, and then down at the mess she had made of her strawberries and whipped cream.

"Suicide! Jesus Christ, Holly, don't even think it. No more about our demise, please, Honey. Look what you're doing to Daddy." The rattled blond tried to console his partner, reaching over to stroke his head. A quaking hand fumbled it away.

"David, I would... I might..." Ted peered down from a precipice with no visible bottom, ready to take the plunge; while Holly's lower lip quivered at the anger aimed at her.

"Theo, don't even think it." David snapped at him to gain his attention, and to stop the impending thoughts, which could create the eventuality. Like a night, very long ago, he had two hands in either one of his, squeezing for all their lives.

"Excuse me, but this is becoming difficult for me to follow, and a little frightening. Let's stop the death scenario, and continue with what Holly said about Spirit, a subject of interest to me. I believe Spirit and Soul are one in the same, needing to be treated with special care and respect for your own self-worth." The interviewer, completely unnerved, changed the odd subject matter. She felt the sadness and earnestness of this child, possibly remembering her mother, and attempting to come to terms with the tragedy verbally. The little girl loved these two men; loss of either would constitute something too grave for one so young.

"The Spirit has to be taken care of and loved by one's own loving. Your Soul and Higher Self must be held in great reverence. They will not be there for you, if you do not. A question, asked of Daddy a while ago, confused him, and he gave the wrong answer. Do you know what she wanted now?" Holly tilted her head; and with the saddest green eyes gazed up at Ted.

"How did you know that? Shit, Holly, you're scaring the hell out of me tonight." Ted fumbled to get his hand back into David's strong clasp.

"Not supposed to say those words."

"I am tonight, and I mean them." Ted grew adamant, remembering his first conversation with Lavender about sacrificing his Soul. He now had fonder memories of that day; but his old teachings suddenly resurfaced; he desperately needed help to conquer his fear of going against those old beliefs. David's grip could not be tighter.

"You said you'd sacrifice your Soul for Christ; and she wanted to know if you had asked first. A Soul can't be handed over to a mere prophet, claiming to be the son of a god, if it doesn't want to go. You can't give away something you don't own." The little girl continued to stare directly into the startled blue eyes, innocently questioning the jumbled thoughts, and trying hard to understand.

"No wonder you pissed her off, and she almost killed you." David arose to stand beside Ted, bending over to hide him from the cameras and prevent him from crying. Between his daughter and his lover, he had to tend to the one who faltered first. He lost control of the conversation too early; his fault Ted and Holly floundered in despair; and yet they spoke their truths. David had to settle everyone, without any idea of how to do so, but let it play through. His partner threw him with his confession of Jamie's forewarning; Ted showed no qualms of ending it, if left on his own.

"I thought it a test of heaven or hell, not knowing any better. David, I didn't know then." Ted wanted to run, but the only place he could hide was in the arms of the person breathing gently into his ear.

"Let it go, Baby. You've come a long way since then. Now relax, take a sip of water, and sit back." Embracing the visible shaking, a kiss to his cheek, and a little rocking, the forever-watchful LaCoix calmed an innocent Spirit ready to depart that moment. David readied himself to administer a pink pill to a very pale person. All remained quiet, while Ted composed himself. The interviewer shook her head in disbelief, while Holly and Willow made subtle eye contact; maybe it was not yet time.

David finally had Ted back to being comfortable, forgetting the rolling cameras while he made the soothing gestures and intimate touches given to a loved one under duress. A beautiful moment of domesticity, the pair showed the world tenderness created by devotion, especially between two men. It proved gentle and caring; no words were necessary.

"Daddy, I'm sorry, we thought you understood."

"It's okay, Sweetheart. You just brought back a recurring nightmare, about how stupid one's Valkyrian attitudes prevent you from moving forward. I refused to listen; and she only wanted to inform me there were other ways to look at my faith; I had choices."

"I don't understand what any of you are talking about; I'm completely in the dark. Holly, you seem to understand this new spiritual belief. Could you explain it to me?" The dark eyes looked straight into the crystal green ones, identical to her father's, and they held the interviewer transfixed. Besides delving deeper with Holly, she could get the cameras off David tending to Barrett.

A hint of red in young eyes, with the look of a cat, flashed suddenly, and then quickly disappeared. Holly started again. "It's easy. You're born with a brand new Spirit every time your Soul decides to reincarnate. Everyone has a Spirit; and it's his or hers alone, so you're right about that. You also have a Higher Self who guards the portals of your past lives. Those lives each have their own Spirit, a different one. The Higher Self takes care of you, protecting each Spirit in turn, especially when the Soul is not around. Just like your Soul, the Higher Self comes from your first life. The difference is the Soul has other things to do, in different times, realms, and dimensions. The magic happens when all three come together, and that's when you get all your good ideas, visions, and dreams. That's the meeting time of your *knowing*, when dreams come true. You have to learn to bring them all together, to walk your own Spirit's path to reach your goals, and then you're at the *Beginning Again*." Holly finished. She gazed at Willow indicating enough had been said, and without another thought, rested her head on the back of her chair.

"Oh Lordy, this child is right over my head. Your path is to set goals. Do you, Gentlemen, agree with this?"

"Absolutely." Again, a word in unison proved one mind could read the other.

David returned to his chair to clarify some of the ambiguity. He doubted anything he said would make sense, his worry overriding his intellect. "Let me barge in here, Holly. The concept is difficult to explain, and what you just heard were Willow's words. When you think about the times you are scattered, and the times you're completely in sync, it's a different feeling."

"Yes, it happens to us all."

"The latter is what we call the *knowing* time. The goals you set are your future; and there lies your answer: powerful, worthwhile goals. Few people have them set in place, putting their futures in jeopardy. We are blindsided by different forms of attack, from environmental obstacles, to society in general, to specific individuals. Unless we keep those goals in sight, and fight like tigers to walk a true path, our future becomes distorted; and we become lost."

"Your philosophical ideas are extremely difficult to comprehend. I feel like I've been run over by a semi." The woman sat back, fanning herself with her napkin, and staring off camera at her director.

"Because they're so simple. I'm sorry that the discussion got away from us; becoming rather fragmented; but please remember the source. It will become increasingly clear, but Willow and Holly are still young, trying to fit the pieces together. We refer to the time coming as the *Beginning Again*, and we try to protect the girls' ideas and manifestations within our home. We, as intelligent humans, have been asleep long enough. Now our secret has been leaked to the world; and whether it be too soon, who knows? Theo and I let our daughters think freely at some risk, as you can see. As fathers, we vowed never to interfere in what they come up with as a philosophy of life. It just happens to coincide with a mystical experience, which Theo, me, and a few close friends experienced. It left us bewitched, bedazzled, and befuddled at the same time; and I'm not making light of the matter. This is very serious." David tried to stop what he thought to be a good idea a few days ago. He could not.

"I can certainly believe that."

They had confounded the interviewer, and with dead air space looming, Ted gathered himself and veered them in another direction. "It's time to put the girls to bed, David. It's getting very late. I'll tuck them in and join you in ten. Let's go, girls. Say good night to everyone, Holly." Exhausted and traumatized by his daughters' words and thoughts, Ted required the break. Only David understood a short respite deemed necessary for his partner; he gave him the opportunity.

"Can you manage on your own?" LaCoix helped him stand, steadied him, and secured Willow in his arms. Ted was too unsteady for his liking.

"I'm fine, and it calms my nerves when my precocious daughters have me totally rattled. It will be nice to get two happy hugs. I won't be long."

After saying a polite good night, Holly eagerly followed Ted with her sister in his arms. The tiny blonde felt very tired, and a little mystified as to why she and Willow needed to bring this matter up so early. They were not ready for explanations. Three LaCoix disappeared into the darkness behind the lights, while cameras kept rolling.

"Well, David, you have an extraordinary family. What comes next?"

"More truths as the girls mature."

"You make them sound like prophets, and you accept it with such ease. It's astonishing and frightening. I'm awestruck by your children."

"As I mentioned, the adult vocabulary and many of her words belong to Willow who exudes the wisdom of an ancient seer. Holly voices her sister's thoughts, yet she is the innocent white rose, with powers of her own. Willow is the black rose with the thorn, and will be the one to come forth as something, but certainly not a prophet. We do not take these terms lightly."

"What would you call them?"

"Messengers, perhaps, like the light and the dark; both sides are equal and necessary. Prophets demand to be heard from a human perspective; their ideals made up in their heads, and not from the main source of wisdom in the universe. This time, it will be the wishes of the real Powers-That-Be, within many realms, realities, and dimensions, whatever you wish to call them. They will soon come forth, exposing themselves to each other and to mankind, turning the Cosmos and beyond into the *knowing*. Everything will change in the years to come. It's easy for me, because I believe, and have been bestowed the great honor of visible proof."

"Are you saying you do not believe in Christ or God?"

"Many beliefs do not. Why should it be a surprise? Christ existed as a man who proclaimed to be the son of a god and the son of man; and John, Mohammed, Brahma, et al, became prophets, choosing one philosophy, listening to no other. Irreversible, their names overwhelm the world, fragmenting us all into warring factions, even when these fractured groups worship the same god. It needs to be mended, as Holly said; and just how my girls are involved, I don't read futures."

"You don't believe in God; yet you state he is the cause of a good number of the world's problems. He has done much to help those in need."

"Only because of those who believe in him and give him the credit for their own actions; a terrible pity, as they also have someone to blame for their mistakes. Good people, unnamed for the most part, do the kind deeds; while the zealots, conversely always known to us, inflict the incredulous horrors, and in the name of the same damn god. How do you know what your almighty has done or not done? People make the decisions to do things in the name of any god. As for my beliefs, they continue to evolve. The power may come from us all; the consciousness, of all beings within the Cosmos, may create a general ruling; and right now, if we take earth as an example, we are sending hate messages by the Starship-Enterprise-full. Perhaps god is actually an elected committee of hundreds of different entities. Ra, Bastet, and Shu may be higher in the pecking order than humans, although I truly believe there are no levels, one being higher or more important than the other. When it comes time for the *Beginning Again,* anything is possible; and that is all we're saying. We do not have to prove our beliefs to others, only to open the portal to keep looking further into our own subconscious minds to find the answers." David sat back down, half-sprawled in his chair. Something certainly did happen with this interview, and it had him wasted and wondering.

"You can't possibly believe all this is true?"

"I do believe. Not many have the proof Theo, Holly, and I have seen and experienced."

"Your daughter is a mystical genius, David."

"As is her more powerful sister." A wicked grin and a wild-eyed look, from under those blond eyelashes, taunted their guest, and the cameras caught the glimmer of something greater, before they stopped rolling. The green eyes flashed a hint of a feline ready to pounce.

Both mentally spent, David and the interviewer settled themselves by the crackling flames ablaze in the beehive fireplace. It filled the room with the unusual aroma of cypress and mesquite, a pleasant woodsy smell with a bitter after-scent. While the crew adjusted cameras and lighting, for one of those fireside chats, Ted made his quiet entrance. David noticed he had freshened up with a few eye drops to remove the red. This had been a bad idea. The older actor shook his head, disgusted at his ten steps backward, to the obnoxious man of riotous notions, just for his strange sense of risk, and the love of tossing it into the establishment's face. The *bad boy* side of David LaCoix returned to play silly games with one who could not cope; and he felt the weight of his shame. He could barely look at his victim.

Ted disguised his short bout of crying, caused by the coming out of many family secrets. Not common knowledge Willow was mute hurt Ted. Not common practice for either of them to show their affection in public hurt Ted. Certainly not common knowledge their daughters were mystical creatures that neither man understood hurt Ted. For the shy man, whose fundamentalist background had been rocked, the conversation forced him to look at other options, which hurt him further. Their daughters had dishonored him in different ways; and David should have shut the conversation down before it started. The controversial subject matter would likely be cut; however, while waiting on his partner, David asked if they could see the edited version before being televised. Shaking her head, only this woman's word of integrity assured him nothing would be used out of context. Of little help, it had been his duty, and his agent's job, to ensure they had contractual approval of final editing. He failed Ted; he failed his daughters; and he failed the *Beginning Again*.

"Hey, Theo, girls asleep?" With an exuberant tone, David tried to add some joy to the winsome face. Although dejected, the slender figure, who belonged to him completely, did not hesitate to approach. Blind trust, David felt unworthy.

"Something's bothering Holly. I'm sure she doesn't see it clearly, but I'm wondering about Willow. She's fussing as well. Maybe I should go back and stay with them in our room."

"Let's finish first; I'll check on them later. They're probably tired after these unusually long days. If it continues, they can stay with us tonight. Come, sit beside me." David reached out to grasp the hand of his responsibility and conscience.

"It scares me, David. What's happening?" Ted curled up on the love seat his partner occupied and cuddled in close, forgetting the cameras, forgetting the woman across from them.

"We'll find out soon enough. You're overtired and lack of food doesn't help." The blond actor played the part of his life, worried to death of what he had done. With some mischief still left in his overactive mind, he quickly snatched the dusty rose-colored afghan beside him, and covered Ted completely with a perfect one-handed toss.

"Gee, thanks. Leave me in the dark; I feel safer in here." A muffled chuckle came from under the fuzzy woolen blanket. The comical maneuver switched the downcast mood immediately, pleasing the doer of the deed.

"Good. The light and the dark walk side by side, one as illuminated as the other. Only the fear of the dark keeps us from seeing our way." David laughed and pulled the covering off Ted's head. "Better?"

"Too bright."

The interviewer delighted in the display of affection between the two men, one so obviously taking care of the other. "You insinuated the girls were both light and dark, David. Does it come from this quote, which seems meaningful to our conversation this evening? Whose words are those?"

"Don't remember. Glad you built a fire. I'm cold." Ted dismissed the reference instantly. They tried not to mention the Mistress all evening; and yet a few hints had slipped out without notice. A difficult task, Lavender had been the start, and they now sensed the preparation of their daughters for the finish. Both men fell into a *knowing* riveted silence, when suddenly interrupted.

"You're cold, Theo, and I'm having hot flashes. Men are so lucky."

"We think so." Ted's taunting smile brightened his gloomy face, to be rewarded with a hug.

"Since you didn't partake in dinner, maybe you should have something to eat or drink. You're teeth are chattering, and you're white as alabaster." David's fingers fixed the hair full of static from the afghan.

The raspy voice sounded sore, particularly in the quiet laughter Ted and their guest shared. "Stop fussing, but some water would be appreciated." The two men sat almost mouth-to-mouth, each in the other's space, chatting intimately as any couple would.

"Change that to hot chocolate and it's yours." David teased in a seductive tone, coming closer to a head growing dizzy with the excitement the voice created. With a smile and nod from his partner, snuggling ever closer, the order was filled, and they all settled back. The conversation went smoothly; clarifying parts of the conversation and the observations, adding a hint of what may be. Warming up to this family was not difficult; their radical concepts of life and visions took greater understanding; precisely the interview she had hoped. With Ted asleep in his partner's arms, the interview wound down to an even more bewildering conclusion.

"I think we have worn him out, David."

"Not a hard thing to do. You saw him at the ceremony. He barely made it through, forgetting every line written, and everything said ad-libbed, straight from his heart." Deep sadness echoed in LaCoix's voice, and seen in his softening face, when he looked down at his partner.

"Theo has a strong character. His words touched everyone, holding an audience spellbound without a writer's assistance. Your wedding was truly beautiful. I thank you for the honor of being included amongst your friends, along with your family and staff. I didn't know what to expect, but it fit you both; masculine yet more loving than many conventional ones I've witnessed."

"Loving--a woman's word--so difficult for any man to say. Although Ted has a very romantic, poetic side, it's seldom heard or seen, except in private and obviously when making vows." David chuckled sadly, remembering the fear in the eyes when his lover rambled out his feelings.

"Have either of you had trouble coming out? It could cause problems considering government and social bickering over legalization, although some states recognize your constitutional rights, just not your marriage."

"So wrapped in contracts, it would be harder for us to separate than a heterosexual couple. We've had little trouble, but then we seldom leave our sanctuary."

"And I hope we can show it in all its beauty. We have several amazing still shots of you and Theo on your special day. My escort happened to be an excellent photographer. With your permission, I would like to place a few in the magazine. One image in particular fits your philosophy, and will definitely excite the girls."

"What did you capture in your treacherous camera?" David squinted suspiciously, and received a huge, teasing smile back.

"Something I now see as very magical." The woman pulled out a folder from her case. A matte 8 x 10 passed between them. An intrigued, teary-eyed man saw himself slightly separating from the passionate kiss with his forever partner. Two very recognizable profiles, totally mesmerized by the other, were clearly visible; one gazed longingly at the other, while the other looked pale enough to fade away. Lips came so close, a fine silver thread could not pass between them; and two entwined circles of fluttering colors danced around their heads and in their hair. Only if one looked hard enough, could you see the mystery of the butterflies. An exquisite watercolor portrait, painted with the softest of pastel strokes, it captured pure magic. David suddenly clued into what he had been living through and in; Awakening Canyon was a La Rosa Negra. Protected here, in a different place and a different realm, with a portal to come and go into the reality of the world in which they worked, their home revealed itself as something very different. A revelation of tremendous importance, David took in a breath, wiped his hand over his face, erasing the shock and continuing without a hint of panic.

"Amazing! Your friend caught one of those fleeting moments when you could not be happier. Ted looks positively ethereal. This captures the day we had hoped. Thank you for our official wedding photo, if you don't mind. I can't believe it. Can we get larger prints?"

"Of course; as many as you like. Besides being an exquisite image of you both, you appear to be crowned with what--fairies or butterflies--perhaps led by Holly's Lady Faery?" She laughed to tease, not to get the serious response given.

"You will know when you meet her Ladyship, and it comes time to publish the December issue." David could not take his eyes off the portrait, wondering if the tiny creatures around each head wanted to be exposed. It would be implanted in the publisher's mind when it came time for a caption. The world may only be ready for friendly butterflies.

"Well, Mr. LaCoix, we've discussed many intriguing things. You have an enchanted, loving home; two brilliant, beautiful daughters; and a handsome, talented partner who looks like he might have a tendency to suck his thumb." They both chuckled softly, and a camera zoomed in on Ted with his clenched hand against his mouth.

"Don't let that get out. An old habit his fist has not forgotten."

"You're worried about him?"

"Always. He's trying so hard. I used to call him an annoying ray of sunshine when we first met. Happy or sad, a ray of sunshine or a gray raindrop, he's mine to protect and hold onto for as long as I can." David pulled the fluffy cover over the fist and eyes to shield Ted from the invasive cameras.

"Theo's a good man, and a courageous one. Perhaps our discussion of his condition should not have been brought up in front of him, but he's proof of the horror within our industry." With sympathy in her expression and weeping tears, she marveled at the man-child lying so still.

"Thanks, but if you didn't start the topic, I would have. It's important and at epidemic proportions. As for this one, we'll make him happy for the rest of his time, no matter the length, and please cut that statement out. He doesn't need to hear more."

"Of course. Is there anything missing in your life, David? Do you have it all: love, fame, fortune, family?"

"Everything I need lies in my arms and sleeps soundly up those few stairs. If I could keep it all, just as is, I could not be happier. The only thing I need is time: a selfish request, but an honest one." David's face again showed the weariness of a man who fought a continuous battle with death over his lover. The soft caresses to Ted's hair made it all the sadder.

"We talked a great deal about spirituality, especially with Holly. What a mystical dynamo that little one is. Can you explain a general view of what she said? You seem to agree with her, and have mentioned something called the *Beginning Again* several times." The woman sat forward, hands holding up her chin, intently studying each word uttered.

"I can't speak for my daughters or Theodore, but I have come to understand, that our growing awareness, of what we once were, is earth's probable future. It's far more than what we discussed earlier, and perhaps only understood by a few who study ancient Pagan philosophies. Not mentioned this evening, the *Beginning Again* is a form of light and thought transference, the power to transform concepts, both material and mental, into an energy field. An example was displayed tonight, with Willow talking through Holly, and Ted and I knowing who said what telepathically. The sciences will innately be understood, considering a thought manifests the reality of what is required. The healing gifts shall return, and people such as Theo, who still does not understand his full power, will mend themselves along with the help from even greater healers. Throughout time, every human has carried some special ability stored within his or her subconscious mind, ready to be taught or simply brought into being with practice. These latent talents will create the diversification to live somewhat more equally, working at what we were born to be and have a passion to do. Humanity will become something wondrous, joining other Cosmic communities, currently undergoing a similar awakening. It all sounds incredible, but Willow and Holly's generation is the start. Contact has already been made with other non-earthly entities and realms of this planet we cannot see. Many will be lost in this philosophical battle, a great sadness that cannot be stopped, but it is time for change, to become better. Always remember, the white rose is the speaker of this new awareness, and the rare black one, with its one thorn, will alter the course of the outcome, whether peacefully or violently. It may make us bleed before we can heal into the *Beginning Again*."

"And you believe this change is starting; and it's philosophical, not theological. All the world's religions will change. Your concepts are very hard to believe, David. Much of this sounds very New Age, and as equally far-fetched as the other new philosophies springing up."

"Exactly. Doesn't it make you wonder why so many new thoughts and ideas are coming forth? The potential for a holy war is foreseen, but one waged amongst gods, other entities, not just humankind; and I use the term *gods* loosely. Religions won't change; they'll disappear. When it's all asunder, and the destruction over, we'll have the peace and life humanity craves. Our future for the planet will be safe within a nurturing galaxy of other beings. Whatever happens, we must accept it with gratitude, for it has purpose, and loved ones will understand death leads only to greater things." David relaxed his unblinking stare, to look down wistfully upon a potential casualty of such a battle.

"My God, David, you have me totally perplexed. Will we be going through another torturous war?"

"I hope not; although it could stop the current ones and the reign of terrorists."

"For one so private, thank you for your candor. Extremely thought-provoking, I await to see what your children have in store for the world."

"Keep your heart and mind open to choices and alternatives, and you shall be on your way. Tolerance and acceptance of common-sense reality, along with the foresight to see the phantasmal as real, will get you through unscathed." A radiant, confident smile reassured her to some degree. David LaCoix had the words to upset and to appease.

"You sound like a preacher." Time to lighten the load, a chuckle came with the judgment.

"Oh, no, not me. Never take us for preaching, but just insights freely given by several wondrous beings, and this amazing man in my arms, who has seen the other side of the stars."

"What a beautiful thought."

"So you're not going to send for men with jackets covered with buckles?" An amused, suspicious look danced from under the blond lashes.

"Houdini could get out of a straight jacket by dislocating joints. You, David LaCoix, would just think it; and it would crash to the ground."

David laughed. "That is certainly a wild speculation on your part."

"Somehow I don't think so. Thank you, and believe me, you absolutely fascinate me, all of you. Perhaps we may talk again in much more detail."

"Your company is always welcome. We have been to the far side of the galaxy tonight, and now can bring you safely back to earth, fair lady." David's charms were unmerciful, flashing a wicked *knowing* wink and chuckling softly, as he maneuvered out of his cramped position, careful not to jostle the body attached to him. With a leech firmly ensconced around him, he pried the tight fists off his shirt and belt, a rather embarrassing situation upon the removal of the blanket. Slowly getting up, he stretched, and then bent down to gain a firm-hold of his sleeping beauty. Not the time to awaken someone who barely slept a few hours a night, the famous actor, and his equally famous cargo, disappeared behind the lights into a distant part of the house, with only one utterance from Ted, calling for his lover on a soft sigh of sweet chocolate breath. Romance also filled this home, creating more wonder.

CHAPTER 51

Thanksgiving came and passed with Jake and Daphne, Ted's family, and the final arrival of David's sons. On the urging of his newly met grandparents, even Tyler enjoyed the first *good start* occasion. Only the Kincaid-Thurgood duo missed the seasonal event, with Steven busy promoting *Brother Mine,* to be released December 1. A fortuitous opening date for *Outlaw's Heart*, it may mean a second lucky happenstance for Kincaid and Barrett's intense new drama. Ted joined Steven on a few interviews the following week, only to return home for David's departure to promote his film opening Boxing Day. With minimal time to relax until after the New Year, they still had Holly's seventh birthday to plan.

Home life steered a tranquil course of a normal family. Ted studied the finished script of *Oberon, the King*, thrilled to be playing the title character. David could only laugh, mischievously thinking of his King Oberon earning his Faery wings. He mused even more at the thought of his villainous role, accepted without the script, only knowing he would be adorned with Elfin wings of a smaller size. All too delightful for him, it did not matter; he looked forward to capturing the fair Titania, not yet cast. After watching a miniseries with Holly, when she was very young, it had broken his heart when the mystical tale ended with the words, *Magic is Dead*. It stuck with him for years, unknowing a mysterious woman would enter his life and alter it dramatically. Having those three erroneous words reverberate through his head continually, he vowed to maintain a mystical world for his daughter; and together, they found it existed.

Opening Night for *Brother Mine* brought an onslaught of media attention for the two, stepping out of a limousine and making their way into the theatre. They both looked *marvelous* according to Holly who watched the couple on an entertainment newscast. Holding hands, the attractive duo glowed in their excitement, to finally experiencing exhilarating happiness. An immediate success, according to their peers and critics, the film opened to long, enthusiastic line-ups, waiting for their first glimpse of three of the *Sexiest Men in the World* working together in a tragedy. It needed no further publicity than the stars themselves. Having been grueling work mentally and physically for Ted, he cried through the Premier, remembering everything each had gone through during months of filming. Each performance was a replica of their individual struggles.

David masked his shock at how truly ill his partner looked on screen. Although Ted's character died in his brother's arms, it looked real to David and Steven. In the darkened theatre, they sat side-by-side, their hands squeezed together in relief Ted seemed better. Tears fell, from the opening scene, but for the stoic few in the audience. It became visible when the famous faces emerged from the theatre with puffy eyes. A hit of the *two boxes of tissue* variety, Oscar rumors started spreading that night, encouraging a nervous Kincaid that his film succeeded in touching hearts, while those same rumors embarrassed Ted with the possibility of a second nomination of his own.

The Premier of Rod Morris' picture also opened to a screaming throng of waiting LaCoix fans. Once again, the famous couple came out of seclusion, to witness the technical marvel of piecing the many thousands of takes into a credible story. No doubt, another brilliant production, the critics raved about the intensity of the star. David's face now competed with both Ted's and Steven's for front-page coverage.

The LaCoix household looked forward to a successful New Year, with both films on their way to making millions. Continuing to enjoy their private life, they rode every day beneath cloudless skies. Ra and Bastet did have them flying; the same feeling experienced during the so-called rockslide. Ted's trouble with his balance kept the beautiful Bastet busy, recovering from any minor mishap with the grace of an acrobat, and those dainty dance steps forcing him to look forward. She appeared to float sideways, to catch the faltering body, as horse and rider became one, with the ever-protective mare loving this quiet human. So gentle and light, she barely felt him but in thought; they heard each other; devotion shared between two unique beings.

Besides Ted busy with a script he liked, another action/mystery intrigued David. With his crazy eyes and wicked smile, those double entendres would be delivered with exactly the appropriate facial expression. Obviously written with LaCoix in mind, it would all come together for the upcoming summer, avoiding any interference with David's part in *Oberon, the King*. The two actors soared professionally and personally.

One celebration, not to be missed, was Holly's seventh birthday, planned for all family members on both sides, to attend in Telluride, Colorado. The fun ski holiday helped her deepening melancholy, turning it into a joyful reunion with her half-siblings. She learned quickly from her Daddy's coaching on the bunny hill, and grew closer to Annie, excited and interested in the new baby soon coming. Besides the second oldest Barrett brother, Raymond and Eleanor joined in, having both families firmly ensconced in their own homes in the Canyon. A week of exercise, fresh air, and sunburned faces had them all invigorated, and travesties once unforgivable strengthened a new family bond.

Ted's courageous attempt at skiing captured the LaCoix boys' admiration. Phenomenal seemed inadequate to describe his grace and skill coming down the hardest of slopes, smoothly and quietly; not showing the tremendous energy expended on his part. Unfortunately, the ear problem gave him some spectacular wipeouts. With too much assistance and concern for his welfare, his athlete's ego lashed out in humorous of fashion. His ski poles took a severe bashing in his attempt to embed them forcibly into the deepest powder, or bend them around an innocent tree. He succeeded in staying upright for the most part, regaining some stability; an important self-confidence builder, participating in something he loved to do; David let him fly free.

LaCoix's abilities, never mentioned, astounded his lover; but considering the man's build and agility, it should not have been a surprise. The deterring factor, from exhibiting his prowess beforehand, lay in his hatred of the cold. A week of balmy late February weather, however, with tons of white fluff to play in, David could handle, and quite enjoyed the thrill of following behind the fresh powder tracks and the graceful sway of his favorite little derriere, especially someone of Ted's caliber. Even more fun, the effort by all to pick up the new mega-star after a spill, became a frenzied wrestling match of giggles to keep Ted's joy of the sport alive. After the first day of falls and anger, David instinctively turned any mishap into frivolity; and no one noticed the one irritating imperfection Ted had in his skiing technique.

Once back in the lodge, the dizziness subsided and another type of playtime began. A steaming outside Jacuzzi, surrounded by piles of glittering snow under the moonlight, with hot toddies warming them, had the men feeling better, dispelling any aches, pains, and nausea. Most of the adults would disappear to party with the younger crowd, while one spent the late evening, telling Annie of their adventures on the hill, while watching two little girls fall away into dreamtime. The last two Spirits would retire, with tender massages, inside and out, and a great deal of soft moans and loving whispers for more attention. David pleasured Ted; and the promised vow returned tenfold. Two men, being the lovers that they had always been, discovered new tricks, new positions, and new exciting erogenous zones, in a strange bed, in a famous lodge.

Returning home, David and Ted climbed to their rooftop hideaway, where blessings floated down on their passion from a far away realm. Feeling dangerously wicked and risqué when performing under the spotlight of the moon, for an audience of stars, the pair fell in love again, their bond growing stronger. With life, adoration, and respect at its peak, they saw only the other; green eyes melted into blue ones, while hands and fingers caressed and played in golden corn silk and rich brown cascading waves. Just breathing in a lung full of air, they could smell the other's intoxicating presence across miles of open space. They were one, and united as such whenever their bodies touched.

Champagne had greeted them at the end of each day at the lodge, and another bottle ceremoniously cracked open with the good news spreading throughout the industry with early wake-up calls. David LaCoix, Theodore Barrett-LaCoix, and Steven Kincaid nominated for Best Actor; Kincaid Productions nominated for Best Motion Picture of the Year; Ethan Peerce nominated Best Actor in a Supporting Role; and Rod Morris nominated for Best Director and Best Motion Picture. Between *Brother Mine* and *Lord Worthington-Smythe*, the competition for Oscars became a riotous wager between the friendly parties involved. The bad omen scenario, of the Golden Globes, had them all scoffing, yet greatly appreciated by Ted for winning Best Actor, and Steven for Best Motion Picture. This did not put the fatal blow to winning Oscars; as those thoughts buried themselves in the depths of eddies encircling the perimeter of their excitement. They remained in the center of their own water vortexes, thinking only the best thoughts for each other. Three friends up for the same award; three friends hoping one of the others would win.

Oscar night and the LaCoix household in Arizona settled in for a victory party. The blonde seven-year-old had become very reclusive and out of sorts, her holiday the only bright part of her life since the wedding. Something lurked in her head; something she could not figure out, while Willow shed tears. Communicating with their fathers on trivial matters, concerned David and Ted who could not reach them telepathically, and decided it had to be the interview, sensing the girls regretted saying too much, or not enough. The edited story presented the family magnificently: beautiful, happy, intelligent, spiritual in their unique way, and completely loving. Nothing Willow or Holly should be unhappy about; it deeply concerned the two men. An Oscar party, with the staff, the Barrett families, and their grandparents, may spark life into their insular little world.

The big event started with the first twosome they loved coming into camera range. Steven Kincaid and Doctor Thurgood smiled at them; and they clapped vigorously, as the younger man bubbled over with non-important verbiage into a microphone. No handholding between this pair, an introduction of your date was shunned unless also in the limelight. Smiles, however, filled Awakening Canyon, seeing their friend aglow with inner excitement and looking better than ever. Even the most shallow minded had to see the dazzling demeanor, which ran deeper than appreciation for the many nominations for his film.

The next two familiar faces came into focus, accompanied by cheers and whistles from the crowd behind the barrier and from the far-off Canyon. The brightest starlets, in the sexiest of multicolored dresses and the gaudiest of Winston diamonds, did not outshine David and Ted. The handsome pair strolled past, hand-in-hand, dressed immaculately in longer-jacketed, formal black suits. David remembered the *marvelous* tag from Holly and Mrs. Morris, and insisted Ted's coat brush his knees, while his own flared out behind him, nearly sweeping the ground. White cashmere turtlenecks replaced the uncomfortable starched shirts, and small, engraved, platinum talismans hung from the most delicate of chains. A perfect match: the tall, lanky blond with the wicked smile and flashing eyes, escorted the smaller, delicate, younger man, with the longer brunet hair, shy grin, and those wide-open, bedazzling sapphires. An extraordinary sight for every woman and gay man in the realm of earth, no one could deny the two men shone brighter than the spotlights.

This night they received only minimal taunting, much to Ted's relief. His fingers ached from crossing them in luck for David. He had his Oscar, and a Golden Globe; this had to be David's; and if visualization could make it materialize into reality, he would do it. Another long evening awaited them for their own category, but it started on a high note for *Brother Mine*, with the first presentation going to Ethan Peerce for his Supporting Role. The kinky abuser had disappeared immediately upon announcing his retirement; but three men saw the sudden burst of purple light caress the statuette and vanish. It had them horrorstruck: Peerce was with Lavender! It turned their world upside down; their assumptions about the benevolent Mistress could be false. The thought haunted them through the night's gala.

Both films vied for a variety of awards, turning their fears into an extravaganza for the foursome. With their category up next, the three friends competing held their breaths. "And the Best Actor... yes... David LaCoix for *Lord Worthington-Smythe*!" The building nearly collapsed with the sudden screaming and clapping. A standing ovation did not stop David from jumping out of his seat and flying like a giant bat onto the stage, while his blue-eyed wonder clapped and cried behind the curtain. At the podium in a few long strides, with the long, black coat dramatically floating from his waist, he rushed to feel the gold-plated, sexually ambiguous knight. The audience full-heartedly endorsed the choice, remembering the force behind the fight to save children from his partner's former church. This man, of such rare talent, had been overlooked too long, only for his wrongfully assumed reputation. Shame, for their mistaken biased attitude, expressed itself on the faces of his peers. It mattered little to David; his large grin and wildly excited eyes flashed honest and true; enhanced by his long, slender hand used to cover a racing heart, exposing the sparkling bonding yellow-green sapphire on his finger.

"It is heavy. No wonder you dropped it, Theo. My Spirit, Higher Self, and Soul thank you. A Genie, of my acquaintance, promised me three wishes; and your appreciation of my work, through this award, is the last granted. My life is overflowing. I do have extremely important people to thank. I dedicate this award to my friend, Rod Morris, who managed to get me through this picture with grand gestures of goodwill during horrific happenings in my life, along with the joyous ones. To the rescuers of my daughter, my partner, and Steven Kincaid: stay well and safe. You, along with all those who risk their lives daily on our behalf, are the ones who deserve our fame and fortune. My gratitude knows no bounds in honoring you. To my forever one, Theodore, the most courageous of them all, I adore you; and you shall always amaze me. Thank you again, everyone, for my last wish you have bestowed upon me. Go to bed, Holly... Willow... Oh man, the names never occurred to me. How did we manage that, Theo?" A close-up of Ted, hiding behind burgundy velvet drapes, showed his surprise; he honestly laughed aloud in a rare moment of silliness.

"Good night, girls. We love you." Off the stage in four giant strides, David reveled in the laughter and whistling ringing in his ears; the standing ovation he had wished for. His excitement soared, with bright eyes glistening yellow-green, as he held his Oscar in one hand, and gleefully swung his partner off the ground with the other arm. Coming to ground, Ted showed off his Hollywood whites, finally able to uncross his fingers and lavish a smoldering kiss to the latest winner. Having just handed out the Best Female Actor award to Mrs. Morris, Barrett-LaCoix's initial appearance on stage had people on their feet, inhibiting him from speaking, much to his embarrassment. He did his duty nervously, including a breathless kiss to the winner's cheek, as he placed her prize in trembling hands, unsure of who shook the most. No longer the appropriate thing to do; nonetheless, she smiled at him in appreciation, giving him a loving hug. With nothing left to be done, he could share David's enthusiasm, enjoying every moment of the man's fantasy of gold. He understood pride for the first time.

After the post-win interview, they were quickly behind one of the many curtains to hear the announcement of Best Director. Rod Morris' name rang out, and *Lord Worthington-Smythe* received its sixth Oscar. For his charitable acts toward his star, the award came to a deserving and talented man. Eyes then turned to witness Kincaid, drumming his fingers on the arms of his seat. His hopes and dreams rested on the next few moments, more unnerving than any other of his many nominations and awards received. He understood how his Scarecrow felt, but vomiting into the aisle had to wait.

"And now, Motion Picture of the year: *Brother Mine*! Kincaid Productions!" Steven and Ted's movie won gold; and Thurgood gathered up his frozen lover from his shocked position and hugged him back to life. Burying his head in the bearded man's neck, he finally pushed away, to run top speed down the aisle toward the podium. His usual cheerful demeanor in public vanished momentarily, to erase the tears streaming down his face; but the famous grin suddenly beamed brightly; and he laughed happily to himself, as if part of one big cosmic joke. Maybe it was.

"This is my lucky day. You've rewarded a film I believe of tremendous relevance, and you've honored many of those involved in our joyous union of creativity. This picture portrayed brotherly love at its highest form in a reversal of roles. I now have such a bond with Theodore Barrett-LaCoix. Thanks, Scarecrow, for a hell of a performance and all your sacrifices. Emotions ran high while filming, and so they are tonight. I have one announcement to end this incredible evening with nine Oscars going to *Brother Mine*. Wow, nine Oscars! Congratulations to my entire cast and crew. It's too much to have even wished for, David." Kincaid looked right, to nod an acknowledgment to his two friends, both standing amongst the many curtains. He drew strength from them; they could feel it. Two hands came together, knowing they may be needed.

"Now, I have another type of love story to tell you. I, oh boy, this is tough, but here goes. Tonight is my one-month wedding anniversary to my new partner in life, Dr. Joseph Thurgood, my soul mate, and a gentle, kind man. The name on the marquee will now officially read Steven Kincaid-Thurgood, thanks to Interpol, and not California and Federal Government discriminatory bodies aligned against us. Maybe we can help change minds, along with David and Theo's stance for what is right. Thanks for the courage, guys, and showing me how to find the right man."

The crowd went still, but starting with one friend walking back onto the stage, clapping vigorously for the brave Spirit, David encouraged one more to stand, and then another. Ted followed, as did the host, and then a few of the winners left in the wings, including Rod Morris.

Louder and louder the roar grew; people stood in homage of another honest man they admired. Steven wiped his tears away with a few thousand dollars worth of Armani light, black wool.

"Thank you for your support of *Brother Mine*; I am deeply touched, and am happier than a person has a right to be. Follow your hearts, everyone. Have a very safe and happy night." Pale-blue, tearing eyes veered in the direction of his partner, and then to Security to escort Dr. Thurgood backstage, where he fell into safe arms and his fears faded, leaving him vulnerable to whatever would befall them. Another admission rocked the world; another heart-stopping Oscar show ended with enthusiastic cheers and tears.

The LaCoixs and Thurgoods fought their way out to find their designated limo. Laughing and hugging all around, they stopped for another cheerful, tightly wrapped, satin body, asking the same stupid questions. While she laughed and giggled, three of the men waved at various friends who passed by, shouting greetings and congratulatory remarks. David did the honors, leaning toward the fuzzy-coated, gray microphone, to quickly respond and get them out of there. He saw it flash in the lights, and he dove in front of Ted with a long agonizing scream. He heard nothing, felt nothing. Where had everyone gone? Why was it so quiet?

Memories returned, slowly filtering through a haze of purple light, turning into the soft pastel colors of his first lavender sky day in the rocks. The Mistress flew toward him, yet unable to grasp his outstretched hands. She hung in mid-air like a soft cloud, her long raven curls dancing in the wind, floating back with a strong force, which aided him in his search for those beautiful, white hands, covered with sparkling gems. Draped in yards of the same pastel blush gossamer, the delicate material whirled and twisted around her, much like the feeling in David's head. She called to him, beckoning him to reach out and grab on. A last look back; he had to look back. The faint noise grew ever stronger; sirens and screams came from behind the rocks. One torturous wail he recognized out of thousands; Ted shrieked like a wounded animal. He could feel the man slowly falling with him, both floating effortlessly to land on the red-carpeted concrete. A cracking sound of a revolver echoed in his head, then another.

'Lavender, help him! Ted's been shot!' He opened his eyes for only a second to catch a flickering of blue frightened eyes, the feel of Ted's hands on his body, and the sound of hysteria, fighting and crying for one word from him. He could not even reach up to caress the autumn tresses splattered with more red highlights. Those eyes were in terror; and David did not want this to be his final image of his forever partner. Closing his eyes, one tear fell, and Lavender reached for his hand. *'No, I'm not going with you. Ted needs us. What are you doing?'*

'It is time to meet your Soul, David. You are crossing to Avalon.'

Ted's hands caressed his dying lover whom lay with a bullet through the heart. Screeching until he could no longer make a sound, a paramedic dragged him away, to have his own shoulder tended to. Pandemonium raged. The crowd first stopped in their horror, only to dive for cover from what might be a crazed assailant aiming at them all. Police arrived *en masse* to dissipate and defend the famous multitude, quickly taking out the gunman. Too many people, too many lives, too much screaming, too much terror, all created by one depraved man.

"Easy, Theo, they have to take care of you as well. You have to give them room to work on David. Please, Scarecrow. Stop screaming, please stop screaming." Steven's voice came from somewhere far away, and he was crying, holding him captive, away from his fallen Knight. The hands would not let go; and Ted felt himself being whisked away by a villainous Elfin creature. No words came out, only torturous shrieks and a rainfall of tears, as his horror mounted, watching men in official uniforms, hooking dozens of hated machines to his lover. Placed on a gurney, it was scoop and run. They hustled LaCoix away and into an ambulance, with blood and more blood spurting from the beautiful chest with every beat of a strong heart.

"David! David! Stay with me! Don't leave me!" Ted's face screwed up in agony; his hysteria escalated when the doors closed in his face. "No, I need to be with him. He can't die alone!"

"Theo, there's no room. They'll save him. The second shot caught your shoulder. Doc, what should we do? This wrapping isn't holding. Should we grab a limo and follow the ambulance, or wait for more paramedics? His heart could give out on us. Christ, Doc, help me." Steven could not hold back his own terror, trying to strengthen the hold on his bleeding friend. He had never seen so much crimson fluid, feeling its warmth from touches to both his friends.

"Settle, Steve, settle. The next limo is ours, to follow the ambulance with a police escort. Push anyone you see out of the way. Theo, where are your pills? Tell me, son. Good boy; let's move." Thurgood picked Ted up easily, and followed Kincaid at an awkward run to the curb. An engine purred quietly; the limo waited with doors open, as Steven pushed his former, obnoxious abuser away, along with his sleazy date, refusing them entry. Steven had no sympathy for the man, just as anxious to get out of the mayhem and a possible third shot. With no thought of that eventuality, he finally knocked the man out cold, while Thurgood lifted Ted carefully into the back of the luxury transport. Two men immediately scrambled in after him, with only one in control. The Professor took over, issuing orders to follow the wailing sirens and flashing lights.

The driver flew to keep pace with the racing paramedics and the four police officers on motorcycles, knowing who lay bleeding in his vehicle. Increasing his speed, he followed dangerously close to the path of red blood that only Ted could see, the streaming scarlet ribbons cascading out of the back of the ambulance. Men in navy blue, with cars and motorcycles, formed a deathly parade, rapidly moving down Hollywood Boulevard. David LaCoix lay dying from a bullet to the heart; his partner cried in his friends' arms, dying from a broken one, and bleeding from his shoulder. The sky suddenly closed in with a downpour of rain.

CHAPTER 52

'What do you want, Lavender? I can hear Ted. What's happened?'

'He will be taken care of. Come and join us in your rightful place.'

'No, this is not the time. I know it, and so do you. Tell me what you're doing?'

'You once offered to assist us; and we are accepting your help, believing you ready to become one of us, one of the Powers-That-Be, as you call us. I am your Soul, David LaCoix, from the moment you were conceived. I regret not having been with you as much as you required.'

'Good one. Keep up the jokes and lies, your Ladyship, while Ted needs us.' LaCoix felt the emotions of anger, fear, and loss, none of which he could understand. Lavender continued to play an infernal guessing game of *Jeopardy* with him.

'My absence almost laid you to waste in your own ego and obnoxious behavior toward your fellow man. I will never forgive myself for leaving you so long. Holly was correct: some of us become too involved in other Cosmic matters, neglecting the one we chose to help. Forgive me for presumptuously thinking you could arrive at this point on your own; but now you have come full circle, free to live amongst the stars as we do, taking care of every realm and dimension beyond your imagination. A flight of fantasy, with tremendous responsibility, you have fulfilled your goal; and eternity is your future.'

David felt himself pulled harder, leaving the warmth of desert rocks under a white sun and lavender sky. She dragged him into her funnel of purple mist, smelling of lilacs and hearing those whispering chimes in his head. Directing him gently to her private chambers, she led him to his final resting place to talk; but he had questions and not long to get answers. He wanted out.

'My God, Ethan Peerce! What in hell are you doing here? I should kill you now, since the Mistress failed to take care of you.'

'Be kind, David. This is not the proper way to start a relationship with us. Ethan granted me a great favor; by giving Stevie a final brutal push into sanity. Our young friend's path grew infirm, becoming gravely apparent that his destructive ways would lead to his untimely death, in a strange place, alone, brutally and grotesquely murdered in some sick, sex game. Ethan volunteered to show him, what his life would be like if he continued; and our plan worked. Think about it, David. How could you possibly defeat a man of Peerce's abilities? You have always known he holds the power of me and Quinlan, yet in your excitement of the night's escapade, you forgot.'

'I didn't forget; I just didn't put the puzzle together fast enough.' David stood his ground, although growing ever weaker.

'In your game of red boys' toys, look at you now; you are a crimson one yourself.'

David looked down to see his heart bleeding, spurting blood from his chest to land in an ever-increasing pool of warm, red liquid around his feet. He had been shot, but felt no pain.

In the speeding black limousine, Kincaid tore up his silk shirt, while Doctor Thurgood gently removed the remaining cashmere stuck to a paling man. The paramedics had done their job, but Ted's agitation and condition negated a sedative, which would prevent him from pulling out an intravenous drip and attacking the bandages in his delirium. Blood seeped out of his shoulder, draining down his white sweater. Thurgood quickly administered first aid, fruitlessly securing the white gauze, with help from Steven's trembling fingers. Maybe they should have waited for the next ambulance, but they chose to follow the important one finally coming to a halt. Carrying Ted, the two men doubled their pace behind the gurney conveying David to the Trauma Unit. To give them room, Kincaid harshly shoved away any attempt to separate his frightened, injured Scarecrow from his lover.

Ted heard the voices, but who said what? A heart had stopped twice en route. Someone was being rushed to surgery. Who were these people? He needed to see David. A sudden uproar in the hallway, they all stopped in mid-stride. People yelled orders, and a crash cart came along side the mobile bed. Once... twice... three times... they took a collective breath, and with a nod from the doctor, with the stethoscope, hurried forward to the waiting elevator. Time ticked past quickly, yet everything and everyone appeared to be in slow motion. Completely lost, Ted screamed just for the sake of screaming.

"Knock that one out with a tranquilizer and get him tended to. Hurry!"

"No, it will kill him." The Professor's voice yelled too close to his ear. Who was he talking to? Who would it kill? Who needed a sedative? Ted's brain shut down in his confusion; his fragile body felt the instant rush of pain. He could smell blood, lots of warm blood, but whose blood? It must be David's; Ted's voice choked with the next wail.

"Someone find him a bed; I need another surgeon. Looks like the banshee caught a bullet in the shoulder. Move it, people." The Trauma Unit's chief doctor shouted orders, as he tried to keep a man alive, long enough to get him to an Operating Room. Another stop of the man's heart; it would be over.

"That's his partner you're taking away." Kincaid begged them to help both men; and the doctor turned sharply, recognizing him instantly.

"Just keep him calm. This must be David LaCoix?" An easy assumption considering the aftermath of the awards played continually on the News, throughout every television in the hospital.

Steven nodded, brushing away the tears that he had not been able to control, and confirming the identity of the one on the gurney that they pushed into an elevator.

"We need to hurry, Mr. Kincaid." The doors shut, leaving Ted behind the cold metal, calling for his Knight.

Several nurses and a few strong-armed trauma team members had Ted and his protectors in a small examining room, away from the noise and chaos of too many people. Claustrophobia overwhelmed him, along with his other fears. Did he say good-bye, good luck, I love you? No, he could only shriek like a crazed mad man. How could someone shoot David? No one had a reason to hate him, and then to try a second shot. Were both shots meant for his partner? Could someone hate his blond Knight for loving him? Ted went quiet, trying to think, while Kincaid gathered him up from the bed to bury him in his chest, arms around the bones shaking loose, rocking him, telling him to visualize. The younger look-alike remembered the pictures David sent to him: a perfect day in the meadow, dancing under the blue sky, amongst the wildflowers full of Faeries and their daughters. It fell away with the thought. "No! Oh, God, no!"

"Easy, Scarecrow, they'll be right back to fix your shoulder, and you'll have to..."

"...have to what? Tell the girls? Holly would have seen it, and Mom and Dad! We have to call! What do I say to them? Help me! Help me!" He pulled away from the supporting arms, attempting to leap off the bed, heading again for some place he did not know. Weak from loss of blood, he fell back into strong arms, which returned him to the bed. His hands covered his ears, and then his fingers ran through his hair, pulling at it for no reason, but giving them something to do. Ignoring his shoulder, his friends' handiwork no longer controlled the crimson flow.

"Doc, please, find a doctor. I'll make the calls." Kincaid pulled out his cellular and dialed the familiar number. Craig answered in tears; and the realm of Awakening Canyon had fallen into turmoil. "How are the girls? Did they see?"

"Yes, sir, along with Mr. and Mrs. LaCoix. They're in shock, but the girls remain unnervingly quiet, both thinking and wondering. It's really strange, Mr. Kincaid."

"Can I speak with Holly? Theo's here and is not in great shape to be talking."

"We saw it all. Be careful with him. Holly's standing beside me, like she expected your call."

"Good, put her on. Here, Theo, it's Holly Jane." Steven passed the phone to a hand, which h barely could lift, and watched his friend, beyond panic, try to slow down.

"Sweetheart, are you okay?" The voice sounded like gravel, hitting the underbelly of a fast moving half-ton wreck.

"We're fine. Are you?" Too cold, too calm, it sent shivers up and down Ted's back.

"No, I'm afraid." His tears fell and continued through the conversation. "They're operating on your Dad now. Do you understand what's going on? Can you and Willow help?"

"We don't know if we should. It just started to rain. How strange, Daddy. I wonder if it's a sign."

"What? What are you saying? Your father is dying; and you're talking about the weather. What's the matter with you? Oh, God, you're in shock. You're not making sense." A blast of a winter wind came through the metal connector, running up his arm and into his brain. Holly's voice felt colder than an Arctic blizzard; and it turned him into something he thought he would never be; his daughters' worst enemy.

"No, we just have to think about it. We didn't know who it would be, or when. Maybe it's supposed to be this way."

"You knew? You knew, and said nothing? You insensitive, inconsiderate, little witch: both of you. You are killing us, little girl. Is that what you want, White Rose? Well, you and that Black Thorn from Hell's Gates had better fucking do something. You're not our daughters; you're not even who you believe you are. You're both frauds..."

"...Give me that. Doc, put a gag in his mouth. Holly? Holly Jane?" The receiver slammed down at the other end. Whether in anger, or a rush to get Willow for help, Steven could only believe it the latter. "What a horrible thing to say to a child. Her father's dying, and you yell at her? For God's sake, Theo, pull yourself together." Steven never showed rage; but this was different; a friend had been vindictive toward his children; he would not tolerate such action.

"God has nothing to do with it, and never has. Witches of the Canyon built by another purple Ogre; they can live their lives alone, rotting together while I fill it with unheard of rain. My would-be daughter thinks this is supposed to be. She'd have to think on it. For Christ's sake, she has to think about saving her father! Don't give me any bullshit about being cruel, Kincaid. I'll seal that rock pile forever. They knew; they both knew; and neither of them gives a damn." Uncontrollable fury poured out with the tears; every strike of anger sent a lightning bolt straight into the Canyon. His tears would drown them all, if he could only sustain it. The powers, he had been feeling, learning, and now controlling, would be unleashed, at whoever came between him and his only reason to tolerate the horror that was earth.

"Theo, that's not true. I know Holly; she won't let her father die."

The medical team returned and stopped the quarrel. They first checked an inflated heart rate, and rectified the coughing fit with an oxygen mask. Doctors had to wrestle with the man to keep him on the bed, attempting to ascertain the damage to his shoulder. Unable to lay still, his naturally induced adrenaline, created by his panic, gave him enough power, even with the loss of blood, for his fists to connect wildly with whoever failed to duck. A serious injury, Ted allowed them little chance to correct the situation. The opportunity presented itself, and an angry Kincaid took the advantage by knocking the crazed man senseless. One sharp backhand across the face worked, and the surgeon started the mending process. Many more operations would be required to make it look picture perfect; and the glass jaw would mend on its own.

In a far off place, David heard Ted faintly through the haze, and with each sob from the raspy voice, a candle flickered out from a single teardrop. *'Lavender, tell me now and fast. I don't have much time, and if I still have some power to make a decision, I'd like to go home.'*

'It is a little early to be fulfilling your future, which will forever continue. My friend and Spirit, you have been chosen to become a member of our High Council: a great honor for a human. You are the first in thousands of earth years to be brought into the powerful circle.'

'And just what will I be undertaking? Sorry, bad choice of words.'

'Something amazing, old chum.'

'Ambrose! Help me out here. I know you're Holly's Sir Lancelot. What's happened to my sweet girl who wants her father dead? Talk to her.' Unable to move, David could not lay a hand on the man who refused to look at him. Quin had to be the one to change Lavender's mind, if he could not.

'It is not of my choosing; I am truly sorry, David. Holly has shut me out since the arrival of Willow; and Theo's daughter will not accept guidance.'

'Enough! You shall become part of the Higher Consciousness, which people, of every faith, pray to. You are now a member of a group of beings who control every aspect of all living organisms in the Cosmos. They are waiting for you to join them; and the unseen realms will be free, from the tyranny of earth forces convinced they do not exist. You will be able to thank your daughters for freeing millions of enslaved and self-imposed exiles. All life will grow into its full maturity, in what we call the 'knowing', and the Faery realm calls the 'Beginning Again'. It starts today, with your physical death. Once you turn into a light entity and are acquainted with the new being you will become, it shall begin. Your girls will take over from there.' Lavender's unwarranted rage showed in her scarlet glowing eyes.

David refused to be intimidated, yet unsure as to why she felt so strongly about snatching him away from his disheveled family. *'Rather demanding of you, your Ladyship, and just why should you be so pissed off? I'm the one dying here; and you appear to be the dictator of my future--and what--this Council of the Powers-That-Be? I did have a private audience with one of them over dinner, now this. Hell, I didn't even want that golden, sexless piece of shit, if it meant losing Ted. As for my girls, they aren't mature enough to cope with this. Show me. Prove to me that this makes sense, that I can make a difference with my dying. I know I'm needed in my own reality.'* David's mind grew clearer as he weakened physically, an unexplainable paradox.

'Your daughters' futures are set in either of two ways. With you dead, they will have Ted's gentle guidance to aid them. With you alive, you may become the lion let loose.'

'And you forgot the third choice, the one where Ted and I survive scenario; because without me, Ted is already floundering. He's not going to make it. Don't you remember our man-child? He can't handle this, not now, not ever. I can hear him, can't you? He's shouting obscenities at our daughters, completely confused at their indifference, as am I. Are they trying to push you into sending me back, or are they helping you finish Ted and me? Do they wish us dead, or not?' David seemed to be drifting between two realities. He had no aspirations as grandiose as the Mistress offered. Ted's sudden hatred of their daughters had him reeling. What was wrong with his girls? Between them, they had the power to save him; and yet he felt them stalling. His heart broke further, adding to the warm, crimson, fluid in which he stood. Who would play his final Fate: Ted, his daughters, the Mistress, or himself? He had to get back, to correct a situation going terribly wrong in his world.

Lavender spread her arms in front of her window; a rush of fresh air filled the room. The clouds cleared, turning the opening into a panorama of the future. David saw the remaining three in the garden. It had to be six years in the future; his daughters, though still children, were serenely walking in robes of white and black, speaking to disciples of the *Beginning Again*. Ted did nothing, but carefully clipped off the dead blossoms from his treasured roses. Another ten years: the garden filled with people, listening to Holly in her flowing white gown; as Willow, in her black, perched on a pedestal, eyes closed, unveiling her thoughts through the mouth of the elegant blonde young woman.

'Go back. Go back to two years from now.'

'As you wish.' Lavender squinted at David with her red eyes, not wanting to grant him what he desired. Bound by duty, however, she allowed the next peek into the future. Rain fell in torrents on their paradise, and it appeared to have been pouring for some time. Severe damage encroached the house, with the gardens already destroyed, and the horses gone. A cold, wet night came next, as the scene moved on. Holly levitated upward to view someone or something in their private lookout. A flying object just missed her, and she floated back to ground level.

'Show me what she saw.' In a panic to defeat time, his life drained from his body too fast. He had to convince them to send him home. The image came into focus. In the pouring rain, Ted sat, curled in a fetal position, soaked to the skin, and hiding in the corner of their rooftop sanctuary. Salty droplets joined the rain, creating a torrential downpour and more destruction of the pastel rock fortress. Ted had gained some control over the girls through his holy tears of grief and fear. Seeing Holly rise before him, he cursed her existence and threw his leather boot directly at her face. The action created a lightning bolt that lit up the Canyon, slowly being decimated.

'No, this can't be right. Show me six months after today.' Awakening Canyon filled with water at its lowest elevations; and Ted sat motionless in the empty stall of Bastet, picking the last petals off a white rose and grinding them into the mud and straw with his foot. He continued to cry; and it continued to rain.

'A year from now, where is Ted, not the girls?'

Unkempt and too weak to stand without swaying, Ted walked slowly into a meeting room filled with a few fellow actors of their acquaintance and Steven Kincaid. The look-alikes came together to quietly exchange words.

"You look awful, Theo. Is it still raining in the Canyon?"

"Not when I'm speaking with you. You're the only one who knows what I'm capable of,

Kincaid. Please, do not open your mind to the girls."

"You have to stop, Scarecrow. You're killing yourself, as they gain more power. They need your soft touch, not your hatred. Come live with Doc and me. Leave the girls to do what they are supposed to do."

"And just what the hell is that, Stevie? They've lost sight of the *knowing*. My tears are all I have left to fight them, to deluge the pile of rocks until it crumbles around us. We'll all drown in the resulting collapse of that den of unmentionable thoughts. They are not the children David and I loved. Willow's crazy with power. You have read of the things she's already destroyed."

"And you are one of them, trying to tear down everything you and David built together. You're attempting to murder your daughters, and commit suicide in the aftermath. You can't do it, Scarecrow. You can't. How can I convince you to stay with us, while working on the film, and to forget this hateful act?"

"That's why I'm here. I can't be Oberon. I can't even read the script, without choking over every word. It's no longer true for me, but you will make it, in all its wondrous brilliance. I believe in nothing but destroying the Canyon. I can't do the picture, for my window of opportunity is small, and you know it. The staff has been dismissed; Jake and Daphne sent home begrudgingly; and the horses disappeared. I didn't want any of them to go, but I had to keep them safe, protecting them from the two I have to deal with, plus the Mistress. I have to put an end to it."

The scene faded when Ted exited the door; and David went berserk. *'No! You're killing him! He's gone mad, along with the girls. He loved that script, and now he chokes on those beautiful words. Look at him. Look at what you've done to your man-child, Lavender. You're torturing him; and he's slowly dying of hatred, wanting to kill our daughters along with himself. Show me those other pictures again, with Ted tending the roses.'* David peered at the sight of the once boyish face, now only bones and big dead eyes. Void of expression, only the mouth clenched tight, as if being forced closed. Those peculiar eyes had stopped crying, without the glitter of sapphires. Only a hint of pale blue in the white, they were blind, unable to see, unable to blink. There would be no more rain without his holy tears; his girls had seen to it. David sickened at the thought of the Black Rose's many thorns, and his own daughter's cruelty.

'The next one, hurry up, where's Ted ten years down the line?'

'He's gone, David.'

'Then he'll be with me.' The green eyes squinted, daring the opposing red ones to give him the answer he wanted. The looks amongst the others told him; and his legs nearly crumbled from under him when the words were spoken.

'He dives off your roof. I am sorry, but it appears impossible for you to remain together. It has to be this way for you to join us. We are unable to discover Theodore's future. With his goals discarded, he lives only day-by-day. We know his power is building, and hope our suspicions are true; but he will take another path, as have the girls for now. We shall take control of them when Ted is gone.'

'No! How tyrannical and callous you've become; and your many titles certainly do not reflect the person I knew as a friend, mentor, and to hell with you being my Soul. Sounds more like you have to correct a major mistake that you're making at this moment.'

'Until we know with certainty, we cannot say. I am sorry you feel such blind hatred without knowing all the details.'

'Oh, I think we've covered your fine details; and they don't mean shit. You're saying the Powers-That-Be have their hands tied. Give me a break. Maybe Ted's first assumption was correct; you're all a group of Satanic sadists.' Taking too long, David started drifting away. He had to remain angry to stay alive in his world.

'You are being dispiteous yourself. We believe we found one of our lost in Theodore; however, his psyche has been damaged beyond repair.'

'Bullshit. You believe, do you? Don't you know? What in hell is the matter with you, Lavender? If he's one of you, then help him become one. You'll be doing that to me without my consent. Where is the loving Spirit, in that inspiring head of yours, and now this vindictive behavior? You once questioned Ted on whether he had asked his Soul if it would agree to be sacrificed for Christ. Well, I'm telling my Soul, that I won't sacrifice my Spirit for you. Understood, Mistress? It's the same choice. Remember Holly's wish to the Faery Realm? You will be destroying her beliefs as well. Now, send me back; fulfill the wish of the Faery rings, before you regret considering me as part of your universal mind, or whatever. I refuse to participate, and if I did, it would be to generate more havoc in this reality than our little Willow is doing in my world. Everything, within my power, I shall destroy, and if I am able, that includes all of you. These girls are not my daughters, but a manifestation of your wickedness. They are out of control and so is Ted. This is not what you wanted, is it? Is it?' Slipping fast, draining of essential life fluid, David only had his rage to keep him on his feet, if he actually stood. He felt nothing; but the others heard his telepathic voice boom through their sensitive hearing range.

'No it is not, LaCoix.'

'Thank you for that, Ethan. Quinlan?'

'No, David, the little girl I know would not participate in these crimes the Black Rose is committing in this future shown to you. Willow is stronger than we thought; and yet it is not her nature to be deadly and malicious either. She has her father's heart and powers.'

'They are starting, my friend. I sense both fighting to bring you back. It is not their fault, but a test designed for your daughters. We took you early for reasons already stated, wanting you even if the girls failed; but these images of the future prove it a mistake. Thank you for demanding to see what we all needed to witness; not what we desired alone. It will be a very different future, and the correct one to send you back. You changed your goals when learning of the meaning of future, allowing you to see Holly and Willow become adults. We, of the Council, respect that goal; and with their passing of our test of heart, we shall return you to your forever partner. Your roses need tending by both you and Theo; balance shall return.' The force of the Mistress grew, and her face softened with human eyes filled with regret.

A round of agreeing nods made no sense to David. Lavender embraced him and led him out of her chambers. *'We are sorry to have put you through this. I cannot explain our reasoning completely, but do know we thought it best. Your children do have heart, and with such power they wield, it was necessary to prove them capable of using it. You can find your own way home, my friend. I am still your Soul and will always be there for you. Take great care in how you deal with the Beginning Again; we now see how fragile the concept is, and how confusing it may become. Stand well back with Theo, and enjoy what your children shall accomplish with your guidance, knowing they love you both. They are not the evil sorcerers our man-child now believes them to be; only young and still learning; they will be a product of your understanding. Help him forgive. Learn all you can from each other, to aid your world awaken to a new future. Do not forget your own powers, and watch for Theo's, which are increasing at an overwhelming rate. They will surprise you one day, when he fully learns of them. You witnessed one develop, within a fraction of time. Good-bye, my Spirit. Call on the wind, and we'll be there.'*

Overtly perplexed by the entire conversation, David only understood he had to find the route out of the labyrinth. One way blocked him with a dead end; another became a junction with both paths leading nowhere. He started calling out for his lover; he heard three voices answer. Ted, Holly, and Willow gave him a sound to follow. Growing weaker, willpower drove him on, through the maze of lights and flying objects, twisted rose branches, and angry tears. Closing his eyes to all the debris, he listened. *'David, you can do it. You are a LaCoix. Follow your babies.'*

David's body had gone through the rigors of eight hours of surgery, putting back the little left of his heart. It seemed to fall apart on its own, while the surgical team struggled to keep pace. It would stop; a time of death pronounced. A flicker of life, and the monitor would start beeping faintly. The superstar Oscar winner tried, while the doctors kept working. Time after time, they informed a grieving man his partner lay dead, only to retract the statement by an excited Operating staff member still attending the body. Hell described the torment of all those involved, including a strengthening David. For Ted, he experienced something far worse than Dante's Inferno.

CHAPTER 53

In the Intensive Care Unit, David LaCoix clung to life. News flashed around a waiting Cosmos; the man had used up his nine lives in one night. His partner sat quietly beside him, in a hospital gown and robe, slippers on his cold feet, a bandaged left shoulder, and IV needles in his arm and leg, one for blood and one for nutrients. Ted's world had become so perfect; and now it lay asunder with grief, pain, anger, love, and hatred.

The Thurgoods were of little comfort to a man in confusion, unwilling to listen or understand. The knots may never loosen, in the tangled skein of this woolen ball. Two hours had passed since David's surgery. The pair, who had wanted to party the success of one's movie and the announcement of their marriage, had gone home to have a frightening cry on their own, to get out of their formal garb, to freshen up, and return to Emergency. They peeked through a window at a fragile creature that had not slept in twenty-four hours or longer, with nothing left but tears. With a tight grip around Steven's heaving shoulders, the Professor took a firm stance to hold his lover together when he asked about the two men; touch-and-go came the response. Tapping quietly on the glass, Ted struggled out with his tubes and bags of life on a stick with wheels. A careful hug came from a bedraggled Kincaid, and then an enveloping embrace from the bearded man who refused to let him go. The youngest gratefully accepted the needed support.

"How is he, Scarecrow?" Steven quietly asked. The tears streaming down Ted's face did not subside, and the other two exchanged glances, more worried and even more fretful. They had called Awakening Canyon repeatedly, unable to get an answer. The telephone lines were down from the rain; flashes of lightning affected cellular contact for reasons unknown. Only Kincaid understood the power of Ted's hatred.

"The same. Waiting's so hard; and they won't tell me anything, except how many times he died. Oh God, Stevie, they say he needs a new heart; his is too damaged to heal itself. They're looking for one now. It scares me to be alone with him. All those machines... they..." Ted held such a tight grip on Thurgood's jacket; they could barely hear the words sobbed into the older man's chest.

"It's very frightening indeed, Theo. You wait here with Steve; and I'll ask if we can wait with you. Would that help?"

"Thanks, Doc, I'm afraid if I blink, that the peaks and valleys will flat-line. I keep talking to him. Do you think he hears me?" The big blue eyes blinked and splashed tiny droplets of water as they gazed up for confirmation

"Of course he does. Deep in his brain, he hears you, son. As for the monitors, the doctors and nurses watch them constantly from over there. Look, Theo, if one miniscule anomaly should occur, they would be in here before you could think. Now, stay with Steve, and I'll see what I can do." The younger man leaned into a familiar embrace of comfort. How many times had he been handed over to Kincaid for safekeeping? They were his only family now; friends to take him away from the evil he would imprison, within the rubble he once called home.

Thurgood returned with good news; the three had permission to enter and sit quietly, promising not to disturb anything. It would be LaCoix's decision to live or die. Steven's lover protected them all from the massive media coverage. The shooting of one night played out, in all its bloodthirsty gore, for family and friends to witness on a cruel, continual basis.

David felt himself back in the light amongst the rocks; their pastel shades became his favorite colors. A raindrop tickled his nose, then another against his cheek. The sun on his skin grew warmer, until he became aware of the intense artificial light over his head, and felt the delicate hand trying to caress his arm. There were voices. Stevie he recognized, talking to another familiar voice, and then he heard Ted; his Teddy Bear whispered incomprehensible gibberish into his ear. David felt the sorrow and the terror he knew waited for him. A flutter of eyelids, the only thing he could move opened. Green eyes focused on two of the world's most priceless sapphires. They turned into liquid pools, and the tears into rainbows. "Ted..."

"David! Oh, God, David, please don't leave me again! Please stay with me! Everything's wrong! I don't know what to do!" Beside himself with the strain, and his own loss of blood, Ted's mental fatigue showed, crying out everything he had said and done. David listened, too weak to notice the tubes and wires coming out of everywhere. Nothing hurt but his Baby's outpourings of sorrow, and they came rushing at him. "I need you, LaCoix. Don't die again. Please, don't die."

"Shush, Baby... everything's okay." David forced himself into his world's reality, with a throat aching for moisture.

"I'm sorry. Does it hurt?"

"Not yet... but I'm sure... it will." His strength gone, LaCoix needed all he could manifest, if only for his distressed young lover.

"Rest, I'll be here when you wake up." Ted's hands stroked back the blond corn silk and wiped the forehead with a cool cloth.

"If you... lie beside me."

"I can't. There's no place for me, with these things I'm hooked to; besides, it's my turn to watch over you." Ted played with fingers too weak to respond with a grip.

"It's good to hear your voice, David. Steve and I will be outside if you need us. Be well, my friend."

"Thanks... Doc? There must... be away to get Ted up... up on this bed... under the covers... I need to feel... to feel life."

Thurgood and Kincaid looked at each other in puzzlement, then back at the bed to hatch a plan. How could they arrange this, and how much trouble would it cause, considering strict hospital rules? Both men hurt, both men exhausted, both men near death, yet both men needed each other more than the tubes in their bodies. Without touching or disturbing David, they gently and quickly rearranged pillows, and a small eight inches of softness held the frightfully thin, younger man. Once in place, they pulled up the sidebar to keep him from falling out. Done in minutes, with Ted's IV tubes secure, he lay on his good shoulder and side, his head pressed against his Knight's cheek. The lazy smile, on the ghostly white face, calmed their fears; it made the move worthwhile.

"You're cold... Baby Bear... Your hands... are like ice." The dry, scratchy voice echoed out a man's concern for someone other than himself.

"I'm okay." The other sore throat could barely be heard; but a few sensible words from David stayed his shaking.

"Just need to feel you breathe. Want to make sure you're safe. What happened? You're hurt." David felt the smaller body shiver and attempt to get closer. Fading fast, he had the lucidity not to increase Ted's fright by falling into oblivion. What had transpired and what condition was

Ted in? He needed to know, and wondered if he looked as terrible.

"I'm okay, David, but I'm afraid I'll hurt you."

"Stay still exactly where you are. You can be my comforting Teddy Bear."

"They told me you were dead four times; and I died right along with you. Someone shot you; your injury is serious."

"Shot, hunh? What a way to celebrate."

"You remember winning? Stevie won and so did Rod."

"I know, Ted. I know everything. We have to set things right. I've seen your other side of the stars, I think, as well as the future in two different ways. There's a third that we must figure out. Sleep now; sleep, Baby."

"Need you so much, LaCoix, stay with me."

"Won't be going anywhere. Shush, now."

Two traumatized bodies succumbed in minutes, neither moving in their shocked state. Both men recovering from different traumas, their combined warmth had them comfortable with the extra blankets placed over them by an attentive Kincaid. The resident doctor came in to check on both. Finding them together, she smiled sadly. It may be their last opportunity to be close; and these two famous figures should at least have one chance. She checked all the equipment, and secured anything that may come loose with her two patients in the same bed. Against all the rules, she left them, carefully watched over by monitors. They never told Ted that David had little chance of surviving the night; his need to be with his lover, when he died, would probably be Theodore Barrett's sorrowful reality.

The attending doctor did tell the Thurgoods, however, and thought they should alert the family for what seemed to be the probable outcome of Mr. LaCoix's severely damaged organ. Sinking hearts touched the floor; and the Professor acknowledged the supposition and thanked her. Once alone, Steven fell apart in his lover's arms, stroked with hands and soothing words, along with an offer to help make the dreaded calls.

Tyler and Bryce had arrived shortly after they saw the carnage on the screen. Their presence upset Ted, throwing him into an uncontrollable rage. Separated from them during his worst bouts of hysteria, he spouted hatred for them both, not being at their wedding when David needed them. They seldom visited the estate, unless free holidays and money dangled before them. The boys tried to help, but nothing could be done or said to appease a man falling into the abyss. Kincaid contacted them first. They had left an hour before to freshen up, and would then return with their mother. With one tortuous call made, Steven gave them some hope, if they could just be there, thinking positive thoughts. They were on their way immediately.

The next call to Jake and Daphne shed endless tears on either end of the line. Shocked at the sight of their two sons bleeding over each other, David's parents could do nothing but follow Kincaid's request to return and help their granddaughters cope with the seriousness of their dad's injury, and the wrath of their daddy. With that understood, and a very fast drive back, Jake went to find Holly. This conversation would be very different. Now late afternoon, Kincaid lived through the worst night and day of his life; his Oscar now meant nothing; neither his nor David's could be found. Someone had stolen them from a dying man and a close friend helping him. His life changed in one excruciating moment of time; and he wondered if a quiet life in Connecticut, playing homemaker, would suit him better. He and his Doc planned to travel; it would get him away from the tortures plaguing him and his friends. Placing the phone to his ear, he sighed and leaned into the only man who could hold him together.

"Hey, Jamie, where's Holly?"

"She's coming. Jake's having a slight problem getting to her."

"Holly will answer when ready. David's out of surgery and said a few words before falling asleep. Ted's resting with him, but it's not good."

"We send our wishes, Mr. Kincaid. One thing, Holly's horse charged into the house, now protecting both girls. The other two fled into the Canyon. We can't find them. It suddenly stopped raining for a few minutes, but looks like its ready to start again. It would be risky, if not very dangerous, if you needed us there."

"The horses understand; let Shu do his job. No need to attempt an impossible trip; indications suggest you would not have time."

"That bad, my God; are you sure you don't want the family there?"

"Things are very fragile at the moment."

"We'll do whatever you say, sir. Here's Holly." One rattled ranch hand held the other tightly, as Jake comforted Daphne.

"We got him back, didn't we, Mr. Kincaid?" Holly whispered in great relief and sadness. Beyond a seven-year-old's responsibility to fight the Fates, she convinced her sister to change a journey gone awry, and to battle her father's purple magic.

"You bet we did, little one. He heard you both to find his way back." Kincaid showed some of his *knowing*, and his powers never discussed. No longer the flighty, beguiling actor of brilliance, he became a new man of strength, at the sound of two shots of a handgun. He pulled himself together for his friends, and accepted the lessons taught by Quinlan Ambrose.

"I know. They think Dad's very special, but he's more special to us. Is Daddy still angry?" The sweet, childish voice tore at his heart.

"Yes, he's very upset and badly hurt."

"Does he hate us? Will he ever come home?"

"Of course, but it will take time for both your fathers to heal; you must continue to fight for your dad's life. He still might not make it, Holly Jane; I'm sorry. We have much work to do in the next couple of days to keep him alive. I'll reason with your daddy, and maybe a reunion at home would be best, while you and Willow focus fully on visualizing your dad in good health. It may distress your daddy to see you right now. He doesn't believe or understand how you helped. In the meantime, your granddad and grandma will stay with you. Please rely on them, little one. They need you as much as you need them. Remember that."

"They're already helping us. We'll send healing power, Mr. Kincaid. We love them, and we're sorry we didn't know what to do. He's my father; I don't want him to die." Finally, a little girl cried heartbreaking tears. It was good to hear.

David brought balance into all their lives; they had to ensure his survival. It surprised Steven that the two treasures of the Cosmos would be left in the hands of a gentle man, whose spiritual ideology continued to interfere in his thinking. Ted tried, but here lay proof of how confused he became; and Kincaid could not let that happen. His look-alike also came close to dying, but for a medical staff who cared. Another death affirmation would have sent Ted hurtling off the hospital roof, leaving him and Joseph to handle the bed of roses at Awakening Canyon: a fearful thought.

Lives would be altered for a while, but the once happy family could hopefully rebuild and adapt to one father's scorn and anger, and the other's long, slow recovery, trying to heal more than his wounds. A future could not be interfered with, not even by the Powers-That-Be; and the *Beginning Again* had started. The ways of the Council also needed a few adjustments. Much had been learned this night of a thousand stars.

The afternoon dragged on for six men and three women pacing outside. The LaCoix family, the Thurgoods, and the Barretts arrived to await the dreaded outcome together. Within the quiet slumber of two men, one precariously on the edge of death, the other wanting to die with him, the visualizations, caused by panic, grew too strong; one forgot the rule. The resident-in-charge came in to check if everything remained secure, and neither patient had interfered with the other. She smiled sadly thinking of the impossibility in their condition. While wistfully pondering the notion of these two sexy men making love, she placed a warmed stethoscope on the exposed neck of the one void of monitors. She heard nothing. An expert touch to the skin; it felt too cold. Pressing the red button on the wall, she hurried to open the doors, hushing the emergency team for fear of alarming the one who they had miraculously repaired. They had to be careful, quiet, and expedient to revive Theodore Barrett. Two lives depended on the next few minutes. They extricated the smaller body, placed him on his back on the hard gurney, and bared his chest.

Immediately upon Ted's removal from David's side, all monitors flat-lined for LaCoix. With the resident-in-charge yelling directions, another crash cart rolled in. Two teams worked at a frantic pace, taking little time for Ted to return to the living, unconscious yet alive. With one heart beating, they whisked the loaded gurney into the corridor, away from the organized mayhem in David's room, where another mobile bed had been pushed expediently through the swinging door. Those waiting outside were now on full alert. En route to another room, the blue team stopped in a flurry of activity to inject Ted with adrenaline straight into his heart. Back on the move, a door slammed behind the first team.

The noise from David's room hummed a cacophony of words that the families did not want to hear. The door flew open at such speed; it toppled Tyler to the floor. They pushed the latest Oscar winner back to surgery; and the voices hinted it would be the end. They needed a heart; they needed it now. The stitches had burst with a sudden, spasmodic beat of a startled life-giving organ, created by the removal of half of it: Theodore Barrett.

Wandering in the pastel light once more, David struggled to get back. What happened to Ted? He grew warm beside him, and then the feel of frosty snow and everything changed. Where was Lavender? She promised him they would go together, but the Lady had not predicted a time. Had they led him on, just to go back and get Ted? He could not hear his cries. His roses called for him, but not Ted. *'Lavender, you promised. Where is he?'*

A silent scream echoed through an unknown canyon; and even the Mistress did not heed his call. He felt her, however, pressing him to return without a word heard in his head. Ethan and Lavender, along with several entities he did not know, frantically tore at him, dragging him back to his hospital bed. Family, friends, and ethereal beings tugged at him with every magical trick up their chiffon and velvet sleeves. Stuck within the craggy rocks of pastel pinks, blues, lavenders, and tans, this was his home, but with no house, no gardens, no family, no Ted. Alone, except for those healing hands, his yells for his lover went unanswered.

The surgical team worked at unheard of speed. A fighter, to what seemed the end; LaCoix would come back to life only to die for a few seconds, then to return. He scrambled for his life, and all he needed was one touch, or a familiar voice. Nothing was heard, until Lavender broke through the barrier between them, pulling him loose from his entrenched position within the rocks. *'Fight, David. You are in the Canyon. Visualize the now, not the past. See the house; be there with Ted. Come on, you arrogant, obnoxious Spirit of mine. Remember I am you; we are one; and you had better start helping me. Now, think it; put your heart back together, piece-by-piece. We can help you, but you have to see it in your mind, and want to be in the world you call home. Visualize what a perfect heart looks like.'*

David could not remember seeing a real working heart. He had to remember; and there it was, in a picture supplied by the Mistress; along with a memory of a film made long ago. He could do this; he had to get back.

The cardiac specialist on call could not believe what he saw. As they stitched bits together, the heart started to beat without spurting red fluid. The holes remained, but they stopped bleeding, long enough to insert gauze into the torn muscle and attach small tubes to the severed ends of each vein and artery. The blood of life began flowing the instant the malleable miracle affixed in place. David became a successful medical experiment, with everything pumping as it should. A new heart may never be needed, as fast-thinking surgeons, along with the visualizations of believers in magic, saved LaCoix to try life again.

Theodore Barrett floated elsewhere, far away from their rock fortress he wanted to destroy. He faced other demons in the darkness; his hatred for his daughters created the horror. Immersed in self-loathing, and facing the truth David may die because of him, he slowly sank deeper into the fire's mouth. He remembered; he saw; the shots were meant for him, not his partner. Judge Matthews wanted him dead; his Knight saved him.

Swirling through the vastness of a giant, black vacuum with no stars, he disappeared into obscurity. He had been living on borrowed time. His heart, that they warned him about, had been given freely to save David. It had attached itself to the other through a self-sacrificing manifestation. Spending countless minutes pretending to sleep, he saw only his partner growing stronger by adding portions of the only thing a man in dementia would think of: his own heart. Every ounce of strength and energy unconditionally filled his beloved with life. It cost him his own; and he could not remember when it faltered.

Physically, Ted should survive the attack. To bring him back to consciousness depended on his own struggle. Still in the dark, twisting and turning, calling only for David, he did not understand they were galaxies apart; and the man could not respond to his calls. He had been alive; he spoke to him. Where was he now? Willow and Holly wanted them dead; and he cut himself off from their power. Even Lavender became his enemy, after berating her in front of Stevie and Doc. It seemed his time; but he would be going alone. He screamed in confusion and terror, while thorns pierced and ripped his body to bleed forever. The treacherous roses and their barbed shrubbery caught him: both the black and the white.

'Theo, wake up. We taught you better than this. Were you not listening as usual, or did you confuse it with some other scripture written by who knows whom. You are stepping backward, waiting for some prophet to save you. Sorry, my fanatical friend, he is busy elsewhere.' Quinlan's stern voice reverberated through the darkness, and his hand reached out to keep Ted from falling further. *'Tell me the line. Remember the line, Lad.'*

Listening to the orders issued, Ted tried to remember, as he peered into the blackness for his teacher. *'What line? Help me, Quin. I'm scared.'*

'You have to say it, Lad. The light and the dark...'

'... they walk side-by-side, one as illuminated as the other. Only the fear of the dark prevents us from seeing our way.' A reminder and he remembered. Imprinted in his disturbed psyche long ago, yet not fully understood, he knew now. He focused into the murky tunnel of oblivion. Images formed in the dark; friendly shadows helped him out of the dank briar patch, as, one-by-one, lights turned on to find happy faces of real people welcoming him back.

'Good, Lad. I am here. Rest, Theo, and do not forget you can do anything, if you see it in your mind and feel it in your heart, even a broken one. You have much power. Use it appropriately.' Quin's voice faded away, but not his warm, blue, healing light.

"Theo, look at me, Scarecrow. You scared us half to death." Kincaid and the Professor held his hands, rubbing warmth into them, while his brothers did the same to his legs. So thin and weak, one wondered how this frail man could survive the wreckage of the past twenty-four hours.

"Stevie..."

'Yeah, it's me, Scarecrow. Your brothers are here too."

"David..."

"Yeah, I know, but he can't be here. You had a heart attack. We have to take care of you as well."

"Where's... where's David?" The dry throat pleaded for his companion; his tears started falling in a conscious effort. Revenge would be his.

"No tears, son. You have to stop. David just got back from surgery. A miracle happened this evening; and there's a great deal of rumor about what took place. I think you and Stevie can guess what happened. Just know this; your Knight is stronger than when he came out of the first operation. He's going to make it, son, and so are you. It's *happily-ever-after* time; and you better get started." Joseph took over the pep talk, one hand wiping the rainmakers from Ted's dark blue eyes, and the other on Kincaid's cheek, also wet from crying.

"I don't... I don't think so."

"Rest, little brother. Think good thoughts about everyone. The girls helped bring David back the first time, and again this second go round, along with the Mistress and all those we know with their powers."

"I... don't believe you... I need to see David."

"Well, you can't. You just have the four of us. Until you're better, you're not moving. Comprende?"

"Comprende."

Days passed, and Ted could wheelchair in to visit David for short periods. Both frightened and unnerved as to their next move, they mutually agreed to concentrate on their full recoveries; mending fences would start immediately after. Conversation shut down on anything to do with their children or the Mistress. It upset them both in different ways. Another time and another place would come, to sort out all the confusion of one man's mind, and the full clarity of it all in the other's. It may be a hurdle too high.

CHAPTER 54

After leaving the hospital, David's toes hit the battle line, drawn across the highly polished rosewood floor of a Malibu mansion. He yearned to be home with his girls and parents, and to take a quiet ride on Ra, hand-in-hand with his partner on Bastet. Their horses returned, yet nervously awaited their arrival, with the mare continuously pawing the ground, letting her own Spirit try to change Ted's mind. Her rider refused to re-enter the Canyon, leaving his devastated partner in a no-win choice: abandon his daughters in Arizona under the protection of his parents and staff, or banish Ted to wander with his demons. He could do neither willingly.

Joining Ted for a week with the Thurgoods, after his release, David came to his decision with his only choice. Responsibility came first, and yet both sides required his protection. Vows made; vows broken; his worst nightmare unfolded. The entire Malibu household became a flight of screaming banshees, let loose from all corners upon his declaration. If Ted declined to accompany him home, David would leave without him; forgiveness would not be forthcoming for his intolerable behavior toward their daughters. Even with an illegal marriage, he had rights; he condemned Ted to a life alone, promising unmerciful public condemnation and dispiteous threats to entangle the younger man, in so much legal paperwork, he would spend the next ten years in civil courts. Steven and the two Barrett brothers unhappily took the girls' side. The million-dollar sapphires closed; no words were spoken; the blond actor's claimed conscience, responsibility, and love of his life were tossed aside; and the shock ricocheted throughout the Cosmos.

Theodore Barrett fell into the silences that day, and like the wild, skittish colt, prophesied by Jamie, he immediately turned his back on everything that went before. Laid to waste and cast adrift, his anger mounted toward his daughters, turning to bitter hatred, and his tears continued to flow. His own child could not touch him, to heal his shattered Spirit. Along with the pain that he could no longer control, his chronic illness returned in full force, his mind failing daily. He did not pack a bag. A cab arrived, before the Malibu household could collect their thoughts. Ted immediately walked out to wait at the gate of Kincaid's mansion, and disappeared into the sinister-looking taxi, without a look over his scarred shoulder.

Unable to walk or stand alone, David sat speechless with the rapid departure. Not given a chance to debate the possibilities, he lost himself in the veil of his purple magic. With nothing to do or say, to stop the man from running, his own tears flowed from tortured green eyes, watching the black car drive away. After waiting several days for the expected return, he sadly departed for home. The special place, where he kept Ted's heart safe and would always love, had been ripped away and trashed during the operations. It vanished, stolen like his Oscar; and he hoped the young man took it with him. His lover had to have some heart.

Partially mended but still bleeding, the last remnant of his mended organ was thrown into his luggage, and David departed for Awakening Canyon. A broken man, with little strength, no hope, and no faith, David LaCoix's proclaimed last Fate pushed him off his path without a handhold in sight. Physically, he had Bernard to help him, and mentally, he had Ra. Bastet, in her confusion, vanished the moment Ted left Los Angeles. Only David knew she searched for her flighty butterfly, her lost love; or she gave up, flying away to her own realm, knowing she had lost him forever. David had.

Nothing could console his distressed mom and dad who became his main support in his grief.

Worse than his fight with the gods of death, he had to explain unfathomable reasons to his daughters. Like David, within their brilliant but immature minds, they could not possibly understand what happened. Daddy hated them, abandoning them to a hurt too deep. Even with their telepathic gifts, they could not sense his thoughts. Gaining sufficient understanding of his innate powers, Ted closed them off; and only during a seldom blue moon, his feelings reached them, slicing like the sharp sting of a paper cut, only to disappear in a flicker of time. Losing their other father in his depression, on occasion David would rally to reintroduce normalcy into their lives; but Jake and Daphne held together the remains of a family gone awry.

The taxi took Ted to a car dealership, where he purchased, in cash, a small, dark green BMW and a matching, cold weather, logo jacket. Heading north, he kept driving, until his hands could no longer release their grip on the steering wheel. He would stop, grab a coffee, purge whatever he might have eaten, if he had, and continue forth. With his thoughts shrouded, thinking only of the open road and his car camouflaged within the trees, he moved at speeds that turned reality into a blur. The route north gave him a lonely road, to end his sojourn of sorrow in a mountainous park in another country. With spring blustering in, the ski hills would close in May, preparing for summer tourists, giving Ted the solitude and freedom of the wild. No one recognized the sickly, scruffy man, whose hair hung well past his collar, while a baseball cap and sunglasses hid his face and famous eyes. They were never taken off.

The stranger obviously had money by the looks of his car, and his attire smacked of designer quality when new. The residents of the small town did not know where he stayed, disappearing for weeks before emerging for a few supplies. He barely kept himself clean and seemed to have only one set of clothes, the ones he stormed out in, and a heavy green parka to match his car. No one bothered him. Someone occasionally spotted the BMW, hidden in the trees near an entrance to an unmarked mountain trail; and they knew the eccentric Spirit wandered alone, high above the timberline. The rangers gave up trying to stop him, referring to him as the Mad Hatter who only opened his mouth to whisper and curse at witches and demons, the darkness and the light. With thoughts scrambled beyond repair, it left Ted unsure of his whereabouts much of the time. During his first month away, he spent curled up in his car, with a new warm blanket and two candles burning to keep him warm; unfortunately, May nights, in the Cascade Mountains, could blow cold and dangerous.

This new day, he enjoyed a hot Indian summer afternoon. The trees told him that, with their colorful display of yellow, gold, and red against a backdrop of dark coniferous green. He perched naked on a large boulder, alone by a waterfall, splashing in a pool, which become a narrow, white water stream. High in the mountains, it remained his hidden place. After washing his only clothes, now drying in the fresh pine-scented air, he sat detached from everything but the intoxicating fragrance, a heady blend of junipers and ferns. The wet reeds, sprouting out of the shallow, calmer waters, looked like long snorkels with a brown-seeded eye; they often caused him paranoiac concern as to who may be spying on him. For now, he squatted on a perfect rock, to contemplate the little breakers, soothing him with their gurgling sound. The smallest of things became all important: to watch the trout swim leisurely through the quieter waters, to look upon the pool's mirrored surface, to smile at the sun laughing at him, and at his own reflected image always framed by tall silver birch and pines. He had taken some nasty falls doing this, fainting periodically. The problem appeared to be healing, with his own powers of intent, enabling him to look down for short periods. As he did when a child, Ted rectified many problems hindering his health, his manifestations growing stronger. His jumbled thoughts turned to what he could do with the talents he had; and a plan had emerged months previously. Practicing on his lone mountain, perhaps he could be of some help before his life ended. With no hesitation in taking risks, his life became a waiting game; it would be a good death.

His mind returned to something forgotten: a celebration of some kind. If consequential, he would remember. This day blossomed in a memory of an English meadow where he met his first Faery. A flower wreath, made of very different foliage and blooms, replaced his baseball cap. Alone on a wilderness track, amongst the wild alpine flowers and gentle animals, with which he shared a forest, filled his need for companionship and love. Even the ferocious ones, and there were many, left him to himself, not bothered by the quiet intruder. Certainly, the black bear, fishing upstream, noticed the odd creature, only to ignore him. Ted merged silently into a place of majesty and beauty. Perhaps his bad heart would give out today; but then he no longer had one. Having given it away, he knew it irreplaceable with his limited talents, and cared little to have it back. Who would want it anyway? Touching the healing but still scarred shoulder to remember, Ted immediately dropped his hand, to drown those times of joy and horror, into the cascading water, sending them to the valley below. A cathartic ritual, he performed it once a day.

Ted wandered in the oblivion of his tranquil hideout: a place to slip away, to remember his last thoughts, allowing him to forget he had two daughters and a partner some place far away, who discounted his existence. They seldom entered the fog surrounding his memories; it just did not matter enough. He stopped crying the day David entered the Canyon, his choice to let the man live, without the rain destroying them all in a bittersweet rockslide of his vengeful creation. With better things to do with his tears, he no longer cared about the *Beginning Again*, experiencing it naturally amongst the forest creatures, along with Bastet who busied herself, sipping fresh water and cooling her dainty hooves in the tumultuous little stream. From his first day's hike up the mountain, she stood waiting for him, never leaving him, except when he descended to purchase a few necessary items. It seldom happened; and she knew where to find him. She protected him from everyone and everything, including the Mistress.

"Theo, my Child! Here you are!" Lavender manifested herself on the rock across from him, her bare feet dangling in the water. Dressed in her denim rigging and her curls piled on top of her head, she scared the life out of Ted. Bastet also spooked at her sudden appearance, jumping sideways, and then pawing at the air, reaching for the sun. "Easy, girl, I shall not harm him. He is one of us, and may never understand until he starts listening."

"Shit, you scared me! Don't you have some place else to go? Surely you have millions of other beings you could be irritating right now." Her abrupt arrival gave Ted a dreadful fright. Being alone for so many months, his solitude and silence had been disrupted by something too harsh on his sense of hearing.

"I have looked everywhere for you. It appears that your gifts have grown tremendously to block us so readily. Maybe you can drop your guard for a short while to talk." She squinted at another disaster, for which, she took complete responsibility. Everything she had wanted to accomplish sped up like a windup toy, only to break the springs. Parts flew everywhere; and she had to find all the missing pieces.

"Doesn't take any special power to let your mind see only what's before you. Listen to no one, no other voices, but the sound of this brook and the wind singing through the pine needles and aspen leaves. Nothing to it, your Ladyship. Didn't think you could be so easily dismissed, did you?" Ted snarled at the woman, angry that he had been found.

"It is certainly not a kind thing to say to anyone, but I suppose I deserve it. I find it difficult to believe your eternal partner and children so easily expendable. You might as well start venting your anger; perhaps you can hurt me further with your words. I never thought I gave you such pain, Theo. Can you forgive me, and explain what I have done?"

"I'm sure the list was long, *once-upon-a-time*. Now, I don't know anymore. My memory fades of long-ago matters. It's a perfect solution to stop being angry, or happy, or guilty, to forget everything in a wonderland of mindless beauty, sound, smell, especially alone. Did you hurt me? Probably in some way, just like everyone else, but then I return the hurt and make it worse. What does it matter? Each new day, the end draws closer for us all."

"An easy way out, my runaway. Single-handedly, you destroyed at least a dozen people, all of whom I have grown very fond of, including yourself. You missed David's forty-fifth birthday, and your own thirty-second. Seems to me, today is a special one they cannot celebrate without you." Lavender flicked some cold water, with her foot, to splash the warm body of the naked nymph.

"What a mean thing to do. It's difficult enough to keep warm. To think of your friends makes me shiver, so please stop referring to them. Why pollute this fresh air with the stagnant smell of the past." Ted's ire flared at the gesture. Being continually cold, this rare hot day gave him a chance to discard clothes, to sit gratefully under a warming sun, blistering his pale skin, while nurturing and nourishing his body.

"Would you not be happier in the warm embrace of David? You may not want to talk about him, but I do, considering you waited a young lifetime for him. How could you leave so easily?"

"His decision, not mine; I just made it easier for him. Your first thoughts are usually better than second-guessing yourself. Besides, this place and being outside makes me feel better."

"Yes it would; but he waited days for your return."

"Who?"

"How petty of you, Theodore."

"Figured he would. Thought he'd send an investigator to track me down. Can't figure out how he missed the cash withdrawal to buy a car." A hint of disappointment lurked between the lines, giving the Mistress hope that it might give her an opportunity to break through.

"He wanted you to return on your own."

"So he sent you instead." Ted lifted his head and growled at her again.

"No, Child, I came alone, wishing for answers you are unwilling to give."

Ted said nothing, but looked away, fully understanding the truth in her thoughts. He could read her now, as easily as blocking her from his mind.

"Theo, who do you think I am?"

"Our first conversation comes to mind."

"Ah, yes, Satan. I am still the apparition created by humankind for humankind, particularly for your former church."

"Don't speak of those misbegotten hate mongers; they have scattered like dust, except those behind bars. I did something no son should have to do. Perhaps Willow should have been raised by another witch of the Christian variety." Ted threw a rock at the Mistress; it passed straight though her clothes and body. A flash of light nearly struck him blind, and then dimmed and trailed away. "How did you do that? What are you?"

"That is my question to you; and please refrain from hideous name-calling. Witches, like other religions, are fine people, helping and saving your world. You must stop confusing things with Satanism, an unreal faith for an icon who truly does not exist. Learn of these things before you judge. Shame on you, Mr. Barrett-LaCoix."

"Who cares, and stop calling me that. I have no name, not a Wagner by birth, not a Barrett made up, and certainly not a LaCoix as a choking device." After so many months of blocking what he knew, Ted slipped, and Lavender caught it. He knew.

"Oh dear, we are unhappy with our life's consequences. Here you are, in the wilds of nowhere, totally unafraid, yet you cannot face those of such great importance to you; and it is only a thought away."

"I don't give a damn, Lavender. Now tell me straight: what just happened? You're not real, even when you feel like flesh and bone. You're full of light. I saw it." The expression dared her to confess; his determination warranted an answer.

With Ted's acknowledged acceptance she was not a hoax, or an illusion, the Mistress sighed, contemplating what to say or how to show him. Today would be an honest one. "This body is a container, Theo, similar but not exactly like yours. Your mind is more energy-focused, because part of you is one of us, trapped within a human shell. If you continue to indulge yourself in this bad attitude, you will never emerge, continuing to battle the Fates who shall forever keep you captive. You have such power, but waste it feeling sorry for yourself. How terribly unfortunate for the world."

"Ask me if I care. Now you're saying I'm like you; probably the reason for the intolerable pain battled a lifetime. Well, thank you very much; it proves you're cruel, as well as a liar. Why would I want to be like you? You've caused me nothing but anguish since we met." Ted grew angrier. Quinlan had taught him ways to use and find his gifts, but never had the man mentioned he might be one of them. He had to figure it out himself, now Lavender confirmed it. Death looked more appealing.

"Oh, Theo, you have forgotten the good things: all the love and all the glory. You will never be like me--similar--but not alike. You revealed yourself, by inferring you were not born a Wagner; that is true. You are human with an immortal being inside, able to travel the galaxy in a flash of conscious effort, to be with David in seconds, or in England with the Faeries in the meadow at a thought; and yet, you refuse to awaken into the *knowing*. Besides eventually turning into light matter, you read minds as easily as your daughters, and have for some time. Because you are inherently human in your needs and thoughts, you refuse to admit that unusual powers grow within you. Maybe it is time you helped others. So few have developed these talents; and you waste what has been bestowed upon you. You better catch up, before David is lost to you forever."

"Is that a threat? David's doing just fine on his own. He's a stronger man than I am, with abilities of his own. What I do with mine is none of your business; they help me survive and clear my conscience in meaningful ways. You spin a great tale, but this light entity crap, show me; prove to me you're something besides what I'm looking at, or your purple cloud." Ted had not moved since her arrival; the Mistress faced the dare with a wicked smile.

"My cloud is another container. If you look at puffs of vapor, you will often see they have soft colors and move in mysterious ways. Your mind once accepted such ideas and wonders, being the Faeries' first contact. You forgot them, but they have never left you."

"Give me a little credit. They surround me here, talking to me when I need to hear a voice."

"Good, at least you retain some knowledge; and I am pleased Bastet found you. She is also very skilled at hiding her thoughts." Lavender looked at the horse, nervously pawing at the water, wondering what the next move would be.

"Enough about Bastet and leave her alone. Let me get this straight. You travel in these containers; and one of them is David's purple cloud. I can then assume, if I lie on my back and look up, I'll see a few of you, grouped together, sharing high tea." Ted laughed at her, still focusing on learning the truth, anyway he could.

"Do not be foolish. Clouds are clouds; and yes, they do contain the power of light. Remember how lightning is created, besides the way you send it hurtling through the Canyon? Look at me and watch closely, my annoying friend. You are so aggravating at times, considering what you have witnessed. I will dim my energy, so you do not fall off your perch in its brightness; and please, if you must speak, do so in a whisper, remembering our abhorrence of loud noises. Are you ready, oh non-believer in magic? Now, I am upset."

"Yeah, right; now we're talking science fic..." Ted stopped. Her bared appendages glowed golden light, interspersed with purple rays, through the natural openings of her clothes. Even her feet turned clear water into glittering prisms, startling the fish yet enticing them to come nearer as she played with them. From her shirtsleeves, colors danced, twisting and turning, like ribbons in the breezy mountain air, changing from one shade to another. Ted felt as if he sat amongst the high peaks of the Himalayan Mountains of Tibet, on that special day they hung brightly hued scarves, in praise of Buddha, and what was to come. They also waited for something.

A fiesta of bright colors and exploding lights, the Mistress performed the impossible. Laws of physics were proven: light rays could not bend unless refracted off a reflective surface; the exception being neon; but Lavender certainly was not a gaudy, flashing, Las Vegas marquee. Leaning back on his haunches and pulling his thighs tighter to his chest, a ribbon of purple wriggled its way toward him and wrapped around his squatting position. His one hand, playing with his toes, stopped, as he watched tentatively at the spectacle, forgetting his entire male anatomy, including the entry to all his delights, remained exposed. Lavender's light felt slightly hotter than warm, and it eased every aching muscle knotted after his cold river bath. Eyeing the ribbons closely, a gala of sparklers flashed from her collar, and she added different colors to twinkle within her favorite purple background, for a finale of fireworks, without the sound of dreaded gunfire. The light grew brighter; he closed his eyes.

He could still see the bright lights through his tightly closed lids, as she caressed him, warmed him, fondled him, and made love to him, like no real woman could. Her energy entered every orifice, including his open mouth, to kiss the inside pleasure of his ticklish palate. Bewitched, he gave in to her, when she filled his rectum with warm light, creating small fountains of his life's essence to spurt into the foamy white rapids of the stream. A small groan of pleasure whistled out of a surprised mouth. He remained in the same position, panting heavily, to look into a smug, teasing face. It felt too erotic to yell rape; and who would believe him. Ted wondered if David experienced the same sensation: probably and many times. His former lover remained smitten with this Fey.

"No, I have not; and he is not. I should have asked, but you seemed to be enjoying the stimulation offered. Better jump into the river again, Theo."

"I... I don't know what to say? Could you feel the intensity? Wow, that was awesome. You may not have entered David, but you've been teasing him somehow."

"Teasing? Certainly not intentionally, only the feelings you both experience come to me; but they are fleeting and hold no consequence."

"Thanks. Too bad you can't feel it physically. You... sorry... we light entities will miss a great deal. I don't think I like that."

"You finally accept who I am: a light entity? You may jest with your remark, but you are still one of us. Now, what does that make me in your terms: Satan, god, the creature from the blue lagoon? Oh, you did mention a purple Ogre once. Who am I, Theo?"

"Satan, no; God, no; maybe one of the other creatures." Ted laughed and threw a sprinkling of water at the reconstructed human container.

"Be careful, as the same term shall apply to you." She smiled at the man slowly returning. A terrible struggle for him since the shooting, his mind never recovered from the horror. Delighted in his first laugh, since the tragedy and the saddest of good-byes, she watched him act the part of a child, splashing to rid himself of his sex. The Mistress let him play, releasing months of anger.

"You'll never tell me, so why should I guess? Could this water put your light out, if I dumped you in, or would you electrocute me?" A hint of mischief from the man, she almost had him.

"The fish were not affected by my light?"

"*Touché*. You're beginning to sound like David."

"Sometimes we are one in the same. I forgot him for a time."

"Like me falling through your cracks, on one of your bad days." Ted continued to laugh, becoming the ray of sunshine so sadly missed. Climbing back onto his favorite rock, he smiled at her, shivered, and took a more discreet sitting position under the hot sun.

"My precocious runaway, you have no idea. You are one of my worst days, actually, many of my worst days. You confuse me, and I you. Fearful of your safety, we treated you and David differently, perhaps an error on our part. He received revelation after revelation to work out himself, and he did, with great expediency. We let you absorb things quietly, without the startling visions, which would have made you work too hard to figure them out. Your first sight of us had you faltering. We initially pushed you, believing you strong enough. Rethinking your reaction toward us, we concluded such further action would be hurtful to you."

"I'm hardly frail, as you can see, living here alone. I have survived, growing better at it."

"Now your inner being is growing stronger inside, and the pain within is increasing. You need to accept who you are, Theo, and what you are to become under Quinlan's guidance."

"I am who I am; a retired actor who has been taught enough. Leave me alone, to deal with what's best for me. My choice, remember?" Melancholy fell over him, like a suffocating blanket; he wanted her to leave. Opening his mind for her to read, she returned the message with a definite *No*.

"I must apologize for disrupting your life with David. My interference nearly foreshortened his glorious future in this reality, by playing his last Fate; never considering I also became the Fate sending you into this cyclone of despair. Please, let me correct it, and get you and your forever one back on your rightful paths."

"Maybe this has always been my goal; to be free and alone from all those who can hurt me. It's always been the need for freedom from something menacing."

"Not from David, Child. You are his, and he yours. You set your primary goal at age fourteen, to be joined forever with your Knight, and giving up puts your future in jeopardy. Look at you now. Is this a very dangerous second choice, or a true goal? I do believe it the former."

"No, your Ladyship, the union is over. I have other pains to deal with."

"You are your worst foe, with no one to help you win this struggle against yourself." Lavender let out a sorrowful sigh, raising her haunted face to stare up at a blinding yellow sun. Remembering Ted's descriptions he expounded upon, she saw the aspen leaves sparkling silver with a mountain breeze. She turned to refocus on the sullen face.

"They don't need this; and they certainly don't need me. I still don't know why you even bother, or how I figure in your master plan." With the wanting expressed, the fear of rejection and the accompanying duress grew greater.

"Perhaps you need never know but one thing: I will always be your Caretaker. What I said is true, and you guessed, or came to understand, we are light entities from a far off place. You shall learn much more. Now, look into the quiet water's mirror. You will not faint; I am here to support you. There is your family in Arizona, doing what they do every day. All are lost in their grief, with no fun, no excitement, no joy, except for little spurts from Jake and Daphne, and the visits of Stevie and Joseph. Your brothers will not return, with their families, unless you are present. David barely smiles at an old joke, or a cartoon he forces your daughters to watch, all too forlorn to enjoy the frivolity. He tries desperately to keep them little girls, in order for them to grow into mature, spirited adults, with brilliant minds. Without your sensitivity to heighten his own, he flounders, Theo. Currently, they are in their usual depressed state, remembering what took place one year ago. Today is your first anniversary; and you have forgotten your glorious bonding. There are your presents from your family and friends. They still wait for you; David forever alone each night, standing on your lookout, wishing to see you come down the road. Your present to them is only yourself, and that, my runaway, is their only wish."

Ted did not respond, but looked into the clearing pool of fresh water. He saw Holly in the garden, drawing her pictures of what only she could see. His hand immediately erased the sentimental image on reaching down to touch the blonde head. It disappeared in a ripple. Another image formed, and Willow walked beside her grandfather, along the road lined with cypress. The runaway looked away, closing his eyes, remembering the intoxicating scent, mixed with roses and eucalyptus, only the musky odor of sex had been washed away in the river. It had made Ted laugh, hearing David's idea to bottle the perfect scent as an aphrodisiac; but there stood a briar patch of roses again, and he hastily washed away the image of his black one.

The picture changed; David leaned against the wall of Bastet's empty stall, sitting in fresh straw, attempting to piece back Ted's first Christmas gift, viciously smashed on his return home. His Knight suddenly started to cry into his bent knees, looking pale and thin when he raised his head to look up at nothing. Ted heard the words; he heard the pain; he refused to hear the love. "Where are you, Teddy Bear? Please come home. Even Bastet is gone; and I have so few reminders of you. Please forgive us all; forgive us for not finding another choice. Please, Ted, just come home." The picture faded; and the Mistress had the sobbing young man picked up, dressed, and in a motherly embrace against her chest. The caressing of a frightened Spirit, by a light form in a warm human container, continued until tears abated.

"Bastet is waiting, if you wish to return. David vowed to give you whatever freedom you require. He has done his part, now what of you? Has it not been long enough, Child? I have tidied you up, but don't be surprised at their shock. You look half past dead." The Mistress fingered his long hair, magically turning it into something presentable. "Do you wish to return?"

"I don't know. What David said; you conjured it up, planting those words in his head."

"Since his return to the Canyon, he sits in the same position, at the same time, uttering those exact words repeatedly. He does not understand why you do not hear him. With his powers increasing, I cannot put ideas into his head; and with your innate gifts, you blocked out the important calls that he shouted from your lookout."

"Things have to change for me to stay there; and I mean no offense to you or what you gave us. I'm killing them all, and that would be the ruination of your game: *the Beginning Again*. I'll do it for who they are, not for what they mean to you." Ted's stature grew with greater gifts than Lavender imagined. She had to be straightforward with him.

"Very true, this certainly could be perceived as a game for our needs; and your decision could jeopardize the start of the *knowing* throughout the Cosmos. Your reasoning is sound, and nothing more can be said. You have always been an honest man, Theo; and it is your decision. Remain truthful in what you say; if you return."

"How do I get back?" Once she admitted to something bigger than helping the handful of them, Ted's need to return consumed him. His car waited at the end of a three-hour walk down the mountain, and the hardest part of his trek. Having to look down the full way, he fell more times than he took a step.

"Bastet will take you. Mount up, close your eyes, hold onto her mane, and think of exactly where you wish to go. Do not open your eyes until she tells you. You have always known your three horses to be unearthly; but stubborn indoctrination of what is real, and what cannot possibly be, gets in your way." Lavender hoisted him aboard and steadied him. "I know you trust Bastet, so do not look down, and keep your eyes closed. The experience will feel wonderful."

"Thanks, Lavender. Let's go home, Bastet." He closed his eyes, his fingers firmly laced in her curly mane. The floating sensation came first, and then the wind entangling his own longer hair within Bastet's even longer mane. They were one, and his magical steed had him open his eyes to view the large wooden gate hidden by the cypress-lined road. He drank in the perfumed air and punched in his code. Taking in the wonders, standing in its full glory, he and Bastet walked slowly to the front of the house. With the damage, created by his tears, repaired, he felt thankful for that. Home in a second, it took only a thought. With magic back in his turbulent life, it gave some peace to an unnerved man who approached a frightening door.

CHAPTER 55

Theodore Barrett had waved good-bye and received good luck wishes from the Canyon's occupants that glorious end of March. He did not see them after the shooting, spending the month of April in and at the hospital. Now early October, those awesome gates appeared bigger, looming over him to ensnare him again. Fear stabbed through the runaway, at what lay behind the only-choice door. Perhaps he and Bastet should continue riding to her realm, or back to the wild forests of the north. Too late for indecision, the frightening portal burst open, silhouetting a tall, thin, blond-haired man, dressed in his signature black, with hope in his sad eyes. Neither man could speak, both frozen in time.

David gathered himself, taking stock of the unexpected appearance that jolted his healing heart. Unsure of what to do or say, he only knew his desperate need for this reunion, if only for answers--what he said, one Oscar night, might be true once more--his life could be overflowing. His strength slowly returned over the long summer; and now with the sight before him, he felt one-hundred percent better. The tortured mess of a heart miraculously mended with the healing hands of Ambrose; although one small rip remained open, to be Krazy-Glued together in the next few minutes, if only he could move his feet, or even smile.

The man, on the Andalusian mare, looked as bewildered. He was home, and yet not. Confused and scared, he could only stare at his forever partner who looked deeply concerned. The slow motion movements seemed surreal; time stopped on one of Salvador Dali's melting clocks. The long, graceful strides, coming toward him, made him swoon in need of a loving word, just a word to let him know the reality of the vision. What waited behind those doors, besides the man coming ever closer, stopped his breathing. Would he be welcome, and what would he say? The ticking of a timepiece deafened him. Why had they put a clock, the size of Big Ben, in the Canyon, to echo endlessly through the rocks? His heartbeat, pulsating in those fine veins in his ears, grew unbearable. He let go of Bastet's mane and covered his head with his hands; it hurt too much.

A yell for help from the man in black had Bernard rushing out the door, only to stop and hold his breath. Bastet stood nervously, carrying a man so emaciated that force-feeding could not cure. The tender drag queen flooded with tears, his hand over his mouth to hold back the gasp, aghast at the sight of a skeleton, and yet one so beautiful. On a magnificent steed sat a wild savage, with the famous eyes, now hauntingly cold and blue, slowly rolling up into his head. The rider fainted; and Bastet helped him fall gently to ground with David's assistance. Burned raw and blistered, Ted looked too sore to touch.

The older man could not yet carry the lightest of loads. It did not stop him from getting on his knees, to lift and embrace the shoulders and head of the lost half of his heart. Kissing every strand of the wild tresses, he continued to stroke and whisper to his runaway who remained unconscious. It took little time for Bernard to help, and carry the smaller man to his rightful place in the master bedroom. His Knight scurried everyone else away, until their lost Spirit had a chance to face his ghosts. Perched on the edge of the bed, David waited for who knew what. Floating down to rest, Lavender sat beside her strikingly handsome leading man, bestowing him with an affectionate hug, a good luck whisper on a breeze, and then to vanish into the vapors. Two men together had to make things right.

"Wake up, Teddy." Uttering the first words, the older man sadly smiled down into the bewitching eyes that flashed open, wild with fear. Not knowing who may awaken in their bed, LaCoix only recognized those blue orbs, habitually turning downward to focus on his toes, unable to meet the green-eyed monster's stare.

Ted fumbled in his mind over his reasoning to return. Lavender told him to be positive, to visualize a correct course, and to be truthful. Truthful: he did not know what it meant, or how to say it if he did.

"I can't believe you left me, Ted. Explain to me what happened; and where you've been all these months?" David bit his lip. Not wishing to sound demanding, the stern questions unexpectedly tumbled out of his mouth. His face froze in anguish, with a deep frown and the saddest smile, while his hands readied themselves to grab the man, if he made a move to run. "Feels like our wedding day; you're not talking. Have you come back for good or just passing through to destroy what's left of this shattered family?" With no reply, a touch to the sunburned face received a cringe. Ted turned away; the dispiteous act meant only one possibility; he had not returned of his own accord. David had lost him again.

"Are you burned this badly all over? I thought you could heal something this simple." Again, no response from the clenched lip, and a flicker of the future dawned on David, remembering the man tending roses. He tugged at the T-shirt, stuffed into the baggy denims, only to have his hand slapped away. "I can't play this game. Bernard will take you to the guest quarters, where he can tend to you. There's no way I can deal with this silence shit." David got up slowly, dejected and ready to burst into tears. Although better physically, he still tired easily; and his massive disappointment, in Ted's attitude, ate away a colossal amount of his energy. Why had Ted come back--to torture and tease him with sadistic games to get even--even for what? David refused to play, even as important as this may be.

He stepped toward the intercom to ring for their nurse. Wiping off his sweating brow, and the tears shed so often in five months, they could never ease the grievous loss of this young man whom appeared still lost. With Ted back to old habits, David would not tolerate the illness to continue under his roof, watching the man slowly die. His heart had been through enough; and now cold silence faced him. A reach for the button, he stopped with the faintest whisper.

"This was a bad idea. I'll get Bastet and move on." Off the bed with a slight wobble, Ted attempted to get past the man blocking his route to freedom.

"She needs to rest. You have some compassion for your friend, or have you changed that much? Can't you stay until she's fed and watered? Perhaps you can tell me what you've been up to before you go. Any exciting adventures I missed?" David returned to sit on the bed. Perhaps not caring would be his best tactic.

"You're right. Forgot how far we came."

"So, what's new? You've obviously been in the sun someplace." David refused to look at anything but his boot tips. His sigh penetrated another lonely Spirit.

"Hiking in Canada. Nearly froze my arse off when I first got there. Nights get so cold in the mountains. This burn is from today. Guess I forgot how intense the sun gets at high altitudes."

"You've been sleeping outside all this time, in the rain and snow? There's some dangerous wildlife lurking amongst those trees; and the sudden temperature changes could have killed you without shelter."

"Built a lean-to when necessary. I leave the animals to their business; and they leave me to mine. Some were comforting to have around, in their special way." Ted shuffled back and forth; something David had missed: the innate, sweet, bashfulness, when the younger man became nervous or unable to answer.

"Is that what you want; to be left alone? Sounds like you should leave. Watching you slowly die would be the cruelest joke of all." David went back to studying his own tan boots. They had been worn the first time on their special day, one year ago, obviously forgotten by Ted. The rip in his heart opened wider.

"I don't know, David. Nothing makes sense to me. So many important things seem to be lost; and I can't find them." Ted slumped beside him, looking as forlorn.

"Like your ring?" The forlorn blond noticed the missing sapphire; his hopes vanished. He twisted his own yellow-green stone around, wishing it would fall off, to shatter into a million pieces. It meant nothing; his love rejected; the deepest wound a mortal faced. He should have accepted Lavender's offer.

"No, it's around my neck. See?" Ted pulled out the leather bootlace from around his neck, which carried tens of thousands of dollars in one perfect sapphire. The intricately engraved pattern, however, had been hammered and beaten, until nothing remained of its bonding symbols.

"You hate us that much. Wish I could forget so easily. A rock to smash a vow of eternity, and I still love you. I must be out of my mind."

"No, it doesn't mean that. Please, David, you are my life and always will be. I just don't want to be here. Come with me--anywhere--let's start again." Ted looked up; and the sunken face of a ghost, with big scared eyes, begged David to run away with him.

"What are you thinking, Ted? It's impossible to start again; something called responsibility is in my way; and I need that control. This is your home; every inch of it is ours. How can you leave Willow behind? You haven't even mentioned your daughter. She's your blood; the only child you'll ever produce; and she's beautiful, inside and out. I don't understand. We have children to raise, friends and family, career commitments, and you want to throw it all away. It's beyond my reasoning." David shook his head, letting it come to rest in his hands, while leaning forward to support the heavy load, with his elbows on his knees.

"You mean more to me than my life, David, but I can't stay."

"Why? This makes no sense." Too distraught, he dared not move to look at this stranger, with such a drastically different attitude.

"Any connection between me and our children was severed with one statement from your daughter and the thoughts of mine."

"What did she say? Nothing could be so bad, to instantly cut your children out of your life. I suppose I shouldn't talk, considering that's what I did with my folks. I'll regret it to my dying day, and so will you."

"I never wanted to tell you, but Holly wasn't sure if they should save you. The sentiment rings in my ears constantly. How could they be so callous about their father's demise? Even bastards like my own, rotting in jail, deserve better than, *'maybe it's supposed to be this way'*. I can still hear the coldness; and it hurts so deep, I can feel it cutting into every part of me, every minute of every day." Ted stood up to pace away his tension, coming to a halt by the window to their courtyard.

"Holly's seven-years-old with no concept of life and death, except someone suddenly disappears from her life, never to return. In a way, you're dead to them both, by disappearing for so long."

"You don't give them enough credit. They know all about death. They know too much about everything. I'm terrified of them. Don't you understand that? I ran, because two little girls scare the crap out of me." Ted turned and snarled at him, disguising his emotions with anger.

"Why didn't you tell me before? Come here, Ted. They're good kids; and whatever happens, we'll make sure they learn what is good and proper. Yes, they do know more about the unreality of our lives; but that's why we're here. Remember Holly telling us she was a new Soul? Think of what that means; both our daughters are blank canvasses to the real world, to be painted in all the colors of earth and its wonders. Holly blossomed in England, learning and seeing, believing in everything. It's your turn to show Willow." David pushed himself to his feet, walked over to a crimson-colored Ted, and gently turned him around to gaze into the confused face. He fell headfirst into the abyss of blue.

"She scares me the most. I can't speak her name without trembling."

"One hug from your raven-haired princess and you'll change your mind. She loves you." David ruffled the hair back out of Ted's eyes, and succeeded without a harsh retaliation.

"Oh, no, not a princess, but a sorceress with other plans; I suppose she's told you this."

"Yes, many times over. You missed her first step, Ted; her first acknowledgment of a fragrance; the first understanding of a feeling; her first touch of a rose petal; and we both missed her first birthday. Only Holly has celebrated these events with her. We come home to find she's suddenly walking, identifying colors, sounds, and so much more. Everything is new to her in this world. What will you miss next: her sixteenth birthday, her first date, her wedding? Maybe she feels more abandoned and frightened than you do."

"My God, her first birthday, and we were in a hospital, fighting for survival. What a horrible anniversary for a child to remember. What have I done?" Ted started to cry, but pushed his partner away, not wanting to be comforted in his shame.

"You ran away and came home. Whatever you need to feel welcome, we'll do. Just tell me."

"I don't know. It's just wrong. We have to make it ours, not Lavender's." Anger and frustration boiled over; and he shoved David aside to rant his bizarre insanity. "Take out every rose in the place; not one is to remain. Fill the beds with happy flowers, besides white and purple blooms, and those with thorns. I want the brightness of a mountain meadow and spectacular desert sunsets, when everything turns yellow, orange, red, and lots of rich blue."

"Is that why you pounded out the design of the ring? By disfiguring our stylized roses, you thought you could destroy all the promises." Confused with the roses, they had become an infusion of their love. Thorns united them in ritual; and now this hatred, for something Ted once loved, seemed such an odd request.

"I don't know, David. When you were shot, I wanted to annihilate this place. I came to realize my strongest power; my tears create rain. Lavender once told me I could change the weather; I guess I can."

"She showed me your gift, and what it can do. It's a thorn requiring great control. I'm glad you vanquished the need to destroy us."

"I couldn't do it, because you came back here. How could I hurt you any more than I had?

When my heart stopped, rose bushes held me captive in the dark. I couldn't get free of them; and the more terrified I became, the deeper I fell into darkness. Only Quin's instructions, and a reminder about the light and dark, brought me into consciousness. From that moment, life for me had to become more vivid, more risk, more excitement. No more paled-out people and lives, floating in celestial visions, and no more hidden thorns to attack you inexplicably and cage you in a briar patch forever. Living in the mountains, the feeling of survival intensified to such an extreme, even colors blazed brighter and the wild sounds made my heart race. I need that, David; and we need a new name for the Canyon. I hate it. Whenever I think of it, I remember who gave it to us and why. She thinks we don't know it's the same as La Rosa Negra. It's not real; and that scares me too. Can't you see this place has never been ours? It belongs to our two thorny roses and the Mistress who arranged our introduction. We're just an option that comes with the property; pawns in an unsolvable puzzle, which Lavender admitted to, in her way." Ted came back in fighting form, speaking his truth in his distressing raving, growing weaker, struggling with the long monologue.

"So, it is a game. I had a revelation about the Canyon some time ago."

"You know as well then. It's some weird game, which I don't want to play anymore. It's not for her I came back, David, but for you."

"Okay, Baby, that's all I needed to hear. Whatever you want to change, we'll rectify. Out with roses, and in with what? Tiger lilies? Bougainvillea? Or do we move elsewhere?"

"This isn't funny, man. It's never been ours; and we have to change it. I told you, when you first saw it, how everything grew by itself. Now we know who manifested every inch of the place. We had nothing to do with it."

"I'm sorry, and I do remember, but we envisioned this together. The house is ours and the gardens are yours. The location however, I think we owe that one to the Mistress. So, whatever you wish to do, go for it. Pink out. Red in. What else?"

"I'm desperate for something new; and I don't know what it is. Maybe it's vibrancy and laughter; anything to brighten the monochromatic world we live in, and the heavy suffocating scent of roses. We need to hear dogs barking; throw Frisbees for them to chase; play hide and seek with the girls in the gardens; kick around a few soccer balls; and take wild, overnight rides outside the Canyon, into the outer desert that we've never explored. What happened to hiking and traveling to find adventure in the smallest of things, as we did in England? We need something bright and fresh, like a spring day, and music: happy, fun, and played very, very loud, instead of chimes. We're not Buddhist monks; we're supposed to be alive, man. And a name, something that's us, not one of Lavender's *knowing* words."

"I thought you liked the Mistress?"

"I do, but I don't want to be like her, or our children to grow into her. They have to be better. I don't know what she meant, but she is part of you, so how could I not like her? Besides Quin, she's the only voice I hear in the dark, when I allow her in. I know I need her guidance as much as you, maybe more."

David gave him a twisted grin, as Ted returned to him in his ranting. He had ignored the man's age, and what made a young man happy. Awakening Canyon was too quiet for a lively ray of sunshine; even their daughters needed something of their generation to idolize. A truce presented itself, all laid out as to what to do, to overcome his partner's fears of their innate gifts. The wicked smile held back the laugh, but he refused to complicate Ted's life further, by telling him he had met his Soul, although his partner felt some connection. "Will you stay, if we change the Canyon and enjoy what comes naturally to we mortals?"

"Another thing, and this really scares me; your eyes sometimes turn feline."

"Don't let out a banshee-like shriek for telling you this, but so do yours; they look like that now." David put his hands cautiously on the surprised, sunburned face.

"No, not me, it's impossible." Ted tried to run for a mirror, but David's feline eyes had him transfixed.

"You have tremendous powers, Baby; you just don't know how to use them fully. If you can change the weather, I'm sure there's more that you're capable of, including showing me those incredible eyes in human form."

"Maybe." The expression yielded more than the word; and David wondered, as he listened further. "She showed me what she really looks like; she's made of light, hiding in clouds and bodies. She said I was one of them, and that's the pain inside. I don't want to be a light entity; it's scaring me to my grave." Ted quivered from head to toe. An embrace carefully secured him, preventing the burn blisters from popping, and confirming the man's humanity with a touch.

"The Mistress told me, Ted, but she didn't mention the reason for your pain. We're all changing here, as they were at La Rosa Negra. Remember the lights in the rocks, glowing from under the robes? Quinlan's a light entity, as you must know. Ethan is also light, and something other than what we were led to believe. Steven may be like you; a light entity trapped within a human body, which gives one all sorts of speculative ideas as to his former behavior. Perhaps, his need for abuse masked the pain through more excruciating agony. The girls are certainly changing, and so are we."

"Why us though? I don't understand. We're all changing from human form, but into what? I'm already one of them, trapped until they let me out. I'm so confused, David, I don't know what to do. I can't take any more. The game's gone too far." Ted clung to the black knit sweater, burying his face in the familiar chest, with blue tears cascading in waterfalls.

"You've been on the edge of believing for so long, you're starting to fall. You're home, Baby Bear, and I won't drop you." Only choking sobs responded, and David continued on a happier note. "Let's do one thing at a time. First, we'll get you freshened up, and say hello to each of the girls, one at a time, and you can stay with them for as long as you're comfortable. I'll be right beside you. They want you home, so much, Ted, and for you to love them again."

"I can't." Ted wept like a baby, his fists pounding against David, whom increased the pressure of his embrace around the heaving shoulders.

"Yes, you can. No negative thoughts, not now, and we'll take everything slowly. While you meet with our daughters, I'll get Paulo to start digging out the roses. He'll be upset about the black one he managed to coax to grow and bloom, but he'll get over it."

"Nothing black. Nothing. Not even your clothes, LaCoix. You'll have to get rid of those you're wearing. No more black and white; not even those old classics we used to watch."

"Slow down, Baby. What about work?"

"Don't be stupid. I won't be seen in public again, ever."

"What about our promise to Stevie? I had to give up the other picture because of the shooting; and I hoped we could do this for Holly and your best friend. What do you say?"

"Maybe, since we'd both be working on it, and if you're up to it. All closed sets though, and no promotional work."

"Works for me; and I know Kincaid wrote the part for you. He feels defeated even thinking about a replacement."

"I must apologize to him. Didn't even say good-bye. Some friend."

"That reminds me, you still haven't finished this. I believe it has some significance to you, if you still want it?" David walked over to the bureau and pulled out a box. Coming directly back and looking rather winsome, he opened the lid for Ted's viewing.

"My scrapbook! It has to be nearly twenty years old. I planned to leave it for the girls when I died: everything special about their dad. I bet it rained here the night I remembered leaving it behind."

"June 4th."

"I did make it rain!" Ted fell back on the bed, his arm over his face. David joined him, side-by-side, a larger hand tightening around a calloused and scraped one, calming the potential torrential storm.

"A sad, gray drizzle came down that night. We sensed you, and marked it on the calendar. You let your guard down for a few moments; and we saw you wrapped in a red blanket with a black stripe. We could do nothing but cry along; you were so frightened and cold. Two tiny lights lit up your face; but we couldn't see where you were, or why you had two small fires."

"You all could see me? A late blizzard blew in that night. I thought I'd freeze to death in the darkness, but my two safety candles kept me warm, and one of those famous Hudson Bay blankets. It's something you always carry in your car up north. They reminded me of my childhood Spirit Keeper. Strange, isn't it, to be thinking about a scrapbook I started as a kid, while suffering through one horrible night I barely survived. The rangers found me in the morning; and I warmed up at the station. They saved me."

"You had many people watching over you, only aware you needed help, but not knowing where you were." A caress of the tangled mane brought out a hint of a grin.

"In a green sports car, too small to sleep in, stuck in a snow bank; and you sensed me?"

"Let's see those human eyes stop crying before you start a flood. That beautiful mouth needs a moist tongue to fix those parched lips. Do you know how much I need you right now?" With the light shining in his favorite eyes, his runaway returned. His embrace grew stronger and the kiss burned like smoldering coals. They walked across the fire barefoot, ignoring the burns, and solidifying a partnership with a sexual savagery two mending hearts could barely tolerate.

Clothes were yanked off in their delirium to feel the other, ignoring the yelps of blisters bursting. Nothing mattered; only the touch of the other became important. Rolling over, David covered Ted's smaller frame, to rub his silken nest of soft brown hair and hard penis against his lover's crotch, igniting both to rise in heat. Violent and needy, they tore into each other in unabashed lust for one to get inside the other as fast as two twisting, frenzied bodies would allow. A lion mauled and devoured a sautéed baby bear that ferociously fought back with nails and teeth. Shrieks and vicious growls could not be heard through the sound barrier created for such ravishment. The bright red skin felt as scorching as the color to the touch; and David reaped its heat, penetrating into his every muscle, now straining for control. He felt a tremendous healing force when the smaller man pressed against the large scar on his once-perfect chest. The flame inside Ted hit David's life force, creating steam within the sensitive rectum, and the eldest lunged wildly into the puckering opening, which craved his succulence. Up as far as his own physical abilities allowed, his first lustful thrust exploded with such urgency, thoughts of seductive foreplay or preparation disappeared in the rapture.

Ted growled, accepting the stinging entry, then hissed his approval of tearing flesh, as David pulled back to assault him again. Scratching and biting, they remained connected, rolling over to deepen the penetration. Two savage male animals displayed their separate energy forces of pure masculine need and fight for power: man against man, man loving man. Sweating and grunting, the union of two wild beasts finished in an explosion of their life essences: the blond inside his runaway, and the brunet covering them both with his own. A battle to the finish, they both won.

Sore and slightly disoriented, Ted pushed away from the bruising kiss, finally to meet the stare of those excited, human, green eyes. He sat on top, still impaled by David's searing spear. It filled him with more pleasure than he remembered; and now he had missed more time with his Knight and his ready lance of passion. If his heart gave out now, he would be forever satisfied. A sudden gush of euphoric proportions went off inside him, and he jerked and shrieked uncontrollably, frantically bobbing up and down, rubbing David's ebbing cock unmercifully against his all-too-sensitive rectum. Another convulsion trembled through his body; and he threw his head back, closed his eyes, and moaned low and long. The blue eyes opened wide with rapture, again feeling David harden, gushing his essence into his cavern and over the intruder. He fell limp on top of the brutally scarred chest.

"Wow! Man, that hardly ever happens, let alone twice. What a rush!"

"I think I'm jealous. You get such a hell of an orgasmic experience. Since I've had little to do lately, I've been reading about this phenomenon. It's a rarity to feel, but it does happen; only with the right technique and interior body sensitivity. Guess you can thank me for having the touch. Apparently, even straight males experience the sensation, but are oblivious unless their partner is erotic enough to play. Very few can release the pleasure like you. Tell me what it feels like?" Captivated by the erotic physical incongruity, David happily enjoyed being the recipient of feeling both his and his lover's semen trickle along his penis in this position. Although never liking the act of being taken up his arse, he had allowed it with the man who skyrocketed him into notoriety; but this pleasure he never felt. He began to rethink it might be fun to try.

"Awesome!" Ted rolled off, and whimpered at the loss of the intruder.

"Did I hurt you? I think your burn is worse from the mauling."

"Yeah, but it felt sensational. Are you okay?" A hand caressed the nasty scar, covering a good deal of David's chest.

"Couldn't feel better. Should be calling you Tiger, not Baby Bear. You sure can use those nails and teeth to advantage, not to mention you almost swallowed my nipple. One's already messed up; I don't need to lose another. You feel incredible, taste delicious, and I've missed you so much, Ted." David turned his head to gaze into the reasons he had adorned this man's finger with a precious sapphire. Too striking for a man, yet now, after the lust had settled, David could only see the skeleton he could have broken in his haste to satisfy himself.

"I missed you, my Knight, although I tried not to. Sometimes I'd be fishing or walking, and I'd just start dreaming about you. Proves I can't live without you, Sir David."

"Didn't do a very good job of rushing to your rescue. Was that what you wanted, your White Knight fantasy?"

"Don't know. Maybe. One thing, I can't find the words for, is how amazing it is to have you inside me. I feel so empty when we're not connected physically; but I guess that's not possible."

"Emptiness is a good word. It does ache, feeling the loss when I slip out of you, but we'd have nothing to look forward to, if permanently attached. Maybe I'll buy you a butt plug, as a belated birthday present."

"How gross is that? Sorry, I only want you in there."

"Joking aside, I'm glad you're back, and willing to try again."

"In the two years since we met, we've both changed. Can we accept that, David?" The anxious blue eyes emphasized the all-important question both men needed to know.

"All we can do is try, and try harder than ever." The mischievous blond gave him a tickle in exchange for a soft giggle he longed to hear. "So, no butt plugs, and the roses have to go."

"Definitely. It has to change. Maybe I'm the only one who has to start again, and like women, redecorating is a form of a new start. We have to become wildly vibrant and alive again. I want to laugh, sing, dance, and run, David; my head filled with something besides death, gods, and mysterious forces. Let's not name the Canyon anything, except home."

"Welcome home, Teddy Bear. Welcome home."

"Happy anniversary, my Knight."

"Are you calling me Oscar?" David chuckled happily.

"Never; he doesn't have your equipment that seems to be reacting to a slow... gentle..." Ted giggled happily; and the ravishment began again.

CHAPTER 56

The Knight won the Spirit so battered, and the Teddy Bear mended a fractured heart. Still loved, still adored by all, Ted came home, gathering his will to resolve the next set of problems. With a great deal of trepidation, two men started over, down a long list of things to be done. For the present, a cool bath for one's burns, and a warm shower for the other, brought both into a known routine. The older man had a surprise to help the red skin, if his returned runaway could forgive further. Clothes left behind were too large, but with a cotton sweater tucked into his softest pants, they sufficed. Much to his distaste, they were faded blue, but preferable over white or black; his old orange, extremely oversized T-shirt, however, lightened his mood. In honor of Ted's request for change, David discarded his signature ensemble of black for navy blue and sunshine yellow: a bright start.

The next step had both men perspiring and a little distracted. Holly came first, being the child who understood the least. Coming around the stables, with David at his heels, Ted halted abruptly when he saw her. His fears evaporated into the dry desert air with the vision of sweetness of his special daughter, quietly daydreaming and doing what little girls did with their horses, playing and being loved in return. With little stacks of straw, meticulously piled in intricate patterns for no reason, they gave her something to do until her Daddy loved her again. Ted and David watched for a moment, while Shu stood protecting the child between his muscled legs. He stood eying Bastet's misguided rider who drew closer.

At the sound of Ted's hesitant stutter, Holly jumped up, ran to greet him, leapt threw the air into his outstretched arms, and grasped him around the neck before he knew it. Their tears mingled, each saying nothing. Kissing and hugging made love return immediately; forgiveness granted unconditionally. Neither man nor the child could relinquish the embrace of a bond solidified long ago in a Gothic, haunted manor. It remained a mystery as to how it had been broken. Of no matter now, Ted saw only love in those familiar eyes and beguiling smile; and Holly could see her daddy's love in the same fashion, perhaps deeper.

Set down gently, Miss LaCoix scrutinized the man up and down. With no discussion, she turned him around, pushed him forcibly toward the house, while studying his slow, awkward movements. A head of longer, silken, blonde tresses shook in annoyance; and her dad grinned his wickedest, waiting gleefully for a small miracle. Ted first refused; but the leaning stance, the tilt of the head, the hands placed determinedly on her hips, and her foot tapping impatiently, his daughter meant business. Without any further argument, the frail body hoisted itself onto the sprawling, dining room table, laid back, and closed sapphire eyes to wait for who knew what. The cooling sensation came as an appreciated surprise from tiny healing hands, smelling of fresh straw, just above his face. Holly took the burning away, magically clearing his skin of scorching redness and oozing blisters, from his forehead to his heels. Without touching him and through his clothes, she soothed with immense power. She had Quinlan's hands.

"Thanks Honey. You can get up Ted, and take a look."

Stumbling over to a mirror, he stood amazed to see the golden tan on his face. Pulling at the collar of his T-shirt, he peaked under to see the same coloration down his chest. The hurting burn and the broken blisters left nary a mark. Holly was a healer, and a good one. "Thanks, Sweetheart. Who taught you this new power?"

"Sir Lancelot."

"Excuse me?"

"Think about it, Ted--a male Spirit Keeper--with an English accent."

"Well, I'm glad your bear means so much to you, and is such a smart critter." Ted turned to wink at her, only to see the face turn sullen again. "Did I say something wrong?"

"No, but you're bleeding inside and have broken bones not healed yet. Why don't you mend them, Daddy?"

"Damn, Ted, I did hurt you. Why didn't you say something?"

"And spoil the moment? Besides, I rather enjoyed the role of a turkey wishbone." Ted grinned bashfully, fully ashamed Holly knew of his bleeding rectum and the location of possible fractures. "Don't worry; I'll tend to them later."

"Finally, after all this time, you admit to your capability of healing and the knowledge of *how to*. If I remember your startling revelation correctly, you and your brothers cure your minor ailments. Moreover, the nurse in England said you didn't need the casts. Damn, Ted, you sped up the healing process: a true self-healer. I wonder if you can rejuvenate any part of your body." David's imagination fully powered up; his smile of amazement lit up the tense but erotic day.

"I don't plan cutting my finger off to see if it will grow back, thank you very much. Let's leave that trick to salamanders. The minor things we cope with, sort of. Whatever it is I do, I guess it helped my severe injuries. Now, if you guys give me time, I'll take care of these minor annoyances later. My rejuvenating ability comes with the aid of a lot of sunshine; and I think I understand why. Now, we have other things to do." Ted started walking away, his scrawny body barely able to walk a straight line. He did not want this conversation, and he managed with what he knew. At the age of six, he had his first experience in mending one of his many breaks; and he got through those agonies without anyone's knowledge. Unfortunately, the scars remained, particularly his grotesquely distorted shoulder, and yet he understood how to rectify them as well. Believing he would never return, he had not bothered, and now he grew weary of blocking his thoughts and newly discovered skills from his family, and more importantly, from Lavender. He would rethink his reluctance, once fully established within the circle, if allowed. Until such a moment, he remained hidden, for the most part.

"You do have powers. You're just afraid of them." Holly's voice showed annoyance

"No more talk of powers, Holly, but thank you for healing my sunburn. What each of us can do remains a secret; and the few I may have will seldom be used."

"Then you'll let yourself keep hurting. Why don't you help yourself?" A valid question brought tears to the child's eyes; and she turned to her dad, weeping into his neck as he scooped her up. Growing taller, and a little heavy for him, while still recuperating, he embraced any sign of a childish side and reinforced it.

"Hush, Honey. Daddy just got home, so let's not make this an unhappy day with so many tears." David squeezed his little blonde clone, and then set her down to help dry the somber face. He looked up at Ted who wiped away the emotional signs with his bare arm, shifted uncomfortably back and forth, and looked down to watch his feet without fainting.

"I'm sorry, Sweetheart. Let's make a deal; you save your energy for people who can't mend themselves. Please try to understand, I don't have the power to snap my fingers to make everything better. I will heal myself; just don't push, okay?" Ted rubbed his hand down over his face, to brush away the sickening feeling he wanted to avoid: the loss of freedom.

Holly walked toward him and held his hands. Looking up, she forced him to gaze into her green crystals, still serious and thoughtful. "Okay, but I know what you can do. A snap of fury sends lightning bolts. Your tears of anger create violent rainstorms that never end. The saddest tears create light gray showers, warm and gentle; and your tears of happiness, like the ones you cried before returning to us, gave us sprinkling showers filled with beautiful sunbows; the same ones you created for Dad in England."

"All right, you caught me. I can change a rainy day into a sunny one, and a bright day into a wicked storm. That's it, Holly Jane, and no medical consultations unless asked. Deal?"

"Deal. I think maybe..."

"Did she learn this from you? You both drive me crazy, never finishing a thought unless it's dragged out of you." David looked sternly at his bemused lover who shrugged, and at a little girl deep in contemplation.

"I stopped because Daddy doesn't want to hear anymore, but I'll finish."

"Good." David had his hands on his hips, doing the LaCoix tilt.

"No." Ted clenched his fists to his sides, dancing the Barrett shuffle.

"Let me finish, Daddy. I think your power is in the creation of things. When he doesn't have anything to do, he creates his own..." She shook her hand as if it would bring out the word she grappled for.

"...misery." Ted sadly filled in the blank of a truth shot into his heart. If not working on something new, his mind collapsed into an abyss of self-destruction. He could generate chaos as readily.

"Perhaps it's the reason you desire to rearrange our surroundings, Ted. Life in the wild is one of constant change, drastic change, and daily. Man, you must have suffocated in your former world." David sympathized with him, but was also surprised at his daughter's insightfulness.

"I had my escape in gardening and climbing. It made the gray disappear; changing it into another place I could dream about." Ted's smile seemed *all-knowing*; and it was noticed. There were many things, which Barrett understood and hid; David would play this particular game.

"You've lived in different realities all your life and only now confessing your secrets. Some are rather blatant, Baby, including the Faery sitting on your shoulder." David nodded at the flimsy, yellow being, awaiting an introduction. No bigger than a damselfly, it had an attitude, standing erect with arms crossed.

"You still with me? Sorry I forgot you, Shaysha. Things happen too swiftly for me sometimes. Didn't even say good-bye to the others. It's becoming a bad habit of mine."

"Where did he find you?" David reached out a finger, as an invitation for two different species to meet.

"In the mountains, and he's an Elf. Holly's images were precise; their wings are smaller. They're also easier to understand, not quite as cryptic. Were you watching David and me? I hope you had the decency to close your eyes." A humming laugh, barely heard, came from the little creature, increasing the size of Ted's smile. His reaction seemed an everyday occurrence. Perhaps his flights of fantasy imitated Holly's; but Ted had veered from the *Beginning Again*, replaced by an unexplainable, radical need for change; and yet, there he stood, accepting the most phantasmal of magic: a bright yellow Elf on his shoulder. His paradigm may have shifted to allow certain possibilities through, but not all.

"Well, Shaysha, you are a welcome new entity to our family. You'll have to show him around, Holly, and teach him the knock rule."

"Nice to meet you, Shaysha; and I'm glad you brought Daddy home. I missed him so much."

"Thanks, Sweetheart, I love you too." Ted did not say *yea* or *nay* to his permanent return, waiting on the whim of another; but his laugher brightened them all, as he whisked his diminutive friend away, to fly off for a cooling drink, and on to visit Bastet.

"I have an idea. If you ever want to leave us again; we'll find something new for you to do." Holly and David joined Ted's gaiety. Clapping her hands together, the child already had a plan to keep him occupied, to help Mr. Kincaid create *Oberon, the King*. Having fallen away, Ted's genius for design, and knowledge of Steven's vision, would ensure its fruition.

Back in the heart of his blonde daughter, and she in his, Ted headed for the nursery, accompanied by an equally nervous LaCoix. "Before we go in, Ted, promise me you'll see her for who she is. I also started a scrapbook of you, including Willow. I would have given it to her someday, and now I can, if you can forgive."

Ted teared up and received a hug of confidence, before slowly opening the door. Waiting tentatively, he looked around for her, and immediately thought this should be the first room to redo. Spotting her caused a little intake of air; no longer a baby, he had missed his daughter's most treasured moments. A heart wanted to fall out and smash to the floor, as his raven-haired cutie pulled clothes from her lower drawers. Having heard her father's demands, she picked out only her black outfits and tossed them toward the trash, willing to sacrifice her favorite color just for him. She felt his presence, sensed his sorrow, and smelled his scent. Turning slowly, Ted's little girl faced her father, sending a shock wave straight through him. Willow's eyes, sparkling of fire sapphires, had changed to those of a cat in structure. They remained the same wondrous dark blue and were larger than Ted's, but it caught him off guard, and fright came back instantly.

She smiled at the distressed, quivering man, and with great excitement and expectation, she ran to him without a stumble. He had her in a moment of time, never to feel as grateful again. She loved him in spite of his madness, sending him thoughts so pure and innocent, he could only cry with her. Two minds met and understood all in a flash. Electricity filled the air with messages back and forth, and not a word spoken to disturb the energy, except for the last few uttered aloud. "I'll always love you, Willow."

David left them alone, to find his own father for much needed guidance. Overexertion, sexually and emotionally, had him hanging onto the wall with one hand and stumbling blindly through the hanging wisteria. A memory of acceptance, and a body pushing against his, had him smiling at the picture, discounting the painful lacerations Ted had inflicted upon him in more places than his back. Chuckling at the lustful, erotic welcome, he treasured every hidden scratch and bite received. They would disappear, quicker than his horrendous chest scar, under the skilled hands of his daughter. Arriving at the guest quarters, Jake met him; and David released his anxieties within protective arms, spilling his tears into an older father's neck.

"It's okay, son. He's back, and he'll stay. Let it out, so you can get on with life that is back to overflowing. He didn't mean to hurt you and the children. Our Ted is as much a confused child as Holly; but we all love him. He's had his run; now he will stay." Jake held his son, rocking him gently and smoothing the blond silk with a light massage. The senior LaCoix had not done this in thirty years; but his forty-five year old boy needed him now, and the special touch of a doting, understanding father.

Daphne, Jake, and David strolled in from the gardens, just as Ted and his girls made their way carefully down the few steps. A happy reunion, Ted clung for long precious minutes within Jake's manic hug, and then a gentler embrace by a tearful Daphne. It became more joyous with the excited staff, offering cheek kisses, body hugs, and handshakes. Life started anew with an order for Paulo to change the garden under Ted's direction, and to pick up paint samples. The gardener laughed, promising he would have dirt and paint under the runaway's nails before dinner every night. Playing in the mud again put a larger grin on the tanned, freckled face. All agreed happily, and life began anew. Awakening Canyon was no more. It would be Home for them all; and it would forever be changing. Paulo removed the sign before the pop of a champagne cork and its contents shared; an anniversary party commenced.

With the house and gardens being modified, costumes and sets revamped, old acquaintances forgiven for taking sides, Ted returned to a ray of sunshine. It shone from the blue sapphire, embedded within a smooth, shiny, platinum band, and an inscription inside, never to be revealed. With his own plans of creation in mind, the family agreed to give him some solitude to work on his mystery project. His self-confidence rose tenfold; and he and David started fresh as the new spring green of an English countryside.

The Thurgoods moved into their new sprawling abode, created by Ted's newly discovered powers of materialization. Along with Joseph and Steven, the Barrett brothers and wives also returned, with a new edition of a newborn boy. All entered with joyful smiles and intense greetings for their runaway brother and friend. Now together, the Canyon became a massive family home, with enough space for privacy.

Special daughters became little girls with Ted's innocent presence; and they grew in maturity daily, but at a slower pace. It pleased both fathers. Back to watching cartoon melodramas every Saturday morning, in front of the forgotten television, they cheered on the good guys and sent raspberries to the bad. Two puppies from the animal shelter soon joined the mix, along with the purchase of a dozen Frisbees. They all played, chased, yelled, laughed aloud, and they did it together, chasing away the constant revelation of spiritual thought, which had nearly destroyed Ted. The shock of the rockslide had initiated a bombardment of awareness rammed into the unprepared younger man, with only fear and little fun. The proclaimed Powers-That-Be had not taken their time with the one who had to make the most dramatic change. A cruel beginning for one so tender, they had to regain his trust and forgiveness; if not, Theodore Barrett, when he put it all together, had powers to destroy the planet with a thought. Only one knew whom Ted may be, and took great care to nurture him with more logical thinking and training. Quinlan Ambrose hovered over Ted, while the Mistress continued to envelop David in her mystic cloud.

One last interview, in their Home, by the same woman, would be their last public appearance. Even for *Oberon, the King*, the contract stated no publicity merry-go-round. The picture became their last acting performance, along with renewed and forgiven friends, with major character assignments for them all. Quinlan Ambrose, since he requested to do one more film, would be the kind Sorcerer, of all the realms of the tiny ones. Ethan Peerce, forgiven by Steven, who now understood the motifs of this immortal being of light, played the villainous Elf who coerced with the King of the Elves. Steven Kincaid-Thurgood became the creator of his own future, by producing the magical film, which hit heights unimaginable, in earth's reality. Theodore Barrett-LaCoix (the last name now permanent) desired one last fling at his second love of acting, starring as Oberon, the King of the Faeries. David LaCoix knew the significance of each man he had fused together, with patience and understanding, became the mad King of the Elves, under the supervision of Shaysha. Five mega-stars collided in a cosmic celebration of magic on the screen, and Steven Kincaid lived happily-ever-after with his Love Doctor, while his fame and rewards drowned him in respect. The group's last picture became another grand success story: Oberon was King.

Once again, around the fireplace, three people chatted about everything in a casual conversation, with no mention of the spiritual. With the girls safely in bed, they would have their turn in the future. This night, with much to ask, seemed like old news of days long past and forgotten. Subject matter included David's recently recovered Oscar, Ted's Golden Globe, the coming out of their good friend Steven Kincaid, the shooting, the surgery, Ted's heart attack, their recoveries, and their new picture earning them greater honors. All questions asked, emoted both concern and joy, were followed by honest answers. With their separation gingerly touched upon, the two men smiled and confirmed the fun of making up, and starting over.

Her final question had them both thinking. "What have you two not done since you met? It seems, for a couple re-uniting, these two and a half years have been a fireworks display of Fourth of July proportions. Awards, rescues, trials, shootings, new spiritual thought, a marriage, a separation, another Oscar winning film collecting untold gold and crystal, and your amazing children, you seem to have put a lifetime into a few years."

"I can't think of anything specifically that we haven't accomplished or at least tried, but missing time I wish I had back. David?" Ted raised his questioning eyebrows, attempting to think of something besides the extraordinary wish to climb K2 with his daughters to find Shambala. He squinted nervously at his partner's smirk. If he had not been sitting, the look would have him doing the Barrett shuffle.

"I can think of one thing we haven't done."

"Do tell, Mr. LaCoix. Come on, Gentlemen, your public awaits another surprise. If it can be shown on television, you must not disappoint us." She laughed, egging them on.

Ted sat nervously, waiting to hear what his partner had in mind. The man in question stood, walked to the entertainment unit, put on a CD, and pushed number six. A haunting instrumental, filled with romance and sensuality, of cellos, harps, and flutes, drifted through the room. A piece of celestial music, which they made love to, had Ted squirming in his chair.

"Is it too loud for the mikes?" David looked up for an answer, while his green eyes sparkled with a dare. With a confirmation that Audio picked it up, LaCoix hit the repeat button for six, and the music floated through the house and out into the night. Long strides strolled up to Ted, and a green-sleeved arm reached for his hand. "Mr. Theodore Barrett-LaCoix, may I have this dance?"

"What?" Stunned, Ted gingerly accepted the hand offered. Whatever David wanted, he would attempt to accommodate with his two left feet. "I've never done this in my life. I don't know how to dance."

"It's romantic, coward. Besides, you know how to shuffle without music; it's time you learned to put a few steps together, two-time Oscar winner. Listen to the music, come closer, and feel my rhythm. Now, close your eyes and float away with me." David pulled him into a light body press to feel the motion; and Ted embarrassingly conceded, attempting not to stumble. Showing elated surprise, the interviewer gently wiped away her happy tears with long-nailed fingertips. The two men merged into one, proving David a natural dancer, graceful and agile, while the smaller man melted into the steps of a slow, seductive waltz. On a whisper of a lip caress, the curtain came down on the LaCoix men. They were gone from the glory they could have claimed as their right. It no longer mattered, waltzing into oblivion, bodies held together with one strong arm, and moving to a rhythm that would always be part of their Spirits. Cameras, crew, and the interviewer vanished from their thoughts, while two men fell deeper into their own magic. The music played long into the night; and Ted learned to dance.

CHAPTER 57

"I don't remember it being so suspenseful." Ted's eyes remained glued to the credits of *Outlaw's Heart*.

"If I remember correctly, you were preoccupied with your first act of love-making and having to watch it later." David laughed, remembering the closeted virgin.

"Nothing has ever compared to those scenes. We know how they were created; and yet the world never guessed what we did as actors. Kind of fun to be remembered for such a steamy film and knowing just how sizzling it truly was." A blush still swept Ted's face after so twenty-years.

"A manifestation of the mind has yet to be discovered, plus accommodating actors and using technology to appease non-believers. Although the next generation will utilize the method, I doubt if actors will go as far as you two went." The beautiful, ageless woman, in the deep green velvet, held her forever goblet, stroking the stem with her fingers.

"You had a singular purpose for our participation, Lavender; and we thank you. Oh, shit!"

"What?" Ted looked at David, catching surprise and embarrassment on his partner's face.

"Why does this still happen to me; and I can't stop it? Since we've known each other for so long, I'll tell you this oddity. On occasion, and at the oddest times, I'm suddenly aroused; and it's such a rush. Not a normal hard-on, I feel physically fondled, as if being stroked by someone. Man, this is uncomfortable, and what a peculiar time to happen."

A goblet dropped. Heavy pewter clanked against the marble floor, ringing throughout the screening room. Ted looked at the Mistress and frowned with his best snarl, trying not to laugh. "Your Ladyship! That's what you've been doing to my partner. I finally caught you."

"Lavender what? She didn't do anything, Baby."

"Oh yes she did." Ted had the biggest grin on his face, which David had never seen. His partner's mouthful of Hollywood whites lit up the dimmed room.

"I certainly did not; a coincidence, I assure you. Now, if you two care to join me, I have a lovely anniversary dinner waiting for you, as well as a viewing of your daughters. Twenty-odd-years today, Theodore Barrett lost his virginity for the entire world to witness." The woman tried, not so subtly, to change the subject.

"Tell him Lavender, or I will; and there's no such thing as a coincidence, remember?" Ted held back his mirth with tremendous difficulty.

"You are becoming tiresome, young man."

"You've said that to me countless times over the years. I'm going to tell him what you've been doing, probably since he was a young stud?" Ted giggled uncontrollably, watching the Mistress brush off the few splatters of deep red wine that would not dare stain her dress. She looked up from under an extraordinary amount of raven curls, and flashed her cat's eyes at him, along with a sly smile.

"What are you two talking about? I hate wasting the little power I have, reading my friends' minds. Damn, it's you and that goblet!" David sat up in his chair, while his mouth dropped in honest surprise.

"Purely unintentional, I have just learned the consequences of a habit. Remember, I am part of you on occasion, David, and have come to understand that my actions stem, pardon the expression, from being your Soul. The stroking of the goblet comforts me, never realizing that I have been playing with you since puberty."

"You've been playing with me all this time?" David smirked behind his hand, withholding just how much pleasure it afforded him. The fondling made him feel particularly virile at the oddest times.

"No wonder you're such a horny bastard. I didn't drop the average; you increased it." Ted continued to chuckle from deep in his abdomen, squeezing into a ball to stop the fit of hysterical laughter.

"Shit, why didn't you just come down, in one of your many velvet gowns, and we could have done it properly? I'm appalled. And how did you know, Ted?" Trying very hard to be sincere, the bemused blond could not keep his mirth from bubbling to the surface.

"Just putting the pieces together; and she's known for some time." The younger man shrugged his shoulders in sly amusement.

"Now I can tell him of your exhibitionistic character, Theo." The Mistress snickered at the nervous feline blue eyes, knowing she had him. Friends for over two decades: learning, laughter, and good times became the norm at La Rosa Negra.

"When have I exposed myself? It's not in my character." Ted unsuccessful failed to sway her. He did not have a hope.

"Of course you have, Child. I believe you can express the pleasure you experienced better than I, considering such a blatant lie."

"Oh, you mean by the river; but it was your choice, not mine." Ted thought he won with the *choice* word; but it kept David intrigued, hearing the inflection in the voice of his grown-up twelve-year-old.

"Looking so unhappy and frightfully exposed, you begged for it. I have seen you naked dozens of times, Theodore; however, that sunny day, when perched on a large rock, you were definitely sitting the wrong way for me not to satisfy that particular human orifice of yours." The Mistress gave him a smug smile, leaned back in her chair, and rubbed her ringed fingers together.

"Okay, so who molested whom, or simply an innocent experience, like I just had? I've enjoyed the pleasure for the better part of my life, by the way." David sat back and waited in fun, watching such a powerful entity match wits with his partner over something so trivial.

"Innocent? Hardly! I think she raped me with her purple light and... Stop that!" Ted jumped out of his chair and straightened at the onrush of another attack to his rectum.

"The wonderful thing about light is it penetrates clothing, and your twitchy sphincter muscles seem to require stimulation a second time. When I finally found you, simple light manipulation up your pleasure zone, for your satisfaction, I thought appropriate. It certainly fulfilled an overdue need from your reaction."

"Actually, it felt pretty amazing. Sorry David."

"So you cheated on me: both of you." David frowned and growled at his long-time lover, then at his friend.

"You've been cheating on me; letting her stroke you like that." Acting like *Peter Pan,* who still emerged from time to time, Ted attempted to switch the wrongdoing that never was.

"Well, she is part of me. I suppose having such a loving Soul has advantages." David finally cracked up, more of an emotional release from his trying day, easing his own tension of an ending drawing closer.

"Enough on such a topic this special night, but I promise never to touch the goblet again. In fact, Mr. LaCoix, if you would be so kind as to pick it up, you can throw it into the water. As for Theo, a moment of pleasure is nothing to fret about. We shall leave it at that, and hasten to hear what Willow and Holly have to say in their first public engagement."

"I don't think I want to touch it now."

"Oh, David, really, it is only a goblet." Lavender smiled, taunting her blond Spirit, who had become her friend.

With great caution, David picked it up with one finger and a thumb, handling the object, as if covered with something more toxic than a woman's fingerprints. He straightened up and graciously held out both arms for each of his companions. They set off to see the world's official awakening of the *Beginning Again*. Strolling out amongst the gardens, the threesome took in the evening's fresh air and all the fragrances from lilacs, to jasmine, to roses, which had become the favored flower again. David's tension evaporated in the vapors, floating over the water that should not be, and absorbing the strange feeling it created. Ted had never seen the spectacle: a last surprise for his forever partner. Lapping pure clean water against a marble staircase, the water was remembered in every detail. A quick glimpse between narrowly spaced columns, he felt pleased to see no changes, except for the addition of one goblet flung into its depths, while he strolled behind the one in luscious green and the other dressed in his long, black-jacket suit. Formal attire seemed a requirement for this occasion.

A day of good-byes and new beginnings, decisions had been made; and two men hid their nervousness at what lay ahead. More disturbing, their last farewell to their grown daughters, hours earlier, broke both hearts. They had taught them well; their girls now faced the world with a power beyond mortals. Tonight would be their last sight of them.

After *Oberon, the King* had wrapped, the couple vanished from public view. Their films, particularly the last four, were now classics; and David had his own cult following, with one of his many movies shown every minute of every day. Two legends were crowned, much to their embarrassment and gratitude. Reclusive, they never received or wanted the riotous attention one public appearance would generate; they no longer needed the adoration. With successful personal lives and retiring at the peaks of their careers, all their wishes had been granted; they only required the company of the other.

Over two decades, David had occupied his time keeping both his daughters from developing too rapidly spiritually, before they matured mentally enough to handle what lay in wait. A task he would never regret, their girls blossomed under both men's tutelage. The two watched the rest of their families expand, fulfilling all their dreams; the guest quarters filled with both the Barrett and LaCoix families, learning and understanding the *knowing*. Dr. Thurgood's continuing presence deemed necessary, teaching the children born within the Canyon, while Kincaid commuted between here and there. Steven's awareness of the *Beginning Again* heightened, participating where and when he could, to push the rising consciousness further. With the Professor by his side, Kincaid learned to live as himself, growing up and remaining one of the more distinguished and respected actors in Hollywood. His star would shine bright until he decided to join them. Joseph Thurgood remained steady, becoming a true participant of the transformation; his future set on becoming a coveted Spirit Keeper, instructing many a wondrous human child of the Cosmos, while other work awaited Kincaid.

Until such time, Lavender left Steven safe with his savior, while drastically altering the course of his first abusive obsession, with a diabolical scheme of interference seldom used. She played a Fate and a dangerous one. Waiting for the moment, she laid to waste the famous figure, exposing the charming demon publicly through his wife, who caught him terrorizing a beautiful young man with one of his Oscars. The bloody scene, of unwanted, torturous bondage, set upon the screaming victim and the salivating madness of her husband, drove the woman to inform the tabloids with everything she knew; and she knew a great deal. Astonishingly, the wife protected Kincaid's involvement, however, she did unleash her abhorrence upon her now ex-mate who never received the forgiveness lavished upon other powerful names of the industry, ones who shone unscathed through their horrific, licentious misdemeanors, and very public ones at that. It remained a disgusting consequence of Hollywood's double standard. The sadist ended his life in disgrace, unable to play his dirty games with young men whom now knew of his decadence.

For the retired couple, far away from Hollywood gunfire, life swept David and Ted away, each developing their own innate skills and powers independently, to burst forth at the appropriate time. The only known fact, a promised kept would bind them together eternally, a time when their own *knowing* would push them to end their lives in Earth's reality. That time had come. With their goals achieved, and their daughters ready to start the last holy war, the couple hoped it would be a peaceful awakening for the sleeping Cosmos. They had accomplished much between here and there.

Tonight, excitement raced through strong hearts, fully healed for the Opening Night of the *Beginning Again*. Willow and Holly started on their quest. To give them a royal send off, their favorite interviewer came out of retirement, once again, to conduct a special for the *Messengers of a New Awakening*. The morning had been a crying fest for two men and their roses, with final farewells, while washing their Home clean with rain. It drizzled softly all that day and continued into the night. One difficult good-bye, the two men stared at the latest in transmission devices. Watching and listening, those expected droplets spilled forth again, while Willow spoke through Holly. All their aspirations, reasons, and warnings of future events were expressed honestly. The *Beginning Again* fell upon a waiting Cosmos.

David and Ted could not be prouder; and a firm embrace, of the Baby Bear by the Lionhearted, helped ease the pain of saying good-bye and good-luck. A beautiful voice came through the screen, with words written by their daughters to their favorite piece of music. Ted fell apart, while David held his emotions together by waltzing the shaking figure around the floor. It felt right on this special night, letting go yet holding fast.

"You both did an excellent job raising Willow and Holly. Their light shines through. Come and we shall feast, while discussing your upcoming journey. The sadness is over; new joys await. The girls can protect themselves, so there is no need to worry; they have armies, from outside sources, ready to defend them and their ideals." Lavender flicked off the viewing screen and turned toward the courtyard, leading to their dinner and the wondrous lake.

"Well, that just scared the hell out of me. Thank you for topping off this stressful day. Show me; I need proof before we leave." LaCoix, having protected their innocence for so long, heard alarms going off. He had hoped the mind-shattering signals would stop after so many years.

"David, you are one for details. Do you not remember a statement you made: *blood would flow before Earth could heal*? Sometimes I wonder if you are a true believer in all you have witnessed; and the explanations you gave in front of millions. Do you want to see this, Ted? I do not think you are prepared to witness your daughters' capabilities." A very distinct warning dimmed the usually melodic voice, which charmed and seldom threatened.

"I don't know; if something goes awry. You've only shown me current things in distant places, never the future." The man looked and acted frightened; he knew instinctively he had reason to be.

"If it's the future, we'll know soon enough. Come on, Lavender, I need assurance that the Barrett-LaCoix girls can handle themselves in a tight situation."

"Things can change, but I will show you six-months from now. They are on tour in France; and it is a wondrous spring morning for spreading the word of choice, and what is to be." The sky above the sea opened, and a different time and place spread before them; a lush garden bloomed with bright new colors. Feeling as if they were present, David and Ted stood high above the large crowd, waiting in anticipation for the regal, fair-haired young woman to speak. She started eloquently, welcoming all, and began her carefully chosen words in perfect French. Ten minutes into the *knowing,* of the light and the dark, a familiar sound cracked the air. Ted shrieked, unable to take a breath with the remembered abomination, and was instantly grabbed, held by a man whose eyes grew bigger and more fearful.

David's beautiful daughter, of earth's new dawning, had been shot. In an instant flash of hot angry light, the White Rose shone in her purest form, and hurled herself in a blazing ray at the assailant in the crowd. Ted's raven-haired beauty quickly raised a finger, looking straight at the man knocked down by the white flash. Willow vanquished him with a thought, using her element of fire, to scorch the perpetrator into a charred human-like form. An agonizing death, dying from the outside in, no light came from the ash remains, to rise as a new enlightened force into the blue sky above. The former human blew away as if he had never been.

Onto the next bullet fired harmlessly into the air, thanks to the lightning strike of the White Rose. Willow terminated the person instantly with her deadly finger of fire. Again, only a charred body turned to dust and the element of air swept it away. A certainty to David, this man and woman would not be entering any realm the two men had witnessed. Lavender confirmed the High Council's new philosophy. With their Spirits and bodies vanquished, by one of the *Beginning Again*, all their past-life Spirits were forfeited along with them. The sequence of events, from the starting of a new Spirit, Soul, and Higher Self, to its last moment, ended with these two, negating any violent traits to pass on to another generation, or to be released into the tranquility of an unaware dimension. They were simply gone.

The white light lashed out again, spotting another sniper targeting the Black Rose. The fire in Willow did its destructive job, and those wondrous sapphire orbs opened wide to scan the crowd for more weapons. Two people ran, only to be caught in a web spun by Holly in search of destructive manmade forces. Only finding frightened witnesses, she gently soothed their hearts and let them go, to settle back down unafraid.

David stood in shock, while firmly holding Ted in his tirade of screaming to stop his daughter and to cry in grief over the demise of his eldest one. Willow could not hear him in the future; and yet in her heart, she would know the disappointment of her fathers; it could not be any other way. To both men's amazement, the white glimmer turned into sunbows; and the elegant container, known as Holly Jane, reappeared unscathed. Her voice became her father's mesmerizing low growl to warn the crowd. Another shock had David reeling; their daughters were already light entities.

"Wanton disrespect of another's pathway, along with other fanatical and sociopathic behavior, in the *Beginning Again*, means immediate retaliation. It will be harsh and violent, if it comes to the terrorism you just witnessed. Premeditated murder, of any living creature, shall not be tolerated, on this glorious planet called home. We cannot allow this trait in humanity to continue, to carry into the Cosmos, and let loose upon unsuspecting life forms. Beware to all; there will be chaos and devastation during the transformation into the *Beginning Again*; before we all speak telepathically and dance in the winds of other realms in peace. You make your own choice; and you have time. We do not ask you to believe in something foreign. Follow through with honorable goals, and be open to the alternatives presented. There are many diverse ways to secure your future with the *knowing* as your guide. It is beyond the façade of beliefs our fragmented cultures have forced us to endure; and generation-by-generation, more of us will see into that shining light and meet the entities hidden in our own world and those beyond. Go in peace, my friends. Learn what is to come from these Unreachables." The girls vanished in two bright rays of light, shooting skyward into the blue, creating whispers of awe amongst their audience. David held onto a sobbing Ted, as Lavender released the future. It would be their daughters' first battle.

"They can't be hurt, can they? They're immortal, just as you are." David's shock intensified, surging through every DNA molecule; he could not stop shaking. His hands quivered, trying to hold Ted's head tight against his frantically beating heart.

"Yes, David, as are you and Theo. That will be Willow and Holly's first rejection. The after-speech was not quite appropriate or truly accurate, but little does it matter at this point. They will handle the next, and the next, with far better words and careful thought."

"No, it can't be; not again. Willow's not a killer. My treasures wouldn't hurt anyone."

"Remember, my Child, Willow strengthened her premature body on her own; and when isolated, she used fire against the rat attacking her. Your daughter understood the *knowing* when only a few months old; she had to aid you, retaining her bruises for the court to see, only to make them disappear when given to you officially. She is *the fire* and *the will* behind the *Beginning Again*."

Ted already grieved the future they had set goals to obtain, not wishing to hear more of his daughter's abilities. It left Lavender to consider whether to grant or dismiss the wish of two roses placed within the Faery rings. Falling away and out of the arms of David LaCoix, Ted stood on the precipice. The last part of the game commenced; it would be Ted's final awakening and admittance.

CHAPTER 58

Lavender's rare ambrosia tasted better with each sip; and the three friends sat quietly on the steps, just staring, unblinking at the horizon of golden water touching a dark sky full of Christmas tree lights. The green velvet gown had turned black, to match the Mistress's change in mood, upsetting both men further. David tipped back his first glass of the precious liquid, and downed the priceless contents in a series of gasping swallows. Ted watched the old habit of steadying the man's nerves with alcohol, while his comfort lay in his lover's hand unceasingly stroking his head, or gripping tightly to his arm. He could not believe what they had started so many years ago, only to come into force this day. Now, his concentration diverted to a greater concern, which he and his partner had to prepare for, and not looking back at what they had just witnessed. Imperative to pull himself together, after crying every human tear he had left for his daughters, something else irked at Ted; something seemed amiss; his hidden secrets of twenty-years told him to duck.

"Are you all right, Theodore?"

"Yes ma'am; just thinking." Like his partner, the younger man felt turmoil brewing, but had to put words together before he could reveal his misgivings of this night.

"I am sorry to have upset you with what may be. What of you, David?"

"You gave us another shock; nothing new about that." Also anxious of what he had seen, LaCoix could not stop shaking. No one should witness the death of their child, only to have that child resurrect herself before your eyes. With a deep breath, to steady his distress, he turned to aid his partner, who needed nurturing to bring love back into his life and new reality. Now in La Rosa Negra, they waited for their promised last instructions and answers. He hoped the rest of the evening would take on a lighter tone, to celebrate good memories in fun, just as the evening had started. It disturbed the older man, however, to see the color change of her Ladyship's gown, which meant a detour and a foreboding one.

Ted tried to open Lavender's mind to him, with an innocuous question. "What is this lake? I sense some importance to you. Feels like a pulling force; and yet, the force is not unwelcome; nor does it need to pull you in." Barrett expressed something David had been unable to do, and did it on his first viewing of the wondrous sea of subtly changing colored mirrors. The younger man felt some peace looking into and across the water, gathering heightened power. Now an urgent need to find the truth, the still very youthful looking man needed to tread carefully this night. Seeing his daughter made him vulnerable in some manner; he readied himself with whatever gifts he possessed. With David's arm around him, he slowed his heart rate and calmed the urge for further emotional release.

"There are many names for the Crossing, Theo, but the other side is of greater importance. Some call the water the Golden Chasm, and the other side Shambala, Shangri-la, the Elusion Fields, Atlantis, the Void, even Heaven. My personal favorite is Avalon."

"You told me Heaven didn't exist." Tentatively Ted spoke, waiting to hear her Ladyship's melodic voice, while gathering his inner resolve to leave that night.

"No, I suggested there may be something higher than heaven and something far worse than hell, remembering they are only names, with mystical imagery surrounding them. Your world, particularly the last 40,000 Earth years, deems a living hell for most. The first people of the *knowing* left earth for elemental reasons; and from the moment of their departure, the Cosmos lost its perfect paradise."

"Who were the first people? Neanderthals certainly couldn't have been part of them, since I read they survived for 250,000 years. It seems too long a time." Ted drew in more energy to be what Lavender expected: someone unafraid to ask. David, meanwhile, hoped the answers would not destroy years of learning.

"Neanderthals were a different species, but certainly close to primitive man who were the scattered remnants of the ones of the *knowing*, or who had contact with their culture. We call the ancients Atlanteans that once crisscrossed your globe, even mating with primitive man, as did Neanderthals, thus the explanation for blond or redheaded, blue or green-eyed humans. As Holly suggested, the Ancients spoke telepathically and could travel on a thought, because they did not evolve from Earth's microorganisms. Your historians and archaeologists have tunnel vision when it comes to humankind's chronological evolution, unable to comprehend that each piece of the puzzle, which they have gathered, comes from every corner of your world, and they belong to one culture: Atlantis."

"They left because of climatic and environmental reasons; and Earth became hell for the survivors. I thought our world had stabilized by that time. How did they leave?" David let Ted speak, allowing his lover's mind to wander away from what they had just witnessed, with a teaching distraction. The three talked about many things over twenty-years, but this piece of history had been touched on only briefly.

"Very astute of you, Theo. Like all planets, Earth continues to pass through readjustments of sorts; like one takes a heavy breath and pauses, and then to repeat the action. A treacherous time of volcanoes, earthquakes, and violent winds created the cataclysm, along with a change in Earth's elemental forces. Survivors forgot their natural, intuitive knowledge, fragmenting all over the planet. Staying alive and continuing to repopulate became foremost; and your idea of hell would have fit their situation. Few were happy; their choices limited. Now, with over seven billion humans populating earth, only the strong can set high goals, but struggle to maintain their footing, and thus their futures. Once again, Earth is under attack; but you know this, learning to manifest a thought to help. As for the original Atlanteans, they left as they came, changing back into light."

"Just as we are about to do."

"A human changing into light is new for us, but very important. When you both desire to use your containers, they will remain with you, but taken care of differently, as they must remain alive."

"And who keeps are bodies alive?" Ted inquired.

"You shall, within your light-form, along with the non-living shells that you will create."

David said nothing, pondering on his acceptance of this new reality. Perhaps, he would not survive the change. Alive because of miracles, he looked and felt too young to give up on the crumbling planet. Barrett, thirteen years his junior, seemed more secure in his silent way. Roles had reversed.

"What about evil Spirits? They die as well. Do they get to reap the benefits of such a place as heaven?" Ted slipped, forgetting an important lesson due to shock over Willow's lethal power.

"It is not the place you perceive it to be, only a starting point, Child, with no pearly gates, and no gatekeeper called Peter. As I said, the Council deemed it inappropriate to pollute the *Awakening,* of the Cosmos, with Unreachables, as is the case with all *knowing* cultures of the universe. They shall be dealt with; the responsibility left to their home planet to weed them out. Before this day, of new beginnings and the changing of rules by members of the Cosmos, they did pass through Avalon, as all beings do, but taken care of in a different manner. In the future, we will not have to deal with such entities so disturbed mentally. The *Beginning Again* is happening throughout the Cosmos; and again, as Holly stated, evil behavior, for lack of a better term, will be perceived and detected early, enabling healers to sort out the problem Spirits before they become a menace. Villains, unwilling to be tolerant and non-destructive, shall be terminated, without a reprieve, as will the zealots of a potential holy war, for they will not believe in the power that could defend them. Besides reducing the current population of your planet, it also benefits us. There lies the choice. It will take many generations, before this rights itself, in all realms. Your daughters have shown you; and I explained what happens after a potential murderer dies."

"What kind of choice is that: submit or die? Who is *Us*? A question I seem to be repeating." Appalled at the finality of deadly retribution, by this entity he thought he knew, David was lost in disbelief.

"The choice is to follow a true, ethical path. It does not matter if I call Avalon Shambala or Heaven; it remains the same place of mystery, understood by few, untouched by decadence, unto itself in every way. It does not matter if I call us the Powers-That-Be, or God, or Allah, or the Universal Mind, it remains the same force, differing only in erroneous linguistics and false imagery. When people get past the name confusion, the hatred will stop; the populace will agree to listen to their own beliefs and knowledge, not just the words taught. Interpretations will differ, but worthy of friendly discussion, with no hidden agenda to change someone else's inner *knowing*. As you predicted, David, religious orders will collapse. Each being maintains full control over their chosen path, undisturbed by the Fates, faulty teaching, false prophesies, and misinterpreted terminology. Discussions, not sermons, will open doors to turn at the correct junction; revelations will induce one to fit the next piece into their own puzzle. You two have been doing this for twenty-years. I dare say you have learned a great deal in that time."

"You're avoiding the main issue. You said *Us*. Okay, Lavender, who are you? Let's finish this." David wanted full disclosure, to his list of many questions, with little time to go slowly.

Ted listened intently; a sudden cold shiver swept through him. He drew closer to his partner. Something was stirring and changing, besides himself and his Knight. Their serene Mistress seemed to be tensing, growing in stature and anger.

"Oh, David, I am a Caretaker, in whatever context you deem appropriate."

"Not good enough. You introduced me to a few of the Powers-That-Be, after the shooting; and now you've added God and Allah. Should we add Caretaker to the list? I need more definitive answers." David grew more insistent, coming close to conclusions that he may not be prepared to accept.

"Have I ever claimed to be anything but one of many? If you wish to know if I have been to Avalon, yes I have. If you want to know of my abilities, that is only for me to know. How old am I? To be honest, I do not know. Time is irrelevant. Life did not start from the moment you believe your god decided to create Earth (just another billiard ball to play with on his vast pool table), nor from your astronomers' meandering, indecisive ideas. Once the *Beginning Again* takes hold, we will no longer have to disguise our identities. We are simply a different life form; light beings who gather energy from every bright star in the galaxy. With plenty to share now, we can go about our own lives. It has been a very long wait for this coming, but it will release us from some of our duties to the Cosmos and the Beyond. My goals were not established by my own free will, like many humans; and there lies my problem and future."

"You are immortal, Lavender, so don't feed me bullshit. Your future goes on to infinity; you probably don't need goals." David finally lashed out.

"We all require the awareness of what we want, need, and how to achieve it. Many of us, just like humans, have appointed duties; and that is the end of the tale." Lavender looked away, allowing the exposition of her own paradoxical situation to anger one and bewilder the other.

"Excuse me, but I have a different question. If everyone turns to light, and can go anywhere, who stays on earth?" The timid man-child returned; and years of learning seemed to evaporate, while his powers of deduction flew away across the mirrored sea. The brilliant actor, he had become, continued to put on a front of gullibility for the others, or at least he hoped. These incidental questions were of concern only to him.

"Many will stay, for it is a familiar environment. Humans will always be, in structure and form, continuing to care for Earth and raise human children, until ready to depart. Some will wish to remain in their containers for a longer time, afraid of losing the intimacy of their partner and family. With other entities arriving, and other dimensions surrounding and within your world, carrying on in the same manner, it is simply a choice. A great deal of mixing and learning of different life forms starts the forgiving and forgetting of past cruelties. I cannot say tigers will stop hunting prey, for that is their way, and the way of their prey: Natural Law. It is not for man to hunt tigers for sport, or to decrease their numbers, which infers murder in Earth's future. If a man, himself, is being charged by the tiger, it then becomes his right of self-defense."

"And what if man attacks man, like our daughters?"

"Willow and Holly will defend themselves against those who wish them harm and act to prevent their demise, thus turning your daughters into the tigers being hunted. The future of a premeditated murderer is inevitable; but we believe such occurrences shall be rare, as the new era progresses and telepathic links correct such pathological incapacitations."

"You mentioned children. What happens to those who die very young? It seems that they have not advanced into *the knowing* until they've learned as much as an adult. You didn't show us a nursery, in which human children can become light."

Lavender looked down, knowing her next words would upset both men. She had never told a lie, but this question required an obscure answer. "You are correct, Theo; children do not have the experience or knowledge to make them even Spirit Guides or Keepers. The Council is pondering the question as we speak."

"You term them to dust! Just like that! How could you ignore children?"

"Have faith, Theo, as there are so many things you do not know about the Cosmos. You must wait, see, and learn, before speculating on such a difficult question."

"So, you won't tell me. I've a strange feeling about your actions, Lavender."

David finally realized the truth in the statement and tried to continue the conversation, without a revelation about human children dying too young or of stillbirth. It was all too much. "Can we at least assume you will give us an answer when we turn to light?"

"Of course, but now is not the time to worry about things of which you know nothing."

Ted switched gears, not wishing to hear something that would drive him into sudden madness. "A really stupid question then: do we eat, or do we just spend time under the sun?" He still had relevant questions for their future, which Lavender was unable to read. His back and forth questions, from a seer to a child, gave him the opportunity to fill the missing pieces.

"It is your dream come true, Child. The energy abounding from your sun will nourish you. If it is inadequate, try the next star for sustenance. You have survived all these years, even when you were not eating, because your growing light entity required only Arizona sunshine to prosper. It saved you from the demons of your childhood, although conversely, it created your horrendous inner pain."

"This is getting weirder by the minute. I'm trying, Lavender, but this seems very far-fetched. What are these realms that exist on earth, and who will Holly and Willow be running into? Who's fighting with whom?" David's turn to forget the magic he lived in for twenty-years; the Mistress faced a difficult decision.

"You already know the many wars humanity continues to endure for one cause or another, usually based on different ideology, or financial gain of important resources. Future battles shall be between species and entities recorded in fanciful tales, some currently unknown by mankind. This new *Awakening* will consume everyone and everything, with no looking back. Your world has many realms existing simultaneously, only in another form, dimension, whatever the term you wish. Your Home is like La Rosa Negra, ever changing and moving through space. Again, linguistics gets in the way; and humans do not have the correct words. An example may help: you are sitting in a park, smelling the sweetness of a rose, and decide to visit another realm of your world. With a thought, you transport to a treacherous mountain terrain, populated with giant-sized entities who can withstand the cold and hostile environment. Seeing a human, for perhaps the first time, but being of the *knowing*, they will welcome you; give you shelter and warmth, until you are ready to leave. Understanding will come through telepathic thought; and who knows, one may return the visit, to smell roses for the first time."

"Now you're being trite." David scolded, in his attempt to comprehend Lavender's words. They seemed to be scattered all over the map this last night; and for one who usually accepted her explanations, even he had problems keeping pace.

"No, because it exists as a possibility. Remember feeling a shudder of a cold breeze lasting a second; the feel of someone brushing against you when no one is there; or a door suddenly opens and slams shut. Two entities pass; unaware they have encountered the touch of another life form, in a different time and space. A portal, between two of Earth's realms, opens for a brief moment, and neither can take advantage of it. Soon it will change; the door forever left ajar." Lavender watched the wheels turn in David's head, and turned to the man-child shuffling his feet.

"What's the greater good of all this? It doesn't make sense for people to bustle around, flitting here and there, and not doing anything productive. None of them will have a purpose; and with humans, I think it's an integral part of who they are. At least that's what we've learned through reading science-fiction." Ted illustrated his new powers, but covered them with his childish reference.

Her young friend's concern, for feelings and needs, gave Lavender hope he understood. Things had to have a purpose for him; it was a very good question. She smiled at him, hearing the word *'they'*. Ted hid a great deal, showing his belief that he may be something other than human. She tried not to laugh aloud at the slip. "Remember me telling you everyone has special talents, and every entity will have its purpose, to use what they know and love best? Visits to other realms will be like taking a yearly holiday, away from chosen tasks. With things still needing doing, work continues, but differently, with a manifested thought, or manually made by one who cares enough to undertake the responsibility. Do you not think I love what I do, although not setting goals in the same sense you did? Achieving a future in one existence does not stop when you decide to leave Earth. Upon departing your reality, you must set new goals to fit your next undertaking. We have selected a task of tremendous importance for you, Child; and David has already been offered membership to the High Council. First, both of you need training in the way things work, and who is who, but you instinctively know what is to be said and done."

"What is it? Don't we have a choice? Maybe my goals differ from yours, Lavender. Will you be separating us? What if we're different colors of light? How do we find each other? What will sex..." *Peter Pan* gibbered incomprehensibly, fighting back for his mistake of a word.

"Yes, you have choices, but this is one we feel is your next future. You may disagree at first; however, we hope you at least try. Now, please trust us, Theo; we shall not separate you from David; and time will be a non-issue for you both. Since your last Oscar, for *Oberon the King*, you have not left the Canyon. You came back to remain captive in your realm called Home, and neither of you have aged. Only several months of filming broke your reclusive natures. You will keep these containers within your energy fields, and can manifest them in your chosen world at any time, simply for a night of human pleasure. Just remember a red sports car waits for all eternity, always parked in its rightful place, fueled, and ready to go. You forgot Quinlan made his classic film twenty-five years before you met, and his container is like mine, entity-made, and ageless. When humans understand how to transform their energy into light, their containers shall also continue unchanged, including the feelings of a human, just as David still feels and appears younger than 43, not 63; and you, Theo, still look sixteen. As for your daughters, they did age as children, a necessity, as who would listen to a child's words. Now in their twenties, they shall decide when to stop aging. They need years of experience, written on their faces, to allow others to follow them, but shining beautiful and bright from within."

"I never thought about it. We haven't changed a bit, and you're still beautiful, Teddy Bear."

"David, stop it. This scares me; and I'm not sixteen or twelve. Never was. Okay, as light entities, how do... how do we..."

"...sexually gratify yourselves? Spectacularly, and you and your Knight have even more to look forward to, always carrying those human feelings in your containers: a wondrous choice."

"That certainly tells us everything we need to know." David's concern increased with Ted's fidgeting and sudden agitation. *Peter Pan* felt something; his panic visibly showed. After twenty-years of watching his partner's mind overload, he knew it would implode without caution.

"Will we have a home? How do I find him? I need to know. There are too many unknown variables before we leave." The rapid-fire questions were all human necessities. Ted did not fear the coming change, only desperately needing information to make a better start. The Mistress felt his panic. David, who at first seemed hesitant, now sounded curious and optimistic to whatever may be, like some grand adventure. She could not keep pace with either man's emotions or thoughts this night.

"I'm sure Lavender will teach us their ways." The soft words calmed the fright minimally.

"There are many places for nomadic entities, such as us, to share romantic love and courtship. As you are aware, a few of us chose human form, enjoying its beauty, taking on the likeness at our leisure. In our unique forms, we also raise families, while some species are purely on their own, being able to reproduce by separating a section of light from their bodies."

"That means nothing! It doesn't pertain to us! We're talking about irrelevant shit, when we need to know about us!" Ted yelled and stood up, almost knocking both Lavender and David into the brink.

"Sit down, Child. You will learn through guidance, once you transform. I cannot explain something you cannot feel or do until you are released from your container." A flash of red in those eyes warned the youngest to behave.

"What do you purpose that I do?" Ted obediently settled down between them. He grew more bashful; unsure of what he had bargained for years earlier. With all this rhetoric, his innate powers backfired on him. Confusion destroyed everything he had come to understand; he had no back-up plan.

"What powers have you learned, Theo?"

"To heal myself, and as you predicted, I can postpone a baseball game."

"You're right about the light energy, Lavender. He could not have survived all these years without something sustaining him. His healing gifts are powerful, like Holly and Willow. My three family members have eliminated all our health problems and old scars."

"Theo did far more, discovering a hidden power of the Ancients, existing within his subconscious mind, and sharing it with his brothers. They intuitively learned from him, and now, all the Barrett offspring are self-healers. You started a dynasty to teach others. Soon, physical problems will disappear unless of a serious nature. For those, you have the likes of Holly. Many healers will develop with each generation, spreading good health with healing hands, hearts, and minds."

"And we watch the population explode further!" Unhappy to hear this news, LaCoix could only foresee disaster. Fire, famine, flood, plague, pestilence, drought, and now elemental calamities, the former means of control had been nullified, with technical and medical advances. Only war seemed the appropriate measure to level the playing field. It seemed too harsh a reality.

"Remember the number who will leave. The planet will be secure with the appropriate populace of each distinct being, which is supposed to live there, every living creature having their own space, and of true importance, understanding the balance of nature."

"That takes care of the physical, Lavender; what of the mentally ill? Who fixes someone like me, who can't come to terms with a carrot?" Ted had not been listening; knowing in his own mind that the planet would survive. Healing matters entangled his thoughts, wishing to hear more of why he could not expand his own paradigm to include his mental distress.

"The mental: what to do about the mind and its many forms of agony and frightening problems." The Cosmos heard her sad sigh, causing stars to dim for a single moment.

"You haven't figured that one out yet? Give me a break." David looked down at his empty glass, wishing for more. It filled instantly.

"We have in some entities, not in others. The human mind is intelligent, creative, fearless, and yet extremely delicate. The terms fanaticism, guilt, lust, vanity, greed, psychosis, all get in the way, with no way around it. This is where Theo's work lies, in a likeness of Pandora's Box."

"You're sending me to the Cosmic nut house! Are you keeping me there, or do you unlock the door to let me out at night?" The thought sent a claustrophobic chill through the man. Nothing could be worse than the implied imprisonment.

"You are not going for your own problems, which have diminished greatly. However, your emotions have produced your greatest power, understanding the frailty of others, and their penchant for blind faith. You have been through a great change, as will the others in your care."

"So I get to come and go. Do the others I visit stay locked up?" Ted thought of his capabilities; he had never asked for any of them.

"No one is caged, *per ce*. It is their choice to be there. How do I tell you this, Theo, without turning your brain into vapor? We have a group of beings, many human, who remain adamantly closed to choice. Some have argued and debated for thousands of years as to who is right and who is wrong; and yet, if you listen closely, they usually are agreeing with each other, but unwilling to hear the other lucidly. No words can describe how astounding this is to us; there lies the problem: linguistics again. With most of your Earth's religions represented, the place is backlogged with followers. After this latest decision by the Council, no more of the Unreachables will ascend to this place. We are overflowing, using much of our energy, space, and time. By being kind, perhaps we became cruel; and thus a far more ruthless rule has been set."

"So what do I do: sit and listen? Do you switch it on and off at your leisure, to learn or to laugh, like you do with rocks and rain?"

"Be respectful, Theo, as these are real entities with serious misconceptions. They must be taught to think on their own, or be terminated. Are you ready for that? I think it wise to hang onto him, David." The eyes said everything. Not a request but a demand, she knew both would be shocked.

"Maybe you shouldn't have asked him yet?" David looked at her with more scorn than she had ever felt. By what he pieced together, it sounded like Ted would be forced to act the part of the Black Rose, annihilating those who refused to play the game. He would not stand for such an eventuality.

Protecting his own, Lavender dismissed LaCoix's anger. "It is too late to turn back, my Spirit, for Theo must learn to destroy, as well as nurture." The comeback enhanced the flash of crimson in her eyes.

"Destroy and nurture what? You are sending me someplace worse than hell!"

"Do not make things up in your head, Child. You know better. Listen and learn before you speak. You shall finally meet Jesus Christ. Participants, still battling religious wars, all those fought and never concluded, continue to wage them in this part of the Cosmos, away from the new order of the *Beginning Again*. These wars are now decreed ended, pronounced by the Council today; and those who do not start believing in their own truths will be dust, terminated into nothingness, giving us peace in this particular section of the Cosmos, to be used for important purposes. Hatred must stop spreading, and members of terrorist groups of any kind, religious fanatics or political zealots, will have serious decisions to make, if they are to participate in the new era. They will lose this battle in agony, for it will involve the true Powers-That-Be. Those, who believe in the peace and tranquility of the *knowing,* will remain unharmed, stronger in their own right of choice. It will be your arbitration and awareness, Theo, to teach the Unreachables that are already in our midst, or vanquish them, no matter whom they may be."

"Me? I'm not an arbitrator, or an executioner! You're out of your mind! I have no powers to do either!" Ted wanted out. It had taken years, but his first thirty still permeated his brain. The thought of Christ, and joking about him, hurt Ted; and the knowledge, that his daughter inherited her skill to destroy, unhinged his mind from his body.

"Your powers are extreme, Theodore; and I shall not hear you lie to me again. Gifted creatively, your innate abilities grow strong enough to deal with such matters, able to save many already targeted for termination. This should be intellectually stimulating for you, if you stay on your path, not overwhelmed with whom you might meet. We have complete confidence in you, so I shall show you. Now, let us see who is currently debating or arguing. I will show them in a form you can recognize." Lavender raised her arms, as the three sat and watched the clouds clear to the left and right.

"My God, is that really..." The sighting shocked even David.

"Which one do you refer to, Christ or Aten, or should I say Atun? It depends on if he is playing the god or the pharaoh."

"It is Jesus! I can't understand what they're saying. What language is it?" Overcome with awe, Ted only saw the one claimed as the divine.

"You disappoint me, Theo. What language should they be speaking: English? You'll understand them telepathically, when you intercede in their sparring matches. No one gets hurt, as these are battles of words; but you must stay impartial, asking the right questions to bring them into the *knowing*. You should now fully understand the phrase your first Faery said to you. Life in all forms is *Beginning Again*, and this group represents the Unreachable who must open their minds to new thought and listen to each other. Willow and Holly are doing that on earth; you shall attempt it here."

"Holy shit! It's him! It's really him!"

"Theodore Barrett, you are treading dangerously close to being terminated yourself, if you do not start listening and reacting sensibly to my words. I shall not repeat myself. Look closely at your prophet. Christ is only a man, with less power than you have; the person you cried out to help you, including the day of the rockslide. Even after that, you called his name. We told you he was busy. Well, there he is, doing what he does with his time, arguing without listening to the other side. Look at the number of Spirits backing him up, unable to understand that they are trapped in his war of theology, when they could be doing something far more useful, like guiding children into the magic of the universe, correcting their own world problems, or revitalizing dead planets. It infuriates me at all this waste of time and energy. He even argues with Moses, a believer in his so-called father. Aten has a large group of followers himself; and they have been here longer than the Christian host. The new terrorists, particularly of Earth, are not part of this scenario, as they fight over different forms of their religion mixed with political hatred. They will be dealt with, along with other zealots, commencing immediately under our new resolution; and many planets, including Earth, shall be in horror at what this one-day may wreak. It is strange, even for us; but measures, to subdue this insanity, have dawdled along with your dove politicians, the self-righteous moral majority, and each group's sympathizers. It is our time to take over."

"What are these two fighting about?" Transfixed, Ted could barely say the words; he certainly did not hear a word the Mistress said; neither had David.

Lavender drew in her breath to give them another chance to listen. Both men seemed incapable of grasping the dramatic events that would transpire on their world within a few days.

"What they are discussing is of no consequence to our discussion. They are simply fanatics who need to learn the reality of an impending disastrous situation. When your time comes, how will you rectify this argument of no consequence?" Lavender's ire rose further over the silly question, when her words should have them thinking of more pressing problems.

"I can't do this. My powers can't compare to the Son of God. You can't call him a fanatic, defending his father and the written word."

"What son of which god? Which written words?" The Mistress boiled over; her new crystal goblet smashed, with all due intent against the marble flooring. Her eyes remained crimson in her frustration; warnings lit up her sky, closing clouds and creating lightning strikes, mimicking the fire set ablaze below.

"Christ of course. Don't make fun of this, Lavender." Ted did not see her change, blindsided by his old beliefs.

"You use his name in the profane, Theo. What am I to think of you? I thought you discarded the prophet, to believe in the expansive thought, which your path has led you. If you are so star-struck, you have wasted my time. I should return you directly to Hollywood, to wallow in the famous names you know there. What will you do when you meet Christ's worst enemy, Mohammed? He is a powerhouse of control and brilliance, with a far larger following than your prophet. Does that simple fact not mean anything to you? Will you turn into a mouse when they clash, or revert to following Jesus who will continue this battle forever? Did you notice his father anywhere? You should be able to find him, if he made man in his own image, a ridiculous, self-centered concept in its own right. Where is he for his son?"

"David, I can't. This is..."

"...Stop. You will do as asked, for this is a serious problem for ninety-percent of the populations existing within the Cosmos, not to mention the Beyond. We need your help, Theodore, to straighten others' pathways. This is your power. Why do you not see Christ the way the rest of the universe does? David, please help us get through to this man."

"What Beyond?" David, who never believed in Christ, still did not grasp the significance of the Mistress's words, but could only view the intriguing debate of incomprehensible dialogue from antiquity.

"That is enough! What has happened to you both?" Lavender stood up, and her hands swirled the clouds in disgust. The black velvet suddenly turned flaming red; and she stomped up the few stairs, smoke billowing from under the long train of the gown. She flicked her wrist; a chair floated from under its place at the table, to be slammed down against the marble floor. There she sat, in grim silence and defeat. Emotionally dejected, defeated with disappointment, she wanted them gone. Her eyes glared at them both. Feline eyes flashed red at the two men who hesitantly approached. "After twenty years of teaching, you have learned nothing. You cannot put two thoughts together, except yourselves, and even that took divine intervention. Thank the Forces-That-Be that your daughters cannot see you back-step so fast. It would spin their heads off."

"We have learned, and we are grateful, Lavender. To be honest with you, I've tried to piece this whole thing together, but I'm having as much trouble as Ted. Why were we chosen for such tremendous responsibilities?" David feared what her Ladyship's ire could create; intuitively knowing they were in great danger. With trepidation and a hand over Ted's mouth, he waited on her answer and contemplated his next move.

"Because of whom you are; and I don't mean pretty boy Oscar winners. Even through your human and enlightened eyes, you remain blind. Perhaps you should mount up, and plod along home to a white picket fence and a house in the valley. You no longer belong in the Canyon. Do not forget the drop when you leave this place." Lavender squinted at Ted, nearly pushing him into the water with the unnerving stare. David caught him, but had to release his mouth to do it.

"Mistress, I do believe in Bastet and Shaysha. Both taught me magic and the unlimited possibilities of the mind. You are coming at me too fast. Please, slow down and help us make sense of this. The first time you took me to your chambers, I was so frightened, and the same thing happened. I came out with only one revelation; I had a choice, a monster step for me." Ted believed he needed to apologize for something that mystified him. He desperately wanted to understand this woman of the Beyond. Unfortunately, his ability to block her thoughts stopped him, not realizing his own barricades were the issue. He had constructed the high-walled paradigm himself.

"At least you learned something; it may save you."

"Do I still have a choice? What you're asking of me is beyond my capabilities." He held onto a steadying arm, slightly hidden by David's protective shield. A common scene since the shooting and Ted's return, his Knight stood firmly in the line of fire, securing the frontal position from attack. Lavender wondered how her man-child ever faced the world as a bubbly imp, full of laughter and old jokes. A fine actor, he may be nothing more. What role did he play now, and was she a fool to believe him? He had learned much, perhaps too much; she pushed through immediately to find her answers.

"Where do you think you are and what have you seen? Both of you sit down and explain to me the existence of Ra, Bastet, Shu, and Isis. Explain to me Shaysha and the Lady Faery. Explain to me the strange colored tornado that tried to terminate Steven and save you at the same time, Theodore. Explain to me how your Home in a non-existent canyon. Explain to me La Rosa Negra and the lake that stretches beyond forever, to a place you may, or may not pass through. Have you not been shown future scenarios, been given Cosmic insights into the *Beginning Again*, learned to think on your own, manifest a thought, and read minds? Both of you changed dramatically into individuals that I respect, like, and love. It is my shame I neglected you for years, David, and to my horror you became an obnoxious son-of-a-bitch, with no goals but to keep working for a hint of glory, and excuse the profanity, fucking everyone in your path. You are no longer that person, becoming kind, gentle, and thoughtful, with the courageous heart of your lion Spirit. Then we have Theo, a misguided follower, manipulating people for your own gain, all rather masochistic, but you let them hurt you anyway. Now you are a thinker, an achiever, a doer of things, even when you are too sick and mentally disturbed to handle the colossal mountains you have climbed. What happened to those men meant to be the grandest stars in my galaxy, shining brighter than they ever did on Earth? Have I misjudged you both, blind to my own feelings toward you and your extraordinary acting abilities? That is all you are to me now--actors--egotistical, self-absorbed actors. Why did I think you could be of relevance to us?" More distraught than she had ever felt, she could not look at her failures.

"Please, Lavender, we need you to slow down. You are telling us things at such a rapid rate, neither Ted nor I can follow. We have a long list of questions, needing only simple answers. Can we reiterate your statements in our own words, simply and to the point? We've been friends for decades; don't give up on us now." David grasped for whatever he could, knowing the red cat's eyes meant they had lost. Something had changed, suddenly igniting such malicious actions and words. The imagery, of being pulverized into dust, swept through his mind.

"Your decades, not mine. Our friendship passed in a blink of an amber eye. I am sorry, David, there is so much to tell, and you planned to leave Earth tonight. Your initial goals were not appropriately set for the *Fathers of the Awakening*, or perhaps, you were never to be part of the *knowing* itself. I assumed a great deal, and more surprises you do not need. Perhaps I should let you discover your own route to wherever it takes you. Therefore, the answer is '*no*'. Leave now, and let me decide what to do with you. You are both too powerful to live in your world, and yet do not understand your capabilities enough to make the crossing. I am in a quandary as to what to do, particularly with you, Theodore, considering you are one of us. You disappoint me beyond imagining. Go now, and do not say one small word." Lavender waved her hand, dismissing them both. Removed from her sight at a flick of a slender, white hand, they stood at the exit gate of La Rosa Negra.

In shock, with what seemed unwarranted anger and the transformation, from a protective guardian and friend to a vindictive Caretaker with tremendous power, David and Ted had been banished from their second home, never to realize exactly what it was. Their only security awaited them: Bastet and Ra. They mounted up, closed their eyes, and their mystical friends winged them homeward. The puzzle presented must be pieced together; and whatever the results, they had to believe in something together. They only had that night.

"Ethan, Quinlan, did you hear?"

"Yes Mistress. You played it well; understandable, yet they became confused with the interruptions of their own thoughts." Peerce emerged out of the shadows, to bathe in the nurturing glory of three full moons created to soothe her Ladyship.

"I must say, the flaming, smoking, red dress lit the match sparking LaCoix's immediate concern. It scared the wits out of Theo." Ambrose always had a twinkle in his eye, finding the lighter side of even the most serious situation.

"We handled this abominably, forgetting they are human, with foibles of their own. They grasped only human needs, not hearing or seeing the catastrophic nature of the situation. Their last test may be too much for them." The downcast look and flashing cat's eyes worried both male entities.

"Remember, your Ladyship, this is a new experience for us; one which we expected, but the timing caught us unprepared."

"We must face facts, Quinlan; we grew weary of the anticipation; and now they are left with very little information. Do you think they can figure it out themselves?" Lavender frowned in anxiety. She had to give David and Ted something to hope for, to make them reach further into their gifts, as she had done with their daughters years earlier. Time was short for two humans on their way to a last leap of faith.

"David is too sharp to ignore details, and puzzles intrigue him, although there are many pieces he has omitted. His list of questions is very long; but he will fight for his own *knowing,* not intimidated by any of us. The man belongs with the decision-making body."

"Thank you, Ethan. Quinlan, what of Theodore?"

"He is too passive to intentionally use the destructive powers he possesses, although he has used them for good. His back and forth conversation makes me believe he understands more than we think. His power to block us, in itself, could be a major crisis. One panicked or angry thought, the *Awakening* ends with the colossal explosion of one small solar system. The loss will be extreme."

"We do have a delicate situation, Gentlemen."

"I am convinced he is very aware of all his talents. Termination would be a waste of such extreme potential, but his behavior, viewing Jesus in action, has me wandering if he would turn and follow." Ethan sat at the ornate table and drank David's portion of the unearthly ambrosia.

"We can conclude LaCoix is not a problem except for one factor; he will not join us without Theo; and if separated, they are walking time-bombs. If they put their heads together, they could vanquish the Cosmos." Lavender settled more comfortably in her chair. She reached for the goblet offered, and stopped; no more surprises for her Spirit, he had other things on his mind.

"Our man-child surprised me as well, at his reaction on seeing the Christ human. As one of our missing specks, along with Kincaid, we must watch them closely. Two more light entities stolen from our nursery, so long ago, and treated atrociously." Ambrose sat down, stretched out his long legs, and sipped Ted's share of the liquid the trio enjoyed when in human form.

"Your hunch appears correct, Quin. It is hard to imagine the pain our babies went through: one hiding it by being abused sexually, while the other allowed physical and mental torture to mask the struggle of a maturing light entity. Remarkable they could ease the inner pain with a physical one. Restrained in such dark, small containers, it is a wonder they survived. Certainly a mistake by the Fates, placing them in human form; they survived with nourishment from their small sun." In another pose of contemplation, Peerce sat forward with his arms crossed, leaning on the table, and puzzling over a problem bigger than they had anticipated.

"It shows the power of Theo and Stevie, suffering in starvation, impeding their growth. I wonder how immature it made our children physically and mentally. They may behave as children, like many of the others we have found, when they turn into their true form." Quinlan watched the whirling liquid in his glass, filling it with a thought.

"There will be much for them to learn, listening to Theo's quaint questions. Definitely childish, but his other queries were worthy of the *knowing*; he is such a contradiction to me. How much easier it was when we could read his thoughts. David, on the other hand, will maintain his own Spirit, and continue to grow in wisdom; but the one to lead him is fighting us for some reason. Our man-child must grow more confident, and quickly. I was looking forward to seeing a new entity emerge." Lavender gazed out her window for solace from her moons.

"Yes, the cautious but accepting LaCoix, my Lady; I hoped his unorthodox conduct and thoughts would spark new debates amongst the current Powers-That-Be. I believe that we have too much power, and now, with the Fates dying out, what will we do with all we know? To be honest, it scares me as well. I sometimes wonder if the entire universe should be obliterated, smashed into tiny fragments to swirl into a new Cosmos. Maybe someone else could do a better job."

"You are a dreamer, Quinlan. Because of what we are, it would only manifest itself again: different faces, with similar vices, demanding power through religion, politics, and greed. It will never happen again to that paradise. We have become preoccupied with the negative, Gentlemen; something we must overcome to help them."

"Of course, for I truly like these two Spirits we sent adrift tonight. This plan you hatched must be something neither can dismiss." The English-accented entity delighted in the scheming of his beloved's mind, so intense and powerful.

"Not only a dreamer, but a devious one; and if they solve the last puzzle, we can deal with the aftermath. It could prove gravely dangerous, but their demise would also cause havoc. They will have to think fast to figure it out; if they do not, it ends where they started; and we begin again."

"Well, my Lady, I shall gather a few members of the Council to discuss Theodore, in case of trouble. There must be a place for him without having to terminate his existence; and he would be frozen in fear at the claustrophobic thought of being one of the Unreachables, especially without David to help him. That would be too cruel."

"Yes it would, Ethan; but it is where he belongs, to spread his knowledge, to stop the fighting, and to eliminate those we no longer have the resources to care for. However, after all his training, he appears unprepared to face the task we chose for him. My current thoughts would leave him with those who believe in him; both the Elfin and Faery Realms would be gentle with Theo and David. The *Beginning Again* cannot be disrupted; and Willow's power is a problem, if something befalls her natural father. The final game begins." Lavender arose; the two men immediately were on their feet.

"Good night, my Lady."

"Your Lordships."

CHAPTER 59

Opening his eyes to the cold and chaos, David nearly tumbled off his horse. They were back to the day that changed their lives. Twenty-years before, Richard Carter barked the same orders. It had been a dream: an illusion. A glance at Theodore Barrett, mounted beside him, said otherwise; the boyish face confirmed the man experienced the same shocking surprise. Those blue eyes rolled up; and a quick as lightning hand reached out to steady him. Without a sound murmured, David LaCoix fell adrift; his mouth opened with words unspoken. If truly a dream, Ted was not his and never had been. He had to communicate the urgency and panic of their situation to someone who may not know anything; his breathing returned with one simple statement heard in his head.

'This isn't Bastet.' Ted shivered from fright, or the cold, since they both sat mounted in a soaking drizzle, staring at a familiar outcrop of rocks.

'This isn't Ra either. Thank the Powers-That-Be that you remember.' David hoped Ted received his message. In overload mode, he searched frantically for an escape to their future.

'I remember everything, David. We have to get back, but those Powers-That-Be, you're praying to, sent us here. We have to return, or...'

'...I understand, Ted. Any ideas? My learned abilities can't send us to where we belong.'

'Mine can.' Ted looked sheepishly at him, out of the corner of his eye. *'This is my fault.'*

'What are you talking about? I know some of your capabilities, Ted, but this, man, she wants us dead; to destroy everything we've accomplished. It sure as hell doesn't look like a second chance.'

'I'm sorry, and I'm scared.'

'So am I. We have to think this out, and bring this game to a conclusion.' David veered his disbelieving eyes forward, looking for a clue.

Following the older actor's lead, Ted also turned dumbstruck and squinted at the same menacing spot. They had to think fast, before the word *Action* was called. *'I could change the weather to a sunny day. It would give us a chance to figure this out.'*

'That would change the future. Can't do that; any change could jeopardize our daughters' lives. If we do anything, it has to be now.' In mortal fear, David could not find a way out; and his life with Ted would have never been. The man, he loved for so long, expressed the same horror in his blue eyes. They were looking through him, as if taking one last look. *'Ted, come on; this is no time to falter.'*

'I can block her; she knows it. She's mad as hell, not knowing what I've been doing. That's why she kept asking me about my powers.'

'No shit? So what else can you do?'

'It's not what I can do, but whether I can get 'you' through it as well. You game, my Knight?'

'Whatever you say; I have no intention of losing you again.'

'Knowing what we know, maybe we should live the twenty years over? It would make it easier this time.' Ted looked down at his wet gloves, desperately wanting to bare his hands and rub his made-up face.

'It does sound appealing; but I don't know, Ted. Everything would be out of balance; and I don't think Lavender is on the other side of the rocks today. That makes it different, and dangerous.' David watched the tremor of the lips, knowing he was right, and wanting to suffocate

the shivering man in his adoration.

'Okay then, LaCoix. It's all in the visualization, our first lesson. It has to be instant, man, and you have to stay focused.' Back to his determined self, Ted assumed the same tone he used on the cliff the day Holly fell.

Relieved to hear it, David nodded. *'No problem.'*

'Yes it is, because one idle thought, disrupting the concentration, will blow it. We have to do the scene exactly like we did that day, with a slight variation. Take my hand when we turn, and as you come back around, lean toward me, kiss me long and passionately, and keep your eyes closed.' Ted had one chance for a death-defying feat he had not tried. Terrified of the possible consequences, of his next action, his front teeth slipped over his lower lip to keep it under control.

'Can't see how that would change the future, except surprise the hell out of Carter.'

'Good, we might be able to do this. I can change into light, David. You know you're also filled with light, but haven't had the opportunity to utilize it. Holly's first attempt will be when she's shot. You remember seeing that in her future. It would be an instant escape for me, as it was for her; but I'd never leave you behind. I'll die here with you first.'

'Don't say that; this is definitely not our time. Just believe it. I think you have much to tell me, so let's get on with what we have to do.'

'Okay then, keep remembering the fog that we rode into years ago, because it was Lavender. Make sure that's in your head. When you kiss me, don't pull away, or let go of my hand. Just keep thinking of Home, the age of the girls when we last saw them, and how you feel about me. See our house the way we left it.' With a deep breath, Ted took over, demanding the bewildered blond to pay attention. David had been his strength, and remained as such, always adding to his power.

'I can only see it in daylight.'

'Fine. Early afternoon after the girls left. Think of riding Home and what it looks like.'

'Shit, what color are the flowers this year?'

'Concentrate! You're the one who remembers obscure details in a crisis. Yellows, reds, and oranges, with lots of greenery: can you see it?'

'You've been changing it constantly. I'm sorry; it just runs together in a watercolor left in the rain. I got it now. Let's do whatever it is you do.' Those frightening alarms echoed through his head, as he released Ted's arm. He had to. It would assure his partner he believed in him. A voice yelled out, reverberating through them and into the past. Life would go on to the end, or it would be over before it began, a rare time of no choices. They heard the cacophony of a megaphone and Richard Carter's voice; the past recommenced on cue.

"Okay, let's get this one, boys. Start slow. When you reach your first marker, make sure you're in the right positions to get your horses into an easy lope. Stunt shots are done, so don't go racing off like lunatics, just to make me mad. Take it easy, and be careful. David, Ted, when you turn, do it slowly. Got it?"

'Man, have we got it this time.' Only Ted heard David and chuckled, giving the older actor a little relief for his headache.

'We had better, LaCoix.'

Close to twenty-years later, the same eleven horsemen set off. Two heads turned simultaneously with the perfect expression, to come around and stare longingly at each other. Visions of Home filled their heads, as a hand clasped the other tightly, and a kiss took them beyond the thickening fog, into the canyon of pastel rocks. The yellow, red, orange, and green mirage merged in the vortex of two men falling in love all over again, their passion captured forever on film, as they rode into the mist, floating as one, oblivious to the sensation of rising above the action around them.

David kissed him gently. Mouths softened and opened to take in the unique taste of the other; the smell of each that excited them both; the touch that awakened their sensuality; and the *knowing* that united their Spirits to meld into one. The vibration of Ted's hum tickled David's lips; the caress blew away the dreary day; and a second once-in-a-life-time became eternity. Each knew every part of the other, after two titillating decades of exploring and fondling. They found the funny little places that made each one shiver; another tiny spot caused hysterical giggling; and all those pleasure points they never knew existed, until the Mistress' divine intervention; and their pretend straight lives turned gay.

Ted's comfort lay in the small of his back; his point of frenzy inside his rectum. The sliding of David's hands, spread around his torso, stroking down his sides, created an instant thrust of his hips, while his sensitive inner thighs, when softly stroked with feather-like kisses, made them quiver and shake so severely, he had to struggle not to come. A gentle playing with his cock, a hand on his crotch through his pants, even a whisper of a touch to any part of him, gave the younger man pleasure, increasing the heat of his arousal, making him feel part of someone else. Once the feeling reached throughout the insecure body, he would purr in rapture, becoming savage. Clawing and scratching turned a sweet kiss into a battle of unnerving euphoria; he sucked on anything to devour his lover. His sensitivity, to all the senses, created a raging wildcat, igniting every inch of the bashful man, until he could no longer hold back a scream of uninhibited euphoria.

David, in his steadfast defiance of the world's contradictory morality, and his acceptance of its unreality, replaced his lover's self-doubt with an open mind. The beautiful colors, fragrant scents, and haunting visions came from the brilliant older actor; and the Teddy Bear would always be grateful to his Knight for allowing him in. Ted opened his eyes when David made love to him, to watch the stars dance in the green crystals, half hidden under seductive blond lashes. Colors sparkled in his head with every touch. It was magic; it was real; and it enhanced his excitement and need. No more ghosts, regrets, or nightmares for Theodore Barrett, only the smell and feel of this wickedly volatile, sensitive father, actor, friend, and lover filled his daydreams and those special visions in the night.

The blond actor, who had become a legend, hungered for his equal in notoriety. Orally and tactilely intense, David lingered with every lick, nibble, thrust, and caress of Ted's body, from the wavy, shagged hair to the tip of his toes. While tasting something delicious on his lover, his hands never stopped massaging, teasing any vulnerable spot he could find. The younger man's beautiful, hard-veined, straining manhood in his mouth gave him a sensation of power, as he purposefully helped it reach full length and breadth by thrusting lubricated, silky fingers into the hot, sensitive rectum. Gently soothing the inner muscles, which always involuntarily attempted to expel his first intrusion, David would taunt Ted's fancy beyond the man's endurance, and send him squirming into a fantasy nothing else could intensify. David would be in fevered bliss, just watching the reaction, and then pushing gently on the small round protrusion, so moist, so seductive; his only thought was to taste and lick its succulence. Sucking Ted's shaft, channeling it down his throat, or filling his mouth with the silky scrotum, hardened with hidden life, had no match for his lust to lick that inner gland within his partner's steamy cavern of surprises. Not to be, he contented himself with reaching it with his fingers or cock.

Visually enthralled, David licked his lips leering at the small, closed, little hole, which one would think impossible to penetrate, as it pulsated in anticipation for the eventuality. Flushing purple in color, its enticement beckoned entry. The blond's ultimate tactile gratification, for his throbbing organ, would push past the double sphincter muscles clamping down hard, only to release his aching snake into a tight, warm portal, leading to everything magical about loving another man. It had his younger lover writhing in ecstasy with his first lunge. Feeling the rhythm of his thrusts, matching Ted's greeting convulsions, he looked down between their slick, sweating bodies, to see a beautiful shaft stretching to find a talented hand. It flipped uncontrollably on the sunken stomach for want of attention. With a simple touch, it sporadically gushed creamy, thick liquid over them both. When he scanned the skeleton body upward, he smiled wily, ready to taste and feel the hardened, burgundy nipples of sweet-flavored raisins, ripened by the sun. The moist mouth and lips were a constant tease, seldom left alone to take in a soft breath and thankful gasp. His last wish would be to die in this position, making love to his Teddy Bear.

Having his own organ played with, by the now very experienced man, electrified his heart, until ready to give out. Fully aroused, his penis down so deep in his lover's throat, had David seeing visions; and he never failed to fill the hungry orifice with his essence. The pure rapture of skin against skin, bone dry or covered with sticky sweat, pressed them together, rubbing seductively, until steam rose off their bodies. Excitement heated with every new experience, using all their senses. Anything that would turn either man into a mass of hysterical moaning and squirming was powerful enough for each to climax, and then re-ignite; just in the taste, just in the feel, just in the smell, just in the sight of the other sent two heads reeling.

Intuitively knowing the other, the intense kiss continued. Both had come several times, with thoughts of the other during their lifesaving caress. Their sense of smell brought them Home, hot dry air filled with cypress, eucalyptus, and sex. The kiss released with a moan; and David looked into those exotic sapphire blue eyes, sparkling with feline satisfaction. With broad smiles of relief, a feeling of victory swept over one, while fear of his next move flooded the other. The grip grew stronger.

Their horse handler looked at the two riders approaching and laughed as they dismounted. "You two must have had some kind of adventure. Didn't have time to unzip your pants, hunh?"

"You have no idea, Jamie." David beamed at him. They made it; and the thankful blond wanted to kiss everything in sight in his joyous relief. Home still existed, remaining steadfast, waiting for them; their sanctuary remained secure for the moment.

Ted blushed in embarrassment at his primal pleasure, immediately wrapping his long dress-coat around the telltale stains, and the terror that created such passion. He brought them back safely, by mere luck; and now he had to tell David the truth. His final admission would ultimately be stated in front of the Mistress. The thought rattled his bones so hard, he thought the sound audible. "We'll be traveling late tonight on a special sojourn, Jamie. Make sure our magical steeds are rested. Maybe you could braid a few blue and yellow flowers into Bastet's mane. You'd like to be pretty when we arrive, wouldn't you girl?"

"You're leaving us, Ted, heading to someplace unknown; the place you disappear at the end of the canyon." All formalities had vanished over so many years, with the two cowboys becoming loyal friends to the family.

Ted could not respond. Busy teasing Bastet's sensitive pink nose with a sweet tasting rose, he left final sentiments to his Knight. He could not break down now.

"Yes, Jamie, it's time Ted and I moved on, taking our last ride you might say. The estate belongs to Willow and Holly now, so take care of everything while they're away, and keep learning of the *knowing*. Listen to the girls, as they love you and Craig, seeing you as caring male role models. You both understand the magic of this canyon, which will remain until you decide your work here is done. You will then join us."

"Thank you for that. We've known the girls pretty much their entire lives, and love them as kin. We'll miss the two of you. It doesn't seem right, looking at how young you both look."

"We may look young, but we're finished here. Take care of our Home for the girls, Jamie; and if you haven't noticed, you and Craig haven't aged either. Now, you two must ensure that the men in their lives are decent human beings."

"We'd be honored David, and certainly interrogate each man appropriately. We never thought we'd have daughters, but now you have entrusted them to us. Thank you."

"They also have uncles, brothers, and cousins to look out for them, but we hope you can support them with your more advanced telepathic powers. You've lived in this special place longer, and without knowing it, you have become part of the *Beginning Again*."

"I guess we have. We'll ensure that love does not blind the girls, although they're powerful enough to know better."

"I certainly hope so. Thank Craig for us as well. We'll see you in the future. Come on, Ted, we have decisions to make."

The two men walked away arm-in-arm, not a word spoken. There was sorrow and there was joy, and either emotion could leave them drained to face the Mistress. Together they showered under a waterfall of kisses and soapy caresses, and dried off with soft seductive strokes of terry toweling. Safe for now, they secured themselves behind a locked door.

David tried not to think of anything that would give Ted away to Lavender. "Time to tell me everything, Baby Bear, and how do I stop my thoughts from being overheard? Talk to me, and not telepathically. I want to hear your breathless, raspy voice to remember for eternity."

"I can block your thoughts, so we're safe for now. I have so much to tell you, and I'm sorry for hiding them from you."

"Come here; I understand why you couldn't. Just tell me straight out, and please, keep the shock level down for this already over-stimulated heart. We'll decide from there what to do."

The two made themselves comfortable on the bed, lying naked in the heat of a desert day; the smaller man encased in the stronger, longer arms. Ted learned much over twenty years, secretly guided by Bastet, Shaysha, and Quinlan Ambrose. His healing powers grew immensely after the shooting and his own heart attack; the life and death experience accelerated not only his heart, but also his fight to survive. His real training started in the mountains of a distant place, by these three very different entities. After years of solitary practice, upon his return to their house, he easily manipulated objects and people, although the latter he seldom thought necessary, convinced it would turn him into an unwelcome Fate. Remembering Lavender's words, he stuck to the non-interference rule, unless specifically called for telepathically. His list of accomplishments stretched the imagination; and his deeds had gone unnoticed by the world, by his eternal lover, and perhaps, by the Mistress.

He exploited his tears of pain and joy for good, using the one power to stabilize the planet, slowly and methodically, turning it into a wonderland of fresh air, clean water, and plentiful bounty. Theodore Barrett had been a busy man with Holly's suggestion to keep him creative, and Lavender's coaxing to save his dramatic trees and keep the ice diamonds crystal pure. It had stopped his potentially self-destructive energies. Only the *Beginning Again* could level the population; a chore left for his daughters. Too extreme a choice for such a soft heart, it became his primary fear of Lavender's proposed desires for him.

David could not believe what he heard. The planet had changed, with the environmentalists and politicians taking the credit. Earth's rebirth constituted one man's thoughts and well thought out plans of drastic situations, considering the changes it caused and had created, particularly politically. Theodore Barrett was that man; and David's admiration for his forever partner grew.

Ted's eating disorder had been diagnosed correctly, with the symptoms, his mental attitude, and the pressure of his agents to stay young accelerating the problem. The doctors, however, saw only the light entity as an over-stimulated physiological energy, and certainly not the reason he remained alive. His condition did prove beneficial for millions, who believed they saw a man dying slowly, and one they wished to save. The ordeal culminated in a healthier trend for natural beauty. In the last ten years, Ted stopped eating entirely, yet remained active and certainly energetic. David came to terms with the idea of the light entity within his lover's body, enabling Ted to exist on the sun's energy alone. Mentally stable, considering his horrendous ordeal of change and acceptance, Ted thought clearly and his concentration level increased. With Quinlan's nurturing support, he came to cope with what he would become. The pain endured alone, for so long, he shared with his Knight who eased the agony by being there and taking his mind off the inevitable. Spending most of his days outdoors, taking in the nourishment of the sun's rays, Lavender's speculation manifested itself.

"It's your turn to discard your container for a few minutes to see how it feels. You might have felt something when we came back." Ted raked his hand through the blond silk of the pale faced man who gazed at him in awe. "You could catch flies with that expression."

The nervous laugh reflected the answer. "I'm not ready. I wasn't ready the last time we were with Lavender." This time David stuttered his way through another surprise. "You certainly took your identity crisis well. I'm proud of what you accomplished with no applause."

"Identity crisis! What an understatement, LaCoix; and I'm twelve again. I like being that age with you, and I've had all the applause I need. What about you?"

"Plenty, but all appreciated. However, my Teddy Bear, after you saw Christ, I thought you'd be babbling prayers to a porcelain idol."

"I know what he is now, and maybe even Lavender. There is a strange sense about her."

"You amaze me at your resilience and acceptance of the phantasmal, compared to twenty-years ago. You're Gandhi and *Peter Pan* rolled into one."

"What an odd mix; and here I thought myself a trapped light entity. It's taken me a long time, David, but it feels good when I change; and it will for you. I'll make it easy for us, my Knight."

"And Lavender?"

"We'll find out when we go back."

"She threw us out, remember? I doubt if she's going to welcome us back into the fold. I didn't think she would try to kill me, being my Soul; but once I'm gone, she's free. It's part of this damn game of hers: first help, and then destroy. It's her motto."

"That's who she is, David. She's black and white, bad and good, light and dark, but there is one thing to remember." A sudden mischievous grin took hold; Ted could not control his giggling.

"What's that? This is serious shit, and you think it's funny." David squinted at the change, from worried vertical lines to happy horizontal ones.

"I think we passed some kind of test; so we can't do anything until we see her. The Mistress kindly reminded us of a hot, red Ferrari though. What do you suppose she meant?" The still boyish face grinned tauntingly, and received a snickering one back.

"One last chance in human form, before we're either light or dust. Don't even get dressed."

"Wasn't planning to."

Two men streaked out of the house and clamored into the expensive antique. With David in the driver's seat, the Ferrari fishtailed through two sets of gates before Ted had his door closed. They were off, whooping and hollering at the world they would soon leave behind. Everything was left in order: their girls safely on their *knowing* path; the planet thriving, yet waiting for an end to political and religious chaos; and close friends and family abounded in happiness on their own rightful paths. Ted would miss Steven Kincaid, but he would grieve later after their *red boys' toy* dream.

Screeching breaks and a 180-degree spin, David leapt out of the car without opening the door. As he scrambled to pull the blanket out of the back, Ted could not stop laughing. "Come on, you. I'm going to love you until all that light energy is flowing in its natural state."

"You haven't said that word in a while!" The giggling continued as David hoisted Ted out of the car and settled him on the blanket. He was David's Teddy Bear, and would always be handled as such. Gentle and kind, his Knight would satisfy him this day beyond even what Ted expected.

"I understand the meaning of it now. Is there anything else you'd like to tell me, before I ravage every part of you?" David sank to his knees, gently pushing the willing, rakish body down. The smile and laughter grew contagious; and he joined Ted's merriment. With nothing left of relevance to do, they spent their last day's adventure together, and in private. What would happen would happen, as it always unfolded; they just had to wait for the usual surprise twist.

"Nothing more concrete than a maybe. I've developed many of Lavender's abilities, and it unsettles her. I don't know why, since she keeps trying to save me. She does love us; I do believe that."

"I wonder why she sent us back to the beginning, still remembering our time together."

"Maybe a reminder we could lose it all." Ted's hands pulled down the blond head, to peer into the startling green crystals, which seemed too deep in thought for this moment.

"Very astute of you, Baby Bear."

"She knows we made it. I can read her mind; and that scares her as well. Now she's blocking me from getting the information we need. This is so damn confusing. I finally understand the things she tried to get through this thick skull; now she doesn't want anything to do with me."

"So, do we leave tonight, to face her down, or stay in the real world a while longer?"

"Curiosity killed the cat; and our eyes have turned completely." Ted laughed.

"They make you look wildly dramatic and seductive: very sexy." David floated on euphoria.

"Sexy, hunh? Tonight then?"

"Tonight." Being bonded for all eternity started with the thought and a gentle kiss of lips. Feeling as if their first time, sweet and innocent, David lay and rubbed himself against the outstretched body he would never forget.

"Breathe your life into me, my Knight." Pulling down the blond head for another touch to his boyish face, it would never be forgotten by the other. A mouth whispered sighs between the younger man's lips; Ted returned a moan of pleasure and acceptance. Every worry line smoothed away with a caress, while noses gently nuzzled into favorite spots, until David groaned for his last measure of human lust.

Ted broke the kiss and put his hands on either side of the handsome face. "I'll never taste you, smell you, or see you again, after we change; it will be thoughts and feelings. Remember me this way, and let me experience all of you. This is our last time, David; it has to be memorable."

"You, my Baby Bear, I'll take in every way possible, and remember it all. If you want to try what I think you're suggesting, let's do it." Unnerved at the request, it still amused David. He hoped that Ted had prepared enough to help him. His excitement increased with the answer.

"We can do this, before Lavender or Quin can stop us." Ted insisted.

"Are you sure about this? Do we know enough; I certainly don't. Besides, I want to start in human form." David blew warm air across Ted's crotch, to rouse the hardening shaft, before engulfing it, accepting the twitching offering he knew he could pleasure. Up and down, twirling his tongue around the heating cock created more whimpers and groans. A few licks to the slit, and opening his throat, the engorged shaft channeled deeply down; and the younger man attacked in short static thrusts. Pulling back, David let the creamy fluid bounce off the now closed throat, to dribble over the straining, hot intruder; a sensation enjoyed by both. The effect brought an instant rush of another quick spurt and a few hip jerks. In the mind of a creative artist, David envisioned those magical vapors rising off the scorching organ, and his equally hot mouth mixed with the slightly cooler semen. Another image he wanted to see, but never would, he made due by firming his fingers around the bottom of the Ted's manhood, giving it a full tongue licking, enticing a gush of the taste he craved, and the feeling of capturing something alive. Moving rhythmically, with just the right pressure of his lips, ever protecting the delicacy from his teeth, the action continued to tease until he swallowed the result and slowly withdrew his last suck. The flavor of his lover would remain forever on his tongue: candy-canes, cinnamon hearts, lemongrass slightly salted, all mixed with something uniquely Ted. No one but David had sampled the enticing taste, oozing from every pore and orifice of his still boyish-looking lover.

David moved off and turned to look down into tearing eyes and a face stained with dripping sweat. Ted panted heavily, while drowning in despair. "Hey, what's all this?"

"Before we leave, I wanted you to experience what I do, when you enter me."

"It's okay, Ted. I've never needed the sensual act; and it's not comfortable for you. I know that. Besides, it's a million to one that I would experience it. Each of us is different in what we enjoy, and how we like to do it. We established our ways of loving long ago. When we're both light, maybe I'll feel it then."

"Why do you get pleasure from it, David? What does it feel like?"

"Besides easing my dick from blowing its head off whenever I'm close to you, the actual act is... that's a difficult question... inside, you're hot, tight, and I rub against soft, tender protrusions, and some very hard ones, like your distinctive tailbone. You feel damp if you have one of your explosions. The combination of textures, and the fact it is not a smooth even canal, drives me crazy enough to almost want to hurt you."

"Wow. I understand the feeling your cock gets, because when you suck and lick mine, I can barely delay coming. Sometimes it frightens me, believing you're a serpent pulling me in, intensifying the pleasure further."

"Your stick is a squirming demon. Feels electrifying, like I've caught something alive and it's fighting back. I ache all over for you, Teddy Bear."

"Even up your butt, like mine feels now?"

"No, but tell me how it feels, so I can take the pain away." David smiled at him, wondering why the sudden interest in describing something so unexplainable.

"It aches so deep, I can feel it straight up my arse, making it contract inside, twisting and shivering, trying to grasp onto something until you're in there. Even my back and pit of my stomach hurt, as well as my dick."

"We better do something about that then." David wiped clean the sorry face of sweat, and pushed himself away, preparing himself for his own need of wanton pleasure.

In his usual dazzling manner of seducing the older man, Ted laid back, never breaking the sultry gaze through those long, dark lashes. Lifting his knees slowly, and then stretching his legs over his head, he spread them out like a curtain, opening for Act I. The spectacle of wishful blue eyes, a hardening crotch, and an orifice already relaxed, opening and closing to the rhythm of each panting breath, mesmerized David, and every inch of him tingled with the viewing. It floated him away to another time and place, reliving a rare and wonderful offering the first night on the rooftop of their Arizona home.

No finger foreplay, he brutally attacked the seductive gesture. The frail body, once impaled, thrashed about on the blanket, until helpful hands lifted his shoulders to secure him. Ted felt the full penetration of David's savage lust; closing his eyes to feel it all; his shriek of satisfaction filled the expanse of their desert. Something was changing; he felt his lover further than he had ever experienced. He knew; and his excitement mounted with another squeal. Letting himself go, with the power he felt bursting within, he stripped off David's armor to bring him into a new miracle of thrills.

Overwhelmed with a strange sensation, LaCoix's ravishment of Ted grew more intense and gratifying. So deep inside, he poured everything he had into the man, infiltrating every molecule in his lover's body. Shooting off rockets at the same speed of his lover's rapturous convulsions, his senses short-circuited; filling him with explosion after explosion of erotic sexual release from parts of his anatomy that he had never felt.

Ted growled deeply, filled with more desire, but without a sound heard, and only David felt the vibration. The youngest floated in space, first full of soft clouds and a warming sun, then to be bombarded by lightning bolts from his lover. If in his human form, he would swear his blond lover came up through his throat, to tickle his lips with the silky ball spilling its essence. Beyond intense, both bodies burned hot; two fireballs fused together to ignite into a flaming pyre of light, streaking gold and silver rays far into the desert sky. A fireworks display of an electrically charged firestorm, of passion and ecstasy, made the daylight a dull background for the spectacle. The screams changed to thunderclaps; each ejaculation skyrocketed assorted colors into the air. Animal need gone berserk, they ended with a grand finale on the hood of their red Ferrari.

Back in human form, Ted lay draped over the front of the car, his head covering the famous logo, while deep-throating David. His lover leaned over him, taking him in the same manner, and neither intended to stop. A final gift, they came together, to swallow copious amounts of each other's life sacrificing essence. David fell to the ground on his buttocks, gasping for air and looking up at a head hanging in front of him. "Is that a smile or a frown? It's hard to tell from this angle." Exhausted, he panted heavily; his taut body covered with sweat, pasting the blond hair to his face and neck. He looked like a victim of a vampire attack.

"A smile; a big one. Ouch! This metal is scorching my back." Ted rolled over and off the car, landing flat on his stomach, and giggling until tears ran down his face. In no better shape, the salty perspiration stung at the sores; and he quickly healed them both of the telltale marks.

"What the hell was that? I'm drained; and you would not believe how incredible you felt."

"Yes I would. You blew me away with what you did, whatever you did, and you're silver." Ted continued to gasp for needed air.

"What?" David gave him the notorious squint, which made him the wicked mystery man to his fans.

Ted adored the look, and melted into those half-hidden bedroom eyes. "Didn't you notice? I'm mainly golden light, while you're silver white, with glittering sunbows, just like Holly."

"You mean I changed?"

"Damn straight; that was the best. You reached in and touched every part of me, every single nerve ending, I swear. Now I can yell *Hi H, Silver* when you screw me." Ted continued his joyously surprised laughter, rolling over on the hard, parched earth, to let his arms stretch out and fall to the ground with a thud, creating a dust cloud that caused a bout of coughing in both men.

"We're screwing now, are we; new word for you, and *Hi Ho, Silver*? You're still a kick, Tonto. Silver, hunh?" David choked on the stirred sand.

"Beautiful, sparkling, white silver, the perfect color for the armor of my White Knight."

"No shit? I felt something different; but this, man, there are no words."

"There aren't supposed to be. Come on, Kemosabe; help me out of the dirt. I think I have sand stuck in places I don't want to feel." Ted glowed in the thrill of the day, never feeling so free and alive. Reaching up, two hands grasped his; David pulled him to his feet to receive another kiss.

"So that's what it's going to be like? I'll be damned."

"Maybe we are; no one would believe this to be pure heavenly bliss, my Knight. I'm just glad you experienced being a light entity for the second time." Again, that wondrous rare laugh had David chuckling.

"Man, I can handle more of that. I just wished I knew how to change myself."

"You did change by yourself. I didn't want it any other way. We can do this, David, just remember: *Mind over Matter*."

"What does silver white mean; and why are you golden?"

"Have no idea. You're the one with all the Pagan thoughts of astrology, numerology, color, and whatever else your New Age women figured out." Ted picked up the blanket, folded it neatly, and returned to the car. He glanced up at the green cat's eyes, seeming to snicker at him in their excitement. "What?"

"Amazing! If we get past Lavender, and into or out of Avalon, we had better be eternally linked like that. I still can't believe the explosiveness of what we just experienced."

"Just remember not to think of our human bodies in space, or we'll die."

"Never thought of that. Good god, how do I not think of you as who you are."

Ted said nothing, just happy to slump into the passenger side of their red pleasure mobile, beside his super-hero. Exhausted and exhilarated at the same time, he celebrated his liberation from everything, which he had been brainwashed into believing. He could defend himself against whatever the Mistress had in store with no fear; his Knight would stand beside him to fight for the good and banish the bad.

They drove home slowly, and once in third gear, it did not change. A hand became more important to hold than a fast slalom course through the saguaros, which continued to entrap the sun in their distorted arms, preventing it from dropping beyond the forever line, until the couple reached Home. One more sunset, and the two men would be leaving. Cleaned up and casually dressed, they watched the final brilliance of orange, purple, gold, and yellow, fading into black. The stars winked at them; a smiling moon shone down for a last look. A wave good-bye to their own magical wonderland, they came down the ladder to head for their exit portal. Good-byes had to be said to their staff, which had remained faithful throughout time, and radiated brilliantly from its benevolence. The only one missing, Bernard, had departed years earlier, to hit Broadway with his one-man show. An overnight smash, he reaped rewards for his tender attention to a special family.

On touching ground, Ted stumbled and groaned. Rushing immediately to help, David frowned at the puzzled, surprised look. "What's wrong?"

"I don't know, but I think I have to change. Ouch! Like right now!"

"What can I do?" David bent over to see a scrunched up profile and teeth bared to hold back the scream. The LaCoix and Barrett families had not suffered from an ailment in years, but for Ted's entity dilemma.

"I don't know; but something's happening; and it hurts. I'm scared; it hurts so badly. Damn, I feel like I'm being punch kicked. Ouch! Like there's a racket ball bouncing inside me."

David picked him up and scurried out to the garden. The moans never let up; and the body seemed to be convulsing in some strange way. He came close to dropping Ted after a spasmodic twitch of tremendous power. "Craig! Craig! Call Jamie to bring our horses here and quickly! Steady, Baby, can you fix it, or turn into light to relieve it?"

"Not until you do. Besides, I don't know what it is to heal. Just because I can turn into light, doesn't mean I know a damn thing about what really happens to us. Help me, David; it hurts. I pissed Lavender off, trying to find the answers to questions like this. Ouch! Maybe my energy field needs to surround this container now, and it wants me to let it out, but I can't seem to change. Hell, I don't know what to do. Ouch! Shit! Man, this is stupid. What's wrong with me?"

A purple mist blew through the garden, and the Mistress' voice issued orders. *'You must hurry. Quinlan and I will escort you to La Rosa Negra.'*

"Hello to you too, your Ladyship. I gather we've been forgiven." David snapped, not moving from his position next to the seated man who held himself together with two arms.

'Now is not the time. Place Theo on Bastet and you on Ra. Move it, LaCoix. Do not argue.' The familiar vapor trailed away, but they felt her urging them on. Upsetting good-byes were exchanged quickly, as three men lifted Ted onto Bastet. Once on the mare, he seemed to gain strength from

her and settled a little. Decked in her flowers of the Faery Realm, she and Shaysha were ready for a quick flight through the vortex to La Rosa Negra. Two men, in the process of change, looked at each other, and with nods of acceptance, rode at a full gallop into the moonlit desert of their *once-upon-a-time* canyon. Heading for the stars, they were gone.

CHAPTER 60

"What's happening? Make it stop, David. Make it stop." Ted flew through the air like a rag doll, crashing into walls of an empty room except for the four human-like beings and a yellow Elf. Each smack, against a wall, cracked another bone; and Ted could do nothing but scream in pain and fear.

"Quiet, Child, it will stop the pounding. You have to change to light immediately!" Lavender and Quinlan scrambled, with whatever powers they possessed, to catch the figure hurtling past them. The speed and force was great; they seemed to be handling the situation too delicately, considering something wanted to kill Ted from the inside. At the flick of her Ladyship's finger, the room softened to pink and the walls to cotton fluff. It eased the next barrage of slam-dunks.

"No! I won't! You won't change me back! David, help me!"

"Ted, I..."

"LaCoix, please; get in the corner, out of the way. Shaysha, stay with him, keep him from talking, and tell him what to do when the time comes." With a single look, Ambrose immediately pinned the frantic blond against the pink cushioning, before returning his attention to the ricocheting body. "Settle yourself, Theo, and do as the Mistress says. Turn into light, and make it pink."

"Pink! Ouch! Shit. I can't control it. Unh! How in hell am I supposed to make it fucking pink? Oh, God, this hurts. I can't concentrate... to turn... into anything. Look out!" During the uncontrollable tirade of anger, Ted slammed against the padded room a dozen more times. Now heading straight for David's corner, he nearly squashed Shaysha, while knocking the wind out of his startled partner.

David's grip had no chance of holding; and the frail body flew against the opposite wall of pink fluff. Ted reached out; but whatever continued the attack from within, snapped him backward like a bungee cord attached to his belt. "Can't you two do something?"

"No!" Yelled in unison, Lavender and Quinlan set David aback, having never heard such an outburst from either of these sedate beings. Never raising a voice, their shout emoted pure frustration, sensed and felt by the human in the corner.

"I must transform, Quin. It is the only way to save him."

"The screaming could damage you. I won't allow it." Ambrose grabbed her arm, guarding her protectively from something he knew as a danger; and uncharacteristically, she did not retaliate. They both ducked at precisely the right time.

"Theo, please try to change. We can help you." Lavender pleaded, and the uncontrollable quiver of anxiety could not be hidden.

"Like hell. Ouch! I don't trust you... after our visit to the past... Uhn! David! David!" The wailing continued, hurting the ears of all those in the room.

"That's enough, Lad. You trust me, don't you? I've taught you how to come in and out of your container. Just think of changing, and for the love of might, stop screaming." Ambrose took control, leaving Lavender's worried thoughts to permeate through them all.

With Quinlan's sharp demand, Ted became quieter; albeit convulsing like a madman, he started to change. David watched in awe at the bright vision of blinding light, shooting off rays in every direction. It had a vague similarity to the afternoon of passion he would never forget.

Something sparkled at the purple center of the golden rays, which shifted to pink as the pain subsided. David heard Ted crying out in his fright, but he could only send messages: silent, loving ones, to soothe the whimpering heard in his head. Lavender and Quin transformed into their natural state, the color of Ambrose's hands and the monk's healing rays. Two blue lights surrounded the pink one, as a single beam emerged from one, to reach in and release the twinkling light from within the pink flashes that were once Theodore Barrett.

'Catch it, David, and don't squeeze. Say nothing. Think loving thoughts.' Shaysha flittered out of the way; as a star, the size of a tennis ball, flew at David, with a toss from one blue light. Caught on the fly, like an outfielder reaching for a potential homer, it warmed his hand at a touch and pulsated through him. He looked up from the improbable object he gently held, to see the three human forms return. Quinlan busily repaired Ted's shattered body, while Lavender held him, trying to console his anger and discomfort. His lover habitually started healing himself, along with two mystical creatures whose concern showed. Terrified, and unable to touch Ted physically, David held firm in his pink corner, carefully placing something of wonder against his heart. It fascinated the older man with the strange sensation it spread through him.

'Are you feeling better, Child?'

"No, I'm sore and angry as hell. What happened?" No worse for the pummeling, Ted came back attacking. Lavender set him down with a thud; and the two entities steadied him on his feet.

'While we are in this room, speak telepathically. Remember how sensitive light creatures are to harsh sounds. In your head, Theo, please. You are giving us headaches, and you are not well yourself.' Lavender brushed away the damp hair, clinging to his sweating face; but he would not look at her. He gazed over to his eternal partner who held the dreaded, hated tumor.

Much to David's surprise, Quinlan stepped between the two and took over. *'We have much to discuss; and you need rest, Lad. You received a severe pounding to your container, and the light source within you. Go with the Mistress, while David and I tend to other matters.'*

"No, that thing tried to kill me. We all go together, including that shiny torture device." Ted took root, determined for battle, while David believed the opposing side had not declared war.

'My chambers then, and if you do not remain silent, Theodore, I can fix that permanently.'

"For the finale, you're going to throw me out your window." Ted crossed his arms in defiance, while David frowned at him, trying to signal him to ease up.

'The way you are behaving, we just might. Come, we shall all take a few moments to relax within my tranquility, and answer your questions.'

"Yeah, right, as if you've ever answered our questions. All you've done is ask them, your Ladyship, or turn them around until they become meaningless." The infuriated young man still refused to obey her commands; and she smacked him hard across the mouth, sending him hurtling into the pink fluff. Even David could feel the affects of the resounding, much warranted action.

'Quinlan, pick him up; if he speaks again smother him. David, place the speck in the softness of the wall; and, Shaysha, stay here, if you would be so kind. Send me a message if you require assistance.' Lavender turned sharply on her heels; her orders were followed. David had no desire to leave the twinkling light he carried so gingerly, and reluctantly left it with the beaming yellow Elf, both snuggled in the candyfloss wall. An unhappy Ted fought like a crazed fool in Ambrose's solid grip, and cursed under his breath. David wondered what possessed his passive partner. Had the power gone to his head? The frantic blond had to calm his beloved, and get his feet back onto

solid ground.

Gaping in amazement at the Mistress' chambers, David remembered few details of the room's opulence and scale, while fighting off a trio of grim reapers. An ancient, throne-styled chair faced outward to a viewing window; the dimensions of which, he could not estimate. Even the ceiling went unseen; it was that high. Seeming to have no up or down, or side to side, only the window and chairs gave him some orientation as to space. The carpeting, of rich dark hued tapestry, hinted that a solid floor lie beneath his feet. Lit by candle fire, thousands flickered into the never-ending space, dancing on the breath of a whisper. Walking directly to the window, he smiled sadly in wonder. "So, this is the other side of the stars, Ted."

"So she claims. Put me down, Ambrose."

"Shut up, Ted. You're acting like a jackass, and our two friends came rushing to help you, from a quandary we know nothing about. Stay beside me and stop fuming, until we hear what they have to say. Whatever you're thinking is probably invalid, considering what you just went through. No wonder I talk to you as if you're twelve. Now, get over here and settle down." David snapped at him, annoyed that this special place was now stained with childish behavior.

"I'm sorry. No, I'm not. I have nothing to be sorry for." Ted spun out of Quinlan's grip, nearly toppling out the window. Saving himself, along with helpful forces too quick to be seen, he unsteadily shoved his way passed his bewildered partner, and slumped exhausted into one of the smaller chairs.

"I don't know what to say, Lavender. I've never seen him act like this."

"Everyone, please sit. Do not worry about the temper-tantrum pouting in the chair. He thinks he knows our secrets, believing he is winning some kind of imagined skirmish against us. Impossible, he shall soon learn the facts." Lavender took up her position on the majestic throne, and motioned for the two standing to take a seat. The breeze wafted its way through the open window, bringing in the scent so familiar. Each curl of her hair ruffled delicately, floating back against the regal chair that could fit three people. The graceful hand came up, and goblets of her treasured wine appeared in their hands. "Where to begin? This has been a long day in coming, and certainly too soon for some things."

All three jumped in, with a question or statement of fact. The Mistress waved her hand for silence. "I shall start, and from the beginning." Making herself comfortable and rimming the top of her goblet with her finger, she let out a disturbing sigh. When those fingers slipped down the stem of the new pewter drinking vessel, David leapt at her, and gently took it away from the surprised perfection in black velvet.

"Let's not do that anymore, if you don't mind. Can you change this from pewter to crystal, or perhaps plastic?" David's eyes twinkled at her, and a bemused smile spread across his face. This he could not deal with, during what appeared to be a major crisis of Cosmic consequences.

"Oh, I am sorry, David; I thought a new one would change that. Let me know if I bother you again." Lavender laughed nervously, comforted slightly by a snicker from Ted, and sly grins on all faces. Crystal immediately replaced pewter, and she gave it a quick stroke. "Better?"

"Can't feel a thing, thanks."

"Good. How odd that is? Not everything is explainable in the Cosmos. Now, are we set? You two have learned a great deal about your world and your own abilities to control its many layers. Now you are in the realm of what you call the Powers-That-Be. It is time to acquaint you with our dimension, and what lies Beyond. We require your trusted help, after you learn to utilize the energy field you shall become, with Quin as your teacher. David, as an evolving new life form, it will take us time to understand your attributes. Ted has always contained one of us; however, the painful he endured went unnoticed too long for us to rectify. We remained incapable of helping until the change tonight, when your pain shall be gone, and we can assess any damage to both your human body and the infant light entity within."

The other three remained silent, with no surprises but a few confirmations. The Mistress identified herself in a practical, historical context, which did not satisfy either man's curiosity, being too outlandish to believe. One of the last of her kind, it fell upon her, as an inheritance, to manage the stability of the known Cosmos. For the most part, Earth remained relatively calm; watching societies grow and expand, fall only to rise again. The last several centuries, of Earth's time, became their nightmare. Although expected, they had become too few in number, unable to handle the tumultuous awakenings to the possibilities of the minds of all species. They searched for leaders, amongst the new forces on all inhabited planets, while continuing to seek out their own life forms, kidnapped by the Fates: the real Fates.

Lavender set down her glass and stared out the window. David chilled at the forlorn, distraught look exuded. He heard Quinlan urging her on; and the ageless face turned to gaze into the eyes of the crazy, longhaired Englishman. A peaceful, sad smile shared, proved their kinship more intimate, along with the thoughts David felt and not heard. Her Ladyship had stated Quin could only bring her happiness; their relationship shone through when helping Ted. Ambrose seemed to take authority when he chose, appearing as a possible equal and protective partner.

The Mistress' species became all powerful, setting forth on a mission to maintain order in an unruly Cosmos, billions upon billions of years before Earth's appearance. Through time, the light entities, thought to be immortal, had their own elemental situation plaguing them. What humans call *'The Big Bang'* has happened twice, but misunderstood by your scientists. Both caused suns to explode and new ones formed. Theories continue to be debated, without conclusive evidence, on all known surviving planets, but the question of what came before still remains. The new suns, from the first cataclysm event, deemed insufficient to sustain them all. Many of their species disappeared into the vapors to find sustenance, leaving only a few to care for what was left. The Mistress was one, along with Ambrose and Peerce, who both spent time on earth, attempting to find their missing. Their treasured lost made up the hundreds of progeny left behind, by those who risked vanishing behind the dangerous veil. With their babies snatched away, *en masse,* via a hideous diversion, they had remained hidden in various guises, for billions of earth years. Many had perished and the count grew. The human form seemed the Fates last hope of succeeding, although never imagining they would erroneously allow their captives access to light. Their only reasoning could be that their own children were also dying without nourishment, and losing them would finally terminate the Fates.

Holly's proclamation that her father was an old Soul, Lavender acknowledged, and confirmed her position as David's Soul. Now his Spirit would be free, with the other past lives she had lived through. This last statement had the man sitting straight, suddenly aware of what she said; he was dead! Both he and his lover were dead, but he felt no different--dead and alive at the same time--without a Soul! Silent words of reassurance that his Spirit would carry him forth, within his new form, did not satisfy his unexplainable fear: not after all this time, after all his lessons, after all the magic he had lived within. Having never used the term himself, perhaps he had always known; and left it for question period, yet still frightened as if being abandoned. He shook himself, wondering where the odd thought came from.

On the other hand, as one of the stolen children, Ted remained a human Spirit nurturing an immature light entity, and had neither a Soul nor Higher Self. He would have no recollection of his consciousness prior to awakening in his current human container. His claustrophobia was a remnant of those times, permanently fixated by abusive human parents. This Ted could not understand, and had to stop the monologue. "I don't believe you. You said I would meet my Soul. You lied."

David got up, pulled the smaller man out of his chair, and harshly set him down next to him. Necessary to stop the rage, he could see Lavender's nervousness in what she had to tell them. His partner sat like a keg of dynamite, sweating under a hot sun; David knew it; Lavender knew it; Quinlan knew it; and the worst scenario, Theodore Barrett knew it. "Shut up, and listen, Ted. This is your last warning. You've opened your mind to all sorts of wonders. Why are you shutting down now?"

"I don't know, but I need answers as to who I am; and why, of all people, I don't have a Soul. Too much is happening; I can't focus; and no one cares." Anger turned into frustration, and then into unfathomable sadness. For Ted, it led to not listening and erroneous judgments.

"I'm sorry, Teddy. You were badly hurt tonight; and we did not show proper concern. I'm equally frightened, with so much taking place in a short time; and you've been the center of it all. You know we all love and care for you." A hug, a seldom-said word, plus a kiss to the forehead, fractionally appeased the nerves of *Peter Pan*. "My Soul forgot me most of my life, and now she's my friend. How weird is that? If you started out as truly human, we'd be in the same situation. Man, does that sound crazy when said aloud. Let's both settle and listen carefully to everything said. This is important to me, and certainly should to you."

"Thank you, David. Now, Theo, I did promise to introduce you to your Soul. I also said you would meet a being with wings, and you have, in Shaysha, the Lady Faery, and their friends. As for your Soul, the absence of one led us to discover who you may be. We light entities do not have Souls; we just are; each unto ourselves, but requiring a partner for an eternal lifetime. You received that gift with David. Unfortunately, I cannot introduce you to something you do not have. I should have known better, but knowing all is impossible. However, your heart and thinking will always be of a human gay male, for you awoke as such; what you are about to become will kindle it further." Lavender puzzled at the astonishingly handsome face, while attempting to blandish some reaction. Nothing but tears filled the still face, quickly soaking into David's sweater.

"A few more questions, Ted, so hang in there. Lavender, we've been through all forms of hell. Do we blame everything on the unseen Fates, and the ones we came to know personally?" Intrigued by all she said, David remained in control for Ted; imperative his lover believed his Knight protected him.

"No, much of it was our doing. The movie created the atmosphere specifically to unite you; there is no mistake of our intention in that regard. As something, you both set goals for, in your different ways, the plan proved worth the risk. You received the love of your life, David; and Ted's dream became his reality, acknowledging his sexuality to be with you."

LaCoix continued to press for more information, while holding a man exhibiting another emotion: severe depression. Ted remained upset, shaking within his arms. To the blond-haired man, it meant a slow, awkward acceptance. To Lavender, it meant something quite different. She forged on emotionlessly, uttering words with a watchful eye on her man-child.

"The Fates held Theo captive since his creation. There is no doubt they inspired his misfortunes, except for those few we felt necessary to develop his belief in the *knowing*. As for your trip into the past, Theo had not prepared you for tonight, David, and we forced his hand. A dire situation had to be created, as we no longer can control his power. Your final test, Child, one in which you had to act fast, used all your abilities to figure out the puzzle. You proved your importance to us, with self-will to rise above it. A severe push necessitated itself to get you to open up, to stop hiding things, to slow down, and to prepare David, but you pushed back. Now, neither of you are equipped to come forth into what is to be. Your futures must be adjusted, due to an afternoon's indiscretion. As for you, David, I must congratulate you on focusing during your predicament, along with trusting in the powers of your partner, which you seldom saw. You will become the first of your kind as a new species--an enlightened human--to sit rightfully on the High Council. There will be more of your kind, which you shall lead and represent when they arrive. Overwhelmed with mass confusion at first, you must come to terms with it, before problems occur."

"A leader! Did you pick the wrong guy. I have no training for leadership. My life has been directors' orders and writers' words."

"And you improvise to perfection, with better ideas than said directors. We saw it, if you recall, so you can cut the humble, egocentric rhetoric, Mr. LaCoix."

"Point taken, I think." David flinched at the sound of a compliment, mixed with a rare attack from the previous night. He saw her soften, however, while hearing the growl from the man in his arms.

"So it was a test of my powers, and you still don't know them all." Ted's nails embedded into human tissue; his mind perceived only fragments of the discussion.

"Pay attention, Child. Once we discovered who you were, we had to let you develop your own potential, aided by Quinlan. Very aware of your achievements, we know how truly powerful you are, and will continue to become. The planet stabilization, perfectly calculated out, showed us your heart could only create beauty and not chaos. You believed us angry, oblivious to your thoughts, actions, and blatant lies; but leaving you to think, that we did not know, helped you grow in strength. Blocking your thoughts deemed very intense training on your part, as we would lose contact with you for short periods; and that, Theodore, frightened us the most: the potential of the Fates stealing you again. Your experimentation, turning into your natural state, though painful and terrifying, you succeeded, even managing to bring an unprepared David along with you, when the proper events were set in motion. You both must learn quickly how to control your light intensity, to make it grow larger or smaller, to create different containers, to translate other languages into telepathic thought. Quinlan will be your tutor. Normally, a young light entity, like you Ted, attends school, to learn everything about the Cosmos, as well as your new form and how it exists. Now, David seems another type of conundrum for us, as he is still unable to turn into light, but tonight he must do it alone. All of this is of extreme importance to both of you: how to conduct yourselves within the Cosmos."

"And there proves the Mistress' point, Lad. You not only brought David into his light, but a mixed entity as well. Neither of you had the knowledge of doing so. Total folly on your part, Theo, not waiting until you understood what a light force is capable of doing."

"What are you talking about, Ambrose?" David felt Ted's shocked body tighten, and wondered what they had done to cause this new disaster.

"The Mistress told you we pair for a lifetime, and in that pairing, we reproduce. While you two played silly buggers in the desert, you mated those few minutes you both turned to light. Too fast to stop, the consequences are irreversible; you produced a speck."

Both men sat motionless; mouths gaped open; breathing stopped. Their shocked expressions delighted Ambrose and upset the Mistress.

"Say again." David whispered, squinting from under the blond lashes.

"A speck! You just had a baby! Congratulations!"

"A what?" Again, a hush of disbelief, David's attention directed itself fully on Ambrose.

"You returned to human form too quickly; and if I recall, it ended with Ted draped over a red convertible. An unfortunate situation, considering a child of light is usually conceived and immediately released. Trying to detach itself and get out of the dark, it felt the pain much like the panic struggle of your own light being, Theo. You have to raise this speck, just as you did with Willow and Holly, as it will have human instincts, with remembrances of touch, scent, sight, and sound. How wondrous this life form will be."

"Quinlan, I think they have heard enough for now. Just know, my friends, you both have to learn quickly how to raise this speck."

"Good god." David fell back into the chair, releasing Ted who sat shivering and stunned.

A trembling, raspy voice, with its sweet sadness and whispered surprise, haunted them all. A child of light, coming to terms with something he was too immature to have created, smashed two light entities conjured-up hearts. "A baby? Our baby? What do we do with it? It's ours, David, yours and mine. I need to see it. Will that happen every time?"

Gathering herself, Lavender could not be gentler with the truth. "No, Theo, but it is where you went beyond your teachings. Knowing the results of your actions, and how to enjoy each other, without reproducing, should have been explained to you. We thought we had time; now Quin and I must teach you both how to control every electron within you. Do you understand our concern now, Child?"

"Yes ma'am. Can we see our baby?"

"It is your right, and it requires your presence. From the look on your face, you need to be with your speck as well. I believe, however, there are still unanswered questions; but you need to rest a while longer, Child." The Mistress could see LaCoix had much more to ask, and yet still in shock to react immediately. Too upset for her liking, Ted needed healing attention, but so much had to be said, and a new speck required their presence.

"Man, this is wild: a baby! We'll learn, Ted; and it's ours--a child of our union--a union of two men. Amazing! I can't believe it, but it felt so perfect in my hands. Wait until you feel it; you'll be ecstatic. I know I am, rambling away with no words to say. This is awesome." David squeezed Ted who shook uncontrollably. Nothing could be done, other than the consoling gesture. With much more on his mind, the protective Knight lovingly stroked the damp hair of his near catatonic partner, but changed the conversation to pose his questions. "It's hard to think after such a pronouncement. In summary, Lavender, your species controls everything within the Cosmos and

Beyond, whatever that means. The Fates are your enemies who you'll destroy during the *Beginning Again*; so, who is in charge? Who manifests wishes and dreams into reality; and conversely, who creates disasters of mass destruction, only to rebuild? Is it one entity, or a host of you, and just what do we Spirits do? Are we a sub-species? If we don't have a Soul, does it mean we have no heart? And then this future thing and staying on your path; that really had us going and still does." David sat still, not looking at anything, only thinking aloud his list of questions, while holding a dwindling Ted, who had stopped listening, pondering his own troubled thoughts.

"I cannot divulge all as yet, but your family is a prophesy coming into reality." The Mistress smiled, regaining her own composure after her confessions. "We are Caretakers of all living entities, whatever the species, wherever the planet. Natural disasters are precisely that, as we do not interfere with Natural Law; unfortunately, one day we may have no option."

"Makes sense, but challenges all theories of evolution and theological thought."

"You have never been told otherwise. All will awaken into the *knowing*, thanks to your daughters. As for Spirits, they are guides for their own species and worlds, with their own power and way of doing things. They are extremely important in their knowledge and understanding. There are no sub-species, and each new life form is represented on the High Council; so far, an amicable group who views the Cosmos as a whole. Meetings are rare, always peaceful, and decisions made democratically. When a rare controversy arises, such as our latest ruling, to leave the teaching or termination of the Unreachables to planetary discretion, was a difficult choice. As each species comes into the *knowing*, the representatives consider themselves 'humanitarians' in your language, thus incapable of terminating those who may disrupt the Cosmos. However, with the decision made, we shall not look back. The many universes, realms, and dimensions will relearn tolerance through the *Beginning Again*; and the Cosmos will continue in harmony." Lavender waited for some acceptance, while watching David absorb more revelations, one cog at a time, still frozen in his position. It appeared the rivets on his chair became his worry beads. Ted assumed the same posture, but his head dropped to contemplate the tips of his boots, and beads of cold sweat dotted his distressed face. In shock and postnatal distress, he had the Mistress worried, wishing David to hurry.

He again interrupted her concern over their man-child. "If I'm changing into light, why haven't I felt the same pain as Ted, and probably Stevie?"

"Trapped specks, trying to gain nourishment, are forceful, demanding influences, which Ted experienced. You developed slowly, your awareness grew, a human turning into light naturally. Your daughters will not feel pain either. You once concluded that Mr. Kincaid masked his pain with more agony, which is true. He also houses a light entity within his human body."

"This is hard to believe. Okay then, what about those Spirits caught in the chaos of religious fanatics you showed us?"

"It is the safest place for them and the rest of the Cosmos; separated from others, including the political zealots, who are held elsewhere, they all must submit or die, as you put it, David. Those in the theological Spirit group remain isolated, until they grow tired of the bantering over abstract gods, goddesses, prophets, and New Age rhetoric. We have great hope that many followers will discover choice, enabling them to leave the dogma behind, as Theo did. The Unreachables, who do not come to terms with freedom of thought, morally and ethically, will be Ted's responsibility to weed out when he has finished his training."

"Can we talk about that later, since Ted can't possibly do what you suggest? The place gives me the creeps; I won't have him being forced into the mêlée." David changed his gaze and looked directly into her feline green eyes.

"The reason, we chose Theo, was because of his innocent yet brilliant mind. Although still biased, he reduces complex problems into simplistic form, thus able to rectify the battles within the chaos, as it is not a choice for a prophet or a son of a so-called god to make. They do not have the power, which solely rests with the Council, whose combination of mental gifts is unimaginable. Unfortunately, we are few, and thus the requirement of assistance. This problem has been left unresolved long enough." Lavender sat calmly, turning her attention to the blue cat's eyes, growing bigger in alarm. She had to catch Ted before he faded away.

"You still want me to do that, and my so-called innocence can battle the likes of Christ, Atun, Brahma; the list is miles long? I can't deal with it. I just need to see our baby."

"Soon Child; Quinlan believes the zealots will have reason to listen to you. Your powers are of us, not of humanity, or any other species within the religious furor. Now, David's final questions: all entities outgrow their need for protection, and when the time comes, and if they believe in the *knowing*, their soul will deliver their Spirit into appropriate hands for teaching, and release their Higher-Self and Soul for other concerns. You, my Spirit, have fallen into the safest hands imaginable; the first of those we have waited for--human changing into light--maintaining the essential essence of what you call *heart* and we call *Spirit*. As I told Ted, he will also retain his human experience."

"And I'm to lead my species into the unknown; moreover, our baby is another species unto itself. Good god." David's brain paralyzed at the thought.

"Your baby was light entity produced with human thoughts and emotions, which leads us to all your other questions, resulting in one. Who does everything else?" The Mistress shifted her position restlessly, wishing to avoid what needed saying.

"Well, Lavender?" David sat ready; Ted did not. The deranged snake, of twenty-years ago, returned to slither its way into a safe haven within his Knight's embrace, while the Lady in black looked at Ambrose, and then out her window to stare at her own worry beads of stars. Her thoughts exploded with the familiar English accent.

"The Mistress is all powerful."

"Holy shit, Ted truly was in your hands when he fell over the cliff! You are God!" David sat bolt upright, releasing his lover, nearly dropping the dazed man out of his nest.

"Please, I dislike that word intensely, as there is no such thing. I am an individual within a species; that is all. We do a job inherited through our families. If I require help, I have others with equal abilities."

"Not quite, your Ladyship."

"Hush, Quinlan. You are not helping."

Lavender rose and floated past them to her window. It led to every corner of the Cosmos, until she could reach through the vapors. Mauve tears stained her face, and dampened the tresses blowing off her face with the forever breeze. How long had she fought the label of deity, ignoring all those who blatantly asked for a particular god or prophet? She granted wishes and prayers when a deity went unnamed, although there seemed always one, in the recipient's mind, who received the credit. There were no gods, only living entities; she just happened to be the one whose birthright gave her leadership. A job her family never aspired to, or wanted; in human terms, she ruled as Chairman of the Board.

Quinlan came around and held her, both looking at and wishing on another falling star. Neither could grant this wish. "I am sorry."

"No need to be. It is who I am, Quin, and I am tired of it." The sorrow filtered through the gray veil into what lay Beyond.

Rising from his chair and pushing a catatonic Ted to his feet, David broke the quiet conversation. His last questions had sent his forever partner spiraling into oblivion. All the younger man's fight dissipated into darkness; but LaCoix needed his own strength to handle what came hurtling at him with deadly speed. Having upset the Mistress of the Cosmos, and thrown Ted a curve he missed, he asked quietly, honorably, and with caution. "What do we call you?"

She turned around and smiled through the tears. "Our species names cannot be pronounced and each light entity has a different one. You shall have billions of monikers to remember. I cherish the nicknames bestowed upon me by a variety of species, but as you turn into light, the only name I hear is *The Mistress*. It appears it has become universal. You will gain our powers; and we shall leave many things in both your capable hands, just as we are training our other surviving specks. Many are very frail and only healing at present, to mature properly, as Ted must do with your help. Do not be afraid of me, thinking I am something other than what you have come to know. Consider my species a family, of which I am the Matriarch."

"What of Quinlan?" David looked at the man who had to be more than the one on the arm to make you look good.

"He is one of us, yet unexplainable, even to me. Quin and I have recently paired in our time, finding each other in this expansive space. We hold the same powers and abilities, like all our species. His eternal partner failed in its attempt to cross the treacherous vapors. Mine let its energy die to nourish our children; a waste of a brilliant mind, for our specks were stolen the moment his glorious light went out forever. My new partner saved me from despair, which I tried to alleviate by using my powers to entertain myself. Very selfish on my part, but even those, who hold the Crown, have bad days. I believe that was your quote, David. Quinlan saved the Cosmos from my wrath, much like you and Holly saved Earth, by refocusing Theo's anger and grief into something wondrously constructive."

"I am her protector, confidant, and lover, nothing more, nothing less." Ambrose released his embrace, only as a courtesy to allow the Mistress to float toward the two stricken humans, with one having much more to ask.

"Humans have different genders, so how is it possible Ted could reproduce? Is he a female light entity?"

"No, for are original species was genderless, allowing either partner to produce offspring. A forever pairing chooses who will carry the speck: Utopia for you, and many of your friends. You two chose to come together as a same-sex couple. Ted is still gay, and his light entity approves to bring forth children. As a new species, David, you shall retain your masculinity in every way; and it gladdens us that Theo has not been harmed in his ability to conceive with you, although far too young to raise a speck." She turned her softening eyes toward her man-child, so precariously on the edge of falling further than the floor. "You have said nothing, Child. How can I help you through this web we have woven around you?" Lavender placed her hand on Ted's face, wiping away the shock with a calming touch.

"I still feel like a man."

"Because you are one, and always will be. Being one of us does not invalidate the fact you are gay, because it was your sexual orientation from the beginning in human form." Ambrose stepped in and took over from David to support the younger man. "Okay, Lad, you have just had two unearthly surprises. It takes time to recover from dying, not to mention giving birth. Shamefully, we have not given you the opportunity to get over the emotional aspect of either, let alone the physical pounding one usually does not have to endure releasing a speck. You must be very tired."

"He is in postnatal shock, Quinlan; something a human male has never experienced. His depression and shock grows. Please wrap him in your warmth." Lavender's face showed her sympathy, wanting to cradle the young man, to gladden his Spirit, to let him rise to his full power, and to let him dance amongst the stars, just for the joy of being who he was, like the fawn kicking up his heels in the excitement of new life.

After what felt like an endless up and down battle with Ted, David gently handed him over to this extraordinary being they considered a friend. It gave him the needed opportunity to stand alone in his wonderment of the omnipotent presence before him, taking in everything done for two stupid humans playing guessing games. With caution, he stepped over to lean against the window ledge, alongside the ageless woman who ruled the Cosmos. His wildest theory proved correct, but he had not believed it possible. What could one say to the pronouncement of such a truth?

"Do not be afraid of your Soul, David. You and I have traveled far."

"It's a little unnerving, you must admit. I still have many questions."

"You shall learn the answers as you go. How are you honestly dealing with this, my Spirit?"

"I don't know. This has been a night of one shock after another. I'm very worried about Ted. He's failing; and I'm terrified of losing him."

"Quin will help, and once you turn into light, things will change for the better. You have something else on your mind. Best to ask now, before the true learning begins."

David stumbled around wanting to ask, but fearing it a stupid question. His mouth opened in spite of himself. "If you are so powerful, why did your species not recreate the universe when it started disintegrating around you?"

"We did not create the Cosmos. It is nature's phenomenon, as uncontrollable as its elements: earth, air, water, and fire. Not everything is explainable or entity-made; something all must learn to stop searching for sensible solutions in wonderland. We, just like humans, evolved out of the mire, and will never be perfect; no entity, mortal or immortal, will ever be. For this reason, we frown on deity names and reverences; no being can live up to such a standard. Certainly not a godly situation to create entities for amusement, and to play with them like pawn pieces, which has become the object of human gods in their abstracted tales."

"A few things I need to know, without Ted overhearing. What do you do with Spirits like Hitler, Caligula, and the rest on the evil list; and how are you perceived as one, yet hearing all?"

"Terminated instantly; dust spewing in the tail of a comet. As for me, I am everywhere, living in every moment, for everyone, and so shall you."

"More insanity. Ted may handle the one answer, but the rest is a mega job for so few."

A deep sigh and Lavender turned to face him. "We are not the only entities with the skills you have witnessed, as others slowly join us, like yourself. It always starts with one. You both are unique individuals: my black rose and my white one. Your goals were set high at the beginning of your journey, to be the best at what you can be, which enlarged your path into something grander, to become legendary as the *Fathers of the Beginning Again*. You will be remembered forever."

"You really are God! Sorry, I just don't know how to put it into words."

"Words will not be necessary when you change. Good luck to you, David LaCoix. Tremendous tasks await you, embracing several new species, remaining a good father, and a loving partner to one of such great importance to us. Ted created another entity with Willow. She is human, with a light entity's education, now turning into energy like you. Your daughters will be under your ruling, as evolved light forms of human background. They grew to be beautiful, sensitive, and intelligent women. I wonder who they got those qualities from." Lavender smiled broadly at him and winked one of those bewitching eyes.

"The looks--clones of Ted and me--but intelligence: as if you had no part."

"I did not; I simply provided them with gifted fathers. Come; let us introduce you properly to your newest creation."

"This baby's the hardest to fathom. Do we stay together as a family? Please give me this one last wish, Lavender, for Ted and myself."

"Of course, but I thought your last wish was to die copulating with Theo, which you did."

"Is that when we died?"

"It was the start. You soon must turn to light, and commence learning. Do not be afraid of the change, as Quinlan will care for you both, holding your focus. Once you gain some simple knowledge, he shall return you here, to rest in your human forms. I will tend to your speck, as it requires a light force to feed. It will feel wonderful to hold an infant within my core. For now, the three of you shall be safe, living and learning, in and out of La Rosa Negra, where Quin and I will guide you. Your new goals need to be set; your workload is great; and you both shall remain together, with your little speck, in a place of your choosing. Even a child of light, with the Cosmos to play in, needs a proper home. As you see, I originally manifested La Rosa Negra to raise my children, which were born light entities, as was I, as was your speck. You will do the same. The Canyon, you gave your daughters, will be maintained for their use, and yours if you wish. Now, a speck waits for its parents."

"I hate you calling our child a speck; it has to have a name."

"I would not have thought otherwise." Lavender smiled at him and took his arm. Turning with a sweeping gesture with her other arm, covered in black velvet and priceless gemmed bracelets, the Mistress of the Cosmos invited them all to join her, to meet the wondrous life two men miraculously and unknowingly created.

Tangled in confusion, from which he could not break free, Ted rushed to David's arms. Turning to face the Mistress, a shaky voice tried to apologize. "Your Holiness... God... no, not that either..."

"Just Lavender for awhile longer." Three of them laughed; Ted did not.

"My God's name is Just Lavender? I'm sorry for acting like... it just seems... I don't know, but I've had a really bad couple of days. No, not all bad, just strange. I think I need to sit down again."

"I know, Child." The Mistress' one arm supported him, while the other held his hand; and as she had done, the first time in her chambers, floated him away effortlessly, without a footfall to ground. "Come, Theo; you are certainly one for understatement. Let us visit this perfect baby you two have produced. It will raise the gray cloud hanging over your head, and let you soar amongst the stars."

The other two followed them out of the mystical chamber of purple vapor and candles. The maze of halls and doors had become familiar to the new arrivals in death; and they soon found themselves in the pink nursery. Peace and silence swept over Ted, giving David hope his forever partner stayed safe mentally. The look on the boyish face softened to wistful happiness, as golden tears sprang from those peculiar eyes. Turning them back into human form, he could gaze at their miracle, to marvel at what he saw, and to remember as a human. LaCoix did the same. With instinctive knowledge, the younger man slipped his hand under the soft, fluffy nest, and lifted the tiny, sparkling star up and out. Cradled gently, yet not touching, Ted held it for both men to ponder. The stalwart blond broke down, weeping openly at the cooing sound he heard in his head from his fifth child; and the whispering chimes sung by an astonished *'mother'*. Their child glimmered as a radiant being of light.

The sight of the three had the other two clinging together in adoration, while the object of their love shone in its happiness. Nurturing thoughts surrounded the speck that reached out its rays to touch warm skin, the hard cold metal of a bonding platinum ring, and the silky texture of the embedded sapphire. The feeling of abandonment disappeared from its immature thoughts; a tiny being discovered a human body that it would feel when creating its own shell. Ted looked up to match tear for tear in familiar green eyes. With the utmost caution, he took one of David's hands, and together they held something so loving, so extraordinary, so beautiful, and yet so frightening. The ecstatic older man reached out with his other hand to cradle his partner's face, his thumb caressing the quivering lips, then leaning over to kiss the tears away. He could not control his own.

The Mistress approached; the first to break into their private thoughts. *'You and your baby are both exhausted and stressed from its attempt to free itself. Return it to its safe nest and step away. Your feelings are so powerful, it felt your love, and will identify you readily.'*

'Is it a girl? Is that why the room is pink?' When lost in the labyrinth of his mind, Ted's innocence reappeared; and Lavender happily watched the depression dissolve and joy return.

'Pink is the color of nurturing, and that is why Quinlan asked you to change. It is the same reason we used the color to break your fall so long ago. We are unaware as to what this little speck will be, but it will be a wonder to see if any human characteristics appear.'

'It's a baby, not a speck. We have a child, David, and it needs a name we can think to it.'

'Aptly put, Child. You can decide between the two of you. Regarding any name, however, it must sound genderless, and extremely unique; something not yet recorded in the Akashic Records. So many humans have the same names; therefore, you must select new ones for yourselves. Perhaps, for David, 'Arizona Fire'; for Ted, 'Ice Diamonds'; thus your speck could be called 'Fire Diamonds'. Something to think about seriously, as it will be important when another entity calls your name. Now, let us leave your baby to rest.'

'I like them all, as they hold meaning for us. Thanks for your suggestions, Mistress.'

'You're welcome, Arizona Fire.'

One last time, four human figures stood by the edge of the ocean of myth. It mirrored their reflections back at them when they looked down, yet knowing they would take these shapes many times, as a resting place, until fully versed in the *knowing*. David embraced Ted, and a kiss and nuzzle calmed both. They had experienced each other in all human forms of a loving union and intense communication; it would last them an eternity.

Quinlan held the Mistress, whispering in her ear. David saw it, and sensed the sudden surge of excitement. Her velvet black merged into the man always donned in the infinity of The Void.

"Are you all right, Lavender?" A stupid question to ask the Almighty, it did show concern; and if David was to find out more, it had to be now. He felt dizzy with the change coming, and all he had heard and witnessed. The explanations required sorting in his head, including another child to raise, a truly immature partner who he still adored, and a contingent of newly enlightened beings to train. He faced a wild, confusing ride; and the most frightening aspect, the commotion would continue forever, unless he made the right choices on his first attempt.

"Yes, David, and I cannot tell you how excited I am. Quinlan has informed me that my youngest two specks survive; and both are well and safely guarded."

"Congratulations, we look forward to meeting them."

"You already know Steven Kincaid." Quinlan smiled at Lavender and kissed the unruly curls.

Those perfect hands, which wielded such power, covered her surprised mouth and quaint gasp. "Stevie is mine? No wonder I cared for him so deeply. This is wondrous news. It has been eons since I showered the Cosmos with an extravaganza, of wild proportions, to express my happiness."

"I look forward to one of your spectacles." Ambrose beamed, able to give the most powerful entity of all the realms something she did not have. "I lived with him, on and off, for two earth years, and recognized your family coding in his light source. These hands do more than heal." Quinlan chuckled at the reaction, and remembered the many times he put Steven back together, after his so-called accidents. He had looked into the body of the man, and found proof of his identity.

"We must bring him to La Rosa Negra immediately."

"It is not time, but very soon. Joseph Thurgood and Steven will join us, once they have the girls and the other children, of the canyon, on their rightful paths. Until then, you have another to love and teach. I am sorry I made you wait nearly twenty Earth years to tell you, but I had to be sure." Quinlan hung onto the woman of wonder, blocking his thoughts from hers, to surprise her again.

"Of course, but who? Do not leave me waiting another eternity."

"Your youngest, my beloved, is your man-child, Stevie's Scarecrow, and David's Teddy Bear."

Another gasp echoed through the Cosmos, and arms flew around the amused entity's neck in a crushing, grateful hug. It lasted a second, until Lavender turned her excited attention to gaze glowingly at Ted. "The night stars shall dance with color this night, for the rebirth of my speck of magic. You truly are my Child, Theodore Barrett, and you are of very great importance to me. How unlike me not to recognize one of my own, never believing it would become an eventuality. I am beyond the Beyond." Two humans stared in awe, listening to the motherly exuberance, so unlike their mystical *Lady of the Rocks*. Light flashed around her, glowing in the fluorescent colors of neon, reminiscent of one Oscar night.

"Theo is the return of Oberon, of magic, of love, and of peace. The King has returned, acknowledged by The Lady Faery and Shaysha's people. Even the adornment of Bastet, with blue and yellow flowers, confirmed his identity for the hidden kingdoms of Earth, as did the wreath crowning his head." Quinlan released the woman he never felt shake as hard, an action that could cause quakes on every star and planet if he could not calm her.

"The legend of so long ago; one child would be the manifestation of their regrouping; and now the journey begins. Theo, we have picked the perfect job for you. As part of me, you will hold immense power over the zealots. I am so thankful for your return, my wondrous Child of Light, my Ice Diamonds, and my lost son." Lavender grew in stature, to clasp her returned speck tightly in her arms.

Ted pushed away, however, to stare at the woman whom he had never seen look so happy. She dazzled him with her glow from within; it terrified him. "What are they saying, David? I don't understand." Ted returned to his Knight's embrace, scrambling to read and understand the two faces shining before him. Blue eyes darted back and forth, frantic to receive an explanation. He felt himself changing, along with his lover, leaving him little time to face this in the form he understood the best. "Tell me now! Help me, David!"

"You are my son, Theo, the true brother of Steven Kincaid."

"Holy shit, please don't place any more on him, Lavender; he's frightened enough." David's face glistened with the perspiration of human shock, understanding the meaning and aghast at the thought. The king references had him bewildered, but the Mistress' last statement created havoc with the forces demanding his body to change.

"It is true, but now you are both rapidly turning into glorious light. We shall meet later for your first lesson in your new form. I love you, my blue-eyed Child, and bless your partnership with your Knight. Welcome to your ancestral home: La Rosa Negra."

"Mother?" Ted could not believe what came out of his mouth, calling out instinctively for her warmth. He had to be sure; the answer pushed him further into David's changing silver light.

"Yes, my Child, you are my youngest offspring. I have searched endlessly for my children; and two have survived."

"What does that make me? I don't understand." Ted's human body began to glow golden, which shimmered in the panic of new thoughts, old habits, and one too many shocks.

Lavender attempted to soften her excitement. "The King of all the layers and realms of the *Beginning Again*, and..."

"...and what?" Ted yelled his last words.

An English accent echoed within their new vibration, giggling in his mischievousness, but being hushed by a beautiful, frantic, female voice. David and Ted heard Quinlan's teasing words the moment of their gold and silver explosion. *'The son of gods, behave accordingly.'*

'No!'

'Shush. Your Knight is here, and you'll always be Just Teddy Bear to me.'

THE END

ABOUT THE AUTHOR

Raven Davies attended university in the faculties of Fine Arts and Interior Design, unfortunately ending up in the corporate world. The well paying job gave this author the means to travel much of the world and to live in other countries. When a 9 to 5 job became too distressing for an artist's mind, Davies discarded the security and started an in-house business, designing and hand-painting ceramic tile, as well as becoming a spiritual guide for seekers of ancient wisdom. Albeit rewarding artistically, spiritually, and mentally, the monetary challenges grew too great, and Davies started writing epic Slash tales under the name 'Ravin' to ease the strain.

A storyteller by nature, Raven creates character-driven fiction to challenge a reader's thoughts, whether it be spiritually, politically, or socially. On a rash decision, and having had overwhelming success as a Slash Fan Fiction writer of five novels, this Canadian renegade packed up a small U-haul, purchased a broken down jeep, and left all behind. While residing in Mexico, Davies wrote two gay novels: *Between Here & There*, a published paperback, and *The PlanetTerra Journals Volume I: WET SEASON* now available in eBook and paperback formats, as well as contributing to two hardcover anthologies. Having returned to Canada, Raven Davies has changed publishers and has now released a Revised Edition of *Between Here & There* in paperback and eBook formats. You will find what and where to buy Raven's writings, along with a free Slash read based on *The Magnificent Seve*n the television series, at www.frictionfictionbooks.com, the home page of Raven Davies.

OTHER PUBLISHING CREDITS

PlanetTerra Journals Volume I: WET SEASON

A gay fiction novel and eBook with a storyline focusing on two men setting out to save the Brazilian rainforest.

The Runaway

A free slash online read based on *The Magnificent Seven TV Series*, formerly entitled *Broken Fences* under my Slash name Ravin. The story now includes references to the entire series and allows a possible ending for the seven men. Available on website www.frictionfictionbooks.com.

The Slash Fanfiction Connection to Bi Men

Contributor of the essay for the anthology: *Bi Men: Coming Out Every Which Way.*

Editors - Ron Suresha and Pete Chvany, Published by Haworth Press

Unleashing Deranged Snakes:

Contributor of excerpt from *Between Here & There* for the anthology *Bi Guys: Firsthand fiction for Bisexual Men and Their Admirers.*

Editor - Ron Suresha; Published by Harrington Park Press, 2005

> *"...The literary tone and styles vary. There are polished pieces by famous writers like Felice Picano and Pat Califia, grittier accounts by relative newcomers, and even a short play.... Attraction is of course very personal, and individual readers will have differences on their own personal inclinations. Myself, a traditionalist, I most enjoyed Larry Lawton's prison story, Simon Sheppard's encounter between two college boys,* ***Raven Davies's depiction of two closeted actors,*** *and Felice Picano's variation on a perennial favorite ... These stimulating stories will satisfy the erotic needs of pretty much all readers. As Ron Suresha explains... the stories are meant to instruct as well as excite. First and foremost, the collection wants to overcome shame - which many bisexuals feel showing characters fully comfortable with their sexuality. The very existence of the volume asserts the importance of bisexuals in society: not only for straight people who are largely ignorant of their presence; but for those gays who think bisexuality dishonest... Whatever the specifics, all stories insist that bisexuality is an authentic human experience, to be pursued without shame.*
>
> *"We can all then be grateful to Editor Ron Suresha and his writers for this collection. Their stories are not only entertaining and stimulating, they introduce to a wide readership a range of bisexual issues and emotions not normally treated in literature, straight or gay. And they deal with these issues positively - with the seriousness and clarity they deserve..."*

Review by David Van Leer in the Journal Edition of BI MEN 2006.

www.ingramcontent.com/pod-product-compliance
Lightning Source LLC
Chambersburg PA
CBHW080925050426
42334CB00055B/2649
9780986674228